MANAGING BAR and BEVERAGE OPERATIONS

Educational Institute Books

HOSPITALITY FOR SALE
C. DeWitt Coffman

UNIFORM SYSTEM OF ACCOUNTS AND EXPENSE DICTIONARY FOR SMALL HOTELS, MOTELS, AND MOTOR HOTELS
Fourth Edition

RESORT DEVELOPMENT AND MANAGEMENT
Second Edition
Chuck Y. Gee

PLANNING AND CONTROL FOR FOOD AND BEVERAGE OPERATIONS
Third Edition
Jack D. Ninemeier

STRATEGIC MARKETING PLANNING IN THE HOSPITALITY INDUSTRY: A BOOK OF READINGS
Edited by Robert L. Blomstrom

TRAINING FOR THE HOSPITALITY INDUSTRY
Second Edition
Lewis C. Forrest, Jr.

UNDERSTANDING HOSPITALITY LAW
Second Edition
Jack P. Jefferies

SUPERVISION IN THE HOSPITALITY INDUSTRY
Second Edition
Raphael R. Kavanaugh/Jack D. Ninemeier

SANITATION MANAGEMENT: STRATEGIES FOR SUCCESS
Ronald F. Cichy

ENERGY AND WATER RESOURCE MANAGEMENT
Second Edition
Robert E. Aulbach

MANAGEMENT OF FOOD AND BEVERAGE OPERATIONS
Second Edition
Jack D. Ninemeier

MANAGING FRONT OFFICE OPERATIONS
Second Edition
Charles E. Steadmon/Michael L. Kasavana

STRATEGIC HOTEL/MOTEL MARKETING
Revised Edition
Christopher W. L. Hart/David A. Troy

MANAGING SERVICE IN FOOD AND BEVERAGE OPERATIONS
Anthony M. Rey/Ferdinand Wieland

THE LODGING AND FOOD SERVICE INDUSTRY
Second Edition
Gerald W. Lattin

SECURITY AND LOSS PREVENTION MANAGEMENT
Raymond C. Ellis, Jr., & the Security Committee of AH&MA

HOSPITALITY INDUSTRY MANAGERIAL ACCOUNTING
Second Edition
Raymond S. Schmidgall

PURCHASING FOR HOSPITALITY OPERATIONS
William B. Virts

THE ART AND SCIENCE OF HOSPITALITY MANAGEMENT
Jerome J. Vallen/James R. Abbey

MANAGING COMPUTERS IN THE HOSPITALITY INDUSTRY
Michael L. Kasavana/John J. Cahill

MANAGING HOSPITALITY ENGINEERING SYSTEMS
Michael H. Redlin/David M. Stipanuk

UNDERSTANDING HOSPITALITY ACCOUNTING I
Second Edition
Raymond Cote

UNDERSTANDING HOSPITALITY ACCOUNTING II
Second Edition
Raymond Cote

MANAGING QUALITY SERVICES
Stephen J. Shriver

MANAGING CONVENTIONS AND GROUP BUSINESS
Leonard H. Hoyle/David C. Dorf/Thomas J. A. Jones

HOSPITALITY SALES AND ADVERTISING
James R. Abbey

MANAGING HUMAN RESOURCES IN THE HOSPITALITY INDUSTRY
David Wheelhouse

MANAGING HOUSEKEEPING OPERATIONS
Margaret M. Kappa/Aleta Nitschke/Patricia B. Schappert

CONVENTION SALES: A BOOK OF READINGS
Margaret Shaw

DIMENSIONS OF TOURISM
Joseph D. Fridgen

HOSPITALITY TODAY: AN INTRODUCTION
Rocco M. Angelo/Andrew N. Vladimir

MANAGING BAR AND BEVERAGE OPERATIONS
Lendal H. Kotschevar/Mary L. Tanke

POWERHOUSE CONFERENCES: ELIMINATING AUDIENCE BOREDOM
Coleman Lee Finkel

MANAGING BAR and BEVERAGE OPERATIONS

Lendal H. Kotschevar, Ph.D.
Mary L. Tanke, Ph.D., CFBE

A nonprofit educational foundation

Disclaimer

This publication is designed to provide accurate and authoritative information in regard to the subject matter covered. It is sold with the understanding that the publisher is not engaged in rendering legal, accounting, or other professional service. If legal advice or other expert assistance is required, the services of a competent professional person should be sought.

—From the Declaration of Principles jointly adopted by the American Bar Association and a Committee of Publishers and Associations.

The authors, Lendal H. Kotschevar and Mary L. Tanke, are solely responsible for the contents of this publication. All views expressed herein are solely those of the authors and do not necessarily reflect the views of the Educational Institute of the American Hotel & Motel Association (the Institute) or the American Hotel & Motel Association (AH&MA).

Nothing contained in this publication shall constitute a standard, an endorsement, or a recommendation of the Institute or AH&MA. The Institute and AH&MA disclaim any liability with respect to the use of any information, procedure, or product, or reliance thereon by any member of the hospitality industry.

© Copyright 1991
By the EDUCATIONAL INSTITUTE of the
AMERICAN HOTEL & MOTEL ASSOCIATION
1407 South Harrison Road
P.O. Box 1240
East Lansing, Michigan 48826

The Educational Institute of the American
Hotel & Motel Association is a nonprofit
educational foundation.

Printed in the United States of America

1   2   3   4   5   6   7   8   9   10   95   94   93   92   91

Library of Congress Cataloging-in-Publication Data

Kotschevar, Lendal Henry, 1908–
     Managing bar and beverage operations/ Lendal H. Kotschevar,
Mary L. Tanke.
          p.   cm.
     Includes bibliographical references and index.
     ISBN 0–86612–05992
     1. Bartending.   I. Tanke, Mary L.   II. Title.
TX950.7.K67   1991
647'.95'068—dc20   91–13954
                                                             CIP

Project Editor: Marj Harless

Editors: Timothy J. Eaton
          John Morier
          Lisa Kloack

Contents

Preface xiii

About the Authors xv

PART I   Introduction 1

1   Introduction to Bar and Beverage Management 2

The Bar and Beverage Business 3

A Brief History • Types of Bar and Beverage Operations • Alcohol Consumption Patterns

Managing Bar and Beverage Operations 10

What Is Management? • A Practical Approach • Marketing and Control

The Future 16
Endnotes 18
Key Terms 18
Discussion Questions 18

2   Social Concerns and Management 20

A Few Definitions 20
Responsibility in Today's Alcohol Market 22

Off-Hour Sales • Serving Alcohol to Minors • Service Involving Intoxication or Alcohol Dependents

Third-Party Liability 25

A Brief History • Changing Drinking Patterns • Health Concerns • Physical Effects

The Industry's Response 35
Serving Alcohol with Care 37

> *The Effects of Alcohol • Alcohol and Other Drugs • Approaches to Server Intervention • Monitoring Drinks*

Endnotes 50
Key Terms 51
Discussion Questions 51

PART II The Business: Planning and Marketing **53**

3 Architecture and Interior Design **54**

Architectural Planning and Construction 55

> *The Four Viewpoints of Planning • Permits, Licenses, and Regulatory Compliance*

Interior Design and Decor 59

> *Establishing a Design Theme • Planning for Space Allocation • Planning for Traffic Flow • Floors • Windows • Walls and Wall Coverings • Ceilings • Furniture and Equipment • Planning for Color*

Interior Environmental Planning 77

> *Air Control and Conditioning • Sound Control • Lighting Control*

Exterior Design 82
Endnotes 83
Key Terms 84
Discussion Questions 84

4 The Bar **86**

Bar Layout 87

> *The Bar Menu in Bar Layout • The Human Factor in Bar Layout • Self-Sufficiency and Security*

Basic Bar Arrangements 91

> *The Front Bar • The Service Bar*

Bar Equipment, Accessories, and Tools 100

> *Ice and Ice-Making Machines • Glassware • Bar Tools and Other Accessories*

Bar Sanitation 105
Endnotes 106
Key Terms 107
Discussion Questions 107

5 The Bartender and the Art of Mixology **108**

The Bartender 110

The Bartender's Role as "Psychologist" • The Bartender's Service Role • The Bartender's Role as Salesperson • The Bartender's Role in Alcohol Awareness

The "Art" of Mixology 117

Cocktails • Drink Preparation Methods

The Bartender's Manual: A Guide to Bartending 126

Work Station Setup

Endnotes 130
Key Terms 130
Discussion Questions 131

6 Service Procedures and Selling Techniques **132**

Service: An Overview 133

A Service Orientation • A Guest-Oriented Approach • How It Works

Establishing Service Standards 136
Basic Service Procedures 137

Table Approach • Taking and Placing the Order • Serving the Guest • Payment/Cash Control

Service Procedures for Beer 143

Serving Temperature • Pouring and Service • Glassware

Service Procedures for Wine 148

Wine and Food • The Sommelier • Preparation • Wine Service

Handling Service Problems 156
Selling 157

Techniques and Strategies • Selling Wine

Toward Successful Service and Selling 161
Endnotes 162
Key Terms 162
Discussion Questions 162

7 The Selection and Training of Human Resources **164**

The Labor Supply and Its Effect on Bar and Beverage Management 165
Job Analysis 166
Job Descriptions 168
Job Specifications 171

Recruitment and Selection 171

    Recruitment • Selection

Orientation Programs 177
Training 178

    Identifying Training Needs • Choosing the Training Method • Training Builds Sales

A Look Ahead 184
Endnotes 184
Key Terms 185
Discussion Questions 185

8 Marketing Bar and Beverage Operations 186

Knowing Your Guest: The Key to Marketing Success 187

    The Changing Marketplace • Market Segmentation • Market Research • Selecting a Target Market and Positioning

Special Considerations in Bar and Beverage Marketing 191

    Marketing Guest Service • Special Characteristics of Service Businesses • Ethical and Social Issues

The Competitive Environment 193

    Competition Analysis • Guest Decision-Making • Forecasting Sales

The Marketing Mix 196
Product and Place 197
Price: Beverage-Pricing Strategies 198

    Product Categories • Sales Value per Bottle • Pricing Methods • Sales Mix • Wine Pricing

Promotion 202

    Developing Promotions

The Promotional Mix 208

    Advertising • Public Relations and Publicity • Sales Promotions • Personal Selling • Merchandising

Marketing: The New Alternative 213
Endnotes 213
Key Terms 214
Discussion Questions 214

PART III Bar Management: Controls 215

9 The Purchase to Issue Functions 216

Selection of Products 217

    The Selection of Beers • The Selection of Wines • The Selection of Distilled Spirits • Purveyor Selection

Purchasing 225

> *Comparing Beverage Purchasing with Food Purchasing • Purchasing to Ensure Control • Establishing a Par Stock • Purchasing Responsibility • Purchasing Bar Supplies*

Receiving 231
Storage 235

> *The Storage of Beers • The Storage of Wines*

Inventory 240

> *Perpetual Inventory • Physical Inventory • Beverage Inventory Turnover • Inventory Control as a Monitor of Sales and Costs*

Issuing 244
Computerization and Product Flow 246
The Ongoing Cycle 246
Endnotes 248
Key Terms 248
Discussion Questions 248

10   Bar Control Systems **250**

The Control System 251

> *What Is Beverage Control?*

Product Control 253

> *Establishing Standards • Preventing Pilferage and Fraud • Automatic Dispensing Systems • Product Control and Banquet Service*

Sales Profitability and Control 269

> *Determining Product Cost • Sales Accountability/Sales Analysis • Pricing*

Cash Control 279

> *Cash Handling Procedures*

Control: A Guide to Profit and Guest Satisfaction 284
Endnotes 285
Key Terms 286
Discussion Questions 286

11   The Legal Jungle **288**

Federal Control 289

> *A Brief History of Federal Regulation • The FAAA • Laws Influencing Internal Operations*

State Control 294

> *Licenses and Permits • Control and License States • Handling Problem Guests • Employment at Will • Miscellaneous State Regulations*

Community or Local Regulations. 298
Potential Liability. 299

*Drinking on the Job • Wine Tastings • Business Liability • Serving
Effervescent Wines*

Words and the Law. 301
The Importance of Prudent Preparation. 303
Endnotes. 303
Key Terms. 304
Discussion Questions. 304

PART IV The Products. 305

12 The Beverage Family. 306

Historical Overview. 307

The Ancient World • The Middle Ages • Modern Times • Early America

Classifications of Alcoholic Beverages. 318

Distilled Spirits • Wines • Malt Beverages

Characteristics of Alcoholic Beverages. 319

Alcohol Content • Calorie Content

Production of Alcoholic Beverages. 322

Fermentation • Distillation • Aging • Blending

Increasing Your Product Knowledge. 335
Endnotes. 336
Key Terms. 336
Discussion Questions. 336

13 Spirits. 338

Grain Spirits. 339

Whiskeys • Grain Neutral Spirits • Vodka • Compounded Spirits

Plant Liquors. 351

Rum • Tequila

Fruit Liquors. 352

Brandy Production • Labeling • Kinds of Brandy

Liqueurs. 359
Aperitifs and Bitters. 360
Judging the Quality of Spirits. 361
Endnotes. 362
Key Terms. 363
Discussion Questions. 363

14 Malt Beverages **364**

Malt Beverage Ingredients 365

Barley • Hops • Water • Yeast • Adjuncts • Additives

Malt Beverage Production 367

Malting • Mashing • Brewing • Fermentation • Pasteurization • Carbonation • Packaging

The Malt Beverage Family 370

Types of Malt Beverages • Alcohol Content of Malt Beverages • Non-Alcoholic Brews

Draft Beer 372
Judging Malt Beverage Quality 376

Appearance • Aroma • Taste • Flavor

Endnotes 377
Key Terms 377
Discussion Questions 378

15 Wine Fundamentals **380**

Basic Wine Classifications 381

Table Wines • Natural and Fortified Wines • Aperitif and Dessert Wines • Sparkling Wines

The Growing and Harvesting of Wine Grapes 383

The Soil • The Vine • The Grape • Geography and Climate • Harvesting

Wine Production 389

Pressing • Fermentation • Aging • Fining • Blending • Bottling and Corking • Maturing • Storage

Regulation and Labeling 401

France • Germany • Italy • The United States • Spain • Other Countries • Recent Trends in Regulation and Labeling

Tasting and Judging Wine 420
Endnotes 425
Key Terms 426
Discussion Questions 426

16 Wines of the World **428**

France 429

Champagne • Alsace • Loire • Burgundy • Bordeaux • Côtes du Rhône

Germany 448

*Mosel-Saar-Ruwer • Rheingau • Rheinhessen • Rheinpfalz • Nahe •
Schaumwein • Eiswein*

Italy 453

*Piedmont • Lombardy • Veneto • Emilia-Romagna • Tuscany • Latium •
Sicily*

Spain 457

Sherry

Portugal 460

Port

The United States 462

California • New York

Wines of Other Countries and Areas 468

*Australia and New Zealand • Austria • Bulgaria • Greece and Cyprus •
Hungary • Israel • Madeira • North Africa • Romania • South Africa •
South America • The Soviet Union • Yugoslavia*

Glossary 477

Bibliography 499

Index 507

Educational Institute Board of Trustees 506

Preface

Creating an environment where people can safely enjoy the pleasures of alcoholic beverages and where you can generate your desired profit is a great accomplishment in today's dynamic bar and beverage industry. Now, more than ever before, success in the bar and beverage business means taking creative risks and meeting new challenges.

New attitudes toward alcohol, as well as accompanying social concerns, make the challenges real. This text addresses both the challenges and how to meet them. Above all, this text stresses a guest-oriented approach, from design to marketing to service procedures.

Part I lays the groundwork, identifying and defining the social concerns and responsibilities and summarizing the management functions.

Part II—Planning and Marketing—begins with pre-operational architecture and design considerations for the building and the bar. It continues with mixology, service and selling techniques, human resources management, and marketing.

Part III focuses on controls. Purchasing and its related functions, pricing, and cash-handling methods and procedures, are operational controls addressed in Chapters 9 and 10. Chapter 11 describes the legal controls.

Product knowledge (Part IV) is the final component of this bar and beverage management package. Product knowledge is a requisite for success. It enables managers to resolve everyday problems and gives them the background they need to take creative risks and meet challenges confidently.

Designed for students as well as beverage professionals, this text combines Kotschevar's product knowledge and research background with Tanke's operational experience and human resources expertise. Our co-authorship developed from a recognized need for such a text in the service economy of the 1990s. It is predicted that almost ninety percent of the total labor force will be employed in the service sector by the year 2000. For the bar and beverage industry, this represents a trend that is waiting to be seized and a need waiting to be satisfied.

We are grateful for the industry input we received from the manuscript review committee. The committee members' advice, suggestions, and support, in addition to the photos and exhibits they contributed, enhanced our efforts and the text's practicality.

The committee members are: Jean-Paul Barat, Director of Food and Beverage at the Walt Disney World Swan, Lake Buena Vista, Florida; Rene Bardel, Division Director of Food and Beverage, Continental Companies, Miami, Florida; George Cashmark, Administrative Assistant, Food and Beverage Department, Stouffers Hotel Company, Solon, Ohio; Professor David R. Grier, Florida International University School of Hospitality Management, Miami; Roger McAleese, Director of Support Services, Opryland Hotel, Nashville, Tennessee; Michel L. Kranz, Director of Food and Beverage, Hilton Fontainebleau, Miami Beach; Glen Reynolds, Director of Food and Beverage, Miami Airport Hilton and Marina, Miami; Regynald G. Washington, Senior Vice President, Concessions International, Inc., Atlanta, Georgia; and Paul Wise, Program Director and Professor, University of Delaware, School of Hotel, Restaurant, and Institutional Management, Newark, Delaware.

—Lendal Kotschevar and Mary L. Tanke
Miami, Florida

Dedication
To Anthony G. Marshall, Esq.
Boss *Extraordinaire*

About the Authors . . .

Dr. Lendal H. Kotschevar, Distinguished Professor in the School of Hospitality Management at Florida International University and the author or co-author of 15 texts, was a pioneer in establishing the discipline of hospitality management.

His broad and distinguished career began when he was trained as a chef by his grandfather, Chef Louis Belanger. Later, in World War II, he served as Director of the U.S. Navy's Commissary Schools. After World War II, he became Civilian Director of the U.S. Commissary Research and Development Facility, where he and his staff were instrumental in food planning research that helped pave the way for the atomic submarine. He left that position to take his doctorate at Columbia University, then went to the University of Montana to become Director of Housing and Foodservices and Chair of the Department of Home Economics. In the early 1960s, he went to Michigan State University as Professor of Food Service Management. He left Michigan State after nine years to devote more time to writing. Dr. Kotschevar served as visiting professor to such schools as the University of Hawaii, the University of Nevada at Las Vegas, Haifa University in Israel, and the Centre International de Glion in Switzerland.

In addition to teaching and writing, Dr. Kotschevar has lectured widely and has served as a consultant to Pope Paul, the Food and Agriculture Organization of the United Nations, and a number of hospitality suppliers. In recognition of his contributions and outstanding service to education, he received the Meek Award from the Council on Hotel, Restaurant and Institutional Education (CHRIE). He is also a diplomate of the Educational Foundation of the National Restaurant Association.

Dr. Kotschevar spends his summers at his cabin on Lake Lindbergh in the Montana Rockies, engaging in fishing, gardening, writing, and socializing. He spends his winters in Miami where he plays golf in addition to writing, teaching, and socializing. His ambition now: to change the phrase "living the life of Riley" to "living the life of Kotschevar."

Dr. Mary L. Tanke is an Associate Professor in the School of Hospitality Management at Florida International University. Her eleven years of teaching hospitality management include two semesters in Switzerland at the Centre International de Glion.

She received her doctorate and a master's degree from Purdue University and a bachelor's degree from FIU. She holds a Certified Food and Beverage Executive (CFBE) designation from

AH&MA's Educational Institute and is an active participant in the Council on Hotel, Restaurant, and Institutional Education (CHRIE). She has co-chaired CHRIE's Accreditation Committee for five years and currently serves as Chairperson for the Accreditation Commission for Programs in Hospitality Administration (ACPHA). It was research stemming from Dr. Tanke's dissertation that led to the formulation of ACPHA.

Dr. Tanke received the Ryder System, Inc., Award of Excellence in Research/Scholarship for her work on accreditation and multicultural management. She is the author of one other text, *Human Resources Management for the Hospitality Industry,* and has developed workshop modules for hospitality industry professionals on the subject of multicultural management.

In addition to her educational background, Dr. Tanke has twelve years of experience in the food service industry. She has been a busperson at Strongbow Turkey Inn in Valparaiso, Indiana; a working chef at the Alabama Hotel, Winter Park, Florida; a cook at Valparaiso University; a manager of the student lab-cafeteria at Purdue University; a banquet chef for Holiday Inn; an assistant to the chef at the Depot, Miami; and a food specialist aboard AMTRAK.

Part I

Introduction

Introduction to Bar and Beverage Management

Chapter Outline

The Bar and Beverage Business
    A Brief History
    Types of Bar and Beverage Operations
        Bars
        Lounges
    Alcohol Consumption Patterns
Managing Bar and Beverage Operations
    What Is Management?
        Planning
        Organizing
        Coordinating
        Staffing
        Leading
        Controlling
        Evaluating
    A Practical Approach
    Marketing and Control
The Future

> Drinking is in reality an occupation which employs a considerable portion of the time of many people, and to conduct it in the most rational and agreeable manner is one of the great arts of living.

> —James Boswell, 1775

Bar and beverage operations have long served the public by providing a place where those who enjoy alcoholic beverages can go and be served. Bar and beverage operations also provide many jobs for those seeking employment, and they provide support to many industries whose materials and products they use. There are bars that serve as centers for social activities and entertainment, and there are beverage operations that supplement a range of dining services.

In short, beverage service remains an important part of hospitality today. We use the word "remains" because many changes have taken place and continue to take place. Beverage service is changing, but indications are it will always be in demand.

New challenges accompany the changes. The service of alcoholic beverages has once again raised the social consciousness of Americans. You will read more about the challenges and changes in Chapter 2, but we introduce some of them here to show how they affect management decisions and functions.

One of the most notable changes has been a decline in the consumption of alcoholic beverages. For example, as you read these words, guests in bar and beverage establishments throughout the United States are probably drinking less than they were the day these words were written. There are various reasons for this decline, but perhaps the primary reason is awareness of the dangers of drinking and driving.

The day a drunken driver struck and killed Candy Lightner's daughter with his car marked the onset of a drastic change in bar and beverage management. Candy Lightner, grief-stricken and angry because the driver who had killed her daughter had been given light sentences for past drunk-driving offenses, formed the organization Mothers Against Drunk Driving (MADD). MADD has become one of the most powerful lobbying organizations for legislation against drunken drivers and for raising the public's awareness of drunk-driving crimes. As a result, many states have passed much stiffer laws against drunk driving. Further, many states assign to anyone serving alcohol in excess third-party responsibility for the actions of those served. (This topic is covered in more detail in Chapter 2.)

What does this new level of social consciousness mean for the management of bar or beverage operations in both the national and international markets? How does this change the role of the bar or beverage manager? The beverage operation has always been considered a profit hub in a wheel of other products and services offered by the hospitality industry. In many cases, products and services with slim profit margins have been offered, with the hope that the high profit margin from the sale of alcoholic beverages would make up the difference. But the days of the three-martini lunch are in the past.

Throughout U.S. history, lobbying groups have pointed to alcohol as the source of many of the nation's ills. The impact of the lobbying groups in the United States has not changed in recent years. Well-organized groups such as MADD have forced changes in state legislation that demand that people assume a social and ethical responsibility for the sale, service, and consumption of alcoholic beverages.

For many Europeans, this social consciousness-raising seems peculiar. Most European countries have long-standing laws imposing tough penalties for drinking and driving. European laws do not place blame for alcohol abuse on the seller and server of alcohol, but on the consumer who gets behind the wheel of a car after drinking too much. "Designated-driver" programs were new to the United States in the 1980s, but in Europe, children have grown up using this concept as a matter of simple common sense. U.S. drinking-age laws make the consumption of alcohol a rite of passage into adulthood. And since it is human nature to want what you can't have, problems with underage drinking are more common in the United States than in Europe.

The realization of high profits in beverage operations throughout the world carries with it a serious responsibility. National and international hospitality companies alike are working hard to ensure that professional, responsible behavior is maintained by their bar personnel.[1] A need exists for different types of management methods and emphases in this new era of social consciousness. Profitability is still feasible, but no longer by selling alcohol in *quantity*. The focus in the 1990s is on *quality* products and services, offered from a guest-oriented perspective. Management of quality, as opposed to management of volume, requires a new approach—a practical approach—to bar and beverage management. This chapter introduces some traditional management functions and suggests a practical focus, in addition to providing an overview of the bar and beverage business.

The Bar and Beverage Business

Bar and beverage operations belong to that vast group of organizations called *business enterprises*. All businesses have organizational goals and perform many functions to achieve them. Not all, however, have the same organizational goals, nor do they function in the same way to achieve their goals. Some businesses are *production* enterprises, engaged solely in the production of goods. Others can be classified as *marketing* enterprises, in that they see that goods are transported to markets where they can be distributed for use by various consumer groups. A third type of business is the *service* enterprise—one that provides such services as communications, surgery, car repairs, and so on. In limited economies, production enterprises assume major importance, but as societies advance technologically, marketing and service businesses assume greater importance.

To which segment would a bar or beverage operation belong? Production? Marketing? Service? The answer: all of these. All bar and beverage operations are engaged in production in that they transform materials into products for sale. They are engaged in marketing to ensure that potential guests know about the products and services they offer. They are engaged in merchandising and selling to ensure that their products are offered to their guests. And they are engaged in service to see that their products are served to the guests.

The three-sided nature of bar and beverage operations can and does cause problems in managing them. To manage a bar or beverage operation successfully, one must be proficient in producing products on demand, merchandising and selling these perishable products, and providing service that meets or exceeds guest expectations. Sometimes management might be proficient in one or two of these areas but be completely lacking in others, and the operation fails.

To better understand bar and beverage management today, a brief review of some milestones in the history of the beverage industry is in order. (Chapter 12 contains a more detailed review.)

A Brief History

It was after the Norman Conquest (1066) that the brewing of ale became something of an industry in England. Abbeys and monasteries typically maintained breweries that catered to their own communities. The first taverns were born on trade routes such as existing roads and waterways. One of the duties of the very early abbeys and monasteries was to provide refreshments and shelter for the travelers. Guest houses, and then annexes to the guest houses, were built to meet the increasing number of guests. These annexes (or inns) served ale or wine as the primary refreshment. Soon, in addition to serving the traveler, they were being used as meeting places for local residents. Hence, the beginning of the bar's use as a center for social activity and entertainment.

Taverns were built in the United States after the colonists settled. These taverns were at the peak of their popularity at the end of the eighteenth century and well into the nineteenth century. But as transportation modes shifted from stagecoach to railroads and steamships, the tavern's clientele dwindled. As the tavern's importance diminished, the temperance movement—an anti-alcoholic beverage crusade—began.

Prohibition—which banned all sales of alcoholic beverages—was legislated in 1920 and lasted for some thirteen years, with disastrous results. Crime abounded, with gangsters moving in to take over this massive industry. Speakeasies—private, secret clubs where liquor could be purchased and consumed—were part of this illegal, underground activity. Enforcement of Prohibition became impossible, and crime rates soared. In 1933, Prohibition was repealed.

During the 1970s and '80s, the beverage industry grew. Alcoholic beverage sales were the primary reason for the financial success of many restaurants. Demographic influences changed the market of many bar and beverage operations. A rise in the number of dual-income families and women in the workplace meant more disposable income. People were staying single longer and having fewer children (or none at all), which resulted in increased leisure time.

Patrons became more knowledgeable at an earlier age and became more assertive in their requests for specific brands. In the 1980s more than half of all drinks ordered were specified call brands, and premium brands became popular. Quality, image, and recognition became critical factors in our guests' decision about which products and drinks to order. The guest was able to recognize quality and was willing to pay for it.

The 1980s also saw an increase in the promotion and popularity of the white goods category of spirits—vodka, rum, tequila, and gin. Vodka was the leader, with imports from Russia, Finland, and Poland carrying particular appeal.

Bar and beverage operations flourished, increasing in numbers and in types.

Today's bars bear little resemblance to this Lansing, Michigan, bar circa 1950. (Courtesy of the State of Michigan Archives)

Types of Bar and Beverage Operations

Classifying bar and beverage operations is not an easy task because there can be so many combinations of features and so much overlap among the various types. Perhaps a broad classification is one using the groupings bars and lounges. There are various differences among the operations in each of these broad categories. There are even other names for these categories; that is, bars may be pubs, taverns, saloons, and so on. Let's take a closer look.

Bars. There are upscale bars, downscale bars, and many types within and at each end of the range. There are bars that serve beverages only, with some offering such snacks as peanuts, pretzels, and chips. Some bars serve a limited food menu, with beverages as their primary offering. There are bars whose trade is local and whose guests are "regulars" who visit often. Bars such as these are gathering places, where good camaraderie and companionship are as much a merchandising factor as the product sold.

There are bars on busy streets and in other areas where passersby can drop in for a beverage. Hotels often have these types of bars (in addition to others) available to guests of the hotel, as well as to individuals not staying at the hotel. Airport bars are similar—sometimes offering only very limited seating in addition to standing room at the bar.

Sports bars and piano bars offer something besides drinks—sports on wide-screen TV, for example, and music played by a pianist who may also sing or lead sing-alongs. Currently, some bars are featuring another type of musical entertainment provided by a Karaoke, which looks like a jukebox and produces recorded backup music for guests who want to sing.

Above: **A casual bar/lounge with a friendly atmosphere.** (Courtesy of Opryland Hotel, Nashville, Tennessee)

Upper right: **A bar/lounge featuring food service and a sprightly decor.** (Courtesy of Strongbow Inn, Valparaiso, Indiana)

Lower right: **A lounge with a club-like atmosphere.** (Courtesy of Stouffer Hotels and Resorts)

Additionally, we have service bars that are operated only to fill orders for beverages to be taken to guests in dining rooms. Mobile bars are often used for receptions and parties. They carry with them a limited amount of stock and can be moved to any location where service is needed. You might even see such a unit in a hotel lobby. Another type of mobile service bar is that used on airplanes.

Other types of bars and bar service include in-room mini-bars in hotels, hotel room service, and recreational bars (those serving golf courses, bowling alleys, and the like).

There is a trend today toward specialty bars—units that serve only a certain type of drink. Thus, there are wine bars where only wine is sold. Some offer a hundred or more wines, including very expensive ones. Beer bars also exist, serving a wide variety of different beers.

Lounges. Lounges differ from bars in that they usually provide space for more tables and chairs and are usually better furnished, often being geared to serve a more sophisticated or upscale type of guest. However, these differences may not always hold; it may be difficult to differentiate a bar from a lounge. Some lounges have a bar where guests can stand or sit and

A luxury dining room featuring opulent settings and complete wine service. (Courtesy of the Willard Hotel, Washington, D.C.)

Nightclubs are lounges with special features. Spectacular lighting and theatrical color add pizzazz to Tremors!, a Livonia, Michigan, nightclub. (Courtesy of Holiday Inn Livonia West, Livonia, Michigan)

Cocktail service in a hotel lobby lounge. (Courtesy of Opryland Hotel, Nashville, Tennessee)

obtain beverages. The tables and chairs provided may be somewhat incidental to the bar business.

Lounges may exist alone, their primary purpose being to serve beverages to guests; but many lounges are combined with a food service operation and exist to complement the dining experience with the service of beverages in a separate area. Thus, a lounge may be placed near the entrance to a restaurant so guests can drop in and have beverages before going on to dine.

Some lounges are very luxuriously furnished and have beautifully designed interiors. They may have soft lighting or rather spectacular displays of lighting or other merchandising features. They may have a dance floor and provide music or some other type of entertainment. Again, these features may not be too different from those of some bars. A bar in an exclusive club may be as beautifully furnished and as well designed as a lounge, but, on the whole, what is indicated here as typical will be true of most lounges. You will read more about the interior design of bar and beverage operations in Chapter 3.

Keep in mind that the terms we use to define operations may be interchangeable with others. Throughout this text, we have used the term **bar and beverage operations** to include all possible combinations of establishments serving alcoholic beverages. When we use the term bar *or* beverage operation, it simply means that one operation is not a bar and beverage operation; it is either a bar, or it is a beverage operation—in other words, a lounge.

Bar and beverage operations are defined by their goals and the type of guests they seek to serve. They are greatly influenced by alcohol consumption patterns.

Alcohol Consumption Patterns

Alcohol consumption patterns have been changing throughout the world since the late 1980s. The primary trends have been a distinct decrease in the consumption of hard liquor, and an increase in requests for premium brands of liquor.[2] In general, throughout the world, people seem to be drinking less, but demanding a higher quality in the spirits they consume. The per capita U.S. consumption of distilled spirits in 1986 was the lowest (at 0.85 gallon per individual) since 1959 when consumption per individual was 0.84 gallon.[3] Simultaneously, there has been a switch to alcoholic beverages with lower alcohol content. This trend includes not only wine coolers and light beer, but "light" whiskey as well. A relatively new product, light whiskey contains one-third the alcohol content and one-third the calories of its "hard" counterparts, with a reduction in proof from 80 to 54.[4]

The popularity of the "white goods" category of spirits continues, particularly with respect to the popularity of imports. Much of this popularity can be attributed to the worldwide focus on Eastern bloc countries. The tearing down of the Berlin wall stimulated an interest in products from these countries that was without precedent. Products experiencing recent surges in popularity include Absolut Citron vodka, Bombay Sapphire gin, and Hiram Walker Red Hot schnapps.[5] Consumers no longer order vodka and tonic, but Absolut and tonic. The image of drinking and drinking establishments must now be upscale to be successful. Consumers are looking for taste in their alcoholic beverages, not just a strong kick.

This emphasis on quality means it is more important than ever for bar and beverage managers to know the products they serve. Product knowledge is so important to management success that Chapters 12 through 16 of this text have been devoted to it. No operation can succeed for any length of time by serving poor-quality beverages. Sooner or later, patronage will decline and guests will go to competing establishments where quality beverages are served. In today's market, patrons are especially sensitive to quality and often will pay more for it.

Managing Bar and Beverage Operations

The purpose of this text is to present material that will lead to the successful management of bar and beverage operations in the dynamic marketplace of the 1990s and beyond. Any framework for understanding management requires a knowledge of the basic functions of management and how they are interrelated.

What Is Management?

Management is variously defined. One definition is, "Management is an operational process involving the functions of planning, organizing, staffing, leading, and controlling to achieve goals."[6] Another definition is, "Management is achieving goals through people." No manager achieves the goals of a business on his or her own. A manager must direct and lead people to these goals.

In addition to planning, organizing, staffing, leading, and controlling, the basic functions of management often include coordinating and evaluating. It is important to note that these functions are not entirely separate and not always sequential; they are closely interrelated and often overlap.

Planning. One of the first things that must be done in setting up a management system for a bar or beverage operation is to establish organizational goals and operational objectives. Achieving these goals and objectives is the reason for the enterprise's existence. Goals and objectives must be realistic, measurable, and within cost parameters. The management system must be devised to reach these goals and objectives.

Once goals and objectives are established, the major management function of planning begins. **Planning** entails consideration of all resources available and their limitations. Basic resources of a bar and beverage operation include people, money, products, time, procedures, energy, and equipment. All are in limited supply.

Planning is often said to be the establishment of a road map that offers the best route to goal and objective achievement. An important part of planning is to see that a proper atmosphere exists so that the staff can perform at its best. Proper planning is also required in establishing how the other management functions are to operate to support the accomplishment of goals and objectives. Thus, planning is an essential component of all the other management functions, especially control.[7] Any failure in planning can show up quickly in operational functioning. Unplanned activities or programs cannot be controlled. Plans must cover long-range and short-range periods, with short-range plans leading to long-range plans.

Part of planning is establishing strategies, policies, procedures, and rules to guide future actions. A strategy indicates a general program of action and the resources that are allocated to support it. Policies are needed to support an operation's goals, objectives, and strategies. Policies should be designed to encourage individual discretion and initiative. Every bar and beverage operation should have written policies and procedures that should be well communicated to the entire staff. Procedures define precise actions and often support policies. Thus, a policy may state that gratuities, in whatever form, will not be accepted from purveyors. A procedure may indicate how such an offer must be handled and how it must be documented or reported. Other procedures indicate how work should be performed.

Functionality of the bar itself is a consideration that must be addressed during the planning stages. (Courtesy of Opryland Hotel, Nashville, Tennessee)

One of the simplest kinds of plans is a rule. Procedures are often groups of rules. An example of a rule might be no smoking on the job. Often, the infraction of a rule requires counteraction. Thus, the first time an employee is caught smoking in a restricted area, a warning might be required, while a second offense might entail a reprimand, and a third may require a discharge. Policies, procedures, and rules form the basis of control systems in bar and beverage operations. Such policies and procedures are discussed at length in Chapters 9 and 10.

One of the most prominent examples of planning in the fiscal area is the budget (management's plan for income and expenditures). There may also be a labor budget that allocates labor resources to specific periods and times in specific amounts. Any budget is limiting in that it establishes parameters for the amount of resources that can be used. Thus, an expenditure budget will specify the amount of money to be spent over a given period for materials, supplies, labor, and other resources.

Planning requires management's active participation. A bar or beverage operation without adequate planning is like a ship adrift in the sea without a rudder; there is no steering mechanism to get the ship to where it must go.

Organizing. An adequate organizational scheme must be set up for a bar or beverage operation if the operation is to function smoothly. **Organizing** is the process of assembling resources and determining the flow of authority and communication. Good organization encourages teamwork and a dynamic operation that moves toward the accomplishment of goals and objectives. Good organization makes the management process easier because the staff members know their jobs and how to do them. The kind of organization established is a result of planning. Planning determines the menu, the amount of business, the type of guests, and the level of service.

Coordinating. Coordinating is the function of using resources efficiently to meet organizational goals and objectives. Assigning tasks and seeing that they are performed correctly and on time are examples of coordinating.

Staffing. Staffing is the recruitment and hiring of employees. Staffing is covered in detail in Chapter 7, which deals with the management of human resources. The importance of finding the right person to fill each job is stressed, as well as the importance of training techniques. Proper staffing means that the people you hire will be able to grow with the organization and support its goals and objectives. Careful selection of your staff is of primary importance. Good selection and training pay off with good performance, which leads to higher retention. Another positive effect of proper staffing is an improvement in service and selling (discussed in Chapter 6), which leads to greater guest satisfaction. Staffing is also a critical management function because it relates directly to maintaining a high level of social responsibility.

Leading. Leading is often defined as "the process of influencing people so they willingly and enthusiastically strive towards the achievement of organizational goals."[8] Leadership is often said to be "followership."

We define a good leader in a business enterprise as one who not only leads and directs but also motivates employees to take specific actions. There is a noticeable trend today toward giving as much authority and responsibility as possible to employees, letting them take the lead. Such a practice relieves management of much responsibility, placing it where the problems really arise and need to be resolved. Action is quicker.

A good leader understands that there are human needs besides money, such as security, companionship, and recognition. The social and physical environment of the workplace is an important component in employee satisfaction and performance. People need to achieve their own personal goals as well as those of the enterprise. Anyone that seeks to lead people should be conversant with some of the major motivational theories.[9] Good leadership is not an inborn trait but an acquired one that needs developing and culturing.

Controlling. The management function of **controlling** has more than one meaning. In one sense, it is the protection of assets and income. In another, it is "the measurement and correction of the performance of activities of subordinates . . . to make sure that all levels of objectives and the plans devised to attain them are being accomplished."[10] A simpler definition is that control is the correction of deviations from standards. This means standards must be established. Examples of standards are those for labor cost or ingredient cost. If the accounting data show we are on target for a standard established for labor or ingredient cost, no action is needed; if there is a significant deviation, management action is required.

A *standard* is a measure with which we compare other things to see if they equal, exceed, or fail to measure up to it. There are many standards in the world. The hour is one, and this standard is maintained in Greenwich, England.

Managers should attempt to establish as many standards as possible. Standards of performance are of benefit to management and workers alike. Performance standards give workers an objective measure of how they are performing.

A Practical Approach

Today's emphasis on quality instead of volume provides new opportunities for the bar or beverage manager. Quality concerns extend beyond the products themselves to the proper ambience, equipment, glassware, and accessories (these topics are discussed in more detail in Chapter 4). Offering high quality in both products and services should stimulate sales figures without increasing guest count or consumption. For the creative bar or beverage manager who truly understands his or her target market, guest check averages do not have to decrease because of the change in consumption patterns.

Bar and beverage managers in the 1990s must look at new ways of marketing and promoting services, alcoholic and non-alcoholic beverages, and other products. (A discussion of the importance of marketing can be found in Chapter 8.)

Guests whose alcohol awareness levels have been raised may be uncomfortable ordering that third drink—some may even hesitate at ordering a second. A single guest who, five years ago, might have ordered a bottle of wine with his or her meal might now order half a carafe, or merely a glass or two. Bar and beverage managers must learn new methods for maintaining their beverage profit margin in an environment which is saying "less, not more" with respect to the consumption of alcoholic products (see Exhibits 1.1 and 1.2).

As a result of these trends, a new and perhaps more practical approach to bar and beverage management must be learned. It is an approach in which every management function, decision, and action must be implemented from the perspective of the guest. This is not a new approach at all, you may be saying to yourself. We agree; not new in theory, but new in practice in the bar and beverage industry, where the traditional approach has been "the more booze poured, the better for the operation." In the 1990s and into the next century, the successful bar and beverage managers will be those who do what is best for the guest.

Rising to the challenge of management from the perspective of the guest will require creativity, a willingness to take risks, and an ability to forget about management solely from the perspective of the operation. It does not mean that bar and beverage operations will no longer be profitable. Rather, profitability will result from non-traditional management styles. What worked previously in a *quantity-focused* management approach will not work toward profitability in a *quality-focused* consumer environment.

Marketing and Control

While researching this text, we repeatedly heard that bar and beverage management consisted of marketing and controlling. Furthermore, food and beverage directors explained that every other management function could be related to one or both of these activities.

Marketing starts as a pre-operative management function and, through promotion and merchandising, carries over into the operative arena. The

Exhibit 1.1   Manufacturer's Ad Promoting Profitability of Non-Alcoholic Products

Courtesy of Blanks Non-Alcoholic Products Co.

operative elements of bar and beverage management focus on controls. Control functions are developed and implemented throughout the purchasing and cash-handling processes. (These topics are covered in Chapters 9 and 10.) And, of course, a critical control arena is "the legal jungle" (Chapter 11).

Successful bar and beverage managers will need to convey this non-traditional management approach to their staffs. Employees will need to

Exhibit 1.2 Non-Alcoholic Drink Recipes

Blanks Non-Alcoholic Drink Recipes

Blanks Creamsicle
1 oz	Blanks Non-Alcoholic Triple Sec
2 oz	Orange Juice
1 Scoop	Vanilla Ice Cream
1 oz	Cream or Milk

Blend ingredients until consistency of a shake. Serve in Stemmed glass. Garnish with Orange Slice.

Blanks Margarita
2 oz	Blanks Non-Alcoholic Triple Sec
3/4 oz	Sweet & Sour Mix
1/2 Cup	Ice

Blend ingredients until smooth, serve in Margarita glass, that has been rimmed with salt. Garnish with Lime Slice.

Blanks New Years Punchbowl
1 Liter	Blanks Non-Alcoholic Peach Schnapps
1 Quart	Orange Juice
1 Quart	Pineapple Juice
1 750ml	Ariel Non-Alcoholic Brut Champagne

Combine ingredients in Punchbowl, float ice ring and slices of orange. (Serves 20)

Blanks Cappacino
1 1/2oz	Blanks Non-Alcoholic Peppermint Schnapps
4 oz	Hot Chocolate
1/4 tsp	Instant coffee
Dollop	Whipped cream

Combine ingredients in stemmed mug. top with whipped cream and shaved chocolate.

Blanks Hot Peppermint Patty
1 1/2 oz	Blanks Non-Alcoholic Peppermint Schnapps
4 oz	Hot Chocolate
Dollop	Whipped Cream

Combine in a mug, top with whipped cream . OPTIONAL: add shaved chocolate.

Blanks Coffee Amaretto
1 1/2 oz	Blanks Non-Alcoholic Amaretto
5 oz	Hot Coffee
Dollop	Whipped Cream

Combine in a mug, top with whipped cream . OPTIONAL: add shaved chocolate.

Blanks Long Island Iced Tea
1 1/2 oz	Blanks Non-Alcoholic Peach Schnapps
1/2 oz	Blanks Non-Alcoholic Triple Sec
1/2 oz	Sweet & Sour Mix
2oz	7 up (or Diet 7up)

Fill with Cola (or diet Cola)

Combine ingredients in tall glass over ice. Garnish with a wedge of lemon.

Blanks Fuzzy Navel
1 1/2 oz	Blanks Non-Alcoholic Peach Schnapps
4 oz	Orange Juice

Combine over ice in rocks glass.

Blanks Pineapple Paradise
2oz	Blanks Non-Alcoholic Peach Schnapps
1oz	Pineapple Juice
1 scoop	Vanilla Ice cream

Blend ingredients until smooth, serve in tall glass, garnish with peach slice.

Blanks Mai-Tai
1 1/2oz	Blanks Non-Alcoholic Peach Schnapps
4 oz	Pineapple Juice

Combine over ice in tall glass. Garnish with Pineapple spear .

Blanks Woo-Woo
1 1/2 oz	Blanks Non-Alcoholic Peach Schnapps
3 oz	Cranberry Juice

Combine ingredients over ice in rocks glass.

Blanks Strawberry Margarita
2oz	Blanks Non-Alcoholic Strawberry Schnapps
1/2oz	Sweet & Sour Mix
1/2 cup	Ice

Blend ingredients with ice until smooth, serve in Margarita glass rimmed in sugar. Garnish with strawberry.

Blanks Strawberry Mai-Tai
2 oz	Blanks Non-Alcoholic Strawberry Schnapps
4 oz	Pineapple Juice
1/2 cup	Ice

Blend ingredients until smooth, serve in tall glass. Garnish with a fresh Strawberry or Pineapple spear.

Blanks Oreo Mint Cream
2 oz	Blanks Non-Alcoholic Peppermint Schnapps
1 regular	Oreo Cookie
1 scoop	Vanilla Ice Cream
2 oz	Milk

Blend ingredients until smooth, serve in Stemmed glass. Garnish with another Oreo Cookie.

Blanks Chocolate Quake
Winner-Third Place
1989-Minnesota AAA Zero-Proof Mix-off
1 oz	Blanks Non-Alcoholic Peppermint Schnapps
1 Scoop	Vanilla Ice Cream
1 Tsp	Chocolate Syrup
1 oz	Cream or Milk

Blend ingredients until consistency of smooth shake, and pour into Stemmed glass. Garnish with Whipped Cream, Chocolate Shavings and a Peppermint Stick.

Blanks Amaretto Stone Sour
1 1/2 oz	Blanks Non-Alcoholic Amaretto
4 oz	Orange Juice

Combine ingredients over ice in rocks glass. Garnish with Orange Slice.

Courtesy of Blanks Non-Alcoholic Products Co.

be able to take the initiative in satisfying guest needs. Innovative approaches to the services and products offered will be the key to future growth in the beverage industry.

Beverage operations can no longer depend on serving only alcohol. Hard work and long hours are no longer the sole requirements for success; rather, a thorough understanding of your target market is needed to take full advantage of every selling opportunity.

From a marketing perspective, the ultimate goal of the bar or beverage operation is guest satisfaction. This goal is met by providing products and services that satisfy guest needs, thereby gaining an advantage over competitors. What are the basics that today's guest is looking for? Quality, value, and service from an operation that conducts business in a socially responsible and acceptable manner.

The Future

The future of bar and beverage management promises to be both exciting and challenging. The management of beverage sales will focus on a guest-oriented perspective. The guests who will return to your operation are those who leave happy and feeling positive about their experiences. An operation's ability to generate a profit will revolve around its ability to provide quality, value, and service to its guests. Innovation will be a key factor in success if we are to combat the neoprohibitionists, as well as proposed increases in liquor taxes.

We asked some leaders in the food and beverage industry for some of their ideas on what the bar and beverage industry will be like in the year 2000. Here are their predictions:

Jean-Paul Barat, Food and Beverage Director, Walt Disney World Swan, tells us:

- Beverage managers will have to be more knowledgeable about wines as consumers become more sophisticated in wine selection.

- Beverage managers will have to become marketing-oriented as the industry becomes more competitive and the customer more demanding.

- Beverage alcohol sales will continue to slump. Bar managers will have to turn up the food sales to satisfy customers who are demonstrating more and more that their appetite is as important as their thirst and usually more so.

Rene Bardel, Divisional Director of Food and Beverage, The Continental Companies, believes:

- The top beverage establishments will be regarded more as entertainment and recreational facilities, as opposed to bars and nightclubs.

- Light cocktails utilizing one-half the alcohol in full-size drinks will be commonplace.

- The revoking of liquor licenses from irresponsible operators will be far more prevalent.

Claude Boudoux, Regional Director of Food and Beverage, Hilton Hotels, says:

Laws concerning misuse of alcohol will be much stricter. [There will be] tighter controls in governing liquors, i.e., lowering the BAC to .05%, resulting in more care and control on the part of the beverage industry in servicing the needs of the public.
The challenge will be how to increase revenues in the marketplace through creative and strategic concepts while maintaining profitability.

From Mike Kranz, Director of Food and Beverage, Fontainebleau Hilton:

- Wines will continue to rise in popularity. The two most popular varietals, Chardonnay and Cabernet Sauvignon, will probably peak-out soon and other varietals will become more predominant.

- Low-calorie beers will gain a greater share in total consumption because people will continue to want the enjoyment of it without putting on too much extra weight.

- Drinking and driving standards will probably become more severe over the next ten years, inducing the public to consume more lower-alcohol beverages.

Roger McAleese, Director of Support Services, Opryland Hotel, states:

Beverage managers will be more knowledgeable concerning the importance of proper human resources. Selective hiring will be important because of a lack of available people from which to pull. Managers will not only be looking for qualified candidates, but candidates who are eager to establish a career in beverage management.

Beverage managers will be more knowledgeable concerning the importance of beverage awareness, the legislation and laws regarding alcoholic beverages, and their ramifications. Beverage management will keep abreast of legislation concerning alcohol consumption and its use and abuse.

Beverage managers will be more creative in dollars and cents and profitability of beverages. . . . The need to be more cautious and critical to capture revenues from the declining market will be urgent.

Social impacts and trends will be important to better manage our resources . . . from people to capital to responsibilities that will be dealt with by the year 2000.

George Cashmark, Stouffer Hotels and Resorts, says:

- Alcohol consumption will continue to go down, especially dark liquors.

- Consumers will continue to request premium wines and liquors (drink better but less).

- Beers, especially premium, will continue to increase in popularity.

And finally, Paul E. Wise, Director and Professor, University of Delaware, predicts that:

Industry technology will retain the taste of distilled spirits but concurrently reduce the alcoholic content (proof). Wine products will emphasize the taste complexities of varietals and also reduce their alcoholic content. Brewed products will reduce caloric and alcoholic levels.

Operators must look more carefully through their guests' eyes. People still need a reason to meet and socialize and will search for fresh new opportunities. Consequently, *entertainment in some form or shape will continue to be the foundation for building a beverage business.* Today it might be "sports bars," "Star in Your Song," or some old idea brought back to life. A basic marketing premise is that people will always have a need to socialize—management must look through the guests' eyes to discover their needs and wants.

Drunkenness will not be a socially acceptable outcome of an evening at the local bar, lounge, or home.

Good management has taken on a new meaning as we approach the turn of the century. Improved marketing and operational techniques, which will be discussed throughout this text, will be essential. Care must be taken in the planning functions to ensure that means are established to achieve the goals of the bar or beverage enterprise.

Endnotes

1. Madelin Schneider, "Raise Profits, Reduce Risks in Selling Alcoholic Drinks," *Hotels* 23 (#11, 1989): 64.

2. Schneider, 62.

3. "U.S. Consumption of Distilled Spirits Hits 27-Year Low," *Wall Street Journal* CCXIV (#103, 1989): A6B.

4. Thomas R. King, "Seagram Taking 'Light' Whiskey to All of U.S.," *Wall Street Journal* CCXV (#79, 1990): B1, B6.

5. "New Brands Show Promising Performance in '89," *Impact*, 19 (#8, 1989): 1.

6. Harold Koontz, Cyril O'Donnell, and Heinz Weinrich, *Management*, 9th ed. (New York: McGraw-Hill, 1988).

7. For additional information on the functions of planning and control, see Jack D. Ninemeier, *Planning and Control for Food and Beverage Operations,* 3d ed. (East Lansing, Mich.: Educational Institute of the American Hotel & Motel Association, 1991).

8. Koontz et al.

9. For information on motivational theories, see Raphael R. Kavanaugh and Jack D. Ninemeier, *Supervision in the Hospitality Industry*, 2d ed. (East Lansing, Mich.: Educational Institute of the American Hotel & Motel Association, 1991), 219–230; and Rocco M. Angelo and Andrew N. Vladimir, *Hospitality Today: An Introduction* (East Lansing, Mich.: Educational Institute of the American Hotel & Motel Association, 1991), 223–229, 267–272.

10. Koontz et al.

Key Terms

bar and beverage operations
controlling
coordinating
leading

management
organizing
planning
staffing

Discussion Questions

1. How did the organization of MADD affect bar and beverage management?

2. How do bar and beverage operations qualify as production, marketing, and service enterprises?

3. Why is it difficult to categorize bar and beverage operations?

4. What are some of the current trends in alcohol consumption?

5. How would you define management?

6. What are the major functions of management?

Social Concerns and Management

Chapter Outline

A Few Definitions
Responsibility in Today's Alcohol Market
    Off-Hour Sales
    Serving Alcohol to Minors
    Service Involving Intoxication or Alcohol Dependents
Third-Party Liability
    A Brief History
Changing Drinking Patterns
Health Concerns
    Physical Effects
The Industry's Response
Serving Alcohol with Care
    The Effects of Alcohol
        Black Coffee and Cold Showers
    Alcohol and Other Drugs
    Approaches to Server Intervention
    Monitoring Drinks
        Special Considerations for the Open Bar

Bar and beverage management has changed dramatically in the last several decades, especially in the United States. It has become more than just providing alcoholic beverages to a public that wants to be served. Growing social concerns about the problems caused by improper alcohol consumption have forced the industry to change its management style and to take steps to see that abuses in consumption do not occur. These concerns have become such an important factor influencing management style that we devote an entire chapter to this topic. In addition, much of the U.S. legal environment discussed in Chapter 11 is closely related to this topic.

Although much of what we discuss in this chapter portrays the potentially negative aspects of alcohol use, do not lose sight of the many positive attributes of alcohol. Alcoholic beverages go well with many foods and can do much to grace a meal. Social drinking is associated with conviviality, friendship, and fraternity. "Sharing the cup" has long been a symbol of hospitality between host and guest and among family and friends. Alcohol is often an important part of religious ceremonies and celebrations such as weddings, holidays, and birthdays. In moderate amounts, alcohol promotes relaxation and comfort. Sometimes, it is actually used medicinally to produce these effects. Alcohol also carries the active ingredients in many medicines. There is some evidence that a moderate amount of alcohol each day can reduce the chance of heart problems.[1] In addition, the alcohol industry is an important sector of our economy. Many people gain their livelihoods from it, and other industries, such as lodging and food service, find the sale of alcoholic beverages an important source of income.

Still, social concerns about the costs of irresponsible alcohol consumption are growing. These social concerns and the actions springing from them have sparked a movement to clearly define the responsibilities of those serving alcohol. Management must assume a leading role in discharging these responsibilities; it should understand the problems and how to cope with them. Policies and procedures must be defined, and employees should be knowledgeable about them and their use. Beverage servers should understand alcohol's physical effects and be able to detect overdrinking and problems caused by it. Such an understanding enables those serving alcohol to make that service a more positive experience.

Servers should also understand their own role in seeing that alcohol is served responsibly. Although we will focus on legal issues in Chapter 11, in this chapter we will look specifically at issues surrounding the responsibility and potential liability of both businesses and individual employees with regard to alcohol service.

This chapter examines the major problems arising out of social concerns that those serving alcoholic beverages to the public face today. It describes ways to detect and handle minors who want to be served. It looks at what the beverage service and alcohol industries are doing to promote greater responsibility in the service of alcoholic beverages. It then discusses how to recognize intoxication, how to monitor guests' alcohol consumption, and how to handle situations when intoxication occurs. Further, it seeks to present briefly some of the reasons these social concerns have arisen and the costs to society that underlie these concerns.

Please note that this chapter does not summarize the law in any specific state or community. You should be aware of all federal, state, and local laws and regulations in your area relating to alcohol distribution and service.

A Few Definitions

Before we continue, though, we need to define some terms that are commonly used in describing those who consume alcohol. Because of confusion about how to categorize those who drink alcohol, the government, the medical profession, and others who deal with problems relating to alcohol consumption have established definitions for certain terms. Although not all authorities use them, these general terms are often used.

An *abstainer* is a person who has not consumed any alcohol for at least a year. A *light drinker* is a person who consumes less than 0.22 of an ounce of 100% alcohol per day. A *moderate drinker* consumes an average of 0.22 to 0.99 of an ounce of 100% alcohol per day. A *heavy drinker* consumes an average of 1.0 ounce or more of 100% alcohol per day.[2]

Drinking over a long period of time can lead to *alcohol dependence.* There are several forms of alcohol dependence. One is the inability to stop drinking until intoxicated. Another is the compulsive need to have a drink at a certain time of day. Yet another is binge drinking; a binge drinker may abstain for months and then drink heavily for days. Alcohol dependence is a disease that can be controlled by physical and psychological therapy. About 6% of all people who consume alcohol develop alcohol dependence over a period of time.

Alcohol abusers are those who, while not manifesting dependence, experience negative social and personal consequences following alcohol use—arrest, accidents, spouse or child abuse, poor job performance, illness, or difficulties with others in personal relationships. *Alcoholism* is the evidence of the beginning of dependence or of actual dependence. An estimated 19 million people over 18 years old suffer from it.[3]

Responsibility in Today's Alcohol Market

Today, there are three primary legal concerns with regard to alcohol service:

1. Off-hour sales/service

2. The sale/service of alcoholic beverages to minors

3. The sale/service of alcoholic beverages leading to intoxication and the sale/service to those known to be alcohol dependents

We will spend much of this chapter discussing the last problem. Let's start, though, by briefly examining the first two.

Off-Hour Sales

Off-hour sales is the easiest of the three problems to control. Hours when the sale of alcoholic beverages is legal are well known. Employees selling them at other times are deliberately violating the law. Such sales are usually made by employees seeking to make some extra money—for example, a hotel bellhop providing a "special" service to a guest who wants a drink during off hours.

A responsible enterprise should have little difficulty in controlling this problem. Management should set up and enforce policies and rules prohibiting it. Bellhops or others who might engage in such activities should

---

State level action urged to curb underage drinking

With surveys revealing that college students under the legal drinking age of 21 are more likely than legal-age students to drink alcoholic beverages, the National Restaurant Association believes every state should have laws against age misrepresentation and should impose reasonable punishment for infractions.

"The onus needs to shift from the restaurant operator to the true offender—the minor who tries to obtain alcoholic beverages under false pretenses," says outgoing association President Harris "Bud" Rusitzky.

*   *   *

The association takes the position that state laws either do not penalize users of false IDs at all, or mandate penalties that are so stiff, such as heavy fines and lengthy imprisonment, that judges refrain from imposing them on minors.

The association is urging legislators in each state to introduce laws against misrepresenting age, with a penalty of suspension of the offender's driver's license for a period of not less than 90 days. It also urges stricter laws governing producers of false identification for minors, calling for jail sentences and/or fines.

Nine states have no laws that penalize age falsification to purchase alcohol. In 18 states and the District of Columbia, there are statutes that include use of false identification. In 23 states, use of false identification is against the law, but penalties are so severe they are seldom imposed.

Source: *Restaurant Show Daily*, May 20, 1990. Courtesy of *Food Management Magazine*, Cleveland, Ohio.

be monitored. House liquor supplies should be put under lock immediately after closing. Storage areas should not be opened until needed for operation. Employees may try to bring in their own liquor and store it in their lockers or elsewhere. Good observation can detect this. A nearby liquor store can also be watched to see that employees do not slip out and purchase alcohol to sell later.

If employees break this law, they should be disciplined or discharged. A firm policy should take care of the problem.

Serving Alcohol to Minors

In most states, minors bear some legal responsibility for falsifying records to misrepresent their age. Nonetheless, minors often misrepresent their age, and their ingenuity in trying to escape detection should not be discounted. Detection and refusal is a challenge to those providing alcohol.

All states have minimum age standards for alcoholic beverage service. Most, if not all, states now set the legal age at 21. It is important to know your state's or locality's age restrictions if you serve alcohol to the public. It is also important that you check ages when in doubt. This involves knowing how to check various documents such as driver's licenses (including international licenses), government or military ID cards, passports, and certain privately issued documents. These identifying documents usually have the individuals' picture on them. Documents without pictures or dates—such as student IDs, birth certificates, or Social Security cards—should not be accepted.

Some IDs use a special characteristic to indicate that a person is a minor. This may be a different colored card or background, a different kind of picture, or words such as "under 21," "minor," or "provisional."

Minors frequently offer falsified documents—documents which have been altered or are counterfeits of genuine ones. Sometimes minors offer a borrowed, stolen, or purchased document as proof of age. Those responsible for checking and verifying should know that the law is often strict. Careless or inadequate checking is sure to cause serious problems for the operation. Some states will excuse a server and an operation if a minor presents a seemingly valid document that is accepted; others will not. Some states have strict laws but do not enforce them.

There are a number of things to look for to verify authenticity. Look for erasures and changes of numerals or other data; some IDs have figures pasted over the correct ones. Take the card and examine it carefully. Look for new data or a newly laminated picture superimposed over old lamination. New lamination can be detected by the presence of a raised surface. Minors sometimes splice information into the original card; you can often detect this by holding the card up to a light and checking for outlines around the splice. Documents with sloppy graphics or substandard lamination should be suspect.

It is not unusual to see manufactured ID cards. On some college campuses, a thriving business exists for making such cards, and they can be extremely difficult to detect. Look for faulty printing, poor photography, incorrect wording, or other telltale signs. A familiarity with authentic IDs will help you to spot these fakes quickly.

An ID frequently gives some description of the person. Does this match the individual offering the ID? Many IDs use the person's birthday as the expiration date. While holding the card, ask the person what date his or her birthday falls on. Minors who have borrowed or stolen IDs often fail to memorize the information on them. Suspect individuals can be asked questions about age, address, ZIP code, birth year, graduation year from high school, and so forth. These should be answered without hesitation. At times, it may be desirable to ask for a second ID or to ask the person to sign his or her name so you can compare the signature with the one on the ID.

Sometimes detection is difficult because some minors appear older than they are or do things to make themselves look older, such as wear makeup or a hairstyle that an older person might have. In such cases, the person's voice can be an indicator. Minors also tend to be somewhat immature, as evidenced by awkwardness, loud talking, giggling, or boisterous laughing. They may act nervous when presenting false identification. Minors also like to move in groups and tend to all dress alike, act alike, and speak similarly using the same slang. They usually do not mix with older groups. A group of teenagers will usually have one or two leaders, often the oldest member(s) of the group.

There are special times when minors might be expected to patronize an operation—for example, when a nearby athletic event, dance, or other function is going on. There might be certain days or nights when minors can be expected. They like to be in places that play the latest music and have the latest trendy entertainment.

Sometimes, minors accompany older persons. One minor in a group can be hard to detect. Sometimes, a minor in such a party may order a non-alcoholic drink, but the others share their drinks with this person or purchase one for themselves and give it to the minor.

Some operations set aside a special section or perhaps even a separate room where minors can order non-alcoholic beverages. If legal drinkers are admitted to this area and allowed to purchase alcoholic beverages, some type of identification (such as a hand stamp) should be used to set these individuals apart from the minors. It may be important to see that minors allowed into such areas do not slip into areas where legal drinkers are; many states prohibit minors from being in such areas.

All operations should have established policies on how to check for proper age and how to handle those who are not able to provide proof or who present falsified documents. Any suspect person who fails to present proper identification should not be served an alcoholic beverage. Such a person should be told that, without proper identification, there can be no service of alcohol. The server can explain that it is illegal to do so and that the server, the person requesting service (if in fact a minor), and the establishment might be penalized if service does occur. The server could add that he or she could be fired for providing service. If any difficulty arises, the server should call a supervisor or the manager. It is important to be firm at all times and to make clear that there will be no service to those under age.

Service Involving Intoxication or Alcohol Dependents

We now come to what in most states is the most significant legal issue currently facing servers of alcohol. In most states today, it is against the law to serve alcohol to a guest to the point of intoxication or to serve alcohol to an intoxicated guest. It is no longer the guest's sole responsibility to know when to stop drinking to prevent intoxication. If an intoxicated person asks to be served additional alcohol, the responsibility for refusing such service falls upon the server.

In addition, the courts of some states have ruled that servers of alcohol have a strong responsibility to recognize and refuse service to an alcohol dependent. This can be a very difficult responsibility to meet because, in the case of someone unknown to the server and seemingly sober, how can the server know? Other courts have been a bit more lenient and indicated that a frequenter who drinks heavily should be considered a potential alcohol dependent. Yet other courts have gone to the point of requiring a record of alcohol abuse.

The stake that an enterprise and its employees have in serving alcoholic beverages to the public in a responsible manner is high. The potential liability for failure to do so is enormous. Courts have imposed fines that have wiped out some businesses. In some cases, criminal convictions have been handed down. Just the cost of insuring against such liability has risen out of reach for some businesses.

Third-Party Liability

In the United States, the liability of businesses and individual employees for harm caused by individuals whom they have helped intoxicate has grown over the years. Long ago, the English, concerned about irresponsibility in serving alcoholic beverages to minors and even to adults, passed laws which made such dispensers liable for their irresponsibility. Since the English pub was also known as a dram shop, the laws became known as

dram shop laws. These laws were designed to stop the sale of alcohol to minors and to protect the families of habitual drunkards and the victims of drunkenness. They held that both the drinkers *and those who served them the alcohol* were responsible for the drinkers' actions.

The U.S. dram shop laws of today stem from these English laws. Dram shop liability refers to the civil liability of those who furnish alcohol to minors, to anyone who is obviously intoxicated or to an alcohol dependent, or to anyone who becomes intoxicated because of such service. These laws (along with common law liability for negligence) are also known as **third-party liability laws** because they hold that a third party can be a contributing factor in the injury of others.

Third-party liability typically arises when someone who is served alcohol to or beyond the point of intoxication then breaks the law or causes an accident (often while driving). The innocent victim sues not only the drinker, but also the licensed establishment and even the specific server(s) that provided the alcohol. All may be liable under the law (although some states do not hold individual servers liable). In some states, this liability arises from statutory laws, while in others it comes from common law liability for negligence.

A Brief History   The laws of the United States are based largely on two codes, English and Napoleonic. Early English colonists brought the English code, which was based on both civil statutes passed by legislators and common or unwritten law that sprang from the precedents set by court decisions over the years. The Napoleonic code grew out of the old Roman law and was largely based on statutes passed by government order or legislation. Today, only Louisiana has this code, and it has been modified considerably by the adoption of the common law system.

Laws relating to alcohol in the United States spring both from common law and from statutes. Dram shop laws are statutory. Even without statutes, however, servers of alcohol may be found liable for negligence under common law. In a number of states, both statutory and common laws affect the alcoholic beverage industry, while other states have just one or the other. In recent years, the number of statutory laws has been increasing.

Every state has different laws, so operators of bar and beverage units should know the laws of their particular state. Local or county governments may also have specific laws that must be known.

The United States has a long tradition of barring the sale of alcohol to minors, supported by either common or statutory law. In contrast, the issue of third-party civil and criminal liability has been more gradual in its historical development. Before Prohibition, the courts tended to view intoxicated drinkers who did harm to themselves, others, or property as liable for any injury or damage they caused—that is, the drinkers were responsible. After Prohibition was repealed, however, laws similar to British dram shop laws began to appear in various states. These laws provided, to varying degrees, that those serving alcohol to or beyond the point of intoxication assumed some responsibility for doing so.

Third-party liability laws became more popular in part because many individuals, organizations, and legislatures grew concerned about the high cost of drunkenness to society. Often, the harmed individuals would not be able to collect adequate damages from the person liable for their injuries (that is, the intoxicated individual); without adequate resources, the injured persons would look to the state for help. In turn, the states looked for relief from the growing burden of these costs and took advantage of third-party liability to bring about recovery. Stiffer laws began to be passed. The movement toward greater and more costly third-party liability was gradual, but unmistakable.

Then, in 1980, an event occurred which transformed this gradual trend into a virtual revolution. A drunken driver by the name of Clarence Busch struck and killed 13-year-old Cari Lightner. Busch had been arrested five times in the previous four years for drunken driving and was at the time out on bail for a drunken driving offense two days earlier. Cari's mother, Candy Lightner, was outraged at the ineffectiveness of a legal system which treated potentially dangerous offenders so casually. Existing laws were virtually ignored or often used merely as a "slap on the wrist." Four days after her daughter's death, she founded Mothers Against Drunk Driving (MADD). Its membership grew rapidly, and the organization began to bring considerable public attention to the problem of drunk driving and the cost to life and property because of it. MADD took two strong positions: that the courts should begin to give stiffer penalties for drunk driving and that stiffer legislation was needed.

MADD was aided in its attempts by a growing public awareness that some steps would have to be taken to correct the problem of driving under the influence and other social and economic problems related to alcohol. Statistics such as the following (selected from a large number compiled by various governmental agencies) fueled the concern:

- Alcohol is involved in 70% of all drownings and in about 30% of all suicides.

- In the last 10 years, as many as a quarter of a million people were killed in alcohol-related motor vehicle crashes. More than 650,000 people are injured in these crashes yearly.

- Over a third of the fatalities in alcohol-related crashes are non-drinking occupants or non-occupants of accident vehicles.

- Most cases of accidental death attributable to alcohol are the result of motor vehicle accidents.

- Teenagers and individuals in their 20s have the highest number of alcohol-related fatalities, accidents, and vehicle crashes.

- In the 1980s, arrests for driving under the influence of alcohol were highest among 21-year-olds, reaching their peak in 1983 with a rate of one arrest for every 39 licensed drivers of that age, compared with an overall average arrest rate of one for every 88 licensed drivers.

In addition, excessive alcohol consumption imposes various costs on society due to crime, non-vehicular accidents, economic losses from lower productivity, absenteeism, poorer health, and more. Exhibit 2.1 presents an estimate of the number of deaths in the United States attributable to alcohol in 1980. Liver damage kills the most people when alcohol is the primary cause of death. Most cases of accidental death attributable to alcohol are the result of motor vehicle accidents. Over half the violent deaths attributed to alcohol are homicides. Exhibit 2.2 shows alcohol consumption

Exhibit 2.1 **Estimated Number of Deaths Attributable to Alcohol in the United States, 1980**

Cause of death	Number of deaths	Estimated number attributable to alcohol	Percentage attributable to alcohol
Alcohol as the main cause			
Alcohol psychoses	454	454	100
Alcohol dependence syndrome	4,350	4,350	100
Nondependent use of alcohol	889	889	100
Alcoholic polyneuropathy	4	4	100
Alcoholic cardiomyopathy	650	650	100
Alcoholic gastritis	84	84	100
Alcoholic fatty liver	1,166	1,166	100
Acute alcoholic hepatitis	794	794	100
Alcoholic cirrhosis of the liver	9,166	9,166	100
Alcoholic liver damage unspecified	1,812	1,812	100
Accidental poisoning by alcohol	218	218	100
Subtotal		19,587	
Alcohol as a contributing cause			
Cancer of directly exposed tissues			
Malignant neoplasm of lip, oral cavity, pharynx	8,553	2,138	25
Malignant neoplasm of larynx	3,412	853	25
Malignant neoplasm of stomach	14,37	22,874	20
Malignant neoplasm of liver	5,618	1,404	25
Subtotal		7,269	
Other diseases			
Diabetes mellitus	35,649	1,782	5
Hypertensive diseases	32,633	1,632	5
Pneumonia and influenza	54,619	2,731	5
Diseases of esophagus, stomach, duodenum	8,734	873	10
Chronic liver disease and cirrhosis not specified as alcoholic	18,645	4,661	25
Subtotal		11,679	
Accidents			
Railway accidents	632	63	10
Motor vehicle traffic accidents	51,930	25,965	50
Other road vehicle accidents	232	46	20
Water transport accidents	1,429	286	20
Air and space accidents	1,494	149	10
Accidental falls	13,294	3,324	25
Accidents caused by fire and flames	5,822	1,455	25
Accidents due to natural and environmental factors	3,194	799	25
Accidents caused by submersion, suffocation, and foreign bodies	10,216	3,576	35
Other accidents	8,744	2,186	25
Subtotal		37,849	
Violence			
Suicide	26,869	8,061	30
Homicide	23,967	11,984	50
Undetermined whether accidental or purposely inflicted	3,663	1,099	30
Subtotal		21,144	
All causes		**97,528**	

Source: R.T. Ravenholt, *Epidemiology* (Washington, D.C.: National Institute on Alcohol Abuse and Alcoholism, 1988), p. 49.

Exhibit 2.2 Alcohol Use Among Convicted Offenders Just Before
Committing Current Offense by Crime Type, United States, 1983

Current offense	Number convicted	Percentage of convicted persons who used alcohol
Total	*132,620*	*48%*
Violent	32,112	54
Murder/attempted murder	3,345	49
Manslaughter	1,188	68
Rape/sexual assault	4,017	52
Robbery	11,945	48
Assault	9,609	62
Other violent[a]	2,008	49
Property	51,660	40
Burglary	17,335	44
Auto theft	2,960	51
Fraud/forgery/embezzlement	5,976	22
Larceny	18,001	37
Stolen property	3,676	45
Other property[b]	3,712	51
Drugs	13,181	29
Traffic	5,469	26
Possession	6,830	30
Other drugs	882	44
Public order	34,036	64
Weapons	2,769	32
Obstructing justice	6,856	43
Traffic	3,734	36
Driving while intoxicated[c]	13,406	93
Drunkenness/morals offenses[d]	4,894	70
Other public order[e]	2,377	28
Other[f]	1,008	40
Information unavailable	623	—

Source: USDOJ 1985.

[a]Includes kidnapping, purse snatching, hit-and-run driving, and child abuse.

[b]Includes arson, destruction of property, property damage from hit-and-run driving, and trespass.

[c]Includes driving while intoxicated and driving under the influence of drugs.

[d]Also includes vagrancy and commercialized vice.

[e]Includes rioting, habitual offender, family-related offenses such as nonsupport or abandonment, invasion of privacy, and contributing to the delinquency of a minor.

[f]Includes juvenile offenses and unspecified offenses.

Source: R.T. Ravenholt, *Epidemiology* (Washington, D.C.: National Institute on Alcohol Abuse and Alcoholism, 1988), p. 54.

among those convicted of various crimes. Exhibit 2.3 illustrates the tremendous costs of alcohol abuse and alcoholism to society. Reduced productivity accounts for nearly 60% of these costs.

The growing public concern, along with MADD's effective work, brought action. Legislators listened and passed stronger and broader laws. Judges began to interpret laws more strictly and to give stiffer fines and

Exhibit 2.3 Economic Costs to Society of Alcohol Abuse and Alcoholism, United States, 1983

Types of Costs	Costs ($ millions)
Core Costs	
Direct	
Treatment[a]	$13,457
Health support services	1,549
Indirect	
Mortality[b]	18,151
Reduced productivity	65,582
Lost employment	5,323
Other related costs	
Direct	
Motor vehicle crashes	2,697
Crime	2,631
Social welfare administration	49
Other	3,673
Indirect	
Victims of crime	194
Incarceration	2,979
Motor vehicle crashes	590
Total	$116,875

[a]For alcohol abuse and alcoholism, liver cirrhosis, other illnesses, motor vehicle crashes, and other injuries.

[b]At 6 percent discount rate.

Source: R.T. Ravenholt, *Epidemiology* (Washington, D.C.: National Institute on Alcohol Abuse and Alcoholism, 1988), p. 48.

penalties. In some states, the blood-alcohol concentration level (discussed later in this chapter) was lowered and the legal age for consuming alcohol raised to 21. Law enforcement agencies and officers began to watch more carefully for people driving under the influence of alcohol or otherwise showing signs of improper alcohol use. The alcohol industry itself joined in with educational programs. Bar and beverage operations began to require all those associated with the service of alcohol to be trained in the proper procedures to help prevent abuses.

Because of the huge sums awarded to individuals who sued some bar and beverage operations for a failure to comply with the law, insurance companies raised their insurance rates, in some cases so high that properties ceased to serve alcoholic beverages. In some states, bar and beverage operators joined together to pool their insurance and thus reduce the cost. The operators also sought relief from legislators and in some cases were successful in obtaining less severe laws. Also, in some states, legislatures have actually repealed some laws. This move to moderate the laws and to make it easier to operate bar and beverage operations has been supported by a feeling among many that attempting to solve social problems by legislation (often called "social legislation") is not the way to go. Thus, the situation is still very much in a state of flux and changing almost daily.

Exhibit 2.4 Apparent U.S. Per Capita Consumption of Pure Alcohol, 1934–1984

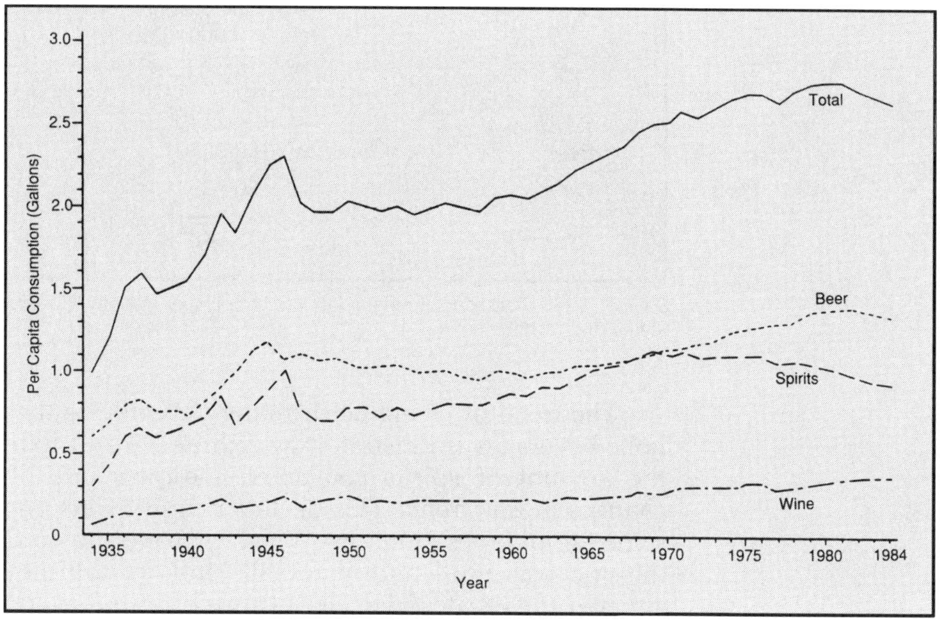

Courtesy of National Institute on Alcohol Abuse and Alcoholism

Changing Drinking Patterns

The overall effect of this public concern and action has been felt not only by those who have fallen afoul of the law, but by society as a whole. The American public has, on its own, taken steps to curb drinking by beginning to change its drinking patterns. Within the last 10 years, there has been a significant change in drinking patterns and in the amount of alcohol consumed. Between 1934 (when Prohibition ended) and the early 1980s, the apparent per capita consumption of pure alcohol typically increased from year to year (see Exhibit 2.4).[4] Then, in 1981, the total per capita consumption of alcohol dropped and did not pick up again. It was not, however, a uniform drop for all alcoholic beverages. Spirits (whose rate of consumption had been declining since the early 1970s) were joined by beer on the downward turn, but wine continued to move upward slowly. Although more recent government figures have not been released, it is evident to those in the business that this downward trend for spirits has continued and that beer may be holding its own, while wine consumption is moving only slightly upward.

In 1984, per capita consumption based on those 14 years old and older was 2.65 gallons of pure alcohol, down from its peak of 2.76 gallons in 1981. Exhibit 2.5 summarizes the apparent consumption of pure alcohol in 1988 from spirits, beer, and wine as reported by the Distilled Spirits Council of the United States (DISCUS). Unfortunately, its figures are based on a *total* population count and not just the population 14 years old and older, so its figures cannot be compared with those previously cited. However, the amount—1.94 gallons of absolute alcohol per capita—may well indicate a continuing drop in pure alcohol consumption.

Exhibit 2.5 Apparent Consumption of Absolute Alcohol, 1988

Type	Absolute Alcohol Total in 1000 Gallons	Absolute Alcohol per Person in Gallons
Spirits	151,319	0.62
Beer	262,085	1.07
Wine	60,436	0.25
Total	473,840	1.94

Source: "1988 Statistical Information for the U.S. Liquor Industry" (Distilled Spirits Council of the United States, Inc., 1989).

The trend of changing drinking patterns for the various kinds of alcoholic beverages is illustrated by Exhibit 2.4 and Exhibit 2.6. The change in the amount of spirits consumed indicates one of the most significant changes in this trend. This decline in spirit consumption has not been the same for all types of spirits. Whiskeys have shown the biggest decline, but this too was not uniform for all kinds of whiskey. American whiskeys suffered the greatest decline because of a shift to lighter Canadian whisky and to lighter scotch. Overall, the decline in whiskey consumption is expected to continue, and by the year 2000 it is expected to be about half the 1960 consumption level.[5]

A recent study found that the consumption of gin, rum, tequila, and vodka has increased, especially vodka and rum, and that this trend is expected to continue at a slow pace.[6] Brandy consumption has also grown slowly, and this trend is also expected to continue. Cordial and mixed drink (cocktail, etc.) consumption has also risen very slowly and is expected to continue growing at about the same pace. However, brandy, cordials, and mixed drinks have a very small share of the overall spirit market.

Another significant statistic that can be used to show changing drinking patterns is the sale of bottled waters. Today, bottled water sales are increasing at the rate of 12% per year. Per capita consumption is at an all-time high of 6.4 gallons.[7] Bottled water is also becoming a year-round drink. Flavored waters are sharing in this rise. Many operations today offer bottled water as a "healthful alternative" and find willing consumers among many of their patrons. Offering bottled water as a "pacer" between drinks also is finding approval. It would be wrong to infer, however, that *all* of this rise is due to changes in alcohol drinking patterns. A very important factor in the sales growth of this product is concern about the safety of municipal water supplies and an interest in health and nutrition.

Some other trends of interest may be found in statistics recently published by the National Institute on Alcohol Abuse and Alcoholism, a research and data gathering body of the U.S. federal government:

- In general, women drink less than men and have fewer drinking problems. However, alcohol consumption among women between the ages of 35 and 54 has increased.

- The age at which people start drinking has dropped, and a surprising number of children in grade school are alcohol dependents. How-

Exhibit 2.6 Proportional Change in Kinds of Alcoholic Beverages Consumed, 1977–1984

Beverage Type	1977	1984
Beer	49%	51%
Wine	11%	14%
Spirits	40%	35%
Total	100%	100%

Source: *Alcoholic Health and Research World* (Summer 1986), p. 63.

ever, the overall consumption of alcohol among children and teen-agers has dropped.

• Individuals over the age of 65 consume less alcohol than younger adults and have a lower incidence of alcohol abuse. The elderly's lower tolerance to alcohol may be a factor in encouraging this lesser use, as may be the fact that alcohol can have greater adverse health effects on the elderly. Some elderly alcohol dependents may become so because of depression, loneliness, or other late-life stresses.

Health Concerns

While the consumption of moderate amounts of alcohol has not been proved to be a health hazard—in fact, it may have certain healthful beneficial results—a substantial toll is taken on the health of heavy drinkers. Among some special population groups, even a small amount of drinking may be harmful. It is important that those who serve alcohol understand what these health concerns are so they can better understand the problem and its influence on their business.

Physical Effects   Heavy drinking over a long period can cause the stomach to secrete too much acid and histamine, leading to severe gastric disturbances, stomach ulcers, and even cancer. Such drinking can also disturb the acid-base balance in the body, opening the door to other health problems. When an acidic condition develops, the body may secrete too much uric acid, bringing on an attack of gout.

Excessive alcohol may also disturb vitamin absorption and utilization and adversely affect protein synthesis. All this can cause a nutritional deficiency that shows up in the form of illnesses, muscle tone loss, and a general deterioration of muscular action and strength. Heavy drinkers may fail to eat properly, further depriving themselves of proper nutrition. Brain damage may result from consuming too many calories in alcohol (and not enough in food), because the brain cannot process the by-products of alcohol metabolism as well as it can the by-products of carbohydrate metabolism. This type of damage may be evidenced by confusion, bizarre ideas, and difficulty in following a logical progression of ideas. Brain damage of this kind is irreversible.

The liver is especially sensitive to excess alcohol because this organ has the job of metabolizing alcohol. It can easily handle moderate amounts, but, if it has to process large quantities, it cannot do so fast enough and passes a lot into the body, where it causes intoxication. Too much alcohol also causes the liver to fail to perform its other functions such as breaking down vitamins, proteins, and fats. When this occurs, the liver eventually fills up with fat, becoming what is called a "fatty liver." This, in turn, can cause health problems and even death. The condition is reversible if the individual stops drinking. If not, the fatty tissues gradually harden and cease to function. This hardening is known as *cirrhosis of the liver*, and the damage is irreversible. A person can survive with a liver partially damaged by cirrhosis, but, if the damage is too extensive, the person dies. As little as five years of heavy drinking may cause cirrhosis; previous liver damage or a liver illness such as hepatitis makes one more prone to develop it. Heavy drinking for 10 to 20 years is a reliable way to make it happen. Some heavy drinkers avoid the problem even after drinking over a long period, but they are not common.

Alcohol dependence develops gradually, without the individual being aware it is happening. Someone may be a light, then a moderate, and finally a heavy drinker. As a result, few people realize that they are dependent on alcohol until they cannot quit. They then find themselves drinking all the time—even waking at night to have a drink—or "just having a few drinks now and then to relax." Eventually, the body fails under the onslaught and treatment must occur. Often, a bout of serious illness or the development of problems such as deep melancholy, remorse, or suicidal tendencies makes it necessary to face the issue. Family intervention may also result in an agreement to seek treatment.

The harmful effects of alcohol to the human body have caused the U.S. government to take steps to try to reduce their occurrence. In 1981, the Surgeon General issued an advisory to caution women who are either pregnant or considering pregnancy to avoid drinking alcohol and to become aware of the alcohol content of foods and drugs. In 1990, a government regulation went into effect requiring all alcoholic beverages to carry the following warning:

> Government Warning: 1) According to the Surgeon General, women should not drink alcoholic beverages during pregnancy because of the risk of birth defects; 2) the consumption of alcoholic beverages impairs your ability to drive a car or operate machinery, and may cause health problems.

This warning is supported by many authorities. One, echoing the opinion of many others, has advised, "Because no assuredly safe level of alcohol consumption has been established, public health officials agree that the safest policy is simply not to drink at all while pregnant."[8]

In addition, a number of laws dealing with alcohol are pending in Congress. We may see more governmental actions and warnings to help reduce the health hazards caused by the improper consumption of alcohol.

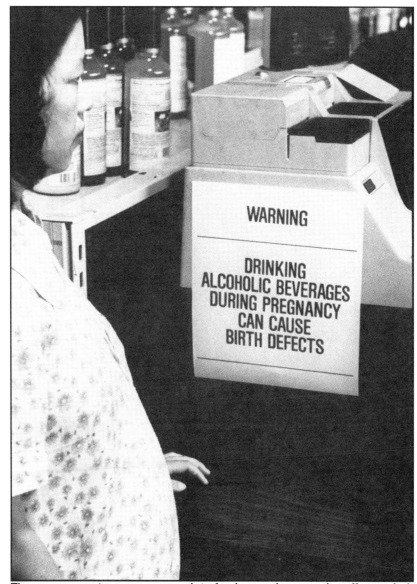

The government encourages point-of-sale warnings on the effects of alcohol on unborn children. (Courtesy of *Alcohol Health and Research World*)

The Industry's Response

Noting all of these trends, the alcoholic beverage industry began to stress moderation and responsibility in its advertising and to give strong financial support to MADD and similar organizations. The industry even formed some groups of its own to combat drunken driving, excessive drinking, drinking by minors, and other alcohol-related problems. It knew full well it was in its interest to do so.

The American Wine Alliance for Research and Education (AWARE) is an example of how the wine industry is attempting to meet the problem. Advertising campaigns like Anheuser-Busch's "Know When to Say When," Miller's "Think When You Drink," and Coors' "Please Drink

Many industries in the alcoholic beverage field are trying to encourage moderation in drinking. (Courtesy of Anheuser-Busch, Inc.)

Safely" are examples of how the beer industry is preaching moderation and responsibility to those who drink. The spirits industry has made similar moves. For example, Joseph E. Seagram & Sons, Inc., produces a program directed to parents and pre-teenagers entitled "Talking About Alcohol." It has had endorsements from educators, the medical profession, and others concerned with alcoholism.

It is not surprising that the movement to interpret dram shop and other liability laws more strictly has brought about significant changes in operational procedures in bar and beverage operations. Such operations are in business to sell alcoholic beverages and carry heavy costs to do so. They have to make enough money to pay these costs and make a profit. If the law places heavy restrictions on them, it becomes more difficult to

Exhibit 2.8 Approximate BAC Levels in Drinks per Hour for Individuals of Different Weights

KNOW YOUR LIMITS

CHART FOR RESPONSIBLE PEOPLE WHO MAY SOMETIMES DRIVE AFTER DRINKING!

APPROXIMATE BLOOD ALCOHOL PERCENTAGE

DRINKS	1	2	3	4	5	6	7	8
100	.04	.09	.13	.18	.22	.26	.31	.35
120	.04	.07	.11	.15	.18	.22	.26	.29
140	.03	.06	.09	.13	.16	.19	.22	.25
160	.03	.06	.08	.11	.14	.17	.19	.22
180	.02	.05	.07	.10	.12	.15	.17	.20
200	.02	.04	.07	.09	.11	.13	.15	.18
220	.02	.04	.06	.08	.10	.12	.14	.16
240	.02	.04	.06	07	.09	.11	.13	.15

Body Weight in Pounds

INFLUENCED RARELY   POSSIBLY   DEFINITELY

Subtract .01% for each 40 minutes or .03% for each 2 hours of drinking.
One drink is 1 1/4 oz. of 80-proof liquor, 12 oz. of beer, or 4 oz. of table wine.

SUREST POLICY IS...
DON'T DRIVE AFTER DRINKING!

Source: Distilled Spirits Council of the United States, Inc.

0.20 to 0.30 induces confusion and stupor or loss of consciousness. At this point, alcohol can act as a poison, causing the drinker to become ill and vomit. A BAC of 0.30 to 0.40 may make the drinker comatose. A BAC of 0.40 to 0.50 can affect the part of the brain controlling respiration and heart action. If this occurs, the person can die. Fortunately, most individuals lose consciousness before drinking this much.

The physical effects of alcohol vary among individuals. People with large bodies can tolerate more alcohol than smaller people. This is related to the amount of water in the body, where alcohol is held. The more water in the body, the less the effect. However, differences can exist even between people of the same weight; people with muscular bodies and little fat tend to put less alcohol into their bloodstream than people with a higher percentage of body fat.

Studies have been done to find out how fast alcohol can build up in the blood. Exhibit 2.8 indicates how fast on average the BAC builds up in people of different weights. One can deduct from the percentage given 0.01 for every 40 minutes that elapses. Thus, a 140-pound person drinking three drinks in a 40-minute period would have a BAC of approximately 0.09 less 0.01, or 0.08. On average, individuals weighing between 150 and 180 pounds add from 0.02 to 0.03 to their BAC for each drink. Thus, an employee serving a 160-pound man four 12-ounce beers in an hour should know he is approaching intoxication or is intoxicated. In light of these figures, servers should learn to estimate the weight of individuals fairly accurately.

However, it must be cautioned that the figures in Exhibit 2.8 are *averages* to be used only as guides. Individuals vary in how they respond to alcohol. Relying solely on a statistical figure as the evidence that a guest is or is not intoxicated is dangerous. The real test is how an individual reacts. Those engaged in serving the public alcohol should be aware of this.

People of different temperaments handle alcohol differently. Some become quiet, while others become volatile. How one feels can also be a factor. Tired or ill people may get a faster effect than a more alert or healthy person. Unhappy or depressed people may get unhappier or more depressed as they drink, while happy people may get happier. Some people have livers that break down alcohol more efficiently than average (which is about 0.75 ounces per hour); these people feel the effects less. Active people seem to be able to "hold their liquor" better than sedentary people. Also, the body can adjust to alcohol intake to a certain degree; people who drink infrequently often may find that they get a quicker and greater effect than people who are accustomed to drinking.

Drinking on an empty stomach intensifies and hastens the effects of alcohol. Food in the stomach can slow the physical effects of alcohol. The food absorbs alcohol and keeps it from passing through the stomach wall. Fatty foods are especially effective because they coat the stomach with oil, making the wall less permeable. Fats also tend to increase the stomach's churning, further reducing the amount of alcohol absorbed through the wall.

Bubbly drinks like champagne take effect faster than still ones. Thus, a 4-ounce glass of bubbly wine will have a faster effect than a 4-ounce glass of still wine.

If drinking occurs in a relaxed atmosphere where there is a lot of conversation, dancing, or other social activities, the rate of drinking is slower. At cocktail parties, beer fests, and other events where people are engaged primarily in drinking, the drinking rate is faster and alcohol consumption is increased.

Black Coffee and Cold Showers. There are several folk remedies about how to sober someone up. Unfortunately, they don't work. The only way to sober someone up is to wait until that person's liver has broken down the alcohol in the bloodstream. Making the person drink black coffee or take a cold shower or walk around the block will *not* speed this process up perceptibly. However, serving coffee may buy some time, allowing the person's natural processes to break down more alcohol before the person leaves.

Alcohol and Other Drugs

Alcohol and drugs often do not mix. Some drugs work to increase the effects of alcohol, while alcohol in turn increases the effects of some drugs. Combining alcohol with depressants such as barbiturates may produce fatal results. Antihistamines, cold tablets, antidepressants, high blood pressure medications, tranquilizers, and sleeping pills depress the central nervous system, as does alcohol, so combining them can substantially magnify their effect. Some antibiotics increase the sedative effects of alcohol; the labels on many such medications warn against taking them with alcohol. When combined with alcohol, stimulants such as caffeine or Dexedrine reduce the depression of the central nervous system, but they do not help motor coordination. The intoxicated person may be more alert (and therefore less likely to fall asleep while driving), but he or she is just as intoxicated and just as physically impaired.

Some people using drugs may show symptoms much like those associated with alcohol abuse. If a guest is acting intoxicated, the server should refuse service even if it is unclear what is causing the behavior. Exhibit 2.9 lists common symptoms of drug abuse.

Medical conditions such as diabetes, epilepsy, and strokes also produce symptoms that may be mistaken for intoxication. People with diabetes or epilepsy often wear a Medic Alert emblem either around the neck or wrist.

Approaches to Server Intervention

Simply knowing the signs and symptoms to watch for is not enough. An explicit server intervention program should be adopted; once adopted, it should be followed. Any program designed to ensure responsible alcohol service should start with a firm commitment by management. Such programs comprise many elements. For example, one program on server intervention encourages:[11]

- Assessment of service practices, making sure they do not promote or encourage excessive drinking. This includes eliminating promotional material that might be perceived as fostering intoxication, providing bar food, providing alternative transportation to someone who has had too much to drink, and fostering a designated-driver program.

- Establishing and publicizing an alcoholic beverage service policy.

- Training all servers in how to recognize falsified IDs and signs of intoxication, and in how to refuse service to those who are intoxicated.

- Introducing point-of-sales material to publicize the message that drinking and driving don't mix.

Once a program is begun, management must then follow through to see that it is implemented and followed.

One of the first things to be done is that management should establish policies and procedures. Such policies and procedures should be aimed at two audiences: employees and guests. Employees need to know what is required of them. Guests should know that a program exists to protect them and to see that they have a pleasurable experience. This can be an important factor in assuring guests who may feel they are being unfairly singled out that management is merely acting to protect them—that management cares. Copies of these policies and procedures should be posted somewhere in the establishment to remind employees of the need to serve alcohol responsibly.[12]

The proper legal age at which alcohol can be served should be added to any policy and procedure statement. There may also be other special features that have to be included in such a statement; special conditions in the establishment or the local area will dictate what these will be. Any policy and procedure statement of this kind should also be reviewed by the

Exhibit 2.9 Common Symptoms of Drug Abuse

General Symptoms
1. Unusual flare-ups or outbursts of temper.
2. Secretive behavior about personal possessions, such as a backpack or purse.
3. Wearing sunglasses when no one else is.
4. Wearing long-sleeved garments in hot weather.
5. Association with known drug abusers.
6. Stealing items that can be readily pawned or sold.

Depressants/Sedatives abuser
1. May seem intoxicated, but no alcohol odor on breath.
2. Staggering or stumbling movements.
3. Falling asleep at work.
4. Loss of interest in former activities.
5. Slurred speech.
6. Dilated pupils.

Hallucinogen abuser
1. Often appears to be daydreaming or in a trance-like state.
2. May touch objects and examine everyday things carefully for long periods.
3. Body image and senses may be distorted, causing the person to panic.
4. Poor perception of time and distance.
5. Paranoid reactions.
6. Dilated pupils.

Marijuana abuser
1. Odor of burned marijuana on clothes.
2. Whites of eyes may appear irritated.
3. May behave more quietly than previously.
4. Increased appetite.
5. Disoriented behavior.
6. Paranoid reactions.

Opiates abuser
1. May have raw, red nostrils if sniffing; needle tracks if "shooting up."
2. Lethargic, drowsy behavior when high; purposive when obtaining money or locating source of drug.
3. Needs money to support habit, more so than other drugs.
4. Constricted pupils.
5. May feel nauseated or have trouble breathing.

Phencyclidine (PCP) abuser
1. Dazed, blank-stare expression; side-to-side eye movements.
2. Poor physical coordination as if drunk, but no odor of alcohol.
3. Sweating, flushed skin, and excess salivation.
4. Change in pupils.

Stimulants/Cocaine abuser
1. Pupils may be dilated.
2. Excessive activity, irritability, nervousness, and aggression.
3. Mouth and nose dry; bad breath; user licks lips frequently.
4. Thin; goes long periods without eating or sleeping.
5. Increased alertness and excitation.
6. Frequent insomnia and loss of appetite.

Volatile substances (glue) abuser
1. Odor of substance on clothes, breath.
2. Runny nose.
3. Irritation around mouth.
4. Watery eyes.
5. Poor muscular coordination; drowsiness.
6. Appears in a stupor.

Source: *Serving Alcohol with Care*, 2d ed. (East Lansing, Mich.: Educational Institute of the American Hotel & Motel Association, 1988), pp. 18–19.

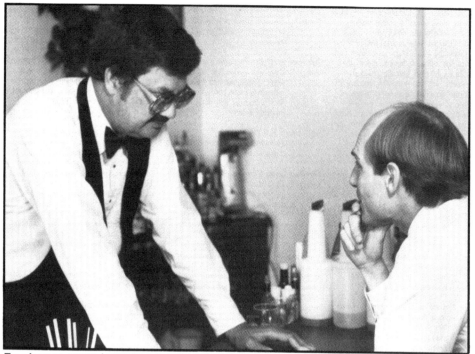

Employees must learn how to "rate" and "relate." (Courtesy of *Alcohol Health and Research World*)

In taking the order, it might be appropriate to ask if there is a designated driver (a non-drinking group member responsible for group transportation) and to point out the menu of non-alcoholic drinks available. However, servers should *not* assume that, when there is a designated driver, the others can then be served over their proper BAC level. The facility and its personnel are still responsible for such service and can be held liable for it.

We mentioned earlier the need for employees to communicate with one another about the state of guests. A popular rating system among many operations classifies guests according to the three colors used in traffic: green, yellow, and red. Green is the go signal indicating that the guest can be served; there are no visible signs of intoxication or other problems. Yellow indicates caution. The guest's actions indicate a potential cause for concern. Proceed with care. Red indicates stop. The guest should not be served any more alcohol because he or she is intoxicated or something else is not right.

When possible, the monitoring of alcohol consumption begins at the start of the green zone. According to the drinks consumed, the frequency and speed with which drinking occurs, and other evidence, servers or others move guests from one light to the next. Do not hesitate to put a guest in the yellow category if there is any doubt. Likewise, hitting the red light should not be delayed if factors indicate that the time has come. The potential penalties for a failure to do so are too great to risk.

Suppose a man and woman enter and order an after-dinner drink after coming from the adjoining dining room. They appear perfectly normal and seem only concerned with relaxing in a pleasant atmosphere, enjoying each other's company, and sipping a drink while they talk. They are "green."

Guests rated "green" may be served additional alcohol, but the server should already be alert to help guard against the chance that the guests will go on and consume too much. Making food or non-alcoholic beverages available can help keep guests in the green stage. In offering food and non-alcoholic drinks, the server can often use personal selling to raise the check total and the size of the tip. If an operation uses entertainers, they might publicize food as an accompaniment to alcoholic beverages. Suggesting a food that goes well with a guest's beverage may actually please the guest more than just serving the beverage alone. After all, alcoholic beverages and food are natural companions, each complementing the other. Remember that fatty foods stay in the stomach longer and also provide a lining over the stomach wall so alcohol is absorbed less quickly.

A "yellow" signal might be given for a number of reasons. Suppose a server sees a sniffling guest take a cold tablet or hears a guest say he or she has done so. There is a good possibility that the cold medication contains an antihistamine or some other compound that reacts with alcohol. The procedure is now one of caution. If a patron is in the "yellow" zone, the server should redouble efforts to try to head off going into the "red" zone. Efforts to sell alternatives should continue. All straight drinks should be served with water on the side. The server should not encourage reordering. Rather, he or she should try to delay it by visiting the table less frequently or by deliberately slowing down service by being busy elsewhere. Remember that for every 40 minutes, the BAC can drop 0.01.

A "red" guest might stagger just a bit before clumsily seating himself or herself. The server could elicit information by suggesting, "You look as if you've been having a good time." If the guest responds, "Yeah, just came from a big smash upstairs," the server needs little more to put the clamps on. The supervisor or manager should be informed, and he or she should decide what course of action to take.

If intervention is called for, the decision about who is to talk to a guest should be made by management. Well-trained servers may be allowed to do this, but often it is best if done by management. It is more authoritative, and guests are less likely to argue or protest.

Whoever does it should do it with tact and good judgment. Do not offend by using phrases like "you're drunk" or "you've had too much." Don't scold or blame. Say rather, "We care about your safety and want to see you get home safely." A server can say, "I'm sorry, but if I serve you another drink I'll lose my job." Soliciting cooperation also may work: "I'm sorry, but I've served you all I can," or "I'd appreciate it if you did not order another drink," or "You might get into trouble; the police are cracking down." Sometimes a show of assistance (such as "Let me call you a cab") works.

The denial should be firmly made. Don't be drawn into explanations, defenses, or arguments. Make the statement and then walk away. Always try to minimize the confrontation. Speak to the guest privately. Sometimes you might even ask a guest seated with others to leave the table for a moment so you can speak privately. Sometimes using peer pressure works—it may be possible to get someone in the individual's group to do the job.

Always keep someone else in the room informed of what is going to be done, so should any serious confrontation occur, some backup can be given and there will be a witness. Sometimes, the individual may try to get a drink from someone else. Everyone in the place should back up the decision once it has been made. It may be necessary to call security or even the police. Servers should know where to contact security in a hurry.

It is advisable to keep a personal record of the incident, so should problems arise later, there is something on record that can be used as evidence. If another person signs it, it is even stronger evidence. Such a record can be used to prove that care was taken and an attempt made to protect the person, others, and property. The record should give the time and date of the event and of the writing of the report and a description of what happened and how and where it happened. Try to get the names and addresses of others involved. These people may later prove to be valuable witnesses. If the police were notified, note this also. The record should be completed as soon as possible, when all details are fresh in the mind. Record only facts, not feelings. The record should be filed in a secure place so it will be available if ever needed.

While it is not always advisable to threaten or create fear, sometimes it helps to remind intoxicated guests that driving while intoxicated is dangerous and against the law. The prospect of an arrest, fines, attorney's fees, and a suspended driver's license may have the desired effect. It may also be helpful to suggest to a guest some alternative for getting where the guest wants to go, such as calling a family member or friend, a local volunteer "safe ride" group, or a cab. Some properties with rooms may have a policy of offering a free room for the night. If an obviously intoxicated person who has little or no driving competence insists on driving, you might call the police. It is better to risk the guest's displeasure than face the consequences of what might happen.

If a physical fight breaks out, move other guests safely out of the way and do not ask other guests to help. Call security or the police or have someone else do it. You might become entangled in the fight. Try to avoid any physical contact unless the affair becomes serious (for example, others are hurt or property is damaged). If any weapons appear, clear the room and notify the police. Unless absolutely necessary, do *not* have other employees enter the fight. Again, keep a record of the incident.

Monitoring Drinks

As part of their monitoring program, some establishments begin by encouraging self-monitoring by guests. They may subtly inform guests about how many drinks they should consume by placing table tents with the information in Exhibit 2.8 on every table. It is unlikely that servers will learn if guests are on any type of medication such as cold tablets, antihistamines, or high blood pressure medication, and it is not proper to ask guests point blank. However, the table tent might also inform guests that certain types of drugs react with alcohol in certain ways. If guests are interested, easily available table tents or cards may be provided that inform them about how gender, body fat, eating before drinking, and other factors can modify these figures. Such a program might also present an opportunity to make a sale of some type of food, which can also help to delay the impact of the alcohol. (These table tents or little cards may be so popular among guests that guests will take them unless something makes it difficult to carry them away in a pocket or handbag.)

Of course, self-monitoring by guests is not sufficient. Servers should also monitor the guests' alcohol consumption. There are two important elements in doing this. One is to count the number of drinks, and the other is to note the time period over which these drinks have been consumed. These observations help give some idea of how the guest is reacting to the alcohol, but, as has been noted, there are other factors that should be considered. No two individuals react exactly the same, so opinions should not be based solely on a norm. Rather, the norm provides a guide to use when considering individuals.

Most servers keep a tab or guest check showing the number of drinks ordered. It is also the policy of some operations to time stamp these when service starts. These written records relieve servers from having to rely on their memories, which can lead to errors. If time stamping is not done, servers can carry a small pad with a page devoted to each table; guests at each table can be assigned a number, and the number of drinks ordered can be recorded after that number. The top of the page should also indicate the time service started and the time when other drinks were served.

When more than one server takes guests' orders, it may be difficult to keep track of the number of drinks ordered or time that has elapsed between drinks. In this case, a system should be worked out so that guest checks or tabs to record information are left at some point where all servers can leave information. Again, remember that such a record is just a guide. Visible signs from the individual must be taken as the main guideline.

It is even more difficult to keep track of guest drinking when there is an open bar.

Special Considerations for the Open Bar. At an open bar, individuals may ask for drinks for both themselves and others. Monitoring is further complicated when there are several open bars in the room. In such a case, it may not be possible to keep a record; floor operation by employees may be the only way to note guests' behavior and reactions and the possibility of developing trouble. If a guest exhibits signs of intoxication, the guest should not be served alcohol. It is important that employees at other service points be notified when this happens. *All* employees must work together in such efforts, not only bartenders and servers.

Open bars are a temptation to drink freely, and many who should know better take advantage of the free liquor and overindulge. One of the ways to bring things under control is to try to limit the duration of open-bar functions. This may be difficult to do, however, since such functions are often a desirable prelude to a dinner with important ceremonies taking place during or after it. Some operations have tried to meet the problem by serving only wine. Serving food may also help in delaying the effects of too much alcohol.

Remember, of course, that too aggressive a program can end up restricting even proper consumption. The program should discourage only improper consumption. Exhibit 2.12 lists suggestions that might be used to control improper drinking at open-bar functions. They should be applied wisely.

The problem of controlling excessive drinking at open bars has led many operations to change operational procedures. When such control can be exercised (that is, when those holding the function allow), guests can be given cards or some other item which they exchange for a limited number of drinks. Alternatively, the bartender can punch a card stating the number of drinks the guest is allowed until the limit is reached. After the

9. Much of this chapter is based on *Serving Alcohol with Care,* 2d ed., a server training program available from the Educational Institute of the American Hotel & Motel Association, P.O. Box 1240, East Lansing, Michigan 48826, (517) 353–5500.

10. The precise amount would be 1.22 drops of alcohol per 1000 drops of blood. The conversion of alcohol by weight to alcohol by volume (and vice versa) is discussed in Chapter 12.

    Some confusion surrounds the meaning of the BAC. Although you will often see it considered and referred to as a *percentage* (as it is, for example, in Exhibit 2.8), it is in fact a *grams percentage*, which is something quite different. A percentage would measure either by weight only or by volume only. A grams percentage uses both measures in stating weight per unit volume.

11. "How to Implement an Alcohol-Awareness Program," *Restaurants USA* (February 1990): 13.

12. The National Restaurant Association's booklet on how to establish an alcohol-awareness program contains a suggested policy and procedure statement that might be used as a guide by those wishing to establish one of their own.

Key Terms

blood alcohol concentration (BAC)
dram shop laws
mini-drink
third-party liability laws

Discussion Questions

1. What are the three primary legal concerns with regard to alcohol service? Which is the easiest to address? Why?

2. What practices should be used to prevent service of alcohol to minors? How do minors try to get around such practices?

3. What are dram shop laws? How are they different from common law liability for negligence?

4. What are the various costs to society of alcohol abuse and alcoholism? What has been the public's reaction to these costs in the last decade?

5. How has the alcoholic beverage industry responded to the changing public attitude about alcohol consumption?

6. What is meant by blood alcohol concentration? How should you use a BAC chart? What must you keep in mind when using such a chart?

7. How useful are the various methods used to sober someone up?

8. How does alcohol interact with antihistamines and cold tablets? antibiotics? stimulants?

9. If service must be denied to a guest, how should the guest be told of this decision? Who should tell the guest?

10. What methods can be used to monitor guests' alcohol consumption? How is this task made more difficult at an open bar?

Part II

The Business: Planning and Marketing

Architecture and Interior Design

Chapter Outline

Architectural Planning and Construction
    The Four Viewpoints of Planning
        The Ownership's Viewpoint
        The Operational Viewpoint
        The Architectural/Engineering/Design Viewpoint
        The Builder's Viewpoint
    Permits, Licenses, and Regulatory Compliance
Interior Design and Decor
    Establishing a Design Theme
    Planning for Space Allocation
        Tables and Seating Arrangements
    Planning for Traffic Flow
    Floors
        Carpeting and Other Floor Coverings
    Windows
    Walls and Wall Coverings
        Curtains and Drapery
    Ceilings
    Furniture and Equipment
        Chairs
        Tables
        Counters
        Upholstery
    Planning for Color
Interior Environmental Planning
    Air Control and Conditioning
    Sound Control
    Lighting Control
Exterior Design

Being part of the planning and building of a bar or beverage operation from the ground up may be a very rare experience for a bar or beverage manager. Nevertheless, knowing the kind of planning that goes into creating a new facility will offer valuable insights.

As a bar or beverage manager, you will more likely be involved in remodeling or completely renovating an existing facility. It might be an existing restaurant or bar where the entire interior is stripped, where walls are removed, entrances and exits changed—practically every imaginable change short of building from the ground up. It might be a building totally unrelated to a bar or beverage operation—a Victorian-era barn, for instance, where antiques were sold. And if you are managing an operation where business is declining, the owners may decide that a top-to-bottom renovation is necessary to attract a new clientele or to take advantage of new market trends (such as the "sports-oriented" bar and lounge).

This chapter, in addition to describing the architectural planning process, provides important information about planning for space, workflow, lighting, sound, air control, and a guest-oriented approach to interior design.

Both technical and design aspects are important in facility planning. The technical aspects include such physical and mechanical factors as construction, HVAC systems (heating, ventilating, and air conditioning), lighting, and plumbing. Design governs the mood or ambience of the facility—how it affects the guests.

Guests often are unaware of the technical factors but, if such factors are lacking, guests notice the lack. In establishing technical requirements, it is important to keep in mind cost, security, wear and depreciation, and many other factors. It is also wise to look ahead. Energy requirements in the future promise to be a much larger cost factor, which means all possible ways of reducing energy costs should be considered.

Many planning decisions cannot be made on a technical basis alone. Design is a major consideration. Design is often defined as the form, scale, color and light patterns, texture, and style of a facility. Design defines the aesthetic quality of a building, and it communicates a mood, inside and out. Sometimes design is called "the art of space utilization." Design should be guided by a unit's functions, and, for this reason, design is often said to be the interpretation of function. One of design's main jobs is to augment and support the technical factors of a building. Guests are usually very much aware of design.

While this chapter addresses the planning and construction sections separately from the sections on interior design, a certain amount of overlapping is unavoidable. Architectural planning, for instance, may specify acoustical (sound absorbing) tile for the ceilings, but more sound may actually be absorbed by interior design elements such as heavy drapery, carpeting, and upholstered chairs.

Architectural Planning and Construction

The proper planning of a bar or beverage operation is essential to its success. Today, the actual architectural planning—whether for a new facility or the remodeling of an existing facility—should be preceded by another type of planning: market research. Without a well-considered marketing plan bolstered by market research, the best-laid architectural plan may not prove to be worth the blueprint paper upon which it is reproduced.

We have devoted an entire chapter to marketing (Chapter 8), but our main thrust in connecting market research to architectural planning is basically the guest: you need to know what types of guests you want to attract to your new or renovated facility because guest-orientation is the single most important factor in the planning process.

Bar and beverage operations succeed by pleasing their guests—by knowing (or anticipating) what their guests want and providing for those wants. Setting the appropriate ambience through interior decoration is only the most obvious of many factors. Planning for guest satisfaction requires a multitude of planning factors which guests may never—at least consciously—be aware of: acoustical sound control built into walls and ceilings and further aided by drapery, and traffic flow planning which allows servers to more quickly serve their guests are but two examples.

Guest orientation is important because guests bring the business and provide the profit. Other planning factors, however, may also affect profit. Good planning provides management with the proper control of inventory, cash, employee performance, and other factors which can affect the bottom line. Poor planning for storage space, for instance, can lead to inventory waste or theft. The improper location of a check payment station can lead to "walkouts" (guests who leave without paying their bill).

Proper planning will reveal how much the proposed facility is going to cost and, subsequently, may lead to consideration of complex financial planning. If careful initial planning doesn't reveal the true or final costs of construction, the owner may be "out of business" before the doors open for business.

The Four Viewpoints of Planning

A successful plan for a bar or beverage facility requires that individuals representing four different viewpoints be involved: (1) ownership, (2) operations, (3) architectural/engineering/design, and (4) building. Each viewpoint is important to the planning process and the ultimate success of a bar or beverage operation. The representatives of these four viewpoints must be able to communicate well with each other in terms which are clearly understood by all.

The planning objectives or needs expressed from each of the viewpoints must be specific, concrete, and, whenever possible, measurable. Objectives such as "fast service," "good drinks," and "pleasant surroundings" are too vague. For instance, the projected time required to take an order from seated guests until the delivery of the order should be stated precisely in minutes, even seconds. A planning objective stating this precisely will help the architect understand where the service bar should be located, where and how wide service workflow aisles should be, and a host of other details which otherwise might not be incorporated into the final plan.

One of the best ways to convey ideas to others is through the use of drawings and specifications. Properly done, these leave little room for misunderstanding. Thus, it is important that representatives of the four viewpoints know how to read blueprints and specifications. The following sections cover the expertise and input required from each of the viewpoints.

The Ownership's Viewpoint. We will be using the term "ownership" to represent all the various types of ownership, including multiple owners, partnerships, and investor groups, whether incorporated or unincorporated. The ownership's viewpoint is naturally the most important one, not only because the owner will provide the money (and the method of financing) necessary for the project, but because ownership provides the basic concept and vision of the proposed facility. And while it is advisable to conduct market research and a **feasibility study** before the architectural planning stage, it is often the vision of an owner that will override every other factor or viewpoint. (How many times have we heard of an entrepreneur creating a huge success while flying in the face of conventional wisdom or "expert" opinion?)

Nevertheless, the ownership's viewpoint must be an informed one, whether through market research or experience. This viewpoint will be the starting place for the planning process and should provide guidelines and details about the kind of clientele desired, what will motivate them to come to the proposed facility, the decor and overall theme, and the size of the building necessary to accommodate the expected patronage.

The Operational Viewpoint. It is advisable to have the manager of the proposed facility represent the operational viewpoint. If that isn't possible, then someone who knows operational needs well should be selected; this person might be a well-known consultant. Having a competent consultant is even more important if the owner is relatively inexperienced in the day-to-day operation of a bar or beverage operation or inexperienced in the type of facility planned (a neighborhood bar owner, for instance, going into a live entertainment nightclub operation). When the manager of the proposed facility is involved, he or she can contribute more knowledge and awareness of day-to-day operational needs: the definition in precise terms of the needs for storage space, production of food and drinks, service, security, and other elements needed to make the facility operate in a satisfactory manner. With ownership focused on the larger picture, the operational viewpoint should keep the planning in touch with such mundane (but extremely important) details as how to handle and get rid of trash or where guests will be able to put raincoats and umbrellas on a rainy day.

In addition, at least one representative of either the ownership or operational viewpoints should know how to read architectural drawings and specifications. In fact, it may be desirable for owner/managers to set up a rough **schematic plan** of what is wanted. Using graph paper with quarter-inch squares and, establishing a scale of ¼ or ½ inch representing a foot of linear space, draw a representative floor plan for your proposed facility. Cut out various shapes of paper to represent bars, counters, equipment, tables, and other major elements (all in the established scale) and move them around while visualizing workflow and guest flow patterns and other design factors. The more ownership and management know— and are able to articulate—what they want, the better the architect will be able to bring those wants to life.

The Architectural/Engineering/Design Viewpoint. Once the ownership and operational viewpoints have been established for the proposed facility, and an overall budget limitation set, the architectural/engineering/design representatives will create the graphic, concrete plans and specifications. Today's architects are fully equipped to supply what used to be considered engineering functions. Not only will the architect provide detailed drawings of the proposed facility, he or she will have on file hundreds of thousands of engineering and government-mandated specifications for every conceivable detail of the proposed facility. Many of these specifications will need to be customized for your particular facility.

Guided by the finished plans and a complete list of specifications, the architectural/engineering/design representatives will be able to inform ownership what types and quantities of materials will be required and establish a tentative construction sequence and schedule. At this point the architect can give ownership an approximate estimate of the final cost of construction. If ownership has chosen an architectural firm with considerable experience in planning bar and beverage operations, that cost estimate will more likely come close to the actual cost. Often the builder's viewpoint will be invited early in the planning stages—especially for exceptionally large projects—because this viewpoint may be more accurate in estimating labor costs and completion dates.

At this time, ownership and management should review all plans and specifications with considerable attention to every detail to ensure that nothing has been left out. Careful checking at this point can reveal blind spots and miscalculations made by any segment of the planning team.

After such review, the plans and specifications are finalized and resubmitted for architectural review. Compromises are always required. A support column may stand in the way of where bar placement is desirable, or appropriate space may not have been provided for certain equipment. Almost inevitably, a certain architectural feature desired by ownership or a functional feature recommended by management will turn out to be more costly than initially estimated. Hard choices must be made: ownership may have to decide whether the desired feature is worth exceeding the budget for, or the architect or builder may suggest a less costly compromise.

The final plan will include not only a floor plan, but **elevations** (drawings showing the front, side, and rear views), specialized drawings (such as lighting and electrical plans), and a perspective drawing of the entire facility—complete with some indication of landscaping and parking lots—as it will appear to the public when finished. The final plan will also be accompanied by thousands of **specifications** that will include everything from the specific density, dimension, and thread type of every screw and bolt required, to the specific model numbers of material and equipment where a particular manufacturer's product is called for.

The architectural firm's job is not finished with the completion of the final plan. It has the further responsibility for overseeing the work of the builder (general contractor) and the work of all the subcontractors to ensure that the actual construction follows the plan and specifications in every detail.

The Builder's Viewpoint. The builder will likely provide helpful suggestions about better or more cost-effective building materials, construction details not clearly indicated by the plan, opportunities for cost savings, and more efficient schedules.

Unless a certain builder has a reputation for successful and cost-effective construction of the type of operation that the ownership has planned, the builder may be chosen through a competitive bidding process. The architectural plan and specifications will serve as a guideline for receiving competitive bids from two or more builders. If ownership, management, and architect have been working effectively as a team, they will examine the bids and the past performance records of the competitive bidders and come up with a collective decision as to which bid will be accepted. Almost as often as not, the lowest bidder will not necessarily get the job. The builder's past performance record and a more detailed and complete understanding of what the project requires will often override a lower bid submitted by a competitor.

Once construction has begun, adding to or changing plans or specifications can be much more costly than if the additions or changes were provided for prior to the bidding process. It is also wise to plan for the possibility of extensive remodeling within a relatively short period of time, say, four to five years. If an operation is in a volatile market situation, the plan should avoid construction that is not flexible enough for major changes.

Permits, Licenses, and Regulatory Compliance

Early in the planning stage, ownership should apply for the proper permits and licenses required by various governmental agencies. Letting such important details go until plans are quite advanced can introduce complications and problems. Depending on the location of a facility, applications may have to be made to every level of government for various permits and licenses.

Local ordinances and licensing requirements can usually be learned by making a few phone calls. In some areas, liquor licenses can be extremely hard to acquire. Some city ordinances may require that bar and beverage operations not exceed an established number within a given area. This might mean that acquiring a liquor license will require waiting for an established operation to go out of business; in other areas, owners may sell their liquor licenses, sometimes for many thousands of dollars. In such areas it would be wise to acquire a license before your first visit to an architect.

Building and construction permits of various kinds will be needed. You will have to comply with zoning ordinances, building codes, health codes, fire and safety codes, and pollution laws, and provide access and parking for handicapped individuals. Your plans may have to be approved by various governmental agencies before construction begins. And after construction begins, you, your builder, and your architect will have to deal with inspectors throughout the entire construction process.

Even where permits or licenses are not required, it would be wise to know about and be prepared to comply with various labor regulations, especially those established by the federal Occupational Safety and Health Administration (OSHA). Compliance may require specific kinds of equipment or practices which will add to the total cost of your operation.

Interior Design and Decor

Interior design is inseparable from architectural planning. Most of what goes into the interior of a new or even renovated facility should be included in the initial plan. This includes the overall color scheme, decoration or decor, paint specifications for different surfaces, different types of flooring for functional as well as aesthetic effect (including finishes and carpeting), types of chairs and tables, as well as their placement, and stationary as well as freestanding and movable equipment—in short, everything in the facility with the possible exception of some minor decorative touches.

As we divide this section into subsections such as "Floors," "Ceilings," "Furniture," and so on, it is important to bear in mind that we will freely intermix elements of functionality and aesthetics, or ambience. We will offer some "rules" or traditional standards associated with interior design, but you should understand that many "rules" can be and are ignored and broken, sometimes with purposeful intent and great success.

Above all, interior design must be guided by the clientele you want to serve. Today, increased competition and rapidly changing market trends often require finding and emphasizing narrow market niches (appealing to relatively restricted kinds of clientele), or, at the other extreme, designing "something-for-nearly-everybody" (incorporating many appealing design features into an integrated conceptual whole). Either way, your interior design should reflect an integrated theme with which your prospective clientele can identify and in which they will feel comfortable.

Establishing a Design Theme

Establishing a **design theme** is primarily a marketing exercise. You expect your theme to attract clientele who will make your operation profitable. Sometimes, the theme selected will reflect the tastes or the dream of the ownership for a particular type of bar or beverage operation. In either case, selecting and thoroughly researching a theme and, more importantly, *following through* on that theme down to the smallest detail is required for success. It is this attention to detail that creates the kind of **ambience** and pleasure in the surroundings that keeps people coming back and bringing their friends.

A nautical theme should have the nets, barrels, anchors, boats, and other items appropriate to that theme. A bodega (Spanish wine cellar or bistro) should follow through completely on this theme even to the extent of providing a small dance floor in the center of the room for flamenco dancers.

Frontier Town on the Continental Divide above Helena, Montana, was built to resemble a frontier town with a jail, restaurant, saloon, post office, and other authentic buildings. In the saloon are saddles instead of bar stools. The bar is a huge pine tree sawed in half lengthwise, with a highly varnished top and extending the full length of the room. Steaks come to the guests branded "rare," "medium rare," or "well." Menu items are burned onto tanned skin stretched between stick frames. Everywhere one looks, the theme is "picked up" and emphasized with hundreds of authentic western frontier objects. It is a place to go not only to get the best in drinks but also to enjoy the atmosphere. It is an experience—which is what a theme hospitality facility should be. No tourist ever came into the area without being told to "be sure to visit Frontier Town." It is also highly popular with the local people.

Planning for Space Allocation

Appropriate allocation of space within the confines of a facility is unquestionably the single most important contribution of effective architectural planning. **Space allocation** has both aesthetic and functional dimensions.

Exhibit 3.6 A Bar with Elevated Dining Floor Plan

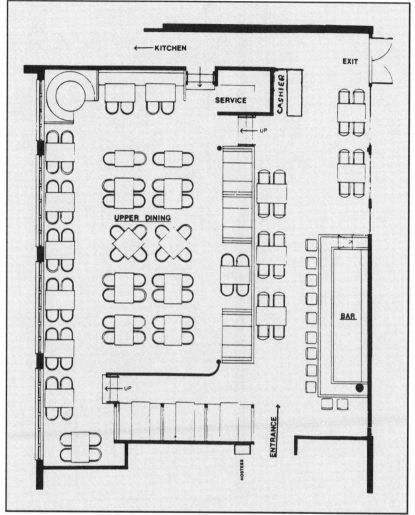

The arrangement of a bar in a dining service area. The bar is located in a good position to attract trade. The raised dining area "separates" the main dining area from the bar. (Courtesy of Di Leonardo International, Inc., Hospitality Design, Warwick, Rhode Island)

Guest flow planning should provide for convenient travel to restrooms. If a coatroom is provided, it should be located in such a way as to avoid congestion at the entrance area.

With our emphasis on guest orientation, don't neglect appropriate planning for workflow patterns. If guests are to receive quick service (and avoid collisions with servers), such planning is important to guests as well as servers. Experienced architects will know how to provide sufficient work space for servers around the service bar area as well as how to balance guest flow and workflow traffic patterns for optimum convenience of guests and servers.

Workflow to and from storage areas is also important if workers are to do their work efficiently and quickly. Chapter 4 goes into more detail

Exhibit 3.7 Barroom in the Center of Floor Plan

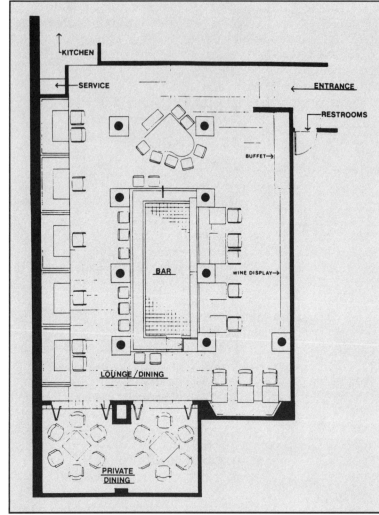

The bar in the center allows service to revolve around it. This makes it difficult to get supplies and materials into the bar without crossing through the service areas. One way this difficulty is overcome is to put in a dumbwaiter that either rises from below into the bar or descends from above. (Courtesy of Di Leonardo International, Inc., Hospitality Design, Warwick, Rhode Island)

with respect to the elements that determine efficient workflow, such as placement of alcoholic beverages, equipment, and so on.

Floors   Types of flooring will differ not only according to different types of operations, but within a single establishment. Cost will be a significant factor because the gap between the costs of linoleum tile, for instance, and an expertly finished hardwood floor laid in a fancy parquet design could be in the tens of thousands of dollars. Maintenance and durability are also important cost factors: wood floors require frequent waxing and polishing; asphalt tile (unless specially treated) will deteriorate quickly when used in kitchens where frequent contact with grease is prevalent.

Exhibit 3.8 A Typical Lounge/Dining Arrangement

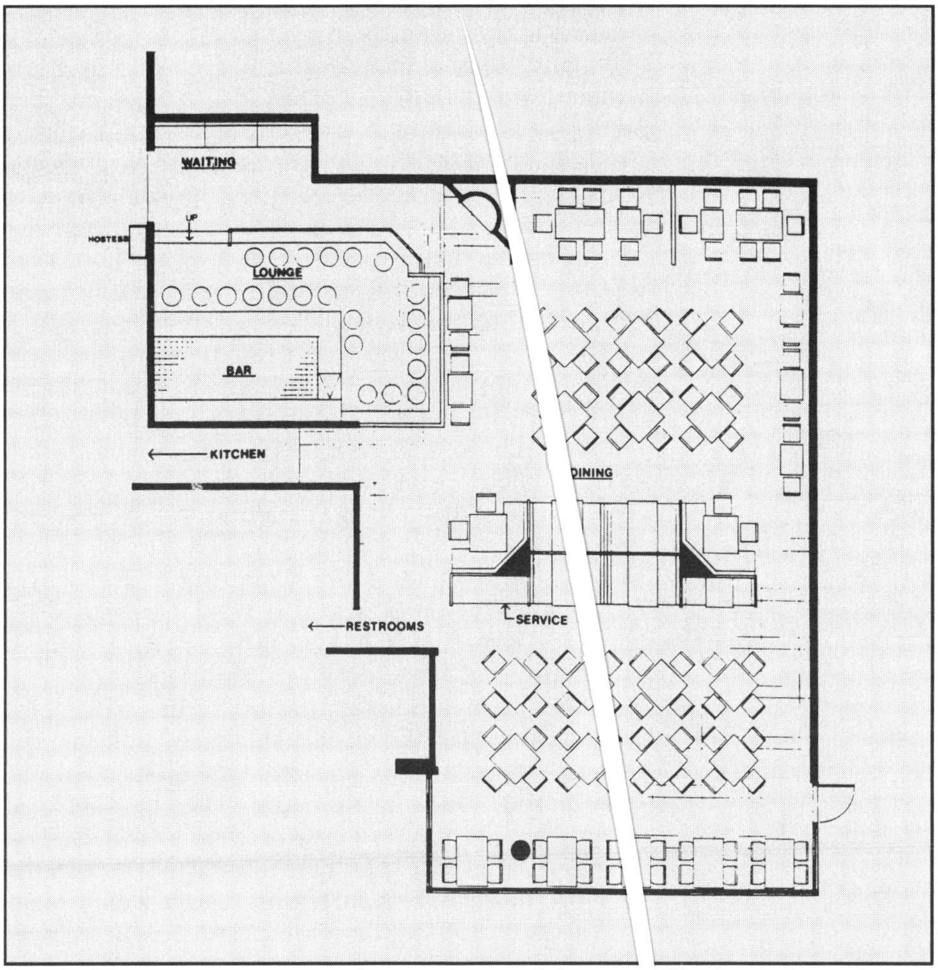

A typical lounge arrangement often put into a dining area. The bar is located close to the entrance so it can act as a holding place when there is an overflow. A waiting space for non-drinkers is provided nearby. (Courtesy of Di Leonardo International, Inc., Hospitality Design, Warwick, Rhode Island)

Costs will be balanced by other considerations such as appearance, safety, durability, cleanability, sound control, and comfort (although the latter two will depend more on floor coverings than the choice of actual flooring material or finish).

In certain places such as around the bar (especially the working area of the bar), flooring should be a hard, durable, non-slip surface that takes heavy wear and can be easily cleaned. Linoleum, vinyl, linotile, ceramic tile, and quarry tile are all more appropriate to the behind-the-bar working areas than expensive wood. Such working areas will most often have some type of removable (for easier cleaning) rubber mat covering whatever flooring material is used (see the next section on floor coverings).

Hardwood floors should generally be finished and/or treated (waxed) with a slip-resistant product. There are always exceptions. The sawdust-covered floor is still a prominent feature in country and western or frontier theme bars. Dance floors require a highly durable finish that *does* provide for some slipping and sliding.

Finally, floors and floor finishes are an important element strictly from the standpoint of decor—color and textural combinations, light reflection and absorption, and so on. A bar or beverage operation with several separate rooms or specially designated areas (fireplace and hearth surrounded by armchairs, for instance) within the same room can make use of all of these elements.

The dance floor is usually located in the center of the seated area or just off it. It should not normally be placed off to a side or in a corner. It is important to ensure that there is easy access to and from it.

The selection of the wood for dance floors should be in keeping with the decor. Maple and oak, if unstained or only lightly stained, give a brightness to the area which may or may not be desirable. Deeper staining or the use of some other hardwoods can give a darker color, if desired. The use of synthetic materials has not been too successful, perhaps for no reason other than that wood is traditional for a dance floor.

Carpeting and Other Floor Coverings. Floor coverings are as varied as floors themselves and are also used for both decorative and functional purposes. Carpeting in heavy traffic areas can look unattractive with wear, so carpeting must be chosen carefully.

Wool and nylon are traditionally more durable than other fabrics, although nylon has the disadvantage of holding the impressions of footprints and furniture marks. There are a wide variety of synthetic materials on the market, and new and improved synthetics are constantly arriving. Such materials may prove to be more cost-effective than traditional floor covering fabrics, and planners should keep current with them.

Short, hard, nubby carpeting resists wear, is more easily cleaned, and provides surer footing than long fiber products. Never place looped, sculptured, or even long yarn carpeting in a traffic area. Such carpeting could be especially dangerous to women wearing high heels and is also hard to keep clean.

All fabric materials used on floors should be specified flame-retardant and treated for stain resistance. Anti-static treatment is also desirable. Heavily patterned carpeting in high traffic areas hides soil and wear.

If carpeting is used in guest areas, it should stop short of the bar seating area and the adjacent area where standing and drinking guests might be expected. Because of the potential for extra wear and soil (spilled drinks, for example), this area should be hard and durable, with an easily cleanable surface. Bar stools are pushed, pulled, and moved around frequently in this area, and a hard surface is the only appropriate flooring.

Floor coverings for work areas should be slip-proof, durable, easily cleanable, and—especially inside the bar—padded to reduce the impact and tiring effect of walking and standing on hard surfaces (see Chapter 4).

Rugs will seldom be used in a bar or beverage operation except in special settings: a small room or a cozy, intimate space (around a fireplace, for instance).

Windows

While windows are not always important factors in bar design, they can help the decor of certain types of facilities and even provide significant marketing appeal. The Images restaurant and bar in downtown Chicago is on the top floor of a skyscraper and overlooks the city in four directions. The architectural planning wisely took advantage of the inherent possibilities with large windows on all four sides. Well-planned seating allows most guests a view of sunsets and the moving panorama of bustling city life below.

Other "penthouse" (top floor) operations have gone so far as to design a circular bar which slowly rotates, giving guests a 180° panoramic view through wall-to-wall windows. Another typical use of windows as a marketing tool is in a bayfront operation.

Windows, however, create other important considerations: they conduct cold or heat and, consequently, increased energy costs. Double or even triple thermopane may be cost-effective in the long term. Open views may be important during the day, but not so important at night. Drapes and curtains may be appropriate in such cases. Drapes may be important to deaden or soften sound (see the section on sound later in this chapter).

Curtains or drapes may be required to reduce the glare at various times of the day or during the summer season. Another option, however, is window tinting. Window tinting can reduce light and reflect heat away from the interior, thus saving on air conditioning.

Finally, mirrors are often an important design element in bar and beverage operations. Often they replace windows, producing the same effects as those offered by windows. If placed properly, mirrors can create more light through reflection and create a feeling of expansiveness in an otherwise small room. Placement of mirrors and lighting should be carefully planned to avoid glare.

Walls and Wall Coverings

Walls are the surface areas most noticeable to your guests. In terms of interior design and decor, then, wall treatment is very important. Walls will more noticeably emphasize the elements of your theme, overall color scheme, and other features of your decor. Walls can also provide for elements that may be considered both functional and aesthetic. Depending on their surfaces, walls can either reflect or absorb sound (see section, this chapter, on "Sound Control"). Depending on their surfaces or coverings, they will reflect or absorb light, or make a room appear larger or more intimate.

Wall surfaces in work areas should be hard and smooth; the covering or finish should stand up to frequent cleaning. Traditional white glazed tile is excellent but not always desirable, because it can give an institutional appearance to the area. However, glazed tile in almost every imaginable color and design is readily available (and is usually much more expensive than plain tile). Oil-based enamels are still the "standby" paint covering for walls that need to be frequently cleaned. However, latex acrylic paints come in semi-gloss and, because they are water-based, will not peel in high moisture areas. Smooth, hard, plastic-coated plywood, a wide variety of plastic materials, and glass fiberboard will also resist moisture and are easily cleanable as well.

Wood paneling is still in use in many bar and beverage operations, but *real* wood (especially hardwoods) is and will continue to be relatively expensive, as hardwood forest areas throughout the world continue to be depleted. Pressed board or fiberboard with an outer layer (veneer) of real wood is widely used and is a less expensive substitute.

Today, science and technology have provided plastics and other synthetic materials of such high quality, durability, and many other desirable physical characteristics, that no interior designer can afford not to keep up with the recent product developments. Plastic materials can create startlingly realistic effects such as stressed wood and textured "old brick" walls, and at a relatively low price.

Curtains and Drapery. Before establishing window covering needs, it is necessary to know the other elements that make up the decor and ambience of an operation. Sometimes just bar windows alone can be highly decorative, especially if they feature a stained glass logo or other decorative touch.

If curtains are used in a place where light is desired, the curtains should be sheer enough to permit a large quantity of light to penetrate. In places where light is not a desirable factor, materials that block out the light should be selected. By selecting the proper materials, you can control the amount of outdoor light entering the place. Sunlight can be a factor in causing curtain deterioration.

Sheer curtains should have a thread count of 76 warp × 64 woof or higher: the better quality materials go higher. A good weave to use is a ninon of 144 threads per square inch. Batiste weaves of combed cotton should be 168 count or higher; if Dacron is used, specify a count of 150 or higher. Also specify double stitching on the inner and outer edges or seams. Curtains should have good draping qualities and be washable. There are drip-dry fabrics that need no ironing. Fiberglass curtains are beautiful and drape well, but with much motion, they abrade and break, except for one kind called Beta Fiberglas. Orlon and Dacron are soft and lustrous and they drip-dry and drape well.

Some good fibers to specify in curtaining are Dacron, Orlon, Saran, Beta Fiberglas, Fortisan, nylon, Chromespun, Celasperm, acetates, and Arnel. Silk is one of the best curtain materials but, because of its high price, is not often used. Rayon is flammable but can be treated to be flame-resistant; it has a beautiful sheen and is quite durable but holds its shape poorly. Some good cotton materials are available: they are not expensive and wash well.

Draperies are made of heavier material than **curtains**, and the weaves are different. There are many types of fabrics. Momie cloth should be made of heavy yarn and be of a 16 warp by 72 woof count. Crash or other heavy cotton draperies should have a count of 68 warp × 76 woof or more. Jacquard weaves should be at least 100 warp × 30 woof.

Drapery materials should have a breaking strength minimum of 35 pounds (15.9 kilograms). Seams and hems should have heavy, strong stitching. Corners should be mitered (cross-stitched) to give them strength. Draperies are given special treatment to hold folds. All window fabrics should be flame-resistant (see also "Upholstery," this chapter).

Ceilings

When properly planned, ceilings can contribute considerably to the overall decorative scheme of the facility. Color, textures, style, decorations, and height, as well as other decorative factors, should be consistent with the overall interior design plan. It is important to remember that bright or light materials reflect light while dark or dull ones absorb it.

Tremors! Nightclub at the Holiday Inn in Livonia, Michigan (Courtesy of Holiday Inn, Livonia)

Sometimes it is necessary to run ducts and various piping or tubing along the ceiling. If so, they should generally be painted to match the ceiling. To further hide them, the ceiling should receive as little reflected light as possible. However, many renovated interior designs have successfully accentuated ducts, piping, tubing, and other ordinarily hidden structural materials—even to the point of painting each of these features in different, bright colors. Fire code-required sprinkler systems are now a reality for most bar and beverage operations, and are yet another ceiling decor element requiring attention. Dark colors tend to make the ceiling appear lower, while light ones make the ceiling look higher. Lighting can also influence the appearance of the ceiling. Conversely, the reflective quality of a particular ceiling material, finish or color will influence the design of some indirect lighting systems. Ceilings may, in fact, be the best place for a great variety of lighting fixtures.

Ceilings should be constructed of materials that are durable, cleanable, and compatible with the decor. Flame-retardant ceiling materials are desirable and often mandated by fire codes.

Finally, ceilings—more than other interior surfaces—may be the most important factor in sound reflection and absorption. So-called **acoustical**

tiles are widely used not just to absorb sound, but to help soften the distorting effects of highly sound-reflective surfaces on music within a room. (See "Sound Control" later in this chapter.)

Furniture and Equipment

A thorough interior design plan will not only locate every piece of furniture and equipment in a facility's available space, but will often specify the type of furniture and equipment to be used. Specifications will often be detailed to the point of calling for a particular manufacturer's product by model number. Every choice will involve a balance between some degree of quality, durability, efficiency, and short- and long-term costs. Naturally, ownership or management should be fully informed and part of these choices.

The increasingly rapid advances in technology, the trend toward getting more efficiency in certain kinds of equipment, and the increasing energy costs have all combined to make getting reliable and up-to-date information about furniture and equipment especially critical. This year's premier refrigeration system may cost thousands more than last year's model, but its energy efficiency may reduce your energy costs by enough to pay for the extra cost within two years.

Trade magazines, trade shows, supplier catalogs and brochures, supplier warehouses, visits to other operations, and talking to other operators are just a few of the ways to get the information you need. Hiring a technical consultant may be advisable. Knowing which manufacturers have the best reputation for reliability, cost-effectiveness, and service is important. In a highly competitive market, these manufacturers will also hire well-informed sales representatives. Talking to representatives of several competitors can often provide as much information as you need to make the right choices.

Some furniture and equipment may have to be custom-fabricated for your operation. Again, selecting a supplier or manufacturer based on reputation for quality, reliability, and competitive pricing could help you make the right choice. However, the more you know about industry standards and cost/benefits, the more likely will your choice be the best possible one.

For the most part, you should select furniture and equipment designed for institutional rather than home use. The former is made to withstand heavy wear and to give the service required in a commercial operation; the latter is not and is often a waste of money to purchase and install.

Every piece of furniture or equipment selected should be weighed from the standpoint of safety. Sharp edges can be a hazard. Be sure the furniture can take the weights put upon it. Inattention to safety considerations can end up in costly personal injury litigation.

One further cautionary note: a new or newly renovated facility will be receiving a lot of furniture and equipment within relatively short intervals, especially during those periods when many other details are commanding management's attention. Nevertheless, it is important that some person or persons be responsible for checking every item and invoice to be sure the items are the ones ordered and that no damage has occurred. Errors and damages must be reported to suppliers immediately. If you are signing a delivery voucher for some items you have received, note on the invoice which items are unacceptable.

Chairs. In selecting chairs, do not get too many kinds. See that chair glides or ball feet are installed so they move easily over the floor. The latter are especially desirable when the chairs are used on carpeting. Legs should be sturdy and the seat should be solid and wide enough to hold a large adult comfortably. The chair should fit under tables without touching any part of the table. Strong back rests are required. Check support for points of stress. See that all parts are well put together and firmly bound together. Metal joints should be strongly welded and even held together by fasteners for additional strength.

See that coverings are washable and proper for the use intended. Coverings and chair design should fit into the decor. A tall-back wicker chair would look out of place in a discotheque.

Chairs may be made of wood, plywood, plastic-impregnated wood, plastic, or metal. Hardwood chairs give good wear and are durable: Birch, walnut, hard maple and oak are suitable. Birch-impregnated chairs are very durable and have good appearance. Bentwood chairs are best made of strong elm. Molded plywood, 7-ply, ⅝-inch thick, gives a strong chair. Often, the backs and legs are made of impact-resistant polystyrene. Fiberglass has good durability. It is possible to combine plastics and woods to get appearance, strength, and durability.

Metal chairs are made of cast aluminum, tube aluminum (square or round), chrome, baked enamel on steel, or covered wrought iron. All metal chairs should have glides. Select glides or chair feet that are suited to the flooring. Some rubber or plastic glides can leave marks. Be sure that metal glides are well rounded and well polished so they do not scratch or otherwise mar the floor finish.

Tables. Tables vary in shape, size, and height. The height range may be from 17 inches (43 centimeters) for some cocktail tables to 26 to 30 inches (66 to 76 centimeters), considered a standard height. Tables need strength to bear the weight of food, drinks, and guests leaning on them. Heavy pressure is often placed on table edges when people get up.

Select tops that are chip-proof and mar-resistant to alcohol, liquids, oils, and other products. Plastic-impregnated wood is good looking, strong, and durable. Specify one-inch, 5- to 9-ply, thick plywood tops covered with ¹⁄₁₆-inch thick high pressure thermosetting, chip- and stain-resistant laminated plastic set with waterproof cement. A similar material can be the same plywood covered with an attractive hardwood with a durable, non-stain finish. Burn-resistant materials are always available and should be specified whenever possible. Include in the specifications that table legs should have levelers. Tables on central tubular stands with levelers free guests to sit comfortably without interference from table legs. Be sure such a table does not tip over when someone leans on it.

Counters. Counters are table tops usually from 34 to 36 inches (86 to 91 centimeters) high; if guests sit on stools, 42 inches (107 centimeters) is usual. Counters are usually 24 to 30 inches (61 to 76 centimeters) wide. Since guests lean on them and give them considerable stress, they should be sturdily constructed, especially at load-bearing points. Watch for sharp edges. Tops should be durable, and burn-, mar-, and chip-resistant. Side panels, if used, should be strong and scuff-resistant.

Counters are often appropriately placed where guests are in a hurry and do not want to sit down, such as in airport lounges. This type of counter is often called a **drink rail**. Drink rails have a surface 12 to 18 inches (30 to 46 centimeters) in depth and about 48 or slightly more inches (122 centimeters or more) high. They are often part of a partition or side wall.

Counters or drink rails are also used in more informal settings where guests move about and mingle with other guests. They are frequently seen near games systems (dart boards, etc.), where guests will set their drinks down while they engage in the game. Counters also make it possible to have more people in a given area than would be possible if traditional seating were employed.

Upholstery. We are treating upholstery separately from chairs for a number of reasons: (1) not all chairs are appropriate for upholstery; (2) upholstery has both functional and aesthetic aspects that will differ according to the particular guest orientation; (3) in addition to chairs, sofas, settees, booths, and banquettes require careful selection of upholstery; and (4) re-upholstering some types of seating units *may* be more cost-effective than replacing the entire unit.

Your selection of upholstery should, first of all, be guided by overall cost/benefit analysis. Will you be able to spend more "up front" for long-term durability and lasting appearance, or will you have to settle for cheaper material now, with the prospect of replacement costs within a few years (or less)?

Next, but no less important, is your guest orientation or target markets. If you want the affluent spenders as guests, the upholstery should be as good as or better than what they are likely to have in their own homes. Expensive soft leather and hard-to-clean fabrics such as velvet are not inappropriate for such clientele.

On the other hand, comfortable (upholstered) seating is important to any type of bar and beverage operation. Fast-food operations purposely install uncomfortable seating—these businesses need to move people in and out to make a profit. You, the bar or beverage manager, want people to stay longer, if only on the basis that they will tend to spend more money and come back more often to places where they feel comfortable.

Your upholstery colors should, of course, match and complement your color scheme.

For most clientele, your upholstery should be easily cleanable as well as comfortable and durable. It may be appropriate to treat the fabric with a stain-resistant spray or to purchase from manufacturers who use stain-resistant fabrics. Another strategy to consider is choosing patterns, such as a Jacquard, which make soiling less apparent.

Many states now require that furnishings and fabrics in places where people congregate (hotels, restaurants, and bar and beverage operations) be flame-resistant. You can ask manufacturers to provide documentation that their products have been treated with fire-retardant chemicals. Dry cleaning companies and other firms specializing in applying these chemicals can also be hired to treat or re-treat upholstery and other fabrics. Some materials also produce toxic gasses when burned. The National Fire Protection Association sets standards on fire retardancy and toxicity. Interior designers usually quote NFPA specifications when they submit their drawings.[1]

Planning for Color   Setting an overall color scheme for your facility is an important part of your initial interior design planning process. Your selection of chairs, tables, drapery, upholstery, and other interior items should take place within the context of the overall color scheme. And your overall color scheme should be guided by the type of clientele you expect to serve.

In recent years, color, and its effect on people's emotions, has been the focal point of hundreds of studies, and a thriving market for "color consultants" has been created. Your architect may have an in-house color expert or may be able to recommend a firm with the appropriate expertise and reputation. In addition, color has many more ramifications, including altering the spatial perception of objects or areas within a room, the highlighting of certain features, and the subduing of other features. Ownership and management may have their own ideas about color but will be well served by some degree of expert guidance.

At times, certain colors are "in vogue" (and become fads); these colors may be appropriate to your clientele, but be prepared to change color schemes when the fad changes. Reds, yellows, and browns—especially when used in proportions that create "earth tones"—tend to create a feeling of warmth, coziness, and security. Combined appropriately, colors such as blues and grays can create a cool and peaceful effect.

Beyond these generalizations, you may notice that in most bar and beverage operations, overall color schemes and color combinations tend to be subdued, with vivid contrasts used sparingly to create special effects or prevent boredom. We come to bar and beverage operations, for the most part, to relax and enjoy the company and the surroundings. However, your expected clientele should be the guiding factor. A youth-oriented operation (such as a disco) may use color to create excitement; you might find garish combinations of wildly contrasting colors to be most effective.

Technically speaking, what we ordinarily think of as color opposites (red and green, for instance) are called **complementary** colors. We use complementary colors for special effect: a bright burgundy vase against a dark green background, for instance. If we wish to reduce the intensity of contrast, we might place a blue-green vase against a red background with some blue in it. Certain colors can be made more intense by being contrasted with other colors. Thus, a blue-green color looks bluer when near a bright green.

Colors blend together when they have the same tonal values. (Tonal value is the degree of lightness or darkness in the color or hue, and is determined by the amount of white or black used to tone down the color.) Areas can be made to look larger or smaller depending upon hues, tonal blending, and contrasting. Light colors make an area look larger, while dark colors make an area appear smaller.

Interior Environmental Planning

The surroundings in which people work and where guests come to be served must be such that both are comfortable and not tainted by undesirable environmental elements. Air must be fresh, of a proper temperature and relative humidity, with no odors or other objectionable or injurious elements. In fact workers and guests should not be aware of air

Enormous potential for creative interior design rests in multipurpose areas such as lounges and bars. (Courtesy of Di Leonardo International, Inc., Hospitality Design, Warwick, Rhode Island)

at all. This requires proper planning for air freshening, heating and cooling, circulation, and exhaust.

Sound control is also an important consideration in environmental planning. In the past few years we have learned a lot about how to control sound and use it to advantage in giving people restful, pleasant living areas. Not all bar and beverage operations will want to control sound by deadening it; a loud and lively atmosphere is just right for the younger markets. Sound control is important in such settings if for no other reason than ensuring good acoustical control over quality music.

A later section on lighting will deal with the importance of lighting to ambience as well as efficiency in work areas. Ownership should be able to articulate work and atmospheric needs to the architect. The architect, in turn, should be able to provide many lighting options appropriate to the building design and the environmental needs of the target markets.

Air Control and Conditioning

With smog and other contaminants in today's air, we hear much about air purity. Bar and beverage units need to have the air flushed out frequently because of the buildup of not only smoke from cigars and cigarettes, but also odors from alcoholic beverages. We all know what a smoke-filled bar or a dining area that smells of cooking grease can do to the pleasure of being there.

It is important that the ambient air environmental system be highly flexible, quickly responsive to controls, automatically controlled within narrow ranges—wide fluctuations are highly undesirable—and as low as possible in cost. The cost factor can be important, especially in areas where there are high or low outside temperatures and where the provision of adequate insulation may increase costs.

Air high in moisture, even though of a proper temperature, does not feel that way because it has little drying effect. Overly dry air is too cooling because it has too much evaporative effect. Normally, inhabited spaces should have an **ambient air temperature** of 65° to 75° F (18° to 24° C) with a **relative humidity** (RH) of 35% to 75% (50% is generally considered ideal).

As a room fills with people, the room warms—a normal adult gives off heat equivalent to that of a 100-watt incandescent light bulb and about 1½ ounces (45 milliliters) of moisture every hour. Exhaust requirements should be set to meet such expectations. If there is equipment in the room, such as a steam table, this has to be taken into consideration. High moisture buildup can be a significant factor in the deterioration of a building. Moisture can collect between walls and floors and start rot.

It is sometimes possible, through structural features, to capture heat and vapor and draw it away before it spreads around. Ceilings can be canopied with an air exhaust duct in the center to capture and take away heat and moisture as it rises.

Air exhaust must be balanced against air input. If less air is supplied than is exhausted, a negative pressure is set up which can draw in troublesome fumes from the kitchen or elsewhere. A slight positive air pressure (greater pressure inside than outside) keeps such fumes from entering. The amount of air that can be recirculated into a room and the amount of new air required to be pulled in from the outside is usually specified by local codes—about 15 cubic feet per minute (425 liters per minute) is usual.

It is also important that proper air velocity and movement be maintained so that air coming into the room does not strike patrons. The system should be designed to give good air spread. Noise of air coming out of or going into a duct can also be bothersome. Proper engineering will prevent these problems. Air velocities of about 15 to 30 feet per minute (4.6 to 9.1 meters per minute) are usual.

In the summer, if the air is around 78° F (25° C) and the RH is about 50%, one will feel fairly comfortable. In some very hot climates, air about 15° F (8° C) cooler than the air outside usually feels comfortable. It should be remembered that air that is hot but quite dry, as it often is in Las Vegas in July and August, will still feel cooler than air in Miami at the same temperature which may have a RH of 90% or more.

In the winter, air is heated. Indoor air at 70° F (21° C), or even a bit below, feels comfortable during this season, especially if the RH is at 50%. Because the RH in a heating system is reduced by the heat, some systems will add moisture to the heated air to bring it to optimum standard.

Sound Control   Sound pollution can cause discomfort for guests and can tire workers. It is often difficult to distinguish conversation from background reverberating noise, especially as people age and lose some of their sense of hearing.

Sound is energy that travels in waves like other energy. The number of waves per second is called the sound frequency or **Hertz** (Hz). The loudness of sound is measured in **decibels** (db) and we indicate them from 0 db on up. Normal office sound is 50 db, normal speech from three feet away is 70 db, and shouting about 90 db from five feet away. OSHA requires that workplaces have an ambient sound environment averaging no higher than 90 db, but some claim this is too high, and 85 db is more appropriate.

Some sound may not be in high decibels but nevertheless is objectionable. The high frequency of a shrill whistle or a jet engine can hurt the ear and, if continued long enough, can do permanent harm to one's hearing. Sound combines; if there are 40 db coming from one direction and they combine with 50 db, the decibels are not 90 but 50.5 db.

Sound waves can bounce off objects the way a tennis ball bounces off a wall, or they can be absorbed by them. The essence of sound control is stopping sound from reverberating by capturing it or diffusing it. Often this is done by using sound capturing materials or devices or by directing sound away from where it is not wanted. Soft draperies, soft furniture coverings, carpets, textured wall coverings—all hold sound. Hard surfaces such as a wooden floor, mirrors, and even table tops reflect sound. Glass will reflect about three times as much sound as drapery hanging near it.

After the completion of a new club in Miami, the bar area was found to be so noisy guests would not stay in it. The back walls were all mirrored with tile between the mirrors. The floor was hard and so was the ceiling. On two sides were complete window surfaces giving an open view of the downtown area of Miami. A small grill area in the room was completely tiled. With hard chairs and hard table tops, the room never had a chance. It was quickly remodeled.

One way of getting rid of sound is to capture it in a concave surface and then direct it away and out of the area. We see this often in outdoor staging where the chorus or orchestra or singer stands in front of a large concave backdrop which catches the sound and sends it out to the audience. Ceilings can be lined with sound-absorbing materials (often called acoustical tile).

The best way to control sound is to stop it at its source. The sound of a motor or a fan can certainly be controlled. Outside sound can be stopped from getting in by sealing the building. Sound can travel along air ducts, pipes, and other connectors, especially if they are metal. It also can be stopped by putting up barriers outside to catch it. A lattice fence with three-inch (7.6 centimeter) squares stops most sound waves over three inches. Barriers from four to five feet (122 to 152 centimeters) high can lower outside sound levels from 8 to 10 db.

Acoustical materials should be selected for their ability to do the job, for appearance, cost, maintenance, and fire rating. They should blend in with the decorative scheme. Codes should be checked to see if they meet with requirements. Moisture-proof materials should be selected. Cleanability is important. Some materials can be scrubbed with a brush, while others abrade easily under cleaning treatment. Check also on their ability to withstand buckling and discoloration. Some acoustical materials are destroyed or can lose efficiency if painted.

Lighting Control

Lighting not only gives light but creates decorative effects and reduces monotony by providing different shadings to a room. Thus, it is important that planning consider lighting's appropriateness in the context of decor as well as the proper amounts of lighting.

Soft, low light may be desirable in some areas, such as in a lounge where guests like to sit and talk while drinking. Such lighting should, however, be sufficient to prevent accidents and to enable people to read a menu. Low lighting that makes seeing difficult is bothersome to many patrons.

In work areas the light should be adequate so there is no eye fatigue. Light can also be used to create a quiet, soft atmosphere or a lively, noisy one. Subdued light creates the former; bright light, the latter.

There are three lighting needs in a bar facility: **task lighting**, **zone lighting**, and **ambient lighting**. Task lighting provides workers with enough light to do their work properly. Zone lighting provides proper lighting for travel into and out of the unit. Ambient lighting provides atmosphere and holds the overall decor of the facility together. Lighting in the lower part of the room is often used to create ambience and atmosphere. Lighting higher up is often used to create task and zone lighting, but will also contribute to atmospheric needs.

Too much light gives a room a stark, "bled" appearance. A large room needs shadows to break it up. Some lounges are highly decorative because of small wall and table lighting. Such lighting can also give a feeling of privacy. Areas of a room can be highlighted while others can be made to seem somewhat secluded just by establishing a proper lighting pattern. Too much contrast, however, can give a chopped up appearance to the room. Use ceiling spots to provide direct and concentrated light on objects or areas. Longitudinal lines of light increase the feeling of length, while horizontal ones increase width.

Fluorescent lighting is a more viable option than ever. The image of fluorescent lighting as stark blue or green and unflattering is a thing of the past. There are some kinds of fluorescent lighting units that give a full spectrum of light almost equal to that of sunlight. **Fluorescent** light has the advantage of being much cooler than **incandescent** and gives five times more light per watt than incandescent. Its disadvantages are a time lag in lighting up and some flicker at times. Mercury lights are somewhat like fluorescent.

If a lot of incandescent lighting is massed in one area, a lot of heat can be generated that might be a problem for air control and conditioning. Often this heat is drawn off by methods other than air conditioning. In some operations, the excess heat is used to warm water.

Select lighting fixtures with care. Fixtures should give the right lighting pattern and the proper amount of direct or indirect light (see Exhibit 3.9). Lighting has advanced to such a point that one can achieve spectacular effects using proper lighting contrasts and colors. In one facility, suspended light fixtures reflected most of the light upward to give a diffused indirect lighting effect below, but each fixture was so made that tiny dots of bright light escaped downward and outward giving an effect of stars shining in the sky.

The positioning of lights should be such that glare is avoided. Objects such as mirrors or stainless steel units should be placed so they do not catch bright light and reflect it as glare. Direct glare can be reduced by increasing brightness behind the light. It is possible to have ceilings reflect so much light that glare results. It is possible to flood a low ceiling with so much light that one walking into the room wants to duck down because

Exhibit 3.9 A Lighting Plan

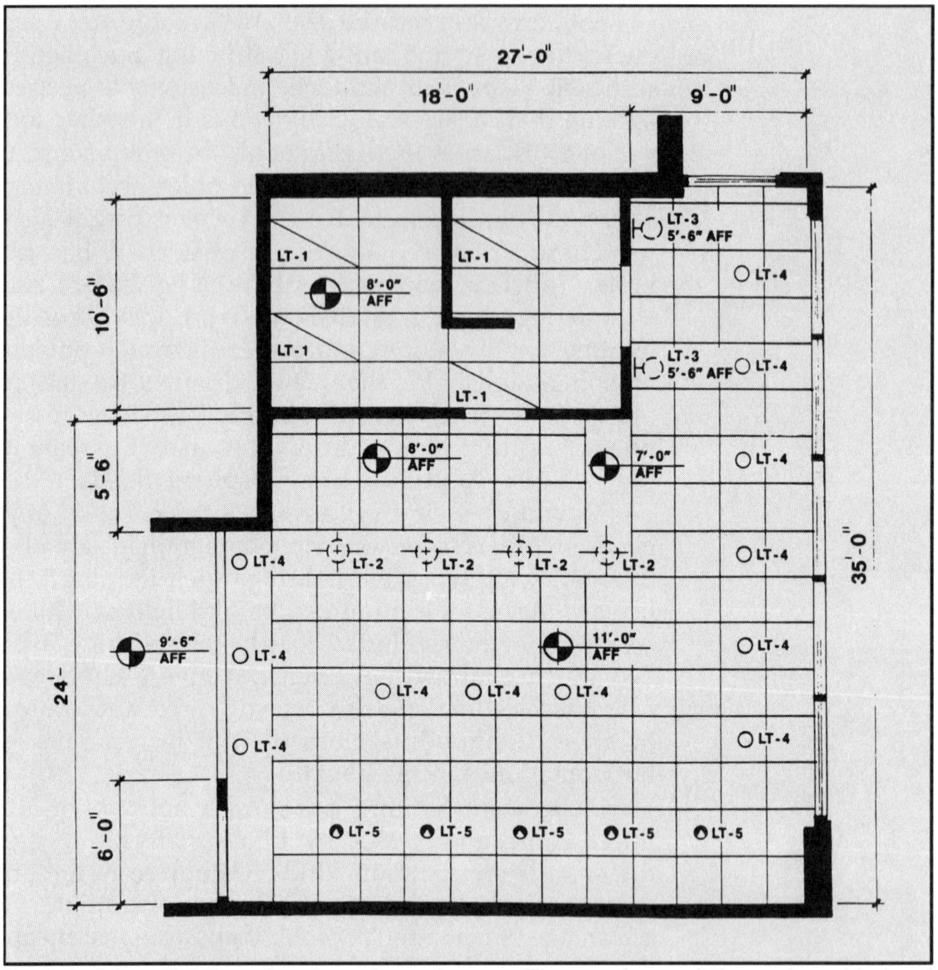

Illustrated is a lighting plan for a large lounge. The numbers of the various kinds of lights (LT) correspond to the lighting specification numbers which accompany the plan.
(Courtesy of Di Leonardo International, Inc., Hospitality Design, Warwick, Rhode Island)

one feels the ceiling is so low. To avoid drawing attention to a low ceiling, do not light it at all from the top. Use lighting from other areas to do this.

Lighting is often measured in footcandles (fc), the amount of light cast by a candle one foot from source. The amount of light needed for a work area is 100 fc or more, while a space where people are seated in a lounge may be 30 fc or less.

Remember, soft light makes people stay, while bright light moves them on. Soft light creates a subdued and quiet atmosphere; bright light creates gaiety and movement.

Exterior Design

While we have covered interior design in some detail, it is appropriate to conclude with a few thoughts about exterior design. As we noted at the beginning of this chapter, it is highly unlikely that you will be part of building a bar or beverage establishment from the ground up. You are more likely to take part in a renovation—which also means that exterior design is even less likely a factor with which you will have to deal in the future. Nevertheless, you should be aware of the basic considerations covered in the ensuing paragraphs.

First of all, it makes a great deal of difference to exterior design if your facility will be freestanding or part of another facility, such as a hotel or restaurant. We assume for purposes of discussion that the facility will be freestanding, because the design concerns will be particular to a bar or beverage establishment and not to a larger entity with overriding design concerns.

Your exterior design should do two primary things: It should attract the kind of customers you have targeted in your business plan, and it should reflect and be in accord with the interior decor. In other words, people should get a pretty good idea about what is inside from what is outside. Signs may be the first thing to attract notice; you will have to decide how much you want to attract passersby to your establishment. On the other hand, a large enough sign to attract passersby might be off-putting to other kinds of clientele. A long-established bar in Sausalito, California, is called the "no name" bar. It attracts a low-key, upper-middle-income crowd, and one of its attractions is that it doesn't need to clamor for attention.

Some degree of landscaping is almost always necessary. Very few exterior designs cannot be improved by the use of trees and shrubs to accentuate building design features. Greenery may be important for practical reasons, such as providing summer shade for window areas (to cut down on air conditioning costs). Trees, shrubbery, and other landscaping elements make a facility inviting to potential customers in a way that is unmatched by the design elements of the facility itself. A word of caution: make sure your landscaping doesn't provide a hiding place for possible criminal threats to your patrons.

Sufficient and efficient lighting is also a security issue. A well-lighted parking lot is essential for the security of your patrons. In addition, entrances and especially any elevations must be adequately lighted for safety purposes. Lighting is integral to exterior design, just as it is to interior design. Lighting can accentuate certain design features, soften others, and tie the building design elements together during the nighttime.

Finally, access to the facility itself and to the parking lot from the street is an important design factor. Access to the building for handicapped patrons is now a matter of law in most states of the United States. Reserved parking for the handicapped is also required in most states. Access from busy streets to the parking lot is crucial; people will tend to stay away if egress or exit is too difficult. Working with city planners prior to architectural planning is important. Often such cooperation may provide solutions—such as turn lanes and traffic islands—to otherwise difficult access problems.

Endnotes

1. Margaret M. Kappa, Aleta Nitschke, and Patricia B. Schappert, *Managing Housekeeping Operations* (East Lansing, Michigan, 1990), p. 248.

Key Terms

acoustical tile
ambient air temperature
ambient lighting
banquettes
complementary (colors)
curtains
decibels
design theme
draperies
drink rail
elevations

feasibility study
fluorescent
Hertz
incandescent
relative humidity
schematic plan
space allocation
specifications
task lighting
zone lighting

Discussion Questions

1. What type of relationship should there be between market research and architectual planning?

2. What planning objectives might ownership and operations want to convey to an architect?

3. How would you use a schematic plan to convey important ideas to an architect?

4. What types of permits and licenses are needed for a bar or beverage establishment, and what are some of the issues of regulatory compliance faced by bar owners?

5. Pick a design theme for "your" bar or beverage establishment; expand on the major elements; include some small details.

6. How do space allocation concerns differ for various types of bar and beverage establishments (discos, lounges, airport bars, etc.)?

7. Describe and discuss various traffic flow patterns—for guests, for staff.

8. Discuss the importance of color in a bar or beverage establishment. Why are color consultants doing a lot of business these days?

9. Discuss elements of air control and conditioning in addition to the obvious cooling and heating factors.

10. What are some of the ways in which sound is "captured," deadened, or intensified (reflected) within a structure?

11. What are the differences between task, zone, and ambient lighting? Give some examples.

12. How would you go about resolving a problem that might arise with respect to access to "your" bar or beverage establishment's parking lot?

4 The Bar

Chapter Outline

Bar Layout
  The Bar Menu in Bar Layout
  The Human Factor in Bar Layout
  Self-Sufficiency and Security
Basic Bar Arrangements
  The Front Bar
    The Backbar
    The Underbar
    A Special Note
  The Service Bar
    Room Service
Bar Equipment, Accessories, and Tools
  Ice and Ice-Making Machines
  Glassware
  Bar Tools and Accessories
Bar Sanitation

In the previous chapter you learned about the architectural and design aspects of the overall bar environment. We examined the lounge area or "room" (as the entire space of a bar or beverage operation is sometimes called) and talked about the importance of architectural design and interior decor in creating the appropriate ambience for the desired types of guests or "target markets." We looked at the importance of architectural design to the overall functionality and efficiency of an operation—traffic flow patterns, for instance—and how to make the best use of whatever space your bar or beverage operation has.

In this chapter we are going to narrow our focus to just one aspect of the room: the **bar.** For purposes of our discussion in this chapter, the bar is that area of a bar or beverage operation in which drinks are prepared and from which drinks are sold. And, most important, it is the profit center of the operation. In small bar and beverage operations, the physical structure of the bar might take up as much as half of the room space. In larger operations the bar might take up just a small percentage of the total square footage.

Small or large, the kind of bar we are most familiar with as guests is called the front bar. The front bar's primary purpose is to serve beverages to guests who may be standing or seated around the bar or sitting at tables in a lounge area.

In some restaurants that serve alcoholic beverages, the bar is little more than a service area where the service staff can order and pick up drinks for the dining room guests. This type of bar is known as a service bar.

This chapter details the functional layout of the bar itself. It includes important information about tools and equipment—their functions and proper placement. It discusses the best use of available storage areas, defines the "backbar" and "underbar," and describes how the proper arrangement of these areas will add to your operation's efficiency. In addition, you will learn about the storage and selection of glassware and proper sanitation of the bar area.

Bar Layout

The layout of a bar depends on the type of operation. Each type of operation presents its own limitations and challenges. For example, the poolside bar at a resort hotel will have special refrigeration and sanitation concerns. An airport bar has to emphasize speed and accessibility in its layout. The layout of a restaurant bar will need to accommodate the storage requirements of wines and champagnes. And most freestanding bars (bars that serve alcoholic beverages as their primary source of income) are so unique it is hard to make any generalizations about them. Even so, there are some general "rules" of bar layout that can guide the functionality and efficiency of most operations.

Many of you may have worked in restaurants that were poorly laid out. If so, you probably encountered such problems as: (1) not enough refrigeration space or too much freezer space; (2) equipment (sometimes impeding the traffic flow) that was never used; (3) equipment that *was* needed but unavailable; (4) not enough shelf space in the salad pickup area for plates; (5) not enough sheet trays to accommodate the baked goods offerings.

Similar layout problems also diminish the efficiency of some bar and beverage operations: the draft beer tap is at one end of the bar and the server pickup area at the opposite end; the servers drop off the dirty glasses in one area, requiring the bartender to carry them to the glass-washing equipment located in another area; the only way for servers to get ice from behind the bar is to go through (or under) the server pickup area or pass the ice over the heads of guests sitting at the bar. Each of these situations can become a nightmare for a bartender during a busy shift.

Perhaps the most important consideration for you, the bar or beverage manager, is the reality that you will often be called upon to manage operations where the original design of the room or the bar area is no longer functional or as efficient as it should be. You may be called upon to manage an operation where the owner or top management has decided to change the marketing strategy to attract entirely different target markets. Your greatest challenge, then, will be to change the layout of the bar and the functions of employees to meet the new marketing requirements.

The Bar Menu in Bar Layout

When we speak of the **bar menu** in this section, we are not using "menu" in accordance with its customary usage; we use "menu" as a conceptual tool that will guide bar layout. The bar menu in this specialized usage is made up of the primary types of beverages you will serve your target markets, in addition to all types of mixed drinks you are prepared to serve, draft and bottled beers, wine, and the specialty drinks you will offer. The bar menu takes into account your target markets and projects their drink preferences. It must also take into consideration what your competition is offering and must have the flexibility to keep up with the latest trends and changing guest preferences.

Ideally, the bar menu should also determine your storage space requirements. In reality, however, your operation will most likely be allocated a pre-determined amount of storage space. The layout challenge, then, is to optimize the amount of space you have available. (Storage space, since it is non-revenue-producing, must be kept to a minimum.)

In an ideal situation—where such things as target markets and traffic flow are pre-determined—the architect can design the layout of the bar with a specific bar menu in mind. Take, for example, an airport food and beverage operation in Orlando, Florida: The owners were given a pre-determined amount of square footage in which to build their restaurant. They had to determine how much of this total space would be allocated for the beverage side of the operation. Since airports have a high traffic flow, with people either in a hurry or waiting for long periods of time, the bar layout had to accommodate both extremes. In general, airport bars do a high volume of business in draft beer, highballs, and simple mixed drinks such as Bloody Marys. Located in a popular tourist resort area, however, the Orlando operation had an opportunity to include tropical drinks as well as the traditional favorites in its bar menu (see Exhibit 4.1).

With the bar menu set prior to the design of the entire operation, the architect was able to design the bar layout and storage areas to accommodate the demands of the menu. The design provided for easy access to the storage area, with plenty of refrigerated space for mixers, such as Bloody Mary mix and bottle beer. The bar layout is such that the bartender does not have to turn around to make a drink unless the guest requests a call

Exhibit 4.1 Bar Menu

CONCESSIONS INTERNATIONAL
OF ORLANDO
Presents

LIBATIONS

LIBERATION

STRAWBERRY HILLS
A combination of fresh
strawberries and rum make for
a fruity delight in this
very berry drink.
$4.75

YELLOW BIRD
Fly away with this delectable
mixture of orange juice, Tia Maria,
banana liqueur and dark rum.
$4.85

GOOMBAY SMASH
Allow yourself to be transported
to the traditional island festival
with this combination of dark rum,
coconut liqueur and pineapple juice.
$4.85

COCO LOCO
Let the creamy taste of pineapple
juice, light rum and coconut drive
you crazy in this luscious
tropical drink.
$4.75

**CONCESSION'S INTERNATIONAL
HOUSE SPECIALTY**

MANGO BANGO
Experience the Caribbean mystique
with the exotic mixture of mango
nectar, orange juice, rum and
banana liqueur in this frothy drink.
$5.30

MARGARITA GRANDE
Try the traditional mixture of
tequila, triple sec and a special
sour mix.
$4.75

TRY OUR SPECIAL COFFEES
Irish—Coffee with Irish Whiskey, topped with
Whipped Cream
Mexican—Coffee with Kahlua, topped with
Whipped Cream
Jamaican—Coffee with Tia Maria, topped with
Whipped Cream
French—Coffee with Cognac, topped with
Whipped Cream
Italian—Coffee with Sambuca, topped with
Whipped Cream
$4.65

FAVORITE COCKTAILS

Bloody Mary	B-52
Manhattan	Long Island Ice Tea
Old Fashioned	Pink Lady
Rusty Nail	Singapore Sling
Martini	Whiskey Sour
Black Russian	

And many more, including your own
specialty, prepared just the way you like.

BAHAMA MAMA
Let this delicious concoction of rum,
sherry and fruit juices take you to
the pink sands of the Bahamas
famous beaches.
$4.85

This bar menu preceded the design of an Orlando, Florida, airport lounge. (Courtesy of Concessions International, Inc.)

brand (those brands that guests request by name). Well brands (those brands carried by the bar and served when guests do not specify brand), ice, mixers, and blending machine are all within easy reach.

Of course, many bar and beverage operations have printed drink menus, that is, a list of the beverages and types of drinks from which guests may order. The detail and extent of such a menu are dictated by the type of operation. It is highly impractical, in most bar and beverage operations, to list every single drink that you can serve. Most operations identify at least a limited listing of the most popular drinks their guests are likely to order.

All bar and beverage operations should provide some list of drink offerings, because of the proven marketing effectiveness of such a list. A list featuring house specialty drinks could, for instance, describe the ingredients in an enticing manner. Another way to "list" specialty drinks is by describing them on an eye-appealing folded card that is placed on every table and at various points along the bar.

The Human Factor in Bar Layout

No less important to the layout of your bar are the job functions of each employee who will be working in and around this area. Job functions are determined through a job analysis which either identifies (in the case of an existing operation) or predicts (in the case of a new operation) the activities that each employee will need to perform in the course of his or her workday or shift. Information from the job analysis determines the specific tasks and duties required by each job. (And, as we will see in Chapter 7, these tasks and duties will lead to the development of formal job specifications and job descriptions.)

In respect to bar design, job analysis is most important when it predicts tasks and duties of each employee necessary for a particular operation prior to the design of the bar. In an established operation, a bar or beverage manager is far more likely to be faced with the task of bringing in more business, hiring more employees to serve that new business, and arranging the flow of employee traffic around the existing bar layout (and changing those aspects of the layout which can be easily changed).

Employee traffic flow is an important human factor in bar layout. Other factors that must be considered are:

- Guest traffic flow patterns in the lounge area

- Volume of business anticipated (to set minimum and maximum staffing requirements)

- Type of business (what kinds of employees, what job functions will be most appropriate?)

- Level (or degree) of service (what kinds and numbers of employees, and job functions will be needed?)

Above all, the human factor in bar layout means placing the equipment, tools, stock, service areas, and other functions within easy reach of the people involved, so that efforts will not be wasted. (You might find it instructive to sit at a bar during a rush period and watch the bartender work. How many steps does it take him or her to mix a drink? Is he or she always reaching or bending for needed items? Does he or she have to travel to three or four different areas to get all the ingredients for a particular drink?)

Self-Sufficiency and Security

Ideally, the bar should be designed to be self-sufficient. That is, it should have its own ice machine, refrigerated storage, and dry storage. Many operational, even security, problems can occur in food and beverage operations that attempt to share equipment and storage space. You want liquor to be stored in accessible areas that can be securely locked up in storage areas. Such cages require a minimal amount of space and are an excellent way to temporarily store the stock that you have moved from your liquor storeroom to the bar area. The overall control system can be greatly strengthened by designing a self-sufficient bar layout. As you will learn in Chapter 10, security and the design of an efficient control system are of paramount importance in bar and beverage management.

Basic Bar Arrangements

Bars come in many sizes, shapes, and configurations. In almost any large urban area you might see "zig-zag" or serpentine-shaped bars—even circular bars mounted on a slowly revolving platform in a circular-shaped penthouse lounge with windows instead of walls. The more common bar shapes, however, include the straight line, the horseshoe or U-shape, the angle, the circular, and the oval.

Whatever their shape, there are basically two different bar types, each of which requires different layout considerations: the **front bar** and the **service bar**. As briefly described in the chapter introduction, the front bar's primary purpose is to serve beverages to guests who may be seated at seats or bar stools around the bar or sitting at tables in a lounge area. The service bar, strictly speaking, is a relatively small bar designed solely to prepare beverages for servers to serve to guests in the dining area.

In the following sections, we will be discussing these two types of bars—their layout, functions, tools, and equipment—as if they were totally unique entities. We do so in order to present the "ideal"; if you, as a bar or beverage manager, have the opportunity to participate in the design or layout of a new or remodeled bar, you will want your operation to come as close as possible to that ideal.

Nevertheless, the real world of bar and beverage management is almost always far from ideal. You will encounter every combination of front and service bar imaginable. Think, for instance, of the owner of a large, successful restaurant, getting a liquor license, and desiring to expand his building and his business. He has only one way to add on, and that is toward the back parking area. Consequently, he has a small lounge and front bar which must also serve as a service bar with a large kitchen area in between the dining area and the bar. Now, the combination front and service bar has only one work station from which, during peak periods, two bartenders must serve guests at the bar, provide the lounge servers with drinks, and provide all the wine and drinks for guests in the three separate dining areas! Pity the poor restaurant servers who have to transport—without spilling a drink—full drink trays close to a hundred feet down a hallway in which guests are coming and going.

The example we have just described is based on an actual food and beverage operation that is very successful and profitable. More commonly, you will see combination lounge/restaurants where one end of a large front bar has a separate work station designated as the "food service" area (see Exhibit 4.2). Much of what you will learn in these next sections can be applied to situations that are far from the ideal.

The Front Bar

The typical front bar serves not only as a place where guests may sit down and order and consume beverages, but as part of a complex work space for the bartender (or bartenders). This complex work space includes storage and display of beverages, tools, and equipment. The front bar can be divided into two basic functional areas, which are described in the following sections.

The Backbar. The **backbar**, as the name implies, is located at the back of the bar, using as much of the entire back wall of the bar as is aesthetically

Exhibit 4.2 Bar Layout

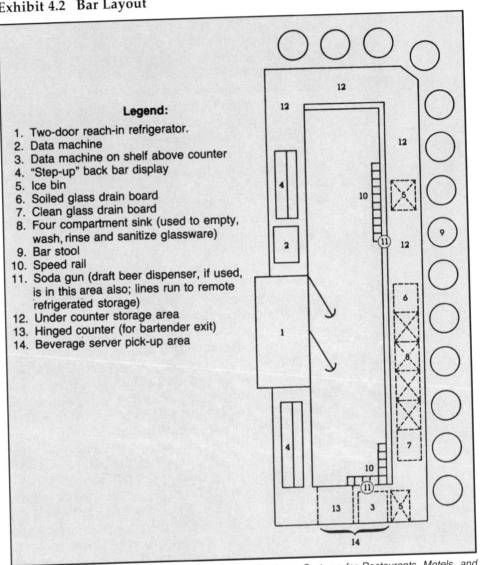

Legend:
1. Two-door reach-in refrigerator.
2. Data machine
3. Data machine on shelf above counter
4. "Step-up" back bar display
5. Ice bin
6. Soiled glass drain board
7. Clean glass drain board
8. Four compartment sink (used to empty, wash, rinse and sanitize glassware)
9. Bar stool
10. Speed rail
11. Soda gun (draft beer dispenser, if used, is in this area also; lines run to remote refrigerated storage)
12. Under counter storage area
13. Hinged counter (for bartender exit)
14. Beverage server pick-up area

Source: Jack D. Ninemeier, *Beverage Management: Business Systems for Restaurants, Motels, and Clubs* (New York: Lebhar-Friedman, 1982) p. 74.

and functionally feasible. In most bar and beverage operations the backbar serves the dual functions of display and storage. Sometimes the back wall display includes mirrors, photographs, or memorabilia—in short, aesthetic or atmospheric decor.

The type of storage space required depends on the type of operation. In food operations with heavy wine sales, specialized refrigerated storage with easy access to all bottles on the wine list is often part of the backbar, but might also require additional space outside the bar area. (There are many types of wire shelving racks designed specifically for refrigerated wine storage.)

Your volume in bottled beer sales will also determine how much refrigerated storage you will need for bottled beers. The draft beer dispensers

Backbars are for display and storage. (Courtesy of Opryland Hotel, Nashville, Tennessee)

are most commonly (and efficiently) located in the front area of the bar as part of the "underbar" (see below). Exceptions to this rule are also common. The restaurant cited above has about one-quarter of a decorative "keg" sticking out of a side wall of the bar area from which specially imported draft beer is drawn. The actual keg is in a refrigerated storage area located behind the side wall.

The storage/display arrangement of the backbar will vary from operation to operation. Some bar and beverage operations choose to display their premium brands on specially designed shelving.

The Underbar. By **underbar,** we mean the primary working space for the bartender. It is that area of the bar that is in front of the bartender as he or she faces the guests and, as the name would indicate, mostly (but not entirely) below the level of the bar itself. The functional aspects of the

A secure controlled-temperature wine storage facility. (Courtesy of Opryland Hotel, Nashville, Tennessee)

underbar are crucial to the success of your operation; its functionality can help or impede the efficiency of the bartender. The front of the bar is for your guests, but the underbar is for your bartender.

The primary piece of underbar equipment in this work station is the speed rack. The **speed rack** contains all of your well brands and should be located in the well under the center of the work station. The speed rack is a stainless steel rack which should be located at about waist level. The bottles should always be set up in the same sequence; this ensures that the bartenders do not have to search for the bottle they are pouring. They know by location where the well bottles are in the rack and can grab a bottle and pour quickly (thus the name "speed rack").

The eight most often used liquors located in the speed rack are scotch, rum, gin, vodka, bourbon, brandy, tequila, and whiskey. In high-volume bars you will find two rails in the speed rack: one for well brands and one for popular call brands. The **ice bin**, which contains a readily available amount of ice (transferred from your ice machine) for drinks, should be located above the speed rack. The ice bin should have a perforated bottom which will drain excess water from the melting ice into your dump sink.

If your bar or beverage operation uses a dispensing gun for sodas and other mixes, it should be located to the right of the speed rack, level with the top of the bar. Juices and other mixes which need to be refrigerated should be kept in refrigerated wells located on the left side of the ice bin.

Right above the ice bin, located on the edge of the top of the bar closest to the bartender, is an area for glasses to be placed while the drinks are being poured. This area is called the **glass rail**. A webbed matting or rubber mat with short protruding knobs is used for the purpose of absorbing any spillage and keeping the top of the bar looking clean.

A backbar display can help promote premium brands. (Courtesy of Opryland Hotel, Nashville, Tennessee)

Depending on the volume of blended cocktails, the blender should be handy without being in the way. Some operations place blenders on the backbar, but a blender is more efficiently placed, in most cases, on the underbar; bartenders then do not have to turn around to use it, saving wasted motion.

In addition to work stations, the underbar area most often includes some type of system for washing glassware. Bar glasses should *never* be run through the food operation's dishwasher. Aside from the breakage, chipping and scratching that can occur, dishwashers also tend to leave a fat or grease residue on the glasses. While this residue can't always be seen, it can affect the taste, consistency, and quality of the drinks you serve.

Some bar and beverage operations use a three-compartment sink. At the front end of the system there should be a dump sink. Then the first sink in the glass-washing system contains a glass brush in the bottom and is prepared with hot water and a special cleansing agent developed especially for bar glassware. The second sink contains a clear, hot rinse, and the third sink contains a sanitizing agent (germicide). At the end of this system is a rubber webbed mat to place the glasses on while they dry. Bar glasses should be air-dried and never wiped with a bar towel (wiping just spreads the dirt around).

If you are managing a large enough operation, especially a combined restaurant and bar, you may find a variety of automatic glassware-washing systems on the market today which could prove to be cost-effective. These systems are designed to operate most efficiently if you have an almost continuous supply of dirty glassware during extended periods of the business day. Another important consideration in selecting a glassware-washing system is the amount of space it will require. A glassware-washing

The speed rack is the heart of the bartender's work station. (Courtesy of Concessions International, Inc.)

machine must be easily accessible to both the service staff and bartender. If not, glasses will pile up and the system will not be used efficiently. Such systems may not be appropriate for the underbar area.

Some kind of cushioned matting should be on the floor of the bar area between the backbar and the underbar. This matting will go a long way toward saving wear and tear on the bartender. It is very tiring to stand and walk in a confined space, such as the bar area, for an eight-hour shift. The matting should be able to be picked up and thoroughly cleaned, preferably every night. This is an important part of sanitizing the bar area. Alcohol, sticky sodas, and juices will be spilled on this matting each day, and if it is not properly cleaned and sanitized after the end of business hours, it will begin to smell very badly. In the early days, these mats were usually wooden slats, but today they are made of cushioned rubber or various plastic materials.

Your draft beer should usually be located above the underbar or on the backbar. Most bar and beverage operations have only one draft beer dispensing system, so its most logical location is as close as possible to the bartenders' work stations. There will usually be one draft "pull" (lever or handle) for each brand you carry. The heads for these pulls, supplied by the distributor of each brand, often have fancy brand logos on them, serving a marketing as well as practical, purpose. The spouts below the pulls are often referred to as "taps."

The beer lines, which run from the tap to the keg, are of critical importance if you want to serve your guests a quality glass of draft beer. These lines must be kept full of either product or water at all times. This is done by disconnecting the line from the keg and running fresh water through it. Then, every two weeks, you should clean the lines with a cleansing agent to remove any sediment that might have accumulated.

A three-compartment or triple sink is often a requirement for glass washing in a bar or beverage establishment. (Courtesy of Opryland Hotel, Nashville, Tennessee)

A Special Note. There are continual improvements and changes in bar equipment, but the fundamental needs seldom change. We have included a bar layout from professionals who specialize in this area (see Exhibit 4.3). Remember that the best design approach is to determine your target market (or markets) and, based on their requirements, prepare a bar menu. Considering these elements before designing your bar or beverage operation is important. Naturally, you will more often than not be required to adapt your layout and service procedures to an already designed operation. And you are more likely than not to encounter layouts that differ from those presented here, but which nevertheless work well and fit the needs of some operations.

The Service Bar

In the real world, there are so many combinations of front and service bars that work well for their particular operations that we will not attempt to examine them all in this text. Instead, we have chosen to isolate a type of service bar that is solely a service bar according to the strictest definition. Such service bars are invariably set up to serve the beverage needs of large restaurants, hotel room service, or table service for large nightclubs or lounges.

These service bars are usually not directly visible to your guests, so your layout concerns can be entirely directed toward the service bar's functionality. Since showmanship is not a consideration in such isolated bars, automatic liquor dispensing units are sometimes used in service bars by managers who would never consider using them in a front bar. These systems are discussed more thoroughly in Chapter 10.

A service bar should be designed for efficiency, so careful consideration must be given to the entire range of drinks your guests will be ordering.

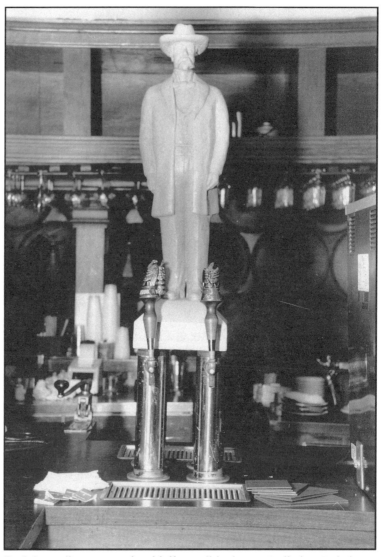

Draft beer dispensers should, if possible, be centrally located above the underbar. (Courtesy of Opryland Hotel, Nashville, Tennessee)

This will largely determine the layout of the equipment in a service bar area. Work flow patterns and sufficient storage space are also important layout considerations.

Typically, the service bar is compact, and the serving area is usually set up along a straight line. Usually, the underbar layout is essentially the same as that discussed in the front bar section.

In many service bar situations, the bartender does not actually handle cash but does have a pre-check machine that rings up the amount of every sale on each guest check. In some computerized point-of-sale systems, the orders are "sent" electronically to the service bartender. Servers can enter their drink orders in the dining room service area and then go to the service bar to pick up their drinks. In large volume situations, this type of system could expedite service.

Exhibit 4.3 Bar Layout

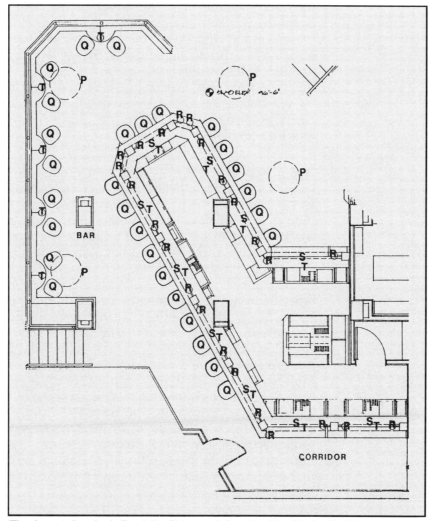

The layout for Jack Daniel's Saloon at Opryland in Nashville, Tennessee—an example of modern design used to create an old-time bar atmosphere. (Courtesy of Opryland Hotel)

Using standard operating procedures for ordering drinks also expedites service. Drink orders are called to the bartender in a specified sequence, and the bartender prepares the drinks in precisely that order. This practice is known as "sequencing." (For more about sequencing, see Chapter 5.) In general, your sequence should take into account that some drinks will "hold" their taste and appearance while sitting (as part of a large order) better than others. Any beverage stored and served at room temperature, for instance, should be prepared first. Draft beer (to keep its "head"), or any mixed drink that can quickly lose its flavor or appearance to melting ice, should be prepared last.

Procedures for the service staff vary from service bar to service bar. In some service bars, the bartenders pour only the liquor when a simple mixed drink is called for: if, for instance, a guest orders a rum and coke, the server calls "rum and coke" to the bartender who then measures and pours the rum into the proper glass and gives it to the server who adds the coke. Whether it is the server or the bartender who puts the ice in depends on where the glassware is located and where the ice bin is.

A lot of "who does what"—server or bartender—can be flexible. If business is light, the bartender *or* the server might add the proper garnish to a drink. If business picks up, it will be more efficient for servers to add the proper garnish, leaving the bartender free to pour and mix drinks.

Arranging the glassware in a particular order is important to the efficiency of the bartender. This means glassware should be set up in the order in which the drinks are called.

Room Service. Service bars in hotels often provide beverages for traditional room service (bellhops or servers transporting drinks from the service bar to guestrooms). A recent trend among many hotel properties has been to provide their guests with a mini-bar in the room itself. A **mini-bar** is a small, under-the-table unit which can be stocked with liquor, beer, and wine. In some cases the mini-bar is a refrigerated unit; in others, the unit is divided into two sections: one for dry items and one for refrigerated items. Sodas, bottled water, candy bars, cheese, crackers, potato chips, and other items are also frequently located in these units. Guests are provided with a key to their mini-bar during check-in and are asked to record on a form the items they consume during their stay. The charges for the items consumed are then added to their room bill. As a control measure, the housekeeper or another designated employee takes an inventory of the mini-bar and reports items consumed to the front desk for billing purposes.

Mini-bars originated for the convenience of both guests and the hotel. Taking single drink orders to the rooms throughout the hotel is not very cost-effective, and during busy meal periods, can cause long delays in room service. However, it should be noted that bottle sales are still an important (and profitable) function of room service. It must also be noted that in-room mini-bars have been criticized for facilitating over-consumption by compulsive drinkers.

Bar Equipment, Accessories, and Tools

This section describes equipment, accessories, and tools common to both front and service bar operations, and focuses on ice-making machines and glassware selection in particular.

Ice and Ice-Making Machines

One important factor in the selection of an ice-making machine for your bar or beverage operation is the size and shape of the ice it will produce. It is the size and shape of the ice that determine its displacement value. Knowing the displacement value of a particular type of ice will inform you how quickly the ice will melt, an important consideration with respect to the quality of the drinks you serve.

The size of the ice can also affect the guest's perception as to how small or large your drinks are. Larger pieces of ice tend to make a drink appear smaller, whereas smaller ones tend to make a drink appear larger.

Ice-making machines can produce many different shapes and sizes. Here are six primary shapes of ice:

Freestanding ice machine with self-contained bin. (Courtesy of Concessions International, Inc.)

- Cube: Comes in a variety of sizes but the smaller, one-half-inch cubes are more frequently used in bar and beverage operations.

- Flake: Melts very rapidly and should not be used in drinks.

- Tube: Comes in a variety of sizes and is used in bar and beverage operations.

- Lens: A very hard, slow-melting ice, which makes it an excellent choice for drinks (however, a pour against the flat edge of the cube will more quickly splash outside the glass).

- Pillow: Another excellent choice for drinks because it minimizes the amount of splash-back from the pour and is slow melting.

- Spiral: A fairly new ice shape, it is recommended more for soft drinks than mixed drinks.[1]

If you are managing a very busy bar or beverage operation, you will be using large volumes of ice. Therefore the selection and location of the ice-making machine will be important layout decisions. The ideal location for an ice-making machine is in a storage area as close to the bar as possible so that the bartender, barback, or busperson can get to it without going through guest-flow paths.

It is also important that the area in which the ice-making machine is located have adequate circulation and that the waste heat from the machine is properly vented. Waste heat can significantly increase the ambient room temperature, making it uncomfortable for employees and guests.

Ideally, the ice-making machine should not be located within the bar area. Aside from the waste heat, the machine can make a lot of noise when

An underbar ice machine. (Courtesy of Opryland Hotel, Nashville, Tennessee)

a load of ice is dropped. However, if storage space is at a premium, there are air-cooled under-counter ice-making machines available on the market. Some operations even prefer these types of ice-making machines because the ice tends to stay colder, melt slower, and thus not dilute a drink as quickly.[2]

Remember that ice requires a temperature from about −10° to +32° F (−23.3° to 0° C). Storage should be dry (moisture dissolves ice), and it should be kept clean. Ice needs to be protected from the possibility of contamination by broken glass, dirt, or debris. If glass is broken anywhere near an open container of ice, *that ice should not be used!*

Ice should be considered a form of edible food. Glasses should always be filled with an ice scoop; never allow servers to use their hands or, worse, scoop up the ice with a drink glass.

Bar glassware comes in a wide variety of shapes and sizes. (Courtesy of Opryland Hotel, Nashville, Tennessee)

You have a wide variety of ice-making machine manufacturers and models to choose from. Freestanding models can produce from 200 to 3,300 pounds of ice per day and can store anywhere from 200 to well over 1,000 pounds of ice at a time. Underbar machines typically produce 23 pounds of ice daily and store about 12 pounds at a time.[3]

Glassware

The selection of glassware should be directed, in large part, by your marketing strategy. The quality and appropriateness of the glassware you select should reflect the image that your bar or beverage operation wants to portray. We will discuss the specifics of selecting beer and wine glassware in Chapter 6. In this chapter we will address more general concerns with respect to glassware selection and the specifics of glassware for distilled spirits, mixed drinks, and cocktails.

The size of the glassware you select is related to the pour size (the standard amount, usually in ounces, of liquor your establishment requires be poured for each drink recipe) you establish and therefore relates to the prices you will charge. Pricing is related to both the marketing and the control of your bar or beverage operation and is discussed from each of those perspectives in Chapters 8 and 10, respectively. By implication, then, the selection of glassware is also related to both marketing and control. From a marketing perspective, you want glassware that attractively showcases the drinks you serve. Additionally, proper glassware selection will determine how your guests perceive the price-value relationship of the drinks they are served (certain types of glassware will make the drink look larger or of such quality as to merit a relatively high price).

Glassware can be an important merchandising tool for a bar or beverage operation. How many times have you been in a lounge and seen a drink being served in a beautiful glass, attractively garnished, and ordered one for yourself because it looked so good? Trader Vic's was ahead of its time when it served exotic, fruity drinks with straws in the 1950s. Today, the rest of the world has caught on to those effective merchandising techniques. A lot of guests order drinks because they look beautiful! Appropriately attractive glassware is important. And don't forget that if glassware is to be effective as a merchandising tool, it must sparkle. A drink will lose its appeal if it is served in a streaked or spotty glass.

The current trend is to upgrade both the quality and stylishness of glassware.[4] Different ways of serving drinks include delivering martinis to guests in small glass decanters so they can fill and refill their own glasses. Using good crystal glassware, in the appropriate setting, can make your guests feel extra special. Long Island iced teas or draft beer served in glassware modeled after mason jars (with or without handles) are often encountered in operations targeting a college crowd. Mugs and steins—traditional beer glassware—are appropriate to the service of imported beers. Sometimes, simply upgrading your glassware can make higher prices for drinks acceptable to your guests.

From the perspective of cost control, the glassware you select has to be able to contain your specified pour size without making certain mixed drinks (highballs, screwdrivers, etc.) taste too weak or too strong. The glassware you select should also be easy to handle and transport, especially during peak periods. Tall, slender glasses might look attractive, but might tip over too easily when carried on a tray.

Where and how the glassware will be stored is another control aspect important to glassware selection. Supplies of all types of glassware must be adequate to meet the needs of your guests during the busiest peak business periods. You don't want your bartenders in the position of having to substitute glassware.

Glassware is expensive; bartenders and service staff should be trained to handle glassware in such a way as to minimize breakage. For instance, bartender and staff should use plastic scoops to fill glasses with ice, make sure the glass is room temperature (and not right from the glass-washing machine) before filling it with ice, and avoid "clanging" glassware together. These careful practices will not only minimize chipping or breaking, but help prevent the possibility that a glass could "mysteriously" shatter while being served to a guest. Glassware that is chipped or cracked must be taken out of service immediately. It is also a good idea to rotate your glassware so that all glasses are used on a regular basis.

Since beverage glassware is available in a wide variety of shapes and sizes, you, the manager, will be responsible for standardizing the glassware that is used in your operation. Many operations will select from seven to nine different types of glassware that are interchangeable for different drinks.

To sum up, the glassware you select for your operation should help foster the image you are trying to create. Glassware can enhance the price-value perception of the drinks you serve and become an effective merchandising tool for your service staff. Selection of glassware must take into consideration the storage space you have available, your glass-washing capability, and the durability that will be needed for the clientele you serve and the services you provide.

Tools of the trade. (Courtesy of Opryland Hotel, Nashville, Tennessee)

Bar Tools and Accessories

A wide variety of hand tools and accessories are used in the preparation of drinks. Exhibit 4.4 lists a variety of small bar tools and accessories that will assist your bartender. How many of these items you need, of course, depends on the volume of business and the size of your bar or beverage operation. Since these tools are invaluable to the effectiveness and efficiency of your bartender, we recommend that you purchase high-quality bar accessories. Good bar accessories will be greatly appreciated by both your bartenders and guests.

Bar Sanitation

As we learned in Chapter 3, all bar and beverage operations must conform to the applicable local, state and federal regulations that pertain to their design and layout. The National Sanitation Foundation (NSF) provides assistance in facility planning and preparation with respect to sanitation code compliance.[5] While not developed specifically for bar and beverage operations, NSF guidelines can be useful because of the close relationship between bar and beverage operations and food service operations.

Additionally, the NSF has developed standards for equipment, products, and services that relate to public health concerns.[6] These standards include basic information on the design and construction of various pieces of equipment that may be used in bar and beverage operations. Compliance with these standards is voluntary; the NSF is not a governmental regulatory agency. Examples of some standards applicable to bar equipment include:

Exhibit 4.4 Bar Tools and Accessories

Bar towels	Juice containers
Blender, electric	Knife, paring
Bucket for moving ice	Knife, serrated
Cocktail picks	Napkins, cocktail
Cutting board(s)	Salt shaker(s)
Fruit tongs	Salt/sugar bowls
Funnels	Straws
Garnish tray/container	Swizzle sticks
Ice tongs	Toothpicks
Ice scoop(s)	

- Standard 7: Food Service Refrigerators and Storage Freezers

- Standard 12: Automatic Ice-Making Equipment

- Standard 18: Manual Food and Beverage Dispensing Equipment

- Standard 29: Detergent/Chemical Feeders for Commercial Spray-Type Dishwashing Machines

Bar and beverage operations, in particular the bar itself, have some special sanitation concerns. Many beverage products, such as juices and non-pasteurized (draft) beer, are especially prone to bacterial infestation. If sanitation practices and procedures are not established and carefully adhered to, bacteria-induced slime and foul odors will come from drip pans, sinks, and storage racks. All beverage spills must be cleaned and sanitized carefully on a daily basis. Remember that you are responsible for the ambience of your operation, the health and safety of your guests and employees, and the delivery of a high-quality product: proper cleaning and sanitation procedures are necessary for each of these concerns.

Endnotes

1. Joseph Durocher, "Ice Makers," *Restaurant Business* 88 (#13, 1989): 181–182.

2. Durocher, 181–182.

3. Cahner's Publishers, "Storage & Handling Equipment: Ice Machines & Dispensers," *Foodservice Equipment & Supplies Specialist* 41 (#5, 1988): 97–98.

4. Ken Frydman, "The Glass Menagerie," *Market Watch* 9 (#7, 1990): 97, 99.

5. National Sanitation Foundation, *Sanitation Aspects of Food Service Facility Plan Preparation and Review* (Ann Arbor, Michigan: National Sanitation Foundation, 1978), iii–iv.

6. National Sanitation Foundation, *Standard Number 2 Food Service Equipment* (Ann Arbor, Michigan: National Sanitation Foundation, 1988), i.

Key Terms

backbar

bar

bar menu

front bar

glass rail

ice bin

mini-bar

service bar

speed rack

underbar

Discussion Questions

1. What are the basic differences between the front bar and backbar?

2. What are the major pieces of equipment appropriate to the underbar?

3. How does the "bar menu" influence bar design or layout? Give examples.

4. How can poor bar layout affect profits? Give examples.

5. What does job analysis bring to bar design or layout?

6. How can inadequate provision for traffic flow affect profits? Give examples.

7. What items should be nearest an ice bin?

8. What are the glass-washing steps for a three-compartment sink? What liquid is in each of the three sinks?

9. What are "mini-bars"? Explain how they work and why they can be profitable.

10. What beverages are especially prone to bacterial infestation?

5 The Bartender and the Art of Mixology

Chapter Outline

The Bartender
    The Bartender's Role as "Psychologist"
    The Bartender's Service Role
    The Bartender's Role as Salesperson
    The Bartender's Role in Alcohol Awareness
        Flaming Drinks
The "Art" of Mixology
    Cocktails
        Mixes
        Garnishes
        Final Preparation
    Drink Preparation Methods
        The Stirred Drink Method
        The Building Drink Method
        The Shake/Blend Drink Method
The Bartender's Manual: A Guide To Bartending
    Work Station Setup
        Bar Sanitation Procedures
        Additional Setup Activities
        Sequencing

Many of us have the impression that a bartender's job is to mix drinks, serve drinks at the bar, convey a jovial personality, and please the guests. We think of a "good" bartender as one who knows most of the regular guests by name. Likewise, those guests know the bartender by name.

The bartender is the most visible employee in many bar and beverage operations. However, the bartender could be the bar owner. He or she could also be the bar manager—entrusted by the owner or top management to hire and fire other employees, order and maintain inventory, and perform dozens of other tasks that guests may never see or know about.

The bartender and his or her skills are so important to the success of a bar or beverage operation that we have devoted an entire chapter to the subject. As a bar or beverage manager, it is more than likely that you will serve at least some time as a bartender, if for no other reason than that of "apprenticeship." However, for clarity's sake, we will continue to assume that you, our reader, are a manager, and we will describe the characteristics and skills of our bartender/mixologist as if he or she were under your management.

Bar and beverage operations are social enterprises as well as places of business. This fact is a unique characteristic of the hospitality industry. Hospitality employees come to work in an atmosphere where, typically, the guests come to relax and enjoy themselves. Nowhere is this truer than in the bar and beverage business. In many bars, the bartender is the employee with whom a guest is most likely to interact. This means that an effective bartender will be a good conversationalist and a good listener. He or she may be a storyteller or something of an entertainer. A good bartender needs to have the ability to establish an instant rapport with everyone—even total strangers.

Above all else, he or she must sincerely like people—sometimes enough to feel like giving them a mental "lift" when they seem down. In fact, a bartender's job is sometimes compared to that of a psychiatrist or priest. Some guests come to the bar and want to tell someone about their troubles; some are lonely and just want to talk.

The effective bartender is a special person with a special personality. While you might be able to train just about anyone to mix drinks, you cannot train anyone to have the personality of a great bartender. That is why hiring, as we will see in Chapter 7, is so crucial to your success— especially hiring a bartender with the right personality.

While the first part of this chapter discusses the various roles of the bartender, another section of this chapter deals with drink preparation, or "mixology," as it is known in the trade. Mixology is both an art and a skill which bartenders must master. To become a master mixologist, a bartender needs good training followed by years of experience. However, your bartender must first learn the basics in order to prepare quality drinks for your guests. Proper terminology, measurements, various mixes and mixing procedures, garnishing, and effective bar setup are just some of those basics.

The bartender plays a role similar to that of a chef, combining different measurements of various ingredients to create the perfect taste combination. Along with knowing how to create historic "standbys" such as the martini and the Bloody Mary, today's bartender must also keep pace with the latest fads and trends. Never before have so many new cocktails (drink combinations) arrived on the scene; a few stay, most are "here today and gone tomorrow."

Bartenders should be able to establish instant rapport with their guests. (Courtesy of Opryland Hotel, Nashville, Tennessee)

In addition to examining the many roles of the bartender and the art of mixology, this chapter deals with the bartender's role in alcohol awareness and intervention and other technical aspects of the bartending profession.

The Bartender

It is estimated that 367,500 bartenders are employed in over 147,000 full-service bars in the United States alone![1] This figure does not include the thousands of bartenders employed in food and beverage operations that operate only service bars. Bartenders have their own national magazine, *Bartender Magazine*, and their own "Bartender Hall of Fame."

The bartender is usually under the direct supervision of a manager (bar or beverage manager, owner, or restaurant manager). The bartender's primary job is to ensure guest satisfaction by the preparation and service of alcoholic and non-alcoholic drinks in accordance with the establishment's policies and procedures. However, the role of today's bartender often goes beyond the mixing and serving of drinks to include inventory control, cost control, sales and merchandising, and mood and ambience enhancement. With today's increasing emphasis on alcohol awareness, the bartender must even take on the role of "watchdog." He or she must be aware of the laws pertaining to the establishment's responsibility for excessive alcohol consumption by its guests. Bartenders should be trained in effective intervention procedures that can be followed when guests have reached their limit.

The bartender is often the most visible representative of a bar or beverage operation. As such, he or she also represents you, the manager. While

Cocktails or mixed drinks (unless they are generally well known, such as a martini or screwdriver) should be identified not only by name, but also by a description of the ingredients. Listing the ingredients is an effective way to encourage a guest to try a new drink. Also, with today's rapid changes in drink fads and inventions, drink names have very little relationship to their ingredients.

Bartenders can also encourage guests to upgrade their drinks by maintaining an awareness of the establishment's premium brands. If a guest orders a vodka tonic, the bartender should ask if the guest would like it made with the bar's most popular call brand; or, receiving an order for a martini, the bartender might ask if the guest would prefer it be made with one of the more expensive premium brands. If a bartender knows that a guest likes a particular type of liquor, he or she might suggest a new drink that calls for that liquor.

Experienced bartenders become good at "reading" their guests, even if a guest has never been there before. "Reading" the guest means that the bartender can speculate what types of drinks might be of interest to particular types of guests. (See also the section on "Selling" in Chapter 6.)

The Bartender's Role in Alcohol Awareness

The political and public outcry over drunk driving has placed a greater responsibility on the bartender to keep an eye on guest consumption and behavior. The majority of guests do not enter a bar or beverage establishment with the sole intention of getting intoxicated. However, serving too much alcohol to even one guest could result in an extremely costly lawsuit for your establishment or—in some states—for the bartender or server directly.

Training for Intervention Procedures by Servers of Alcohol (TIPS) is a program established and administered by the National Bartenders Association. It goes beyond alcohol awareness training to teach employees and management actual intervention techniques requiring active involvement with guests.[3] Another organization dedicated to combatting drunk driving is Bartenders Against Drunk Driving (BADD). Here are some steps which some bar and beverage operations follow to discourage over-consumption:

- Do not encourage guests to order **doubles** (double the standard measure of alcohol in one glass) by charging less than twice the price. Some bar and beverage operations either forbid the sale of doubles altogether or give their bartenders training and the power to forbid doubles (especially late at night) at their discretion. Experienced bartenders know that guests who order doubles are often drinking for the purpose of getting intoxicated.

- Do not allow guests to order **backup drinks** (two drinks purchased at one time by or for one guest), especially at **last call** (just before closing).

- Serve snacks or hors d'oeuvres to all guests (this won't discourage over-consumption but will somewhat lessen the *effects* of alcohol on those guests drinking on an empty stomach).

- Serve all alcoholic drinks with **water on the side** (a separate glass of water).

- Train your bartenders to be alert for the more subtle signs of intoxication; many drinkers become legally drunk before becoming obviously intoxicated. (Many bar and beverage operations have established in-house alcohol awareness programs for their employees.)

- Do not give bartenders an incentive compensation based on a percentage of sales in addition to their wages. To do so might encourage your bartenders to increase sales by allowing guests to get intoxicated and become drunk drivers. You will better serve the interests of your establishment by paying the bartender a higher wage to begin with.

- Give bartenders and servers full support in handling problem guests.

A growing national trend among safety- (and liability-) conscious bar and beverage operations has been to eliminate **drink incentives** (two drinks for the price of one, half-price drinks, etc.) during so-called **happy hours** (periods of time, usually between 4:00 and 7:00 p.m., during which bar and beverage operations attempt to bring in customers after work and before they go home). Other operations offer half-price drinks, but not two for the price of one, because research has shown that consumers will have a better idea of how much they are drinking if they order only one drink at a time. Many such establishments also offer, instead of drink incentives, a wide variety of hors d'oeuvres and work to create a happy hour ambience for their guests.

Remember that both bartenders and servers have more than the right and responsibility to refuse service to any guest who is intoxicated or in danger of becoming a drunk driver. They may be held *personally* liable according to the law.

Flaming Drinks. The question of liability brings up another risk for bar and beverage operations: *flaming drinks*. Throughout the years, drink trends have included at least one popular flaming drink. A flaming drink usually consists of one or another of certain **liqueurs** which is poured into shot glasses and ignited or "flamed" just before serving. Because the alcohol in these drinks ignites and flames at a *relatively* low temperature, the drink can be consumed quickly without the drinker feeling excessive heat.

What most bar and beverage operations have found, however, is that if you play with fire, you might get burned in court. Juries are not sympathetic to owners and operators who permit the use of flaming alcohol. For this reason, many hospitality companies have prohibited the preparation and service of flaming drinks. The problem, however, is that these policies do not always work their way down to the operations people. A regular guest comes into the bar, orders a flaming drink (perhaps giving the bartender a large tip), and the bartender makes the drink, prompting similar requests from other guests. The more flaming drinks a bartender makes, the higher the probability of a serious accident. And remember, the higher the proof, the higher the flammability.

One showy practice associated with flaming drinks is for the drinker to put his finger in the flaming drink, hold the flaming finger in the air for about one or two seconds, then extinguish the flaming finger in his or her mouth. Another "game" has the bartender light the drink then slide it down the bar, yelling, "Fire!" The dangers inherent in such practices are apparent: (1) after one or two seconds (at most) in contact with the skin, the flame can get hot enough to cause serious burns, and (2) spilled, the flaming drink is out of control, with the possibility of igniting flammable clothing or highly flammable hairspray. And when one customer gets the practice started, it soon catches on with others.

Some liquor manufacturers warn that their products should not be used for flaming (see Exhibit 5.2). If a manufacturer tells you not to use a product in a certain way, don't! The manufacturer has good reasons for making such prohibitions: safety and liability. Ads such as the one in Exhibit 5.2 might influence the courts in deciding that the burden of reasonable care be shifted from the manufacturer to the bar operation.

In short, serving flaming drinks is a potential menace to the health and safety of your guests and employees, and an unnecessary and costly risk to your bar or beverage operation. The practice is prohibited by many individual establishments and by many hotel and restaurant chains. Nevertheless, this prohibition may not overcome the temptation of a bartender to serve a flaming drink to a guest who offers a large tip. Where in effect, the prohibition of flaming drinks should be highlighted in training and bartender manuals and emphasized regularly by managers.

The "Art" of Mixology

Bartenders are sometimes referred to as mixologists, and the knowledge and skills required to prepare drinks known as **mixology**. Bar and beverage professionals like to think of mixology as an art because it requires a high level of skill and knowledge and, sometimes, style and creativity. A variety of books is available to help you acquire the requisite skills and provide the standard recipes. One is the classic red-covered *Mr. Boston Official Bartender's Guide*, first published in 1935. With more than nine million copies in print, it is still widely used.[4] Another is *Grossman's Guide to Wines, Beers, and Spirits*. Harold J. Grossman was one of the first people to research alcoholic beverages after the repeal of Prohibition.[5]

Cocktails   Cocktails are made of two distinct types of ingredients, a base and a modifying agent or agents. A modifying agent may be as simple as one other alcoholic beverage or a combination of other modifying agents, including more than one alcoholic beverage (including several varieties of aromatic bitters which modify smell as well as taste), water, carbonated water, popular soft drinks (colas, etc.), special coloring, foaming or flavoring agents, milk, cream, juices, eggs, vegetables, and commercially prepared **pre-mixes**.

The base, or predominant ingredient, of the cocktail usually consists of a single **liquor**. (Throughout this chapter, "liquor" refers to those unsweetened, high-alcohol-content beverages such as gin, vodka, rum, and the various whiskeys, including scotch.) The base is often the distinguishing taste feature of the cocktail: For example, in a daiquiri, the flavor of rum is predominant; in the martini, the predominant flavor is overwhelmingly that of gin or vodka—hence the term "dry martini," which means little more than a drop or two of vermouth added to the base. For the majority of cocktails, however, the objective of mixing a cocktail is to blend

Exhibit 5.2   Bacardi Ad Warning About Flaming Drinks

Courtesy of Bacardi Imports, Inc.

the ingredients into a smooth, palatable drink with no one flavor over-shadowing the other.[6]

Modifying agents other than those containing alcohol have a variety of purposes, among them: (1) creating a distinctive taste (fruit juices, for instance); (2) creating a distinctive texture in addition to taste—a smooth texture in the case of milk, cream, and eggs—or the unique texture created

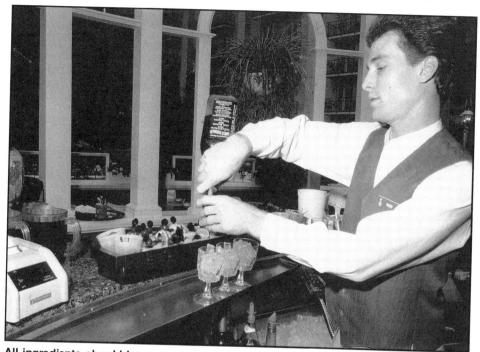

All ingredients should be measured for every drink the bartender prepares. (Courtesy of Opryland Hotel, Nashville, Tennessee)

by finely crushed ice in drinks such as frozen daiquiris; (3) creating a distinctive color as well as taste by using fruit syrups such as grenadine or cherry juice (although many of today's popular cocktails use a wide variety of colored liqueurs).

The quality of a cocktail depends on the quality of the ingredients. To mix mediocre orange juice with a premium vodka, for instance, will leave guests dissatisfied with the screwdriver they ordered.

Remember also that most cocktails use ice which, as it melts, will affect the strength of the drink. Therefore the use of proper glassware and careful selection of ice-making equipment is imperative to the mixing of a good cocktail.

A tested **standard recipe** should be used to ensure day-after-day consistency—guests who have a special cocktail favorite should be able to get the same quality of taste in their favorite every time they return. In addition, some type of measurement device or devices should be used to ensure that all ingredients are measured precisely. While experienced bartenders may be able to measure by eye, this is not a sound control practice, as you will learn in Chapter 10.

Sometimes, bartenders think they are doing guests a favor by **overpouring** (putting in more alcohol than the standard recipe calls for). A *strong* drink is not necessarily a *quality* drink; quality means a good-tasting drink, and this requires the consistency provided by the standard recipe measurements. Furthermore, the practice of overpouring doesn't promote the kind of clientele that you want in your bar (see "The Bartender's Role in Alcohol Awareness" earlier in this chapter).[7]

Ordering a drink "**neat**" has traditionally meant ordering a straight shot of liquor without ice. More often than not, this older word is being

A lemon peel (twist) is twisted over a drink for flavoring from the lemon oils. (Courtesy of Strongbow Inn, Valparaiso, Indiana)

replaced with the term "**straight up**," meaning any drink served without ice. With ice, the commonly used term is "**on the rocks**." A **water back** or a **soda back** means that the drink ordered should be served along with a separate glass of water (or "soda"—carbonated water) on the side. A **back** could also refer to any beverage which a guest orders to be served in a separate glass along with his or her drink. A drink ordered with a **twist** refers to the practice of twisting a piece of lemon rind over a drink so that the oil from the lemon rind gently flavors the drink.

Simple syrup is used to sweeten most drinks instead of granulated sugar, which takes too long to dissolve in alcohol. One notable exception: an "old fashioned" prepared correctly mixes *extra fine* granulated sugar with fruit (orange slices and cherries) by a crushing technique known as **muddling**. Simple syrup is prepared (sometimes by the bartender) by dissolving powdered sugar in water, bringing the mixture to a boil, and cooling. The mixture should then be stored in the refrigerator. Simple syrup is also available in pre-mixed gallon containers.

Mixes. Only quality mixes, properly prepared and stored, can make quality drinks. There is a wide variety of mix products available on the market

Providing carbonated mixes for mixed drinks through a pressurized dispenser system is economical and an almost universally accepted practice. (Courtesy of Concessions International, Inc.)

today, including pre-mixes such as Bloody Mary mixes that only require adding the vodka. Selection of the mixes you will use for your operation requires careful taste-testing. In carbonated mixes the amount or degree of carbonation is critical. Many bar and beverage operations use the small, individual bottles of club soda and tonic water because they feel that the quality of the product outweighs the lower cost of buying in larger containers.

Most bar operations, however, use a pressurized dispenser system for their carbonated mixes that include popular soft drinks such as cola and ginger ale in addition to soda and tonic. These products are dispensed through a "gun" that has a separate button for each mix. The bartender simply pushes the appropriate button while holding the gun over the glass. The tank of the pressurized dispensing system requires syrup, usually in bulk 5-gallon Cryovac bags that can be stored away from the bar area.

The syrup is mixed with carbon dioxide under pressure in the dispensing system and is carried to the bar area through plastic tubing to the

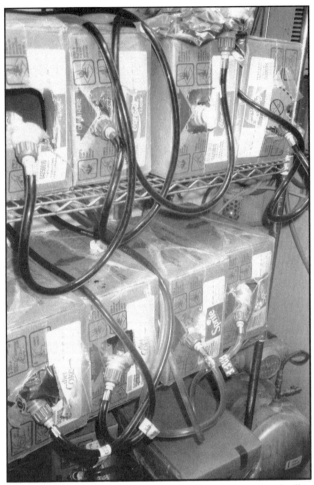

The syrup and carbon dioxide for pressurized dispenser systems are stored in an area remote from the bar. (Courtesy of Concessions International, Inc.)

dispensing gun. Because you are buying product in bulk and without bottles, the pressurized dispenser method is the most economical way to purchase carbonated mixes.

Other mixes needed in a bar are juices: orange, lemon, lime, grapefruit, tomato, and pineapple. Lemon and lime juice are usually purchased in frozen or powdered form. (Rose's Lime Juice, required for a type of drink called a "gimlet," is not true lime juice since it contains other distinct ingredients as well.) Grapefruit, tomato, and pineapple juices are usually purchased in cans, but they should never be stored in open cans; always transfer them to closeable plastic or glass containers to keep them safe and sanitary. Orange juice is best when fresh but is most commonly purchased in refrigerated or frozen containers. Cream, milk, and eggs (refrigerated and checked every day or every shift for freshness) are also required for a complete bar setup. A variety of condiments and other additives are also needed to have a well-stocked mix inventory. These include bitters, bitter lemon, grenadine syrup, nutmeg, Orgeat (almond-flavored) syrup, pepper, salt, sugar, Tabasco sauce, and Worcestershire sauce.

Carefully garnished drinks have the eye appeal that increases sales.

Garnishes. Garnishes require special care in both preparation and storage. This is particularly true of fresh fruit garnishes such as lemon twists, lemon and lime **wedges** (sections of the whole fruit), and lemon, lime, and orange slices. Additional garnishes which are required in a well-stocked bar include maraschino cherries (with the stems), green olives, cocktail onions, and celery stalks. All fruit and vegetable garnishes should be fresh and crisp. Usually, the bartender cuts up a supply of fruit garnishes at the beginning of a shift in anticipation of the expected business. One way to keep them looking crisp and fresh is to store the pre-cut garnishes on ice in containers which will drain the melted ice into a sink. There is nothing less appetizing than a drink served with a dried out, droopy garnish.

Maraschino cherries are purchased in jars in syrup and stored at room temperature. Crushed or discolored cherries should be discarded. Green olives may also be stored at room temperature in their own brine. Cocktail onions must be refrigerated, although a small quantity at a time, in their own juice, may be set in a garnish tray for easy access during busy service periods. Onions not used that day should be discarded and never returned to the refrigerated container. Celery stalks should be cut fresh daily and, for optimum freshness and crispness, stored in ice water.

Final Preparation. Eye appeal is the final, but very critical, aspect of drink preparation. In some bar and beverage operations the bartender is responsible for adding the mixer and garnishes to the drinks; in other operations

Careful, quick stirring minimizes the dilution of a drink from the melting ice cubes. (Courtesy of Strongbow Inn, Valparaiso, Indiana)

that responsibility falls to the service staff. Since the server is the last person to see the drink before it is presented to the guest, it should be his or her responsibility to see that the drink he or she is about to serve is attractive. That means making sure that the appropriate glass has been used, that the garnish looks good and is properly placed, and taking care that the drink contents have not spilled over the rim of the glass on the way to the table. An attractive drink not only makes the drink taste better, but can also serve as an effective sales tool.

Drink Preparation Methods

The drink preparation methods we will study include the **stir method**, the **build method** and the **shake/blend method**. We will also discuss hot drinks and punches as their preparation require somewhat different methods.

The Stir Method. If the cocktail is mixed with either fruit juices or aromatic, it is stirred. Cocktails which contain liquors and clear ingredients require only stirring with a bar spoon for proper mixture. Cocktail folklore has it that a good martini is stirred and not shaken to prevent the gin from being "bruised." Setting aside the question of how gin can be bruised, however, the clear reason for stirring instead of shaking is to mix the ingredients and cool them with the minimum amount of dilution from melting ice. The stir method simply means stirring the drink ingredients with ice in a mixing glass and then straining out the ice through a wire strainer. Martinis and gimlets served straight up are examples of drinks prepared in this manner.

Care must be taken that the drink is stirred enough so that the cocktail is properly chilled and the ingredients thoroughly mixed. Too much stirring, however, will cause the ice to melt to the point of diluting the cocktail.

If the same type of stirred drink is being made for more than one guest, the drinks are made in one batch. When the batch is poured, the glasses—lined up in a row—should each be filled to about the middle of the glass. The bartender should then go back to the first glass and finish pouring the first glass to the proper level, then the second, and so forth. If the ingredients have been measured properly, each glass in the batch will be filled to the same level with nothing left over in the mixing glass when the last glass of the batch has been filled. However, if the bartender is working under the pressure of a very busy bar, he or she will often fill each of the batched glasses to midpoint, then pour a little into each glass, moving and pouring quickly until each of the glasses has been filled to the *same*, if not ideal, level.

The Build Method. Building drinks, if the "building" is done on the rocks, is the easiest method of drink preparation. Building a drink requires the ingredients to be poured into the glass in which the drink will be served.

The proper procedure for building drinks on the rocks is to place the ice in the glass first, add the liquor, and then add the mixer. Highballs and Collinses are examples. These drinks are served without mixing or stirring. However, the bartender will often place a **swizzle stick** (a thin plastic tube) in the glass so guests have the option of stirring the drinks themselves.

The **pousse-café** is a classic example of the build method and a high expression of the art of mixology. It is built by very carefully floating one layer of liqueur on top of another. Liqueurs have different levels of specific gravity (different weights and densities compared to water); those of lower specific gravity will float on top of those with a higher specific gravity.

A pousse-café can be as simple as two layers or as complex as seven different layers, each with a different color. Building them is a skill which requires patience and time. The pousse-café is made by *carefully* pouring equal layers (usually ¼ oz.) of liqueurs, each with a different color and with no intermingling between each of the colored layers.

The Shake/Blend Method. Cocktails prepared by this method use cream, eggs or fruit juices (along with the alcohol portion of the recipe) which cannot be mixed to the desired texture (usually smooth and foamy) by stirring. Many cocktails requiring the shake/blend method can either be shaken by hand with a cocktail shaker and mixing glass or with an electric blender. The increasingly popular frozen daiquiris and ice cream drinks, however, must be mixed in the blender.

In bar operations where showmanship is emphasized, guests prefer to see the drinks shaken by hand. When shaking drinks by hand, the mixing glass should be placed tightly just inside the top of the shaker, then shaken

An electric blender, essential for today's popular frozen and ice cream drinks, and an old-fashioned shaker with strainer. (Courtesy of Strongbow Inn, Valparaiso, Indiana)

hard and fast to ensure proper blending of all the ingredients and the appropriate texture. The ice should be added to the shaker first, followed by the modifying agents, and finally, the liquor. The ice not only chills the drink but also acts as an agitator to mix and foam the ingredients. After shaking, the drink should be strained and poured into the appropriate glass and, if required, garnished before service. In the past, all shaken or blended cocktails were served straight up as a matter of course; today, the bartender will usually ask if you want the blended cocktail straight up or on the rocks.

The Bartender's Manual: A Guide to Bartending

A well-planned and organized bartender's manual can be a vital asset to your bar or beverage operation. It can serve as a guide to training, a compilation of policies and standard operating procedures, and as a source of specialty drink recipes. The bartender's manual should be designed and organized so that it can be used conveniently—as a reference source—at the bar. No bartender can be expected to remember every policy, procedure, and recipe all the time. Bartenders are entitled to have immediate access to the tools they need to perform their job effectively and efficiently. A good bartender's manual is such a tool, and it is management's responsibility to provide it.

The bartender's manual will necessarily vary from operation to operation. The following are among the topics and items often included:

- Job description and job specifications
- Philosophy of service statement
- Beverage department inspection sheet
- Rules of conduct (no drinking on the job, etc.) and dress code
- Alcohol awareness statement and/or policies
- Station setup procedures
- Drink preparation methods
- Table of measurements and portioning
- Glassware, garnishes, and bar mixes
- Pricing structure and cash handling procedures
- Cleanup and sanitation procedures
- Stocking procedures and responsibilities
- Scheduling policy
- Standard recipes (although these are sometimes placed in a separate manual in a format that is easy for the bartender to use during peak periods)

The specifics of each of the policies and procedures in your manual depend on the type of bar or beverage operation you manage and the services you offer. For example, very different procedures and policies will be required for an operation that has only a front bar, as opposed to one that has a front bar and a service bar.

Many of the elements identified here will be discussed at length in future chapters in this text. In this chapter, we will examine one of the elements of the bartender's manual that deals directly with the bartender's job—the work station setup.

Work Station Setup

An efficient work station setup is important for the efficiency (and therefore the profits) of your operation. During peak business periods, the bartender doesn't have time to search for products or tools and equipment. All items in the bar area must have designated places and be immediately returned there after being used.

Once a setup is established for each work station, it should always be maintained. This means that well bottles should always be racked in the same order and the bottles on the backbar arranged and stocked in the same manner.

Cleaning the bar area is an essential part of work station setup. (Courtesy of Stouffer Hotels and Resorts)

The first duty of the bartender is to arrive in enough time to set up the bar before hours of operation begin, if he or she is the opening bartender. If the bartender is on the second or third shift, he or she must arrive early enough to double-check the bar setup to make sure everything is in order. One of the main responsibilities of work station setup is to ensure that all the necessary products and brands are fully stocked for the upcoming work shift. When the bar is busy, too much business can be lost by running back to the storage area for a bottle when there is no readily available backup. (Chapter 9 will thoroughly discuss appropriate procedures for requisitioning and stocking bottles in the bar area.) Juices, mixes, fruit, cream, sugar, and other additives and condiments must also be well stocked. An adequate supply of such items as cocktail napkins, drink stirrers, and straws should also be available for each shift.

Bar Sanitation Procedures. The importance of good sanitation in bar and beverage management is stressed throughout this text. It is also a very important responsibility in the work station setup. The very nature of alcoholic beverages—as well as the mixes, garnishes, and condiments that

Keeping the stock replenished before each shift is important to efficiency (and sales). (Courtesy of Concessions International, Inc.)

accompany them—demands the strict enforcement of established sanitation practices and policies.

In addition to daily cleaning procedures, weekly cleanings are recommended. Cleaning the entire bar area is part of station setup. Cleaning the bar top, ashtrays, glassware, hand tools, equipment, coolers, backbar, and underbar are typically the responsibility of the bartender. Not only should the bar area be spotless—with glassware and equipment sparkling—it should also be free from odors. Many beverage products contain ingredients which can spoil, causing bacteria and fungus growth and foul odors.

Additional Setup Activities. Additional station setup activities include filling or replenishing ice bins, cutting and preparing fruit for garnishes, setting up the glass washing station or equipment, and straightening out and checking the arrangement of chairs, tables, menus, and other physical items necessary to successful operations. The final preparations involve setting up the point of sale system (cash register) and retrieving the bank (opening cash) from management—operations which are dealt with in Chapter 10.

Sequencing. Once the work station is set up, bartenders have one more responsibility that is especially important in busy bars: **sequencing**. Sequencing means establishing a system by which servers order batches of drinks in a particular sequence, and bartenders coordinate the ordering sequence with the sequence in which they prepare those drink orders.

Bartenders all have their own unique ways of sequencing drink orders. Experienced bartenders will usually have worked out a system that minimizes the motions required to fill the orders. For example, if an order is placed for six drinks and three require gin, the bartender will sequence the drinks first by product and then by preparation method. If the drinks were sequenced by preparation method, the bartender might have to pick up the gin bottle four times instead of once. The service staff must be trained to call all product drinks in order.

Another decision to be made in sequencing drinks is which product should be called first; i.e., should the server call gin drinks first and then scotch drinks or vice versa. Most bartenders want their drinks called in the same order that the well stock is set up, working from left to right. Frequently that order is from clear to darkest liquors. Hence, the server would call drinks in this order: vodka, gin, scotch, bourbon, liqueurs, and beers.

Another system of sequencing drinks is by preparation method, and in very busy bars this method has the advantage of increasing the bartender's speed. A typical sequence by preparation method would be straight shots, highballs, mixed drinks, shake/blender drinks, liqueurs, and beers. It is important that the servers and bartenders both understand the sequencing system to be used as well as the terminology. If not, both ordering time and mistakes will increase.

Endnotes

1. Carolyn Hughes Crowley, "What makes a bartender great?" *Restaurants USA* 10, (#2, 1990): 27–29.

2. Crowley, 28.

3. Neal J. Scott, "Management Training," *Nation's Restaurant News Bar Management Supplement* 21, (#3, 1986): 46.

4. *Mr. Boston Deluxe Official Bartender's Guide* (Boston: Mr. Boston Distiller Corp., 1979).

5. Harold J. Grossman, *Grossman's Guide to Wines, Beers, and Spirits*, revised by Harriet Lembeck (New York: Charles Scribner's Sons, 1977).

6. Grossman, 384.

7. Scott, 45–46.

Key Terms

back	mixology
backup drinks	muddling
build method	neat
call brands	on the rocks
call drinks	overpouring
doubles	pousse-café
drink incentives	pre-mix
happy hour	sequencing
last call	shake/blend method
liqueurs	simple syrup
liquor	standard recipe

stir method

straight up

swizzle stick

twist

water (soda) back

water on the side

wedge

well drinks

well stock

Discussion Questions

1. What are some of the positive psychological roles a bartender can play? Discuss some that are inappropriate.

2. What constitutes "good service" from a bartender?

3. How can the bartender be an effective salesperson (without necessarily pushing more drinks)?

4. How can a bartender reduce the chances of a guest getting intoxicated?

5. What are flaming drinks? How are they sometimes a problem?

6. What are the consequences of overpouring?

7. Why are garnishes important, and what procedures do they require?

8. How do the stir, build, and shake/blend methods differ?

9. What items should be readily available at a well-stocked bartender's work station?

10. What is *sequencing*? Give some examples.

6

Service Procedures and Selling Techniques

Chapter Outline

Service: An Overview
    A Service Orientation
    A Guest-Oriented Approach
    How It Works
Establishing Service Standards
Basic Service Procedures
    Table Approach
    Taking and Placing the Order
        Drink Preparation and Transport
    Serving the Guest
    Payment/Cash Control
Service Procedures for Beer
    Serving Temperature
    Pouring and Serving
    Glassware
Service Procedures for Wine
    Wine and Food
    The Sommelier
    Preparation
        Serving Temperatures
        Decanting
        Glassware
    Wine Service
        Sparkling Wines and Champagne
Handling Service Problems
Selling
    Techniques and Strategies
        Product Knowledge and Substitution
    Selling Wine
        Merchandising
        The Wine List as a Sales Tool
Toward Successful Service and Selling

▬▬▬▬▬▬▬ We now come to the very heart of our business—service and selling. This is where you, the bar or beverage manager, are in the driver's seat. This is where you can best lead and influence your employees and impress your superiors with increased profits.

A successful bar or beverage business depends on service and selling. Pleasing ambience, fancy decor, and efficient bar design won't count for much unless your employees have a thorough understanding of proper service procedures and selling techniques.

It is not only the responsibility of bar and beverage managers to promote and maintain quality service and selling in their organizations, it is the key to their success within the organization. Employees who know how to sell and serve beverages can enhance guest satisfaction and help increase profits. Guests may not know whom to credit, but owners and top management do! They know that their manager has taken the time to learn proper service procedures and effective sales techniques and, as a good manager, has consistently reinforced those skills in his or her employees through proper training programs and follow-up evaluations.

In this chapter we will take a brief but important look at why "service" and "a service orientation" have been such hot, much-discussed topics in every service industry worldwide. We'll see how a service orientation works in the bar and beverage business and how a guest-oriented approach takes service orientation a few steps further.

Most of all, however, you'll learn from this chapter practical, day-to-day (and night-to-night) beverage-serving procedures such as "pulling" a draft beer like an expert (and why the right-sized "head" is important to the taste of the beer as well as to guest satisfaction). You'll learn how to present and serve a *Premier Cru* with all the style and panache of a polished sommelier. And much, much more. We will offer a variety of personal selling techniques and strategies. By the end of this chapter, you will see how—in bar and beverage operations perhaps more than in other businesses—quality service procedures and personal selling techniques are inextricably linked to your success and the success of your establishment.

Service: An Overview

There was a time in the not-too-distant past when the talk about service in the United States was along the lines of: "Where is it? Where did it go?" And: "Doesn't anybody remember old-fashioned service values anymore?"

Well, there are still pockets of terrible service in America, but the tide has changed. Increased worldwide competition helped open the eyes and minds of top management. Increased competition, coupled with a dramatic shift from a predominantly industrial to a service-based economy, virtually forced management in every industry to search for every possible competitive edge. Progressive managers began to see that a total top-to-bottom dedication to service quality and to the actual needs and desires of customers was (and is) *the* competitive edge.

For many businesses and industries, service orientation has been more than a competitive edge; it has been the key to survival. Nowhere has this been truer than in the hospitality industry.

With more leisure time, guests have a greater opportunity to use the services we offer. (Courtesy of Opryland Hotel, Nashville, Tennessee)

A Service Orientation

Never before in the history of the hospitality industry has service been examined, debated, and questioned to the extent that it is today. Our guests have become more knowledgeable in correct service procedures and therefore more demanding in their expectations. People today have more leisure time, more disposable income, and therefore more time and money to spend on the services offered by the bar and beverage industry.

Let's face it, each of us likes to go to a bar or restaurant that provides great service. From recognizing you when you enter the door ("where everybody knows your name," as the "Cheers" TV theme goes), to correctly opening the bottle of wine you order with dinner or putting the appropriate garnish in your mixed drink, quality service greatly enhances our enjoyment. The more enjoyable our experience as a guest, the more likely we are to stay longer and to return again.

A service-oriented staff is the key to whether your guests have a positive experience and return along with their friends, or a negative experience that they will share with anyone who will listen. Many observers believe that the level of service your staff provides is a direct reflection on you, the manager.[1]

Service-oriented employees are public relations specialists, representing both you and your organization to the guest. Service-oriented employees make things happen—from greeting the guest to selling and serving the products you offer. They make the guest feel welcome and carefree for the short period of time the guest is in your establishment; they know the guest is always right.

Service-oriented employees act as if the establishment they work in is their own home and the guests their personal friends. They don't view their job as a form of servitude, but as a profession; they take pride in learning the skills of their trade and applying those skills to meet the needs of their guests. The skill to anticipate needs, listen, and smile convincingly are as necessary as remembering drink ingredients and preparation methods.

Selecting the right people and training them is only the beginning in creating a service-oriented staff. You, the manager, must demonstrate your complete support. Without their service skills there will be no sales, no profits, no paychecks. The success of your operation as well as your personal career goals depend on service-oriented employees.

A Guest-Oriented Approach

In the hospitality industry, service orientation is called a guest-oriented approach. And the reasons for that distinction apply equally to our corner of the hospitality industry—bar and beverage operations. Other industries and businesses might offer a multitude of services and shower their customers with attention, but our industry and business goes a step further: To be successful, we do everything in our power to make our customers feel like cherished guests—distinct, individual personalities, much like our own friends.

Let's take a look at our guests in this light. What might they be looking for when they enter one of our establishments? Many guests are not looking for a drink. They may be looking for a place to relax where they can socialize with their peers. After all, they can buy the same beverage and consume it at home for a lot less money. Perhaps our potential guest has had a bad day at work. Perhaps he or she is going out to celebrate a holiday, a promotion, or some other special occasion. Our guest might be looking for companionship, a place where he or she will not be alone. He or she could be a businessperson meeting someone for a business appointment. Perhaps the guest is traveling on business and prefers the atmosphere in your bar to the decor of his or her hotel room.

Guests enter bars and restaurants for many different reasons. This means that guest-oriented service must not be routine, but must be customized or individualized to best meet the needs of each particular guest. A guest's reaction to service is often emotional, rather than based on his or her knowledge of proper service procedures. Knowledgeable service is defined by each guest that enters your establishment according to the guest's own perceptions of service and atmosphere. Therefore, to provide great service, your employees must focus on guests as individuals and be flexible, as opposed to sticking to one unwavering pattern of behavior. Each of us has been in a bar or restaurant where a standardized greeting (such as "Hi, my name is _____; I'll be your server tonight") is delivered with little eye contact and no enthusiasm.

The service staff's ability to be flexible is critical in meeting guest expectations in bar and beverage operations. Learning how to become flexible in one's service style comes from experience, but even experienced employees need to be reminded of the importance of staying adaptable to different guest expectations. Adaptability is also a reflection of management's hiring and training skills. To be adaptable, your employees need the basic knowledge and tools to perform their jobs. But adaptability also stems from your ability to effectively coach and motivate your staff in developing an honest, sincere, and flexible guest-oriented approach to service.

How far should you go to ensure that your employees maintain a flexible, guest-oriented approach? Satisfaction Guaranteed Eateries, Inc., of Seattle turned guest complaints to their overall advantage by putting both the responsibility and the authority for an absolute guest satisfaction guarantee in the hands of the service staff. What this means in practice is that no longer do employees have to chase down a manager to resolve a guest complaint; the responsibility is their own. They are given the authority to "comp" (offer free) drinks or desserts or even the entire meal ticket if *they*, the employees, feel it is appropriate.[2] This approach has given all employees the feeling that they truly are part of the company they work for. They no longer look for excuses to explain why a guest wasn't happy or try to place blame. Additionally, this policy identifies service weaknesses that can be quickly corrected.

How It Works

In the 1990s, quality service is clearly becoming a strategic factor in the attempt to increase sales. To make it work, management must take a close look at its guests and identify guest needs. We will examine the concept of target marketing in Chapter 8, but it is important to connect guest-oriented approaches within the context of identifying, developing, and managing service procedures. Maintaining a guest-oriented approach means keeping the following five factors in mind:[3]

- The guest defines guest satisfaction, not management.

- Your service staff knows where the guest service problems are in your organization.

- Every employee within your organization has a guest, even if the guest is internal; that is, everyone has someone to whom he or she is responsible—a supervisor, manager, etc., and for those who aren't servers, whomever they have to please is like a guest.

- The commitment to guest-oriented management begins with top management.

- A guest-oriented approach must be part of all aspects of the organization's planning.

The more you know about your guests (and potential guests—the target markets), the better equipped you will be to make the crucial decisions required in developing and managing service procedures and selling techniques. This is especially true in a highly competitive environment. One of the first areas of decision-making in a guest-oriented approach is the establishment of service standards.

Establishing Service Standards

There are many factors that come into play when establishing quality service standards and procedures (see Exhibit 6.1). Some of these were introduced in Chapter 5 as we discussed standard drink recipes and the importance of a control system. Others will be discussed in future chapters. Our focus in this chapter is on the procedures themselves.

employ in your wine service procedures should be guided by your guest-oriented philosophy. Never should they be intimidating or threatening or too showy for the environment you have created for your guests' comfort.

Before we go into the finer points of wine service, let's look at some basics:

- Bringing the bottle to the guest who ordered and showing the label to him or her *before* the bottle is opened simply ensures that the guest is getting exactly what he or she ordered.

- Servers should be *practiced* in opening the bottle—and in all other wine service procedures—so that the process is unobtrusive. Guests should be able to continue their conversation without having to witness the server struggle with the proper service procedures.

- Pouring a first taste for the table host or person who ordered is practical—there is no other way to determine whether the wine has "turned" or soured. It is also symbolic. The act says, in effect: "We are perfectly willing to take this bottle away and bring you another in order to ensure your complete satisfaction."

Not all of the following service procedures are appropriate for every establishment. Details vary from one operation to another. Guests in some restaurants may be overwhelmed by the full treatment; guests in other types of restaurants will be upset if you leave out a single detail.

Step 1. The first step is to present the wine to the guest. This need not be done with any airs of overbearing pride; the purpose is simply to make sure that the wine you are about to open is the wine the guest intended to order. It's better to find this out before the cork is removed. Exhibit 6.11 illustrates wine presentation and wine-opening procedures.

Step 2. Place the bottle on a solid, level surface. Then, cut the metal or plastic band approximately one-fourth inch below the tip of the bottle. The cut should be low enough so that you can pour the wine without having it touch the band, as this may affect the wine's taste. The neck of the bottle should then be wiped with a clean cloth napkin to remove any deposits that may have collected under the cap during storage. These deposits are quite normal in most cases, but should be prevented from falling into the guest's glass.

Step 3. The objective of this step is to remove the cork from the bottle of wine without causing it to crumble or be pushed down inside the bottle. There are many types of corkscrews available today. In some operations, the choice is based on the preference of individual servers. It is important that the corkscrew chosen be of high quality and of a design that each server is comfortable with.

To ensure complete removal of the cork, insert the corkscrew exactly in the middle of the cork. Give an extra turn once you see that the tip of the corkscrew has emerged through the bottom of the cork and then pull out slowly. After the cork is removed, leave the cork on the table. The bottle mouth should be wiped with a clean cloth to remove any sediment that might fall into the guest's glass when the wine is poured.

Exhibit 6.11 Opening a Bottle of Wine

a. Present the wine to the guest. b. Cut the plastic cap below the top bulge of the bottle neck. c. Wipe the cork and exposed glass rim with a napkin. d. Twist the corkscrew into the cork until it is through, and hook the lever on the bottle rim. e. Draw the cork out and remove it from the corkscrew. f. Place the cork on the table.

It should be noted that corks sometimes fall apart through no fault of the server. A bad cork is often impossible to remove in a proper fashion.

Servers faced with a bad or crumbling cork should excuse themselves from the table and return with a fresh bottle of wine. If the cork has been badly damaged during storage, it is highly likely that the wine itself has lost many of its characteristics or has gone completely bad. In any case, such wine can be returned to the purveyor for credit.

Step 4. After the cork has been properly removed, a small amount of wine should be poured into the glass of the table host or person who ordered so that the wine may be tasted. The purpose of this step is to make sure the wine has not gone bad, and also to allow any cork particles to fall into the host's glass. If this occurs, the host should immediately be given a fresh glass. To avoid dripping wine on the table, the server should give the bottle a slight twist just before raising it from the pouring position. The server should avoid wrapping a napkin or towel around the bottle, as this hides the label (unless, of course, the server has just removed it from an ice bucket). The server or sommelier should taste the wine if asked.

Step 5. Once accepted, the wine should be poured for the remainder of the party, often women first, then men, to the right of the host, moving around the table counterclockwise and holding the bottle so that each guest may view the label as the wine is being poured from the guest's *right* side. Care should be taken not to touch the glass with the neck of the bottle when pouring. The host or person who ordered the wine is served last.

The wine glass should never be filled completely. Rather, enough room should be allowed at the top of the glass for the wine's aroma to be appreciated as the wine is drunk. Usually, depending on its style and size, the wine glass should be filled to only one-half or two-thirds full. Wine glasses should ordinarily not be removed from the table when filling or re-filling as this can unnecessarily warm a glass, disturbing the effects of a chilled wine.

Step 6. After all the guests have been served, the wine bottle should be placed in an ice bucket if the wine is white and on the table to the host's right if the wine is red. While the host may sometimes want to serve refills, it is ordinarily the server's duty to do so, and thus the server should observe the table frequently for this purpose.

Sparkling Wines and Champagne. The proper serving temperature of between 45° and 50° F (7° and 10° C) is very important in the service of champagne. Champagne that is opened at too warm a temperature will gush out too quickly and uncontrollably. Serve champagne too cold and the taste will be flat. If the champagne has been left in an ice bucket after it has been opened, care should be taken that the champagne has not chilled too much. It is also a good practice to remove the champagne from the bucket for a few minutes before pouring to take some of the chill off and maximize the subtlety of the champagne's flavor.

Opening a bottle of champagne is similar to opening a bottle of wine, with a few notable exceptions. First, great care should be taken not to shake or jar the bottle. It should be placed at a 45-degree angle and maintained at that angle throughout the opening process. Keeping it at this angle distributes the carbon dioxide throughout the entire bottle rather than concentrating all the pressure at the top, causing the wine to gush out when it is opened.

All sparkling wines have a foil cover over a soft metal or plastic hood held in place by a wire harness over their corks to prevent the cork from accidentally exploding. First the foil should be cut approximately 1/4 inch below the tip of the bottle. The cut should be low enough so that you can pour the wine without having it touch the foil, as this may affect the wine's taste. The purpose of the foil is to prevent dripping when the sparkling wine is poured. Next, the metal or plastic hood must be loosened by undoing the wire harness. The lower end of the harness will be twisted underneath the lip on the neck of the bottle. Untwist the wire slowly with one hand, while keeping the palm of your other hand firmly over the cork. Extreme caution should be exercised during this step so that the cork does not explode accidentally from the bottle. Also, for this reason, make sure that the neck of the bottle is pointing away from any people, either servers or guests. Please note that once the wire harness has been loosened, the hood should not be removed separately from the cork—this is a common, yet dangerous, service practice.

Next, the cork and the wire harness and hood should be removed at the same time. Firmly hold the base of the bottle with one hand and the cork and hood with the other. Slowly twist either the cork or the bottle until the cork is loosened and pulls out from the neck of the bottle. The cork should *ease*—not pop—out when this procedure is done correctly.

The procedures for serving sparkling wines are the same as those for other wines (although the sample taste is optional for champagne), but extra care should be taken not to pour sparkling wine too quickly or it will bubble over the rim of the glass. How much to fill the glass is dictated by the type of glassware used by your operation. Generally, tulip glasses are not filled as full as flute glasses, since flute glasses hold less by volume (although they appear to hold more). The standard pouring range is between two-thirds and four-fifths full. Since warm champagne is not appealing, you are better off pouring less rather than more.

Handling Service Problems

The service of alcoholic beverages is carefully regulated by federal, state, and local laws. You—the bar or beverage manager—have a responsibility to make sure that you are fully informed of, and in compliance with, all applicable legislation. Dealing with intoxicated guests has never been easy. Today, it can be extremely costly. If one of your staff serves alcohol to a guest who later is found to have a blood/alcohol percentage above the legal limit *and* who has caused injuries in an accident, your establishment—even the individual server—might be found liable for such injuries in a court of law. The so-called "Dram Shop Acts" have become a stark reality for many bar and beverage managers. And, as you already learned in Chapter 2, there are some very specific procedures your service staff can follow to prevent alcohol abuse by the guests in your bar or restaurant. How delicately and judiciously your staff handles such problems will also affect other patrons and the atmosphere of your establishment.

There are a number of other problems and mishaps that sometimes occur. It is a good idea to be prepared (backed by a written policy in your manual) for such situations. For instance:

- What should a server do if a drink is spilled on a guest?

- What should a server do if a guest falls in the bar?

- What should a server do if a guest vomits on the table or bar? If it spills onto another guest?

Your procedures need to cover the routine as well as the occasional-but-difficult situations—such as handling a guest's complaint about "not enough booze in a drink" or handling an order for a cocktail that is unfamiliar to the bartender.

Selling

The service staff is also your sales staff. Without your staff's sales skills, many of the products and services you offer would not be sold. It is your responsibility to see that your employees, in addition to knowing about the products and services your establishment offers, learn some selling techniques and strategies. A good *service* staff knows how to be courteous, the products they serve, and the proper service procedures. A good *sales* staff knows how to increase sales, and how to do so responsibly.

Do your guests have to "trip" the server to get a second drink? Are your guests too intimidated to order a bottle of wine? Perhaps your employees need to appreciate the fact that exercising their dual role as service and sales staff will bring direct financial rewards in the form of better tips.

In our business, service and selling are often virtually indistinguishable. For instance, being friendly, upbeat, easy to talk to—establishing a rapport with your guests, in other words—is good service. It's also a good selling technique because guests who relate well to that kind of personal service tend to stay longer, spend more money, and come back more often. Finding and hiring people with the right characteristics and abilities is the subject of the next chapter. Honing these characteristics and abilities is part of your responsibility in developing your sales staff (see Exhibit 6.12).

Techniques and Strategies

Developing selling strategies depends to a great extent on anticipating your guest's needs and desires. Through a process of market research and analysis, market segmentation, and related marketing techniques (see Chapter 8), you will identify a "target market" (briefly defined—a certain type of guest with specific needs and desires). Market analysis will direct your basic selling strategies.

One strategy you can provide without market analysis is an employee selection and training strategy that adds selling techniques to the service training. Remember that a good service staff takes the order, a good sales staff "sells" the guest.

This means starting with a positive approach. Instead of starting out with that tired old greeting: "Will you be having cocktails tonight?" how about trying: "If you're considering cocktails before dinner, we're offering (brand name) champagne at a special price tonight." This technique is

Exhibit 6.12 Characteristics of a Good Server/Salesperson

Shows awareness of responsible alcohol service

Displays enthusiasm

Communicates effectively

Is guest-oriented

Displays initiative

Has integrity

Knows the products

Knows the operation and the company

Knows service techniques

Is personable, friendly, and well-groomed

Organizes work well

Uses effective selling techniques—does not act "pushy"

called **selling by suggestion** or **suggestive selling.** It means putting your sales approach, statement, or question in such a way as to avoid an automatic "no" and to encourage a "yes" response.

One very effective approach to suggestive selling is to suggest personal favorites: "I just tried the bartender's Long Island iced tea last week, and it is the best I've ever tried. May I bring you one?" Or, "I just served a second round of our daiquiris to another table. Would you like to try one?"

Another method of suggestive selling is to use brand names if possible. Your employees should be given an opportunity to taste all house specialty drinks. Knowing your menu is an integral part of suggestive selling.

Good sales techniques mean good service in general. Good managers offer their servers the following advice: Don't rush your guests. Take the order and deliver the drinks promptly, but don't give your guests the impression that they should hurry up and leave. Don't wait for the guests to ask you for a second drink; you should be at the table suggesting another round before they are finished with their first drink unless there is reason to believe they have reached a point where slower service might prevent over-drinking. Suggestions should be made sincerely. The guest should never feel pressured to buy. Avoid negative questions such as, "Do you want anything else?" Good selling techniques involve assistance and persuasion—not high pressure sales tactics.

Product Knowledge and Substitution. As we mentioned earlier, a thorough knowledge of products and services offered gives a solid foundation from which to create sales by suggestion. When bartenders or servers are faced with being unable to supply a particular brand requested by a guest, they have an opportunity to exercise some old-fashioned "salesmanship." For example, if a guest asks for a well-known 12-year-aged scotch whisky, and it is unavailable, the bartender or server should be able to suggest an adequate substitute that will please the guest. (A word of caution: *Know*

Product knowledge is as much a part of training as service procedures. (Courtesy of Opryland Hotel, Nashville, Tennessee)

what you're talking about; if you don't have an adequate substitute—especially for something as specialized as an aged scotch—you are much better off saying so. Honesty *is* the best policy.)

Selling Wine

Nowhere is product and market knowledge more important than in the "art" of selling wine. If guests seem hesitant about making a wine selection, your service staff should be able to offer immediate assistance. The more knowledge your sales staff has about the wines you offer, the more confident they will feel in making wine suggestions to their guests.

Your servers will be faced with many more opportunities for substitutions where wine is concerned. To be able to say with authority "Our Cabernet Sauvignon has a somewhat fruitier bouquet" tends to inspire confidence.

In order to obtain full service staff cooperation in your wine sales efforts, you should provide a wine sales training program. The program might consist of a series of short (15-minute) training sessions and tastings, conducted on an ongoing basis. Wine tastings should be limited to two per session and should focus on what you want the servers to understand about the wines so that they can better describe them to your guests. Whatever wines your staff tastes before their shift will be the wines you sell the most of during that shift, so be prepared.

The training program should follow a logical sequence, perhaps beginning by reviewing the proper procedures for opening a bottle of wine and by tasting the house wines. Organizing each training session so that a service technique is reviewed and two wines are tasted and discussed is a good pattern to follow. Encourage your staff to read up on wines and share what they have learned at the training sessions. As a manager, your attitude and knowledge about wines is critical to the success of a wine sales program. If the service staff knows that you are interested in and knowledgeable about wines, they are more likely to take learning about wines and champagnes more seriously.

Exhibit 6.13 Pronouncing Wine Names Correctly

TONGUE TWISTERS

Pronouncing The Names

Some white wines:

CHARDONNAY (SHAR-DONE-NAY)

SAUVIGNON BLANC (SO-VEN-YON BLAWNK)

FUME BLANC (FOO-MAY BLAWNK)

CHENIN BLANC (SHEN-IN BLAWNK)

JOHANNISBERG RIESLING (YOE-HAN-ISS-BERG REES-LING)

GEWÜRTZTRAMINER (GHU-VERTZ-TRA-MEE-NER)

Some red wines:

CABERNET SAUVIGNON (CA-BER-NAY SO-VEN-YON)

MERLOT (MARE-LO)

PINOT NOIR (PEE-NO NWAR)

ZINFANDEL (ZIN-FAN-DELL)

BEAUJOLAIS GAMAY (BOE-JAH-LAY GAM-MAY)

Courtesy of Opryland Hotel, Food and Beverage Training Department, Nashville, Tennessee

There are a variety of resources available to you as you plan these wine training programs. Wholesalers and distributors have experts on their staffs who would be eager to assist you and your staff in becoming more knowledgeable. There are also regional, national, and international organizations that serve as representatives of the wines produced in their regions. These organizations can provide printed and audiovisual materials to assist you. In-house seminars are usually productive. In addition, there are a variety of periodicals devoted solely to the study wines. While learning about wines does take time and requires continually reviewing the products available, there is no better way to increase wine sales in your bar or beverage operation.

Merchandising. There are many ways to merchandise your wines and thereby assist your sales staff. These include setting up attractive wine displays at the entrance of your operation; using a mobile wine cart to display several varieties of your wines and champagnes; placing bottles of wine, unopened, on the tables; or setting the dining room tables with wine glasses.

The servers should be prepared to make appropriate wine suggestions for each phase of meal service and know the importance of encouraging the guest to "trade up" from house to premium wines. They should be able to pronounce each of the wines on your wine list (Exhibit 6.13).

Servers must also know how much wine (what size of bottle) to suggest. A **split** contains about 6 ounces (187 ml) and is suitable for one person. A **half-bottle** contains approximately 12.5 ounces (375 ml), adequate for two. A **full bottle** usually contains approximately 25 ounces (750 ml), which could adequately serve three to four persons, but is not too much for two people over the course of a full meal.

The Wine List as a Sales Tool. The most effective way to use your wine list as a sales tool is to make it attractive and informative, and to organize it in such a way as to make it easy for your guests to use. You might group the wines according to their uses, such as appetizer wines, white wines, red wines, dessert wines, and champagnes or sparkling wines.[6] Another way of organizing the wine list is to place the white wines in the order of driest to sweetest and the red wines in the order of lightest to fullest-bodied.[7]

One method of listing wines identifies the country of origin, the name of the wine, the vintner, the vintage, the price, and an assigned number (which could be helpful to guests having difficulty pronouncing the name of a particular wine). Universally, wine lists are organized as either "domestic" or "imported," with the imported wines classified by country of origin and by wine-producing region (Bordeaux, Burgundy, etc.).

In the United States, in years past, domestic wines were invariably considered inferior to imported wines. Today, many American wines, especially from certain estates in the Napa Valley of California, are praised by critics the world over. In building the domestic side of your wine inventory, the wine list should reflect the growing prestige of American wines.

Your wine list should work for you. If you are trying to increase wine sales (and profits) in a restaurant whose guests are relatively unsophisticated when it comes to wine, consider including appealing descriptions of wines: "This slightly dry Chenin Blanc varietal with a subtle fruity bouquet comes from the award-winning _____ estates in Sonoma, California." The wine list can also be designed so that it relates both the wines and food you offer in your operation to each other.

Your wine list should be kept in an easily accessible location, and kept in good condition without products and prices crossed out. The print should be large enough to be read in the lighting atmosphere of your establishment. The wine list should be brought before or with the food menus at the beginning of the service process.

The wine list is a sales tool and can be an important factor in generating revenue. Remember that the quality of the wine list is a reflection of your establishment. Present it with pride.

Toward Successful Service and Selling

The success of your bar or beverage operation can be enhanced by the manner, appearance, and expert service of your staff. No matter how excellent the products you serve, your guest's experience can be ruined by poor service. The guest must come first, and last.

Proper service procedures enhance not only the quality of your service, but the quality of the products you serve as well. As you have learned, many alcoholic beverages are very delicate products and must be handled with care during service.

Better service does lead to better sales. Higher sales bring greater profits both to the operation and to the server. Your service staff also becomes your sales staff performing the function of selling. In selling, the guest's desire to purchase more often depends on how he or she feels about the individual serving him or her. The best sales technique is your staff's ability to interrelate with your guests. Suggestive selling, when done properly, shows your guests that you are taking an active interest in their needs.

It is up to you as manager to make your service staff feel responsible for the success of the operation. You must treat your service staff as professionals. The better they do their job, the more successful everyone will be. If selling wine and champagne is part of their job, then part of your responsibility is to see that they have the proper knowledge base, through training, to do their jobs effectively.

Quality service can never be taken for granted. What we perceive as quality today may be mediocre tomorrow. Guests' needs and expectations are dynamic and constantly fed by dynamic competition! Outperforming your competition and improving profits will be even more difficult in the years to come. Higher quality standards of service will be the competitive edge.

Endnotes

1. Darryl Hartley-Leonard, "Service Begins at the Top," *Newsweek* CXIII (#20, 1989): 4.

2. Timothy W. Firnstahl, "My Employees Are My Service Guarantee," *Harvard Business Review* 89 (#4, 1989): 28–32.

3. Lee Weinberger, "Five Steps for Staying Close to the Customer," *Newsweek* CXIV (#14, 1989): 12.

4. Charles G. Burck, "The Whiskey Distillers Put Up Their Dukes," *Fortune* 109 (#9, 1977): 155–156.

5. Alexis Bespaloff, "The Wine-Chill Factor," *New York* 26 (March 1984): 82, 84.

6. The Wine Institute, *The Sale of Wine in Restaurants* (San Francisco: The Wine Institute, 1979), 28.

7. Bill Main, "Selling Wine the Easy Way," *Restaurants USA* 10 (#2, 1990): 32.

Key Terms

beer-clean glass	sediment
decanter	selling by suggestion
decanting	sommelier
full bottle	split
half bottle	suggestive selling
level of service	wine steward

Discussion Questions

1. What characterizes a guest-oriented approach to service?

2. How is it possible to provide too much service?

3. What are the major steps in serving cocktails?

4. How should beer be poured from a bottle?

5. How should a draft beer be drawn?

6. What are the general procedures for opening and serving a bottle of wine?

7. What are the basic guidelines for wine serving temperatures?

8. What overrules any guidelines that pair wine with food?

9. What are some examples of effective suggestive selling techniques?

10. What are the benefits of wine training and tasting sessions?

The Selection and Training of Human Resources

Chapter Outline

The Labor Supply and Its Effect on Bar and Beverage Management
Job Analysis
Job Descriptions
Job Specifications
Recruitment and Selection
    Recruitment
        Identification of Available Labor Pools
        Methods of Recruitment
    Selection
        The Interview as an Effective Selection Tool
Orientation Programs
Training
    Identifying Training Needs
    Choosing the Training Method
    Training Builds Sales
A Look Ahead . . .

Exhibit 7.2 Sample Newspaper Ads

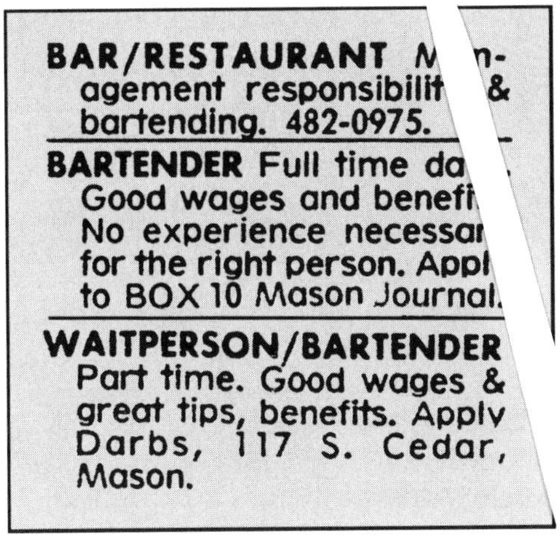

BAR/RESTAURANT Man-
agement responsibilit &
bartending. 482-0975.

BARTENDER Full time da
Good wages and benefi
No experience necessar
for the right person. Appl
to BOX 10 Mason Journal.

WAITPERSON/BARTENDER
Part time. Good wages &
great tips, benefits. Apply
Darbs, 117 S. Cedar,
Mason.

Bar and beverage operations often use newspaper advertisements to recruit applicants.

to use internal or external sources or, as most companies do, a combination of both. **Internal recruitment methods** seek to determine whether qualified individuals are available within the company. A common internal method is **job posting**. All job vacancies are communicated to current employees via postings listed on bulletin boards, in circulated newsletters, or in special publications which list vacancies. These postings provide information on the job, including a job description and a specification indicating the necessary qualifications. Any interested employee possessing the necessary qualifications can apply for the posted job vacancy.

Another method of internal recruitment is the use of **employee referrals**. Current employees can recommend friends or family for job vacancies. This is a very effective recruitment method in a labor shortage and generally proves to be quite reliable. Employees are not likely to recommend someone whom they would not be proud of or who might damage their reputation with your organization. Perhaps because of this, good employees generally recommend better candidates than bad employees. Another advantage is that, since your employees already have an insight into your corporate culture, management expectations, and job requirements, they tend to encourage only people they think will fit in. An employee referral program is also a very cost-effective recruitment method. Sometimes, companies apply some or all of their savings to employee referral incentive programs. Cash, savings bonds, and/or employee discounts are offered to employees who make successful referrals for job vacancies. A "successful" referral is generally defined as one who is hired and performs satisfactorily for a specified length of time.

With **external recruitment methods,** management looks outside the company to fill job vacancies. This can be much more expensive and difficult than recruiting internally. Advertising campaigns, placement agencies, and unsolicited walk-ins are the primary methods used by bar and beverage operations. Advertising is done through the media, primarily radio, television, newspapers, and trade magazines. Newspaper advertisements are the most common form of advertisement (see Exhibit 7.2). Placement or employment agencies can be expensive and are used primarily for managerial job vacancies. Unsolicited walk-ins should not be dismissed as a poor recruitment source. If your bar or beverage operation has earned the reputation of being a great place to work, walk-ins may be of very high caliber.

In the United States, the Immigration Reform and Control Act of 1986 makes it unlawful for any person to hire undocumented immigrants. This law makes the employer responsible for verifying the right to work of *all* employees hired since November 7, 1986. An I-9 form must be filled out for every such employee and signed by management stating that the appropriate documentation has been checked.[5] Managers who have had experience with the **Immigration and Naturalization Service (INS)** recommend that copies of all documentation and the I-9 form become part of the employee's file. They will be helpful if the INS ever questions the legal status of one of your employees.

As recruitment becomes increasingly difficult, a strategic recruitment plan becomes imperative. It is no longer enough to place a help-wanted ad in the newspaper and wait for the job applicants to stream in. In large companies, human resources departments are being asked to develop creative strategies for recruitment and to devise training and development programs that will assist in employee retention. In smaller operations, these responsibilities are frequently left up to the bar or beverage manager. The more creative your approaches to recruitment are, the likelier you are to fill your job vacancies with highly qualified people. By establishing a sound recruiting program, a bar or beverage operation ensures its ability to develop sources of applicants for its job positions.

Selection

Selection is a process in which all job applicants are screened (in compliance with all legal restrictions) to identify the best candidates from the available applicants. Since the success of an operation is heavily dependent on the quality of its employees, the selection process should instill a measure of quality control. If screening determines that none of the job applicants are suitable for the job, the recruitment process should be repeated.

The criteria for selection are found in the job specification for each job position. Management must determine how heavily to weight each of the required qualifications in making a selection decision. For example, how important is job experience? Some bar and beverage managers want to hire only bartenders who have several years' experience. Other managers feel that the best bartenders are those whom they train, and want job applicants to have no experience. In most bar and beverage operations, the amount of experience desired is somewhere between these two extremes. All bar and beverage managers would agree, however, that applicants for job vacancies in the bar need to be personable and highly motivated. With the high degree of guest contact that bar and beverage employees have, these qualifications are a must!

There are a variety of screening methods used in selection. An application should be required of all persons interested in a particular job vacancy. Information requested on an application must, by law, be job-related. This prohibits asking any question that relates to age, race, marital status, height, or weight unless you can prove that the topic is a **bona fide occupational qualification (BFOQ).** To show that a qualification is a BFOQ, you must prove it is necessary in the performance of the job duties and responsibilities. The fact that your guests prefer male cocktail servers would not be accepted as a BFOQ. However, an applicant's sex would be a BFOQ when hiring a restroom attendant.

The verification of references is another method of screening job applicants. Many bar and beverage operations are becoming reluctant about releasing information regarding former employees because of the threat of litigation for slander and defamation of character. Answering questions regarding performance levels, work behaviors, or reasons for leaving may make a previous employer vulnerable to such litigation. However, questions that verify employment dates, job positions held, and duties are perfectly acceptable. In fact, there is no liability to the potential employer for asking job-related questions—the liability is restricted to the company and people answering the questions.

The Interview as an Effective Selection Tool. The interview is conducted only after the screening process has narrowed the list of job applicants to those who meet the qualifications identified in the job specification. The interview process is time-consuming. Management should not waste valuable time interviewing applicants who do not meet minimal qualifications.

Conducting an effective interview requires skill on the part of the interviewer. The interview allows the interviewer to further explore information on the job application and to evaluate the applicant's communication skills, personality, and job knowledge. Generally, a review of the application form will suggest many questions that can then be addressed in the course of the interview. Depending on the size of the organization, the job applicant might go through a series of interviews. At a minimum, an interview should be conducted by the bar or beverage manager and, if different, the position's immediate supervisor.

Care must be taken in the development of interview questions to ensure that they elicit the information you will need to make a final selection decision. We recommend that you develop a list of questions along with a set of answers that you find acceptable well in advance of the actual interview. The Equal Employment Opportunity Act prohibits employers from asking job applicants questions that do not relate to the specific job being interviewed for. During an interview, it is illegal to ask questions pertaining to the following areas:

- Participation in fraternal or benevolent organizations

- Age

- Religious beliefs

- Nationality

- Marital status

- Military discharge status

- Credit history

- Race

- Arrest record

In deciding whether a question is illegal, ask yourself, "Is it job-related?" If the answer is no, don't ask the question.

The interview is an effective selection tool.

To obtain the most information, it is best to ask open-ended questions, as opposed to those that can be answered with a yes or no response. Give interviewees as much time as they need to answer the questions. Often, interviewees will provide more information than you are asking for if you give them time and listen carefully. In bar and beverage operations, your employees need to be very sociable. They must be comfortable working with strangers and must like to serve other people. Questions should be developed that will help you determine if the job applicant has these characteristics.

Good interviewing is a skill which a bar or beverage manager needs to learn. How you handle interviews will determine whether you will be able to select the best job applicant. Your goal in the interview is to learn as much as possible about the interviewee. You should listen 70% of the time and talk only 30%. Listen carefully to the applicant. Even though you have a list of questions prepared, do not hesitate to pick up on information you hear and delve deeper if it is relevant to the position.

Body language can also tell you a lot about applicants. Are they alert, upbeat, and interesting? If you find someone a bore in the interview, where most applicants are trying to impress you, it is highly likely that your guests will find him or her boring as well.

In most situations, you will have made a hiring decision before the interview is over. It is generally wise not to make an offer at that moment,

3. William B. Martin, *Managing Quality Customer Service* (Los Altos, Calif.: Crisp Publications, 1989), 35.

4. For more information on job analysis, see Lewis C. Forrest, Jr., *Training for the Hospitality Industry,* 2d ed. (East Lansing, Mich.: Educational Institute of the American Hotel & Motel Association, 1990), chapter 2, "Job Analysis and Development."

5. David P. Berry and Jeff T. Appleman, "Policing the Hiring of Foreign Workers: Employers Get the Job," *Personnel* 64 (#3, 1987): 48–51.

Key Terms

bona fide occupational
   qualification (BFOQ)
employee referrals
external recruitment methods
Immigration and Naturalization
   Service (INS)
internal recruitment methods
job analysis
job description
job incumbent

job inventory
job posting
job specification
on-the-job training (OJT)
orientation program
position descriptions
position guides
recruitment
selection

Discussion Questions

1. How are world demographics changing? How do these changes affect individual bar and beverage operations?

2. What is job analysis? What role does it play in the strategic planning of human resources management?

3. How do job descriptions help both employees and their managers?

4. How are job specifications used in the recruitment and selection process?

5. What effect does a positive or negative reputation have on an operation's ability to recruit?

6. Why do most operations use a combination of internal and external recruiting methods?

7. What types of questions are illegal during the selection process? Under what circumstances might normally illegal questions be acceptable?

8. What information should be covered in an orientation program? How do well-developed orientation programs save money?

9. How does training affect turnover?

10. What types of training methods are commonly used?

8 Marketing Bar and Beverage Operations

Chapter Outline

Knowing Your Guest: The Key to Marketing Success
    The Changing Marketplace
    Market Segmentation
    Market Research
    Selecting a Target Market and Positioning
Special Considerations in Bar and Beverage Marketing
    Marketing Guest Service
    Special Characteristics of Service Businesses
    Ethical and Social Issues
The Competitive Environment
    Competition Analysis
    Guest Decision-Making
    Forecasting Sales
The Marketing Mix
Product and Place
Price: Beverage-Pricing Strategies
    Product Categories
    Sales Value per Bottle
    Pricing Methods
        Bar Type
    Sales Mix
    Wine Pricing
Promotion
    Developing Promotions
        Budgeting
        Selecting and Developing the Idea
        Establishing a Timetable
        Selecting Your Media Strategy
        Delivering What You Promise
        Evaluating the Results
The Promotional Mix
    Advertising
        Print Media
        Television, Cable, and Radio
        Word-of-Mouth Advertising
        Criticism of Alcohol-Related Advertising
        A Word About Media Selection
    Public Relations and Publicity
    Sales Promotions
    Personal Selling
    Merchandising
Marketing: The New Alternative

A well-planned marketing effort is essential to achieving your operational goal of guest satisfaction. **Marketing** is a management planning activity whose purpose is to generate sales by conducting business from the consumer's perspective. The marketing of bar and beverage operations is guest-oriented—focused on the needs and wants of guests, not on the operation itself or its products and services. For example, you sell Long Island iced tea because your guests want to purchase it, not because it's the food and beverage manager's favorite drink. Anything the operation does that influences a guest's decision to buy can be related to marketing.

A marketing plan should examine a 12-month period and identify goals to be achieved and specific promotional opportunities to be developed throughout the year. Marketing goals are achieved through such planned activities as positioning, product selection, promotion, merchandising, pricing, public relations, advertising, and personal selling. This chapter will describe these important marketing tools and explain their roles in the overall marketing plan.

There are several considerations in developing a marketing plan. For example: Who are your competitors? How successful are they and why? How does your operation rate in comparison?

Marketing planning, like other aspects of bar and beverage management, must take into account the ethical and social issues surrounding the sale of alcohol. The consequences of drinking and driving have forced many bar and beverage managers to rethink their marketing activities. This chapter will describe how some operators have used this issue to actually attract guests to their operations.

In developing a marketing plan, it is important to remember that the hospitality industry is a service industry. The marketing plan should be based on the premise that guests often patronize bar and beverage operations for the intangible services they receive, not the tangible products they could easily consume at home.

This chapter explains the importance of guest-oriented marketing in bar and beverage management and describes the variables that affect the guest profile. Market segmentation, target marketing, and positioning are defined, and the uniqueness of service industry marketing is explored. Other marketing terms and concepts described in this chapter include competition analysis, sales forecasting, and the marketing mix.

Knowing Your Guest: The Key to Marketing Success

In a competitive environment, only those bar and beverage managers who listen to their guests will direct successful operations. Knowing what your guests want and enjoy and then delivering it to them is the key to success. Guest-oriented marketing is a much broader approach to marketing than simply being sales-minded. While bar and beverage managers in the past were able to conduct business from the seller's perspective, today's ever-changing marketplace demands the flexibility of a guest-oriented approach.

Quite simply, what we will do in this chapter is provide you with the marketing tools that should be used when formulating your marketing strategy. These marketing tools (or planned marketing activities) will help you define your markets, identify your guests' needs, and compare those needs to what your bar and beverage operation is selling.

Exhibit 8.1 Guest Profile Variables

Age	Type of Housing
Education	Income Level
Ethnic Mix	
Expectations	Occupation
Gender	Social Habits
Marital Status	Values
Family Size	Activities

Before you can determine what products and services your guests want to purchase, you must first identify who your guests are and try to learn as much about them as possible. What you need to develop is a **guest profile**—a list of characteristics that your guests have in common. Exhibit 8.1 lists some of the variables affecting guest profiles. The guest profile helps you identify which market segments you appeal to; it can also be used to define segments you would like to attract.

Consider how each of the factors listed in Exhibit 8.1 might affect your bar or beverage operation. For example, what kinds of products and services might you offer to a clientele of primarily college students? What might you have to change in order to attract a different segment—for example, the after-five executive crowd?

Ethnic mix is becoming an increasingly important consideration in the hospitality industry. Bar and beverage operators must be aware of the ethnic diversity surrounding them as they select the products and services they will offer. The ethnic mix will directly affect the variables of expectations and values. Guests who are predominantly Japanese Americans, for example, might have different expectations than guests who are African Americans. What do each of these ethnic groups consider important in life? What do they hold sacred? What is forbidden? Bar and beverage managers should develop an understanding of cultural differences in relation to hospitality and the service of alcohol.

The Changing Marketplace

The first step toward knowing your guests is understanding the constant market changes in the bar and beverage business. People move in and out of your location, they age, their incomes change, they get married, they have children, and their children leave home. Each of these changes affects your guests' needs and therefore the demand for the products and services you offer. Considering the fact that a bar and beverage operation's potential market increases every day as people reach legal drinking age, managers must be able to respond readily to market trends.

Many changes have occurred over the last decade. More women have entered the work force, many as heads of households and many as part of a two-paycheck family. The latter situation is becoming increasingly common, and while in many cases a second paycheck is necessary to pay the bills, it often becomes discretionary income, which allows the family to lead a more comfortable lifestyle.

Household size has decreased since 1960, and all data indicate that this trend will continue. In general, smaller households spend more money per capita on food and beverages away from home than do larger households. One- and two-member households (singles and couples without children) usually have more opportunities to go out. Demand for food and beverages becomes more elastic as household size increases; that is, large households spend a higher percentage of their disposable income when they go out than smaller households. This is all good news for the bar or beverage manager who targets these markets and effectively meets their needs.

The "graying of America" also affects the bar and beverage business. By the year 2000, the median age in the United States will be 35. U.S. population growth will likely continue to be zero, which means potential markets will continue to grow older. The graying Americans tend to be better educated and less concerned with high-status positions than their younger counterparts. The older consumers consider other things in life just as important as, if not more important than, going to work each day.

Market Segmentation

Market segmentation is the process of dividing the broad market into various groups of potential guests who share common wants and needs. No bar or beverage operation can expect to attract every potential consumer in a given market area. Market segmentation seeks to attract one or more particular groups—**target markets**—into the operation.

The question in market segmentation is which segments do you appeal to, or hope to appeal to? The interior design of your operation, the music or entertainment you offer, the products you choose to serve, the uniforms your employees wear, the type of glassware you select, and the type of service you offer all depend on the particular market segment you want to attract. The guest who wants to see wide-screen sports events is not in the same market segment as the guest who wants to dance to ballroom music. In this case, the choice between these two forms of entertainment is based on which segment you want to attract. Perhaps neither is satisfactory for your operation.

Unlike product-driven or operationally driven businesses, the bar and beverage business is market-driven. Market-driven companies must examine the following considerations:

- What specific market are we trying to serve?
- What should we offer the guests in that market segment?
- What products should we provide?
- What services should we provide?
- What environment should we create?

Given what we have already learned about the changing marketplace and consumer needs, it is imperative that we know who our guest is. And we need to realize that there are different guests with different needs representing different segments of the market. Demographic market segmentation looks at income levels, occupations, age levels, marital status, and so on. Psychographic market segmentation looks at such variables as personalities, lifestyles, attitudes, and interests.

Exhibit 8.2 Potential Markets

Businesspeople	Shoppers
Conventioneers	Dancers
Tourists/Travelers	Entertainment-Seekers
Local Residents	People-Seekers
Sports Enthusiasts	Nightlife-Seekers

**Market
Research**

How do you go about compiling a guest profile? First, you identify the needs of the market segment that your bar or beverage operation currently satisfies, and second, you identify the target markets that *could* be served by your operation. Exhibit 8.2 lists some potential target markets. The process of gathering this type of information is called **market research**.

Market research can be conducted in a variety of ways. Carefully developed guest surveys can yield much information on the type of guest your operation currently serves. In addition to revealing guest profile information, a survey can indicate how your guests perceive the quality of your operation's products and services. This information is essential to the success of the marketing plan.

You can obtain useful feedback about your operation by talking to your guests as they arrive or leave, or by having an employee do it for you. To ensure consistency, the person at the door should be trained to ask a specific set of questions. Your employees can be valuable sources of information, as guest satisfaction is in their best interests. Informal meetings at the end of each shift usually provide better data than do employee suggestion boxes. Bartenders should be questioned about the types of drinks and product brands that are requested. Managers need to respond quickly to the rapidly changing needs of their guests.

Market research on existing guests should identify their needs, expectations, and wants, including product brands, level of quality, atmosphere, price, service, and entertainment.

Research on potential markets should attempt to answer the following questions:

- How many potential guests does your operation have?

- What markets do these guests represent?

- What are their ages? their income levels? their employment status? their household structure? their expenditure patterns?

- What do your potential guests think about your operation?

- What trends operating in these markets might have an effect on your operation?

**Selecting a
Target Market
and Positioning**

As we stated earlier, no single bar or beverage operation can be all things to all people. Each manager must decide, based on market research, what particular market segments the operation wants to attract. The process of selecting these target markets is called **target marketing.**

Target marketing is based on the assumption that products and services can be more effectively marketed toward groups of people who share common characteristics. Once an operation selects its target markets, it can make an effort to meet the specific needs and wants of each group. Target markets should be analyzed continually; trends in the bar and beverage business are highly volatile and managers must anticipate them, rather than react to them.

As a bar or beverage manager, it is important to determine how your operation is going to compete for the target markets you have identified. This strategy is known as **positioning**. Positioning involves trying to attract target markets by offering products and services designed to meet their wants and needs. Positioning allows an operation to control, to a certain extent, the types of guests it attracts. For example, by offering high-quality products and services, you can attract guests who are affluent enough to pay for such quality.

The objective of positioning is to give your operation a competitive edge over other bar and beverage operations targeting the same consumers. Positioning efforts should therefore focus on offering products and services that are superior, in the eyes of your potential guests, to your competitors' offerings. (Competition is discussed further in a later section of this chapter.)

Special Considerations in Bar and Beverage Marketing

Marketing Guest Service

Services are the fastest-growing economic sector in the United States. By now, many of you have heard the U.S. Department of Labor's projection that, by the mid-1990s, nine out of ten jobs will be provided by service industries.[1] This increase in service jobs has been occurring gradually since the 1950s, when the United States began changing from an industrial economy, based on the manufacturing of products, to a service economy, based on the provision of services. Much of this change has been the result of an increase in technology. It is not that people are demanding fewer products, but that it takes considerably fewer people to produce the products.

Bar and beverage operations are service businesses because guests do not *need* to leave home to consume the beverage products and are thus paying primarily for service. With the exception of bars in some airports, trains, ships, and other isolated locations, most operations do not have a captive market. Our primary offering in the bar and beverage business is *service*.

Special Characteristics of Service Businesses

Most bar and beverage operations are not primarily product-driven; they are not in the beer business, the wine business, or the liquor business. Product knowledge is important, but product knowledge and service knowledge are *not* the same, and service knowledge is essential for effective service marketing.[2] Because service is intangible, it is more variable than a product. It is also more difficult to evaluate. For example, you can train a bartender to properly garnish a drink, and you can easily determine, by looking at the drink, whether the product is being presented correctly. However, mere observation does not always reveal whether the services you offer are being delivered properly. You cannot follow each cocktail server to every table. The abstract nature of service presents bar and beverage managers not only with a quality control challenge (discussed in Chapter 10), but with a marketing challenge as well.

Dealing with people in a service business is different from dealing with products in a manufacturing business. And because of these differences, it stands to reason that the approach to marketing must be different. As we pointed out earlier, our approach to marketing must be guest-oriented. A guest enters a bar or beverage operation with certain expectations. Service quality may be defined as the degree to which the actual service conforms to these expectations.[3] Whether we meet, exceed, or fail to meet those expectations depends on the guest's perception of the service he or she receives.[4] This, in turn, determines whether the guest will return to the operation. Consistent service (and the repeat business it produces) is essential to the success of any bar and beverage operation because service is perishable—an empty chair (and lost sale) today cannot be made up tomorrow.

Bar and beverage operations are high guest-contact businesses; marketing efforts should therefore focus on selling this guest-employee interaction. The importance of these interactions should not be underestimated. Much of America watches the interactions between bartenders and patrons shown on the hit TV series "Cheers." And, as we pointed out in Chapter 7, the selection and training of our employees is critical to the success of bar and beverage operations.

Inconsistent service is an undesirable factor in service businesses. Guest expectations of service are on the rise. We have all heard, and possibly said, "I'll never visit that place again—the service is terrible!" One of the marketing decisions that you will need to make involves the level of service your bar or beverage operation will offer. Providing this level of service consistently is one of your most important managerial responsibilities. If service expectations are not met, it is unlikely that your guests will return.

Ethical and Social Issues

Your duty as a manager to act responsibly in the sale and service of alcoholic beverages is discussed throughout this text under a variety of topics dealing with social and ethical responsibilities. These ethical and social responsibilities also apply to the marketing of alcoholic beverages.

Ethical responsibilities are different from the legal responsibilities discussed in Chapter 11. Frequently, the culture of a particular hospitality organization will dictate the boundaries of ethical responsibility. In most situations, however, there are no general rules, and managers must rely on their own judgment. Understanding the social issues surrounding the sale of alcohol can help you make informed decisions in this highly controversial and emotional area.

Dictionary definitions of "ethics" include such phrases as "moral principles" and "rules and standards governing a group of people." If we apply those definitions to the bar and beverage business, we must ask ourselves, "Whose rules and standards are we governed by?" Are we solely governed by our guests? By the beverage industry (the producers of the products we sell)? By consumer activist groups such as Mothers Against Drunk Driving (MADD)?

Bar and beverage operations are a high guest-contact service business. (Courtesy of Fontainebleau Hilton Resort & Spa, Miami Beach, Florida)

MADD has been very effective in its marketing efforts, targeting voters, legislators, jurors and judges, the police, and drivers. It was as a result of MADD's marketing campaign that tougher legislation was passed regulating drunken driving. The American public has a greater awareness today of the dangers of drinking and driving than ever before. Even the producers of alcoholic beverages promote an awareness of the dangers of drinking and driving (Exhibit 8.3).

The marketing of bar and beverage operations must take into account the safety and social, as well as the economic, concerns of the day. By behaving in a socially responsible manner and making sound ethical decisions, bar and beverage managers can work toward satisfying both the needs and expectations of guests without placing others in danger.

The Competitive Environment

Competition Analysis   How many bar and beverage operations compete with yours? Any operation that takes a prospective guest away from your operation should be considered competition. One part of a successful marketing strategy is keeping an eye on your competitors. **Competition analysis** gives you an advantage by enabling you to anticipate your competitors' actions and capitalize on their weaknesses through positioning. Competition analysis should be an ongoing management activity.

Exhibit 8.3 Bacardi's Ad Promoting Awareness of the Dangers of Drinking and Driving

You can analyze your competitors merely by visiting their operations. Observing and asking open-ended questions (questions that can't be answered by a simple yes or no) can provide a good deal of information about such particulars as:

- Drink price policy
- Drinks, food items, and services offered
- Methods of presentation
- Cleanliness
- Decor, ambience, layout, and design
- New products and services offered
- Guest profiles
- Current promotions and their effectiveness
- Cover charge policy
- Music/entertainment format
- Parking facilities and cost

You should compare this information with data gathered from your own operation. Further research can provide additional information for the competition analysis, such as age of operation, management expertise, sales volume, beverage cost percentage, labor cost percentage, and reputation.

Guest Decision-Making

Once inside a bar, lounge, or restaurant, guests need to determine which products they are going to purchase. During this decision-making process they may consider such questions as: Do we want to order a bottle or carafe of wine, or wine by the glass? a drink before dinner? a snifter of brandy or cordial after dinner? Or shall we order a basket of chicken wings with a pitcher of beer?

Social factors are influential. The days of the three-martini lunch are over. Dinner parties that used to order two bottles of wine with dinner will stick with one. Guests who used to order two drinks before dinner will order only one. Designated drivers will be requesting a wide variety of non-alcoholic beverages. Guests who visit bars just to drink alcoholic beverages are becoming fewer and fewer.

One of your challenges as a bar or beverage manager will be to determine what motives your guests have, not only for entering your operation, but for making the product decisions that they make. Understanding guest behavior and motives will be essential to offering the products and services that satisfy guest needs.

Forecasting Sales

Sales forecasting is an important element in the marketing planning process. A **sales forecast** indicates the amount of a product the operation expects to sell over a specific time period. Sales forecasts provide information that can help an operation select target markets. They are also useful in positioning since they point out opportunities for new products and services.

Managers use sales forecasts to develop budgets for advertising and promotions and to anticipate future cash flow.

Sales potential refers to the maximum amount of product that an operation could possibly sell to a given market segment during a specified period. Sales potential can be determined by breaking down the economic forecast of industry sales. Market forecasts are available from industry trade associations and published in industry trade publications such as *Market Watch, Wine Spectator, Restaurant Business, The Wine News, Food and Wine,* and *Gourmet.* How much of the sales potential is forecast and then actually captured by the operation depends on the different levels and types of marketing efforts.

The Marketing Mix

The marketing effort would be simple if every guest patronized an establishment for the same reason, such as the best-priced pitchers of beer in town, the most extensive selection of California wines, or proximity to the dorms on a major college campus. Guests, however, have a variety of reasons for purchasing the products and services an operation offers. The reasons a guest selects your particular operation over all others can be influenced by a group of variables or tools known as the **marketing mix.**

The marketing mix is one of the most frequently discussed topics in marketing literature. The term was first used in 1964 in an article by Professor Neil Borden, although the concept had been practiced for years.[5] Borden's original list contained 12 major elements:

1. Product planning

2. Pricing

3. Branding

4. Channels of distribution

5. Personal selling

6. Advertising

7. Promotions

8. Packaging

9. Display

10. Servicing

11. Physical handling

12. Fact finding and analysis[6]

Borden's list has since been condensed into four major elements known as the four Ps of marketing: product, place (channels of distribution), price, and promotion. This definition of the marketing mix, now commonly accepted, includes all of Borden's original elements in a simplified scheme. For example, advertising, promotions, packaging, and display all fall into the promotion category.

The importance of the marketing mix lies in the interdependence of its elements. For example, the decision to add a new product (such as a new label of wines) may increase the cost of product (all wines), resulting in a price increase that may in turn reduce sales. Your target markets will guide the design of your marketing mix. Each element of the marketing mix must be measured against the needs of your target markets.

Product and Place

The term **product** refers to what you sell. In bar and beverage operations, the product can be either an actual product or a service. In order to market the product effectively, you must identify precisely what that product is.

In the guest-oriented bar and beverage business, the product consists of whatever your guests are looking to buy—ambience, music to dance to, a place for romance, good service, an extensive wine list, lavish hors d'oeuvres, the latest drink fad, or champagne by the glass. Thus, decisions about what products and services to offer should be governed by the needs and wants of your target markets.

Determining what products and services to offer is not easy. The greater the amount of competition, the more difficult such decisions become, unless you are offering a product or service that is unique to the marketplace. It is important to remember that people do not *need* to leave their homes to drink or to pay cover charges to do so. People do not *want* to be embarrassed by a wine list they do not understand. Offering products and services they need and want will ensure your competitive position in the marketplace.

Managers must decide which brands to carry and the types and sizes of drinks to serve. Combining this information with an operation's standard recipes will allow management to later establish fair prices.

How are these decisions made? By using a guest-oriented approach to marketing. Brand preference, drink preference, and drink size are all determined by your target markets; decisions surrounding them should be based on target market research. Built-in profit margins set arbitrarily by management won't reap any profits if your potential guests are sitting in your competitor's bar.

Because services are intangible, it is often difficult to define and market them effectively. Valet parking and taxi, limousine, or other transportation for intoxicated guests are examples of services that might be overlooked as marketing opportunities. It is important to carefully identify not only the products your operation offers, but its services as well. This information will later help you make decisions about promotions, merchandising, and personal selling.

It is improbable that many bar or beverage managers will have decision-making responsibilities regarding the operation's location. While place is a critical component of the marketing mix (it determines how easy it is for your potential guests to find you), site selection is usually a preliminary planning decision made during the early stages of development.

The remaining Ps—price and promotion—are so important to successful bar and beverage management that we cover them in greater detail.

Price: Beverage-Pricing Strategies

Pricing is an important marketing tool; it is also a very difficult management responsibility. There are a variety of methods and approaches to this arduous task. However, the task can be simplified by remembering the basic purpose of pricing: to design a price structure that will maximize the operation's return on investment while meeting its guests' perceptions of value. The following are among other pricing objectives:

- Standardize the price structure.

- Define a range of possible prices.

- Maintain a competitive edge.

- Build fairness and equity (every guest is charged the same price for the same drink).

- Provide methods of control to monitor employee efficiency.

- Consider the sales mix in establishing prices.

Price is driven by marketing and controls. In this section we will examine pricing strategies from the perspective of marketing. In Chapter 10 we will view pricing as a control measure. Pricing strategies cannot be independent of other marketing activities. Pricing affects and is affected by advertising, public relations, and personal selling.

Setting prices requires first an analysis of costs. The dollar amount needed to cover fixed and variable costs is a good starting point to determine pricing strategy. It is relatively easy to determine the cost of producing a drink: add the raw costs of the ingredients, including garnishes, to the calculated amount of labor required to produce the drink. Determining the cost of an intangible, like the services you provide, is more complicated, but it can be done.

As a bar or beverage manager, you must also consider the hidden costs of doing business. While a guest may see only the quantity and quality of the martini in front of him or her, you must consider the cost of storing the gin, vermouth, and olives (or onions or twists) that go into the drink. You pay wages to the bartenders, the servers, and perhaps a purchasing agent; in addition, you incur glass-washing expenses and the cost of replacing broken glassware. If the martini is served on the rocks, its hidden costs include maintaining the ice machine. Spillage and spoilage add to the hidden costs of doing business. Although the typical guest is unaware of these costs and may wonder why a martini costs three or four dollars, managers must nevertheless include these costs when calculating a fair drink price.

How much guests are willing to *pay* for a drink depends on a number of factors other than the operator's costs, including availability and competition. For example, guests will pay more for a beer in an airport lounge than they will at a neighborhood bar because there is no competition in the airport. One concessioner usually operates all the bars in a single airport. Although the airport authority regulates the lounge operator's prices, the beer is still more expensive than it would be if travelers could purchase

Exhibit 8.4 Bar Product Categories

Well Stock	Draft Beer
Call Stock	Non-Alcoholic Drinks
Premium Stock	Wine by the Glass
Super-Premium Stock	Highballs
Domestic/Imported Bot-tle Beer	Cocktails
	After-Dinner Drinks

it elsewhere. Pricing can be used as a competitive strategy, as we will soon see. Likewise, competition can significantly influence pricing.

In setting prices for services, price-quality relationships are important. Nowhere is this more evident than in the price of wines. People who drink wine at home are well aware of the actual cost of a bottle of wine. If these guests are to pay twice the cost (or more) of the wine to drink it in a bar or beverage establishment, they must perceive the service quality as high enough to warrant the extra cost. As a manager, you must identify the level of service your guests expect for their money.

Product Categories

Because of the large variety of products and brands that are found in bar and beverage operations, products are usually categorized to facilitate pricing and control. Can you imagine trying to train a bartender to remember the prices and brands of well over a thousand different drinks and products? Can you imagine the confusion of your guests when they receive the bill and every single different drink has a different price? Generally, categories are based on type of drink and cost—either the raw product cost or the cost of labor in either preparation or service. For example, not only do ice cream drinks have a higher cost in raw ingredients, but they also take longer to prepare (labor cost) and require more expensive glassware for their service and presentation. Exhibit 8.4 identifies some of the typical ways of grouping drinks.

Sales Value per Bottle

As you will learn in the next chapter, keeping a record or inventory of products will give you information regarding the cost of every bottle in your liquor storeroom. Such information gives you a starting point for categorizing products for the purpose of establishing drink prices.

The **sales value per bottle** of liquor is determined by multiplying the number of drinks each bottle provides by the price of each drink. This allows you to forecast your expected revenue from specific brands. Your calculations must be based on how each of your products is used. Computer technology has simplified this task; guest checks or computer records can identify how each product is served over a given time period.

The sales value per bottle multiplied by the total number of bottles you expect to sell yields a projected sales figure for each brand. By adding these figures together, you can determine a total expected sales figure. You can then compare projected sales with actual sales periodically. While some spoilage and spillage can be anticipated, any major deviations between anticipated and actual sales could be cause for alarm. Are your bartenders overpouring? Is there some theft occurring in your operation of which you are unaware?

Pricing Methods

A pricing method should be selected only after careful consideration of all of the marketing factors discussed so far in this chapter. Management must then decide on the amount of markup necessary to ensure a profit or desired percentage of return on investment. There is no industry standard for this markup.

The simplest method of pricing is based on the categories of beverages you serve. Typical categories were identified earlier in Exhibit 8.4. The more categories you divide your beverages into, the more complex your pricing structure will be. The fewer categories you break your beverages into, the simpler your pricing structure will be.

You should divide your beverages into at least four categories for pricing: beer, wine (house), liquor or distilled spirits, and non-alcoholic beverages. To divide into five categories, you would separate cordials and liqueurs from liquors or distilled spirits; to make six categories, you would consider specialty drinks separately. The categories you select may be influenced by your point-of-sale system.

One common pricing structure places call or premium brands at a set limit over well brands. Another scheme divides beverages into house (well) brands, call brands, premium brands, and super-premium brands (such as cognacs and brandies); drinks from each group are generally priced at a set amount higher than the previous group, although there are some exceptions. The base price of your house brands will be dictated by the target market and the competition.

With the wide variety of products available, careful categorization is a complex process. For example, beers may be categorized as domestic and imported or draft and bottled. In order to promote alcohol awareness and designated-driver programs, non-alcoholic beverages must be presented as a good value to your guests.

Bar Type. The type of operation you run will affect your method of pricing. A catering or banquet bar, for example, often has fixed prices: beer and wine might sell for $2.00, mixed drinks for $3.00, and soft drinks for $1.00. The airline industry uses a similar pricing method for coach passengers because it expedites service and simplifies the cashiering job. In many catering or banquet bars, however, the guest paying for the function pays the entire bar tab, either by the drink or by the bottle. Under this arrangement, the guest is charged for the total amount of beverages consumed, based on inventories before and after the function.

The type of service and entertainment you provide is an important factor in selecting a pricing strategy. For example, lounges with expensive sound systems, lighting, or live entertainment must see a return on investment for providing such extra services. Cover charges help offset some of these costs; often, however, drink prices are also higher. Sometimes the drink prices are significantly higher, depending on the type of establishment. Again, how much your guests are willing to pay depends on their value perceptions and what your competition is doing. If the services and entertainment you provide are extraordinary, your guests may not object to paying more for the products you serve them. If, on the other hand, your guests think that you are taking advantage of them or that

Exhibit 8.5 Calculating Product Costs

Martini Made with Flying Frog Gin

Price of gin per liter	$65.00 ÷ 12 liters/case = $5.42
Cost of 2% spillage	$5.42 × 0.02 = $0.108
Actual cost of liter	$5.42 + $0.108 = $5.528
Cost per ounce	$5.528 ÷ 33.8 oz/liter = $0.163

Cost of drink:

2 oz gin @ $0.163/oz	$0.326
Vermouth	0.134
Ice/olives	0.015
Total Cost of drink:	$0.475

Selling price per drink based on a 20% beverage cost percentage (see Chapter 10):

$$\$0.475 \div 0.20 = \$2.375 \text{ or probably } \$2.50$$

---

there is no value for the dollar they spend, it is unlikely they will return to your establishment. The cost/value relationship is important whether you charge $2.00 or $7.00 for a shot of vodka. The actual price is not the issue; the cost/value relationship is the most critical pricing factor.

Sales Mix

The term **sales mix** refers to the ratio of categories of drinks you are selling to total sales. The sales mix is constantly changing with the ever-changing wants and needs of your guests. This information can be useful in determining prices. What we need to know is the ratio of sales of each product category to sales of another and/or to total sales. What is the ratio of beer sales to wine sales, to liquor sales, to non-alcoholic beverage sales? Or what is the ratio of house brand sales to call brand sales, to premium brand sales, to super-premium brand sales? Suppose you offer four categories of liquor: house brands, call brands, premium brands, and super-premium brands. Typically, you would expect house brands to be the biggest-selling product category, call brands to be the second highest seller, and so on. A breakdown of the number of drinks sold might look like this:

Product	Sales
House brands	50% of all sales
Call brands	20–30% of all sales
Premium brands	10–20% of all sales
Super-premium brands	10–15% of all sales
	(Total sales = 100%)

The next step is to calculate the actual product cost of each drink by brand. Using Exhibit 8.5 as an example, if Flying Frog gin were your house brand and you were to pour a 2-ounce shot, with Flying Frog gin costing

$65.00/case (or $5.42/liter), it would cost you $.321 per Flying Frog gin drink. However, figuring a 2% factor for spillage would increase the cost per liter by $0.108, making the actual cost per liter $5.528. This means that the real cost of a 2-ounce shot is $.326. If a guest wants a martini, you must add the cost of vermouth, at $.179 per ounce for our example. Our recipe calls for three-fourths of an ounce of vermouth, so we add $.134 to the cost of making a martini. For the purposes of our example, the cost of ice and olive for garnish is $.015. Hence, the total cost of making a martini with our well brand is $.475.

The most effective way to determine the sales mix is to cost out every drink by brand and average your costs for drinks in each product category. This information, combined with the projected sales value per bottle and your competition's prices, can help you calculate selling prices. (See, for example, the discussion of beverage cost percentage in Chapter 10.)

Wine Pricing

Despite the growing popularity of wine in America, many Americans do not order a bottle of wine when dining out unless the occasion is a special one. In most European nations, the question is not whether to order wine, but which wine to order. The general public in Europe is very knowledgeable about wines, and many Europeans debate at length their wine preference for a particular meal—not whether red or white, but rather which region, which label? In many places in America, helping people identify the wine they want is an important part of increasing wine sales.

Pricing wine is equally important, if not more so. For many Americans making wine selections, price is a major determinant of their choice (after, perhaps, the decision between white and red). The price/value relationship discussed previously is especially important in pricing wines.

Two methods are often used to calculate the menu price of wines. One method is to double the cost and add a constant dollar amount. For example, if a bottle of wine cost you $10.00 and your constant were $5.00, you would price that particular bottle of wine at $25.00 ($10.00 × 2 = $20.00 + $5.00 = $25.00). The constant amount is based on overhead and labor costs. The other method is to use a range of markups when pricing bottled wines. For example, low-cost wines might be sold at four times the wholesale cost. Medium-cost wines might be sold at between two and a half to three times wholesale, and high-cost wines might sell for two times wholesale or less.

Wine sold by the glass should be priced carefully, based on your competition and your positioning strategy. Some guests will not pay $3.50 for a glass of Chardonnay when they can buy a bottle of Chardonnay for $6.00 on the way home. Some hotel markups are between two and three times wholesale cost plus $1.00. The range allows individual hotels to account for competitive conditions, guest perceptions, and cost considerations.

Promotion

Promotion can be thought of as any form of communication between you and your current and potential guests—or any special activity you provide for them—that persuades them to buy your products and services. Exhibit 8.6 lists some examples. Promotional decisions usually are made after decisions about product, place, and price.

Exhibit 8.6 Examples of Promotions

Advertisements	Freebies (give-away food, recipes, glassware, etc.)
Newspaper	
Magazine	Grand Openings
Radio	Holiday/Seasonal Specials
Television	Introduction of New Product, Service
Directories	
Brochures	Press Releases
Fliers	Coupons
Direct Mail	Price Discounts
Outdoor Billboards, Posters	
T-Shirts	Sampling
Celebrity Appearances	Special Events
Contests, Games	Theme Evenings

A promotion is developed to accomplish a specific purpose, such as increasing wine sales, introducing a new product (see Exhibit 8.7), introducing a new brand to your well stock, or attracting a new target mix. There are many reasons to develop promotions; you might consider promotions when you want to:

- Stimulate the interest of your current target market

- Increase bar check averages

- Increase business during "off" periods

- Offset new or current competition

- Introduce new services

- Re-energize your staff

- Acknowledge holidays or local special events (such as home football games)

- Attract new guests

- Build or reward guest loyalty

- Break monotony

- Influence product mix

- Introduce a new operation

Knowing the needs and wants of your target markets is the key to developing successful promotions. The promotion of intangible services is often more difficult than the promotion of a tangible product. It is helpful if you understand why people enter an establishment like yours. Exhibit 8.8 suggests some of the reasons.

Exhibit 8.7   A New Product Promotion

Courtesy of Hiram Walker, Inc.

Developing Promotions   Because promotions are such an integral part of the marketing process, they should be carefully planned and budgeted. Some guidelines for successful promotions are shown in Exhibit 8.9. In order to develop a successful promotion, you must first specify the promotional objectives, based on information about your target markets and your competition. Defining promotional objectives will help you select promotional activities and tools. The promotional objectives must be measurable. The best way to ensure measurable objectives is to state them in monetary terms—either as percentage or dollar increases in sales. There are six major activities in developing a

Exhibit 8.8 Some Reasons for Guest Visits

Entertainment	Food and Drink
Change of Environment	Business/Social Purposes
Company of Others	Relaxation
Celebrations	Curiosity
Enjoyment	To Be Seen

Exhibit 8.9 Sample Guidelines for Developing Successful Promotions

1. *Set a Goal.* Fix an objective, whether it's livening up Tuesday nights or increasing cover counts. Then allow sufficient time to coordinate a professional approach.

2. *Promote Food and Beverage Consumption.* Based on your goals, promote your lounge, your restaurant, your catering services, your room service; promote a drink, a menu item, a contest; anything that best helps you to achieve your goals. Promote a drink to liven up Tuesdays in the lounge, offer a discount on an entrée to increase guest covers in your restaurant. Consider regional preferences, season and taste trends. Keep the promotion simple. Don't complicate it.

3. *Train Your Staff.* Make them part of your promotion. Invite their participation from creation to implementation.

4. *Get the Proper Tools.* The correct merchandising aids—buttons, posters, table tents, fliers, etc.—to help create awareness.

5. *Implementation.* Prepare for increased traffic, volume. Monitor sales and record any outside influence such as weather or events that would have an impact on guest traffic.

6. *Follow-Up.* This is a crucial step. Analyze your sales records. Did you achieve your goal? Did you discover ways to improve the promotions? Record these observations for the next promotion.

Courtesy of Stouffer Hotels and Resorts (adapted from "Six Secrets for Successful Promotions")

promotion: budgeting, developing the idea, establishing a timetable, selecting media, delivering what you promise, and evaluating the results of the promotion. Each of these activities is discussed below.

Budgeting. How much does it cost? It is essential to carefully budget a promotion. A single promotion can involve many expenses, all of which must be planned and monitored. Some of the expenses might include:

- Advertising
- Special decorations
- On-site merchandising
- Additional labor
- Additional or special entertainment
- Reduced profit margin
- Higher liquor cost percentage

The selection of a particular promotion will be partially determined by how much you want to spend. Local purveyors are sometimes willing to sponsor promotional events. They might, for example, provide printed promotional materials, which could reduce your out-of-pocket expenses. However, keep in mind that there may be legal restrictions on their assistance.

Selecting and Developing the Idea. This is a creative process. Choose a catchy name for your promotion, one that will give your potential guests an immediate idea of what the promotion is all about, what is being offered, and why you are offering it. This name should be used throughout the life of the promotion—in your decor and in all your advertising and merchandising efforts. The promotional idea should be innovative and appeal to the target market for which you are developing your marketing program.

Select special features for your promotion that fit into your theme. Order any special items necessary for the promotion—such as costumes, decorations, and special menus—well in advance. Sometimes such items can be ordered from producers who are promoting certain products (see Exhibit 8.10). Make sure that your inventory is sufficient to satisfy what you promise in your advertising campaign. Develop a checklist to keep track of all the necessary details.

Establishing a Timetable. Decide well in advance when the promotion will begin and end. Be sure to allow yourself enough time to prepare thoroughly—at least two months. Make arrangements for pre-promotion advertising and the delivery of any printed materials that will be used.

The timetable should include a detailed schedule of all the activities that you have planned throughout the course of the promotion. It is a good idea to check on other special events in your area on the dates you select. Any major events—social, sporting, or others—might draw people away from your promotion.

Your employees should of course be involved as far as staffing needs are concerned; it is also wise to invite their participation in the development of promotions. Their creativity should supplement your own; the more involved they are in the planning, the more enthusiastic they will be during the course of the actual event. The staff should be kept fully informed throughout the planning process. Hold regular staff meetings for the purpose of explaining details of the promotion as the planning proceeds.

Selecting Your Media Strategy. Choose the media that will most effectively reach your target markets and that fit into your budget constraints. You should carefully evaluate the different media.

Delivering What You Promise. You have promised your guests a certain experience through your promotional efforts. In doing so, you have raised their expectations of your operation, with respect to either the products or services you offer. Failure to deliver what is promised can be a major reason for a business failure.

Exhibit 8.10 Example of a Producer-Sponsored Promotion

Sip the fun!.....with COCO–RHUM.
Shake up your profits with Hiram Walkers new tropical blend.

As the sun rises, it will dawn new light on higher profits with Hiram Walker Liqueurs intrusive new blend – COCO–RHUM, so go ahead and tempt your customers with a taste of the tropics and watch your profits flourish. COCO–RHUM is an eloquent combination of smooth, light Puerto Rican and other Rums and tangy, rich Coconut to provide unique year round fun.

In proven research consumers thought our contemporary COCO–RHUM blend was a premium quality, up–scale Rum specialty. It had a superior taste appeal with a higher purchase interest over competitors.

COCO–RHUM'S bar kit, including t–shirts, buttons, drink shakers and table tents all feature the unique brilliant tropical logo, and will allow your employees to create a sultry spirit and encourage customers to enjoy the fun, with COCO–RHUM. The attractive drink shaker is a unique way to prepare and serve COCO–RHUM creations to your customers. The table tents display three delectable combinations, for both cold and warm weather sipping.

So to get your profits shining, *Sip The Fun* with new tropical COCO–RHUM. Another premium brand by Hiram Walker Liqueurs.

Kit Code No. 800-0127-070

HIRAM WALKER LIQUEURS—20%–45% ALC./VOL. (40-90 Proof) Liqueur. Hiram Walker Incorporated. Farmington Hills, MI   800-0127-040

Courtesy of Hiram Walker, Inc.

Evaluating the Results. Was it successful? You should measure the success of each promotion in relation to its stated objectives. For example, if the objective was to increase the sale of specialty drinks, an increase in the number of specialty drink sales during (and hopefully after) the promotion may indicate success. You can also analyze the promotion while it is in progress by observing your guests' and competitors' responses to it.

It is a good idea to keep a written record of each analysis; this information can be invaluable when planning future promotions. Details of both the negative and positive—what worked and what didn't work—should be recorded. Was the promotion profitable? Did it accomplish its stated objectives? Why or why not? What could you have done to improve the promotion? The answers to these questions form the starting point for future promotions.

The Promotional Mix

The **promotional mix** comprises the promotional communications and activities discussed above in addition to advertising, public relations and publicity, sales promotions, personal selling, and merchandising. These components of the promotional mix should be viewed as the tools you will use to achieve promotional objectives.

When planning a promotion, you must decide how much of the budget should be spent for each category in the promotional mix. Not every promotion will require the use of all five categories. In some cases, advertisements and personal selling will be all that is needed; for others, a different mix may be required. What you are trying to achieve is the best combination of the mix for each particular promotion that you plan. Let's look at each component.

Advertising

Advertising is a spoken or written announcement designed to attract business from the public or a specific market segment; most forms of advertising require payment. The purpose of advertising is to attract potential consumers into your bar or beverage operation and convert them into guests. It is not until that happens—that is, until you have actually generated sales, not merely inquiries—that the advertising can be considered successful.

Advertising can play a very large role in an operator's success. You might attribute your success to having the best entertainment in town, the most efficient and courteous staff, or the most beautiful decor. Indeed, these factors may *seem* to account for your guests. But unless your guests see or hear an advertisement of some sort, they enter your operation merely by chance. Basing the management of your bar or beverage operation on chance is no way to succeed. Your business needs to be advertised to succeed. Effective advertising can persuade a potential guest that your operation is more desirable than any other.

Like all of the other elements in the marketing process, advertising requires thorough planning. You must establish your advertising objectives, create an advertising plan, prepare an advertising budget, and then actually develop the ad. Some managers contract for the services of an advertising agency. Advertising agencies can also help you with other aspects of the marketing plan. Although good advertising cannot compensate for bad products, bad advertising can certainly do much to negate the great products and services you offer.

Print Media. Broadly defined, print advertising can be any form of advertising dependent on printed messages, and print media can include newspapers, magazines, directories (such as restaurant guides), billboards, posters, fliers, and direct mail. Print advertising is a good alternative to the high cost of television advertising. It can be effective in reaching potential guests who have no knowledge of your operation by making them aware of the products and services you offer.

There are many advantages of advertising in print media. It is typically considered highly cost-effective; that is, the cost per contact is low. Print media can disseminate information to unknown target markets. By selecting your print media carefully, you can also target a specific audience.

It is extremely important that you select a medium that will effectively reach your target market. You should also consider your budget when choosing print media, as some cost more than others. Bar and beverage operations in lodging properties need to keep in mind the effectiveness of in-house posters and direct-mail fliers (for use in billings, catering correspondence, other correspondence, newsletters, etc.).

Once you have selected the particular form of print media you will use, the development of the ad can begin. A good advertisement should contain the following elements:

- Strong message impact

- Complete message (don't forget address, location, phone number, and any other pertinent information)

- Appropriate message (of appropriate length) for the target market

Television, Cable, and Radio. For most independent bar and beverage operations, the initial expense of television advertising is cost-prohibitive. However, because it reaches such a large audience, TV advertising has a low cost per contact. Television is a prestigious medium that reaches its audience quickly.

One disadvantage of television advertising is the competition for the audience's attention. Most people are annoyed by or indifferent to the many commercial interruptions that occur in the course of a 30- or 60-minute television program. A commercial must be special to stand out in viewers' memories. There is also some controversy over the effectiveness of television relative to that of other advertising media. Some market areas face a lack of available airtime, but with the increase in the number of cable channels, this problem has subsided somewhat.

Despite the disadvantages, the impact of television and cable cannot be denied; the use of a combination of both sound and sight to persuade potential guests to visit your operation is most effective. Television offers high visibility and the ability to select specific target markets by running your ads during certain programs.

Radio can also provide you with access to specific target markets. One advantage of radio over television is the ability to change your message more often. Radio messages also reach a large audience; practically every home and car in America has a radio. Although radio advertising might not carry the prestige of television advertising, it is less expensive. One disadvantage of radio advertising is its limited impact; radio often serves as "background noise," and the message is usually unnoticed or quickly forgotten.

Word-of-Mouth Advertising. Positive word-of-mouth advertising is unquestionably the best advertising medium available. Personal endorsement of a product or service carries more weight than any single advertising medium. One way to evaluate this informal advertising medium is to ask new guests how they happened to visit your operation. If they respond that a friend, business associate, or relative told them about it, you know that word-of-mouth advertising is working for you. Although the guests may have heard your radio or TV spot or seen your ad in the Sunday newspaper, the real motivating factor in their visit is the fact that someone they knew had been there, liked it, and shared the experience with them.

Criticism of Alcohol-Related Advertising. Earlier, we discussed the ethical and social responsibilities of marketing alcohol products and services. A great deal of controversy surrounds advertisements promoting alcohol. The federal government has responded by proposing a bill mandating health warnings for all alcohol beverage ads.[7]

The college market is particularly controversial; beer and wine distributors have historically advertised heavily in both college newspapers and local newspapers in college markets. In addition, distributors have commonly sponsored campus activities such as concerts and sporting events. Bar and beverage operations in college towns often hang posters and banners in sports stadiums and arenas, advertising such promotions as happy hour and post-game specials. Spring-break visitors to the Florida beaches are likely to see airplanes pulling banners across the skyline advertising a variety of promotions in area bar and beverage operations that evening.

The problems of underage drinking and alcohol abuse among college students, however, have prompted many colleges and universities to ban alcohol-related advertisements from student publications. In addition, severe restrictions and even bans are being placed on liquor distributors that sponsor campus events.

The liquor industry—in particular, the beer industry—has responded to this and the Surgeon General's criticism of alcohol-related advertising by increasing its public-service budget.[8] Additional criticism has come from the Center for Science in the Public Interest. The liquor industry is concerned about this criticism, and many companies are trying to stress alcohol awareness and moderation in their ads. Local bar and beverage operations are also promoting the message of responsible drinking in their advertisements. Advertising such as this can have a positive effect on the reputation of your operation by exhibiting your social responsibility toward alcohol consumption. To be indifferent to the consequences of alcohol abuse could be very harmful to bar and beverage operations in the 1990s.

A Word About Media Selection. No amount of advertising can help a bad product. The purpose of an advertising campaign is to do more than merely create an image or build awareness; its ultimate aim is to create a desire that will motivate people to action. You should select advertising media that will bring the highest number of guests into your operation at the lowest cost. Most operators find that a mix of media alternatives works best for them. The question you must ask yourself is, "What is the most effective way to sell the products and services we offer?"

Public Relations and Publicity

Public relations is the process of obtaining public goodwill toward an operation; **publicity**—one form of public relations—is written or spoken communication about an operation that is given at no cost to the operation. While advertising is a service for which a bar or beverage operation contracts, publicity is free. It is often generated by human interest news about an operation, its employees, or the products and services offered. Publicity can promote awareness of your products and services, and it can enhance your operation's image. Operation-generated news releases, press conferences, letters to the editor, and feature articles are all examples of publicity. An operation can create its own publicity by sponsoring such community activities as a local road race or a sports team. Any of these activities will establish positive relations with the community and improve the public's perception of the operation's image.

Sales Promotions

A **sales promotion** is a promotional activity that influences guest behavior and requires guest action. The behavior that you hope to bring about is the act of purchasing your products or services. Sales promotions offer guests an additional incentive for making a purchase. Perhaps the guests get a choice of appetizers at 50% off when a drink is purchased during specified hours, or perhaps they are given a coupon for a free glass of wine, redeemable upon a subsequent visit.

Sales promotions can be used to introduce a new product (for example, if guests buy a certain new drink, they get to keep the glass) or to respond to increased competition. Sales promotions can also reinforce your advertising messages. Though not a replacement for advertising or personal selling, sales promotion makes both more effective. In fact, without advertising and personal selling, most sales promotions would fail because potential guests would never hear about what you are offering.

Purveyors sometimes sponsor sales promotions to stimulate the sale of their particular brands. Often, these sales promotions can be offered at little or no cost to your operation. Beer distributors, for example, might sponsor a sales promotion in which a contest is staged or a drawing is held for a free trip to the spring-break location of the winner's choice. This might be an effective sales promotion in a university town. The beer distributor not only covers the cost of the award (in this case, the trip) but may also supply you with point-of-sale materials and some local advertising.

Before implementing a sales promotion, you must establish the promotion's objectives and its budget. You should analyze the competition, as well as records from previous sales promotions. Sales promotions are marketing activities that are intended to have a direct impact on the purchasing behavior of your guests. As guests continue to expect more value for their dollar, the use of sales promotions in bar and beverage operations is likely to increase.

Exhibit 8.11 Forms of Merchandising

Backbar Displays	Water List
Wine and Liquor Displays	Wine Menu
Wine Carafes on Tables	Entertainment
Blackboard Messages	Unique Glassware
Calendars of Events	Souvenir Place Mats
Competitive Pricing	Souvenir Glasses or Stirrers
Original Drink Garnishes	Table Tent Cards
Menu Clip-Ons	Posters
Drink List	Yard of Ale

Personal Selling

To your guests, each of your employees is a representative of your establishment. Employee selection is of critical importance (see Chapter 7). Training these employees in the techniques that are unique to the beverage services you offer is one of your most important management responsibilities. (These service procedures and the art of suggestive selling are discussed in Chapter 6.)

Personal selling is a promotional activity in which a salesperson (a staff member) becomes a persuasive communication tool in the sale of your products and services. The quality of your staff's personal selling efforts is a direct reflection on your operation. Personal selling depends upon anticipating the guest's needs and wants.

Unlike many salespeople, bar and beverage employees do not have to seek out customers. If the other components of the promotional mix have been effective, guests should be walking in the door with some idea of the products and/or services that they are interested in. A personal selling program should be part of the overall marketing plan, with the goal of establishing long-term relationships with your guests.

Personal selling objectives should be developed, and they should then serve as guidelines for your service training program. Objectives may focus on increasing the quantity of products sold or on introducing a new product; specific selling decisions will be influenced by the promotional mix. Remember, too, that the personal selling program you establish becomes very closely tied to the human resources management functions of recruitment, selection, and training.

Merchandising

Providing guests with good drinks and an enjoyable experience is what bar and beverage operations are all about. The marketing process is concerned with selecting a target market, making appropriate pricing decisions, and using the promotional mix to attract potential guests. **Merchandising** is the in-house promotion of products and services. Merchandising is often more cost-effective than sales promotions and thus generates a greater profit. Exhibit 8.11 identifies some forms of merchandising. Merchandising ideas need to be re-evaluated constantly because they can quickly lose their effectiveness with your regular guests.

Many bar and beverage operations are focusing on merchandising low- and non-alcoholic products. Specialty coolers, margaritas, and daiquiris are sometimes offered without the alcohol for a reduced price—for example, $2.00 less than their alcoholic counterpart. Ice cream drinks without alcohol can also be merchandised effectively; other non-alcoholic products include bottled waters, malt beverages, wines, champagnes, and sparkling ciders. A strong merchandising program featuring these products can revive sales that are lagging because of the alcohol awareness movement in the United States. Merchandising techniques allow you to adapt quickly to your guests' changing beverage preferences.

Marketing: The New Alternative

Today's competitive environment, coupled with changing consumer tastes, requires the bar or beverage manager to carefully define target markets and keep a close watch on the competition. Using intuition, mimicking your competitors' strategies, or merely duplicating what has been done in the past is sure to lead to less than satisfactory results in the marketing process. Systematic market research and planning is the new alternative to the hit-and-miss strategies of the past and is essential to your operation's success.

The marketing process begins by carefully identifying your target markets and identifying their expectations, needs, and wants. Your establishment cannot be everything to every person. Clearly targeting segments and designing your products and services to suit those segments improves the possibility of both guest satisfaction and operational success.

Using a planned marketing approach in establishing your pricing structure can lead to improved profits and greater guest satisfaction. The old beverage-pricing strategies based solely on product cost and intuition have given way to the modern school of thought, which first considers the target market and the competition and *then* the costs. Price determination in the nineties is a guest-oriented marketing activity.

Effective marketing requires the proper promotional mix. Advertising, personal selling, and merchandising are the most commonly used types of promotion in the bar and beverage business. You must be prepared to do exactly what your promotions promise, or the promotions will do more harm than good to your reputation. Promotional techniques are numerous and limited only by your imagination.

Marketing is not exclusively a pre-opening effort. When marketing stops, opportunities are missed. Marketing is an ongoing process that is critical to your present and future success.

Endnotes

1. Jean Berger, "The False Paradise of a Service Economy," *Business Week* (March 3, 1986): 79.

2. G. Lynn Shostack, "Breaking Free from Product Marketing," *Journal of Marketing* 41 (April 1977): 73–80.

3. Leonard L. Berry, David R. Bennett, and Carter W. Brown, *Service Quality: A Profit Strategy for Financial Institutions* (Homewood, Ill.: Dow Jones-Irwin, 1989), 26.

4. A. Parasuraman, Valarie A. Zeithaml, and Leonard L. Berry, "A Conceptual Model of Service Quality and Its Implications for Future Research," *Journal of Marketing* 49 (Fall 1985): 44.

5. Neil H. Borden, "The Concept of the Marketing Mix," *Journal of Advertising Research* 4 (June 1964): 2–7.

6. Borden.

7. Steven W. Colford, "Ad-Basing Is Back in Style," *Advertising Age* 61 (#18, 1990): 4, 58.

8. Francine Schwadel, "Anheuser Raising Public-Service Budget After Surgeon General's Criticism of Ads," *Wall Street Journal* CCXIII (#125, 1989): B6.

Key Terms

advertising

competition analysis

guest profile

marketing

marketing mix

market research

market segmentation

merchandising

personal selling

positioning

product

promotion

promotional mix

publicity

public relations

sales forecast

sales mix

sales potential

sales promotion

sales value per bottle

target market

target marketing

Discussion Questions

1. What is the purpose of a guest profile?

2. Why are bar and beverage operations described as service operations?

3. What types of information are helpful in analyzing your competition?

4. What is the basic purpose of pricing?

5. What is the most critical pricing factor?

6. Under what conditions, or for what purposes, might you consider implementing a promotion?

7. After specifying objectives, what are the six major activities in developing a promotion?

8. When can advertising be considered successful?

9. How does the effectiveness of word-of-mouth advertising compare with the effectiveness of print and broadcast advertising?

10. What merchandising techniques might be used to revive sales that are lagging because of the alcohol awareness movement?

Part III

Bar Management: Controls

The Purchase to Issue Functions

Chapter Outline

Selection of Products
  The Selection of Beers
  The Selection of Wines
      House Wines
  The Selection of Distilled Spirits
  Purveyor Selection
Purchasing
  Comparing Beverage Purchasing with Food Purchasing
  Purchasing to Ensure Control
  Establishing a Par Stock
  Purchasing Responsibility
  Purchasing Bar Supplies
Receiving
Storage
  The Storage of Beers
  The Storage of Wines
Inventory
  Perpetual Inventory
  Physical Inventory
  Beverage Inventory Turnover
  Inventory Control as a Monitor of Sales and Costs
Issuing
Computerization and Product Flow
The Ongoing Cycle

Selecting, purchasing, receiving, storing, inventorying, and issuing products are all critical, interrelated functions in successful bar and beverage management. The variety and number of decisions which a bar or beverage manager must make involving these operational functions are astounding.

The process by which products move through an operation is cyclical, as can be seen in the flow chart in Exhibit 9.1. The decision-making begins with your selection of products, including beers, wines, distilled spirits, mixers, and condiments. Next, the product orders are actually determined and placed with the selected purveyors. Note that the purchasing function is tied directly to your inventory system, as the par you establish will determine your purchasing needs. Third is the receiving function, which is followed by storage. Inventory procedures and issuing are ongoing activities which relate back to your selection and purchasing decisions.

The decisions you make with respect to these functions both affect and are affected by the other elements of bar and beverage management. These interdependent relationships need to be fully understood. We talked in Chapter 1 about the importance of good planning for effective and efficient bar and beverage management. The operational functions discussed in this chapter must be viewed from the perspective of the planning functions.

The selection and purchasing of products depend on the type of bar or beverage operation you manage and the target market which you are trying to attract. Receiving and storage depend on the architecture and layout of the operation with respect to storage space and distances. Inventory procedures and issuing also depend on the design and layout of the bar and, in some operations, even on the type of service procedures and selling techniques the employees use.

Each of these components is directly related to the topic of control. It is for this reason that **separation of duties** will be emphasized throughout this chapter. Separation of duties means that no one person has responsibility for more than one function in the process. Hence, the person responsible for purchasing is not responsible for receiving, storage, inventory, or issuing. The more people involved, the less chance for misuse of trust. In small bar and beverage operations, the separation of duties is not always possible. When that is the case, the owner or manager should perform the functions discussed in this chapter.

This chapter explains effective selecting, purchasing, receiving, storing, inventorying, and issuing procedures. When differences exist between how beer, wine, and distilled spirits are handled, the procedures are discussed individually. The need for the establishment of standards as control tools and for the separation of duties is also stressed.

Selection of Products

Bar and beverage managers are sometimes responsible for selecting products to be served in their operations. This means choosing both the type of product and the brand. This is a critical difference between food purchasing and beverage purchasing. When food is purchased, product selection depends largely on the menu. Most often, whether you select iceberg lettuce or romaine lettuce is not a purchasing decision, but rather a selection dictated by the recipes for your menu items. Your role in

Exhibit 9.1 Cyclical Product Flow

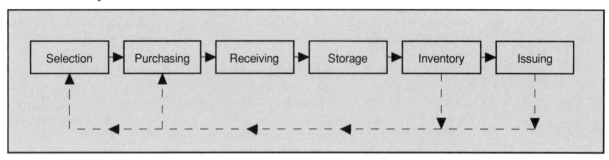

purchasing food involves selecting a product which meets your standards of both price and quality and then choosing a purveyor.

Although the selection of beverages is also dependent on the menu (for example, some operations may sell only beer or only wine), it is much more dependent on the target market. In bar and beverage operations, the guest dictates the product and brand selection. While some specialty drinks may require you to carry a product not typically carried, a bar is generally expected to carry a full range of products. As you will learn in Chapter 11, the types of products your operation is permitted to carry—that is, beer, wine, and/or distilled spirits—are dictated by state and local regulation and the availability of licenses.

So the decisions you must make as a bar or beverage manager do not involve whether to carry gin or vodka, but which brand(s) of both gin and vodka to purchase. Since we are viewing bar and beverage operations from a guest-oriented perspective, the selection of products is a *marketing* decision (as we saw in Chapter 8).

When you select products and brands, you determine what will be available for your guests. Therefore, selection decisions must be made with the guest foremost in your mind. And in few businesses do trends and fads come and go as rapidly as in the bar and beverage business. This means that selection of product is not done just once and then forgotten. Every product and, more importantly, every brand you carry must be constantly re-evaluated in terms of its contribution to your sales mix. Liquor inventory is expensive to carry. When you walk into a liquor storeroom, each bottle represents cash sitting on a shelf earning you zero return on investment until it is poured and sold. No bar or beverage operation can afford to have stale (unmoving) product or brands. The best way to avoid this is to listen to your guests and watch your sales!

The Selection of Beers

Selecting beers has become more complex in the past several years. With the increase of brands, imports, premiums, standards, lights, and drys, it is increasingly difficult to stock the specific brands and types of beer products your guests drink in their own homes. Since beer is a perishable product, you must be careful not to overselect, and thereby overstock, your beer offerings.

Again, the type of bar or beverage operation you manage and your target market will dictate your product selection. Beers may be purchased in bottles, cans, barrels, or kegs. Management must decide what system it wants to use. Typical bar and beverage operations stock both bottled and

Exhibit 9.2   Considerations in Wine Selection

Brand (winery) recognition	Price variations within each category
Choice of vintages	Proportion of red to white
Fits in the style of operation	Quality recognition
Interesting bottlings	Reasonable markups
Local as well as worldwide varieties	Shelf life of wines
Matches cuisine of the operation	Storage availability
Matches guests' knowledge of wine	Value perception

keg (draft) beer. Bottles have the advantage of being easier to inventory and store; their disadvantages include breakage and the need to return or dispose of them. Draft beers generally have a better taste and higher profit potential, but kegs are hard to handle and draft systems require careful maintenance and sanitation to maintain product quality (see Chapter 14).

The Selection of Wines

The selection of wine essentially translates into the development of a wine list. Whether this responsibility will be yours depends on the operation you manage. Since some bar and beverage managers make the decisions on wine selection, we will present you with a few general guidelines. In Chapter 6, we described developing the wine list as a sales tool. Here, we will look at wine list development in terms of the types of wine you choose to promote and sell. Note, however, that developing a comprehensive wine list can be a very complex task requiring a knowledge base that goes well beyond the scope of this text.

Information about wine is available from distributors and in a variety of reference books. Still, most wine experts agree that the best way to learn about wines is to taste them. Only then can you truly understand the subtle differences among the choices available and begin to appreciate the qualities of fine wine. Attending wine tastings is a good way to learn how to recognize by both sight and smell the basic characteristics of wines.

Ultimately, of course, the tastes of your guests and their degree of wine sophistication will determine your wine selection. A well-developed wine list should not exasperate, embarrass, or intimidate your guests. Rather, it should lead them to a selection of their own choosing. Exhibit 9.2 identifies some considerations in wine selection.

We suggest that you start your wine selection by determining the scope of your list. Will you offer 10 wines or 130? The number of wines you can offer might be limited by the amount of available storage space. As we will see later in this chapter, the proper storage of wines requires some very specific conditions. The length of your wine list might also be affected by your operation's initial capital investment, as wine inventories can tie up a lot of cash very quickly. How quickly you want your wine inventory to turn over is directly related to this decision. A turnover rate of eight times the dollar value per year is often cited as desirable, but if you put wines down to mature, your turnover rate will be lower.

Next, you should identify the types of wine (for example, Chardonnay, Sauvignon Blanc, Pinot Noir) you will offer, including the proportion of

Exhibit 9.3 Partial Wine List

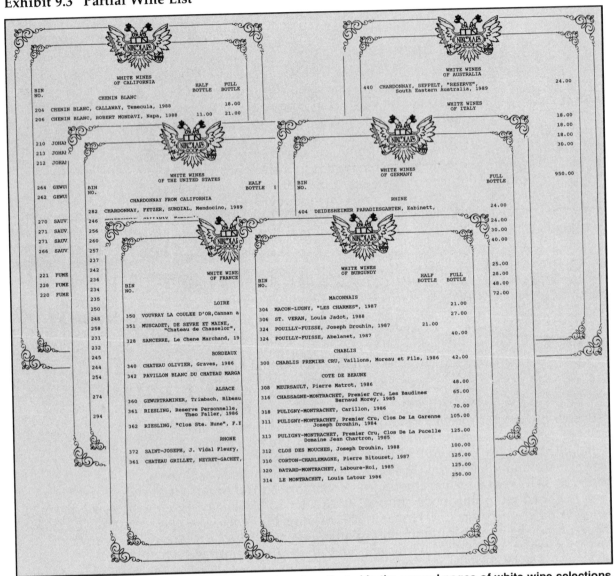

The increasing American preference for white wines is reflected in the several pages of white wine selections on this partial wine list. (Courtesy of Atlanta Hilton and Towers)

red to white. Americans today are showing a preference for white wines. Most wine lists reflect this trend (see, for example, Exhibit 9.3) unless the operation's target market or menu offerings require a greater proportion of reds. If the beverage operation is part of a food operation, then wine selection must also complement the menu offerings.

The selection of brands or wineries that produce the wines is your next decision. You need to determine what products will attract your target markets. This decision must be based on a careful analysis of your guests' knowledge of wines. In some target markets, your guests' knowledge of wineries might be limited to those that they see frequently advertised or on grocery store shelves. In other target markets, guests might think a large selection of grocery store wines is insulting. As your target market becomes more sophisticated in its wine tastes, you should upgrade your wine selections.[1]

Again, we stress that you should not intimidate your guests. If your wine list is filled with unfamiliar brands, even your most effective servers will have great difficulty selling these products. The wine list should be easy to understand and select from. Carrying glamour wines is no longer seen as being as important as carrying good wines that drink well.[2]

It is important to remember that product selection and pricing go hand in hand when selecting wines. Along with deciding on how many wines you will offer, you must also decide on a price range that you want your wine list to cover. Begin by determining your low and high prices. Since most of your wine sales will stem from the wines priced between these two extremes, that is where the majority of the wines you select should fall. We recommend that these moderately priced wines make up 60% of your wine selection.

Remember also that many guests enter your operation with a limit on how much they want to spend on their evening out—for example, $20 per person. In such cases, the guest's choice of wine is made on the basis of the meal price plus the wine. If the meal price is $14, that leaves $6 to spend on cocktails and wine.

You must also decide whether to purchase wines suitable for immediate service or cellar wines (fresh wines that will benefit from aging) that might not be added to your wine list for years. Cellar wines are generally less expensive than wines that already have some bottle age on them. Aged wines such as Bordeaux and Burgundies cost more because someone has already taken the time, energy, and expense to age them. This decision is generally dictated by the type of operation you manage and the organization's cash flow. Few hospitality organizations can afford to have their cash tied up in a wine inventory. One famous club once faced a serious cash shortage because an over-enthusiastic manager laid down too many wines to mature.

Bar and beverage operations wanting to carry large inventories and wine selections will do best by hiring a wine expert to develop their wine list. Buying cellar wines can be risky and there is no substitute for experience when buying wines. Sophisticated wine lists can take years to develop. For most operations, the simpler the wine list, the faster the wines you stock will turn over—assuming, of course, that they are not overpriced. When your clientele wants a specific wine but the wine moves slowly, you should order by the bottle instead of by the case.

House Wines. Historically, most house wines offered by the glass consisted primarily of American and Italian red and white jug wines or wine products. Sangria, Lambrusco, rosé, and Burgundy were once common house wine selections which were offered by the carafe, half-carafe, or glass. The selection of wine by the glass has improved in most beverage operations with the advancement of bar equipment which can maintain the quality of bottled wine once it has been opened.

In the early 1980s, as Americans became more knowledgeable and the trend turned away from spirits to lighter alcoholic drinks, there was a proliferation of wine in the American market. Wine by the glass no longer meant the house jug wine. Rather, it became a way for guests to taste truly fine bottled wines affordably. Today, many operations promote this type of sales strategy by tying their wine selections to by-the-glass promotions. This trend has raised the quality of house wines.

One way of joining the popular trend of by-the-glass promotions is to offer the most popular bottled wines from your wine list by the glass. Even though guests have become more knowledgeable about wine, many remain intimidated by ordering a bottle of wine with dinner. A by-the-glass program encourages these guests to sample wines that they feel uncomfortable ordering by the bottle. Additionally, it allows your guests to experiment with a variety of labels. This can be an effective merchandising tool.

Building a wine list requires that you first educate yourself about the basic characteristics of wine and how wines relate to various geographic locations (see Chapters 15 and 16). Even though many people are at first intimidated when learning about wines, you owe it to your guests and your organization to be as knowledgeable as you can be about the products you serve. The wines on your wine list are certainly no exception.

The Selection of Distilled Spirits

How do you determine which brands you will use for your house or well brands? How do you determine which brands will constitute your premium or call brands? Should you consider pouring a premium well? Which brand(s) of cordials should you pour? These are all product selection decisions concerning distilled spirits.

Well brands are those liquors which are poured when the guest does not specify a particular brand. **Call brands** are those liquors which your guests request by brand name. For example, the guest who orders a martini would be poured a drink using the well stock. Another guest requesting a Beefeaters martini would be poured a drink using Beefeaters gin and would be charged more, since a premium or call brand costs more. Some companies even have three different pricing and quality structures of liquor: house, call, and premium.

The selection of well brands is an important one from the standpoint of price. These are the products you will pour, and therefore purchase, most frequently. Availability and price become major factors in the selection decision. Not only does the selection of your well brands help establish your cost/price standards, it also establishes quality standards. Judging the quality of distilled spirits is further explained in Chapter 13.

Some bar and beverage operations have done away with the dual pricing structure and dual inventory of having a well and call system. These operations have adopted the practice of pouring a premium well. Instead of stocking well brands which have virtually no name recognition, these operations pour nationally recognized brands instead. While this is more expensive, many operations have found this to be an effective merchandising tool. Pouring and merchandising a premium well denote that your operation serves only products of excellence. Since most people like being associated with quality, the premium well can draw guests into your operation. Servers can also take pride in informing their guests who request a call brand that "we pour that brand from our well."

The selection of brands is also important from the perspective of your guests. Typically, guests have specific brand preferences. Some guests can become very unhappy if they learn that you don't carry their favorite brand. This emphasizes the importance of conducting a thorough analysis of your target market. While it is impossible to carry every brand and

Pouring a premium well does not cost very much more than stocking only well brands. (Courtesy of Hiram Walker Inc.)

please every guest, a careful market analysis will enable you to satisfy the maximum number of guests possible.

A well-trained staff will also bring to your attention any brands which are being requested regularly which you do not stock. It is a good policy to have bartenders keep a record of any requested product which you do not carry, so that you can make good product selection decisions on an ongoing basis.

Exhibit 9.4 Purveyor Selection Factors

Credit/payment policy	Price factors
Delivery policy/schedules	Quality
Location	Services offered
Minimum order requirements	Stock available
Price discounts for volume orders	Storage techniques

With the thousands of beverage brands on the market today, product selection can be overwhelming. A good starting place is to ask your purveyors for a list of their best-selling items. You can then test them in your own operation.

Purveyor Selection

Purveyor selection is often determined by your brand selection; in many locations, only one purveyor will carry a particular brand. Exhibit 9.4 lists several topics to consider when you select purveyors. Not all of these factors will be important to every operation, so you should determine which ones are important to you. For example, if your operation has very limited storage space, the delivery schedules will be more important to you than receiving price discounts for volume orders.

In some countries, liquor purchasing, as well as sales, is governed by laws and regulations. As a bar or beverage manager, you must investigate the regulations pertaining to your operation. For example, purchasing regulations in the United States vary by state and sometimes even by community. States allowing you to choose which purveyor you want to work with are known as **license** or **open states.** In such states, liquor wholesalers, distributors, and manufacturers are licensed by the state to sell their products. Characteristics of open states are:

- Price competition, although not always on all products

- Discounting

- Generally available credit (30 days only)

- Lower prices due to competition

Even license states, however, exercise some control over liquor purchasing. Regulations governing the sale of distilled spirits may be different from the regulations governing the sale of beer and wine (see Chapter 11). Also, you must always carefully investigate the local laws, which may override state legislation. There are still "dry" counties—that is, counties or regions which prohibit the sale of alcoholic beverages. Since the degree of control varies widely, the efficient bar or beverage manager must carefully research the laws governing his or her operation.

In **control states,** also known as **monopoly** or **closed states,** there is no price competition among retail liquor stores. In these states, identified in Exhibit 9.5, all liquor must be purchased from state stores. Some characteristics of control states are:

Exhibit 9.5 Control States

Alabama	Montana	Utah
Idaho	New Hampshire	Vermont
Iowa	North Carolina	Virginia
Maine	Ohio	Washington
Michigan	Oregon	West Virginia
Mississippi	Pennsylvania	Wyoming

- Reduced brand selection
- One price
- No credit
- Problems with supplier stock-outs
- Reduced order options
- Limited delivery options

Even in control states, the degree of control varies. For example, Montana controls only alcoholic beverages above a certain percentage of alcohol but leaves others, like malt beverages and table wines, to be sold by any licensed purveyor. Some states allow many distribution locations, but will wholesale all products themselves and perhaps even set the retail selling price. Other states control all distribution centers and operate all retail outlets.

Not all of these controls should be viewed as negative restrictions. While they reduce your options in both product and purchase decisions, they also protect you from unscrupulous purveyors and price wars.

Purchasing

Sound purchasing practices become the cornerstone for both the quality and control aspects of your bar or beverage operation. **Purchasing** is the ability to obtain the right quality of products in the right quantity at the right time from the right purveyor at the right price. This definition of purchasing leaves us with many questions. What are the objectives of beverage purchasing for your operation? How can you guarantee the quality of the products you order? What are the variations in both quality and price among the various brands? Who will be responsible for purchasing decisions? For ordering decisions? As we have seen, sometimes the manager has little choice regarding either price or purveyor.

Comparing Beverage Purchasing with Food Purchasing

Managers who have experience purchasing food should not assume that all the same procedures and concerns apply to purchasing beverages. There are several differences between purchasing food and purchasing beverages. As we saw above, one difference is the manager's freedom to choose purveyors. Also, purchasing beverages is less dependent on specifications, since products are ordered by brand rather than by using grade and quality terms.

Another distinction concerns controls. In food purchasing, the control aspect must be concerned with both preventing theft and maintaining product quality. For example, if fifty pounds of shrimp is delivered to your food operation, it may spoil or be stolen if proper control procedures are not implemented immediately. However, because of the more perishable nature of food products, it is more difficult, although not impossible, for your employees to steal them. Fifty pounds of shrimp delivered in the morning will not always keep in the back of someone's car until the shift is over.

In beverage purchasing, the controls are primarily concerned with theft. Although alcoholic beverages, particularly beer and wine, can lose quality if not stored properly, in most cases they would still be drinkable. (A notable exception is keg beer, which can spoil as quickly as the stolen shrimp mentioned above if left unrefrigerated.) Since the profit potential from alcohol sales is higher than that of food sales, the loss of alcoholic beverages through theft can have a significant impact.

Let's examine how this higher profit potential operates. Assume that you are aiming at a food cost of 40% and a beverage cost of 20%. This means that you mark up each food item by 2.5 times and each beverage item by 5 times. If your food cost for providing a 16-ounce Porterhouse steak dinner is $4, you will charge approximately $10 ($4/.4) for the dinner. In contrast, $4 worth of scotch would sell for approximately $20 ($4/.2). As you can see, a pour cost of 20% provides a much better return on your investment. This gives you a more favorable ratio with both sales and profit.

Purchasing to Ensure Control

We mentioned earlier the importance of separation of duties. This means that the person you designate to do the purchasing will not receive, store, or issue the products he or she is responsible for ordering. When inventory is conducted by teams, the purchaser may be allowed to participate, but only when no other alternative is available. One of the most important management responsibilities related to purchasing is the establishment of **standards** for the purpose of control.

Standards are used to ensure that each step is conducted in the same manner every time an order is placed. This establishes consistency which leads to predictable costs, quality, and profit. Any deviation from the standards you establish signifies a control problem which you should act upon immediately.

The purchasing function operates as a unified control system which establishes rigid standards for each step of the process. To operate effectively, your operation must maintain the standards of each step. If at any point the standards are modified or sacrificed, you will lose the element of control which you have spent much time establishing. This control system should be supported by written records at each step.

Establishing a Par Stock

The management of every bar or beverage operation must determine how much liquor to order and keep in the storeroom and how much to keep at the bar. Both amounts are known as **par.** In the storeroom, the goal is to store just enough product that you don't run out between deliveries; storing more than this amount unnecessarily ties up cash in inventory. At the bar, the goal is to avoid running out of a product in the course of a shift or a day. Establishing a par for both the storeroom and the bar is known as

two tier par stock. Using a par system makes it easy for the buyer to determine how much to order. It also makes it easy for you or the bartender to determine how much liquor to requisition from the storeroom for the bar area. The answer to "how much?" in both of these situations is "to par." We will discuss bar par further under issuing and in the next chapter.

The storeroom par is basically equal to the amount of product you expect to sell between deliveries, plus a safety factor added to deal with unexpected increases in sales and other unforeseen events. There is no industry-wide formula for establishing a storeroom par because each operation has its own unique needs. Expected sales should be determined from a careful analysis of perpetual inventory information (discussed later). The safety factor should then be based on expected sales in some way. Rather than basing the safety factor on a generic, arbitrary percentage of expected sales, we recommend basing it on your own operation's historical data reflecting reliability of deliveries, product mix, volume, and other appropriate factors.

There are a number of factors which you should consider when establishing your par. These are:

- Availability of deliveries—depending upon your location and volume, suppliers' delivery schedules might be limited.

- **Lead time**—that is, the amount of time between when you order products and when they are delivered. A management objective is to reduce the amount of lead time, so as to reduce the size of the inventory.

- Anticipated volume—this can be particularly important for operations with banquet business, where par can change from week to week.

- Size of your storage facilities.

- Marketing mix and guests' drink preferences.

- Amount of cash flow—how much cash can your operation afford to tie up in liquor storage?

In practice, par systems can vary. In one approach, whenever you order, you build up your inventory to the established par for every item. Look at Exhibit 9.6. For brand A, with an established par of 20 bottles, there were 10 bottles in the storeroom on 11/20 when the order was placed (as represented by the figure above the diagonal line). To build up the inventory to par, an order was placed for 10 bottles (as represented by the number beneath the diagonal line). On 11/25, when the order was placed, there were 8 bottles in the storeroom, so an order was placed for 12 bottles.

Another approach is known as the minimum/maximum par system. In addition to identifying the par (called *maximum par* in this system), management identifies a *minimum par*, that is, the amount below which stores should never fall. When your inventory reaches the minimum par level, the product is ordered to the maximum par level. When a lengthy lead time is required, the reorder point occurs before stores fall to minimum par to allow for delivery time. In contrast to the first approach, then, an item that was below maximum par would *not* be ordered if it had not

Exhibit 9.6 Sample Par Order Grid

Brands	Established Par	11/20	11/25	11/30	12/5	12/10	12/15		
A	20	10 / 10	8 / 12	18 / 2	15 / 5	5 / 15	4 / 16		
B	5	5 / 0	4 / 1	3 / 2	4 / 1	1 / 4	2 / 3		
C	50	10 / 40	2 / 48	12 / 38	5 / 45	2 / 48	0 / 50		
D	25	25 / 0	15 / 10	10 / 15	5 / 20	5 / 20	1 / 24		

fallen to its minimum par (or its reorder point). Management would not order everything to par every time an order is placed.

A third approach combines elements of the first two. Although a specific minimum par is not established, there may be times when certain products—most typically, cordials and premium brands—are below par, but not by very much. The manager may decide to "ride the par" for another ordering period (usually one week), especially if the supplier or state has minimum order requirements that would take the supply substantially over par. This decision will be based primarily on recent usage rates. In this approach, most items are ordered to par every time an order is placed, but exceptions based on informed decisions are relatively common.

It is important to make a few other points about par. First, appropriate par levels can change, sometimes rapidly. It is not unusual for your guests' drinking patterns to change seasonally as well as in response to new trends. You must closely watch your usage rates. You should keep a **dead stock list** (a list of all products and brands which guests no longer request) and watch products or brands which have either slow or fast movement.

In Exhibit 9.6, for example, note that this operation ran out of brand C, with a par of 50 bottles, on 12/15. This should not have been a complete surprise, since stock had fallen to only two bottles twice in the previous four ordering periods. Also note that the usage of brand D has increased dramatically over the six ordering periods shown, with stores falling to a single bottle on 12/15. Management should consider raising the par for brands C and D. In fact, if this operation has a two-day or longer lead time, it will also be in danger of running out of brand A before delivery. You can review the appropriateness of your par stock levels by analyzing the sales mix of your products. Computerization has made such analyses much easier to perform than they were in the past.

Another point is that, in some operations, pars may change not only due to changing demand in the bar, but also due to the number of banquets and other special events offered. While pars for bar usage may be relatively steady in the short run, the amount and types of alcohol needed for special group events can vary greatly from week to week. Setting pars in operations offering such services is more difficult, but it can be done. Historical information about the group (when available) or similar groups can be analyzed. Also, the event's sponsors may indicate what they want or expect to use. Anticipated needs, again with a safety factor, can then be added to the pars needed for the bar to produce the overall par for that ordering period.

Still another important point is that par is a guide rather than an absolute standard. At times, it could be good business practice to violate your established par. This might occur when the supplier or the state imposes minimum order requirements. In Exhibit 9.6, for example, the supplier for brand A might require that this product be purchased by the case. In this situation, an order for 12, rather than 10, would have to be placed on 11/20.

Another situation which might cause you to disregard par would be the availability of discounting. **Discounting** is a price reduction given by the purveyor when you purchase large volumes. For example, your purveyor may offer you a discount of $10 a case on your well gin if you purchase at least five cases. Discounting availability varies from state to state (license versus control). It also depends on the purchasing power and sales volume of the bar or beverage operation. You must decide whether you can afford to tie up capital by ordering over par. You also need extra storage space. A good rule of thumb for distilled spirits is that it is acceptable to purchase up to a six-month supply if you get a good price reduction. Ordering more than a six-month supply ties up too much capital in inventory. Don't be pressured into purchasing large quantities of liquor merely because you save a few dollars per case. Take time to evaluate all the hidden costs associated with discounting practices, such as the potential for theft, tied up capital, and the costs of storage.

Par can be established by the case or by the bottle, depending on the volume needed. In general, well brands have a case par and cordials have a bottle par. In addition to being a method of determining how much product should be ordered, par is also a control device.

Purchasing Responsibility

Management, through the establishment of par stock and selection of purveyors, makes the following purchase decisions:

- What to buy (including what brands to buy)
- How much to buy
- Whom to purchase from
- When to buy
- Vintage dates (for wines)

Through the use of the par stock system, order decisions become very simple and do not have to be made by management. The person responsible for ordering merely needs to check the inventory sheets and order up to par using a **purchase order** (see Exhibit 9.7). A purchase order is a form used to record the products ordered and to standardize the information about those products. Think of the purchase order as the first internal control tool in the purchasing process. A purchase order should be written for every order. Minimally, it should state the item (brand) ordered, the

Exhibit 9.7 Sample Purchase Order

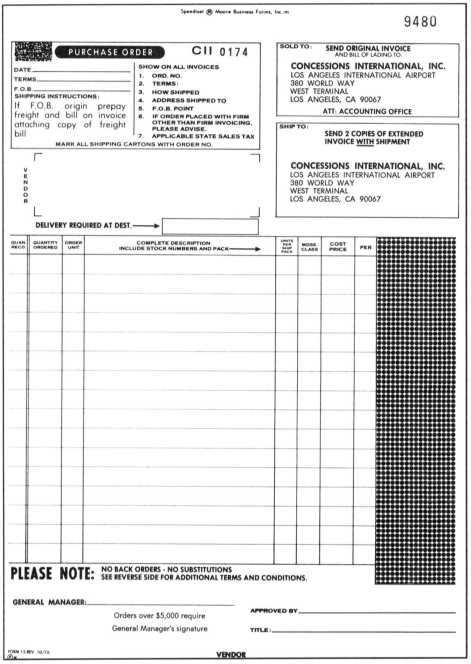

A purchase order should be filled out each time an order is made. (Courtesy of Concessions International, Inc.)

date ordered, the price quoted, the unit size requested, and the quantity ordered. Purchase orders should be properly secured; access to them should be limited.

Ordering is generally done weekly. The person responsible will vary depending on the size of the operation. In large properties, a centralized purchasing office might purchase all items, including food, beverages, and

Exhibit 9.9 Sample Purveyor Invoice

NATIONAL WINE & SPIRITS CORPORATION
P.O. BOX 1602 • INDIANAPOLIS, INDIANA 46206

	IN LIQUOR PERMIT	IN WINE PERMIT
INDIANAPOLIS	W49-09133	W49-15036
MERRILLVILLE	W45-86016	W45-86017
SOUTH BEND	W71-87478	W71-87479

CUST # 56365
LICENSE # RR64-12434

3388-6?

NATIONAL wine & spirits corporation

CD

		1-800-	
INDIANAPOLIS	(317) 636-4880	1-800-	772-7347
EVANSVILLE	(812) 867-7441	1-800-	742-3910
FORT WAYNE	(219) 484-2654	1-800-	552-0878
MERRILLVILLE	(219) 769-0601	1-800-	552-4095
SOUTH BEND	(219) 232-3001	1-800-	552-2571

A Wn: 2

CUST. NAME STRONGBOW TURKEY INN INC
CUST. D.B.A. STRONGBOW TURKEY INN
ADDRESS U S 30 E

VALPARAISO   IN 46383

INVOICE DATE 06 29 90   PAGE: 1   918 97

DUE DATE ON THIS INVOICE 07 14 90
IN ACCORDANCE WITH INDIANA LAW

INVOICE NUMBER 621774

SPECIAL INSTRUCTIONS

TO ASSURE PROPER CREDIT PLEASE INCLUDE INVOICE NUMBER WITH PAYMENT

SALESMAN'S #	4793	4793	4793
	4793	4792	4792
	7060	4793	

LOC	QUANTITY CASES / BOTTLES	SIZE	DESCRIPTION	SLS	ITEM NUMBER	WAREHOUSE LOCATION	UNIT PRICE	DISCOUNT	NET PRICE	AMOUNT * INDICATES TOTAL
G21	✓ 2	750ML	CHAT STE MICHELLE JO RIESLING	3	054074 023	1653	4.26	.00	4.26	8.52 Y
AQ33	✓ 1	750ML	KAYSER PIESPORTER MICHELSBERG	3	009484 020	1102	5.65	.00	5.65	5.65 Y
FF59	✓ 2	750ML	CHAT STE MICHELLE CHARDONNAY	3	054124 022	1137	7.82	.00	7.82	15.64 Y
ZZ99	✓ 1	750ML	CHAT DE LA CHAIZE BROUILLY 88	3	008294 001	7832	7.45	.00	7.45	7.45 Y
	**********	750ML	CHATEAU GREYSAC 1985		016934 006		SORRY, STOCK TEMPORARILY DEPLETED			
ZZ99	✓ 1	750ML	SARTORI BARDOLINO	3	008154 015	8331	4.18	.00	4.18	4.18 Y
ZZ99	✓ 1	750ML	FREEMARK ABBEY CAB SAUV 1986	4	028184 016	8341	9.04	.00	9.04	9.04 Y
ZZ99	✓ 1	750ML	MONDAVI FUME BLANC	4	028234 017	7545	7.14	.00	7.14	7.14 Y
ZZ99	✓ 1	750ML	CLOS RESSIER POUILLY-FUISSE 88	3	014764 021	9031	9.31	.00	9.31	9.31 Y
ZZ99	✓ 2	750ML	STERLING CABERNET SAUVIGNON 87	3	033014 024	7831	11.32	.00	11.32	22.64 Y
Z9??	✓ 2	2.0L	SUN COUNTRY MELON BERRY	3	016662 014	1264	18.97	.00	18.97	37.94 Y
									TOTAL	128.01

Courtesy of Strongbow Inn, Valparaiso, Indiana

Exhibit 9.10 Sample Credit Memo

NATIONAL WINE & SPIRITS CORPORATION
P.O. BOX 1602 • INDIANAPOLIS, INDIANA 46206

	IN LIQUOR PERMIT	IN WINE PERMIT
INDIANAPOLIS	W49-09133	W49-15036
MERRILLVILLE	W45-86016	W45-86017
SOUTH BEND	W71-87478	W71-87479

CUST # 56365
LICENSE # RR64-12434

3388-6?

NATIONAL wine & spirits corporation

CD

		1-800-	
INDIANAPOLIS	(317) 636-4880	1-800-	772-7347
EVANSVILLE	(812) 867-7441	1-800-	742-3910
FORT WAYNE	(219) 484-2654	1-800-	552-0878
MERRILLVILLE	(219) 769-0601	1-800-	552-4095
SOUTH BEND	(219) 232-3001	1-800-	552-2571

A Wn: 2

CUST. NAME STRONGBOW TURKEY INN INC
CUST. D.B.A. STRONGBOW TURKEY INN
ADDRESS U S 30 E

VALPARAISO   IN 46383

INVOICE DATE 06 29 90   PAGE: 1   918 97

DUE DATE ON THIS INVOICE 07 14 90
IN ACCORDANCE WITH INDIANA LAW

INVOICE NUMBER 621774

SPECIAL INSTRUCTIONS

TO ASSURE PROPER CREDIT PLEASE INCLUDE INVOICE NUMBER WITH PAYMENT

SALESMAN'S #	4793	4793	4793
	4793	4792	4792
	7060	4793	

LOC	QUANTITY CASES / BOTTLES	SIZE	DESCRIPTION	SLS	ITEM NUMBER	WAREHOUSE LOCATION	UNIT PRICE	DISCOUNT	NET PRICE	AMOUNT * INDICATES TOTAL
	<<<<<< ******		RE: 610550		****** >>>>>>					
119	1-	1.0L	GORDON'S VODKA 80PR	2	077023 001	1010	72.87	11.80	61.07	61.07- Y
133	1-	1.0L	GORDON'S GIN	2	077053 002	2001	89.80	13.90	75.90	75.90- Y

CREDIT MEMO

SPO   TOTAL   136.97- *

Courtesy of Strongbow Inn, Valparaiso, Indiana

Exhibit 9.11   Losses Preventable Through Good Receiving Practices

Breakage in handling, during or after delivery

Damaged products in sealed cases

Errors in billing

Shipment errors (wrong item in delivery)

Shortages in shipments

Stealing from unattended deliveries

Substitutions

- Check for broken bottles, spillage, and leaks.

- Check for broken seals.

- Check for required stamps on cases or bottles.

- Always count bottles, even if you must open a sealed case.

As you can see, receiving agents *must* be familiar with the products they check in. Exhibit 9.11 identifies some of the losses which effective receiving practices can prevent.

The receiving agent should fill out a **beverage receiving report,** such as the one in Exhibit 9.12. This provides your accounting department with a detailed breakdown of what is received on a daily basis. Generally, all that the receiving agent needs to do is transfer the information on the purveyor invoice and credit memos to the receiving report after the order has been carefully checked and moved to storage.

The delivery should not be left unguarded. After it has been received, it should be placed in the locked storeroom or refrigerated areas immediately. This is quite different from food receiving, where many items go directly from the receiving dock into the kitchen production areas. In no situation should beer, wine, or liquor be allowed to go from the receiving dock to the bar. Many of your control devices will be circumvented if you allow this to happen. Again, separation of duties calls for the person who receives the order to be different from the person who maintains the storage areas.

As an additional control device, many bar and beverage operations have special stamps created which are placed on every bottle as it is stored. This permits stolen bottles to be easily identified. It also allows you to check bottles being issued and those on the bar to ensure that none of your staff is bringing in his or her own liquor and selling it to your guests.

The higher the standards you establish in your receiving procedures, the better your control advantage. The more thorough your checks, the less likely it is that you will be intentionally cheated by your purveyors. Delivery persons will quickly recognize that they can't slide short orders through your operation or make brand substitutions without first discussing them with the manager. When they notice that strict receiving procedure standards are the same each time they deliver to your operation, they will take their inferior products and short cases to your competitors' doorsteps.

Exhibit 9.12   Sample Beverage Receiving Report

```
        C O N C E S S I O N S          I N T E R N A T I O N A L
        ~~~~~~~~~~~~~~~~~~~~~~          ~~~~~~~~~~~~~~~~~~~~~~~~~~~~
    RECEIVING LOG                 DATE:   FEBRUARY 7, 1991

    PAGE ONE OF ONE
    |                         |AMOUNT OF |INVOICE/ |   MERCHANDISE        |
    |      RECEIVED FROM       |INVOICE  | BILL #  |   DESCRIPTION        |
    -------------------------------------------------------------------------
    |                         |         |         |         |            |
    -------------------------------------------------------------------------
    |                         |         |         |         |            |
    -------------------------------------------------------------------------
    |                         |         |         |         |            |
    -------------------------------------------------------------------------
    |                         |         |         |         |            |
    -------------------------------------------------------------------------
    |                         |         |         |         |            |
    -------------------------------------------------------------------------
    |                         |         |         |         |            |
    -------------------------------------------------------------------------
    |                         |         |         |         |            |


    -------------------------------------------------------------------------
    |                         |         |         |         |            |
    -------------------------------------------------------------------------
    |                         |         |         |         |            |
    -------------------------------------------------------------------------
    |                         |         |         |         |            |
    -------------------------------------------------------------------------
    |TOTAL                    |   0.00  |         |         |            |
    =========================================================================
```

Courtesy of Concessions International, Inc.

Storage

A well-designed storeroom allows for order and cleanliness and has adequate space. Ideally, it should be close to the bar, yet still permit tight security. Unfortunately, many bar and beverage operations are less than the ideal. In the real world, you must often make do with the situation you have. Storage space for your beer, wines, and distilled spirits is no exception.

Since specific storage requirements are necessary for beer and wine, we will discuss these in greater detail. There are, however, some general practices of good storeroom management which apply to all of the products you store, including distilled spirits and non-alcoholic beverages. All beverages must be carefully handled and stored to preserve their quality. Alcoholic beverages represent a large capital investment and should be treated with respect. Although beverages are not as highly perishable as some foods, poor handling methods and storage procedures can still damage them and affect their flavor. Also, with a few exceptions, alcoholic beverages do not improve with age.

The objectives of liquor room storage, be it room temperature or refrigerated, are as follows:

- Maintain product quality by ensuring proper temperature, humidity, light, and adequate security.

Exhibit 9.13 Sample Bin Card

Name _____		Par _____	
Bottle Size _____		Reorder Point _____	
Date	Received	Issued	Balance

Bin cards can help maintain storeroom organization and assist in inventory control.

- Maintain proper rotation of stock.

- Maintain accessibility of products.

- Maintain knowledge of product in stock by proper inventory procedures.

- Maintain cleanliness and order.

- Prevent pilferage.

To ensure that these objectives are carried out, management should design the storage areas so that each product has its designated place on the shelves. Products in the same beverage category (well brands, call brands, cordials, and so forth) should be stored together and in the sequence in which they are listed on the inventory sheets. This will save time during issuing and inventory procedures. The storage system you devise should conform to the needs of your operation. Products that turn over more quickly should be in easy-to-reach locations with plenty of storage space for both bottles and cases. Some products, such as cordials and brandies, might need room for just one bottle.

The use of **bin cards** helps to ensure that the product arrangement you devise for your storage areas will always be used. Bin cards are standardized forms (see Exhibit 9.13) attached to the shelf where the product is stored. They maintain a record of product received, product issued, and sometimes most recent cost. They may also list the product's par and reorder point or, in a minimum/maximum system, the minimum and maximum that should be on hand. Many bar and beverage operations have

Storage areas for both alcohol and bar supplies should be designed so that all products have their designated spaces. (Courtesy of Concessions International, Inc.)

replaced bin cards with computerized bin cards. The storeroom order is still maintained to correspond with the electronic bin cards.

Thermometers should be used in both dry and refrigerated storage areas as temperature can affect the quality of alcoholic beverages. Dry liquor storage should not be located in a warm or hot area. Beverage storerooms should be separate from food storage areas due to humidity, temperature, and security concerns. Excessive humidity leads to label deterioration and may affect the cork in wine bottles (discussed later). The opening and closing of refrigerated areas which is required in food storage areas can cause large temperature fluctuations. This can cause a rapid deterioration of both wines and beers, especially kegs. Keg beer that gets too warm produces too much foam and may even sour. Wines are particularly sensitive to vibrations. Purveyors can often be very helpful in identifying the specific storage needs of the products they sell.

All liquor storage areas should be kept locked and the keys should be tightly controlled. Typically, no more than one or two people need to have keys to these areas. Since items are issued only once a day, this policy should not be a problem. We recommend changing locks on a periodic basis, especially if you have high turnover among employees with access to these areas. Bartenders are generally not allowed access to the liquor storage areas. They should requisition needed products, which should be issued to them on a daily basis by a member of your management team.

The importance of security in these areas must not be underestimated. The rules and standards which you establish surrounding your liquor storage areas are an important element in an effective control system.

Adequate space is also a major concern. The amount of stock of each brand and type will be determined by your par. This information translates into the amount of shelving you will need in both your dry and refrigerated areas. There are no generic formulas for space requirements. Each operation has different target markets desiring different product mixes and therefore different storage needs.

Sanitation concerns must also be considered in the design of storage areas. Requirements are determined by both local and state codes. These vary from state to state and location to location. Storage areas should be well-ventilated and bottles should not be allowed to get dusty.

The Storage of Beers

The shelf life of beer is shorter than that of any other alcoholic beverage. Therefore, care must be taken to avoid overstocking and to maintain proper storage conditions. Beer does *not* mature with age. Without proper handling and storage, it actually begins to deteriorate once it is packaged. While we will give you general guidelines for handling beer and related products, you should check with your purveyor to see if there are any specific storage requirements for the brands you purchase.

When deliveries of beer are received, they should be stored behind the existing stock, which should be sold before the new beer is sold. This same procedure should be used when beer is issued to the bar. This system, called the **first-in, first-out (FIFO) system,** should always be the standard for handling beer products.

Ideally, the storage area should be designed specifically for beer. The room should be dry, dust free, and, when unoccupied, kept dark. Cases should not be stacked directly on the floor, but rather placed on raised, slatted platforms that will allow for proper air circulation. Excessive humidity or dampness can destroy or distort the labels and reduce your guests' perceptions of quality.

When bottles are served, a place for empties must be provided. In those states that prohibit keeping empty alcoholic product bottles on the premises, it may be necessary to provide for broken bottle storage. Some bar and beverage operations use a chute that runs directly from the bar to the empty bottle storage area below. This keeps the bar area from being cluttered with empty bottles which pose both sanitation and safety problems. In operations which sell a high volume of bottled beer, storage space and procedures for handling empties must be clearly planned.

Beer products are delicate and have many enemies, including time, light, and heat. Good brews with a wonderful flavor and delightful aroma can quickly go bad under the wrong combination of elements.[3] Beer must be stored where it is not exposed to heat or light, and must be used in a relatively short time—draft beer within 45 days of packaging at the brewery, and bottled and canned beer usually within 90 to 120 days of packaging. For this reason, it is best to order beer on a weekly basis so that your stock is always fresh. Leaving packaged beers too long, even under good storage conditions, can cause problems. Even chilled beers which stand for long periods develop a gray sediment from protein deterioration. This can build up into a gray lump on the bottom of the bottle and look like a small, dead mouse. Such bottles are not likely to impress your guests favorably.

Beer in clear glass bottles should be kept in its closed cartons to keep the light away. A skunky flavor can result from light striking beverages containing hops. This is why most brewers put their products in dark bottles. The shorter the time that beers are exposed to light, the better.

Beers should not be shaken or handled roughly, as this can bruise them. Non-draft beers need a storage temperature between 40° and 70° F (4° and 21° C), even those for which the producer does not require constant refrigeration. It is all right to move beer from warm to cool storage, or from cool to cool, but never should beer be moved from cool to warm and then back to cool. The product is so delicate that it requires an even temperature in a cool range for maximum quality. While beer must be kept cool, it should not be allowed to freeze. This can cause flake-like solids to form. If beer is frozen too hard or too long, these flakes are irreversible. If the product is only slightly frozen, it should be allowed to thaw slowly. You should then lightly mix the beer by carefully inverting the bottles or cans and, as carefully as possible, shaking the product until it is clear and may be served.

If beers are served too cold, they will gush out of their container when opened. If beers are served too warm, they can be wild and can lose foam and carbonation too quickly. If you are going to serve beer in unchilled thin-shell glasses, you can expect a two Fahrenheit degree (one Celsius degree) rise in temperature when the product is poured into the glass. If you use unchilled heavy-shell glasses or mugs, you should expect a four to five Fahrenheit degree (two to three Celsius degree) rise in temperature.[4]

Draft beer should be stored between 36° and 38° F (2° and 3° C). Since this product is not pasteurized, it is highly perishable and must be kept cold at all times. Storing above 45° F (7° C) will cause a change in flavor and the product will become cloudy. If held too long at a high temperature, the beer will actually become sour. Hence, kegs of beer should be taken to the cooler as soon as they have been checked in at receiving. Sitting on a loading dock on a hot summer day can cause serious quality problems.

Management should place a reliable thermometer in the cool storage area and check it routinely. Putting the thermometer in a glass of water probably gives a more accurate reading, since the air temperature in a cooler can vary as doors are opened and closed. Thermometers may be checked for accuracy by placing them in cold water that contains melting ice. The temperature should register 32° F (0° C).

The Storage of Wines

Wines represent a large capital investment. For that reason, you should choose the location and conditions for the storage of your wines with great care. A well-kept wine cellar can be a source of great pride to a bar or beverage establishment. Some operations even make their wine storage facilities part of the decor and ambience, allowing guests to see the well-maintained stock. The location should be secure, accessible, and have adequate space to meet your needs. Unlike distilled spirits, wine bottles should be stored on their sides to prevent the cork from drying out and affecting the quality of the product.

The storage area for wines should be neither too dry nor too moist. If too dry, the corks will dry out and the wine will oxidize. If too moist, the labels may deteriorate and mold may appear. Either condition can significantly reduce the quality of your wine products. The ideal humidity for wine storage is between 60% and 70%. This is too dry for the growth of fungus and moist enough to keep the corks fresh.

The best temperature for wine storage is 55° F (13° C) for reds and slightly lower for whites.[5] For proper serving temperature, white, rosé, and sparkling wines should be stored at 50° F (10° C) and red wines at 65° F (18° C).[6] Temperature changes and extreme temperatures are especially harmful to wines. A steady cool temperature is best. Underground storage cellars are good because they tend to maintain a steadier

Wine storage areas can be highly decorative or purely functional. (Courtesy of Strongbow Inn, Valparaiso, Indiana)

temperature. However, the humidity in underground cellars must be carefully monitored.

Wine should be stored away from light, as light causes the product to deteriorate. This is why many wines are bottled in dark glass.

Wine is fragile. Care should be taken not to slam storage area doors or disturb storage racks. Once stored, wines should be moved as little as possible. This is because vibrations can cause wine to throw off its sediment too soon. Place bottles in and remove them from storage carefully, avoiding shaking or a lot of motion. Wines should be moved at least 24 hours—and preferably longer for wines with lees on the bottom—before service, carefully placed upright, and allowed to settle and rest before opening. Well-matured wines should be given the most care in handling and the most time in resting. Red wines need more care and rest than whites. Wines should not be served immediately after delivery, but rather should be allowed to rest. Shipment can cause wines to get "shipment sickness," a temporary loss of flavor and other quality characteristics.

Inventory

Inventories are a critical component of product control. An **inventory** is a count of the product you have on hand at any given time. Inventory

Exhibit 9.14 Sample Computerized Perpetual Inventory Form

```
LIQUOR  ON  HAND                            NEXT    INVENTORY  DATE: 2-22-9X
        FOR DATE: 2-6-9X          UNIT    COST                          UNIT      COST
                    UNIT  QUAN    COST    EXTS.                  UNIT QUAN  COST   EXTS.
========================================================================================
                                  0.00    0.00 BARTLES&JAYMES RED  CS        0.00    0.00
JIM BEAM            LTR           0.00    0.00 BARTLES&JAYMES WHT  CS        0.00    0.00
                                  0.00    0.00 BURGUNDY PONY       CS        0.00    0.00
BUSHMILL           LTR           0.00    0.00 BURGUNDY    4LTR     EA        0.00    0.00
CANADIAN CLUB      LTR           0.00    0.00 CHABLIS KEG         EA        0.00    0.00
CROWN ROYAL        LTR           0.00    0.00 CHABLIS PONY        CS        0.00    0.00
EARLY TIMES        LTR           0.00    0.00 CHABLIS     4 LTR   EA        0.00    0.00
JACK DANIELS BLACK LTR           0.00    0.00 CHAMPAGNE PONY      EA        0.00    0.00
                                  0.00    0.00 DRY SACK            LTR        0.00    0.00
SEAGRAMS 7         LTR           0.00    0.00 DUBONNET            LTR        0.00    0.00
SEAGRAMS VO        LTR           0.00    0.00 HARVEYS BRISTOL     LTR        0.00    0.00
WILD TURKEY        LTR           0.00    0.00 ROSE PONY           CS        0.00    0.00
                                  0.00    0.00 ROSE        4 LTR   EA        0.00    0.00
CLAN MAC GREGOR    LTR           0.00    0.00                                0.00    0.00
CHIVAS REGAL       LTR           0.00    0.00 BECKS               CS        0.00    0.00
CUTTY SARK         LTR           0.00    0.00 COORS               CS        0.00    0.00
```

Courtesy of Concessions International, Inc.

controls need to be established both at the point of sale and in the storeroom.

The purpose of taking an inventory is to determine the amount of product you have on hand at any given time. Inventory procedures really begin when you establish your par stock. Remember that par establishes a set number of bottles of each product to be in your inventory at all times. Your bar par is stated in terms of specific number of bottles.

Inventory procedures maintain controls for *all* alcoholic beverages in your operation, not merely the relatively expensive wines and distilled spirits. Even though a bottle of beer costs less than a bottle of scotch or wine, the quantity of beers sold is frequently much higher. Although the process is tedious, a close count should be kept on your bottled beers, including domestics, premium domestics, and imports. Draft beer is easier to control from an inventory standpoint, as the amount of beer in kegs can be inventoried by weight.

Perpetual Inventory

A **perpetual inventory** provides a record of all product you have in your bar or beverage operation without your actually counting it. It helps you to determine your beverage inventory in terms of both dollar value and number of bottles. This system uses either perpetual inventory cards very much like the bin card shown in Exhibit 9.13 or a computer program that records similar information on a screen or printout such as that shown in Exhibit 9.14.

Perpetual inventory cards or programs allow you to record the number and purchase cost of bottles issued and received whenever they are issued from or delivered to the storage area. By adding the number of bottles received to the number of bottles on hand and then subtracting the number of bottles issued, you keep a running balance of how many bottles *should be* on hand. The number of bottles indicated on the perpetual inventory record should match the number of bottles in the liquor storage area. In order to maintain tight control over your inventory, we again emphasize that under no conditions should alcohol products be taken from receiving to the bar area. This practice circumvents the perpetual inventory procedure and makes your operation susceptible to theft.

Perpetual inventories can also be used to track how well or poorly each of your brands is selling. Carrying stock which does not sell is expensive, so slow-moving products should be eliminated from your inventory and replaced with other brands. Over time, perpetual inventory information also provides an accurate historical analysis of your bar or beverage operation.

Physical Inventory

In addition to maintaining a perpetual inventory, you should conduct a **physical inventory** at least once a month. The physical inventory is performed to verify the information on your perpetual inventory records. If it does not, discrepancies should be tracked down immediately! When discrepancies arise, it is advisable to conduct physical inventories more frequently, perhaps even weekly, until the problems are resolved.

Of course, a physical inventory can be taken whenever you feel there might be a control problem. Some bar and beverage operations notify their bartenders that occasional spot-check inventories will be taken. In spot-check inventories, a manager randomly selects several brands to inventory before the end-of-the-month physical inventory. This can catch control problems before they get too serious and start affecting the bottom line.

Again, for obvious reasons, the person taking inventory should not also maintain the storeroom, receive, or purchase. There would be too many opportunities to falsify records so that the inventory sheets (Exhibit 9.15) matched the perpetual inventory cards, receiving sheets, and purchase orders. It is best not to have operational people responsible for inventory whenever possible; rather, assign this task to someone in your accounting department. We also suggest, as an additional control measure, that two-person teams—each with one manager—conduct physical inventories. One person should count and call and the other record.

The physical inventory of the storeroom is relatively simple compared with the physical inventory of the bar stock, which deals with open bottles. There are a number of ways to handle the counting of open bottles. One system simply ignores any open bottles, counting only those that are full. The philosophy behind this system is that there is a constant amount of liquor in the open bottles over a period of time. Hence, the open bottle inventory evens itself out.

A more common method of counting open bottles is to estimate the contents by tenths (9/10 full, 8/10 full, and so on). This system works quite well as a consistent measure of the product you have in stock in open bottles at your bar.

Beverage Inventory Turnover

You must never lose sight of the fact that your liquor inventory represents cash. The amount of product you can purchase and even your selection of brands depends on the capital investment you are willing to make in your liquor inventory. The objective of this process is *not* to keep the liquor in the storage areas, but rather to convert these physical assets back into cash as quickly as possible. The more quickly you can turn your inventory into cash, the higher your return on investment (ROI).

Exhibit 9.13 Sample Physical Inventory Sheet

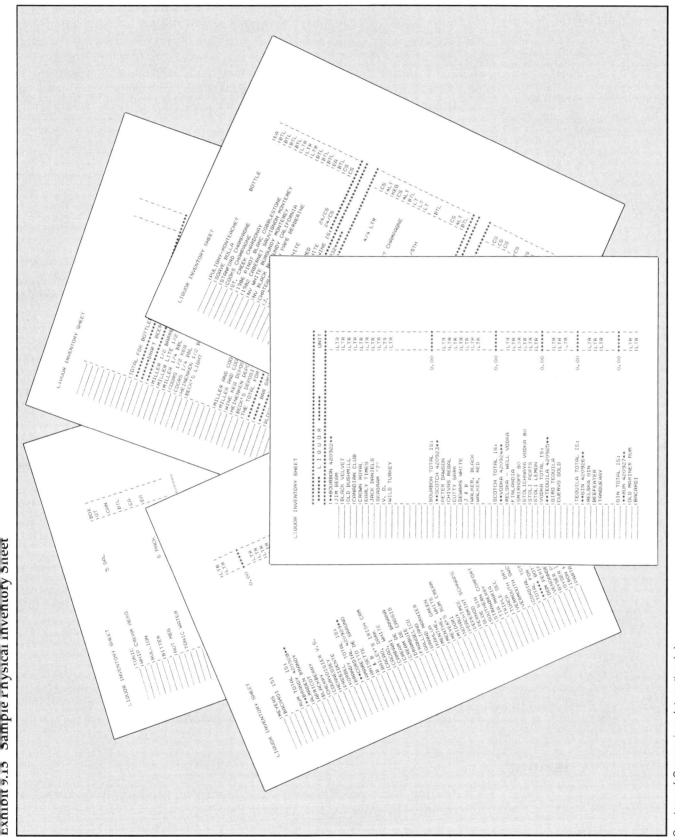

Courtesy of Concessions International, Inc.

Your **beverage inventory turnover** is a reflection of how efficiently you convert your liquid assets back into cash. It is calculated by dividing the cost of beverage sold by your average inventory. Assume for the following example that opening inventory is $7,000, closing inventory is $6,200, and the cost of purchases is $8,600. Your cost of beverage sold (or used) is calculated by taking the opening inventory plus the cost of purchases minus the closing inventory:

$$\$7,000 + \$8,600 - \$6,200 = \$9,400$$

Average inventory is computed by adding the opening inventory and the closing inventory and dividing that figure by two:

$$\frac{\$7,000 + \$6,200}{2} = \$6,600$$

Given these figures, your inventory turnover ratio is $9,400 ÷ $6,600, or 1.42, which is in the desirable range of 1 to 2. If your inventory turnover ratio is over 2.0, you are carrying insufficient inventory to meet the needs of your operation. It is very likely that you are running out of product and creating dissatisfied guests. If, however, your inventory turnover ratio is less than 1.0, you are carrying too much stock and should reduce your inventory.

Managers should watch for fluctuations in this turnover figure. If the figure drops, then the operation's return on investment is falling. If the figure rises, the liquor on your shelf is being turned to cash more quickly. This is positive as long as you are not always running out of the product or brands that guests request.

This step needs to be carefully and consistently monitored. As target markets and guest needs change, so will your forecasts for product selection and purchases. The accuracy of your forecasts directly affects your inventory. Ideally, bar and beverage operators would like the purveyor to hold the product for as long as possible while still being able to meet the daily demands of guests. Of course, inventories need to protect against unforeseen surges in business and delays in delivery.

Inventory Control as a Monitor of Sales and Costs

The purposes of taking inventory are to maintain control over the product and to provide information about the sales of particular brands over time. Accurate inventories and requisition sheets are critical. The paper trail associated with the flow of product through an operation has been devised to permit the accurate monitoring of beverage sales and costs. From the purchase order to the issuing requisition form, this system allows you to track your liquid investment from the back door to the bar.

Inventory is an essential part of a control system and, as such, should be conducted regularly and with care. Following strict guidelines will help ensure consistent accountability for all products.

Issuing

Issuing is the procedure involved in moving products from storage to the bar area. In order for any alcoholic beverages to be moved from storage, a requisition form, such as the one seen in Exhibit 9.16, must be filled out. Under no circumstances should product be moved without a requisition. In

Exhibit 9.17 Sample Computerized Inventory Sheet

STRONGBOW LIQUOR INVENTORY -- 7-15-90

Item Description	Vndr	Size	$/Btl	Beg. Inv. #	Beg. Inv. $	+ Receipts #	+ Receipts $	- Usage #	- Usage $	= End Inv. #	= End Inv. $	Par Stock #	To Be Ord.
Blackberry Brandy	01	LITER	$7.95										
Blue Curacao	01	LITER	$7.57	4.1	31.04					4.1	31.04	1	-3.1
Canadian Club	01	LITER	$11.34										
Canadian Club - 2nd	01	LITER	$11.71	5.6	65.58	4	46.84	2.0	23.42	7.6	89.00	8	0.4
Cardhu Scotch	01	750 ML		1.0						1.0			-1.0
Chambord	01	750 ML	$14.73	1.2	17.68					1.2	17.68	1	-0.2
Cherry Brandy	01	LITER	$6.31									1	-0.2
Cherry Brandy	01	LITER	$7.95	1.2	9.54					1.2	9.54		
Courvoisier - 2nd	01	LITER	$22.08	2.0	44.16					2.0	44.16		
Courvoisier	01	LITER	$20.97									2	
Creme de Banana X	01	LITER	$7.37										
Creme de Banana	01	LITER	$7.51	3.0	22.53					3.0	22.53	2	-1.0
Creme de Cassis	01	LITER	$7.55	2.4	18.12					2.4	18.12	2	-0.4
Creme de Cacao-Dk X	01	LITER	$7.79										
Creme de Cacao - Dark	01	LITER	$7.92	2.1	16.63					2.1	16.63	2	-0.1

Courtesy of Strongbow Inn, Valparaiso, Indiana

control, your employees will learn to appreciate the products you serve and will serve those products with great pride.

To begin with, select products that reflect both your target market and level of service. Your selection of the beer, wines, and distilled spirits helps determine your operation's image. Efficient purchasing will save money and set the tone for the type of control system you have established. Your standards for control begin with the purchase order and are carried systematically throughout the paper trail surrounding the flow of product through your operation. The purchasing of alcoholic beverages is sometimes strictly controlled by local and state practices. In some states, product may only be purchased in government stores, while in others only one purveyor is allowed to represent a particular brand.

Sound receiving practices are very important. The receiving agent must be familiar with beers, wines, and distilled spirits. The purveyor invoice must be matched against the purchase order and then against the actual products delivered. It is best if beverage shipments are scheduled at designated times so that the care and attention the procedure deserves can be observed. It is a good control practice to stamp the bottles with a special stamp so that stolen bottles can be recovered and employees are discouraged from bringing in their own bottles to sell from.

After the products have been received, they should be taken immediately to the appropriate storage areas, which should be separate from food storage. Products should never be left unattended before being stored. Ideally, storage areas should be located close to the bar. Storage areas must be securely locked and the proper temperature and humidity requirements maintained.

Inventories, both perpetual and physical, must be conducted on a consistent basis. Inventory sheets should be set up to conform to the storeroom arrangement, thereby expediting the inventory procedures. The beverage inventory turnover can be useful in determining the appropriateness of both the brands and amount of product you carry. This figure relates directly to your operation's return on investment. Carrying a large inventory means a low turnover ratio and a low return on investment.

The final step discussed in this chapter was issuing. By watching what products sell, management can make informed decisions about whether to change product selections.

Endnotes

1. Ronn R. Wiegand, "Profit from the Growing Wine Market," *Night Club & Bar* 5 (#8, 1989): 14, 16.

2. John F. Mariani, "Short and Simple Restaurants Trim Wine List Inventories," *Market Watch* 9 (#7, 1990): 80–82, 84, 87.

3. *The Modern Beertender* (Anheuser-Busch, Inc., no date).

4. In the United States, the recommended serving temperature for beer is 40° F (4° C). However, this temperature preference is by no means universal, even within the United States. Throughout the world, beers are served at various temperatures depending upon cultural preferences. These varying preferences again point to the importance of understanding and responding to your target market.

5. Alexis Bespaloff, "Buying and Cellaring," *New York* 18 (1985): 88–89.

6. Brian K. Julyan, "How To Store Table Wines," *Restaurants USA* 10 (#2, 1990): 30–31.

Key Terms

beverage inventory turnover
beverage receiving report
bin cards
call brands
closed states
control states
dead stock list
discounting
first-in, first-out (FIFO) system
inventory
issuing
lead time
license states

monopoly states
open states
par
perpetual inventory
physical inventory
purchase order
purchasing
receiving
separation of duties
standards
two tier par stock
well brands

Discussion Questions

1. What role does the separation of duties play in controlling the flow of product through an operation? How do small operations differ from large operations in this regard?

2. What are some of the factors that affect the scope of a wine list?

3. How has the selection of house wines and wines by the glass changed over the last few years?

4. What benefits can be gained by pouring a premium well?

5. What topics should you consider when selecting a purveyor? Why would some factors be more important than others for any given operation?

6. What factors should you consider when you establish a par stock?

7. What procedures should be followed when products are received? How is receiving alcoholic beverages different from receiving food?

8. Why is it important to use the FIFO system when handling beer products?

9. How do perpetual and physical inventory systems differ? What is each used for?

10. What does the beverage inventory turnover indicate? What does it mean if it is less than 1.0? greater than 2.0?

10   Bar Control Systems

Chapter Outline

The Control System
    What Is Beverage Control?
Product Control
    Establishing Standards
        Standard Recipes
        Portion Control Tools and Procedures
        Glassware
        Par Levels
        Service Procedures and Operating Policies
        Prices
    Preventing Pilferage and Fraud
    Automatic Dispensing Systems
    Product Control and Banquet Service
Sales and Profitability Control
    Determining Product Cost
    Sales Accountability/Sales Analysis
        Gross Profit
    Pricing
Cash Control
    Cash Handling Procedures
Control: A Guide to Profit and Guest Satisfaction

██████████ **Controlling** is the management process of comparing actual performance with established standards and, when necessary, taking corrective action to bring performance up to standards. Control systems in bar and beverage operations use a variety of methods, each with a specific control objective. Bar control systems involve establishing and maintaining standards for product control, sales and profitability control, and cash control. The planning and operating functions discussed in the first two parts of this text all serve to support the maintenance of the bar control systems you establish. Managers of successful bar and beverage operations repeatedly emphasize that practical bar and beverage management *is* controls.

Regardless of how well you have planned and organized your operating functions, bar and beverage operations seldom work out precisely as planned. Envision your operating functions as a path that you travel down to reach the perfect combination of guest satisfaction and organizational profitability. Bar control systems enable you to keep your strategic plans moving down this path with only slight deviations. Bar and beverage managers who develop and consistently monitor a control system are more apt to reach their established goals.

This chapter examines various bar control systems. It identifies the three primary control systems found in bar and beverage operations and describes the various standards which need to be established to maintain quality control. It looks at the different methods which can be used to control the pouring costs in your bar or beverage operation, describes control methods to prevent theft and pilferage, and identifies the advantages and disadvantages of automated dispensing systems. It describes the use of pricing as a control tool and discusses proper cash handling procedures to ensure effective control.

The Control System

It is management's responsibility to establish the systems of control. Well-designed control systems enable you, as the bar or beverage manager, to maximize the time you spend with your employees and guests. Control systems should not be viewed as a paper trail of insignificant data and recordkeeping. Rather, they are information systems that should be used in an ongoing effort to achieve guest satisfaction and organizational profitability.

Many of the planning and operational functions discussed in earlier chapters are closely linked with bar control systems. Good hiring practices can help reduce the problem of employee theft before it begins. Proper training helps establish product consistency and staff adherence to cash handling procedures. Good bar and facility design improves the effectiveness of the bar control systems you establish by improving efficiency and reducing the possibility of theft. For a bar's profit potential to be fully realized, its management must recognize and understand all aspects of the operation that are related to the control function.

All control activities eventually focus on profitability or the bottom line. As a bar or beverage manager, don't get so caught up in the day-to-day running of things that you forget your control responsibilities. A good control system should be used to affect positively the performance of all your employees. It is not a negative management tool (that is, a means of discipline used to keep employees in line) nor should you present it as such to your employees. It should make your staff more quality conscious and better equipped to serve the guests and should enhance the sense of hospitality your operation has to offer. The establishment and maintenance of a control system is not a contradiction of our guest-oriented management philosophy.

Control systems are closely related to the operational planning process. In the planning process, objectives are established for performance. These objectives set the standards to be used by the control system. The control system should be designed so that corrective action can be implemented whenever necessary. If your control system indicates a deviation from standards, take corrective action immediately, not a week or a month later. The cause of the deviation from standards should also be investigated to determine if adjustments need to be made in the training program or the purchasing process. Not only do control systems tell you what happened, they also provide you with information on what *should* happen. Beverage costs represent a significant expenditure in most bar and beverage operations. Nothing should be left to chance.

What Is Beverage Control?

Controls ultimately deal with money either paid out or received. There are three primary control systems needed in bar and beverage operations. They are:

- Product control

- Sales and profitability control

- Cash control

Product control is established to protect physical assets. An essential part of product control is developed throughout the purchasing process (see Chapter 9). Purchasing and marketing functions work hand in hand to see that guest demand is met. A second, but equally important, component in product control is the protection against leakages due to either improper handling or pilferage. Concerns about improper handling and pilferage involve not only the storage and security considerations previously discussed, but also handling the product after it has been issued to the bar. The effectiveness of the standards you establish in product control is closely related to the efficiency of the layout of the bar and lounge area. A third factor in product control is quality assurance, that is, making sure that the guest's drink is the same quality time after time.

Sales and profitability control revolves around the bar or beverage operation's bottom line and profits. Here we determine sales potential through the use of a sales analysis, evaluate the cost of product, compute the sales mix, monitor sales volume (the generation of profit), and make pricing decisions. Sales and profitability control deals with the hard realities of establishing and maintaining cost control measures.

Cash control looks at an entire system of cash handling procedures. A key control tool should be a cash handling manual which discusses detailed procedures for every aspect of handling cash in an operation, from setting up the opening bank to handling voids to filling out the cash deposit slip at the end of the shift. Cash handling procedures tell all employees who is responsible for every activity involving cash and what the correct actions are for accomplishing each task. Cash control is closely

Quality control means that the guest's drink should look and taste the same each time it is ordered. (Courtesy of Strongbow Inn, Valparaiso, Indiana)

linked with a training program for all employees that emphasizes consistency in maintaining established procedures.

We will now look at these three control systems in more detail.

Product Control

The two basic objectives of **product control** are to assist in the control of quality and of costs. In beverage operations, the product—a case of vodka, a bottle of cognac, a case of champagne—is expensive and deserving of very rigid controls. In comparison with food, beverages are relatively easy to control. In most situations, beverages are delivered by the case or the bottle. It is not difficult to tell if a case or a bottle is partially empty. And when the bartender pours a drink, it must be measured so it is easy to determine if the amount sold is equal to the amount poured. This ease of control is not always possible in food operations. For example, in a recipe calling for a "wedge" of lettuce, one salad prep's idea of a "wedge" may vary from the next person's.

The product control system is supported by numerous standards established by management. Standards are built into the control system to ensure that your guests always receive quality drinks at a fair price and that ownership receives a fair return on its investment. Performance is compared to each of these standards to see if deviations exist. If deviations are present, then procedures for corrective action need to be implemented immediately.

Establishing Standards

Standards define the level of performance that management expects. For example, assume that you have established 1.5 (fluid) ounces as the standard pour size for drinks in your operation. The level of performance that you expect from your bartenders is a consistent 1.5-ounce pour for every drink they make. Establishing levels of performance allows you to project potential

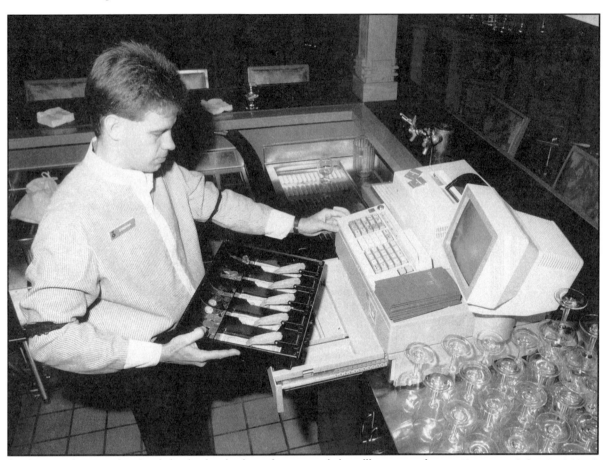

Setting up the opening bank is the beginning of your cash handling procedures. (Courtesy of Opryland Hotel, Nashville, Tennessee)

sales and profit for each shift. Based upon a 1.5-ounce pour and knowing how many drinks were sold, you can determine how much alcohol should have been used. To determine what the sales figure should be for that bartender's shift, multiply the number of drinks sold by their respective prices. Information is provided daily to management through sales reports which reveal deviations from standards by indicating if more alcohol was used than should have been, based on the number of drinks sold. If there have been no deviations from standards, you can then determine your profit for that shift or day. If there are deviations, immediately take corrective action. Begin by analyzing the cause of the deviations. Is it a training problem (for example, the bartender was never told the correct pour size)? Is it sloppy procedures (for example, the bartender is *trailing* the drinks—that is, continuing to pour liquor into the glass after the shot glass or jigger is full)? Is it a theft problem? Your analysis of the deviation will point to the corrective action needed.

It is management's responsibility to establish and maintain standards. Let's now examine some of the standards which need to be established for bar and beverage operations.

Standard Recipes. Recipes are standardized so that all drinks are uniform in both taste and appearance. Establishing standard recipes includes de-

Exhibit 10.1 Sample Standard Drink Recipe

> *Wild Turkey Strut* $3.50
>
> In a blender cup with ice:
>
>   2 shots Wild Turkey
>
>   1 ounce lemosa
>
>   2 teaspoons sugar
>
> Blend, strain into martini glass.
> Orange and cherry.

Courtesy of Strongbow Inn, Valparaiso, Indiana

termining **drink size**, which is the amount of alcohol (in fluid ounces) that is poured into each drink (not the size of the completed drink). Drink size ranges from three-fourths of an ounce to two ounces. Drink recipes also specify any other ingredients, the correct method of preparation, the appropriate garnish, and the correct glassware (see Exhibit 10.1).

Portion Control Tools and Procedures. Portion control tools and procedures help you standardize your drinks. If your control system is to be effective, the size of your drinks must be the same every time. Today, there are a variety of options, from the shot glass to highly sophisticated computerized systems, for controlling the amount of liquor your bartenders pour. Each of these options has its advantages and disadvantages with regard to the product control they provide.

Just about every other option is preferable to the **free pour**. The free pour is an unmeasured system where the bartender simply pours freely into a glass (see Exhibit 10.2). Some bartenders will attempt to convince you that their free pour is as accurate as using a shot glass. They will tell you that they can pour an ounce or an ounce and a half on command and may even give you a demonstration of their skill. Using a measuring device, they may claim, hinders their performance skill and speed. Perhaps so, but allowing your bartenders to free pour removes virtually all control over the amount of product poured and greatly reduces the overall effectiveness of your total control system.

Measured pouring may be done using a shot glass, a jigger, or a measuring device which is part of a pouring spout you can attach to each bottle. **Shot glasses** may be either plain or lined and are used for measuring the liquor required for a particular drink. Plain shot glasses are filled to the brim, while lined shot glasses are filled to the line etched on the glass. **Jiggers** are double-ended measuring devices typically made of stainless steel (see Exhibit 10.3). Each end of the jigger holds a different amount (for example, three-fourths of an ounce and either an ounce or an ounce and a half). In mechanical **pourers**, ball bearings allow the bartender to dispense whatever pour size you have determined is appropriate. Each time the bartender tips the bottle, the predetermined amount of alcohol is dispensed. Pouring is still fast with a pouring spout and you reduce the

Exhibit 10.2 Free Pouring

The free pour is not part of a solid bar control system; this is a demonstration.
(Courtesy of Opryland Hotel, Nashville, Tennessee)

spillage which can occur when pouring directly from the bottle. Pourers can be color-coded to denote different price levels or different pour sizes.

Automatic or computerized bar systems became more popular in the 1980s. Drinks are dispensed from a gun (see Exhibit 10.4) or a pouring spout at the touch of a button. Many of these systems dispense mixes as well, assuring your guests of a consistent drink each time the button is pushed. Some systems are attached to the point-of-sale system (see Exhibit 10.5); these systems can provide you with an instant tally of drinks sold by server, brand, product, or sales dollar. They can also be tied into your inventory system, automatically deducting the amount of product sold from your beginning inventory each time a drink is dispensed. We will discuss these systems at greater length in our discussion of sales and profitability control.

Glassware. The size and shape of glassware used for each drink must be standardized. One of the most effective control tools available is the selection of glassware. The glassware should also be appropriate for the drink to be served in it. You wouldn't serve a drink ordered neat in a rocks glass or vice versa, nor would you serve a highball in an elaborate glass designed to show off your frozen drinks. (Glassware was discussed in Chapter 6.)

Par Levels. The maintenance of a daily par level at the bar is a key link in your control system. It is a way to monitor the flow of product from issuing to your guest. The par level for the bar is based on the amount of product used on the busiest day of the year plus a safety margin of 50%.

Exhibit 10.3 Jiggers

Exhibit 10.4 Dispensing Gun

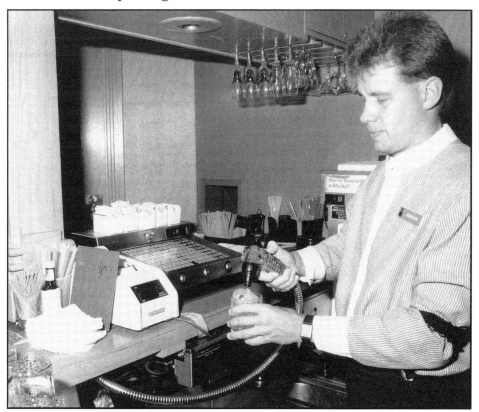

Drinks may be dispensed from a gun in automatic bar systems. (Photos courtesy of Opryland Hotel, Nashville, Tennessee)

Exhibit 10.5 Schematic of a Computerized Bar System

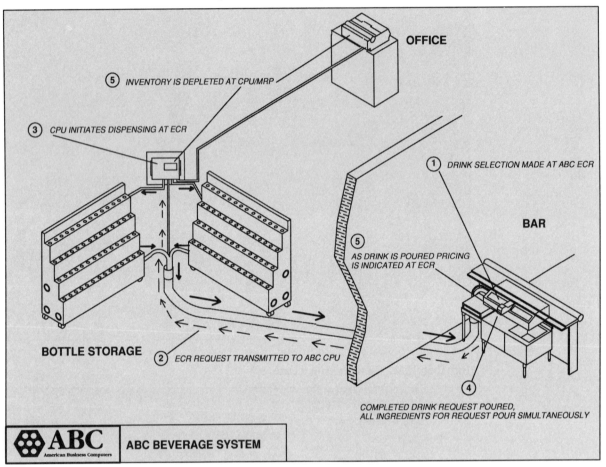

OFFICE

⑤ *INVENTORY IS DEPLETED AT CPU/MRP*

③ *CPU INITIATES DISPENSING AT ECR*

① *DRINK SELECTION MADE AT ABC ECR*

BAR

⑤ *AS DRINK IS POURED PRICING IS INDICATED AT ECR*

BOTTLE STORAGE ② *ECR REQUEST TRANSMITTED TO ABC CPU*

④

COMPLETED DRINK REQUEST POURED, ALL INGREDIENTS FOR REQUEST POUR SIMULTANEOUSLY

⊕ABC
American Business Computers | **ABC BEVERAGE SYSTEM**

Courtesy of American Business Computers

Liquor is requisitioned at the end of the shift or day by the bartender by comparing the inventory on hand with the par. An even simpler procedure is to use the empty-for-full replacement method. In this method, all the bottles emptied during the day are saved. The amount of liquor requisitioned equals the number of empty bottles of each brand. Some states require that bottles must be broken once they are emptied. Some operations adopt this policy to ensure that bartenders cannot refill old bottles with their own liquor. In this case, the requisition would be filled out to bring the bar inventory up to par. In situations where the entire bottle is sold by the server, as with wine sales, the use of a **full bottle slip** should be implemented. When a full bottle is ordered, management or the point-of-sale system issues a full bottle slip to the bartender to exchange for the full bottle. To requisition these bottles (since there is no empty), the bartender attaches the full bottle slips to the daily bar requisition form.

Keeping a tight handle on your par through frequent inspection also discourages bartenders from bringing in their own bottles and selling drinks from them while pocketing the proceeds. This is a good reason to use a special stamp to mark the bottles once they have been issued from the storeroom.

an innovative, dishonest bartender. Management can deal with this problem by counting the money in the tip jar, moving the tip jar, or doing both.

Bringing in their own bottles. Bartenders may set up their own bar business in your establishment. They pour drinks from their own bottle (so your inventory is not affected) and pocket the money from the sales. While you're not losing product, you are losing something much more important—your sales revenue! Using a bottle stamp can help to discourage this practice.

Watering down the contents of your bottles. Adding water to bottles increases the number of drinks the bartender can pour from a bottle. He or she can then pocket the money from the "extra" drinks sold. Both you and your guests get cheated in the process. Watering down your products can also cause you to lose your liquor license if the Alcoholic Beverage Commission finds your liquor is underproof. Closely watching your inventory and comparing your actual sales with your projected sales can curb this problem. Alcohol can also be tested periodically to determine if its labeled proof is accurate.

Collusion between the bartender and service staff. The bartender and server can work together in a variety of ways. They might pad the check of a large party, collectively keep track of substitutions, underpours, or under-rings, or even trade liquor for food in the kitchen. The use of **spotters** or **shoppers** (people hired to observe the bartender and servers while posing as guests) can help you discover collusion problems.

Skilled bartenders are a valued human resource, but honest skilled bartenders are a true asset.

Automatic Dispensing Systems

Automatic, electronic, and computerized dispensing systems improve portion control, inventory control, and quality control, as well as the accuracy of guest checks and the adherence to standard recipes. An automatic dispensing system's most obvious function is to pour liquor. As we have seen, control over the pouring of liquor is critical in the development of an effective control system. Some operators believe that the method you use to pour liquor might be the most important management decision you will make. The method you choose, be it to use free pour, shot glasses or jiggers, pourers, or some type of automated dispensing system, depends largely on the operation you manage.

The accountability achieved through using automated dispensing systems is hard to beat. Some additional advantages of these systems include the following:

- The accuracy and consistency of product is improved.

- There is less spillage and guest service is faster.

- The need for bartender training is reduced because the recipes and prices are all programmed.

- Prices can be easily changed to accommodate special pricing periods such as happy hour. Pricing decisions are totally under management's control.

- Almost all of the theft problems we identified previously are eliminated. The security of product inventory is improved as there are no bottles at the bar. The bartender never handles the liquor bottles.

Exhibit 10.8 Keyboard for an Automatic Dispensing System

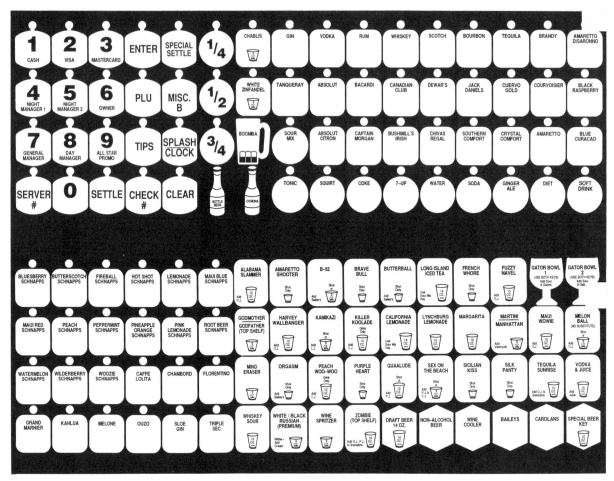

Courtesy of American Business Computers

Each guest is provided with an itemized receipt at the end of each sale. The system maintains dollar totals for cash and charge sales.

- Sales and profitability control is improved.

- A more accurate and up-to-date inventory is available any time it is requested.

- Mixes, bulk wines, and draft beer can be incorporated into the system.

- The system eliminates much paperwork.

There are a variety of automated dispensing systems on the market today. Not all of them provide you with all of the advantages presented above. Nearly every bar and beverage operation can afford the investment in at least a basic system. Higher priced systems should be more sophisticated and provide greater control.

Automated dispensing equipment typically has computerized or electronic control mechanisms attached to each bottle that monitor and control

Exhibit 10.9 Storage Racks for Automatic Dispensing System

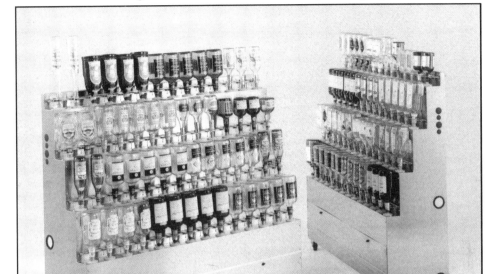

Liquor is stored in a rack in a locked storage area when an automatic dispensing system is used. (Courtesy of American Business Computers)

the amount of alcohol dispensed. The bartender requests a particular drink from the pouring station by pushing a button on a keyboard such as the one shown in Exhibit 10.8. The liquor and other mix ingredients travel from the liquor storage area (see Exhibit 10.9) to the pouring station through hidden plastic tubing. The system dispenses the drink when the bartender holds the glass under the pouring nozzle. The drink is then garnished and served to the guest.

Product control and quality are emphasized in all aspects of this system. All liquor is stored in racks in a locked storage room. Sodas and other mixes are also stored in this room. When the bartender requests a drink, the liquor and necessary mixes travel to the pouring nozzle through separate lines to maintain quality and taste. Most people wouldn't want gin or bourbon traveling through the line prior to their ordering a vodka tonic. Specific drink portion sizes and prices are all programmed by management and stored by the automated system. The pouring station from which the drink is dispensed may be connected to a guest check imprinter which records every sale as the drink is dispensed. On some systems, the guest check must be inserted into the imprinter before the drink will be dispensed. Such systems eliminate over-rings, under-rings, and forgetting to ring the guest check.

Automated systems also generate control reports. Many systems provide complete sales and inventory records. Sales reports can be generated that include the product category, time of day, server sales, and tips from charge slips as well as the sales for each pouring station. Sales can be broken down into regular versus happy hour totals. Voids and complimentary drinks are all accounted for. Inventory reports can include brand name, bottle size, bottles poured, and even ounces poured. Exhibits 10.10 and 10.11 present two samples of reports.

With all the advantages, affordability, and ease of operation, why doesn't every bar and beverage operation use an automated dispensing system? One of management's biggest criticisms is system breakdown. Remember that the more sophisticated the system is, the more control it maintains and the less control the bartender has over product. A malfunction in a system which controls every liquid you pour can literally shut down your bar operation until you either switch the system onto bypass or bring in bottles from the storeroom. In the worst case scenario, the system goes down on a busy Saturday night and your bartenders can't dispense drinks. You put the system on bypass so you can dispense drinks, but in doing so you lose practically every aspect of product control.

Another frequent criticism stems from a marketing viewpoint. Guests in the 1990s are brand conscious. They want to see the bottle, with the label, from which their drink is being poured. And some guests simply like the showmanship and ambience of a bar which pours its drinks from bottles as opposed to a dispensing gun or pouring spout. In response to this criticism, some manufacturers have created automatic dispensing systems in which the bartender uses bottles at the bar. Bottles are fitted with a special nozzle which itself then fits into a unit (either stationary or hand-held) that measures the drinks and records the sale.

Other bar and beverage operators believe that, despite manufacturers' claims, there simply is no system on the market which an innovative bartender can't beat. Some of these operators even feel that automated dispensing systems are seen as challenges to otherwise honest bartenders who feel that you do not trust them enough to handle the product they are selling. The challenge then is to beat the system. If they can't, they can deliberately cause the system to fail so that it has to be placed on bypass. Then, they can rob you blind because you have virtually no product or sales control features in place.

Most systems cannot mix all drinks. This is especially true for the wide variety of specialty and ice cream drinks which are popular today. Therefore, some drinks still need to be made by the bartender.

As a bar or beverage manager, you must weigh the advantages and disadvantages of these systems in light of your own operation. Whether you choose an automated dispensing system or not, one thing that bar and beverage operators do agree upon is that automated systems are not a substitute for good management and the establishment of high product control standards. They should not be seen as a cure-all for your control problems or be used to cover up for bad management.

Product Control and Banquet Service

Managers who are responsible for bar service during banquets and catering functions have a special set of control problems to deal with. Since the bar service will be customized to meet the needs of the guests, there are a variety of different selling methods which might be used.

In a **cash bar,** each guest pays for the drink as it is ordered. This type of bar should operate with the same type of controls as your main bar. In

Exhibit 10.10 Sample Automatically Generated Report: Sales Mix by Major Product

SAMPLE ABC COMPUTERBAR MANAGEMENT REPORT
REPORT #6 — SALES MIX BY MAJOR PRODUCT

Ring Off #22 — 2:52 a.m. 1/06
Accumulators Cleared — 8:01 a.m. 1/05

Sales Mix By Major Product	STATION 1 SALES	STATION 2 SALES	STATION 3 SALES	STATION 4 SALES	TOTAL SALES
Scotch	30.00/ 12	46.00/ 22	45.00/ 18	15.00/ 6	136.00/ 58
Chivas	.00	.00	12.50/ 6	.00	12.50/ 6
Cutty	.00	.00	4.50/ 2	.00	4.50/ 2
Dewar's	46.75/ 17	30.00/ 12	36.50/ 14	46.75/ 17	160.00/ 60
J&B	11.00/ 4	8.25/ 3	32.00/ 12	.00	51.25/ 19
JW Black	8.25/ 3	13.75/ 5	2.75/ 1	2.75/ 1	27.50/ 10
Bourbon	47.50/ 19	15.50/ 7	21.50/ 9	5.00/ 2	89.50/ 37
Granddad	.00	5.25/ 3	.00	.00	5.25/ 3
WildTurk	5.50/ 2	8.25/ 3	.00	.00	13.75/ 5
JDaniels	74.25/ 27	90.75/ 33	65.25/ 27	35.75/ 13	266.00/100
Seag 7	52.50/ 21	15.00/ 6	13.00/ 6	30.00/ 12	110.50/ 45
MakrMark	5.50/ 2	18.25/ 7	2.75/ 1	11.00/ 4	37.50/ 14
Seag VO	22.00/ 8	40.00/ 16	45.75/ 17	27.50/ 10	135.25/ 51
Cr Royal	13.75/ 5	19.25/ 7	2.75/ 1	.00	35.75/ 13
C Club	8.25/ 3	82.00/ 32	35.75/ 13	8.25/ 3	134.25/ 51
Tanquray	60.50/ 22	46.75/ 17	51.00/ 20	22.00/ 8	180.25/ 67
Beefeatr	2.75/ 1	2.75/ 1	8.25/ 3	.00	13.75/ 5
Gin	25.00/ 10	10.00/ 4	7.50/ 3	2.50/ 1	45.00/ 18
Bombay	11.00/ 4	.00	.00	.00	11.00/ 4
Absolut	16.50/ 6	38.50/ 14	16.50/ 6	2.75/ 1	74.25/ 27
Vodka	145.00/ 58	130.00/ 52	205.50/ 85	45.00/ 18	525.50/213
Stoli	46.75/ 17	40.25/ 15	76.00/ 28	19.25/ 7	182.25/ 67
Smirnoff	24.75/ 9	13.75/ 5	.00	.00	38.50/ 14
Rum	30.00/ 12	5.00/ 2	28.00/ 12	5.00/ 2	68.00/ 28
Bacardi	.00	.00	.00	11.00/ 4	11.00/ 4
Trip Sec	.00	2.50/ 1	.00	.00	2.50/ 1
Peach	75.00/ 30	27.50/ 11	5.00/ 2	17.50/ 7	125.00/ 50
Sloe Gin	.00	2.50/ 1	.00	.00	2.50/ 1
Dom Beer	428.25/191	321.00/145	218.25/ 99	119.25/ 53	1086.75/488
Imp Beer	41.25/ 15	51.25/ 19	18.25/ 7	24.75/ 9	135.50/ 50
Tequila	5.00/ 2	.00	12.50/ 5	2.50/ 1	20.00/ 8
Cuervo G	2.75/ 1	24.75/ 9	5.50/ 2	.00	33.00/ 12
Gr Marn	.00	6.50/ 2	19.50/ 6	6.50/ 2	32.50/ 10
Brandy	12.50/ 5	.00	.00	.00	12.50/ 5
Menthe L	17.50/ 7	.00	7.50/ 3	.00	25.00/ 10
Menthe G	.00	.00	2.50/ 1	.00	2.50/ 1
Cacao Dk	2.50/ 1	.00	.00	.00	2.50/ 1
Drambuie	19.50/ 6	.00	6.50/ 2	.00	26.00/ 8
Di Saron	6.50/ 2	.00	3.25/ 1	.00	9.75/ 3
Amorita	19.50/ 6	.00	7.75/ 3	.00	27.25/ 9
Frngelco	.00	.00	3.25/ 1	.00	3.25/ 1
Chrdonay	.00	3.00/ 1	.00	3.00/ 1	6.00/ 2
Kamora	32.50/ 10	.00	4.50/ 2	.00	37.00/ 12

continued

Sales Mix By Major Product	STATION 1	STATION 2	STATION 3	STATION 4	TOTAL SALES
Midori	3.25/ 1	.00	.00	.00	3.25/ 1
Chablis	5.25/ 3	15.75/ 9	21.75/ 13	8.75/ 5	51.50/ 30
Sambuca	.00	26.00/ 8	45.50/ 14	.00	71.50/ 22
TiaMaria	.00	.00	7.75/ 3	.00	7.75/ 3
Zinfndel	21.00/ 7	21.00/ 7	36.00/ 12	6.00/ 2	84.00/ 28
Soda	.00	.00	1.75/ 5	.00/ 3	1.75/ 9
LemLime	1.75/ 2	.00	1.75/ 1	.00/ 1	3.50/ 4
SeagCool	.00	12.25/ 7	1.75/ 1	.00	14.00/ 8
Cola	.00	1.75/ 1	10.25/ 6	1.75/ 1	13.75/ 15
Tonic	.00	1.75/ 1	.00/ 1	.00	1.75/ 2
Diet	.00	5.00/ 3	1.75/ 1	7.00/ 6	13.75/ 10
Martini	10.25/ 3	13.75/ 4	21.25/ 7	78.75/ 23	124.00/ 37
Manhattn	3.25/ 1	3.25/ 1	40.25/ 13	.00	46.75/ 15
Mai-Tai	11.00/ 3	11.00/ 3	.00	.00	11.00/ 3
Wh Sour	5.75/ 2	28.75/ 10	15.50/ 5	.00	50.00/ 17
TCollins	5.00/ 2	7.50/ 3	10.00/ 4	.00	22.50/ 9
Daiquiri	13.00/ 4	.00	1.50/ 1	3.00/ 1	4.50/ 2
Bl Russn	.00	2.25/ 1	2.25/ 1	.00	17.50/ 6
Rusty Nl	19.50/ 6	.00	6.50/ 2	.00	6.50/ 2
Stinger	.00	.00	.00	.00	19.50/ 6
Kamikaze	85.00/ 34	85.00/ 34	27.50/ 11	.00	197.50/ 79
Spritzer	1.75/ 1	3.50/ 2	17.50/ 10	1.75/ 1	24.50/ 14
Ice Tea	26.00/ 8	32.50/ 10	26.00/ 8	9.75/ 3	94.25/ 29
Lemonade	.00	6.50/ 2	.00	3.25/ 1	9.75/ 3
W Cooler	1.75/ 1	1.75/ 1	1.75/ 1	.00	5.25/ 3
Margrita	12.50/ 5	2.50/ 1	.00	.00	15.00/ 6
PeachDaq	.00	3.50/ 1	.00	.00	3.50/ 1
B-52	52.00/ 16	6.50/ 2	3.25/ 1	.00	61.75/ 19
V Hammer	.00	.00	7.00/ 2	7.00/ 2	7.00/ 2
LaBoomer	.00	.00	3.50/ 1	.00	3.50/ 1
Spec Ctl	58.50/ 18	9.75/ 3	35.75/ 11	.00	104.00/ 32
Totals	**1686.75**	**1415.25**	**1371.00**	**590.00**	**5063.00**

Sales Mix By Product Lookup	STATION 1 SALES	STATION 2 SALES	STATION 3 SALES	STATION 4 SALES	TOTAL SALES
Moet Chandon	38.00/ 1	38.00/ 1	.00	.00	76.00/ 2
Cajun	.00	.00	6.95/ 1	.00	6.95/ 1
Barb Chick	6.95/ 1	13.90/ 2	.00	.00	20.85/ 3
Wild Mush	.00	6.95/ 1	.00	.00	6.95/ 1
Brie	.00	.00	4.95/ 1	.00	4.95/ 1
Thai Chick	6.95/ 1	.00	.00	.00	6.95/ 1
Reuben	.00	5.95/ 1	.00	.00	5.95/ 1
Mush Pep Sau	5.95/ 1	29.75/ 5	11.90/ 2	.00	47.60/ 8
Totals	**57.85**	**94.55**	**23.80**	**.00**	**176.20**

ACCUMULATORS ARE CLEARED

ABC Version JOT6A   *ABC ComputerBar*™

Courtesy of American Business Computers

Exhibit 10.11 Sample Automatically Generated Report: Product Usage

SAMPLE ABC COMPUTERBAR MANAGEMENT REPORT
REPORT #7 — PRODUCT USAGE

Ring Off #22 — 2:52 a.m. 1/06
Accumulators Cleared — 8:01 a.m. 1/05

Product Usage	Bottle Size	Ounces Poured	Bottles Emptied
Scotch	1.75 L	77	1
Chivas Regal	1.75 L	7	
Cutty Sark	1.75 L	2	
Dewar's	1.75 L	82	1
J&B	1.75 L	24	
JWalker Black	1.75 L	17	
Bourbon	1.75 L	54	1
Jack Daniels	1.75 L	130	2
Jim Beam	1.75 L		
Makers Mark	1.75 L	17	
Old Granddad	1.75 L	3	
Wild Turkey	1.75 L	6	
Canadian Club	1.75 L	64	1
Crown Royal	1.75 L	17	
Irish Whiskey	1.75 L	1	
Seagram's 7	1.75 L	60	1
Seagram's VO	1.75 L	73	2
Gin	1.75 L	43	1
Beefeater	1.75 L	6	
Bombay	1.75 L	5	
Tanqueray	1.75 L	92	1
Vodka	1.75 L	414	7
Absolut	1.75 L	34	1
Smirnoff	1.75 L	18	
Stolichnaya	Liter	111	3
Rum	1.75 L	66	1
Bacardi	1.75 L	5	
Myers's	1.75 L		
Tequila	1.75 L	15	
Cuervo Gold	1.75 L	15	
Brandy	1.75 L	15	
Apricot	Liter		

Almond	Liter	4	
Cacao Dark	Liter	3	
Cacao Light	Liter	1	
Menthe Green	Liter	1	
Menthe Light	Liter	15	
Midori	Liter	2·	
Peach Schnaps	1.75 L	68	1
Sloe Gin	Liter	1	
Triple Sec	1.75 L	42	1
Di Saronna	1.75 L	3	
Amorita	Liter	27	
Drambuie	1.75 L	12	1
Frangelico	750 ml	1	
Grand Marnier	1.75 L	19	1
Kahlua	1.75 L	4	
Kamora	Liter	29	1
Sambuca	750 ml	28	1
Tia Maria	Liter	15	1
Chablis	1 Gal	234	1
Chardonnay	1 Gal	10	
Wht Zinfandel	1 Gal	159	1
Margarita Mix	5 Gal	2	1
Sour Mix	5 Gal	138	
LemLime Syrup	1 Gal	32	
SeagramsCoolr	1 Gal	7	
Cola Syrup	1 Gal	36	1
Tonic Syrup	1 Gal	40	1
Diet Syrup	1 Gal	9	
Soda	1 Gal	799	6
Water	1 Gal	42	

ACCUMULATORS ARE CLEARED

continued

ABC Version JOT 6A   *ABC ComputerBar*™

Courtesy of American Business Computers

remote locations, the use of automated dispensing systems is highly unlikely, so pouring methods and standards will need to be established.

In a **hosted bar,** the host or hostess pays for all the drinks consumed by the guests at the end of the event. The price, agreed upon ahead of time, may be per bottle, per drink, or per person. When the price is per bottle, a special par stock is set up just for that function and the amount of liquor consumed is computed by subtracting the ending inventory from the par. If payment is to be made by drink count, then the bartender must use some method determined by management to keep track of the drinks poured. This can provide for loose product control if you are not very careful. Some bar and beverage operations have a cashier sell tickets which then can be given to the bartender in exchange for a drink. This eliminates the need for the bartender to handle cash, permitting faster service and tighter controls. A cross-check can be made with product inventory by subtracting ending inventory from the banquet par stock. The number of ounces consumed should match with the drink tickets sold *and* collected. Exhibit 10.12 shows a sample banquet beverage control sheet.

Sales and Profitability Control

Sales and profitability control looks at the relationships among costs, sales, and profit in the bar or beverage operation. These relationships form the basis for your cost control measures. The objective of any beverage control system for sales and profitability is to keep costs as low as possible. Many of these control procedures begin in purchasing and must carry through to the sale of the product.

Cost control information allows you to look at your operation both historically and currently to determine the action plans needed for future success. The better your cost control information, the quicker you will be able to take corrective action to prevent serious harm from being done to sales and profitability. This is the reason we call this control system **sales and profitability control** as opposed to cost control. Costs are indeed what we seek to control, but only as they have an effect on sales and profitability. Let's now examine the various components of this second primary control system.

Determining Product Cost

Costs are the expenses we incur in providing the products and services we offer. The **actual cost** of our liquid assets is the amount of money we paid to buy them. This is considered to be a **direct cost** since it can be charged directly as a cost of doing business. That is, generally speaking, as sales go up, so does the cost incurred in buying liquor. As sales go down, so does the cost of buying liquor. The cost of beverages is also called a **variable cost** for the same reasons. The cost of product varies with sales.

The formula for calculating the beverage cost for a specified period is as follows:

$$\text{Beginning Inventory} + \text{Purchases} - \text{Ending Inventory} = \text{Cost of Product Consumed}$$

In food and beverage operations which commonly transfer food products such as juices, fruit for garnishes, and so forth to the bar, adjustments need to be made to the gross cost. Similar adjustments must be made for any products transferred from the bar to the kitchen, such as wine for cooking. In these cases, the gross beverage cost would be adjusted as follows:

$$\text{Gross Beverage Cost} + \text{Transfers to Bar} - \text{Transfers from Bar} = \text{Net Beverage Cost}$$

There are also indirect costs associated with selling alcoholic beverages. Realistically, consideration should be given to storage costs including space/equipment, labor (handling), and the cost of maintaining your inventory. Don't forget that the money you have invested in inventory could be earning interest dollars elsewhere. The successful bar or beverage manager

Exhibit 10.12 Banquet Beverage Control Form

OPRYLAND HOTEL		BANQUET BEVERAGE CONTROL								

FUNCTION _____ DATE _____

ROOM _____ B.E.O. # _____

TYPE BAR: CASH   HOSTED □ _____ TIME: _____ AMOUNT $ _____

	OPEN STOCK	ISSUES			TOTAL ISSUED	UNITS RETURNED	CONSUMED			
							UNITS USED	DRINKS USED	SALES AMOUNT	COST AMOUNT
PREMIUM										
Jack Daniels Black	LIT.									
Smirnoff Vodka	LIT.									
Beefeater Gin	LIT.									
Canadian Club	LIT.									
J & B Scotch	LIT.									
Bacardi Rum	LIT.									
Kentucky Tavern	LIT.									
DELUXE										
Stolichnaya (or) Absolut	LIT.									
Tanqueray	LIT.									
Crown Royal	LIT.									
Wild Turkey	LIT.									
Bartles & Jaymes	12 oz.									
Concannon Vintage White	1.5									
Concannon Burgundy	1.5									
Concannon White Zinfandel	1.5									
Michelob	12 oz.									
Michelob Light	12 oz.									
Corona	12 oz.									

SALES RECAPITULATION

UNITS ISSUED	DRINKS BTL.	DRINKS SERVED		DRINK PRICE	VALUE	% COST
LIQUOR	X		X			
WINE	X		X			
BEER	X		X			
BARTLES & JAYMES	X		X			
SODAS	X		X			
	X		X			
	X		X			
	X		X			

Bar Opened & Closed _____

Bartenders _____

Barboys _____

Remarks: _____

TICKET/CHECKS

COLOR			
LAST NO. USED			
STARTING NO.			
SOLD			
USED			
NOT USED			

RECAP

Units Consumed as Per Iventory		
Unit Used as Per Ticket Sales		
Difference	Over	
	Short	

WHITE—BANQUETS
YELLOW—ACCOUNTING
PINK—CATERING

FORM 3785

Courtesy of Opryland Hotel, Nashville, Tennessee

must consider in detail every aspect of beverage cost from the time a beverage leaves the purveyor to the time it reaches the guest.

In addition to the factors just discussed, several other factors can contribute to high beverage costs:

- Poor pricing
- Too large an inventory
- Purchasing brands which are too expensive
- No audit of invoices and payments
- Excessive spillage or breakage
- No check on use of standard recipes
- Overproduction (failing to adhere to standard recipes)
- No forecast of sales or costs

Sales Accountability/ Sales Analysis

In addition to keeping costs as low as possible, you must make sure that the bar or beverage operation receives all of the income it is supposed to receive. Beverage operations present unique product control challenges since so many of our employees have access to the products we sell.

The starting point for controlling sales accountability is having some idea of how much income should be coming in. The simplest way to determine total bar sales is to multiply the number of drinks sold by the selling price. Daily cash register receipts will tell you the actual number of drinks sold at each selling price. The next step is determining the beverage cost percentage, calculated by dividing the net beverage cost by total bar sales. For example, if net beverage cost were $6,722 and total bar sales were $38,994, the beverage cost percentage would be:

$$\$6,722 \div \$38,994 = .172 \text{ or } 17.2\%$$

The **gross profit** on sales in the above example is almost 83%. Is that good? It depends on your particular operation. The computation above shows your **actual beverage cost percentage.** Let's compare that percentage with the **potential beverage cost percentage.** This is calculated by determining the sales value per bottle (that is, the number of drinks per bottle times the selling price per drink). For example, if drink size is 1.25 ounces, one liter (33.8 fluid ounces) will yield approximately 27 drinks; if drinks sell for $2.50, the sales value per bottle is $67.50 (27 × $2.50).[1] The cost of the bottle (let's say $6.22) divided by the sales value per bottle equals the potential beverage cost percentage:

$$\$6.22 \div \$67.50 = .09 \text{ or } 9\%$$

Your potential beverage cost percentage should then be compared against your actual beverage cost percentage for wide variations. In the above example, the actual beverage cost percentage was 17.2%, while the potential beverage cost percentage was 9%. Given sales of $38,994, this variation between the potential and actual beverage cost percentages cost the operation a minimum of $3,213—the difference between actual beverage costs of $6,722 and potential beverage costs of $3,509 ($38,994 × 9%). In fact, since at least some of the variation is probably caused by failure to take in all money that was due for drinks served, the operation has also lost sales revenue. Variations such as this call for immediate analysis. While there is no industry standard stating how large a variation should be acceptable, you should seek to minimize or even eliminate the variation.

Because distilled spirits, wine, and beer each sell at different cost percentages, you should calculate them separately to see a true beverage cost percentage. Any fluctuations in the beverage cost percentage indicate a potential control problem that requires immediate analysis to determine if corrective action should be taken. The types of information found on your cash register receipts depend largely on the sophistication of your point-of-sale system.

Gross Profit. There is no one right number we can give you for gross profit that will guarantee your success. What is good or acceptable for one operation might be considered very high for another. We can tell you, though, that mixed and premium drinks generally yield the largest gross profit. Compared to well brands, call brands can add an average of 28 cents to the gross profit of a mixed drink.[2] To determine your total gross profit, you must first calculate your cost per drink:[3]

Ounces/drink	Drinks/case	Avg. $/case	Cost/drink
1.25	324.5*	$74.63	$.23

$$*\text{Drinks/case} = \frac{\text{fluid ounces/liter} \times 12 \text{ liters/case}}{\text{fluid ounces/drink}}$$

$$= \frac{33.8 \times 12}{1.25}$$

Suppose that the above example is for well brands which make up (let's say) 35% of the total number of drinks you sell. Assuming 1,000 drinks are sold, you would calculate the total gross profit as follows:

$$
\begin{aligned}
\text{Total Gross Profit} &= \left(\begin{array}{c} \text{Drink} \\ \text{Selling} \\ \text{Price} \end{array} - \begin{array}{c} \text{Cost} \\ \text{per} \\ \text{Drink} \end{array} \right) \times \begin{array}{c} 35\% \text{ of the} \\ \text{Total Number} \\ \text{of Drinks Sold} \end{array} \\
&= (\$2.50 - \$.23) \times 350 \\
&= \$794.50
\end{aligned}
$$

The records that you compile on a daily, weekly, or monthly basis will use the information we have discussed so far to assist you with your control of both sales and profitability. These records can be used to reveal inconsistencies between potential and actual sales and costs. Not only does this information allow you to monitor the performance of your bar or beverage operation, but it can also assist you in maximizing profits by allowing you to correct problems as quickly as possible. To achieve this, both dollar and percentage figures are calculated. The most effective bar and beverage managers do not wait to see their operation's monthly reports; they check weekly, even daily, if they feel close monitoring is warranted. A **sales analysis** measures whether the sales objectives or projections have been met for a designated period of time. This is done by comparing the actual sales figures against the potential sales. A number of factors could be responsible for a variance between actual and potential, including:

- Spillage

- Theft

- Incorrect pouring size

- Not following standard recipes

- Improper documentation of voids

- Ringing incorrect prices

- Incorrect inventory

Sales and profitability controls allow the bar or beverage manager to monitor the effectiveness of each bartender. The use of guest checks, point-of-sale systems, automated dispensing systems, and pre-check registers are all tools which assist you in this process. Variations between projections and actual sales figures probably indicate a slippage in the established standards.

Pricing   Pricing was discussed in Chapter 8 in reference to its relationship to your competitive factors. Obviously, how much competition you have and what it charges for its drinks are both important considerations. For example, an up-scale lounge in a five-star hotel might be able to get $5 for its mixed drinks because guests want to stay in the property. Your local neighborhood bar might consider itself lucky if it can get $2 because there are several bars in the area. Airports can charge $3 for a draft beer because most travelers don't have time to leave the terminal in search of a cheaper price.

While competitive factors are important to pricing, a pricing strategy does not begin with the competition. Nor does it begin with product cost or theoretical pricing formulas. Rather, it begins with the economic environment found in your particular operation. The word "strategy" implies that you are trying to devise a plan. But "strategy" also implies a conceptual element. Accordingly, the following discussion provides a conceptual framework which will lead you to sound pricing decisions. While relying solely on theoretical pricing formulas certainly makes the calculation of prices easier, it also wrongly suggests that pricing decisions can be made irrespective of management judgment. There are *no* magic formulas for pricing in the bar and beverage business.

Good judgment in pricing should not be mistaken for intuition or a trial and error approach. Rather, it is a thorough understanding of the operation you manage and your market—what it wants, how to satisfy it. The most important components of an effective pricing strategy are those related to the economic environment. Costs must be covered, a profit must be made, and guests must be pleased so sales are good. Goals must be established so management can design strategies (plans) to reach them. This takes someone who really knows the business. Pricing is not a job for amateurs.

While management judgment is more important than formulas in pricing, management still uses theoretical pricing formulas. In fact, management often uses theoretical pricing formulas as one of its tools to achieve a targeted total revenue figure. Such formulas provide prices which management can then modify and consider in relation to other factors to help ensure that the total revenue goal is met. Thus, theoretical pricing formulas are used as broad guides.

There are a number of factors which might make management modify a price based on a theoretical formula or what we will call here a "formula-based price." A competitor's price for the same drink might be such that a formula-based price cannot be used. Or management may find that its guests have become so used to a price that they strongly resist any increase to a higher formula-based price.

A common method of using management judgment to supersede formula pricing is called "charging what the market will bear." Sometimes management knows its market will take a much higher price than the formula-based price. In other cases, it knows that the formula-based price is too high for the market and must be scaled down. Where you can go above the formula-based price, you usually have what is called a **high gross item** (because of the high gross profit it provides); where the price has to be scaled down, you usually have a **low gross item.** Management tries in merchandising and through other means to balance out high and low gross items in its sales so that the total revenues goal is approximately reached. In setting up a list of available drinks, management commonly puts high gross items at the start or end of a column because these items stand out. High gross items may also be highlighted on a menu by some means to call attention to them. Servers may be told to push high gross items.

Management may also modify formula-based prices as a promotional activity. Often, management will advertise some special promotional plan. Prices might be lowered on some or all drinks for advertising purposes. The formula-based profit margin goal is not met, but management charges off the difference to advertising. Management also uses special promotions to increase business during known slow periods—certain hours of the day or certain days or nights. Formula-based prices are reduced because management wants to bring in guests at this time. In the end, management profits because this extra business takes care of labor and other costs that would be incurred anyway. The result is worthwhile even though you do not achieve your desired pour cost or profit margin on the products sold. (In the past, happy hour promotions were used for this purpose, but such promotions have fallen into disfavor because of their tendency to encourage overdrinking and their use has declined greatly.)

Whether an operation sells only beverages or sells both food and beverages, the basic principle of pricing mentioned here applies. Formula-based pricing is modified by management judgment in both cases. Exhibit 10.13 is a short summary of some pricing formulas used in pricing either food or beverages. This is not a complete listing of methods used.

The cost percentages for food and beverages typically differ. It is common to see drink prices based on ingredient costs of around 20% to 25%, while the target will be set higher for food ingredient costs, usually 35% to 40%. Where drinks and food are both served, it is common to keep separate accounting figures for each, as well as combined totals. This

Exhibit 10.14   Summary of Sample Pour Cost Calculation

	Amount	Percentage of total sales
Return on investment (net profit)	$ 35,000	6.2%
All non-ingredient costs	405,000	71.8
Total profit and non-ingredient costs	$440,000	78.0
Total sales ($440,000 ÷ 0.78)	564,100	100.0
Pour cost	112,820	20.0
Balance for meeting change	11,280	2.0

alter each beverage type's percentage. Informed management judgment is needed.

Your next pricing strategy decision involves determining how you can be competitive with your desired pour cost. Since marketing drives sales, the prices you charge must be competitive and guest-oriented. It is the guest who will determine if your prices are fair. Hence, your prices must take into consideration how much your target market is willing to pay. This is known as the guest's value perception, the way he or she relates the price of the drink to the value he or she receives from ordering and drinking it at your establishment.

The fact that price affects guest demand for products and services highlights a problem with the budgeting and pricing processes. The budget, based in part on expected sales, determines the amount of sales necessary to meet the desired profit. It also produces a beverage cost percentage that is used to set prices. However, how can estimated sales be used to set prices when those prices will affect actual sales? More to the point, what happens when the beverage cost percentage leads to prices that guests refuse to pay? In such cases, you will need to cut costs, raise sales, and/or accept smaller profits. The most difficult and mysterious element of pricing is predicting the effect of pricing on demand.

The goals of an effective pricing strategy are to ensure that all guests are charged the same price for their drinks and to guarantee operation profitability—that is, protect the bottom line. Therefore it is extremely important that drink prices be standardized and that all bartenders and service staff know the pricing structure. Because it is impractical to charge slightly different prices for the hundreds of drinks your operation may serve, drink prices are generally standardized within categories by calculating the average selling price of drinks that fall in each category. Typical drink categories for purposes of pricing are:

- Straight drinks, well

- Straight drinks, call

- Cocktails, well

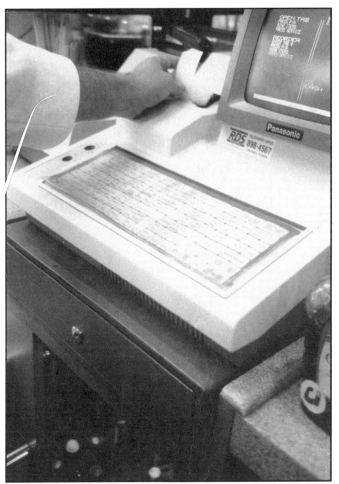

Computerized point-of-sale systems are essential for cash control. (Courtesy of Strongbow Inn, Valparaiso, Indiana)

- Cocktails, call

- Frozen and specialty drinks

- Beer, domestic

- Beer, imported

- Wine, house

- Wine, premium

- Non-alcoholic

The categories you select for your bar and beverage operation will be based upon the products you sell and your target market. Bartenders and servers must be trained in the importance of maintaining the price structure you establish and should *never* be allowed to determine the price that will be charged for a drink.

Spotters or shoppers can detect both theft and a failure to follow standard operating procedures. (Courtesy of Concessions International, Inc.)

agement with all the information needed for accurate decision-making. There are three primary areas under which all controls fall: product, sales/profitability, and cash. The two objectives in each of these areas are the control of quality and the control of costs.

In large bar and beverage operations, a controller and staff will assist you in establishing and maintaining cost control. In smaller operations, however, the bar or beverage manager will be totally responsible for maintaining the control system. There are many decisions which you will need to make. From establishing pouring procedures and standards to handling cash, each of these decisions will affect the profitability and the quality of the operation you manage.

Endnotes

1. If a bottle of liquor is used in drinks with different drink sizes and prices, you will need to determine a weighted average for both drink size and selling price. This involves adding up the number of drinks sold over a given time using a given liquor (vodka, for instance) and the number of ounces of liquor used in those drinks. The number of drinks sold divided by the number of ounces used gives you your average

drink size. This number divided into your bottle size equals the average number of drinks per bottle. You then multiply this number by your average selling price (total sales of vodka drinks divided by number of vodka drinks sold) to get your potential sales value per bottle.

2. Distilled Spirits Council of the United States, "Making a Buck on Booze," *Lodging Hospitality* 13 (#44, 1988): 13.

3. We have not computed an allowance for spillage in this example for purposes of clarifying our emphasis on gross profit. As was discussed in Chapter 8, many bar and beverage operators do figure a percentage for spillage in their calculations. This is a management decision upon which opinions vary. This example has been further simplified by excluding the cost of the garnish and mixer. If the recipe called for products in addition to the alcohol, the cost of those products would need to be included.

Key Terms

actual beverage cost percentage	hosted bar
actual cost	jiggers
automatic/computerized bar systems	low gross item
	measured pouring
bank	potential beverage cost percentage
bottom-up approach	pour cost
cash bar	pourers
cash control	product control
check control sheet	sales analysis
controlling	sales and profitability control
direct cost	shoppers
drink size	shot glasses
free pour	spotters
full bottle slip	variable cost
gross profit	void control sheet
high gross item	

Discussion Questions

1. How does establishing a standard pour size for drinks contribute to your control system?

2. Why should bartenders not be allowed to work out of an open cash drawer?

3. What functions can spotters or shoppers perform in a control system?

4. What are the advantages and disadvantages of using automated beverage dispensing systems?

5. How would you determine your actual and potential beverage cost percentages? Why would you want to do this?

6. What does a sales analysis measure?

7. How are theoretical pricing formulas best used in setting prices? How should they *not* be used?

8. What is meant by "backing into" your pricing structure? What are the advantages of doing this?

9. What role does a void control sheet play in cash control?

10. What are several possible characteristics of a tight cash control system?

The Legal Jungle

Chapter Outline

Federal Control
    A Brief History of Federal Regulation
    The FAAA
    Laws Influencing Internal Operations
        Employment Laws
            Civil Rights Act
            Sexual harassment
            Gender
            Alien employment
            Wrongful discharge
State Control
    Licenses and Permits
    Control and License States
    Handling Problem Guests
    Employment at Will
    Miscellaneous State Regulations
Community or Local Regulations
Potential Liability
    Drinking on the Job
    Wine Tastings
    Business Liability
    Serving Effervescent Wines
Words and the Law
The Importance of Prudent Preparation

The variety of laws governing and affecting bar and beverage operations throughout the world is enormous. It is not possible in a single chapter to discuss completely those of even one country, much less every country. Still, to give you some idea of the scope of the laws you may have to deal with, we will focus here on providing an introduction to the nature and complexity of U.S. law.

The alcohol industry is perhaps the most regulated industry in the United States. The tremendous number and variety of laws within the United States is due largely to the fact that, in addition to the federal government, each state and thousands of local communities enact their own laws and regulations. Anyone dispensing alcoholic beverages to the public must be aware of and responsive to all applicable laws. The failure to comply with such laws can lead to adverse court decisions, court and attorney's fees, fines, penalties, and even criminal indictments. Furthermore, the publicity given violations sometimes harms a business more than the court-imposed penalties. It is wise to consult good legal counsel if you want to operate in what is often thought of as the legal jungle.

Our judicial systems may also differ from state to state because of the code differences on which each state's legal system is based. Some states are what we call **common law states.** Common law is not passed by legislatures. Rather, in these states, major emphasis is placed on using previous court decisions as the basis for saying what the law is. Many central and western states are common law states. This does not mean that such states have no laws created by legislation—they all do—but rather that they give emphasis to common law. Common law came to the United States from English law. In contrast, some states are what we call **statutory states.** In these states, largely in the East and South, the emphasis is on laws created by legislation.

Louisiana differs from all other states in that it relies on the Napoleonic Code. Its laws are largely based on legislative passage, but also come from a traditional code that grew out of old Roman law.

In this discussion we attempt to differentiate between federal, state, and local laws. However, there are sometimes no clear lines of demarcation. A federal law may address a topic that is also addressed by state and/or local law. Jurisdictions often overlap, for example, with regard to taxes, sanitation, and health laws. In addition to discussing laws which must be directly obeyed, this chapter will look at a legal environment which affects businesses more indirectly by suggesting areas which need policies to address them. To reduce or avoid potential liability, for example, operators may set policies that are not legally required, but which represent prudent action in the face of such potential liability.

Federal Control

Federal law covers three basic areas: the sale of alcoholic beverages to the public, internal operations, and the dealings between the retailer and wholesaler. The first of these topics—selling alcohol to the public—presents many legal pitfalls to the unwary or careless operator. Because of this topic's prominence in today's public consciousness, we devoted part of Chapter 2 to an examination of many of its elements—serving minors, serving to or beyond the point of intoxication, third-party liability, off-hour sales, and so forth. Laws governing internal operations and retailer/wholesaler relations are not similarly in the public mind today, but the failure to obey them can often be very costly.

A Brief History of Federal Regulation

The first U.S. federal law controlling the production, marketing, sale, and taxation of alcoholic beverages was passed in 1791. It proved to be very unpopular, as evidenced in part by the Pennsylvania Whiskey Rebellion in 1794. In this rebellion, Pennsylvania farmers refused to pay a liquor tax on their home-distilled liquor and attacked (both singly and in an apparently organized "army" of around 500 people) federal agents attempting to collect it. President Washington sent in federal troops, which effectively quelled the uprising and established the right of the federal government to tax liquor. Still, the law's unpopularity led to its repeal in 1802. In 1813, Congress tried again, but in 1818 again had to repeal the law. It was not until 1862 that a law was passed that endured. In the same year, the Office of Commissioner of Internal Revenue of the Treasury Department was created and given the responsibility of administering the new regulations.

The FAAA

Today, federal regulation and control comes largely from the Federal Alcohol Administration Act (FAAA) of 1935, Title 27, U.S. Code, and its corresponding regulations. (Copies of the FAAA are available from the Bureau of Alcohol, Tobacco and Firearms, or BATF.) The FAAA requires all establishments producing, warehousing, or bottling alcoholic beverages to be federally licensed and to operate under federal law and regulations. Its far-reaching provisions govern how the alcoholic beverage industry must be operated. In the discussion that follows, we mention a number of provisions in this law that affect retailers, called **on-premise retail dealers** by the federal government. Control over this area has been placed with the BATF of the Treasury Department.

The BATF is responsible for the prevention, detection, and investigation of violations of this law. One of its jobs is to ferret out and stop the sale of alcohol upon which no tax has been paid. Its agents are the well-known "Feds" prominent in law enforcement for their detection of hidden distilleries in Kentucky and Tennessee, where some of the spirit of the Whiskey Rebellion still exists.

A major element of federal taxation of alcoholic beverages occurs at the production or bottling level. Exhibit 11.1 indicates the federal tax schedule as passed in 1990.

Standards of identity under the FAAA state exactly what a product must be to bear a particular name. To be called a gin, a bourbon, a wine, a lager, or anything else, an alcoholic beverage must meet precise BATF definitions. These standards are discussed in the following chapters under the different kinds of alcoholic beverages. When we provide definitions in this book, they either match or are not substantially different from the federal standards.

The FAAA requires enforcement of regulations governing how business is to be conducted between an on-premise retail dealer and wholesalers who supply alcoholic beverages to this dealer. Retailers must know these regulations and how they can invite criminal prosecution if violated. Retailing includes not only selling packaged take-out goods in a liquor store, but also dispensing drinks to the public from a bar, lounge, restaurant, hotel, or other establishment. The following discussion looks at some

Exhibit 11.1 Federal Excise Tax on Alcoholic Beverages

Distilled Spirits	$13.50/proof gallon*
Wine	
Still wines not more than 14% by volume	1.07/gallon
Still wines over 14% but not more than 21% by volume	1.57/gallon
Still wines over 21% but not more than 24% by volume	3.15/gallon
Artificially carbonated wines	3.30/gallon
Champagne or sparkling wines	4.30/gallon
Beer	18.00/barrel**
Small brewers producing not more than 2,000,000 barrels per year:	
First 60,000 barrels	14.00/barrel
Barrels over 60,000	18.00/barrel

*A proof gallon is one gallon (231 cubic inches) containing 50% ethyl alcohol by volume.
**A barrel holds 31 gallons.

of the major provisions of the FAAA. However, this is only a summary; it is not meant to be a substitute for reviewing the law itself and consulting an attorney.

It is unlawful for anyone selling alcoholic beverages to the public to require an on-premise retail dealer to purchase such products from a "sole source to the exclusion of other sources," even a minimum quantity for a limited time. For example, an enterprise, say a race track, cannot require a concessionaire with a contract to serve alcohol on the enterprise's premises to purchase alcohol supplies only from a designated source. It is also illegal to set up a sales contract through competitive bidding that requires a retailer to purchase from a sole source or from limited sources. Any threat, act of violence, or coercion to force a retailer to purchase from certain sources is illegal, as is offering a bonus, a premium, compensation, or some other thing of value as a bribe.

It is also illegal to make what are called **tied-house agreements**. For the purpose of gaining a tied-house agreement, a supplier may not (among other things):

- Help a retailer get or pay for a license.

- Have a legal or financial interest in the business.

- Rent or purchase space in the seller's operation or furnish free warehousing.

- Extend credit over 30 days.

- Give, furnish, rent, lend, or sell equipment or supplies to a retailer, except for items like product displays, wire racks, and inside signs if these items do not cost the supplier more than $127, not including transportation or installation costs (a few other exceptions are noted below). No outside signs, even on buildings near the establishment, may be furnished.

A supplier may not require a retailer to take or dispose of any quota or brand of alcoholic beverages. It is also illegal for a supplier to list in advertisements the name and address of a retailer that purchases the supplier's products unless (1) no retail price is given, (2) the listing is the only reference to the retailer, and (3) the listing is relatively inconspicuous in relation to the whole advertisement.

A consignment sale is an arrangement in which the retailer is under no obligation to pay for items received until they are sold. Usually the retailer can return any unsold products. Any consignment arrangement is illegal in the alcoholic beverage business. It is also illegal to exchange one product for another conditioned upon the acquisition of other products in addition.

Generally speaking, a supplier can furnish posters, window signs, decorations, placards, or items carrying advertising matter such as coasters, trays, napkins, thermometers, ash trays, printed recipes, blotters, can or bottle openers, postcards, and so forth, if the value of what is supplied does not exceed $62 per year. With certain limitations, a supplier can also:

- Give, rent, loan, or sell printing cuts (engraved blocks) for advertising or give or sponsor educational seminars for employees.

- Sell beer tapping supplies, glassware, or carbon dioxide gas or ice at cost or above, if the price is collected within 30 days of the date of sale.

- Furnish, give, or sell a beer coil cleaning service.

- Give product samples to a retailer who has not purchased the brand from that seller, limited to three gallons of any malt beverage, 500 milliliters of a distilled spirit, or three liters of wine (some state laws limit this—check to see what is allowed in your state).

- Conduct tasting or sampling activities in the retailer's establishment.

- Supply customer coupons redeemable at the retail establishment, if the coupon does not specify the retailer or retailer group as redeemers.

- Offer contest prizes, premiums, or refunds directly to the consumer through advertising at the retailer's establishment.

Suppliers can assist a convention of a retailer's association by displaying products, renting advertising space, providing their own hospitality independent of association-sponsored activities, purchasing tickets to functions, and paying registration fees (if not excessive) or making payments for advertising at the retailer's functions if the total payments do not exceed a specified amount per year.

Laws Influencing Internal Operations

There are a wide number of laws that govern how a business is to be conducted. Some of these apply only to bar and beverage units, while others apply to all businesses. Because of their scope, we summarize only the major laws below.

Employment Laws. There are many employment laws which must be observed. These include provisions in the Civil Rights Act, National Labor Relations Act, Fair Labor Standards Act, Immigration Reform and Control Act, Equal Pay Act, Age Discrimination in Employment Act, Federal Wage Garnishment Act, and Americans with Disabilities Act, as well as various elements of public policy.[1]

Civil Rights Act. The Civil Rights Act of 1964 brought about significant changes in the manner in which individuals were to be employed and treated on the job. Today, an employer can easily run afoul of the law's provisions. Under the Civil Rights Act, employment discrimination on the basis of race, color, sex, religion, or national origin is prohibited.

Sexual harassment. In 1980, the Equal Employment Opportunity Commission (EEOC), the agency charged with enforcing Title VII of the Civil Rights Act, published some guidelines on what constitutes sexual harassment. It defined sexual harassment as:

> [U]nwelcome sexual advances, requests for sexual favors, and other verbal or physical conduct of a sexual nature . . . when
>
> 1. Submission to such conduct is made either explicitly or implicitly a term or condition of a person's employment; or,
> 2. Submission to or rejection of such conduct by a person is used as the basis of employment decisions affecting such person; or,
> 3. Such conduct has the purpose or effect of unreasonably interfering with a person's work performance or creating an intimidating, hostile, or offensive working environment.[2]

A number of sexual harassment court cases have favored the plaintiff and imposed substantial penalties. Some of these have involved complaints by cocktail service personnel asked to wear abbreviated costumes or "hot pants." Because the employees had been discharged for refusal to wear the required dress, they were reinstated in their jobs with full back pay, payment of the claimants' court costs, and reasonable attorney's fees. In a court case in the state of New York involving discharge for refusal to wear an objectionable costume, the judgment was for $33,141.75 in back pay and interest and $90,899 in attorney's fees. You can offer a specific kind of uniform to a worker, but the worker should willingly accept wearing it without any coercion whatsoever.

Gender. It has also been found that it is illegal to make employment decisions based on gender, unless it is "necessary for the purpose of authenticity or genuineness . . . as a bona fide occupational qualification, e.g., an actor or actress."[3] Thus, it is illegal to specify that only male bartenders are to be used for a specific party. After a court case involving Pan Am Airlines, men won the right to be airline hosts even though passengers might prefer hostesses for the job. Gender discrimination even applies to guests. Under a different statute, it is illegal to have an "all males night" or "a ladies only night."

Alien employment. The Immigration Reform and Control Act of 1986 prohibits the hiring of aliens not authorized to work in the United States.

Employers are made responsible for verifying that every person hired after November 6, 1986, is authorized to work in the United States. U.S. citizens must prove identity and citizenship. Aliens must prove identity and authorization to work. Authorization to work can be granted by the Immigration and Naturalization Service (INS). If an authorized alien loses authorization, you may no longer employ the person. There are stiff penalties for violating any of the law's provisions.

There is a grandfather clause in the law that allows aliens hired before November 7, 1986, to continue to work. They do not need permits to work. The employer does not have to have on file a Form I-9 for any employee hired before that date.

All new employees must give proof of identity and of work authorization. A U.S. passport, certificate of citizenship or naturalization, unexpired foreign passport with work authorization, or alien registration or resident alien card with a photograph are examples of acceptable documents for proving both identity and work authorization. Separate documents may also be used to prove identity and work authorization. A driver's license, voter's registration card, U.S. military card, and various other documents are acceptable as proof of identity. A social security card (as long as it does not say "not valid for employment purposes"), an unexpired re-entry permit or refugee travel document, a birth certificate, an INS employment authorization document, and various other documents are acceptable as proof of work authorization. A Form I-9 must be completed and put into the employee's file; it verifies that the new employee has submitted satisfactory proof of identity and work authorization. Do not ask for such information until after you have offered the applicant the job. Asking before you offer the job may leave you open to claims of discrimination from those applicants who did not get hired.

Wrongful discharge. Wrongful discharge is another area in which problems arise today. Under the Civil Rights Act and various other pieces of employment legislation, no discharge may be made on the basis of race, color, sex, religion, or place of national origin; for performing jury duty or participating in unions or in collective bargaining; for filing a complaint based on the wage and hour laws; or for a handicap, for wage garnishment for a single indebtedness, or for age if the employee is 40 years old or older. The penalty imposed for wrongful discharge can be re-employment of the employee, payment of back wages with interest from the date of discharge until re-employment, court costs, attorney's fees, and, in claims based on public policy or outrageous employer conduct, punitive damages. It can be expensive. We will return to wrongful discharge when we discuss state laws later in this chapter.

State Control

Each of the 50 states also has its own laws and regulations governing the alcoholic beverage industry. There are sometimes wide differences between them, and you should consult counsel in your state. However, there are some general elements in common. These are largely covered in the material that follows. Where a standard regulation exists, such as that governing the sale of alcoholic beverages, the major differences will be pointed out.

Licenses and Permits

All states have some type of regulation or law that requires a license or permit to sell alcoholic beverages. There is often little difference between a license and a permit. The effect of both is to allow the selling or dispensing of alcoholic beverages to the public. A license often gives the right or privilege, while a permit is an allowance to act in a certain manner. An establishment meeting required standards may be licensed and/or issued a permit to operate. Often, this grant must be placed where it can be seen. Licenses and permits are usually granted for one year and must be renewed annually.

In some states, a specific number of licenses are granted according to a set population count, say, one for every 4,000 people. In such cases, licenses can become very valuable possessions. When more businesses want them than can get them, a current owner can often get a high price by selling to the highest bidder.

In some states, the issuance of permits or licenses depends more on the type of business than on population restriction. Some states may have a population restriction, but also allow the issuing of additional licenses to special kinds of operations. In a few states, only certain kinds of operations can be licensed. Thus, in a state where only clubs can sell to the public, hotels, restaurants, and other businesses may seek and be allowed to operate a "club" within their operation. A nominal fee to guests allows membership.

Before being allowed to buy permits or licenses, the prospective buyer must meet the state's criteria. These may concern the character and financial resources of the holder as well as the kind of operation, location, and so forth.

The charges for licenses and permits may or may not be based on a flat fee.

Control and License States

As discussed in Chapter 9, *control states* require all alcoholic beverages containing over a certain percentage of alcohol to be sold in state stores. Bars and others selling such beverages must purchase from the state. Some control states do not restrict retailing of table wines and beers, but require purchases of alcoholic beverages with over a specific percentage of alcohol to be made in state liquor stores. *License states*, in contrast, control these operations through licensing. Businesses can buy from whomever they wish, but sometimes there are regulations covering the way such purchasing can be done. In 1991, there were 32 license states and 18 control states. The District of Columbia is a license district. Some states, such as Mississippi and Wyoming, are a combination of control and license. They require purchase from state-controlled sources at the wholesale level, but allow the public to purchase from any licensed or permit-holding dealer.

The kinds of alcoholic beverages that can be sold in commercial operations are often controlled by permit or license. Some permits or licenses allow only the sale of packaged beers and wines below a certain percentage of alcohol. Some allow the sale of both packaged and by-the-drink spirits, while others allow only packaged sales. Some go so far as to allow the sale of packaged liquor by commercial operations if it is purchased from a state store operated on the premises.

Handling Problem Guests

In Chapter 2, it was indicated that at times problem guests might have to be asked to leave the premises. Normally, management or an authorized management representative should do this unpleasant job. Care must be taken not to violate the guest's rights or to cause a fight or some other more serious problem.

Every state has laws which indicate how matters of this kind should be handled. The management of an enterprise should know what these are and what limitations they impose on handling such guests. Before you attempt to forcibly throw someone out, make sure you know the applicable laws.

State laws usually require that prostitutes or pimps soliciting in an operation or others engaged in illegal acts must be excluded, as must anyone carrying arms of any kind. In such a case, it is usual to call in law enforcement officials and have the individual removed. However, it may be proper before doing this to request the offender to leave. In some states, a pimp or prostitute cannot be asked or forced to leave until some overt solicitation is made. Often, an effective way to handle the situation is to have security sit as close as possible to the person and speak loudly several times over a walkie-talkie about security matters. The person often gets the message and leaves.

Other laws may indicate that the operator of a public place may refuse service to a guest who is, for example, "intoxicated, immoral, profane, lewd, or brawling [or who otherwise uses] language or conduct which disturbs the peace and comfort of other guests or which injures the reputation, dignity, or standing of the establishment."[4] It is also possible to remove or cause to be removed guests who are carrying on this way. Usually, the law will go so far as to indicate that it is possible to remove or have removed someone whose presence in the operation is undesirable. You must be sure, however, that there is a bona fide reason for such an opinion and that you can prove it. Under no circumstances should such removal be based on race, creed, color, sex, physical disability, or national origin. One can run afoul of various laws if this occurs.

The proper way to handle the matter is to tell the guest that the operation no longer desires to entertain him or her and that the person should leave. If you wish to be sure that there is proof of such a request, it can be in writing. Florida law indicates that such a written notice should read: "You are hereby notified that this establishment no longer desires to entertain you as its guest, and you are requested to leave at once. To remain after receipt of this notice is a misdemeanor under the laws of this state."[5]

Some states allow a person to be taken into custody (placed under citizen's arrest) and detained for a reasonable time if there is reason to believe that the person is engaging in disorderly conduct and that such conduct is a threat to the safety or life of the person or others. A police officer should be promptly called in. You should know, however, that making such an arrest may expose you to suits for false imprisonment and false accusation. This is not an action to be taken lightly. Some states provide protection in some circumstances against civil or criminal liability if this is done. Such a citizen's arrest is usually not possible if the individual is only a trespasser.

Very often, when removing a guest, you must identify yourself as management or a designated person with the authority to act for management. A failure to give such identification might impair management's rights in the matter; the individual could even resist a citizen's arrest and not be liable. Again, it is strongly advised that you know the law and act strictly in accordance with it.

In some cases, a guest may only be a nuisance. Less drastic action must then be taken. Still, management or its representative should be alert to nip in the bud any incident of this kind, since it might end up in an altercation or some other undesirable incident. Others may become so annoyed that they try to take matters into their own hands and discipline the annoying person. The person in charge of the area should set matters straight immediately, leaving no room for an incident to occur.

The responsibility of an establishment to a guest is often clearly defined in one or more of the laws of a state. A Florida Court of Appeals decision in a case of this kind read in part:

> A tavern and bar may be likened to a place of amusement to which the public is invited. As to such places, the owner or proprietor is not an insurer of the safety of his patrons, but must exercise due care to maintain the premises in a reasonably safe condition for the customary and reasonable uses to which they may be put by the patrons, to use ordinary and reasonable care for the safety of his patrons and to guard against subjecting them to dangers of which he is cognizant or which he might reasonably foresee.

The operation and even its employees may be liable if there is an awareness that an individual is intoxicated and this individual harms someone. A court might well decide that the operation could have reasonably foreseen that such an individual might present a danger to patrons. In a Kansas case, the judge decided that if it becomes apparent that there is impending danger or even that there are dangers which one might reasonably foresee, management is liable if steps are not taken to warn patrons or to protect them.

In most states, the law will take the view that when the public enters a place of business for the purpose of doing business there, the management is generally:

> liable to members of the public for any physical harm caused by accidental, negligent, or intentional harmful acts of third persons or animals. . . . [Management] is also liable for failing to exercise reasonable care to discover that such acts are being done or are likely to be done; or to warn visitors so they can avoid the harm or protect themselves.[6]

Employment at Will

Once, the U.S. system of employment was one in which a person took a job and worked on it until he or she wanted to quit. The employer was free to fire the employee at any time for any reason; the employee had no say in the matter. Conversely, the employee was free to quit the job at any time for any reason; the employer could not force an employee to stay on a job against the employee's will.

This idea that either party can end an employment relationship—called by the courts **employment at will**— still exists in some of our states, but in about 30 of them there has been a change. Both courts and state legislatures have established that employees can at times be wrongfully discharged and the employer may be held liable for this.

In some decisions, courts have held that discharging an employee for refusing to do something illegal or for reporting illegal actions of other employees was illegal because it was "against public policy." In other cases, the courts have held that a discharge was a retaliatory action by an employer or was motivated by an intent to do harm to the employee. Of course, the proof has to be there. If an employee can prove that an employer discharged him or her in bad faith, the courts will often find wrongful discharge.

Employees in other instances have won favorable judgments by claiming that the employer violated a contract of employment by a breach of fair dealings, good faith, or just cause. Some employees have won by showing that they were discharged for protesting that the employer had failed to honor statements in an employment application, employee handbook, or other written materials. Some courts have held that such written materials constitute a written contract; if their provisions are not observed, it is a breach of contract.

Because states vary on the definition of unlawful discharge, employers should check the laws of their state. However, the trend is clear. In 1985, a Justice of the Supreme Court of Texas wrote in an opinion, "Absolute employment at will is a relic of early industrial times, conjuring up visions of sweat shops described by Charles Dickens. . . . The doctrine belongs in a museum, not in our law." Whether or not you agree with employment at will, its validity is clearly eroding in many courts.

Miscellaneous State Regulations

There may be many other regulations and laws governing either all businesses in the state or bar and beverage operations only. Operators should be aware of those of the state in which they operate. Such laws or regulations may cover building requirements, days and hours of permitted operation, age limits of employees, minimum age limits of guests, employment, and so forth. A wide number of these spring from common law and not from statutory law.

With regard to days and hours of permitted operation, the sale of alcoholic beverages on transportation that crosses state lines may be controlled. For example, suppose one state allows the sale of alcohol on Sundays, while a neighboring state does not. A passenger on a Sunday train might be able to purchase an alcoholic beverage a minute before passing the state line, but not be able to do so after entering the second state.

Some states regulate whether one may charge a bill for alcoholic beverages. In some states, hotels and others may allow credit on a bill to be paid later. Other states forbid credit of any kind. Regulations on the kind of advertising permitted also are found in some states; often, these are more detailed than the federal law. Many states not only have a sales tax, but also tax certain kinds of beverages. In these cases, an operation must keep records on the amount of sales of various kinds of beverages sold and submit reports and tax payments based on them.

Community or Local Regulations

As we have seen, some counties, communities, or other local units may completely forbid the sale of alcoholic beverages. They are known as *dry* areas. In most other places (where the sale of some kind or another is allowed), there will be regulations governing what, when, where, and by whom sales can be made.

"What" regulations may govern such matters as allowing only the sale of wines and beers below a certain percentage of alcohol. Others may permit only the sale of some kinds of packaged goods. Certain operations may be allowed to sell some defined kinds of beverages by the drink, while others may not. The size of a package may also be defined—for example, a requirement to sell only miniature bottles.

"When" regulations often follow those of the state, but some local areas may have different, more restrictive laws and regulations if the state has granted them the authority. Thus, while state law may allow the sale of alcoholic beverages on Sunday, a community might not. Hours of operation different from those of the state may also be in effect.

"Where" regulations control the location where a sale can be made. Bar and beverage operations must not only conform to normal zoning laws applying to all businesses (that is, the location must be zoned for business), but may also have to follow regulations which do not allow them to be located within a certain distance of a church, hospital, or school. The type of establishment may also be specified. Thus, alcoholic beverages may in some communities be sold *only* in establishments also selling food. Sometimes, food sales must be greater than alcoholic beverage sales.

"Who" regulations are also common. These frequently have more stringent requirements regarding who can own and operate an establishment. They may even require an operator to be licensed to operate, as well as the establishment. Additional permits or licenses may be required. The charge for these may be a flat fee, or a fee based on the percentage of business done (with a ceiling), the kind of establishment, the size of the operation either physically or in terms of sales, or a combination of these.

In addition to these what, when, where, and who regulations, there will be several building codes (see Chapter 3). Local health regulations may also be in effect. Thus, a transportation company like a railroad or airline that crosses over state lines may find that it must undergo federal, state, and local health inspections. Local regulations may also cover matters such as advertising, promotions, signs, and so forth. In some communities, there may be a special sales tax in addition to that of the state.

Normally, all businesses are required to maintain adequate accounting records so local, state, or federal authorities can check on financial and other matters of the business. Bar and beverage operations may have to maintain even stricter records. The matter of having to report the amount of different alcoholic beverage sales and pay taxes on them has been mentioned, but there may be others. Local law enforcement authorities may also require that certain records be maintained on unusual incidents that occur in the operation. Thus, if someone is forcibly ejected, the matter might have to be written up and the police notified. Other regulations not pertaining to records may be enforced so the local police are better able to know that the business is being conducted in a proper manner.

Potential Liability

As we have seen in previous chapters, there are a number of ways in which a bar or beverage establishment can suffer from alcohol-related liability. We often do not realize that there may be a potential for liability until an event occurs, a suit is brought, and a court decision interprets a law in a new way, establishing a new type of liability.

Some sources of liability are fairly evident. One is management's responsibility for allowing or condoning drinking on the job and for the drinking employee's actions. Another is the third-party liability of an establishment that conducts or sponsors such events as wine tastings. Other sources of liability may not be as evident, but management should be aware of the potential.

Drinking on the Job

It is common for some drinkers at the bar to "buy the bartender a drink." Should this be permitted? The answer is no. As a general rule, the courts have ruled that an employer (master) is responsible for the actions of employees (servants) while acting within the scope of the job. This ruling comes from a legal theory known as *respondeat superior*. An employee who drinks on the job can easily lose control and become a problem to guests and the employer. If such an employee injures someone, the injured party may have a cause of action against the employer.

It should be company policy that alcohol or drug use is not permitted on the job. When a patron asks to buy a drink for an employee or wants an employee to drink with him or her, the employee should indicate that drinking on the job is against company policy and, while he or she appreciates the thought, it cannot be done. In some operations, the bartender may accept the patron's offer but pour a non-alcoholic drink. In other cases, the bartender may be allowed to accept the patron's money for the drink as a tip.

The policy prohibiting drinking or using drugs while on the job should be in writing. It should be written in consultation with an attorney. Every employee should receive a copy and acknowledge that violation is cause for suspension or termination. The policy should be rigidly enforced. An employer cannot risk allowing an employee to commit acts which could be disastrously costly to the employer. Such a policy is one way to try to stop it.

Wine Tastings

Wine tastings are enjoyable gatherings often given to promote wine which one wants to sell. A wine merchant might give the tasting for your establishment. Even if there is no charge to you and someone gives the affair for you, you still face potential liability, as does the wine merchant. In most states, it is not necessary to *sell* an alcoholic beverage to be liable. Giving it away can also create liability. It is the *service* that creates the liability.

An event of this kind should be carefully monitored. Age should be checked when you suspect someone is a minor. The condition of guests and, of course, the amount of drinking that goes on should also be watched. Suppose an adult drinks to the point of intoxication or someone who has come is already inebriated and is served. In some wine tastings, a considerable amount of wine is poured during an evening. There are many different wines and the portions are not "tastings" but glasses filled with wine. The event often becomes one of drinking rather than tasting. In some cases, guests are given a complete bottle and allowed to pour as much as they desire from it. If one of these guests later injures someone or themselves or destroys property, management may be liable as a third party (recall the discussion of third-party liability in Chapter 2). Such events should be treated with the same degree of caution that must be exercised in the regular sale of alcoholic beverages.

Business Liability

Business organizations, including bars, restaurants, and hotels, often give functions for employees where alcohol is served. In many cases, certain employees are expected to attend these. They are there not of their own volition but rather as part of their job. If such an employee at such a function becomes intoxicated and is in a traffic accident while driving home, the business can be held liable. The view is often taken that it was the business's function, the employee was required to be there, and the business should have used more care in seeing that excessive drinking did not occur. It has become more well defined that, if an employee who had to be there was injured, the individual qualifies for workers' compensation.

Serving Effervescent Wines

We looked at the dangers of and potential liability for serving flaming drinks in Chapter 5. This is not the only way an alcoholic product can physically injure someone. A bottle of effervescent wine can also be a dangerous weapon. Usually, the bottle must withstand a pressure of 110 pounds per square inch (compared, for example, with the 24 to 40 psi typical in automobile tires). For this reason, such bottles must be specially built of thick glass with a special shape to hold in the pressure. The cork is also held in by a wide, tapering base plus a wire cage called an *agraffe.* Both the cork shape and the agraffe help to hold the cork in the neck bottle against terrific pressure.

Careless handling or trying to serve a bottle of warm effervescent wine can cause the bottle to shatter. If the bottle is given a sharp rap against a hard object, the bottle may literally blow up, sending glass in all directions. Because warm wine is under greater pressure, just a sharp *movement* may cause the bottle to shatter. For this reason, servers should be taught to take care in handling effervescent wine and to see that it is *thoroughly* chilled before trying to open it.

Also, the agraffe should be removed carefully with the cork. The bottle should be pointed away from anyone so, if the cork does blow out, it will not strike and possibly injure someone. Sometimes, effervescent wine bottles which have had their agraffes removed outside the service area are placed onto a cart or tray and then rolled or carried in. An experienced server will cover such bottles with several heavy wet towels so that, should one or more blow up, the damage can be contained.

Operations that want to avoid injury to guests and costly lawsuits see to it that everyone serving effervescent wines knows how to do the job properly. Failing to train servers in such service may be a costly omission.

Words and the Law

Even though laws are usually carefully written—each word is weighed by legislatures—there can be wide interpretation later as to exactly what a law means. Lawmakers sometimes find that the law they thought they had written to mean an exact thing does not convey this meaning in practice. This is because every law must be interpreted by many, many people, each of whom may have different ideas about its exact meaning. Often, the courts are then forced to try to interpret the true meaning of the law and to see that its application is what the lawmakers intended. This whole matter of ambiguity and interpretation has built a huge industry of lawyers, courts, and accompanying factors. Interpretation is what most law is about today.

This issue can have a direct bearing on you. Earlier, we quoted a law barring "immoral" and "lewd" behavior. In today's world of changing moral standards and acceptable conduct, what *is* immoral or lewd? The answer will probably vary depending on whether the person asked has conservative, moderate, or liberal views. What might be offensive and immoral to one group may be perfectly acceptable and normal to another. A given legal interpretation of a term might not fit the meaning that some people attach to it. For instance, the manner in which a woman is dressed might not conform to acceptable conservative patterns of dress, but it might be acceptable and even something to be envied by one who holds a more liberal view.

A person who is a "nuisance" is by general definition someone who is offensive or annoying to individuals or to the community. But this too can vary. One woman might find a man's attention from another table very annoying and offensive, while another might not. To some, the kissing and fondling of two adults might seem lewd, while to others it is "wonderful to be in love." Where such differing viewpoints are held in society, courts have great difficulty in deciding what the law should be.

When even the courts are sometimes unsure of how to interpret laws, how do those who must obey the law exactly know what is required of them? Bar and beverage managers should consult an attorney to get the best possible opinion. They should realize, however, that this opinion is no guarantee that the courts will not later interpret the law differently.

Thus, perhaps you should think twice before asking a young woman to leave because she is wearing what seems to you to be a provocative, abbreviated dress. If she refuses, you perhaps should think three times before escorting her out against her will. A claim later that the dress was offensive, indecent, and annoying to other patrons might not hold up in court.

The best advice is that, when doubtful situations arise, remain calm and work out some strategy to minimize the incident as much as possible. In the above example, if getting the woman to sit down would make the dress less obvious, it would be politic to seat her in a far corner away from others. If she insists on standing at the bar with her escort, you might explain the situation and offer to serve free drinks at a table.

Another common word subject to varying interpretation is "knowingly" as in the phrase "knowingly serving an intoxicated person" or "knowingly serving an addicted person." Certainly a common, simple explanation of the phrase would be that the server knows he or she is serving someone who is intoxicated or habitually addicted. But how can the server always know when a patron is intoxicated or addicted? Some intoxicated people can hide the fact and seem to be in full possession of their faculties when they are not. However, using this as a defense in a court case—that the server could not tell—may not work. The view is often taken that it is up to the server to know or to ascertain. Any suspicion deserves full credence and as much of a check as possible. In some states, the courts have said that if you know that someone is "habitually addicted," you could be liable for serving such a person alcohol. The drinking pattern of an individual can be a warning. Furthermore, in some states the courts have held that a server need not be put on notice that the individual is habitually addicted. It is up to the server to know. Just how the server is supposed to know, the courts do not say.

The Importance of Prudent Preparation

Take advantage of legal opinion. Contact an attorney who knows the area and have him or her explain where the liability and potential liability areas are in your state and community, as well as ways to avoid them. Such information will be helpful when you establish policies and procedures for handling problems. These written policies and procedures should be given to all employees who may interact with guests purchasing alcoholic beverages so as to minimize or eliminate areas of liability exposure.

It is also advised that you conduct meetings where you discuss the policies and how employees should implement them. Explain in detail the procedures which should be followed when problems arise. Give emphasis to critical points. Use demonstrations, lecture, role playing, and other training devices to get the points across. Check to see that employees know and understand the policies and how to implement them. It may be a good idea to consider having law enforcement officials come in to speak at training sessions. It is important to follow through on policies and procedures and to check frequently to see that employees are performing adequately. It is better to build a good defense in trying to avoid problems than to try to think of a good defense after you must go into court.

The attitude that management should take in all of this is that the facility, its employees, and its guests *must strictly* obey the law. A straight, no-quarter-given attitude of complete compliance with the law and a follow-through to see it is observed is considered the best policy. Trying to cut corners and shade a bit here and there eventually can be a trap and a costly one.

Endnotes

1. For more detailed discussion of most of these laws, see Mary L. Tanke, *Human Resources Management for the Hospitality Industry* (New York: Delmar, 1990) and David Wheelhouse, *Managing Human Resources in the Hospitality Industry* (East Lansing, Mich.: Educational Institute of the American Hotel & Motel Association, 1989).

2. EEOC Guidelines on Sexual Harassment.

3. 29 C.F.R. Section 1604.11 (1987).

4. Florida Statutes Chapter 509.141.

5. Florida Statutes Chapter 509.141.

6. Elio C. Bellucci, J.D., "Protect Patrons from Third Party Assaults," *Southern Beverage Journal* (January 1989).

Key Terms

common law state
employment at will
on-premise retail dealer
standards of identity
statutory state
tied-house agreement

Discussion Questions

1. With regard to the sale and service of alcoholic beverages, what three primary concerns are addressed by federal law?

2. What types of federal taxes are levied on producers and sellers of alcoholic beverages?

3. What are tied-house agreements? Are they legal?

4. Who must supply proof of identity and work authorization? What documents are acceptable for such purposes?

5. What types of restrictions are sometimes placed on the availability of licenses and permits?

6. What should you know before you attempt to forcibly remove someone from your operation's premises?

7. What is wrongful discharge? How does it relate (if at all) to employment at will?

8. What types of regulations are often imposed by local communities? How do these regulations relate to state and federal regulations?

9. Why is it sometimes difficult to anticipate where liability may arise?

10. Who may suffer from third-party liability laws for wine tastings given on your premises by a wine supplier? Does it make a difference if you give the wine away rather than sell it?

Part IV

The Products

12 The Beverage Family

Chapter Outline

Historical Overview
    The Ancient World
    The Middle Ages
    Modern Times
    Early America
        The Saloon
        Hotels and Inns
        Restaurants
        The Temperance Movement
        Post-Prohibition
Classifications of Alcoholic Beverages
    Distilled Spirits
    Wines
    Malt Beverages
Characteristics of Alcoholic Beverages
    Alcohol Content
    Calorie Content
Production of Alcoholic Beverages
    Fermentation
        Weight Changes
        Yeast
        Congeners
        Fermentation of Distilled Spirits
        Fermentation of Malt Beverages
        Fermentation of Wine
    Distillation
        Types of Distillation
        Rectification
    Aging
        Aging Spirits
        Aging Wines
    Blending
Increasing Your Product Knowledge

██████████ Product knowledge is a prerequisite to successful management of a bar or beverage operation. This chapter provides a basis for understanding the in-depth product information presented in the chapters that follow. It presents a historical overview that sets the stage for an introduction to the alcoholic beverage family. The chapter also describes beverage production processes and defines many of the terms you will encounter as you proceed.

Knowing more about the products your operation offers will sharpen your management skills in many areas—among them: purchasing, storing, selling, service requirements, guest relations, and employee training. Such knowledge should lead to an even greater appreciation of the complex and fascinating nature of the bar and beverage business.

Historical Overview

The Ancient World   Alcoholic beverages were known to man long before recorded history. The earliest records reveal that in many cultures wine or fermented brews had long been in use and played significant roles in social institutions such as medicine, religion, marriage, and government.[1] Alcoholic beverages were also an important element of public and private ceremonies such as national feasts, weddings, births, and burials. Wine or brews were consumed regularly in the daily fare. They were often much safer to drink than the water, as well as being highly palatable, relaxing, and intoxicating. No one knew what fermentation was; all they knew was that something caused some foods or beverages to foam and turn into desirable, potable drinks.

The first fermented product was probably a brew. One can only guess how it was made. Perhaps early man gathered grains for food and left them where they got into a liquid in a warm place, and wild yeasts did the rest, fermenting the mixture and producing a liquid that tasted good.

Reference to a fermented product is found in Assyrian cuneiform records over 7,000 years old. The people, perhaps of Sumerian origin, were engaged largely in agriculture and had a fairly advanced Stone Age civilization. The knowledge of making brews and wines came later to ancient Mesopotamians, Babylonians, and Egyptians. Exhibit 12.1 shows a nearly 4,000-year-old recipe said to have been handed down to the Mesopotamians by their god Enki. In these ancient countries, laborers received part of their pay in rations of brew. Historians have called beer the ancient national drink of Egypt—the Egyptians called it "hek"—and a number of drawings inscribed in tombs show beer-making (see Exhibit 12.2).

The Babylonians, according to records, made 16 different brews from barley or other grains. There is archaeological evidence of later civilizations in Asia Minor and Egypt indicating that their methods of making brews and wine were quite advanced. Barley had become the preferred grain for brews, and certain varieties of grapes began to be chosen for their wines.

Wine was the preferred drink of the wealthy and influential because it was usually more costly. Beer was usually the drink of the common people. From the number of huge jars of wine stored in the tomb of Tutankhamen (d. 1352 B.C.), one can conclude it was a highly important substance to be taken into the heavenly world. Wine in those times was also important in medicine, being used as an antiseptic to treat wounds,

Exhibit 12.1   The First Recipe for Brew

Around 1750 B.C., scribes worked with pointed utensils on slabs of wet clay to inscribe history's first-known recipe for a brew. The slabs were excavated at Nippur, Iraq, and are today housed in the University Museum, University of Pennsylvania. (Courtesy of Anheuser-Busch)

to anesthetize, to make water safer to drink, to cause sleep, and to help create an appetite and assimilate nutrients. The Egyptians also ascribed to wine some supernatural powers. The tenth tablet describing the life of the Babylonian king Gilgamesh tells of his hunting for immortality in an enchanted vineyard. Wine was also an important item of trade in those times. Herodotus, the great Greek historian, said that much wine was floated in

Exhibit 12.2 Signs of the Times

(a)
(b)
(c)
(d)
(e)

(a) Drawing of ancient Egyptians sowing barley, harvesting it, making it into a brew, and tasting it.
(b) Drawing of Queen Shu-bad of ancient Mesopotamia using long golden straws to reach from her throne into a large container of brew.
(c) Tomb inscription of pharaoh's brew inspector sampling wine.
(d) Old Roman coin depicting barley's importance.
(e) To the ancient Sumerians, the symbol on the left represented a clay vessel, and the symbol on the right was a vessel filled with brew. (Courtesy of Anheuser-Busch)

skin boats down the Tigris and Euphrates Rivers to be traded in the river cities. Traders carried the wine in huge jars called amphoras.

The grape is one of our oldest plants: some say over 60 million years old. It was found in ancient times in many places in Asia Minor, and wine is thought to have been made in Mesopotamia or Caucasia around 6000 B.C. Ancient Persia also grew the grape, making a considerable amount of wine from it. The ancient Chinese were fond of their *kiu*, a brew made of millet and later rice, sorghum, or other products. One legend tells of a king who ordered a small lake built and filled with *kiu*. That evening the king gave a feast and, at a given signal, the monarch and his guests waded in and had a grand splash party! Needless to say, many staid Chinese did not appreciate such antics, and this dissolute king was soon replaced by a more temperate one. India at one time produced a lot of alcoholic beverages but, as Buddhism became prevalent, consumption languished.

One of the pillars on which the Jewish culture rests is wine. It has always been important in their laws, literature, religion, and social life. The Christians also paired wine with religion. The Bible mentions wine

165 times. Beer, too, played a biblical role. At the ancient site of Nineveh, the place where—according to the Bible—Noah's ark came to rest, some ancient baked clay tablets have been found indicating beer was something Noah included in his provisions to stand the rigors of his long voyage. One of the first things Noah did after disembarking from the ark was to plant a vineyard.

The Phoenicians are credited with having spread the grape around the Mediterranean. The island of Crete in the Minoan Age (3000 to 1100 B.C.) had a thriving wine-producing and -trading industry. Wine was being made in Greece around 2000 B.C. It was Thucydides who wrote, "The peoples of the Mediterranean began to emerge from Barbarism when they learned to cultivate the olive and the vine." Much of the culture of the Greeks also put heavy emphasis on wine. Wine was a common thread that ran through their art, literature, religion, and national and social life. Taverns, inns, and markets sold wine and other fermented products. The Greeks liked to drink their wine diluted with water. It was a common drink in social gatherings and meetings. The term "symposium" is derived from Greek words which mean "to drink together."

Sicily was making wine around 1500 B.C. The Greeks, finding that the grape grew well in Italy, called Italy "Oenotria," the land of wine. The Etruscans in central Italy were expert vintners, raising the art to a high level, and their conquerors, the Romans, carried their knowledge throughout the Roman Empire. They also began to identify areas where superior products were made each year, presaging the later development of *crus*, or growth areas, in France. They also began to distinguish between vintages. Glass bottles were invented, and they plugged them so air could not enter and spoil the wine.

The wine industry grew, and wine became an important item of trade. Galen, physician to Emperor Marcus Aurelius, wrote a book on wine production and its use as a medicine. Excavations at Pompeii reveal that over 100 *tavernas* existed at the time of the Vesuvius eruption, most of them open-air dispensaries. The wine was stored in huge urns near the counter and covered with oil to keep air from turning it into vinegar. The Romans also liked their brews and inscribed their coins with sheaves of barley.

When the Romans occupied Britain, they found the Celts and Druids producing a type of beer made from grain. Farther north, the Vikings were making mead from honey and other brews from grains. Their Norse gods are frequently portrayed holding up in triumph a mead-filled hunting horn. The Huns, who overran Europe in the Dark Ages, and the Mongols, who later conquered China, drank a brew called *koumiss*, made from mare's milk. They were seldom without, since they were cavalrymen often riding on their own manufacturing plants. History reports that Mohammed drank a wine called *nabidh*; it was made from dates.

The Middle Ages

During the Middle Ages, production of fermented beverages improved and increased, largely under the holy orders of the Roman Catholic and Greek Orthodox churches. Monasteries produced large quantities for their own use and for sale to the public. They further refined production techniques and shifted wine- and beer-making from a mystique to a science. Sulfur, when burned to create sulfur dioxide, was found to be excellent to introduce into casks to help destroy destructive yeasts and other organisms, thus helping to preserve the wine. In the time of Charlemagne (742–814), France and Germany began to emerge as dominant wine-producers in Europe. Later, a number of knowledgeable treatises on wine- and brew-making appeared, such as *Liber Commodorum Ruralium* (1303) by Petrus de Crescentiis, *Liber de Vinis* (1311) by Arnaldius de Villanova, *Secretum Secretorum* (1378) by the monk Geoffrey of Waterford, and *Lo Crestia* (14th c.). The monastery brewers found they could make a better beer by malting barley than by using an unmalted grain. Later, they took over an idea from the Dutch of using hops to improve the flavor of beers and help preserve them. Thus, modern beer was born. They also were able to improve fermentation and wine-aging techniques. Exhibit 12.3 shows some interesting medieval wine-making equipment and processing procedures.

One of the holy orders that did the most to advance the knowledge of winemaking was the Cistercian order under the famous St. Bernard. The saint was given a piece of land in Chablis when he founded the order in the twelfth century. He ordered the first plantings of the Chardonnay grape, and it prospered. So did its wine under the strict, sanitary, and careful winemaking procedures he developed. The order spread, and soon in Europe there were over 2,000 Cistercian monasteries producing the finest of wines. They were the first to set forth the modern concept of the *cru*, an area where each year superior wines were very likely to be produced. They also experimented with different grape varieties, adding to the knowledge of how specific varieties contributed to specific qualities in wines. In a sense, they were the originators of the system later developed in France called the *appellation contrôlée*.

It is not known who first discovered how to distill alcohol from its mother liquid. Some authorities believe the process was known to the ancients. Aristotle refers to it in his *Meteorology*, writing that "sea water can be made potable by distillation; wine and other liquids can be submitted to the same process." The ancient Gaelic words *uisce beathadh* and *uisge beatha* are credited by *Webster's Third New International Dictionary* as the forerunners of our word "whiskey." However, as we have seen, until the twelfth century or even later, the common drink of Europeans was a brew or wine or both. Distilled spirits were not commonly produced until the sixteenth century.

One early written reference to a distilled spirit was made by an Arab alchemist named Albukassen in the tenth century. Around this time the Chinese were distilling their rice beverage into a spirit. It is believed the Chinese learned of distillation from the Arabs. There is reason to believe that the Moors, who had settled in Spain in 711, transmitted knowledge of the distillation process to Europeans. Around the twelfth century, the Moors were using a still called the *alembic* to capture the essence of flowers so they could make perfumes. A short time later in Armagnac, France, this same still was being used to make brandy. It is still used today in Armagnac and Cognac and the name is still alembic. Note in Exhibit 12.4 that the English called one of their old stills an "alembick." It is of interest also that the word alcohol comes from the Arabic word *alkuhul*.

There were few, if any, inns in the Middle Ages. Monasteries served in their place, springing up along the main travel routes. During the Crusades, monasteries provided a safe and comfortable place of rest for those devout adventurers who sought to free the Holy Land. In other places, hostelries and way stations appeared along world travel routes. Remnants

Exhibit 12.3   Old-World Winemaking Processes and Procedures

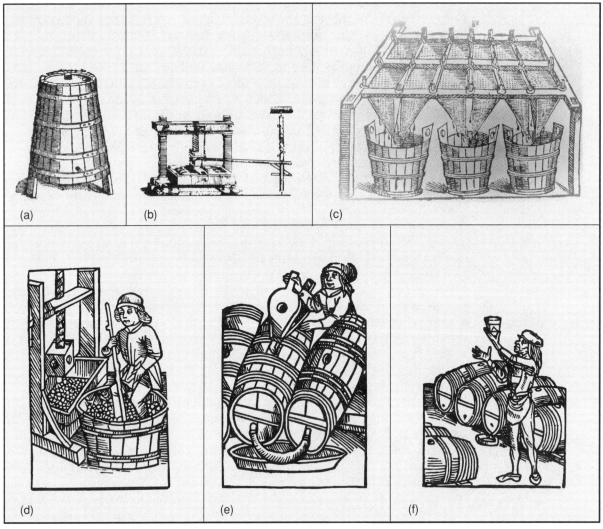

(a) An old fermenting vat. (Courtesy of the Italian Trade Commission of New York)
(b) An old winepress. (Courtesy of the Italian Trade Commission of New York)
(c) Eighteenth-century filtering system using hemp sacks. (Courtesy of the Italian Trade Commission of New York)
(d) Treading grapes. (Courtesy of the German Wine Institute)
(e) A fireplace bellows saved work in casking wines. (Courtesy of the German Wine Institute)
(f) A wine master judging his product. (Courtesy of the German Wine Institute)

of some of these havens are still preserved along the arid roadways of the Old Silk Road—the long, tortuous route over which Marco Polo traveled to and from China. The remnants tell us much about the way such places served weary travelers and their caravans of camels, donkeys, and horses. Wine and brews were not missing in the fare these places offered to their guests.

Trading in wine became much more important. At first, Genoa and then Venice took the wine-trading lead, spreading wine throughout the known world—even as far as England, Ireland, and the Scandinavian countries. Vintners who wanted to sell wines in far-off lands had to see that the right wine was produced and that it was made properly, because

Exhibit 12.4 Old Drawing of a Distilling Operation

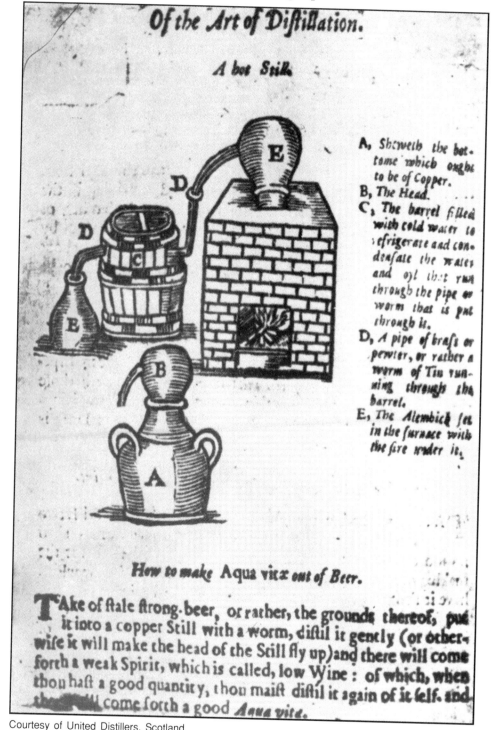

Of the Art of Diſtillation.

A hot Still.

A, Sheweth the bottome which ought to be of Copper.

B, The Head.

C, The barrel filled with cold water to refrigerate and condenſate the water and oyl that run through the pipe or worm that is put through it.

D, A pipe of braſs or pewter, or rather a worm of Tin running through the barrel.

E, The Alembick ſet in the furnace with the fire under it.

How to make Aqua vitæ out of Beer.

Take of ſtale ſtrong-beer, or rather, the grounds thereof, put it into a copper Still with a worm, diſtil it gently (or otherwiſe it will make the head of the Still fly up) and there will come forth a weak Spirit, which is called, low Wine : of which, when thou haſt a good quantity, thou maiſt diſtil it again of it ſelf, and there will come forth a good *Aqua vita.*

long-distance shipping could damage the wine. The fragility of the wines of Cognac made them poor candidates for long voyages. This prompted enterprising vintners of Cognac to distill their wines into spirits which could take the long voyages, thus starting the famous brandy industry of Cognac.

Modern Times

There was no sharp demarcation between alcoholic beverage production at the end of the Middle Ages in the sixteenth century and at the beginning of what we call modern times. The movement toward improving production and marketing continued slowly. Glass bottles began to replace stoneware jugs and wooden casks. Corks replaced wood plugs or glass stoppers, giving a more air-tight seal. The lagering of beer became commonplace and preferred in Europe. (Lagering will be discussed in Chapter 14.)

In the seventeenth century, estate wines came into prominence. The wine Haut-Brion from Bordeaux was one of the leaders in this field. Vintages began to be much more important in the marketing of wines, with buyers seeking out those wines that came from the better years. Dom Perignon and some others began perfecting the *méthode champenoise*. The first account of the use of the "noble mold" *Botrytis cinerea* to develop a higher sugar content in the grape was reported in 1617. In 1755 Portugal established production areas called *ramos* where only domestic wines could be produced and other areas called *fist orias* where wine for export could be made. New scientific information helped upgrade the quality of alcoholic products. Pasteur unfolded the mystery of fermentation and showed how yeasts made alcohol from carbohydrate products. Other scientists such as Lavoisier made important discoveries which also advanced the industry. Advances in horticulture improved grape strains, resulting in higher-quality grapes and higher yields. In general, as more and more control was exercised over natural processes, products improved. New information was also compiled on how to make better distilled products.

Many countries began to become known for special beverages. France, Italy, Spain, and Portugal—in that order—were wine-producing countries, while Germany began to gain prominence in making both brews and wines. In England in Shakespeare's time, beer and ale rivaled wine as the national drink.

A number of excellent treatises on the making of alcoholic beverages appeared. André Jullien's *Topographie de Tous les Vignobles Connus* is still considered a classic. Other important books were Cyrus Redding's *History and Description of Modern Wines*, Jean-Antoine Chaptal's (chaptalization is named after him) *Traité sur La Vigne*, and Abbe Rozier's *Dictionnaire d'Agriculture*. These texts plus others indicated that the beverage industry had come of age.

Early America

When Leif Eriksson first visited the New World, he found the shores laden with grapes and was so impressed by their abundance that he called the new land Vinland (land of the vine). The American Indians undoubtedly ate the fruit and knew its juice would ferment to make wine. Columbus later discovered these native Americans making a brew "made of maize (corn), resembling English beer." Subsequently, Cortez brought the European grape to Mexico, and, to further its planting, required landholders to plant 100 vines for every Indian living on their land. The grapes prospered, and soon the New World was shipping so much wine to Spain that the Spanish government forbade further imports to save its own wine industry.

The first colonists on the eastern seaboard were not without their brews or wine. The Pilgrims' voyage was shortened to stop at Massachusetts and not Virginia as intended, because, as one passenger wrote, "We could not now take time for further search . . . our victuals being much spent, especially our bere." (The word beer comes from the old Anglo-Saxon word "baere" which meant barley). John Alden's job on the Mayflower was to maintain the beer barrels; he was a cooper. Later, the native Americans taught the Pilgrims to make a brew from corn, so they did not run short of it.

The first American brewery was built in New Amsterdam (later to be called New York City) in 1630. Later, Roger Williams built one in Rhode Island in 1637. Many of America's founding fathers were either brewers or strong advocates of alcoholic beverages. William Penn pioneered brewing in Pennsylvania, building the first brewery there in Bucks County in 1683. Thomas Jefferson had an elaborate distillery, brewhouse, and winery at Monticello. He collected all the books he could find on alcoholic beverages, adding them to his extensive library. He made a valiant effort to grow the European grape *Vitis vinifera*, but failed. He thought it was because the grape was not acclimated, but the cause was the phylloxera, a variety of plant lice that later destroyed most of Europe's grapevines (of which we will read later). He finally turned to native grapes. Samuel Adams, called the father of the American Revolution, was a brewer by profession. George Washington, whose handwritten recipe for making beer is shown in Exhibit 12.5, had seven stills on his property for making spirits; he made wine as well.

Brews and wines were favored over spirits by legislatures and Congress. It was thought the more moderate drinks were better for the populace than the stronger ones. A Budweiser pamphlet detailing the early history of beer notes that a Massachusetts act encouraged the manufacture of "strong beer, ale and other malt liquors. . . . The wholesome qualities of malt liquors greatly recommend them to general use as an important means of preserving the health of citizens of this commonwealth."

Throughout the colonies, it was common to see a tavern every 20 to 25 miles on main routes of travel. This was just about the distance of a half day's travel for a fast stage or a day's travel for a slow one. During the American Revolution, the taverns became centers for patriot gatherings. After the Revolution, the taverns moved with the settlers, springing up along travel routes and in towns and cities. As in Europe, the taverns became the centers of political, economic, and social life.

The Saloon. The Industrial Revolution and the subsequent growth of cities fostered the development of a new type of drinking place: the saloon or beer hall, which appeared in the 1880s. These new drinking places made fewer pretenses of serving food than taverns, existing largely for the sale of alcoholic beverages. However, in some, light lunches could be obtained—often free with a nickel glass of beer (hence the term "free lunch"). Pool halls often housed saloons or beer halls. These businesses were established for the common working man. Most served only male patrons, although a few had separate rooms with separate entrances for escorted female patrons.

Many of these new kinds of places were located in poorer areas where workers and their families lived. Some would let a guest drink too much—in fact, encourage it—so he would spend a goodly share of his paycheck,

Exhibit 12.5 George Washington's Beer-Making Recipe

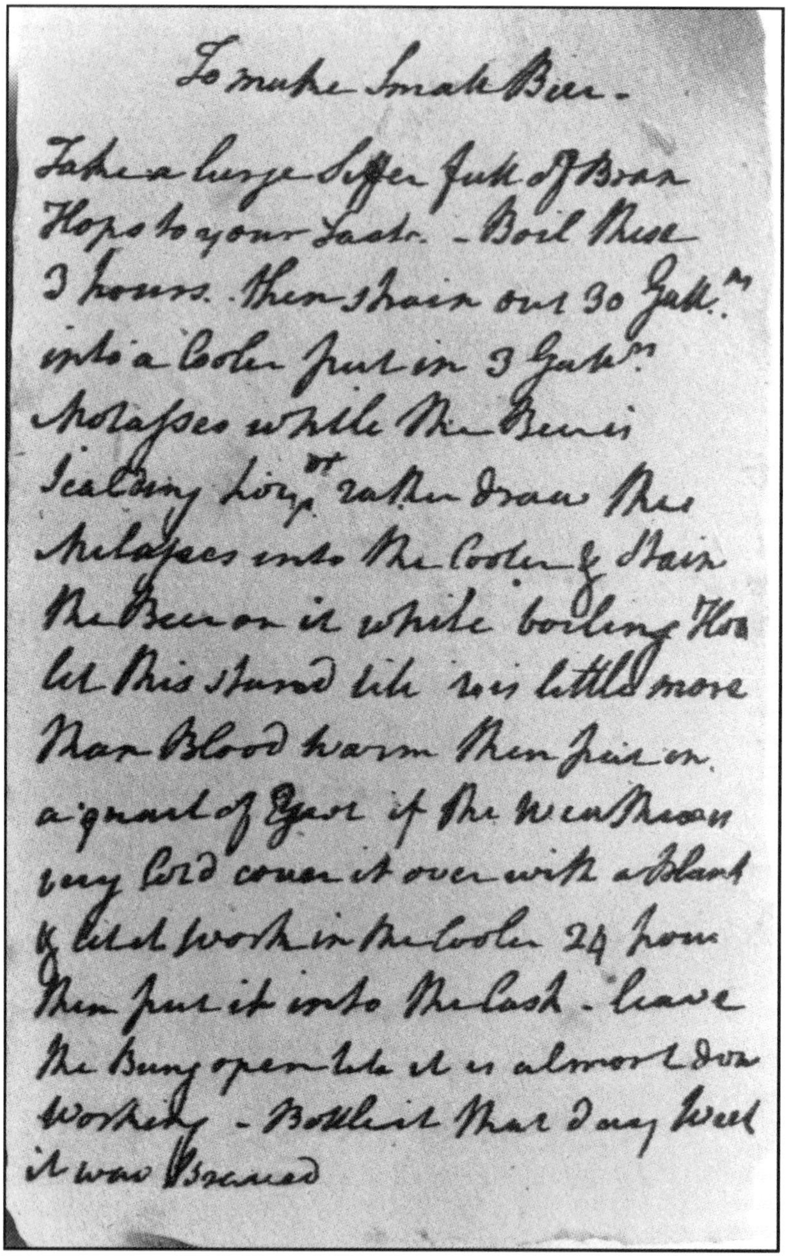
To make Small Beer.
Take a large Sifter full of Bran
Hops to your Taste. – Boil these
3 hours. Then strain out 30 Gall.
into a Cooler put in 3 Gall.
Molasses while the Beer is
Scalding hot or rather draw the
Molasses into the Cooler & Strain
the Beer on it while boiling Hot
let this stand till it is little more
than Blood warm Then put in
a quart of Yeast if the Weather is
very Cold cover it over with a Blanket
& let it work in the Cooler 24 hours
Then put it into the Cask – leave
the Bung open till it is almost done
working – Bottle it that day Week
it was Brewed

Courtesy of Anheuser-Busch

leaving little to support his family. Prostitution and other crimes often developed around these operations, giving them an unsavory reputation. Because of these conditions, many people began to believe that such operations should not exist. Gradually these people joined together and formed the Temperance Movement.

Hotels and Inns. With the advent of the railroad, hotels and inns appeared near railroad stations in cities and towns. Most were small and primarily served traveling salesmen, the occasional business traveler, and some visitors in the area. However, many offered food and drink as well as lodging. In the larger urban areas, luxurious hotels appeared—the Waldorf-Astoria Hotel in New York City, the Brown Palace in Denver, the Palmer House in Chicago, and the St. Francis in San Francisco. These hotels became famous for their elegance and the way they catered to the elite, the powerful, and the wealthy. Many a sumptuous banquet, toasted freely with champagne and other fine wines, was additionally graced by beautiful ladies in fancy gowns and brilliant jewels. All over the country, duplicates of these famous places were built; many of them are in business today, open to a larger segment of the public.

Restaurants. Before World War II, the restaurant industry was small. The restaurants that existed served the wealthy who could afford to eat out, travelers, and others who had no other place to eat. They were not patronized by common working people as they are today. Many restaurants did not bother to obtain liquor licenses because the demand for alcoholic beverages was low. However, restaurants patronized by those who could afford the price did offer alcoholic beverages. After World War II, the food service industry grew rapidly. By the late 1940s it was the sixth largest industry in the country, accounting for around six percent of the gross national product. More people had disposable income to spend in restaurants. Serving alcohol became profitable, and many operations added bars and lounges. Dining rooms also began serving alcohol.

The Temperance Movement. Opposition to alcohol is probably as old as alcohol production, and even though the consumption of alcoholic beverages has been worldwide, not all cultures approve of it. Religious groups like the Buddhists and Muslims have long condemned and even prohibited their use. In the United States, Seventh Day Adventists, Mormons, some Methodists, and some Baptists opposed the use of alcoholic beverages. The social ills which became associated with saloons led many others to question the desirability of the sale of alcoholic beverages. This opposition to alcohol grew with time, and soon the Temperance Movement had many adherents, many of them women. One woman, Carry Amelia Nation, became the national leader of an aggressive temperance group. She and her followers gained notoriety for themselves and the movement by destroying saloons with hatchets.

In the early 1900s, many temperance groups and religious organizations joined together to press for the passage of laws that would prohibit the sale of alcohol. World War I had brought about a shortage of grain, and the adherents of the temperance movement pointed out that because grain was used to make spirits and brews, prohibition would help the war effort by saving grain. In 1920 the Eighteenth Amendment became law. It forbade the production, sale, or consumption of any alcoholic beverage over 2.25% alcohol by volume. The amendment was ratified by 46 states (all except Vermont and Rhode Island). Thus, the United States became an officially "dry" nation.

However, the nation became dry in name only. An illicit industry quickly sprang up, and the hidden manufacture and sale of alcoholic beverages became widespread. In the "Roaring Twenties" it became fashionable to defy the law by patronizing speakeasies or producing homemade alcoholic beverages. Homemade wine, homebrew (beer), bathtub gin, and other beverages were common. "Rum-running," the illegal importation of alcoholic beverages, increased dramatically. Law enforcement officers were unable to enforce a law which so many refused to support. Organized crime gained a foothold in the lucrative alcohol market. The consumption of alcoholic beverages increased, and there were more establishments selling alcohol than there had been before Prohibition.

The situation got so bad that supporters of the Eighteenth Amendment now admitted that it was a failure. President Coolidge gave it a subtle death blow when he called it a "noble experiment." The amendment was repealed in 1934.

Post-Prohibition. Although Prohibition failed, it helped clarify the need for alcohol regulation. Individual states established laws controlling the industry. For example, 17 states became monopoly states, meaning that packaged alcoholic beverages above a specified alcoholic content must be purchased in state-controlled liquor stores. Some of these states allowed the sale of alcoholic beverages from other than state-owned stores, if the stores purchased these beverages through state-owned stores. Many of these states in various ways also controlled the sale of alcoholic beverages by the drink. Some states, counties, and communities established stricter regulations; even today there are a few "dry" areas in the United States.

States that did not become monopoly states became license states, meaning that anyone selling alcohol had to be licensed to produce or sell alcohol. Some license states had certain kinds of control on the sale of alcohol either as packaged goods or by the drink. Thus, in the state of Texas until 1960, if one wanted to drink in public, one had to buy alcohol by the bottle and then pour it into a glass provided by the establishment. "Setups," which included glasses and soft drink accompaniments, were also sold for this purpose. In 1990 there were 18 monopoly states and 32 license states; the District of Columbia is also a license area.

Classifications of Alcoholic Beverages

Alcoholic beverages can be classified as distilled spirits, wines, or malt beverages. Distilled spirits may be further divided into spirits and liqueurs (cordials).

Distilled Spirits

Distilled spirits are liquors obtained from the process of distillation; the term is often used synonymously with liquor. Distilled spirits include whiskeys, rum, brandy, gin, vodka, ethyl alcohol, and others, or any dilution or mixtures of these, used for human consumption. Distilled spirits do not include mixtures that are half or more wine, such as wines fortified with brandy like sherry or dessert wines.

Wines

Wine is the fermented juice of fruit, usually grapes; wine made from other fruits (berries or citrus fruits) must be labeled to show the type of fruit. Thus, a wine made from grapes may be labeled "Spanish Red," but a wine made from peaches would need to be labeled "peach wine." Wine made from apples or pears may be designated cider or perry, respectively. Labels must identify wines made from raisins or other dried fruits. Wine can also be made from the residue of grape pressings, fruit, or other agricultural products mixed with water.

Malt Beverages   The Federal Alcohol Administration Act of 1935 states that a **malt beverage** is one made with some barley malt and hops; it may or may not contain other malted or unmalted cereal products or other carbohydrates, or products made from them. In addition, other wholesome substances suitable for human consumption may or may not be used. The addition of carbon dioxide is permitted.

Malt beverages are named variously according to their ingredients, brewing method, or historical uses. They may be labeled "beer," "lager beer," "lager," "porter," "stout," or a variety of other names as long as they contain a half percent alcohol or more by volume. For tax purposes, *sake* and some other alcoholic beverages made from unmalted products are classified as malt beverages. Some malt beverages are labeled "half and half," which means they are an equal blend of two different malt beverages. Half and half is popular in Great Britain.

Characteristics of Alcoholic Beverages

Alcohol Content   The word **proof** refers to the alcohol content of a spirit and is derived from the Latin word *probare,* meaning to prove or test. At one time, there was no reliable way to test the amount of alcohol in a spirit. One could water down a spirit and sell the diluted product as "the real stuff." It was difficult to prove otherwise. However, an inventive Englishman discovered that gunpowder mixed with a spirit would fire and that a spirit lower in alcohol content than a certain percentage would not fire. The lowest alcohol content at which a spirit would fire when mixed with gunpowder was adopted as the British standard. If a mixture of gunpowder and spirit fired, it was considered *proof* that the spirit had been diluted only to the legal standard. The standard was termed "100 proof"; anything over proof (OP) was over 100 and anything under proof (UP) was under 100. The British retain this system, although the original test of firing to check the content is rarely performed.

Other standards are used to indicate alcohol content: the European Gay-Lussac standard and the American standard. Both are based on the percentage of alcohol by volume. The Gay-Lussac standard is based on the actual percentage of alcohol, while the American standard is twice the actual. Exhibit 12.6 compares the three standards.

U.S. law requires that all spirit labels state proof and that imported spirits be labeled in American proof. Malt beverage labels need not indicate alcohol content. Wines must be labeled with the percentage of alcohol by volume. Exhibit 12.7 shows two examples of alcohol content labeling.

In the United States, spirits (except cordials) are usually from 80 to 100 proof; cordials are usually 36 to 60 proof. Regular beers are 3.2% by weight. Table wines are from 7 to 14% alcohol by volume, while dessert and aperitif wines range from 14 to 24% alcohol by volume. There are exceptions; for example, some rums are 151 proof, and a neutral spirit like White Lightning may be 190 proof.

The amount of alcohol by weight differs from the amount of alcohol by volume. The weight of water is 1.22 times that of ethanol; conversely,

Exhibit 12.6 Comparative Proof Standards

	British	Gay-Lussac	American
Pure alcohol	175	100	200
	100	57	114
	88	50	100
	79	45	90
	75	43	86
	70	40	80
	65	37	74
Pure water	0	0	0

the weight of ethanol is 0.82 that of water. Thus, while a liter of water weighs 1,000 grams, a liter of alcohol weighs only 820 grams. The following rules convert alcohol content by one measure or the other:

- To convert alcohol by volume to alcohol by weight, multiply the alcohol volume by 0.82.

- To convert alcohol by weight to alcohol by volume, multiply the alcohol weight by 1.22.

The alcohol content of distilled spirits is stated in proof, which is the percentage of alcohol by volume multiplied by two. Without going into precise mathematical calculations, you can convert proof to the approximate amount of alcohol by weight by dividing proof by two and multiplying the result by 0.82. Using this approximation, a distilled spirit of 80 proof would be 33% alcohol by weight ([80 ÷ 2] × 0.82 = .328 = 33%).[2] The alcohol content of wine is stated in percent by volume. A wine of 11% alcohol would be 9% by weight (.11 × 0.82 = 0.09 or 9%). The alcohol content of malt beverages is stated in percent by weight. Thus, a 3.2% beer would be 3.9% alcohol by volume (0.032 × 1.22 = 0.039 = 3.9%, rounded to 4%).

Calorie Content

Alcohol packs a fairly good wallop when it comes to calories (see Exhibit 12.8). A pure carbohydrate (like starch or sugar) or protein as found in meat, eggs, or cheese has four calories per gram, and fat has nine, with alcohol in between at seven calories per gram. Because alcohol's caloric content is so high, many who consume a considerable amount of alcohol are overweight.

To calculate the calorie content of an alcoholic beverage, the alcohol content must be expressed by weight because the caloric value is measured by weight. For example, two ounces of 80 proof (33% alcohol by weight) scotch would contain about 129 calories, calculated as follows: 33% (alcohol by weight) × 56 grams (number of grams in 2 oz) × 7 (calories per gram) = 129.36. The *alcohol content* of a 4-ounce glass of 12% (alcohol by volume) dinner wine contributes 77 calories, calculated as follows: 4 oz × 28 grams (per ounce) × 0.12 × 0.82 × 7 calories/g = 77 calories; but since the wine has *other caloric items* in it, you add five calories per ounce, which gives about 97 calories. If this were an 18% (alcohol by volume) dessert wine, you would add an extra eight calories per ounce because of the extra

Exhibit 12.7   Labels Showing Alcohol Content

Courtesy of Berry Bros. and Rudd Ltd., London, England, and Brittany Imports Corp., Miami, Florida

sugar such wine contains. For the non-alcoholic ingredients in beer, add about 4.5 calories per ounce. A 12-ounce can of 3.2% (alcohol by weight) beer would contain about 129 calories (0.032 × [12 × 28 grams per oz] × 7 = 75), plus the extra calorie calculation of 12 oz × 4.5 = 54.

Mixed drinks are often higher in calories because of their non-alcoholic ingredients. For example, the alcohol in a martini made with two ounces of 80 proof gin and a half ounce of 20% vermouth contains 129 + 18 or 147 calories. Add the olive and the non-alcoholic calories in the vermouth and you get between 160 and 165 calories. A manhattan made with two

Exhibit 12.8 A Comparison of Alcoholic Beverage Caloric Values

Alcohol and Calories	PRODUCT	SIZE of Drink	ALCOHOL in Drink	CALORIES in Drink
Fact v. Perception	**Distilled Spirits** 80° Proof (40%)	**1½ oz.**	**.6 oz.** (.4 alcohol x 1½ oz.)	**†100.5**
†Highballs: club soda and most diet sodas add 0 to 1 calories	**Table Wine** 12%	**5 oz.**	**.6 oz.** (.12 alcohol x 5 oz.)	***120**
*Light wine 72 calories **Light beer typically 95 to 105 calories. SOURCE: ABP and industry data.	**Lager Beer** 5%	**12 oz.**	**.6 oz.** (.05 alcohol x 12 oz.)	****130–140**

Courtesy of Beverage Media

ounces of 80 proof rye whiskey, a half ounce of sweet 20% (alcohol by volume) vermouth, and a cherry contains about 157 calories:

Rye whiskey	129 calories
Vermouth (alcohol)	16 calories
Vermouth (non-alcoholic substances)	4 calories
Cherry	8 calories
Total	157 calories

Carbonated beverages containing sweeteners have, on the average, 10 calories per ounce; some, such as colas and Tom Collinses, contain 12 calories per ounce. A drink containing two ounces of 80 proof gin and five ounces of tonic water would contain 179 calories—129 from alcohol and 50 from five ounces of tonic water.

Production of Alcoholic Beverages

Making an alcoholic beverage is a simple process. All you need are some fermentable materials in a warm liquid, and nature does the rest. However, making the kinds of alcoholic products available today takes a lot of knowledge, skill, and application. It is imperative that the correct materials be used. The fermentation process must be proper for the product and must be controlled to give the unique qualities wanted in the various kinds of beverages. A distilled spirit must be made from the right materials, be properly distilled, and (depending on the spirit) be flavored correctly. Many products require a carefully controlled aging process. And some products need blending and/or rectification to be ready for consumption. All this takes expertise, and today such expertise is demanded by the market.

Fermentation

All alcoholic beverages are the result of fermentation or the presence of a fermented product. Different fermentation processes are used to produce distilled spirits, wines, and malt beverages. The differences help preserve each product's unique qualities. Fermentation is a natural process. To achieve desired results, however, the correct yeast, temperature, environment, and handling are necessary. **Fermentation** is a process in which yeast changes a sugar, glucose, into ethyl alcohol (ethanol) C_2H_5OH) and carbon dioxide (CO_2). Heat is developed in the process. The enzyme zymase, which is carried in the yeast, facilitates the chemical change. Other enzymes may be needed to reduce some starches and sugars to glucose so the yeast can feed on it and convert it to ethanol. Examples of such enzymes are diastase (found in wheat) or maltase (found in barley). The chemical process may be shown as follows:

$$C_6H_{12}O_6 \xrightarrow{\Delta} 2C_2H_5OH + 2CO_2\uparrow$$

(glucose)   (ethanol)   (carbon dioxide)

The triangle above the arrow indicates heat is formed; the arrow pointing upward after the CO_2 indicates the carbon dioxide is a gas which escapes. In some fermentations, the heat developed can build up to a point where it must be controlled by circulating cold water, ethylene glycol, or another cold liquid around the fermenting vat or in coils placed in the fermenting solution. The carbon dioxide may be trapped and retained as it is in champagne. Some brewers also capture the carbon dioxide and re-incorporate it later to give effervescence to malt beverages. Yeast will grow in temperatures ranging from around 50° F (10° C) to 115° F (46° C), but it does best at human body temperature (98.6° F, 37° C).

Under favorable conditions, the desired fermentation may take from several days to over a month. Fermenting time depends on the amount of glucose produced, the temperature, and other factors. Yeast multiplies during the fermentation process; in a week of good fermentation, it may increase fourfold or more. Fermentation ceases when conditions are no longer favorable—when the temperature gets too low or too high, when the alcohol content reaches 14 to 15%, or when the yeast runs out of glucose. A solution that contains more than 55% sugar is also not fermentable.

Not all fermentable liquids contain glucose; yeast contains enzymes that change other kinds of carbohydrates to glucose. For example, grapes contain fructose; the enzymes in the yeast must change this to glucose. Yeast also converts complex carbohydrates such as starches into glucose. However, this process is more complex and slows fermentation, impeding some of its favorable actions. To avoid this, producers often facilitate the change themselves by sprouting barley and some other grains, a process in which enzymes in the sprouting plant change starch to maltose. They may also add enzymes to change starch to glucose. Yeast easily attacks maltose, splitting it into two glucose molecules. Some grains or other carbohydrate substances can be finely ground and then cooked into mashes; this hydrolyzes and gelatinizes the starches and some sugars, making it easier for the yeast to attack them. Before yeast can do this, however, other enzymes such as diastase or maltase must break these starches and more complex sugars down into glucose.

Weight Changes. A chemist might say that glucose has a weight of 180 units; ethyl alcohol, a weight of 46 units; and carbon dioxide, 44 units. In fermentation, one glucose molecule splits up into two ethanol molecules and two carbon dioxide molecules, which arithmetically can be shown as $180 = (2 \times 46) + (2 \times 44)$. Since the carbon dioxide is a gas, it escapes, leaving only ethanol, so the mixture gets lighter by that amount. This is the reason for saying that for every 2% of sugar, fermentation yields 1% of ethanol. Thus, a grape must that is 22% sugar can ferment down to an 11% alcohol-by-weight wine. (A **grape must** is the juice of grapes obtained from pressings before fermentation; it contains small amounts of seeds and stems.) It will be a dry wine with little or no sugar left.

Yeast. Wild yeasts are abundant and only need food and a favorable environment to reproduce. They can easily drop from the air into a warm, liquid food and start to ferment it. For this reason, fermentation was once thought to be a spontaneous action, but Louis Pasteur and others refuted this idea when they proved fermentation was caused by yeast and identified many of the substances that fermentation produced.

For many years, wild yeasts were used for fermentation. Brewers, vintners, and others eventually developed yeasts which would produce specific results. Brewers developed cultured yeasts that would ferment malt brews near the surface. Others developed yeasts which fermented beer slowly at the bottom of the fermenting vat. The two beers that result are quite different. Vintners today use various strains of the yeast *Saccharomyces cerivisiae* to produce specific results. However, wild yeasts are still used. *Mycoderma vini*, a wild yeast found in the Jerez area of Spain, ferments from the top, forming a thick film over the liquid and producing the desired flavor of sherry.

Various methods are used to stop wild yeasts from getting into brews. A sterile mash is used to make a distilled spirit or a malt beverage. Both are inoculated with a special yeast so fermentation takes place quickly before wild yeasts can establish themselves. Vintners kill wild yeasts in the fermenting vat and the surrounding air by burning sulfur to create sulfur dioxide gas, which is lethal to them. The desired cultured yeast is then added.

Congeners. In some fermentations, as much as 5% of the sugar may be turned into substances other than ethyl alcohol, such as acids, glycerine, phenolics, butyl alcohol, propyl alcohol, and fusel oil. These fermentation products are often called **congeners** or components and may be desirable or undesirable.

Glycerine is a congener that makes wine taste smooth. Its presence in any quantity can be detected by whirling wine in a glass; the tiny legs or rivulets on the sides of the glass are caused by it. Small amounts of propyl, butyl, amyl, and other alcohols, also formed during fermentation, enhance a wine's fruity aroma, as do aromatic substances such as fragrant aldehydes. Esters form during fermentation when alcohol and an acid combine; they too can be highly aromatic. Fragrant aldehydes and esters are important constituents of perfumes.

Distilled spirits and malt brews develop far fewer congeners during fermentation than wine does. The development and importance of congeners in distilled spirits and malt beverages are discussed in Chapters 13 and 14, respectively.

Fermentation of Distilled Spirits. The liquid distilled for spirits is often called **wort** or **distiller's beer**, the latter because it is produced by the same method as beer. Wort is produced from a cooked mash made from carbohydrates which have been converted into sugars, such as glucose,

Making wort for American whiskey in fermenting tanks. (Courtesy of Makers' Mark Distillery)

maltose, or some form of dextrin. Special cultured yeasts are added and fermentation takes place at temperatures around 70° to 80° F (21° to 27° C); the process takes from two to four days. The resulting wort is usually 6 to 7% alcohol, although it may go as high as 10%. At this point the wort is ready for distillation.

Fermentation of Malt Beverages. Two fermentation processes are used to produce malt beverages: top and bottom. Top fermentations are fast, usually taking no more than a week. A special kind of yeast is used and the temperature is kept high. The resulting product has a slight yeast flavor and is not as smooth as some other brews. British brews such as ale, stout, and porter are top-fermented.

Bottom-fermented brews are fermented slowly at low temperatures for much longer periods of time—sometimes as long as several months. This process produces a smoother, softer brew than top-fermented brews. Bottom-fermented brews are called **lagers.**

Fermentation of Wine. Under favorable conditions, yeast grows rapidly in a wine must. In a large vat of fermenting must, the yeast activity is violent and produces a sound much like a railroad train passing by. Outdoor vats may attract fruit flies which carry bacteria that turn alcohol into acetic acid (vinegar). Because fermentation requires oxygen, the fermenting liquid cannot be sealed to exclude these fruit flies. Many vintners therefore prefer an indoor fermenting room.

Grape skins of red grapes are sometimes fermented with the must to produce the red color in wines. These skins, along with some stems and seeds, form a thick cap on the surface of the fermenting liquid. This cap must be broken up periodically to secure desirable fermentation.

Red wines are quickly fermented. It usually takes five to seven days to completely ferment all the sugar, producing a dry wine. The temperature is kept between 70° and 90° F (21° to 32° C). These temperatures foster the development of desirable congeners such as acids, tannins, glycerine, and other substances which help to preserve the wine or enhance its quality.

Fermentation produces some undesirable components such as fusel oil and excess acids and tannins. **Thermovinification,** a recently developed process, helps reduce the formation of such substances in red wines. In this process, the must and skins are heated to 156° to 160° F (69° to 71° C) for about 30 minutes; this extracts the necessary red color. The skins are then removed and fermentation proceeds without the skins and other substances. Removing them in this way reduces tannin and often acid, resulting in a smoother, softer, and fresher-tasting wine.

White wines are fermented more slowly and at lower temperatures (45° to 60° F, 7° to 16° C) than red wines. This process retains volatile aromatics and reduces acid formation, producing a more delicate wine. Fermentation lasts from 10 to 14 days. The temperature must be at least 35° F (10° C) for this to occur.

A rosé wine is produced by leaving the skins with the fermenting must for about 24 hours; this gives it a light tint of pink or red. The skins are then removed and the wine is fermented much like white wine. Because the skins are often left overnight, rosé is often called *vin de nuit*—wine of the night.

Sweet wine is produced by stopping fermentation before the yeast converts all the sugar or by having some sugar left when alcohol stops fermentation at about 14%. The wine is then passed through filters fine enough to remove yeasts, bacteria, and other microorganisms. Such filtration is called **sterile filtration;** no further fermentation can occur because all organisms that might cause it have been removed.

Tartaric acid (cream of tartar) is the primary acid formed in wine fermentation. Chilling precipitates tartaric acid; much of it settles to the bottom of casks in cold storage as a precipitate. Some tartaric acid also precipitates when wine is matured in the bottle, forming lees on the bottom.

Tart (high-acid) grapes do not necessarily produce a high-acid wine. Alcohol tends to precipitate tartaric acid; thus a wine high in alcohol decreases in acidity as it ages and matures. Most of a grape's sugar turns to alcohol, so a grape high in sugar is high in alcohol if fermentation is left to go on naturally. Thus, a high-sugar, high-acid grape (such as the Pinot Noir) can make a fairly low-acid wine, and a low-acid, low-sugar grape (such as the Gamay) may produce a wine of higher acid content.

Vintage. Sometimes it is desirable to know the year an alcoholic product came into existence. A vintage date indicates the year a wine was fermented. The term is not used for other beverages. A vintage designation can indicate wine quality because the grapes and other conditions can vary from year to year, causing better wines to be made in some years than in others. In addition, the vintage year gives an approximation of how long the wine has been maturing in the bottle, since most wines are bottled in the spring following the year in which they were fermented.

Distillation

Distillation is a process in which a fermented liquid is heated to separate the ethanol from it. The liquid is usually mainly water, which vaporizes at 212° F (100° C), while alcohol vaporizes at 176° F (80° C). Thus, by heating a liquid containing ethanol above its vaporization point, but not to that of water, the vapor can be captured and cooled to become a liquid separate from the water, which never vaporized because the heat was not high enough. It is now in a very concentrated form. It does contain some water as well as other congeners. The device in which the liquid is heated is called a **still.** Cooling of the ethanol vapor is done in what is called a **condenser.** Some type of container must be provided to catch the distillate after it condenses.

Thus, the basic parts of a distillation system are the still in which the liquid is heated until the alcohol and its accompanying substances vaporize, and a condenser in which these vapors are cooled down to a liquid state. Other equipment components include the container into which the distillate is deposited and sometimes a **gin-head** through which vapors are passed to pick up flavor.

Types of Distillation. There are two types of stills: pot stills and patent or Coffey stills (also called column or continuous stills). Each type is used to produce a distinct kind of distilled product.

A **pot still** is a rounded pot with a tapering funnel at the top where rising vapors can be collected and then be carried off to the condenser through a tube. After each distillation, the still must be emptied of spent material and cleaned before being filled with new distilling material. The still is heated from underneath. In some cases, the old method of building a wood fire underneath is used, but most stills today are heated by controlled heat. Distilling temperatures are held down so distillates come off usually at about 110 to 160 proof. This allows more congeners to vaporize with the ethanol, thus heightening the spirit's flavor and body.

In pot distillation, it is common to separate the distillate obtained into a first part (head), middle part (heart), and last part (tail). Only the middle part is used to make a spirit. The first and last parts are put back into a liquid about to be distilled and redistilled (see Exhibits 12.9 and 12.10). Many times the middle part is redistilled. For example, malt scotch is distilled twice, and Irish whiskey is distilled three times. Redistillation is done to clean and improve product quality.

Exhibit 12.9 Drawing of a Pot Still

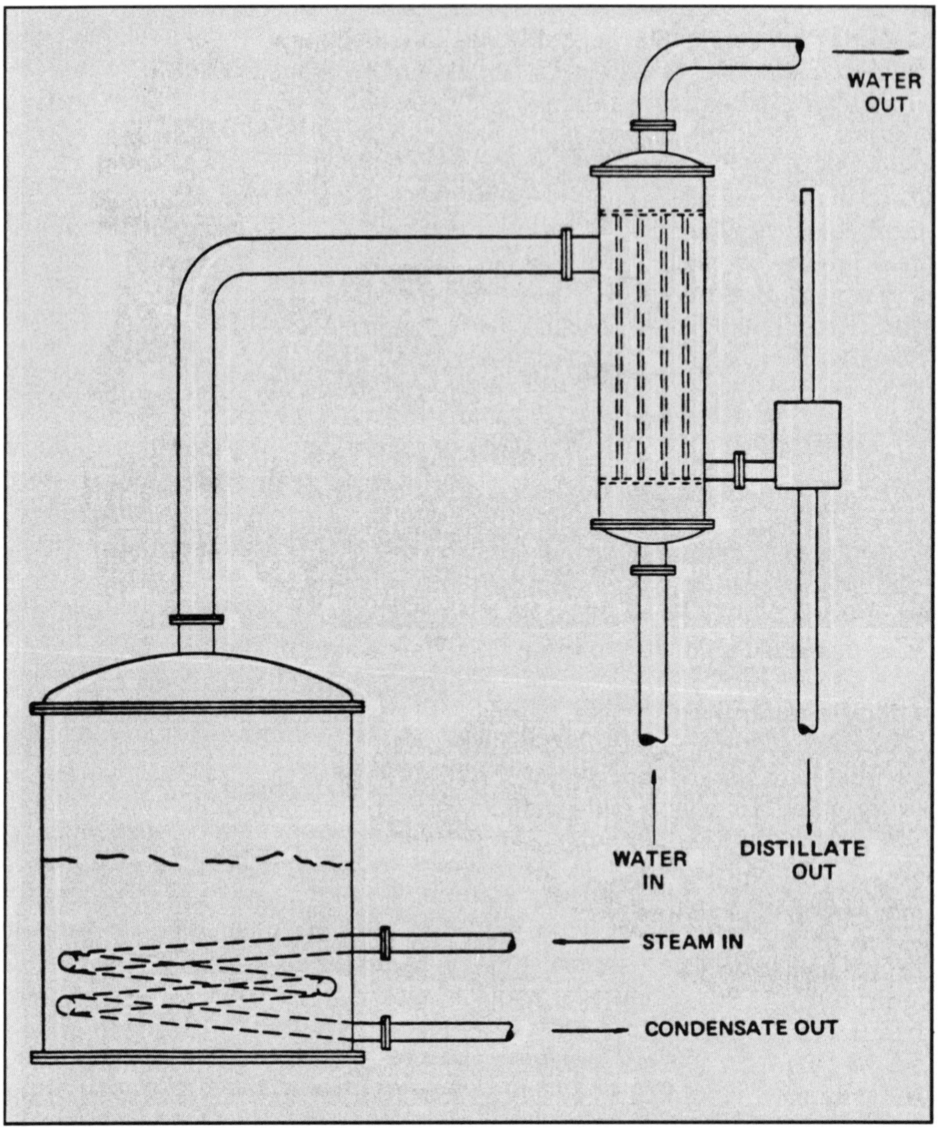

WATER OUT

WATER IN

DISTILLATE OUT

STEAM IN

CONDENSATE OUT

Courtesy of Hiram Walker & Sons, Ltd., Canada

A **patent still** is both a vaporizer and condenser; its condensing system consists of a number of condensing spaces placed at strategic points in the still. Most patent stills are single towers or cylinders several stories high, but some are set up as two cylinders. Exhibits 12.11 and 12.12 show drawings of these two arrangements.

The process is one in which preheated wort or fermented liquid is introduced at the top of the cylinder while steam to heat it is introduced on the bottom. As the liquid falls, it strikes baffle plates, where it is heated until the ethanol vaporizes. It is then possible to get different temperatures between baffle plates so a much purer ethanol is obtained, because many of the components do not vaporize at exactly the same temperature as the ethanol. These components are condensed at different points in the cylinder and drawn off. Some, like fusel oil, have value; fusel oil is used as a paint

Exhibit 12.10 Pot-Still Arrangement Used for Distilling Scotch Twice

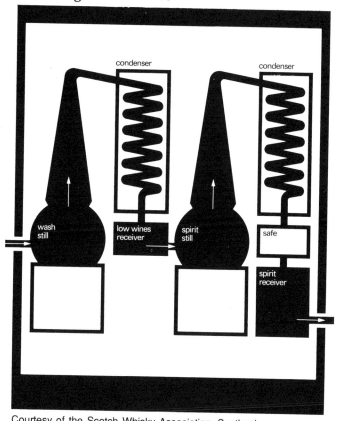

Courtesy of the Scotch Whisky Association, Scotland

solvent and for a number of other purposes. The ethanol comes out of the still at 190 proof or slightly below it. The spent liquid falls to the bottom of the cylinder and is drawn off. Thus the process can be continuous, with spent liquid being drawn off at the bottom. Almost all spirits in the United States are made by using the continuous patent-still method; only some brandies and a few other spirits are distilled by the pot-still method.

Patent-still products made from grain are called grain neutral spirits. Tasteless and colorless, they can be used to make vodka or flavored spirits such as liqueurs and gin. They are also used for blending. In Scotland, grain scotch is used to blend with malt scotch. Patent-still spirits are rarely redistilled, and they are less costly to make because patent stills can make more alcohol in a given time. Also, patent stills are less costly to operate in terms of labor. In Scotland there are hundreds of pot stills and only seven patent stills, but these seven make far more alcohol than all the other pot stills combined.

Rectification. To rectify, in the language of the distiller or bottler, is to redistill a spirit. **Rectification** is usually done to improve a spirit's quality. However, to the U.S. government, rectification means blending a spirit with anything other than water. Thus, what is called a blended whiskey in the United States is, by government definition, rectified. When cordials are produced by adding flavors, sugar, and perhaps coloring, the process

Exhibit 12.11 Single-Cylinder Patent or Continuous Still

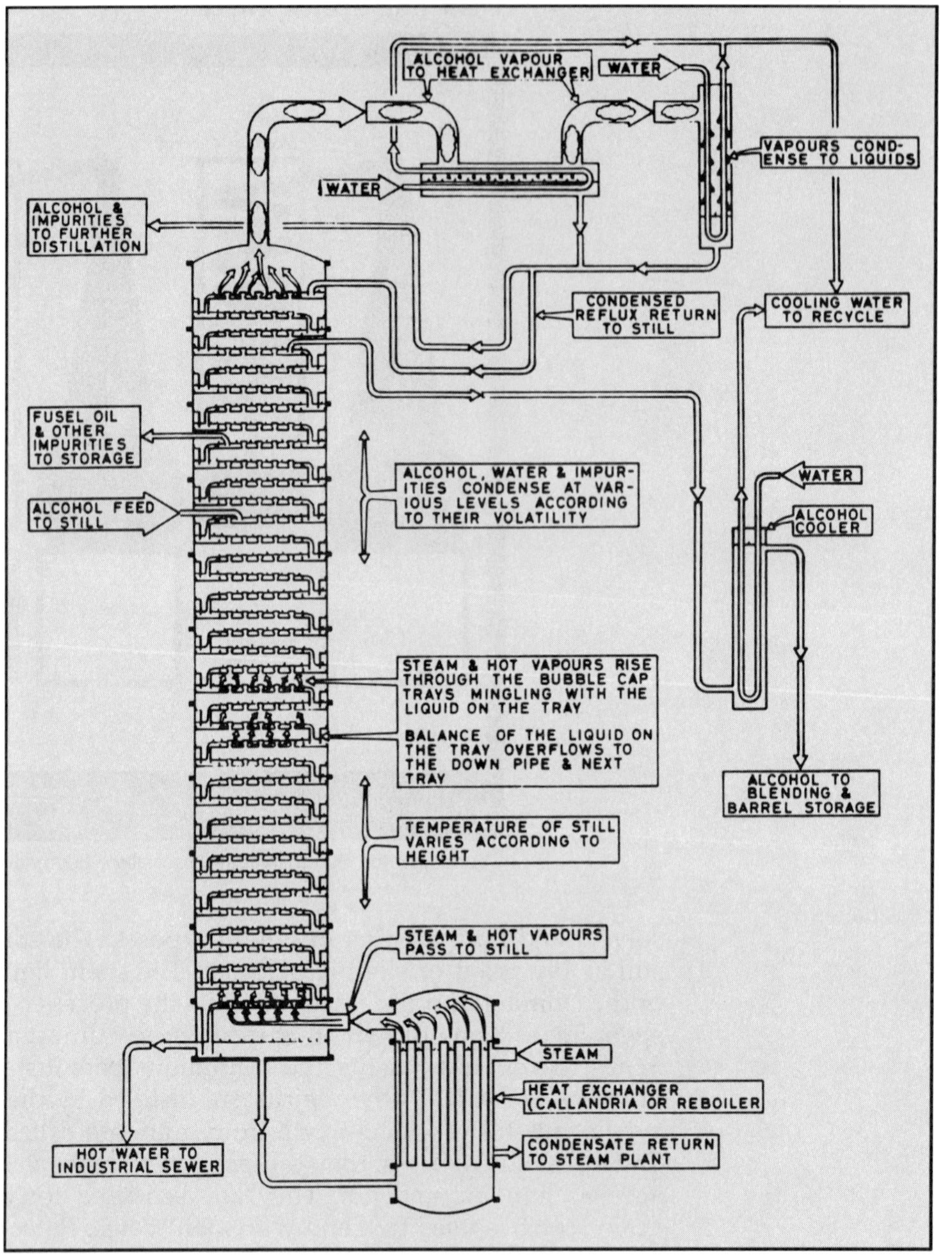

ALCOHOL VAPOUR TO HEAT EXCHANGER | WATER

VAPOURS CONDENSE TO LIQUIDS

WATER

ALCOHOL & IMPURITIES TO FURTHER DISTILLATION

CONDENSED REFLUX RETURN TO STILL

COOLING WATER TO RECYCLE

FUSEL OIL & OTHER IMPURITIES TO STORAGE

ALCOHOL, WATER & IMPURITIES CONDENSE AT VARIOUS LEVELS ACCORDING TO THEIR VOLATILITY

WATER

ALCOHOL COOLER

ALCOHOL FEED TO STILL

STEAM & HOT VAPOURS RISE THROUGH THE BUBBLE CAP TRAYS MINGLING WITH THE LIQUID ON THE TRAY

BALANCE OF THE LIQUID ON THE TRAY OVERFLOWS TO THE DOWN PIPE & NEXT TRAY

ALCOHOL TO BLENDING & BARREL STORAGE

TEMPERATURE OF STILL VARIES ACCORDING TO HEIGHT

STEAM & HOT VAPOURS PASS TO STILL

STEAM

HEAT EXCHANGER (CALLANDRIA OR REBOILER)

CONDENSATE RETURN TO STEAM PLANT

HOT WATER TO INDUSTRIAL SEWER

Courtesy of Hiram Walker & Sons, Ltd., Canada

is rectification. Adding flavor to gin by running it though a gin-head is also rectification. The U.S. government taxes all rectification processes.

Aging   Wine and spirits are usually aged before bottling. Malt beverages are not aged; they should be consumed after a short adjustment period in the bottle. Some malt beverages undergo a type of aging called lagering during fermentation. (Lagering is discussed in Chapter 14).

In general, a long aging period produces a better alcoholic beverage. However, this is not always the case. Some delicate wines begin to lose

Exhibit 12.12 Two-Cylinder Patent or Continuous Still

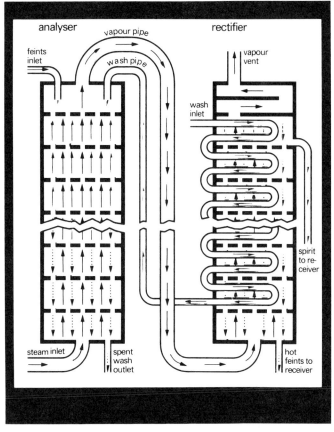

Courtesy of the Scotch Whisky Association, Scotland

quality if aged too long; such a wine is said to be "going downhill." Some whiskeys cease development after a certain period of time and may even begin to lose quality. Some alcoholic products become flavorless after too much aging.

Aging Spirits. Spirits under 190 proof are aged in wooden barrels. Aging time varies: some light rums may be aged only a year, while the best brandies may be aged over 20 years. The best scotch is aged for about 15 years. After this, it is apt to take on a woody flavor from the cask.

The Scottish government requires that scotch be aged at least three years. Some rums and most whiskeys are aged to make them mellower and smoother.

Spirits aged in an oak cask absorb flavor from the wood. Wood also allows a small amount of air to come in contact with the spirit, and there is a slow physical and chemical change that improves quality. Wooden barrels are often charred inside, and the activated charcoal in the charred material changes some of a spirit's constituents. It also adds color. Scotch is often aged in old sherry casks to give it added flavor.

This old distillery at Cardhu is still in operation. (Courtesy of United Distillers, Scotland)

Spirits aged in wood generally mellow with age, losing some of their raw, sharp, and biting characteristics. Aged spirits become smoother. We can account for some of these changes. Aging in casks usually decreases the alcoholic content of spirits slightly. Spirits evaporate (about 2% each year) when aged in casks.

In the United States, **bonded spirits** are those aged in bonded warehouses—warehouses under government supervision. A company placing its spirits in bond gives up control of the product for the storage period, receiving a certificate indicating the company has the quantity and type of spirits described in the certificate. These certificates serve as a type of loan collateral. The company must present the certificate to get back its bonded product. The government will certify that the spirits have been aging in bonded storage for the time they are under bond.

Modern pot stills in the stillhouse at Cardhu Distillery. (Courtesy of United Distillers, Scotland)

A spirit must be stored at least four years in a government-bonded warehouse to be certified as bonded. The use of a green stamp to indicate a bonded spirit has been discontinued, as well as use of the pink stamp to indicate a blended one. Instead, companies are now placed on their honor. They blend and bottle without government supervision, report to the government periodically on the amount they withdraw from bonded inventory, and pay the tax due. The label indicates whether the spirit is a bonded one.

Spirits labeled as bonded must be produced from a single distillation, be distilled at 160 proof or less, be bottled at 100 proof, and be unblended, which means the spirit is a straight whiskey.

Bonding does not guarantee quality. Poor-quality spirits can be bonded. However, when a liquor is bonded, it usually indicates that the aging period improved the original quality of the product.

Aging Wines. After fermentation, wine is often placed into casks for aging. The casks are stored in caves or other cool areas. The cool temperatures help to precipitate tannins and other congeners, and the wine clarifies, becoming more brilliant. In oak-cask aging, some "hard" tannins precipitate out of the wine, and "soft" tannins from the oak take

Barrels of malt scotch stored for aging in the Glenkinchie, Scotland, warehouse.
(Courtesy of United Distillers, Scotland)

their place. The former give wine a harsh astringency, while the latter give wine a softer one. Most wines are aged over the winter and removed from the casks in the spring, often for bottling. Some are blended with other wines before bottling.

As a result of aging, some acids are reduced, making the wine less tart. Other subtle changes occur. Fortification—increasing the alcohol content by adding spirits—stops fermentation and can prevent some wine from aging further. When wine ages in the cask, it purifies itself through air exposure and other natural processes. Cool aging temperatures precipitate tannins, tartaric acid, and other congeners.

After bottling, wine continues to have some minute contact with air through the cork. This can cause further changes. In addition, some chemical and physical changes occur, causing the wine to mature.

Blending   Many spirits are blends. A **blend** is a mixture of two or more similar products, such as two or more of the same kind of spirits or two or more wines. Most scotches are a blend of grain and malt whiskeys. Irish whiskey is also blended. Sherry depends a good deal upon blending for its character. Most champagnes are a blend of different wines from different grapes and often from different years. U.S. wines are mostly blends. Most brandy is blended. What is called blended whiskey in the United States is a straight whiskey (whiskey from one distilling) blended with grain neutral spirits in a ratio of up to 20:80.

The White Horse blending and bottling plant in Glasgow, Scotland. (Courtesy of United Distillers, Scotland)

Blending is usually done to produce desirable flavors, body, or other characteristics in the final product. For instance, southern France produces a good but somewhat ordinary wine. It is therefore blended with a heavier-bodied North African wine to create a more balanced wine. Blending is not an indication of a lack of quality. In fact, blending may make top-quality products out of lesser ones. The clarets produced by merchants or shippers called *négociants* are often compared favorably with the best wines from Bordeaux.

After an alcoholic beverage is blended, it is allowed to rest for a time to completely mix and unify. The process is called **marrying.**

Increasing Your Product Knowledge

This chapter has provided a basis for understanding the in-depth product information presented in the chapters that follow. The historical overview and introduction to beverage production processes presented herein, along with definitions of many of the terms you will encounter as you proceed, should enhance your study of the individual product categories.

Chapter 13 covers distilled spirits; Chapter 14, beers, ales, and malt liquor; Chapter 15, wine fundamentals; and Chapter 16, wines of the world.

Endnotes

1. In this text, brew refers to an undistilled fermented beverage made from fermentable products; thus, beer, ale, *kiu*, *sake*, and similar beverages are brews.

2. A more precise calculation to obtain the percentage of alcohol by weight must consider the fact that, because alcohol is lighter than water, a liter of 80 proof spirits (40% alcohol by volume) would weigh only 928 grams (600 grams of water and 328 grams of alcohol). The true percentage of alcohol in this mixture would be 35% rounded (328 ÷ 928 × 100).

Key Terms

blend	malt beverage
bonded spirits	marrying
condenser	patent still
congener	pot still
distillation	proof
distilled spirits	rectification
distiller's beer	sterile filtration
fermentation	still
gin-head	thermovinification
grape must	wine
lager	wort

Discussion Questions

1. The ancients used beer and wine for what purposes other than drinking?

2. In the Middle Ages, what role did monasteries play in the production of beer and wine?

3. In what century did the production of distilled spirits become commonplace?

4. What was Prohibition? What were some of its effects?

5. What are three classifications of alcoholic beverages?

6. What are the rules of thumb for converting (a) alcohol by volume to alcohol by weight, and (b) alcohol by weight to alcohol by volume?

7. Is it true that mixed drinks are often lower in calories because of their non-alcoholic ingredients?

8. What are the basic products needed for a fermentation?

9. What are the basic parts of a distillation system?

10. How does a patent still differ from a pot still?

13 Spirits

Chapter Outline

Grain Spirits
    Whiskeys
        Scotch Whisky
        Irish Whiskey
        American Whiskey
        Canadian Whisky
    Grain Neutral Spirits
    Vodka
    Compounded Spirits
        Gin
        Aquavit
Plant Liquors
    Rum
    Tequila
Fruit Liquors
    Brandy Production
        The Grape
        Distillation
        Aging
        Blending
    Labeling
    Kinds of Brandy
        Cognac
        Armagnac
        Calvados
        Other European Brandies
        American Brandies
        Synthetic Brandies
Liqueurs
Aperitifs and Bitters
Judging the Quality of Spirits

The federal government defines a **spirit** as any alcoholic beverage containing a significant amount of distilled ethanol. Spirits are classified according to either their alcoholic source or their processing method. The five major groups of spirits are grain, plant, and fruit liquors, liqueurs, and bitters. Spirits made from grains include whiskeys, vodka, grain neutral spirits, and compounded liquors such as gin and aquavit. Rum and tequila are the major plant liquors. Brandies are the most important fruit liquors. Liqueurs or cordials are made from a base of grain, plant, or fruit spirits or their combination. Aromatic or fruit bitters are highly flavored spirits containing bitter substances such as quinine.

This chapter describes the five major types of spirits, as well as different products within each group and how and where they are made. It also explains federal requirements for spirits. In addition, the chapter discusses the origin and development of certain spirits and offers guidelines for judging spirit quality.

Grain Spirits

Whiskeys

As noted in Chapter 12, the word whiskey comes from the ancient Irish-Gaelic words *uisce beathadh* and the Scottish-Gaelic words *uisge beatha*, meaning "water of life." Somehow *beathadh* and *beatha* were dropped and *uisce* became "whisky," the spelling used by the English, Scots, and Canadians. The Americans and the Irish spell whiskey with an "e," but U.S. government publications use the British form, a vestige of America's colonial heritage. This text uses the American spelling except when using the term "Scotch whisky" (wherein the S is capitalized) and in the sections about scotch-making and Canadian whisky in this chapter. The first known use of the modern English form "whisky" is found in the Scottish Exchequer Rolls of 1494.

Whiskeys vary depending on the source of grain, type of fermentation, distillation method, and processing after distillation. Exhibit 13.1 shows the steps in making a whiskey, and Exhibit 13.2 shows differences in distillation and bottling proofs. The discussion that follows focuses on the major whiskeys—Scotch, Irish, American (rye, bourbon, corn), and Canadian.

Scotch Whisky. Scotch production methods have not changed since the spirit was first produced many years ago.

> The origins of Scotch are as misty as the fogs that hung over the sites of the first stills, believed to have been built by Christian missionary monks who settled in the now famous Dufftown, Islay and Mull of Kintyre regions.
>
> In the monasteries, they used the local barley, sparkling water and peat fires to produce the *aqua vitae* as it was then called. They perceived its recuperative powers as a divine gift and began a cottage industry that spread to farms the length and breadth of Scotland.[1]

The U.S. government defines **scotch** as a distinctive spirit from Scotland manufactured in compliance with British laws.[2] If the spirit is a mixture of Scotch whiskies, it must be labeled "Blended Scotch Whisky"

Exhibit 13.1 Steps in Making Whiskey

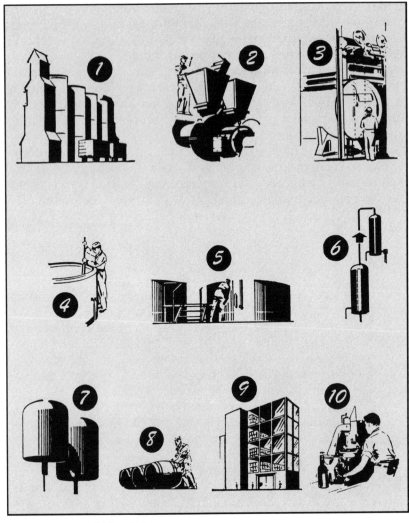

1. The grain is harvested, inspected and stored.

2. It is ground into mash.

3. The mash is cooked with malt, converting the starch to sugar.

4. Yeast is prepared and added to mash in the fermenting vats.

5. Fermentation changes the grain sugars to alcohol.

6. Still separates the alcohol from the mash by vaporization, the vapors are caught, condensed and drawn off as new whiskey.

7. The new whiskey is stored in a cistern room.

8. The whiskey is reduced in proof and drawn into barrels.

9. The barrels of whiskey are stored for aging.

10. The aged whiskey is adjusted in proof and bottled as Straight Whiskey. . . . Aged whiskeys are blended with spirits or light whiskey.

Courtesy of Hiram Walker & Sons

or "Scotch—a blend"; unblended malt scotch is labeled "Single Malt Scotch Whisky" (see Exhibit 13.3). U.S. imports must be at least 80 proof (scotch is bottled at 80 to 115 proof).

There are two kinds of scotch: malt and grain. Malt scotch is made from 100% barley malt while grain scotch is made from malt combined with unmalted barley and corn. Malt scotch has a heavier flavor and body than grain scotch because it is pot-distilled and comes off as a fairly low distillate (120 to 140 proof), giving it a number of flavor components. The greater amount of malt also gives it a heavier flavor. Grain scotch is the result of continuous distillation. Because it comes off at 180 to 188 proof, grain scotch has fewer congeners to give flavor, body, and other character to the spirit.

Grain scotch is often blended with malt scotch at a ratio of 40 to 60. Such blends are lighter and more delicate than malt scotch and have

Exhibit 13.2 Distillation and Bottling Proofs

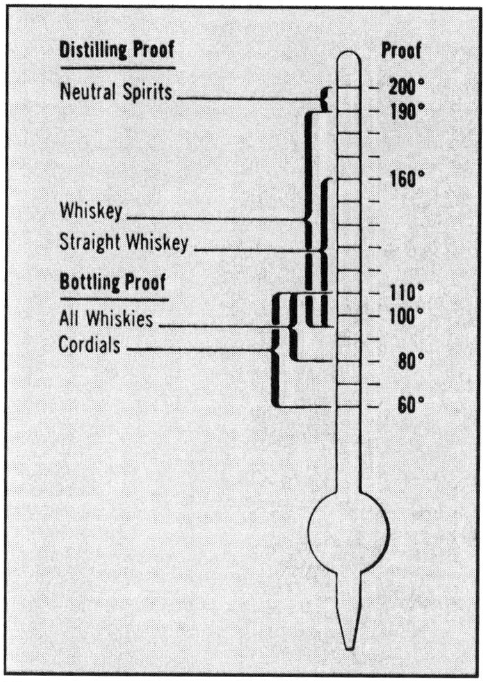

Distilling Proof		Proof
Neutral Spirits		200°
		190°
		160°
Whiskey		
Straight Whiskey		
Bottling Proof		110°
All Whiskies		100°
Cordials		80°
		60°

The proof at which whiskey and other spirits are distilled determines their character. The proof at which product is bottled determines its potency but bears little relation to quality. (Courtesy of Hiram Walker & Sons)

increased the popularity of scotch in America and elsewhere. No distillate other than a true malt or grain scotch can be used in a blend.

Most grain whiskies are produced in the Lowlands of Scotland, south of a line drawn between Dundee and Greenock. Malt whiskies are produced in several areas. Highland malts are made in the Orkney Isles; Campbeltown malts are produced in the Mull of Kintyre in the south. Islay Island on the west coast of Scotland is another source of malt whiskies. Speyside malts are made in the area around the River Spey.

The process of making scotch is unique and was developed over a period of many years (see Exhibit 13.4). Scotland's cool climate favors the cultivation of barley, and this grain gives scotch part of its distinctive character. The kind of barley is carefully selected—one of the requirements is that it contain at least 60% starch. The barley is cleaned and then placed in warm water to sprout. When barley sprouts, an enzyme called diastase converts most of the starch into a sugar called maltose, which yeast can easily change into glucose and ferment. The sprouting also produces the "malty" flavor which, to some extent, carries over into the spirit.

When the development of maltose is complete, the sprouting is stopped by drying the sprouts over burning peat, lending a smoky flavor that also carries over into the spirit. The dried sprouts are then ground to make what is called a grist. The grist is mixed with fairly warm water in a tank called a mash tun, and any remaining starch then develops into maltose. The grist, now called draff, is drawn off and sold for cattle feed.

Exhibit 13.3 Four Labels of Single-Malt Scotch

Courtesy of Schenley Industries

The remaining liquid, called wort, is fermented for about 40 hours, during which time the maltose changes to alcohol and carbon dioxide, with an alcoholic content of 7.5 to 10%.

Malt scotch is pot-distilled twice, and only the middle distillate is retained. The first and last distillates (the foreshots and feints) are combined with a new wort for redistillation. Grain scotch is patent-distilled once; this method produces a spirit adequate for blending.

Most scotch is aged five or six years. Premium scotch is aged for eight years or more. Scotch usually benefits from aging up to 15 years, after which it can take on a woody flavor from the barrel. Old oak American bourbon barrels are often used, as well as old oak sherry barrels. Scotch matures during this aging, developing smoothness and improved character. While aging may also produce some color, caramel coloring may be added later. A blend labeled with the age of the scotch must indicate the age of the youngest scotch in the blend.

The exact formula used to produce a given scotch blend is kept secret. Every blending company has its own formula, which may include as many as 50 different scotches. This variety is necessary to produce consistent blends, as changing climatic conditions result in slightly different whiskies

Exhibit 13.4 Steps in Making Scotch

1. The barley is selected and screened to remove foreign material.

2. It is then steeped two or three days in tanks after which it is spread out on a malting floor and allowed to germinate 8 to 12 days. (The more modern way is to germinate the barley in a big drum or malt kiln called a *Saladin* box where the temperatures can be controlled by blowing cool air through the germinating barley.)

3. The malted grain is dried over peat.

4. It is next ground into grist, and then mixed with hot water to dissolve the maltose developed during germination; the grist is strained away leaving a liquid called wort.

5. The wort is fermented for several days producing a wash or miller's beer, which contains low-strength alcohol, some unfermentable matter, and some congeners.

6. The mixture is then distilled by the pot or patent-still method. Two distillations occur when pot-distillation is used.

7. The new spirit is put into oak casks to age or mature; malt whisky takes longer to mature than grain whisky.

8. After aging, malt whisky is blended with grain whisky and the blend reduced in strength by the addition of soft water. (Some pure malt whisky is sold which is not blended with grain whisky.)

9. Bottling of the blend now occurs, after which there is a short period of rest given to allow the blend to marry; in some cases, the blend is shipped in barrels and bottled at the receiving point.

each year. If a certain malt is not available, a similar one can be substituted from a library stock so that the blender's distinctive flavor is maintained. Thus when a guest orders a particular brand of scotch, he or she always expects the same thing.

The scotch blender selects his whiskies like a careful host selects party guests, inviting a variety of "personalities." Some contribute good conversation or good listening, while others are just good minglers or agreeable people. Each has something to contribute to make the party a success. For example, scotch produced in the Lowlands is said to be gentle and affable, like the climate and land in the Lowlands. Whiskies produced in this area mix well in a blend.

Highland whiskies are said to reflect their more rigorous environment, and may be somewhat volatile and unpredictable, but true scotch.

Islay Island takes quite a beating from the rough seas. "The winds are often violent and the peat takes on the tang of the sea. This is reflected in the Islay malts, which are altogether more peaty, more highly flavored, with more than a whiff of the sea air."[3] To many scotch drinkers, Islay malts also possess the true character of what scotch ought to be.

The Spey River Valley is somewhat protected, thus its environment is not nearly as rugged and harsh as that of the Highlands and Islay Island. Speyside scotch reflects this more sheltered terrain, imparting a gentleness to blends. This scotch may be likened to a good listener who furnishes an audience for others, or a good speaker who holds an audience together.

Nations other than Scotland have tried to make scotch with no success. Some attribute this failure to the water, since water is an important ingredient; others say that the Scots possess a certain magic that enables them to produce a whisky all their own.

Scotch is perhaps the most universally known liquor. If you order a whisky anywhere in the world, you're most likely to get a scotch. As far as many are concerned, there is no other whisky.

Irish Whiskey. The Irish produce whiskey much the same as the Scots do. There are, however, some differences. The Irish use sprouted barley and other cereals to make wort, and the sprouts are dried over peat without absorbing a smoky flavor. Irish whiskey is pot-distilled three times. Only the middle distillate is retained, producing a liquor that is very smooth and mellow. The mandatory aging time is three years, but the usual period is five to eight years in old sherry casks.

Irish whiskey is produced both in the Republic of Ireland and in Northern Ireland. The regulations in each place are similar. Irish whiskeys are often blended to make them lighter. Blends are labeled "Irish Whiskey—a Blend" or "Blended Irish Whiskey."

American Whiskeys. The United States produces three different kinds of whiskey in addition to whiskey blends: bourbon, rye, and corn. Bourbon is by far the most extensively produced.

Bourbon. The first bourbon is reputed to have been made in 1789 in Bourbon County, Kentucky, by a preacher named Elijah Craig. Evan Williams had built the first commercial distillery in Kentucky in 1783. Together, these two started an industry that still thrives. Most bourbon today is produced in Kentucky (see Exhibit 13.5). Bourbon is also made in Tennessee, Illinois, Indiana, Ohio, Pennsylvania, and Missouri.

Tennessee "bourbon" is called sour mash whiskey instead of bourbon. Tennessee whiskey is filtered through maple charcoal after distillation, which gives a delicate smoothness and flavor. Sour mash is a spirit made from a regular sweet mash brew mixed with some soured old mash brew in a ratio of about two regular to one sour. Federal regulations require that a whiskey labeled "sour mash" have at least one part sour to three parts regular mash. The sour mash gives a heavier body and finer flavor to the bourbon, lending it a bit of sweetness and delicacy. Most bourbons are sour mash, although their labels may not indicate it.

Federal regulations require that bourbon be made from a mash containing at least 51% corn, mixed with other fermentable products such as rice, rye, or wheat. The usual ratio is 60% corn, 28% rye, and 12% barley malt. The grains are ground, cooked into a mash, and fermented. Bourbon is distilled by the continuous method. Most bourbon distillates come off at 110 to 130 proof.

Bourbon must be aged at a proof of at least 125 for at least two years in charred oak barrels. Most bourbons are aged four to six years. (The time a whiskey spends outside a barrel does not add to its age.) The barrels help create some of bourbon's distinctive character. Charring produces a reddened, resinous surface on the wood which provides special flavor constituents.

Bourbon has a rich body and the full, distinctive flavor of corn. Most of its color develops during aging, although color may be added. Bourbon is bottled as bottled-in-bond straight, a blend of straights, or a blend of

Exhibit 13.5 Labels of Two Straight Whiskeys (Kentucky Bourbons)

Courtesy of Old Evan Williams Distillery and James B. Beam Distilling Co.

straight bourbon and grain neutral spirits. "Straight" indicates an un-blended whiskey of one distillation. Blends must be 20% or more straight whiskey. Bottled bourbon has an alcoholic content of between 80 to 110 proof (see Exhibit 13.5).

Rye. During colonial times, rye whiskey was the primary liquor made in the United States. Rum took over gradually, then, as corn and other grains became important in U.S. agriculture, bourbon replaced rum.

Rye whiskey must be made from 51% or more rye grain. Like other American whiskeys, it must not come off distillation at more than 160 proof. Rye whiskey is produced by continuous distillation. It is usually bottled and sold at 80 to 110 proof, although some ryes are higher in alcohol content. Rye must be aged at least two years in new charred oak casks. Pennsylvania and Maryland produce the most rye whiskey.

Corn whiskey. A whiskey bearing the name "corn" must be made from a mash containing at least 80% corn. It is distilled by the continuous method. It need not be aged in charred oak casks and therefore may lack color. Corn whiskey must go into the aging cask (oak) at 125 proof or higher. Its flavor is definitely that of corn, and the body is light.

Canadian Whisky. Canadian whisky is lighter in body and more delicate in flavor than American bourbon. There are several reasons for this difference. Corn is the primary grain, usually mixed with additional fermentable products such as rye and barley malt. Canadian whisky is distilled in a Coffey still. Precise separation of the congeners and alcohol eliminates the fractions (parts of the distillate) that give a heavier body and flavor. The Canadian government allows distillates to come off at 150 to 185 proof, also resulting in a spirit light in flavor and body. (The American government limits whiskey distillates to 160 proof, which allows more flavor and body congeners to come over.)

Canadian whisky is aged primarily in old oak barrels, which help to produce a delicately flavored product. The normal aging time is six years. Canadian whiskies are blends of whisky and grain neutral spirits, modifying the flavor toward the lighter end. They are labeled "Blended Canadian Whisky" or "Canadian Whisky—A Blend." The U.S. government defines Canadian whisky as a whisky from a distillate coming off below 90% alcohol (190 proof) produced according to the laws and regulations of the Canadian government. It can contain no spirit less than three years old.

Grain Neutral Spirits

A **grain neutral spirit** is a distilled spirit made from a grain mash. It is produced by continuous distillation, removing a number of harsh congeners in the process. The distillate comes off at 190 proof and is colorless, odorless, and tasteless. If a similar spirit is made from a non-grain mash, it must be labeled as a neutral spirit—the word "grain" cannot be used. Grain neutral spirits are used in making vodka and gin; they are also used in blends with other spirits.

Vodka

The Russians and Poles drank **vodka** for centuries before it became popular in the United States. Today it is the leading spirit in America, holding over 20% of the market. Because it lacks flavor and has a soft, mellow character, it mixes better than any other alcoholic product. Vodka may also be popular because it leaves no alcohol odor on the breath.

Vodka was known to the Russians and Poles as early as the twelfth century. It was then called *zhizenennia*, meaning water of life. It was a rather flavorful, raw, harsh liquor, and remained so until a man named Smirnoff discovered that running vodka through activated charcoal removed many of the harsh congeners, leaving a smooth-tasting liquor. This is today's vodka.

The U.S. government's Standards of Identity define vodka as "neutral spirits, so distilled or so treated after distillation with charcoal and other

A modern fermenting floor.

A number of distillates are placed into barrels for aging.

Courtesy of Hiram Walker & Sons

Rolling in the barrels for storage in the aging room.

Bottles of Canadian whisky coming off the bottling line.

Courtesy of Hiram Walker & Sons

A modern pot still with gin head on top. (Courtesy of Hiram Walker & Sons)

materials, as to be without distinctive character, aroma, taste or color."[4] Some vodka is centrifuged or distilled by a special process to remove congeners; congeners may also be removed by filtering the vodka through a bed of fine sand or other material. However, most vodka is treated by charcoal filtering or by steeping it in charcoal.

The quality of a vodka depends upon the quality of the grain neutral spirit used to make it. Vodka is distilled at 190 proof. Water is then added and the spirit is bottled at between 80 and 110 proof. Vodka need not be made from grain spirits but almost always is. The claim that vodka is made from fermented potato mash is not true, although it might once have been produced this way in Poland and Russia.

In the past, vodka was flavored to help camouflage its harshness. Today's Zubrowka vodka is a carryover from those times. This vodka is steeped with zubrowka (buffalo) grass seed, which gives it a marked bouquet, a slightly bitter flavor, and a light yellow color. The Russians have Pertsovka, a spicy, flavored vodka, made fiery-hot with cayenne and other substances. Pertsovka is aged several months to allow the flavorings to blend in. Okhotnichya, also called hunter's vodka, is a similar product. It is sweet, flavored with ginger, juniper, anise, orange and lemon peels, and other herbs and spices.

Absolut is a Swedish vodka, one variety of which (peppar) is highly seasoned with jalapeno peppers and paprika. Limonnaya is a vodka flavored with lemon peel. Several sweetened vodkas are on the market, often flavored with orange, lemon, mint, grape, or other ingredients. These products are usually bottled at 70 proof. Flavored vodkas are very popular today; some say chilled vodka will be the drink of the nineties.

Compounded Spirits

Some spirits are flavored to produce compounded liquors. There are several ways to incorporate the flavors. Flavoring agents may be added to a brew before distillation so that the essential oils in the flavorings vaporize and come off with the distillate. Another method is to expose the alcohol vapors to the flavoring substances at the top of the still in a gin-head. The spirit may also be percolated over the flavorings or steeped with them (often called maceration).

Since many flavoring ingredients vary from season to season, some distillers flavor spirits with essential oils instead of the actual substances. In many cases, essential oils can be added directly to the base spirit. Grain neutral spirits or brandy usually form the base for such compounded liquors.

Gin. Gin is a compounded spirit. There are basically two kinds of gin: "dry" and "heavy." Dry gin is light in flavor and body; the term "dry" indicates a light, somewhat delicate spirit that mixes well with other substances. Dry gins are often labeled "dry," "extra dry," or "very dry," although there is no real variation among dry gins. Heavy gins are high in flavor and body and carry with them a slight suggestion of malt. They do not make good mixers and are often consumed "neat" over ice.

The Dutch invented gin, but its name derived from the French word *genievre*, meaning "juniper." Dutch (also called Holland or Netherland) gins are heavy and are usually divided into three types—all are heavy: Holland, Geneva (Jenever), and Schiendam. However, the differences between the three are small. Dutch gin is sometimes called schnapps.

Dutch gin is made from a mash containing several grains, usually barley malt, rye, and corn. The resulting brew is distilled into a low-proof substance called malt wine, heavy in body and rich in flavor. The malt wine is pot-distilled at low temperatures so that the resulting distillate of 100 to 110 proof retains its rich flavor and heavy body. During the last distillation, the alcohol vapors pass through juniper berries in a gin head, picking up a heavy juniper flavor. Some distillers may also use other flavoring ingredients (called botanicals) such as cassia bark, licorice, coriander seed, orange peel, cardamom, or angelica, but Dutch gins have fewer of these flavorings than gins made in other countries.

English gins are dry. They are produced from grain neutral spirits distilled at 180 to 190 proof. English gins are flavored either by adding juniper berries and other botanicals to the liquor before distillation, or by means of the gin head. English gins vary depending upon the botanicals used.

Some American gins are made by steeping the flavoring ingredients with the final distillate. Some American gins are produced like English gins. One method uses a glass-lined vacuum to lower the vaporization temperature of alcohol to about 90° F (32° C), resulting in a very delicately flavored gin. Only gins flavored during distillation may be labeled as "distilled gin." American gins have less character than English or Dutch gins because they are produced from a high-proof grain neutral spirit that lacks flavor congeners.

Few gins are aged; if they are, they usually take on a golden color and may be sold as "golden gin." No claim of age can be made for a gin in the United States. American gins must be bottled at no less than 80 proof.

There are several sweet, flavored gins, including mint, orange, lime, or lemon gin. Old Tom is a sweet English gin. Sloe gin is not a gin; it is actually a liqueur flavored with sloe berries, and is usually a heavy pink to reddish color.

Aquavit. This Scandinavian spirit still retains a part of distilled liquor's original Latin name, *aqua vitae*. It is made from neutral spirits (usually from a grain mash), distilled at 190 proof and then redistilled with caraway seed either in the spirit or through a gin head. After distillation, it is reduced to about 86 to 100 proof. Aquavit is usually consumed straight in a small shot glass; it is considered proper to toss it down in one gulp.

Plant Liquors

Many plant liquors are produced around the world. However, most are consumed only locally or nationally and, even though they may be consumed by millions (as are Chinese distilled spirits made from sorghum or rice), they are not prominent worldwide. **Rum** and **tequila** are the only plant liquors to have attained this status. A few others are gaining popularity.

Rum

Columbus is said to have brought sugar cane to the Caribbean islands, where it became an important agricultural product. Sugar production leaves a by-product, a fermentable substance called rum-bullion, which in the seventeenth century became a popular drink in Europe and, until recently, a product of issue in the British navy. Rum was an important ballast on slave ships. Many ships carried slaves to the sugar-producing islands, then brought molasses to New England (where rum was made); these ships then transported the rum to Europe.

Sugar cane contains sucrose, which yeast converts into carbon dioxide and alcohol. The fermented molasses or sugar-cane brew is distilled to 190 proof (160 proof for New England rum). The distillate is aged in uncharred oak casks and thus has little color. Color is added to some products. Most rums are blends, ranging in body and flavor from heavy and pungent to slight and brandy-like, and in color from light to dark. Blending produces a rum distinctive in aroma, taste, body and color. Rum is usually bottled at 80, 86, or 151 proof. Labels must indicate a rum's area of origin.

There are two basic kinds of rums, light-bodied and heavy-bodied, although there are many variations among them. Light rum (also known as silver or dry rum) is most popular in the United States. Light rum is usually produced by the continuous distillation method and comes off as a high-proof distillate. This method eliminates a number of flavorful congeners but gives a smoother product with only a slight rum flavor. Light rums usually bear a white or silver label. They are mild and slightly sweet in flavor. Most light rums are aged for one year. Some, however, are aged as long as brandies; they may be shipped under brand names and may command higher prices than common rums. The label may bear the term *añejo* ("old") or *muy añejo* ("very old"). Most light rums come from Puerto Rico. Cuba, the Dominican Republic, Haiti, Venezuela, Mexico, Hawaii, and the Philippines also produce light rum.

Heavy-bodied, more pungent rums are produced in Jamaica, New England, and British Guiana (Demerara, Trinidad, and Barbados). These rums have a heavy bouquet resulting from their basic ingredient, the rich skimmings from sugar boilers. Natural yeast ferments the brew; the result is what is called a product of "spontaneous fermentation," a rather violent and fast process producing many congeners which give a very richly flavored rum. The sediment from a previous brew is often added to help start fermentation, much like the sour-mash process. Much of this rum is often sent to England and other countries for aging and consumption. The label and product are nearly as dark as molasses.

Santiago rums are prized because of the special care taken in their production. A finely cultured yeast produces a rich flavor and full body. The Island of Batavia also produces a rich, highly aromatic rum called Batavia Arak or Arrack. It is aged three to four years in Batavia and then sent to Holland for four to six years of additional aging. Arrack has a heavy, brandy-like quality.

There are a few medium-bodied rums produced in the Virgin Islands and New England. These rums range in color from tan to rich mahogany and usually bear a gold label. They are more pronounced in flavor and sweeter than light rums.

Tequila   Only Mexico produces **tequila,** a distinctive liquor distilled from the fermented juice of the blue variety of the agave plant *(tequilon weber cactus)*. It is a special type of **mezcal,** the primary Mexican spirit, and is produced in a legally defined area around where it originated. The Mexican government regulates the making of tequila under the *Norma Oficial Mexicana de Calidad*. A tequila label bears the letters DGN if the product conforms to these regulations (see Exhibit 13.6).

The heart of the agave plant (the *piña*), which may weigh between 50 and 200 pounds, contains a sweet juice called *aguamiel* (honey water). This sap is removed, often fortified with sugar, and then fermented. It is distilled twice, coming off at 104 to 106 proof with many flavoring agents. The distillate is then filtered through charcoal.

When tequila is aged, it develops a gold color. White tequila is a new product shipped without aging; silver tequila is aged up to three years; gold tequila is aged in oak casks for two to four years and may carry the name *muy añejo*. Some tequilas may be artificially colored, so buyers must know what they are buying. Some tequilas are aged quite long and are expensive.

Contrary to popular opinion, tequila is not bottled with a worm. Genuine mezcal, however, does contain a worm which is said to be delicious.

Fruit Liquors

Brandy is the primary liquor made from fruit. Any distilled spirit made from fruit or fruit derivatives qualifies as a brandy. However, only a spirit distilled from grapes can be called just "brandy"—if distilled from other fruit, the type of fruit must precede the word brandy: thus "pear brandy."

The word brandy (short for brandywine) comes from the Dutch word *brandewijn* meaning "burnt wine," referring to the fact that the wine was

Exhibit 13.6   Tequila Label

Courtesy of Maidstone Importers

distilled with heat. It was once thought that the distillation of wine would produce a concentrate—the "soul" of the wine—which could be reconstituted and thus restored to its original state. Although this idea proved false, the resulting product—brandy—caught on.

Brandies are usually marketed at 80 to 84 proof. They can be distilled up to 190 proof. Most American brandy is the result of continuous distillation, but most imports are distilled by the pot method.

Brandy Production

Brandy is known to have been produced in Cognac, a city in France, sometime after the 1300s. Records indicate that it was being made in France's Armagnac district in 1422.

The character of a brandy is influenced by the kind of grapes it is made from, the climate and soil they are cultivated in, cultivation and harvesting methods, fermentation and distillation processes, aging, and blending. Each factor is important and all have an impact on the type and quality of a brandy.

The Grape. The variety of grape used to make brandy must be low in sugar and rather acidic. It should also produce a fruity wine, high in aldehydes and flavor esters. The low sugar content means that a lot of wine must be distilled to produce the distillate, increasing the congeners which come over with the alcohol. The acid content helps with aging. Some of the favorite va ⁓eties of grapes grown for brandy are St-Emilion (called the Ugni Blanc in Ca ⁓ornia and Trebbiano in Italy), Folle Blanche, and Colombard.

The soil eed not be rich; some excellent brandies come from grapes grown in poo soil. However, certain characteristics in a soil influence the brandy produ 'd. In Cognac, some of the most favorable grape-growing areas for brand making have soil with a high calcium content, often coming from anciei oyster beds. The lands around Cognac with the least amount of calciu in the soil produce grapes for the poorer brandies. On the other hand, th soil of the Armagnac region is a bit different. The areas with less calcium the soil produce better brandy-making grapes than the areas with high -calcium soil.

The climate mus be favorable for grape cultivation. It cannot be too cool, as warm tempera ires and sun are necessary to produce a sufficiently juicy, flavorful grape w h adequate sugar. The grapes must be completely ripe when harvested to nsure full flavor development.

After careful selectio the grapes are brought to the press where the must (juice) is extracted, en fermented.

Distillation. Brandy must ι distilled at fairly low temperatures to produce a low-proof distillate w h many congeners. The French regulate the maximum proof of distillates be used for brandy. The final distillate for cognac cannot be over 144 pi of. Pot-distillation is preferred, although some brandies are made by a s ni-continuous or continuous method.

Brandy may receive only one distillation, but it is often distilled twice to improve quality. The first dist ation is a low proof and thus high in congeners. Only the middle part o the distillate is retained. The first and last parts may be used for other pu ooses or may be returned to a brew to be redistilled. (Cognac comes ove in the first distillate, called *brouilli*, at 27 to 35% alcohol.) The final disti te, called *bonne chauffe*, is about 69 to 71% alcohol. Distillates coming ov · at higher alcoholic content lack distinctive flavor and are often used to ortify wines.

Aging. Brandy is aged in special oak casks, from which it extracts flavor. The wood also absorbs some undesirable components from the brandy. In addition, the cask allows a bit of air to seep through, causing a very slow oxidation. Thus the wood is an important factor in a favorable aging process.

Most cognac producers think the best oak for aging casks comes from the Limousin forest, although some believe that oak from the Troncais Forest in mid-France is just as good. By law, Calvados must be aged in casks of Limousin oak. Armagnac brandy is aged in casks made from the blackish, sap-rich, tannin-rich Monlezun forest oak. The staves for these casks are specially carved to expose more surface.

Aging brandy is stored in special warehouses, where it loses about 2½% of its volume each year. This loss, called the angel's share, can be sizable—up to a fourth of the original distillate in a long aging period.

The fumes escaping from the casks encourage the growth of a black fungus, called *torula*. In Cognac, one can easily identify warehouses where cognac is being aged because the tiled roof turns a sooty black. In Armagnac, the sides and ceilings of aging caves are blackened by the same fungus.

Several components develop during aging, including aromatic aldehydes and polyphenols such as tannins, gums, and lignin (wood)

rapidly, becoming an inferior product. The brandy is marketed in fairly large quantities after 3 years of aging.

The French government allows Armagnac labels to carry a vintage year, which indicates the year it was distilled.

Calvados. Normandy is a province in northern France with a climate unfavorable for grapes. However, Normandy produces excellent apples that are used to make its famous apple brandy called calvados. There are three types of calvados; the one produced in central Normandy is considered best and is called Calvados du Pays d'Auge. It may bear on the label the words *appellation contrôlée,* which means "name controlled by law." It must be made in the same manner as cognac.

Brandy called simply calvados, though not the best, is considered a fine product. There are ten areas surrounding the Pays d'Auge region tha' produce calvados. The label may carry the words *appellation réglement/* meaning "regulated control." A rather plain brandy made from apple˖ ˖n the rest of the province may be called eau-de-vie de cidre; it may also ˖ate on the label *appellation réglementée.*

The Calvados du Pays d'Auge brandy is pot-distilled twice, r˖ ulting in a distillate of about 140 proof. Only the middle part is retained ˖ r aging. It is aged for at least one year; sometimes for many years, l˖ ˖ cognac. Calvados brandy is distilled by the continuous method at lo˖ r temperatures, so many congeners come off. It is aged only two or ˖ ee years.

Other European Brandies. Other countries in Europe pro˖ ˖ce well-known brandies, many of which are of very high quality and ˖ ˖ prized as after-dinner drinks. Many possess unusual and distinctive ˖ ˖vor and character that make them highly interesting. These brandies a˖ made either by fermenting the fruit and then distilling it or by soakin˖ ˖nely chopped fruit in a high-proof neutral spirit or brandy (a process cal'˖ d maceration), and then carefully distilling at low temperatures to ensure ˖ ˖e fruit flavors come over with the alcohol vapors. Brandies produced '˖ y this method do not improve with aging, so they are bottled and m˖ ˖keted soon after distillation.

The following is a short summary of s˖ ˖ne of these brandies and their major characteristics.

Marc is a French brandy made fro˖ ˖ grape pressings; it is relatively unaged and so possesses a fiery, raw fl˖˖vor and a rich, fruity taste. Grappa is the Italian counterpart of Marc.

Kirsch or Kirschwasser is made from a cherry that grows in Germany, Switzerland, and France. (In German, brandies are identified by the name of the fruit compounded with either *wasser,* meaning water, or *geist,* meaning spirit. The Germans also call kirsch *Schwarzwalder.*) French kirsch is lighter and more delicate in flavor than German or Swiss kirsch. The flavor is distinctive and heavy, with overtones of the cherry and its pit. It is the product added to a Swiss cheese fondue, giving the dish a special flavor.

Poire Williams is a distinctive Swiss brandy that is sometimes marketed with a fully grown pear inside the bottle. A young pear is placed in the bottle and allowed to grow; the stem is then cut and the bottle is filled with pear brandy. Poire Williams is so named because it is made from Bartlett pears, called William pears in Switzerland. The brandy, also called William Birnenbrand, carries the rich odor of ripe pears. Its taste is somewhat fiery and lacks pear flavor.

Framboise is a raspberry brandy produced in the Alsace region of France. It is highly regarded for its delicate flavor and rich raspberry aroma and taste. The Swiss and Germans make a similar brandy that is not as rich in raspberry flavor as the French product. The French also make a strawberry brandy called *fraise* which has the flavor of strawberries and many of the same characteristics as framboise.

German brandies are usually a bit drier and more delicate than French brandies. One traditional product of some repute is *asbach uralt*. Italy produces some excellent brandies, slightly richer and harsher in flavor than French brandies, because they are not aged as long. Two respected brands are Vecchia Romagna VSOP and Stock 84.

Slivovitz is a well-known yellow plum brandy from the Balkans. It is usually aged, sometimes up to 12 years, giving it a yellowish or straw color. Slivovitz has a rich plum taste and aroma and is somewhat fiery in nature. The French make an excellent brandy (Mirabelle) from a yellow plum, which may also be aged. The same plum is the source of a similar brandy made in Germany and Switzerland. Quetsch (French) or Zwetsch-genwasser (German) is a brandy made from a purple plum in Alsace; it has a dry, spicy, plum flavor and pale color. This product is sometimes mistakenly called slivovitz.

Ouzo is a brandy of Greece and the Near East with the flavors of anise and licorice. It tastes similar to the Near East liquor *arak* and turns a grayish white when mixed with water. Metaxa, the most famous brandy of Greece, is a slightly sweet, greenish-tan beverage. It is somewhat fiery but has great depth of flavor and aroma and is respected worldwide.

Apricots are used to make a richly flavored brandy in Austria and Hungary called Barack Palinka.

Spanish brandies are usually made from a blend of wines. They have a heavier flavor and sweeter taste than French brandies. Carlos I and Fundador are two high-quality Spanish brandies; there are others, but it is a good idea to check quality before purchasing. Because of their heavy flavor, they are not usually good for mixed drinks.

While not of European origin, pisco bears mention. This brandy is made in Peru and is named for Pisco, a seaport near where it is made. It is full-bodied and has a strong, distinctive flavor. It is usually marketed in a black bottle in the shape of an Inca god's head. Pisco is used to make Pisco punch.

Any country producing a fairly good wine also produces a brandy. For example, New Zealand, Australia, Mexico, and Chile, to name a few, market brandy products. However, these brandies are not well known in international markets.

American Brandies. Americans are not traditional brandy producers or consumers, although in some parts of the country brandy is popular in mixed drinks like manhattans and whiskey sours. The manufacture of American brandy began in California, and most American brandy is now produced in that state.

American brandies are generally light in flavor and body and make good blending spirits. Most are somewhat sweet. There are some flavorful, aged American brandies suitable as after-dinner drinks. Most American brandy is produced by continuous distillation, although some better products may be pot-distilled.

Pisco from Peru comes in this black, smiling face bottle modeled after one of the ancient Inca gods.

American brandies are usually made from grapes not used to make wine, such as the Thompson seedless, Flame Tokay, or other table grapes. The fermented brew of raisins is occasionally used to make brandy as well.

The distillate usually comes off at 190 proof, containing few congeners but producing a smoother product. American brandies must be aged two years or more in oak barrels. Some straight brandies are marketed as bottled-in-bond; they *must* be aged four years to qualify for this designation. Most American brandies are blends.

Applejack is a brandy distilled from fermented apple juice (cider). It may be bottled-in-bond. An applejack blend must consist of apple brandy aged at least two years combined with no more than 80% grain neutral spirits. Applejack blends are much lighter in flavor than straight applejack.

Synthetic Brandies. Some flavored spirits are marketed as brandies but do not meet U.S. requirements for this designation. They are usually neutral spirits or brandies flavored by the addition of a fruit product. Although such products are liqueurs or cordials by U.S. definitions, they may be labeled as brandies in Europe. In the United States, these spirits must bear labels indicating that they are flavored products.

Liqueurs

Liqueurs, also known as cordials, are compounded spirits flavored in various ways. Liqueurs contain at least 2½% sugar usually added as syrup;

Exhibit 13.8 Infusion, Percolation, and Distillation Methods of Flavoring

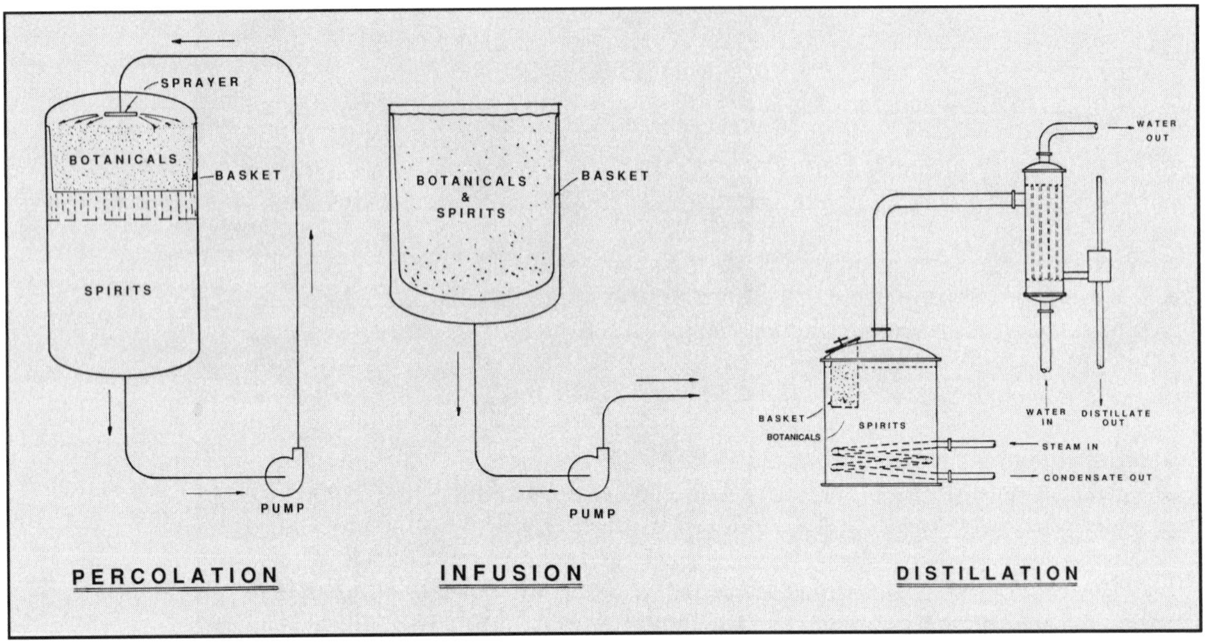

Courtesy of Hiram Walker & Sons

most contain more syrup. The sugar content of a 2½% sugar liqueur is equivalent to about a half-teaspoon of sugar (eight calories) per two-ounce drink. Liqueurs are flavored with many different substances, including herbs, spices, fruits, mint, coffee and licorice. The processing method, the quality of the flavorings, and the basic ingredients influence the final quality of each liqueur.

Most liqueurs are made from grain neutral spirits, but there are exceptions—bourbon is used for Southern Comfort, Scotch whisky for Drambuie, Irish whiskey for Irish Mist, and rum for Tia Maria. The flavorings are incorporated by either infusion (maceration), percolation, or distillation (see Exhibit 13.8). Some infusion processes may take as long as six or more months. Concentrated flavors may be added to the spirit and syrup. (Liqueurs containing artificial flavoring must be labeled as such.) All liqueurs are usually aged so that the flavor, spirit, and flavorings can marry.

Liqueurs are often used as after-dinner drinks. Some (such as Triple Sec) are used as flavoring ingredients for mixed drinks.

Aperitifs and Bitters

Aperitifs are spirits consumed primarily as appetizers. They may also be mixed with other alcoholic products. Many aperitifs, also called "digestives," are flavored with ingredients that give them a bitter taste.

Some aperitifs, including vermouth, are fortified wines; dry vermouth is used in martinis and sweet vermouth in manhattans. Vermouth is also consumed straight. The fortified wines of Dubonnet and Lillet are both used as mixers and served straight.

Campari, an Italian liquor, is a well-known aperitif with a very sweet, bitter flavor. It is a rich red and lends a pleasing color to mixed drinks.

Amer picon, a brandy, is a similar product produced in the Balkans; it is flavored with quinine, the same substance that gives tonic water its bitter flavor. When quinine was discovered to be a preventive against the malaria virus, it became a popular addition to many mixers, offering the incentive of enjoying a drink while taking your medicine. Amer picon also contains orange and is quite sweet. Fernet branca is another sweet, bitter spirit. It has a reputation of being a good remedy for hangovers.

Some liqueurs are used like aperitifs, often adding a spicy, bitter flavor to mixed drinks.

Bitters are used only as flavoring ingredients; in many recipes, a dash or two produces just the right flavor. Bitters are usually made from roots, spices, bark, berries, fruit, or herbs steeped in or distilled with a neutral spirit. Bitters have a highly flavorful, aromatic, bitter taste. Some of the better known include Angostura, made in Trinidad from a very old secret formula; Abbot's Aged Bitters, made by the same family for years in Baltimore; Peychaud's Bitters, made in New Orleans; and Orange Bitters, made in England from the dried peel of bitter Seville oranges.

Judging the Quality of Spirits

Every type of spirit has its own distinguishing characteristics, and within types there are differences that clearly separate products. For example, some rums are light and delicate while others are heavy and robust. These differences are the reasons for consumer preferences. Some people like the smoky flavor of scotch; others prefer vodka. Scotch drinkers may have a preference for one brand over another. Even vodka drinkers can be staunch advocates of one brand, although vodka is supposed to be colorless, odorless, and tasteless.

Evaluating spirit quality is not easy. Spirits are perhaps the most difficult to judge of all alcoholic beverages. A good judge must be able not only to identify the elusive factors that make up quality, but to remember these factors and compare them to a standard.

A glass used to judge spirits should be straight or have slightly outwardly-sloping sides. Only a finger's depth of room-temperature spirit is poured into it.

The first thing to do is examine the appearance of the spirit. Watch it as it is poured and note the color. Some spirits carrying a brown or caramel color may be as pale as citron, others will be mellow amber, and others may be brownish with a flash of burnished brass. Vodka must be colorless; gin and tequila should also be colorless unless they are aged. Rums vary in color from clear, light tan, and delicate amber, to an almost blackish brown. Chartreuse, a liqueur, may be green or yellow. Crème de menthe, another liqueur, comes in white or green. The judge must know what the proper color should be. Part of evaluating appearance is noting clarity and brilliance—two important quality factors.

The next step is to judge body. Body indicators can be observed by rocking the spirit gently in the glass or giving it a gentle whirl and noting how it holds together as it moves. The appearance of rivulets (called "legs") also indicates body. Body is judged further when the spirit is in the mouth; the sensation is called "mouthfeel," and should be pleasant. The density, viscosity, and other physical properties of the spirit should be evident. There will be body differences between spirits. For example, a liquor with a high sugar content will have a heavy body while a light vodka will have little or no body, disappearing quickly in the mouth.

The "nose" (aroma or odor) of the beverage is one of the best indicators of spirit quality. Your hand should warm the spirit slightly so the aroma rises in the glass. The swirl should also release it. Put your nose into the glass and sniff, pulling the aroma up into the nostrils. You should detect mellowness, harshness, fruitiness, or other characteristics of the spirit. Is there a proper carryover of the basic ingredients from which the spirit is made? Some spirits made from malt may have a sweetish odor, while spirits made from other grains may have a "dry" aroma. Scotch should smell smoky, but the intensity of this peaty odor is an important factor. The judge matches the odors detected with what he or she knows the spirit should smell like. Odors should blend together smoothly, and the final sensation should be pleasant.

When tasting spirits, some judges like to add a bit of pure room-temperature water (ice lowers the taste sensations and should not be used). The characteristic flavor of the spirit should immediately appear and develop into both taste and odor. It should then fade and disappear. The proof of the spirit makes a difference; high-proof spirits have a bite. Various components should be evident. Is there a muskiness, a flavor of malt, corn, rye, or other ingredient, and is this what it should be?

A liqueur should possess the true flavor of its main flavoring ingredient. Some flavors linger for a time on the palate, while others disappear quickly—a good indicator of the quality of the product if what happens is typical of the flavor. The total flavor should be full-bodied, balanced, harmonious, and smooth. In liqueurs, especially, the flavor should be unified (that is, not give way or fall apart) and should continue or last.

Finally, one judges the aftertaste or what is often called the "finish." The aftertaste should echo the spirit's flavor and be harmonious. Everything should be in agreement.

While an expert judge may be able to taste as many as 400 spirits in a day, the average person should not try to taste more than 4 or 5. An expert judge never swallows the spirit. Pure, tasteless, room-temperature water is used often to cleanse the palate. It can be non-sparkling spring water. Some judges also eat a low-salt or no-salt cracker to remove former flavors. Others say they should not be used. Items that have a flavor carryover should not be used to cleanse the palate.

Endnotes

1. *Scotch Whisky: Nature's Bounty and Blender's Art Make It the World's Most Valuable Drink* (New York: Scotch Whisky Information Center, 1989).

2. The British government defines scotch as a spirit from a fermented brew containing some malted cereal, distilled and aged in Scotland for at least three years.

3. *Scotch Whisky.*

4. U.S. Treasury Department, *Laws and Regulations Under the Federal Alcohol Act (FAA), Title 27, U.S.C.* (Washington, D.C.: U.S. Government Printing Office, 1977).

Key Terms

aperitif	rum
bitters	scotch
brandy	spirit
gin	tequila
grain neutral spirit	vodka
mezcal	whiskey (whisky)

Discussion Questions

1. What are the five major types of spirits?
2. How does scotch differ from other whiskeys?
3. What are the distinguishing features of bourbon?
4. How does gin differ from vodka?
5. How does tequila differ from mezcal? In what country are they produced?
6. What spirit is distilled from sugar cane?
7. What does VSOP mean? On what products is it used?
8. What is angostura and how is it used?
9. What are the processes by which flavorings may be incorporated in liqueurs?
10. By what means could you properly judge a spirit's quality?

14 Malt Beverages

Chapter Outline

Malt Beverage Ingredients
    Barley
    Hops
    Water
    Yeast
    Adjuncts
    Additives
Malt Beverage Production
    Malting
    Mashing
    Brewing
    Fermentation
    Pasteurization
    Carbonation
    Packaging
The Malt Beverage Family
    Types of Malt Beverages
    Alcohol Content of Malt Beverages
    Non-Alcoholic Brews
Draft Beer
Judging Malt Beverage Quality
    Appearance
    Aroma
    Taste
    Flavor

The U.S. government defines a **malt beverage** as "a beverage containing 0.5% or more of alcohol, brewed or produced from malt, wholly or in part, or from any substance thereof."[1] The definition further states that beers, ales, stouts, and porters are part of the malt beverage group. In this chapter, the term "brew" is often used to refer to the entire beer family, which includes the products listed above, as well as bock and *sake.* Malt beverages are brews that have malted barley as a main ingredient.

Almost every culture produces a brew of some sort. The Crimean Tartars make a brew from millet seed, as they have for centuries. *Kvass,* a brew still consumed in parts of Russia, is made from kvass seed. The present-day *Weissbier* of Germany is descended from a brew originally made from wheat. Arabians, Ethiopians, and a number of African tribes produce brews from native grains such as teff, millet, grass seeds, and others. The Chinese make their centuries-old brew, called *kiu,* from rice, sorghum, or other fermentable products. Fermented brews are also made in the South Pacific regions, some from coconut milk. Many of the Central and South American countries produce brews from fermentable substances at hand; as noted in Chapter 12, Columbus found the native Americans making a beer from corn, much like English brew. It is possible that, overall, brews have been consumed in greater quantity and more universally than wine.

In the United States, over 5.5 million gallons of beer were consumed in 1980—ten times the amount of wine consumed. Today, more brew is consumed around the world than any other alcoholic beverage.

Malt beverages are very socially acceptable products. Because their alcohol content is low, they are appropriate given the current emphasis on drinking in moderation. Brews are popular among all age groups; it is common to see people choosing beer over stronger alcoholic beverages at social events. It is even proper to serve beer with a specific course in a meal in which a progression of wines may also be served.

Because malt beverages are so popular, bar and beverage managers should know these products well and know how to serve and merchandise them. This chapter describes the ingredients of malt beverages, explains what they contribute to the various types of brews, and discusses methods of brew production. It covers the different kinds of malt beverages, including their individual characteristics and where they are produced. The chapter also includes a discussion of draft beer—how to care for it and how to operate the draft beer equipment to preserve a high-quality product. The chapter concludes with suggestions for judging the quality of malt beverages.

Malt Beverage Ingredients

The type and amount of ingredients used to produce a malt beverage greatly influence the quality of the product. Today's brews are produced from malted barley, hops, water, and yeast, as well as adjuncts, which support fermentation, and some additives. Each of these components is discussed in detail below.

Barley The term **barley** as used in the discussion of brews actually refers to the seeds of the barley plant, of which there are several varieties. Certain varieties produce better brews than others. Barley used for beer production should have a high starch content, a low protein content, and little flavor. Two-row barley—barley which has two rows of seed on its head—is considered best; however, four- and six-row barley, which are cheaper, are used for less expensive brews. In the United States, barley grown in the north central and northwestern regions is the most suitable for making beer.

Hops

Hops are the dried, scaly fruit of the vine *Humulus lupulus.* Hops are added to malt beverages for several reasons: to give them a slightly bitter and "hoppy" taste, to produce a more stable and softer foam, to supplement aroma and body, and to help preserve the brew. Some claim that hops also lend clarity to a malt beverage.

The best American hops come from the West Coast states. Those from Yakima Valley in the state of Washington are preferred. Bohemian hops, considered the best in the world, are grown in the Bohemian area of Czechoslovakia. Some German hops are also highly respected.

Many brewers use a blend of hops to produce the desired flavor, but premium brews are usually made with Bohemian hops. Because light—artificial or natural—can cause a brew containing hops to develop a "skunky" flavor, hops are often treated to remove the substance that causes this reaction.

Water

Water is critical to the quality of a malt beverage, and a water that is good for one kind of brew might not be suitable for another. Lager beers are generally produced from water with a low mineral content. Yeast is sensitive to the type of water used, a factor which must be taken into consideration when selecting water for brewing.

Many brewers make claims of superiority for their beers because of the water used to produce them. Coors, for example, plays up its bubbling mountain water, and the labels of products from the Olympia Brewery in the state of Washington carry the slogan "It's the Water." While natural spring or mountain water is suitable for some beers, water from any source can be rendered as pure as these waters, or more so.

Yeast

Yeasts are living organisms which need food, moisture, and the right temperatures to reproduce. Most yeasts grow best at temperatures between 68° F (20° C) and 113° F (45° C); many prefer an environment at human body temperature (98.6° F or 37° C). Yeasts feed on a simple sugar called glucose and often use their enzymes to convert starches or other sugars into glucose. In the process of metabolizing glucose, yeasts produce carbon dioxide and ethyl alcohol. Some brewers save this carbon dioxide gas and add it back to the brew before packaging, thereby producing the bubbles that give a brew its zesty character.

Each brew requires its own special kind of yeast. Some brewers grow their own yeast to ensure its consistency. Anheuser-Busch became so involved in yeast production that the company began to market its yeast, eventually becoming one of this country's largest yeast producers.

Adjuncts

In the United States, it is common practice to use a cereal, called an **adjunct,** in addition to malt to make a brew. The additional grains include rice, corn, and wheat. Soybean flakes, potato starch, and even sugar are sometimes used as well. The use of adjuncts is allowed in some countries, but prohibited in others. Adjuncts are finely ground, cooked to swell the starch granules, and then heated with malt during the mashing process.

The use of adjuncts results in a brew that is light in color, flavor, and body—beer qualities that are popular in the United States today. Some light American brews are produced with reduced amounts of malt and adjunct, so they contain less alcohol; other light beers have a normal alcohol content.

Some very good malt beverages in this country contain adjuncts accounting for up to 30% of the brew's fermentable ingredients. However, some premium brews contain only 5% adjuncts. Some brewers claim that adjuncts develop desirable properties. One brewer uses rice to produce a crisp-tasting beer. The use of adjuncts reduces the cost of brewing, and some brewers may use them for this reason alone.

Additives

An **additive** is anything added to a product that is not strictly necessary for making the product, but which facilitates the production of or enhances certain qualities considered desirable by the producer. For example, salt or sugar added to a food is an additive. Brewers use additives to produce certain characteristics in their products, such as more stable and softer foam or greater clarity. Enzymes are sometimes added to encourage the conversion of starch to sugar or to expedite the fermentation process. Additives may also function as preservatives, enhancing a brew's stability and extending shelf life. Many good brews are made without the use of any additives.

Additives must be approved by the Food and Drug Administration, which lists approved substances in the GRAS (generally regarded as safe) list. Additives not contained in the list are prohibited.

Malt Beverage Production

The basic steps in the production of malt beverages are malting, mashing, brewing, fermentation, pasteurization, carbonation, and packaging. Each of these steps is discussed in detail below (see also Exhibit 14.1).

Malting

Except for brews made from wheat, all malts are barley malts. Most brewers buy their malt in a dried or roasted form; many cheaper beers use a malt extract. Some brewers, however, make their own malt. The first step is cleaning and steeping the barley in warm water to encourage germination or sprouting. Sprouting is necessary to produce malt enzymes—principally *diastase*—which convert the grain's starch into **maltose**, a fermentable sugar. When the maximum amount of maltose has been developed, sprouting is stopped at the precise moment by drying the barley in intensely hot kilns. The sprouts are then roasted according to the brewer's special instructions. The precise time and temperature of roasting will affect the dryness, sweetness, and color of the final product (malts for the lightest brews will be roasted at the lowest temperatures).

Mashing

The **mashing** process begins when the barley malt, ground into a grist, is placed in a mash tun, along with measured amounts of pre-cooked adjuncts and water heated to about 154° F (68° C). Some brewers, however, heat the water to near boiling. The resulting mash is then mixed and cooked from one to six hours, during which time the malt enzyme *amylase* converts

Exhibit 14.1 "From Barley to Beer"

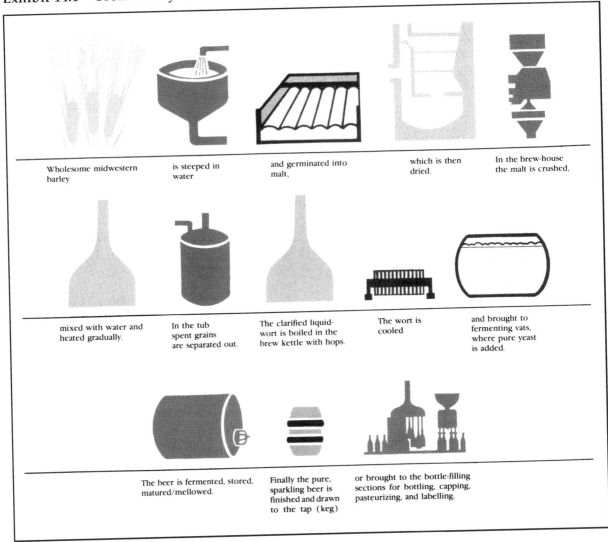

Wholesome midwestern barley

is steeped in water

and germinated into malt,

which is then dried.

In the brew-house the malt is crushed,

mixed with water and heated gradually.

In the tub spent grains are separated out.

The clarified liquid-wort is boiled in the brew kettle with hops.

The wort is cooled

and brought to fermenting vats, where pure yeast is added.

The beer is fermented, stored, matured/mellowed.

Finally the pure, sparkling beer is finished and drawn to the tap (keg)

or brought to the bottle-filling sections for bottling, capping, pasteurizing, and labelling.

Courtesy of Brewing Systems, Inc.

the adjunct's starch into maltose, and the enzyme *protease* breaks down the proteins for clarity in the brew.

The mash is then strained through a mash filter (to remove any grain residue) into a lautering tub. *Lauter* means "to make clear" in German, and that is precisely what happens. The clear, warm, sugary fluid, called wort, is now ready for brewing; the remaining solids are sold as cattle feed.

Brewing

The **brewing** process is relatively simple. The wort is placed in huge copper or stainless steel brew kettles, and hops are added to the liquid, a process called **hopping.** The mixture is then boiled to sterilize the wort and extract the flavor of the hops so essential to the taste of beer. The hops are drained off and the wort is cooled—for ales 50° to 70° F (10° to 21° C) and for lager beers 37° to 49° F (3° to 9° C).

Fermentation

Fermentation—the conversion of the sugars in the wort into alcohol and carbon dioxide—begins when the proper yeast is added. As noted in Chapter 12, there are two types of fermentation: top and bottom.

Top-fermentation is fast and vigorous; it takes only a few days and produces a heavy foam on the top of the brew. The wort is fermented at temperatures ranging from 50° to 70° F (10° to 21° C). After fermentation, the brew is filtered, carbonated, and packaged for immediate marketing. The most common top-fermented brews are ales, porters, and stouts—brews originating in the British Isles and, for the most part, consumed there.

The slower process of bottom-fermentation is called **lagering,** a term derived from the German *Lagerbier,* meaning "beer to be stored." The process originated in Bavaria in the eighth century as a method of preserving beer, which soured quickly during the summer without refrigeration or pasteurization. An enterprising brewer fermented some beer in cold mountain caves, hoping it would keep. Not only was the beer preserved, but the flavor became smoother and more mellow. The cold fermentation process also improved sedimentation, producing a more sparkling beer.

The process was gradually improved. Brewers discovered a yeast which better facilitated the slow fermentation at low temperatures. All of Germany soon adopted the process, and its neighbors followed suit.

In lagering, the yeast works slowly at the requisite low temperatures. Actual fermentation takes place at the bottom of the tank and is visible only by the few tiny bubbles of carbon dioxide that float to the surface. The slow pace results in fewer congeners and a more mellow product.

Pasteurization

Canned or bottle brews must undergo **pasteurization** (exposing them to 140° to 150° F [60° to 65.5° C] heat in order to kill bacteria which cause spoiling) before they are packaged. Draft beer is not pasteurized. It is thus perishable and must be stored at temperatures between 36° F (2° C) and 42° F (6° C).

Draft beer is sometimes bottled or canned. In order to preserve the draft flavor, the brew is not pasteurized but rather passed through fine filters to remove spoilage bacteria. This process, called sterile filtration, results in a brew with the shelf life of a pasteurized beer and the fresher taste of a draft. However, refrigerated storage is often recommended by the brewer.

Even with pasteurization, bottled and canned beers have a limited shelf life. For this reason, some brewers mark each package with a **pull date**—often three to four months after packaging. Others provide codes with the date of brewing. Rotating your stock to serve the oldest dates first is good practice.

Carbonation

Carbonation, the addition of carbon dioxide gas to malt beverages, is responsible for their spritzy, zestful character and the rich, fine collar of foam on the top of a glass. A brew with insufficient carbon dioxide is said to be "flat."

Carbonation methods vary somewhat. Some brewers carbonate their beer before packaging by pumping the gas under pressure into the product. Other brewers save the carbon dioxide given off during fermentation and restore it to the brew during packaging.

Krausening is a method of adding carbon dioxide by putting the brew through a second fermentation in a pressurized tank. Fresh wort is added to an already-fermented brew; the mixture is allowed to ferment under pressure, locking the gas in the beer.

Malt beverages are fermented and carbonated in tanks lined with glass or plastic or made of stainless-steel, inert materials which do not affect the flavor of brews. Wooden tanks are never used, as wood harms a brew's flavor. However, one brewer adds beechwood chips during krausening to enhance the beverage's clarification.

Packaging   Malt beverages are packaged in various containers (see Chapter 12); the most popular size is the 12-ounce can or bottle. Beer cans are coated inside with tannish lacquer, a substance which seals the metal to prevent it from reacting with the brew. Glass, because it is an inert substance, does not require this treatment.

Most beer packaged in kegs is sold to bars and restaurants. Although kegs are made of strong metal, they must be handled with care. (Draft beer is discussed more fully in a separate section.)

Packaging is also important from a marketing standpoint. The producers of malt beverages are well aware of this and spend a considerable amount of money to discover what type of package sells best.

The Malt Beverage Family

There are many types of malt beverages made around the world, and many are imported into the United States. For the most part, these imports are German, British, or Dutch brews. However, beers from Mexico, Australia, and Japan are doing well in the United States. Malt beverages from many other countries are also available.

Some of the most common types of malt beverages are described in the following sections.

Types of Malt Beverages   **Ale** was developed by the British and is still popular in Great Britain. It is top-fermented at high temperatures. Ale usually contains more hops than do most beers, resulting in ale's characteristic bitter taste. It has a pale, bright, yellow-tannish color. Ale is sometimes mixed with lager beer to produce **cream ale.**

Porter is a brew named for the English porters (servers) who first served it at Coventry Garden. It became very popular among the British, although it has now lost much of its popularity. Porter is made from malt roasted at high temperatures, which gives it a dry, bitter taste and a darker color than beer. It resembles ale but is sweeter with less hoppy taste. Porter is top-fermented and can contain as much as 8% alcohol by weight.

Stout is similar to porter but got its name by being more "stout"—that is, higher in alcohol content than porter. It is top-fermented and has a dark color, acquired from roasted unmalted barley. Stout has more of a hoppy taste than either porter or ale. There are two kinds of stout: dry stout, such as Guinness and other Irish brands, and the sweeter stouts popular in Britain.

Bock is a German beer that is darker, richer, and higher in alcohol content than regular 3.2% beer. It is also somewhat sweet. Bock is brewed in the spring, usually for festivals; for this reason, it is associated with Easter and often referred to as "Easter beer." Bock was first brewed in Einbeck, Germany, around A.D. 1200 and was called *Einbecker Bier.* At some point the brew was renamed *Bockbier,* which has been shortened to bock.

Doppelbocks are full, rich lagered bocks of high alcohol content, ranging from 6% to 10.5% alcohol by weight. One Bavarian doppelbock (Kulminator) is 10.5% alcohol.

Dark beer is similar in color to bock but is not as sweet. It has a rich, creamy taste. Like bock, dark beer gains its dark color and pronounced flavor from malt sprouts roasted at high temperatures.

Pilsner (or pilsener) is a light, rich, and mellow lager with a dry, crisp, hoppy flavor and a light color. It is made from hops grown in the area around Pilsen, Czechoslovakia (now Plzen), reputedly the finest hops in the world. The original brew became so famous that it attracted many imitators. Many brewers producing pilsner today obtain only part of their hops from Plzen.

Bavarian beer, also called Münchner, is a lager made from the hops of Bavaria, which possess good flavor characteristics. It is light in body and darker than pilsner, getting its full, rich flavor from heavy malt. There are two types of Bavarian beer: light (*helles*) and dark (*dunkel*).

Dortmunder, produced in Dortmund, Germany, is a beer of a character between pilsner and Bavarian beer. It has a dark color and full body.

The Germans also produce a brew much like British ale. It is called *Alt,* the German word meaning old.

Weissbier and *Weizenbier* ("white beer" and "wheat beer," respectively) are made from varying proportions of malt and malted wheat. They are thus less malty than brews made from straight malted barley. These brews are top-fermented and krausened, which gives them a creamy, delicate character.

Malt liquor is made (or should be made) from straight malt with no adjuncts. It has a more pronounced malt flavor and is slightly darker than regular beer; it usually has a higher alcohol content, ranging from 3.2% to 8% by weight. It may also be a bit sweeter than regular beer. Some malt liquors are a blend of regular beer and malt wine.

Steam beer is a malt beverage brewed predominantly from malt with very little adjunct, originally made in San Francisco. It is top-fermented and receives a second fermentation which produces a creamy foam and high carbon dioxide content.

Alcohol Content of Malt Beverages

The alcohol content of malt beverages is stated by weight rather than volume. Thus, a beer which is labeled as 3.2% alcohol contains 3.2% alcohol by weight or 4% alcohol by volume (see Chapter 12 for information on how each measurement is determined).

The amount of adjunct and malt used to make a malt beverage is one factor determining its alcohol content. The production methods are also a factor. In general, top-fermented products are higher in alcohol than bottom-fermented ones, but not always. Some German lagers (doppelbocks), for instance, contain as much as 10.5% alcohol by weight. American light beers are about 2.4% to 2.8% alcohol by weight. Most German brews range from 3.6% to 4% alcohol by weight. Ales, American premium beers, and Dortmunder are about 4% alcohol; German bocks are higher. Malt liquors usually have the highest alcohol content, about 6.4% by weight. Alcohol content is not a mark of quality. Some premium brews have a lower alcohol content than brews of lesser quality.

As noted in Chapter 12, the U.S. government prohibits the inclusion of alcohol content on malt beverage labels unless required by state law.

Non-Alcoholic Brews

Non-alcoholic brews, often called "near beers," have come into their own.[2] Many people who want a cold, non-alcoholic drink ask for these products instead of soda pop or carbonated water; they can thus enjoy the taste of beer without its intoxicating effect. The variety of brands on the market today reflects this demand, which is growing (see Exhibit 14.2). In 1989, Americans consumed about 9.6 million cases of non-alcoholic beer, an increase of 15% over the previous year. Sales are expected to increase even more in the 1990s. By contrast, alcoholic beer has experienced relatively flat growth; sales increased very little from 1988 to 1989, a trend which will probably continue.

Non-alcoholic beers, available in bottles and cans and on tap, have fared well when taste-tested against regular beer. Most have been ranked as equal, while some have even been ranked higher. Non-alcoholic beer is produced with the same ingredients and by the same methods as beer with alcohol; methods of removing the alcohol differ among brands.

Government regulations require that non-alcoholic beer contain less than 0.5% alcohol by weight. One company advertises its product as having less alcohol than orange juice. While it would take a great many bottles of non-alcoholic beer to get intoxicated, most authorities on alcohol addiction warn that even 0.5% alcohol (or the familiar beer taste) can trigger relapses in recovering alcoholics.

Draft Beer

Dispensing brews from bottles or cans is not difficult, but dispensing from a draft system demands a bit more knowledge and attention. Draft beer is usually purchased in half- or full barrels or kegs. A full barrel holds 31 gallons; half-barrels are more popular.

The keg is connected by a hose to a pressurized cylinder (1,000 psi) containing either carbon dioxide or air. The pressurized gas forces the brew out through a line connected to a serving tap or faucet.

A pressure regulator controls the amount of gas released into the dispensing system. A gauge indicates the pressure. The system should have a pressure release mechanism so the pressure can be dropped if some part of the system malfunctions.

There are several methods of connecting barrels to a dispensing system, a process called **tapping.** Clearly visible warnings that tapping can be dangerous when the pressure is too high are always printed on kegs.

Draft beer is not pasteurized; it is therefore perishable. It must be stored at temperatures between 36° F (2° C) and 42° F (6° C).

Draft beer is usually krausened or carbonated so that the pressure is stable at about 12 psi. The pressure gauge at the cylinder head should register about 15 psi in order to hold the carbon dioxide gas in the brew. (It takes half a pound of pressure per square inch to dispense a half-barrel of brew.) Too much pressure will make the beer frothy and give it a gassy flavor; too little pressure lets gas escape, resulting in a flat brew. The needle on the pressure gauge should be stable. Gauges should also be inspected

Exhibit 14.2 Non-Alcoholic Beer

The growing popularity of non-alcoholic beer reflects a recent trend toward re-duced alcohol consumption; the demand has brought many new brands to the market. (Courtesy of Anheuser-Busch, Inc.)

to ensure that the regulator is functioning properly. A fluctuating needle usually indicates a leak in the regulator, which must then be replaced. Over time, the pressure in the cylinder drops; the pressure gauge should therefore be monitored and pressure increased.

Exhibit 14.3   Changing the CO$_2$ Gas Cylinder of a Beer Dispensing System

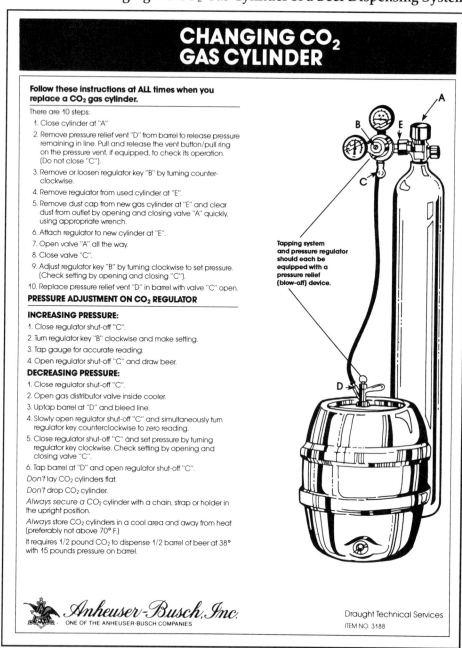

CHANGING CO$_2$ GAS CYLINDER

Follow these instructions at ALL times when you replace a CO$_2$ gas cylinder.

There are 10 steps:

1. Close cylinder at "A"
2. Remove pressure relief vent "D" from barrel to release pressure remaining in line. Pull and release the vent button/pull ring on the pressure vent, if equipped, to check its operation. (Do not close "C".)
3. Remove or loosen regulator key "B" by turning counter-clockwise.
4. Remove regulator from used cylinder at "E".
5. Remove dust cap from new gas cylinder at "E" and clear dust from outlet by opening and closing valve "A" quickly, using appropriate wrench.
6. Attach regulator to new cylinder at "E".
7. Open valve "A" all the way.
8. Close valve "C".
9. Adjust regulator key "B" by turning clockwise to set pressure. (Check setting by opening and closing "C".)
10. Replace pressure relief vent "D" in barrel with valve "C" open.

PRESSURE ADJUSTMENT ON CO$_2$ REGULATOR

INCREASING PRESSURE:

1. Close regulator shut-off "C".
2. Turn regulator key "B" clockwise and make setting.
3. Tap gauge for accurate reading.
4. Open regulator shut-off "C" and draw beer.

DECREASING PRESSURE:

1. Close regulator shut-off "C".
2. Open gas distributor valve inside cooler.
3. Uptap barrel at "D" and bleed line.
4. Slowly open regulator shut-off "C" and simultaneously turn regulator key counterclockwise to zero reading.
5. Close regulator shut-off "C" and set pressure by turning regulator key clockwise. Check setting by opening and closing valve "C".
6. Tap barrel at "D" and open regulator shut-off "C".

Don't lay CO$_2$ cylinders flat.

Don't drop CO$_2$ cylinder.

Always secure a CO$_2$ cylinder with a chain, strap or holder in the upright position.

Always store CO$_2$ cylinders in a cool area and away from heat (preferably not above 70° F.)

It requires 1/2 pound CO$_2$ to dispense 1/2 barrel of beer at 38° with 15 pounds pressure on barrel.

Tapping system and pressure regulator should each be equipped with a pressure relief (blow-off) device.

Anheuser-Busch, Inc.
ONE OF THE ANHEUSER-BUSCH COMPANIES

Draught Technical Services
ITEM NO. 3188

Courtesy of Anheuser-Busch, Inc.

Methods of replacing empty cylinders vary from system to system (see Exhibit 14.3). In general, the pressure at the cylinder and at the keg is closed off. After the pressure regulator has been removed, the cylinder is disconnected from the system and a new one is connected. The pressure is then turned on at the cylinder head and at the barrel.

Because the cylinders are filled with pressurized gas, they must be handled carefully. Do not drop them or tip them over. They should be stored upright in a clean, dry room at about room temperature.

Exhibit 14.4 How to Clean the Lines

1. Mix brewery approved cleaner in a bucket of water according to manufacturer's directions.

6. While you're waiting, scrub tap and beer faucet parts with brush—inside and out.

2. Disconnect tap from both barrel and tubing. Remove beer faucet and take apart.

7. Put the small sponge in the line at the faucet cleaning attachment.

3. Put tap and faucet parts in bucket to soak.

8. Reconnect coupling and pump sponge through beer line. This cleans out sediment. For perfect cleaning, run sponge through again.

4. Put on faucet cleaning attachment. Connect coupling to cleaning attachment.

9. Assemble rinsed faucet parts and connect faucet. Fill bucket with fresh cool water. Connect pump hose and beer line using twin male coupling. Pump the fresh water through the beer line system to remove cleaning solution.

5. Pump solution from bucket through line (with bucket-type pump) until it starts to flow out beer line. Continue to pump the cleaning solution through the system for several minutes to thoroughly clean the beer lines.

10. When crystal clear water comes through, you're ready to retap barrel. Draw the water from the beer line. Now you're ready to serve beer.

Cleaning your draft beer lines as frequently as every two weeks is necessary to prevent spoilage from bacteria. (Courtesy of Anheuser-Busch, Inc.)

Lines from the keg to the dispensing faucet should be flushed daily with fresh water and cleaned thoroughly at least every two weeks to remove sediment, which affects flavor (see Exhibit 14.4).

Judging Malt Beverage Quality

To judge a malt beverage, you must first know what qualities the brew in question should have. For example, a top-fermented brew should have different characteristics than a lager. Likewise, ales, porters, and stouts all differ from one another, as do different brands of the same type of beverage. Many factors influence the quality of a brew, including the fermentation method, the amount of hops and malt used, and the ingredient handling practices. As noted earlier, even the water gives a brew certain quality characteristics.

Appearance

As with wine and spirits, malt beverage evaluation begins with the eyes. As discussed in Chapter 6, a beer-clean glass should be used for judging purposes. Note how the brew pours into the glass. Brews are about 95% liquid; the 5% of solids gives body to the brew, so it should not flow thinly like water, but rather roll into the glass. Malt beverages are not clear as they are poured. Carbon dioxide bubbles rise, producing a whitish cast which clears rapidly.

The color should be typical for the product being judged—either light yellowish-tan, tan, golden, amber, copper, brownish-tan, brown, deep brown, or blackish-brown. Regular 3.2% beer is usually amber gold; dark brews such as bock are the result of longer roasting at higher temperatures during the malting process. Porter is darkest in color because of longer roasting of the malt.

Some brews should show a brilliant clarity, with no sediment or cloudiness. Some high-malt brews, on the other hand, may be slightly murky because of the protein in the malt. Too much cloudiness is undesirable.

As the brew is poured, a foam (head or collar) should form at the top, usually from an inch to two inches high. It should be dense, creamy, and fine, and should not dissipate quickly. Tiny bubbles should begin to rise in the glass. Large bubbles indicate a product that will go flat quickly. The bubbles should not form on the side of the glass but should drift lazily from the bottom up to support the foam. There should be many fine bubbles. As you drink a brew with good carbonation, the foam should cling to the inside of the glass in thin circles.

Aroma

Next, smell the brew. The odor should be fresh and clean, not sour, tainted, moldy, or cured (an odor of ham or canned meat). The odor of hops should be evident, the intensity dependent on the amount of hops used to make the brew. **Dry-hopped** beer (dry-hopped meaning the hops have been soaked in the brew without boiling to extract a lighter, less bitter flavor and better aroma) may give off the odor of spice, pine, mint, or thyme; these odors should be very delicate.

The brew should also have the aroma of malt, readily identifiable in most brews. The odor, which varies in intensity depending on the amount of malt used, should be clear and sweetish, without a trace of rankness, sourness, or rawness.

As you smell the brew, you should hear the faint, sharp click of bubbles bursting.

Taste

The first taste sensation should be a slight acidity on the tongue; top-fermented brews will have more of this characteristic than bottom-fermented brews because the former method produces more acid. There should be no salty taste. Some brews may be dry, while others may be definitely sweet. High-malt brews are often sweet because the malt is primarily from the maltose sugar.

A malt beverage should have a distinctive bitter taste; the degree of this bitterness depends on the amount and kind of hops used in making the brew. Roasted malt sometimes lends additional bitterness to a brew.

Flavor   Flavor is the combination of aroma and taste. Good brews have a delicate flavor, even though it may be pronounced. Of course, the balanced combination of the taste and odor of the hops and malt should be present. There should be no harshness, rawness, or indication of spoilage.

Brews can develop off flavors in the fermenting process; top-fermented products are more prone to this than lagers. In any fermentation, some butanol or butyl aldehyde can form. Either of these substances may change to butyric acid, which has the soapy flavor of rancid butter or fat. Acetone may also form, especially when a corn adjunct is used. These substances have the odor and perfumed taste of nail polish. Lactic acid—the acid that sours milk—may also form during the production of alcoholic beverages. While some lactic acid may be typical and desirable, too much destroys the mellowness and balance of flavor of a good brew.

Evaluating the flavor of a malt beverage is an extremely subjective experience. Although this section has attempted to present some guidelines, the taster must rely primarily on his or her experience and judgment.

Endnotes

1. Federal Alcohol Administration Act of 1935.
2. Non-alcoholic brews may not be labeled as "beer" in the United States.

Key Terms

additive	krausening
adjunct	lagering
ale	malt beverage
Alt	malt liquor
barley	maltose
Bavarian beer	mashing
bock	pasteurization
brewing	pilsner
carbonation	porter
cream ale	pull date
dark beer	steam beer
doppelbocks	stout
Dortmunder	tapping
dry-hopped	top-fermentation
hopping	yeasts
hops	

Discussion Questions

1. What are the six types of ingredients used in making malt beverages?

2. What are the seven major processes in malt beverage production?

3. What is the chief difference between top-fermentation and bottom-fermentation?

4. What is another term for bottom-fermentation?

5. How does pasteurization affect the shelf life of beer?

6. What is a pull date?

7. How does ale differ from beer?

8. What are some of the major concerns in dispensing draft beer and in maintaining the dispensing system?

9. What is the definition of non-alcoholic brews by U.S. standards? What are some of the reasons for their growing popularity?

10. How would you begin to judge the quality of a malt beverage? What are the succeeding steps?

15 Wine Fundamentals

Chapter Outline

Basic Wine Classifications
    Table Wines
    Natural and Fortified Wines
    Aperitif and Dessert Wines
    Sparkling Wines
The Growing and Harvesting of Wine Grapes
    The Soil
    The Vine
    The Grape
    Geography and Climate
        Local Growing and Weather Conditions
    Harvesting
Wine Production
    Pressing
    Fermentation
    Aging
    Fining
    Blending
    Bottling and Corking
    Maturing
    Storage
Regulation and Labeling
    France
        The Appellation Contrôlée Label
        The VDQS Label
        The Vin de Pays Label
        Other Labeling Regulations
    Germany
        Producing Regions
        Quality Levels
        Origin
        Wine Name
        Vintage Year
        Sugar Content
        Grape Varieties
        Testing
    Italy
    The United States
    Spain
    Other Countries
    Recent Trends in Regulation and Labeling
        Organic Wines
        Sulfur and Sulfites
        Non-Alcoholic Wine
Tasting and Judging Wine
    Preparing to Judge
    Judging the Wine

A knowledge of wine fundamentals is essential to the education of a bar and beverage manager. As we have noted in Chapter 12, wine is by far the most complex beverage in the annals of human history: the variety of hauntingly elusive flavors is, by itself, staggering. The methods that produce these flavors are an odd combination of centuries-old nature-dependent processes, stainless steel vats, and computer technology. The subject of wine is further cloaked in mystery and romance and obscured by millions of words written by "experts" in heated disagreement with one another. Getting the fundamentals in one chapter is no easy task.

Nevertheless, your success in the bar and beverage management arena may well be defined by the extent of your wine knowledge. In a bar or beverage operation with little or no food service, you will need relatively little knowledge. You will stock dry and sweet vermouth for mixes (martinis and manhattans), perhaps some champagne or other sparkling wine in full bottles, half bottles, and "splits" (about $6^1/2$ ounces), some traditional wine-by-the-glass offerings, brand name aperitif wines like Dubonnet and Campari, and dry and sweet sherries.

In such operations you will be guided more by market trends and brand names than by a knowledge of wine fundamentals. For instance, Americans over the past few years have created a trend toward drinking white wine instead of cocktails—usually a Chablis or Chardonnay with a small degree of sweetness. Part of the reason for this trend lies in a growing societal disapproval of conspicuous alcohol consumption—white wines *generally* (not always) have less alcohol by volume than reds or other wines. Wine "spritzers" (usually white wine with carbonated water added) further reduced the alcohol and led to the marketing of "wine coolers"—sweet, artificially carbonated, fruit-flavored beverages with a wine base—sold by the bottle like beer. Although wine lovers will be quick to point out that wine coolers are little more than alcoholic soda pop, a bar or beverage manager would be wise to keep some brands in stock to satisfy the demand by younger customers (a demand fueled by millions of advertising dollars).

The primary reason for knowing wine fundamentals is the use of wine to enhance a meal. As a bar and beverage management professional, you can aspire to no higher (and richer) calling than that of a manager of a great restaurant with a great wine inventory. Even if you don't have such aspirations, consumers are becoming more and more sophisticated about wine and you will need to keep ahead of their demand for good wine with their meals, not only by learning wine fundamentals, but by keeping up with a rapidly changing marketplace.

In this chapter we will start with a brief overview of some basic classifications of wine, move to the growing and harvesting of wine grapes, through various production methods, on to an understanding of the regulation and labeling of wines, and end with a brief primer on wine tasting.

Basic Wine Classifications

Table Wines

Table wines make up the largest category of wines and, as the name suggests, include wines primarily suited to accompany food, but not limited to such purpose. On a wine menu, table wines will be further classified by color as *red*, *white*, or *rosé*. However, these colors are approximations: "reds" run from purple to slightly red-tinged brown to clear, light red; "whites" run from clear as water to green-tinged, varying shades of yellow through gold, and light brown. Although rosé wine is generally described by its rose color (light pink to light orange-red), it is made by leaving the skins of red grapes in the fermentation process for a short period, then removing them. Its taste characteristics (which vary widely) are more to the point. Color *is* an important distinction when wine with the same name comes in both red and white. A Graves is a famous white wine from the Bordeaux district in France; there is a red Graves, however, which is a fine wine but is neither well-known nor particularly important.

Natural and Fortified Wines

Most table wines are **natural wines:** basically the product of grape fermentation without the addition of alcohol or sugar (beyond a small amount allowed for certain wines under specified conditions). Natural fermentation stops when there is no more sugar to convert to alcohol or when the alcohol reaches 14% by volume. Thus, table wines may have as little as 7% alcohol but never more than 14%. (Many table wines, however, are created by stopping fermentation by *unnatural* means—by heat, by adding sulfur dioxide, and by removing the yeast through sterile filtration.)

Fortified wines, on the other hand, may range in alcohol content from 14% to 24%. Alcohol—usually in the form of a brandy distilled from wine—is added to a wine during fermentation. Adding alcohol produces two results: the extra alcohol brings the alcohol content beyond what is naturally possible; the unfermented sugar stays in the wine, producing a sweet wine. Some fortified wines (such as sherry) allow for complete fermentation of the sugar, adding the brandy (and often a sweetener) after fermentation. Port and vermouth are other examples of fortified wines.

Aperitif and Dessert Wines

Aperitif wines (from the French, *apéritif*, meaning "appetizer") are wines that are traditionally served before meals as an appetizer or cocktail. They are often fortified and herb-flavored (vermouth, for instance, is both fortified and flavored with herbal ingredients). Besides Dubonnet and Campari (mentioned earlier), other brand names include Punt e Mes and Lillet. Dry sherries are often included in this category.

Dessert wines, as the name implies, are meant to be served after dinner with dessert or *as* dessert. Dessert wines are often fortified—the sweet varieties of sherry ("Cream" and "Oloroso," primarily) and port are examples. Madeira is another. Natural wines, such as some varieties of Sauternes and many German wines classified as *Beerenauslese* or *Trochenbeerenauslese*, are sweet wines that are often used as dessert wines.

Sparkling Wines

Basically, any wine can be made into a sparkling wine by the addition of carbon dioxide under pressure. However, sparkling wines are usually made by re-fermentation. The already fermented wine is made to ferment a second time by the addition of yeast and sugar with the resulting carbon dioxide trapped instead of released. In the classic **champagne method**, the second fermentation takes place in the bottle in which it is sold—a laborious and exacting process which accounts for the high price of the best Champagne. Less expensive methods include the *transfer process* (the wine is transferred through a filter to another bottle) and the **Charmat** or **bulk process** in which the second fermentation takes place in a vat and the wine is later filtered and bottled under pressure.

The most famous of the sparkling wines is, of course, Champagne. Champagne, by law, can only come from the Champagne district of France. American "champagne" must be identified as "American champagne," "California champagne," or "New York state champagne." The Italian word for "sparkling" is *spumante*; the German word is *Schaumwein* or *Sekt*.

The Growing and Harvesting of Wine Grapes

All grapes are basically vines, members of the *Vitis* genus, *Vitaceae* family. These vines were climbing trees or sprawling shrubs for millions of years before they were cultivated expressly for wine production by human beings. The growing of grapes for wine goes back to our earliest records of human activity—to the Bible and the hieroglyphics of early Egyptian dynasties.

The main sugar in grapes is fructose (often referred to as grape sugar) which, like all sugars, can be fermented. Even so-called table grapes can produce a wine, however unsavory. However, one species of *Vitis—Vitis vinifera*—stands out as the great European wine grape. From it have come more than 4,000 named varieties of wine grape.

North America has its own species, *Vitis labrusca*, which withstands the cold winters of New York state, as well as Ohio, Michigan, and other cold-winter areas. However, the varieties of *vinifera* are by far the most used in making wine. Although we don't know where or how the first varieties were brought into existence, selective breeding is still going on. A cross between the Riesling and Muscadelle varieties created the Emerald Riesling, the grape used in the production of the fruity, soft, lively Emerald Dry wine produced in the United States.

The story of how wine grapes are grown and harvested is a fascinating one. The immense complexity and variety of wine starts with the many different areas and growing conditions in which the wine grape is grown. We will explore this process briefly in the following sections, from the ground up.

The Soil The French swear by the attributes of soil as being responsible for great French wines. The physical attributes of soil—texture, porosity, drainage, and depth—are probably more important to growing than the chemical content. Oddly, good wine grapes do not prosper in a rich, loamy soil. Such soil holds too much moisture and nutrients and, consequently, the roots of the vine don't have to develop in their search for moisture. A gravelly or rocky soil provides good drainage, causing vine roots to "chase" after moisture during dry periods. This process ultimately gives the vine the stable root support needed for good grape production.

The soil of the famous Chianti Classico region of Italy looks like nothing but gravel and rocks. Yet, the grapes prosper. Such a rocky soil is also beneficial because it absorbs a considerable amount of heat in the daytime which helps to keep the roots above 50° F (10° C) at night. (The roots do not function well below this temperature.)

The soil must, however, contain enough fine material to carry adequate nutrients. A good source of nitrogen, phosphorus, and other nutrients must be present. If not, fertilizer must be added to provide them. Many vintners make sure that stems and pressings of the grapes are returned to the soil where these materials can break down and provide needed nutrients such as nitrogen.

A grape vine can live for 50 years or more, producing a big crop of grapes each year. However, the soil in which it grows must receive proper care. The soil must be tilled, weeded, and cared for just like any ordinary agricultural crop. If you ever drive by a vineyard, you will see how well-manicured and cared for it is.

The Vine

The vast majority of modern European vineyards consist of selected European *vinifera* vines grafted on to a selected American rootstock (*Vitis labrusca*) which is naturally resistant to the deadly, vine-killing **phylloxera**—a variety of plant lice. In the middle of the last century, phylloxera was carried to Europe on *labrusca* rootstock by some English vintners who thought that the hardy American grapes would prosper in England. Crossing the channel, the phylloxera virtually wiped out all the vineyards in France, Germany, and Italy. The discovery that grafting the branches of the *Vitis vinifera* on to the rootstocks of the *Vitis labrusca* would cancel the destructive power of phylloxera revitalized the shattered European wine industry. Today, virtually all of Europe's vines grow on American roots.

Grafting of vines (called scions) to different rootstocks is now common practice for other reasons: In California, a grower can decide to change his grape crop to adjust to market trends by sawing off a vine which has been in production for many years and "T-bud" grafting another variety scion in its place. Within two years the grower will have a producing vine of a totally different variety.[2]

The other major vine care activity is pruning. Expert pruning is required to train grapevine growth to desirable patterns. In hot climates, vines are pruned and trained to grow on high trellises that serve to shelter the grapes from ripening too soon under the leaf growth. In Germany, the opposite is required. Many vineyards are trained to a height suitable for mechanical harvesting.

Pruning takes place every year in the winter, and is usually very thorough—90% to 95% of new growth is cut back. Central to the objective of pruning is the notion that "the greater the quantity, the lower the quality." While this notion is overstated, the principle is correct—the more grapes on a given vine, the more competition for sunlight, nutrients, and moisture. While pruning is, traditionally, a job for experts, mechanical pruners (with some follow-up hand pruning) have been in use for about 10 years. Carefully monitored results have shown little difference in the quality of the next year's crop whether mechanical or hand pruning is used, with mechanical pruning costing just 15% that of hand pruning.

The Grape

The grape, of course, is the essence of wine. Not only do wine grapes provide a multitudinous variety of wines, but every part of the grape can have an effect on taste; even stems are sometimes purposely kept in the fermentation (see Exhibit 15.1). Wine is made from the juice of one variety of grape or a blending of the juices of two or more varieties. Both by custom and by government regulation, certain wines can only be made from one variety of grape or a blend of the juices of specified grapes. Thus, the

Training the vine is an exacting and often painstaking job. (Courtesy of Glen Ellen Winery)

Nebbiolo grape alone is needed to make the rich, red Barolo wine of Italy; the Chardonnay grape to make a French Chablis; and only the Palomino grape gives a proper sherry. A wine coming from just one grape variety is called a **varietal** wine.

Wine made from a blend of wines to resemble a particular wine of a region such as the Rhine is called a **generic** wine. U.S. federal law calls such wines *semi-generic*, and requires that the place of origin be included on the label (as in "California Burgundy"). However, blending is commonly practiced, and the assumption that blended or generic wines are inferior to varietals is erroneous. Wines are blended for increased complexity—the blend often superior in taste to either of the blend components alone. French Champagne is almost always a blend of grape varieties. Brand name wines are blends which rely on the bottler's reputation for consistency, quality, price, and value.

In some countries such as France, a varietal wine must be made from 100% of the grape variety. In the United States, a wine may be identified as a varietal with only 75% of the grape variety actually used. In either case, a varietal wine may or may not be an indicator of quality. In California, with its wide variety of great wine grape growing areas, the best growers have produced wines primarily from one variety and have so identified their products. This has led to a consumer identification with varietals as "high-quality" wines.

Exhibit 15.1 Longitudinal Cross Section of a Grape

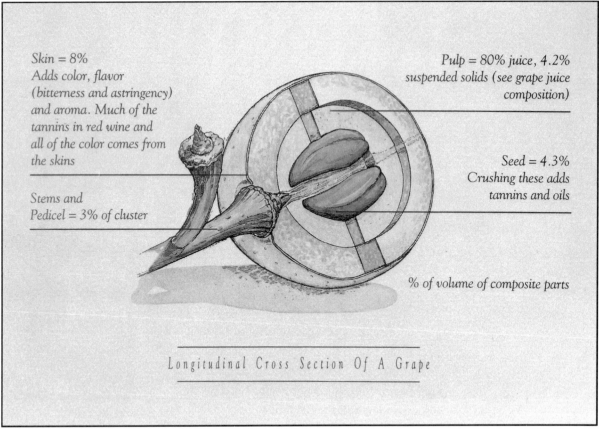

Skin = 8%
Adds color, flavor
(bitterness and astringency)
and aroma. Much of the
tannins in red wine and
all of the color comes from
the skins

Stems and
Pedicel = 3% of cluster

Pulp = 80% juice, 4.2%
suspended solids (see grape juice
composition)

Seed = 4.3%
Crushing these adds
tannins and oils

% of volume of composite parts

Longitudinal Cross Section Of A Grape

Courtesy of Sonoma County Wineries Association

Hybridization is an important factor in growing wine grapes. New grape varieties are constantly being developed through crossbreeding. The cross that created the Emerald Riesling mentioned earlier was developed in California to make the parent Riesling grape more adaptable to warmer growing conditions than are found in the part of Germany where the Riesling originated. German *viticulturists* (wine grape growers) are still trying to develop a Riesling variety which will ripen earlier (and avoid autumnal killing frosts) and still retain the taste characteristics of the parent. However, the great parent varieties were naturally developed over thousands of years, and the wine-buying public is relatively slow to accept new varieties.

Geography and Climate

The wine grape likes to grow in a temperate area, not too hot and not too cold. It grows poorly, if at all, below 50° F (10° C), and does well up to just over 90° F (32° C). Thus, the Champagne, Loire, and Alsace regions in France and the region starting about mid-Rhine in Germany are about as far north as the wine grape will prosper. England, north Germany, and northern France are a bit too cold for it. On the other hand, the Italian peninsula is just about one vast vineyard with its abundant sun and warmth. However, parts of Sicily are almost too warm for good wine production. Northern Algeria, Israel, and many countries of the Near East are not too warm for wine production.

A similar band of climatic conditions in both the northern and southern hemispheres favors grape growth. Thus, in the southern hemisphere, the land band formed by Chile, Argentina, South Africa, Australia, and New Zealand, the wine grape grows well. In the northern hemisphere, certain areas of the Near East, Iran, and the United States also produce good wine grapes.

Warmth and sun are needed not only for the vines to grow, bloom, and produce a healthy, plentiful crop of grapes, but also to develop adequate sugar for the production of enough alcohol to give a good keeping wine. In certain areas, the warmth and sun are so abundant that the grapes produce an excess of sugar, so sweet wines like the Tokaji Aszú, Sauternes, port, or Madeira are possible.

There is an old German saying that "the soil is the mother of wine, the vine its father, and the climate its fate." The spring, summer, and fall must be sufficiently long for the grape to leaf out, send out new roots, blossom, grow a rich, full, juicy, and fully ripened grape. Around 120–150 frost-free days are needed for this cycle.

The regions of Alsace and the Rhine have about the minimum of frost-free days, and their wines are dry and crisp and are not high in alcohol content because the grapes ripen without sufficient sugar; all the sugar in the grapes *have* to be fermented to get a minimally acceptable amount of alcohol. On the other hand, some very warm wine-growing areas such as southern Spain or Southern California have more than enough sun and warmth to fully ripen the wine grapes. However, wine grapes in such areas will often lack sufficient acidity for good table wines—all wines require a certain amount of acidity to retain character.

Too little or too much rain can be a problem. Too little can be solved by irrigation—Australia and Chile rely on irrigation for their considerable wine industries. However, too much rain can be devastating. Grape vines need to develop long taproots that often extend to 15 feet or more as they search for deep groundwater (see Exhibit 15.2). Too much rain can keep these taproots from developing. Ideally, rain should be adequate during vine and leaf growth, but sparse during the ripening of the grapes.

Winters must also not be too rugged. Young vines cannot stand a hard winter. A state like Montana is not favorable for grape production, because the young vines are often killed by the low winter temperatures there. However, a period of several weeks or even more when the ground remains frozen is not harmful. In fact, some good winter chill drives the sap down out of the vine and makes for a more sturdy plant in the growing season.

Local Growing and Weather Conditions. Various local growing conditions throughout the world may be more significant than geography, especially when it comes to growing the truly great wine grapes. It is generally accepted among viticulturists, for instance, that the slopes of hills are best for wine grape growing. Not only does the angle of an incline capture more solar radiation, but cold air, accumulated during the nights will roll off the slopes more quickly. A south slope is almost always ideal, but local growing conditions (an autumnal morning fog, for instance) may favor a western slope because the sun won't break through the fog until the afternoon. French wine will often carry names prefixed with *côtes* or *coteaux* which means "slopes." The world-famous Côte d'Or (literally, "slope of

Exhibit 15.2   The Root System of a Grape Vine

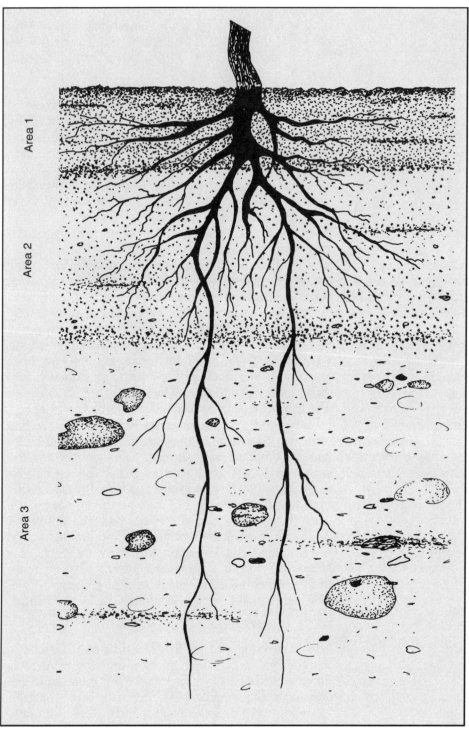

In Area 1—about 8 inches of topsoil—there are few roots; this area is tilled to remove weeds. Area 2 often extends to two feet and is the area with the most extensive root growth. Most of the vine's food and water will be supplied from here. Note the long taproots extending down through Area 3. These taproots provide low-lying ground-water during times of drought.

gold") in the Burgundy district of France produces some of world's greatest wines on its south- and east-facing slopes.

Also part of the magic and mystery of wine growing is the specific climatic conditions (often referred to as "microclimates") in various growing areas. These areas (and the famous *côtes* are good examples) seem particularly favored not only by their slopes and soil, but by their receiving the right amounts of sun and moisture at the right times more consistently than less favored areas. Such areas are singled out in the French classification system as *crus* or "growth" areas (as we shall see later in this chapter). Microclimates can so affect small areas—even individual vineyards—that a **good year** (a year in which the grape crop receives the optimal sun and moisture) can vary even from one part of a region to another.

Harvesting

Just as vines are pruned on the basis of "the higher the quantity, the less the quality," so also do most wine-producing countries limit the yield per acre that can be harvested (the United States is a notable exception). In France, the highest quality *crus* limit the harvest to about two tons per acre. Before reunification the Federal Republic of Germany (West Germany) allowed an average of 5–6 tons per acre.

The German wine-making emphasis is more on achieving the right balance between sugar and acidity at the time of harvest than it is on limiting yield. This balance and the natural sugar content of the grape is tested in the vineyards: Before a wine can bear various quality designations on its label, it must pass government tests for specific sugar content before the grapes are harvested.

In fact, the balance between sugar and acidity is the critical element in the harvesting of all wine grapes. As the grape becomes more ripe, its sugar content begins to outweigh its acidity. There is no one "right" ratio, but each type of wine will have a ratio appropriate to its particular taste characteristics.

Some grapes may be left on the vine for a long time in the fall until they are overripe, developing a large concentration of sugar. In late fall, the morning mists and afternoon sun create ideal growing conditions for a mold called *Botrytis cinerea* or, more commonly, "**noble rot**." It is called "noble" because it creates some of the greatest, naturally sweet wines.

The traditional method of harvesting is to send pickers out into the field with special cutting knives or shears, carrying baskets which are filled with 35 to 50 pounds of bunches of grapes which are mostly ripe. (Picking individual ripe grapes is a relatively rare practice and limited to some very expensive types of wine). These filled baskets are dumped into carts, called *gondolas*, to be moved to the pressing room. Hand picking is still the preferred method because human judgment can be used to select desirable grapes while rejecting undesirable ones. However, machine picking is catching on, especially in California, and may become more common in the years to come.

Wine Production

The basics of fermenting grapes—as related in Chapter 12—are utterly simple. Squeeze the juice from the grapes and the yeasts which grow naturally on the grape skins will cause the juice and skins to ferment. White

Harvest time in California. (Courtesy of Glen Ellen Winery)

skins produce white wine and red skins produce red wine. However, thousands of years of tradition and experimentation would fill volumes on the subtleties of making thousands of varieties of wines. And today, with stainless steel vats, computer-assisted controls, genetic research, and other technological developments, the production of wine worldwide is reaching unprecedented heights of quantity *and* quality. The following sections offer the bare basics of winemaking. (See Exhibit 15.3.)

Pressing   The gondolas filled with grapes are brought to the presses where the grapes are washed and gently crushed to begin the process of removing the juice, which is called **must**. Some of the juice obtained is what is called *free run*. This is the must that runs off after the grapes are crushed but before they are pressed. Most of the must coming from the pressings is retained for wine, but some of it may not be fermented for wine—a portion may be fermented separately and distilled into brandy or used for other purposes, such as making wine vinegar. The final pressings in the making of sherry

Exhibit 15.3 Winemaking

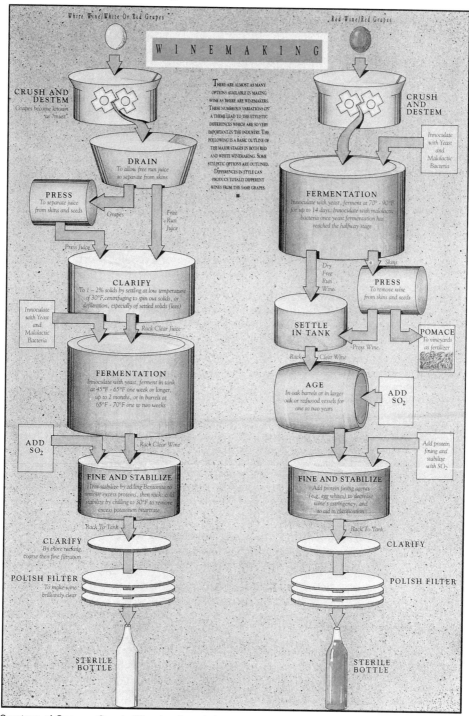

Courtesy of Sonoma County Wineries Association

are separately fermented and then distilled into brandy for use in fortifying the sherry wine.

Pressing must be done with care, since rough or heavy pressing can extract undesirable components. Thus, the crushing of the seeds can give an excessively bitter wine. In the past, grapes were pressed by bare feet, which gave just about the right pressure and action to remove the juice without getting undesirable substances into the must. However, today's presses are so designed as to just about duplicate the pressure of human feet. Modern presses are more efficient than bare feet in extracting must but tend to leave a higher proportion of solids such as skins, flesh, pips, and dirt in the must. For this reason, the must (especially for white wines) is cleaned before fermentation—by allowing the solids to settle out, by a powerful vacuum filter, or by careful centrifugal pumping.

Fermentation

Almost universally, the first thing vintners do before fermentation is to add a small dose of **sulfur dioxide** (SO_2) to the must. The amount used is regulated by law. It is used to kill the wild yeasts present on the skins of grapes and thus prevent premature and uncontrolled fermentation; it is also used to prevent oxidation.[3]

The next basic decision required is whether sugar should be added to the must—a process called **chaptalization**. This process is often necessary when weather conditions prevent grapes from ripening fully and developing enough natural sugar to convert into the amount of alcohol prescribed (often by law) for certain wines. In some countries, chaptalization is controlled and some wines may not be allowed to be chaptalized. (Some expert tasters say they can tell by the aftertaste if a wine has been chaptalized.)

All wines also need some acidity. If acid is lacking, the vintner can blend in grapes with enough acid to make up for any deficiency. Pickers may also be instructed to pick enough unripe grapes to give the required acidity.

The proper fermentation temperature is different for different kinds of wine, and individual vintners have sharply differing views on proper temperature. A vigorous chemical process, fermentation develops heat and may have to be controlled so the temperature does not rise too high and develop undesirable substances. Wood and concrete vats are very poor conductors of heat; for this reason alone, stainless steel vats are now in wide use.

Red wines are fermented at temperatures usually from 70° to 90° F (21° to 32° C) and whites at from 45° to 65° F (7° to 18° C). The lower temperature for whites is used to give a more fresh and fruity flavor to the wine. The usual cold fermentation temperatures are from 65° to 70° F (18° to 21° C) for reds and 44° to 59° F (7° to 15° C) for whites.

Fermentation occurs only as long as there is sugar to ferment. When it is used up, fermentation stops. It also stops when the alcohol content rises to 14%, because the alcohol at this point kills the remaining yeast. If sugar remains with alcohol at this percentage, the wine will tend toward sweetness—a wine of 2% sugar content is sweet.

Red wine is red because it is made with red (or black) grapes and fermented *with* the skins. The red in grape skins is made up of *anthocyanins* which are soluble in alcohol and some other organic substances, but not in water. Thus, as the must ferments and alcohol is produced, a red color pervades the ferment. When skins are left in, a thick cap develops on top of the fermenting wine which hinders fermentation by blocking oxygen. Either this cap must be broken up frequently or wine must be pumped from the bottom and run over the cap so oxygen is available.

Stainless steel fermenting tanks. (Photo by Lenny Siegel)

White wines are made from white grapes or red and black grapes with their skins removed so they do not color the wine. Many French Champagnes are made from mostly black or red grapes with the skins removed—the so-called *grand noir* Champagnes.

A rosé wine is made by fermenting the must with the red skins for only a short period, usually overnight. For this reason a rosé is often called *le vin de nuit* (the wine of the night).

Malolactic fermentation can easily occur in the fermentation process. This is a bacterial change and a breakdown of malic acid into lactic acid and carbon dioxide along with other minor substances. Malic acid is much more tart than lactic acid so the overall result is less tartness. Since the wine becomes smoother, malolactic fermentation is generally considered a favorable fermentation reaction. However, in warm areas such as California,

Chardonnay fermenting in 60-gallon French oak barrels. While most white wine is fermented in stainless steel tanks, fermenting (and aging) in oak provides unique and complex taste characteristics. (Courtesy of Clos du Bois Winery)

malolactic fermentation must be controlled—it tends to remove too much acidity—acidity needed both for preservation and for character. Malolactic fermentation can be controlled by filtration (see below) or by the addition of sulfur dioxide.

Some wines (primarily reds) are produced by a fermentation process called *carbonic maceration*. Uncrushed grapes are vatted in a sealed chamber and fermentation starts. The oxygen is used up and only carbon dioxide now fills the chamber. Without oxygen, the wine produces less acid and a rich, fruity flavor and brilliant red color. This relatively new process has been particularly successful with wines—such as the Beaujolais Nouveau—which are intended for consumption when very young.

Aging   **Aging** of wines is the storage of wines that takes place after fermentation, but before bottling; its purpose is to allow further chemical reactions with a small amount of air, with suspended particles in the wine, and sometimes, with the storage medium itself (as with oak casks). Most wines are aged after fermentation, usually by being placed in casks and then stored in a cold area. Caves, which are quite cold in the winter, were adequate cold storage areas for the more northerly wine-growing regions. (The advent of refrigeration greatly enhanced winemaking, especially in the warmer growing regions.)

During the aging period, flocculent (suspended) material in the wine settles to the bottom of the cask or vat as sediment or **lees** (which includes some tannins, and some tartrates). At various times after the settling out of the above substances, the wine is carefully run off the lees into another container, a process called **racking**. Racking removes some acidity; the color of the wine becomes more brilliant; the fermented wine becomes less astringent due to the reduction of tannins. During aging, flavors also blend together and smooth out. Glycerine develops, giving additional smoothness and more body.

Aging wine in small oak casks is favored for some wines because the wood encourages certain desirable changes in taste and texture. Some aging specifies *new* casks, because new wood imparts stronger wood flavor to the wine; some vintners scrape the insides of the casks after many years of use to achieve "new wood" effect. Wood may actually add tannins, but these tannins are described as "soft" while the tannins in grapes (which partly settle out) are called "hard" and give a harshness to wine. The end result of aging in casks is usually a smoother, softer wine.

Aging today may not always occur in small oak casks. Instead, huge oak vats may be used. Also, concrete, glass-lined, or stainless steel vats may be used. These may be sealed so there is little oxidation or other changes from the air. Whites and rosés are often aged in vats which are lined with inert materials. Some wine is lost during aging from evaporation and, to keep casks filled, additional wine is added—called *topping off*—to fill the cask and prevent excessive oxidation.

It is important to prevent excessive oxidation since it can destroy the wine. Another undesirable oxidative change is caused by the fruit fly. It carries a bacterium which, in combination with oxygen, changes alcohol into acetic acid (vinegar). During fermentation and subsequent handling—even through bottling—it is important to keep fruit flies away from the wine.

Aging can develop quality up to a certain point and after that the wine may not improve and may even deteriorate. Most wine is aged just over the winter, and bottling takes place in the spring after the harvest. Other wines are aged several or more years, just as they may be left to ferment over a long period. Some others, like the robust and more stable reds, may be aged in casks for a long time. Aging, in this case, encourages more and more development. In some cases, specific aging times are required by law if certain terms are used on the label. (We will discuss such terms later in this chapter and in Chapter 16.)

After a wine is aged, it is possible for wine experts to make a final judgment as to what the quality of the wine will be. Up to this point all indications may point to a great or a good year, but it is only after the wine is aged that the experts make their final determination. In some years, the aged wines may only be described as *ordinary*; in a slightly better year, the wine may be said to be *medium*; in a better year, described as *good*; if still better, the wine is described as *great*, and the very best is said to be *exceptional*. Thus the vintage year shown on a label of such wines is important, because a buyer will have a basis for judging the value of the wine. Exhibit 15.4 shows a vintage chart for wines of France. Note that the wine qualities do not stay the same in the same year between different areas. Thus in 1982, the reds of Bordeaux were the only ones called "exceptional," while other areas obtained only a "medium" rating.

Fining   **Fining** is a process that removes certain microscopic solids still remaining suspended in the wine after racking. Fining gives the wine more clarity and brilliance; it also removes materials that might give undesirable properties to the wine. Filtering the wine through very fine filters is one way of

Exhibit 15.4 Comparison of Vintages for the Wine-Growing Regions of France

★ EXCEPTIONAL VINTAGES: 1921, 1928, 1929, 1945 ★										
VINTAGE	Red Bordeaux	White Bordeaux	Red Burgundy	White Burgundy	Côtes du Rhone Growths	Alsace	Pouilly-Loire Sancerre	Anjou Touraine	Beaujolais	Champagne
1947	★	••••	••••		★			★		
1949	★	••••	★		••••			••••		
1955	★	••••	••••	•••	••••			••••		
1959	••••	••••	★	•••	•••	★		★		
1961	★	★	★	••••	••••	••••		•••		
1962	••••	••••	•••	•••	••••	••		•••		
1964	•••	••	••••	•••	•••	•••				
1966	••••	•••	••••	•••	••••	••••				
1967	•••	★	•••	•••	••••	••••				
1969	•	••	••••	••••	•••	•••		••••		
1970	★	•••	•••	★	★	•••		••••		
1971	••••	•••	••••	••••	••••	★		•••		
1973	•••	•••	••	••••		••••		••		
1974	••	•••	•••	•••		••		••		
1975	••••	••••	•	•••	••••	•••		•••		
1976	•••	••••	••••	••••	••••	★		••••		
1977	••	••	••	•••		••		••		
1978	••••	•••	★	••••	★	••		•••		
1979	••••	•••	•••	★	••••	••••		•••		
1980	••	••	•••	•••	•••	••	•••	••	•	
1981	••••	•••	••	•••	•••	••••	••	•••	•••	
1982	★	•••	•••	••••	••	•••	••••	••••	•••	
1983	••••	••••	••••	••••	•••	★	••••	••••	★	
1984	••	••	•••	•••	••	••	••••	•••	••	
1985	Abundant harvest of very fine quality									

Average vintage	Medium vintage	Good vintage	Great vintage	Exceptional vintage
•	••	•••	••••	★

These appreciations are based on averages; the exception proves the rule.

Courtesy of Wines of France

Checking the purity of a new white wine after filtering. (Courtesy of Glen Ellen Winery)

doing this, and can be very effective since only pure liquid remains. In fact, filters may remove too much, including colloidal suspensions that give a wine special character and taste. For this reason, a vintner may use a fining agent to remove only some suspended particles.

Some fining agents work by carrying negative electrical charges to attract positively charged suspended particles that are undesirable. Others are gels to which flocculent materials attach themselves, causing the combined mass to sink to the bottom. Egg white, colloidal silica, bentonite, gelatin, and even animal blood are some of the products used for fining. Centrifuging can also be used for such clarification.

Blending

Many wines are blends. **Blending** refers to the use of different grape varieties in making one wine, but more often describes the practice of blending different wines (wines from different years or with different taste characteristics) to create one brand of wine. True Champagne (from France) is always made from a blend of wines, sometimes from different growers/wine makers, often from different years, almost always from more than one of three specified grape varieties. Many clarets (dry, red Bordeaux wines) are the result of wines purchased at different wineries by *négociants* (wine merchants) and blended by them for a consistent taste.

Traditionally, American wines are blends of different grape varieties. As we noted earlier in this chapter, U.S. regulations allow wines to be labeled as a varietal with up to 25% from other grapes. (However, the best varietals are 95% to 100% of the grape specified.) Vintners in the eastern part of the United States may purchase California *vinifera* wines and blend them with their *labrusca* wines to reduce the grapy flavor.

Blending allows the bringing together of desirable components in different wines to make a better product; it is seldom a dilution of a good wine by a poorer one. One wine may lack the necessary tannins for good taste and keeping qualities, while another wine may have an excess of tannins and be too astringent. By blending the two together, a vintner may produce a very good wine.

Bottling and Corking

By the spring following the fall harvest, most wines are ready for bottling (the fine red wines being a notable exception). Traditionally, this is the time that wine merchants will visit the wineries, sample the wines, and make their purchases. The casks will then be shipped to the bottler's establishment for bottling. More and more wineries, however, are bottling their own wines.

"Estate bottled" has a certain cachet because the wine grower can usually be expected to protect his or her reputation with a high-quality wine. In France, growers who bottle their own wines have a legal right to put *"mis en bouteille au château"* or *"mis en bouteille au domaine"* on their labels. In former years only the very rich vineyards and prominent vintners such as the Rothschild family could afford to have their own bottling plant. Today, portable bottling operations in large vans can service many less affluent vineyards; the *mis en bouteille* label is no longer synonymous with quality.

Glass is by far the preferred container for holding wine and is often colored to keep the wine from being affected by light. Different shapes are traditionally used for different kinds of wines and especially to signify the wine-growing region (see Exhibit 15.5). From the bottle shape and color, one can often tell at a glance where the wine comes from and what type it is.

Some sparkling wines of many nations are marketed in standard French bottles and bottle sizes for sparkling wines. Exhibit 15.6 gives the metric and ounce sizes and the name of the container used for sparkling wines. Most of these bottles must be made of heavy, dark glass and be specially built to withstand the heavy pressures built up by the carbon dioxide gas inside.

After bottling, many wines must be left to rest for a time to recover from what is called *bottle sickness*. During this period, the wine stabilizes and regains its full flavor and character.

Cork has been found to be one of the best materials with which to seal a bottle of wine, although some of the new plastic materials do just as well—they probably would be used more if it were not for the fact that cork seems to have some romance attached to it as well as a long tradition in winemaking.

The cork tree is an oak which develops a thick, spongy, semi-hard bark several inches thick. The tree does not start to produce cork until it is about 40 years old; and then only about every nine years can the bark be removed. Portugal produces the best and the most cork; Spain produces some and Italy a little.

A high-quality cork can last about 50 or more years, but many experts suggest re-corking after 25 years. Crumbly, porous cork allows air

Exhibit 15.5 Different Bottle Shapes for Different Regions

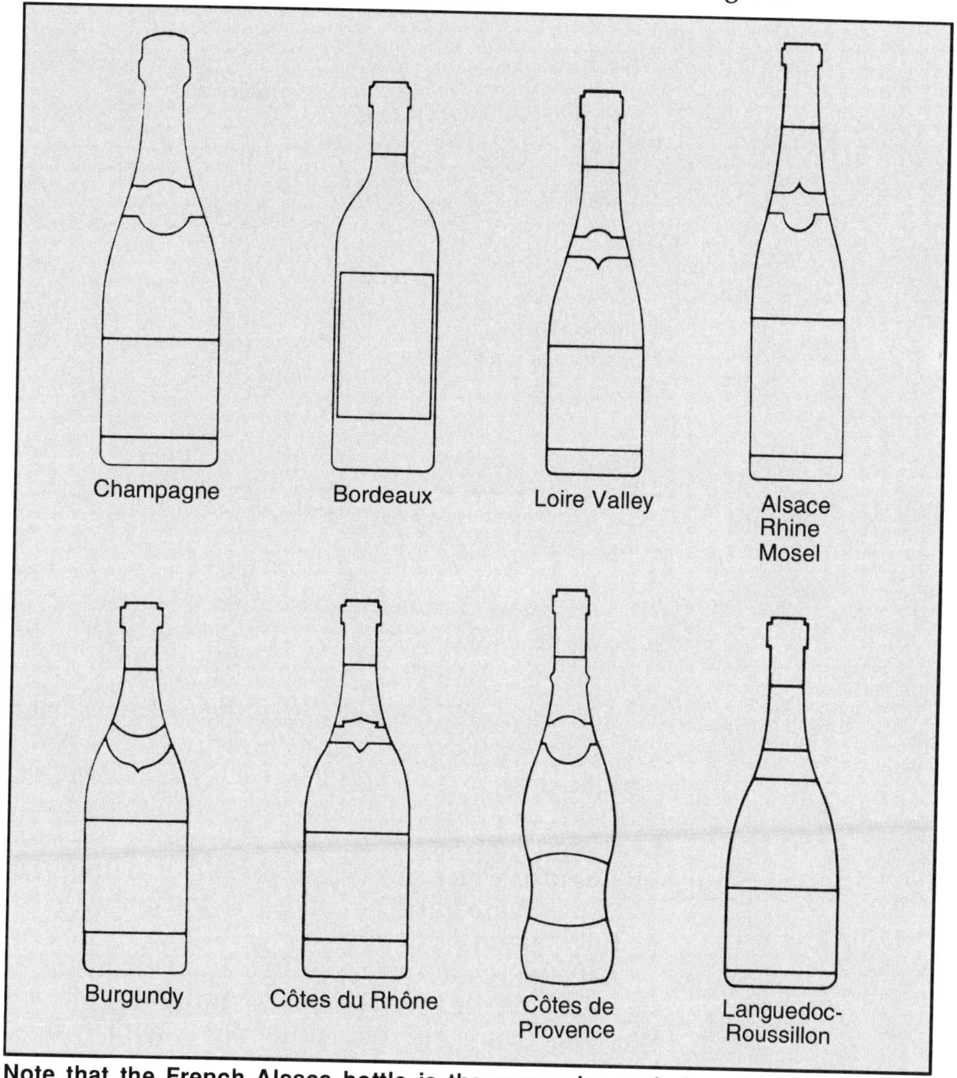

Champagne   Bordeaux   Loire Valley   Alsace
Rhine
Mosel

Burgundy   Côtes du Rhône   Côtes de
Provence   Languedoc-
Roussillon

Note that the French Alsace bottle is the same size and shape as that used for the German Rhine and Mosel wines; the Alsace was formerly part of Germany and many of its best wines are made from traditionally German grapes. However, Rhine wine bottles are brown, while Alsace and Mosel bottles are green. (Courtesy of Wines of France)

to penetrate into the bottle. On rare occasions, a cork containing fungus cells can deteriorate and give the wine a "corky" flavor.

Corks often have imprinted on them a logo or some information about the wine such as place of bottling, kind of wine, vintage date, place of production, and so forth.

Special corks must be made for sparkling wines and these must be quite thick with broad bases so the inside pressure does not force them out. In addition, the cork is wired down to the bottle by a helmet called a *muselet*.

Screw-top caps are often used instead of cork or plastic for some wines that do not have to rest on their side, such as sweet dessert and fortified

Exhibit 15.6 The Bottle Capacity of Various Champagne Containers

Bottle Name	Bottle Capacity	
	Metric Measure	U.S. Equivalent (oz.)
Nebuchadnezzar	15 L	540.93 (4.23 gal.)
Balthazar	12 L	432.74 (3.38 gal.)
Salmanazar	9 L	324.46 (2.53 gal.)
Methuselah	6 L	216.37 (1.69 gal.)
Rehoboam	4.5 L	156.00 (1.22 gal.)
Jeroboam	3 L	108.19 (3.38 qt.)
Magnum	1.5 L	54.09 (1.69 qt.)
Bottle	750 ml	25.4
Half-bottle	375 ml	12.7
Split	187 ml	6.76

Source: U.S. Bureau of Alcohol, Tobacco, and Firearms

wines. Screw-top caps are sometimes used for sparkling wines. They seem to do quite well.

Maturing

It is often said, "Wines age in the cask, but mature in the bottle." Wine is the only alcoholic product that matures in the bottle. **Maturing** is the term used for aging in the bottle; it is usually associated with complex, full-bodied reds such as a good red Bordeaux or Burgundy, or a wine primarily from a Cabernet Sauvignon or Pinot Noir grape. However, young white wines can improve with some degree of bottle maturing. Champagne and vintage port are matured almost entirely in the bottle, but tawny port and sherry are fully matured in casks.

Different wines mature differently in the bottle. Some mature fast and after that, lose quality. Others can improve up to 50 or more years. We say of a wine that is old, but still improving, that "it is still going uphill."

A good acid-tannin balance is needed for a wine to continue to improve over a number of years, as one of the finer Bordeaux or Burgundy reds might do. Young reds of good promise start out quite fresh but somewhat harsh and raw in flavor due largely to an overabundance of tannins and acid. They lack smoothness and finesse. Gradually, however, they lose this character and begin to develop a soft mellowness and depth of flavor that begins to approach the characteristics of what might be called "a great wine."

Some wines are not meant to mature for a long time in the bottle. Many German whites lack the staying power to last much over eight years. An ordinary Beaujolais red is a wine that also does not take aging too well. Thus, one must know which wines take age and which ones do not, and to move inventories when one sees that the wines in one's cellar are beginning to reach a point at which they might begin to go downhill.

During maturing, it is possible that a wine will cast a lot of lees. These usually are on the side of the bottle, if it is properly stored on its side. Before such wine is consumed, the bottle should be *carefully* put upright so the lees slide down into the bottom. Careful pouring may make it unnecessary to decant the wine. However, in some cases, the wine may have to be decanted to remove it from its sediment. Allowing the sediment to mix with the wine spoils not only the wine's appearance but also its flavor.

Wine—particularly white wine—may form a crust at the place where the wine surfaces in the bottle or around the lip of the bottle. This is a harmless and natural consequence of tartrate crystallization; with careful pouring it should not cause problems.

Storage
The storage area for wine should not be too dry nor too moist. If too dry, the corks dry out and the wine oxidizes. If too moist, the labels deteriorate and mold may appear. The temperature should be about 55° F (12.8° C) for reds and slightly lower for whites, if possible. Where both reds and whites are stored together 50° F (10° C) should be ideal. Temperatures above 65° F (18° C) can be harmful to wines as are widely and frequently fluctuating temperatures. A steady, cool temperature is best.

The storage area should only be lit when one needs to see. Light is harmful to wine. This is the reason that many wines are put into green, brown, or other colored glass bottles.

Most table wines should be stored on their sides so the wine is always against the cork, preventing it from drying out. Fortified and sparkling wines do not have to be stored on their sides, although some feel sparkling wines have less chance of a dry cork if stored on their sides.

Once stored, a wine should be moved as little as possible. Remove bottles carefully and avoid shaking them. Some wines are best moved some time before service and allowed to rest. One needs to be aware that wine is fragile and must receive proper care to be a good product.

After a shipment of wine is received, it should be carefully stored and allowed to rest. Shipment can cause wines to get "shipping sickness," losing flavor and other quality characteristics. They usually recover after a short rest.

Regulation and Labeling

In the material that follows, the major features of laws controlling the wine industries of some of the leading wine-producing nations are presented. For the sake of brevity, many details of these laws are not covered, but the factors important for those who work in the alcoholic beverage industry are included. Special attention has been given to those factors which govern information given on labels, since it is from labels that information essential to good purchasing, good merchandising, good menu planning, and good pricing and other factors covered in beverage management is derived.

Until the nineteenth century, the wine industry in Europe operated for the most part on a *laissez faire* system. There were no general standards covering the entire industry; standards were the province of individual vineyards and winemakers. As a result, buyers of wines were never sure of the source of the wine, its purity, sanitation, quality, or other factors that might indicate what they were purchasing. Buyer approval or rejection of some wines and pressure from retailers and even some producers brought about some attempts to regulate wine production. Gradually, governments

Exhibit 15.7 The Grand Cru Classé Designation

This classification, ranking the châteaux of the Haut-Médoc among France's greatest wines, comes from a decree issued in 1855 by Napoleon III. (Courtesy of Wines of France)

began to set up regulations to bring about a more stable and reliable industry.

France

In 1854, Emperor Napoleon III of France set up a committee of experts and wine brokers to officially rank the wines of the major châteaux of two great Bordeaux districts—the Haut-Médoc and Sauternes. The purpose was to give special distinction to these wines at the Exposition Universelle to be held in Paris in 1855. This committee tried to establish their ratings based on the opinions of experts, but disagreement was so furious that the committee had to base its choices on those wines which had historically commanded the highest prices. The wines were given one of five *cru* (growth) classifications: Premier Cru, Deuxième Cru, Troisième Cru, etc. Collectively, all five are referred to as the Grand Crus and, today, a wine in any of the five classifications will likely bear *Grand Cru Classé* on its label (see Exhibit 15.7). Only 60 wines of the Médoc and 22 of the Sauternes were included in the classification; one outside these areas (Graves) was also rated.

Since that time the 1855 rankings have remained much the same (Château Mouton-Rothschild was added to the original four Premier Crus—Châteaux Lafite, Latour, Margaux and Haut Brion—in 1973). Since then other regions have been similarly rated, giving prospective purchasers a reliable, but not infallible certification of quality.

The problem with the 1855 classification is that it left the erroneous impression that Premier Cru wine was first in quality and all the other *crus* second rate. This was not the case, since all the wines of the original classification came from the top class, the elite wines of the region. Another problem was that many fine wines were omitted. Most of these "orphans" were identified by the label *Cru Exceptionnel*, *Cru Bourgeois*, or *Cru Bourgeois Supérieure*.

Nevertheless, the classification of 1855 was a beginning of some sort of recognition and ranking of quality. During the ensuing years as more and more regions were classified, the need for more regulation became apparent. In 1936, France was first to establish and enforce a strict and broad set of regulations covering its alcoholic beverage industry. It worked so well that many other nations followed suit.

Today, France and the rest of Europe are beginning to feel the effects of European Economic Community (EEC—commonly known as the "Common Market") regulations on their respective wine industries. The EEC regulations, designed to establish uniform quality standards for all member nations, have already caused some European governments to change their national standards in order to compete. However, long-standing national standards still predominate, although the future may see EEC regulations supersede them.

The Appellation Contrôlée Label. The laws passed in 1936 in France to regulate its alcoholic beverage industry were given to the *Institut National des Appellations d'Origine* (INAO) for administration. The laws are known under the collective name *Appellation d'Origine Contrôlée,* and the short form stands for **appellation contrôlée,** which means, literally, "name controlled." In effect, *appellation contrôlée* (AC) on a label means that the wine is among the highest classification of French wines and that whatever appears on the label is strictly regulated by the INAO. Requirements for AC labeling are complex and standards differ from one major wine region to the next. Nevertheless, one or more of the quality control standards listed below must be met to receive the coveted AC label.

Production area. Geography is fundamental to AC classification. The most important geographic areas are still the designated *cru* or growth areas established in 1855. However, since that time the INAO has raised some wines to a higher *cru* rank while dropping others. It has also added some wines while eliminating others. In 1954 it completed a ranking for the St. Emilion district in Bordeaux, dividing the 76 most famous vineyards into two classes: *premier grand cru* and *grand cru.* Where the wine comes from is the main point of *appellation d'origine contrôlée*: the more narrowly defined the origin of the wine, the higher the quality is a good "rule of thumb" in selecting quality wines (but is far from foolproof).

- The most precise name in indicating location is the name of a château or vineyard. Thus, a wine bearing the label *Château Margaux* accompanied by the term *appellation contrôlée* means that the grapes were grown at that specific location and the wine is bottled there.

- Labels can state location as that of a defined growing district such as *Appellation Pomerol Contrôlée.* Pomerol is a small area in the Bordeaux region which has a limited number of recognized high-quality vineyards; in any given year such a wine *might* be better than that from a specific château but should definitely be better than the next, broader designation.

- A broader area would be a limited general growing area defined by AC within a wine region such as Bordeaux, and the designation on the label might be *Appellation Bordeaux Supérieur Contrôlée* or *Appellation Premières Côtes de Bordeaux Contrôlée.* In Burgundy, such a designation might be *Beaujolais Villages,* which includes some 39 villages and is more likely than not to indicate indifferent quality in comparison to a wine from a single town or village.

- The least knowledge of where the grapes were grown and wine was produced under an AC classification is indicated by a label which identifies the wine only by the major wine region it comes from, such as Bordeaux (generally with the *appellation contrôlée* designation directly underneath). Some of these wines can be undistinguished or even poor in quality. However, a number of excellent wines come under this last category. Champagne, for instance, is made from grapes grown anywhere in the Champagne region.

Grape variety. Certain wines can only be made from specific grapes. Thus Champagne can only be made from a mixture of Pinot Noir, Pinot Meunier, and Chardonnay grapes. The best Burgundy reds must come from a Pinot Noir, a Beaujolais from the Gamay grape, and a Chablis from the Chardonnay.

Viticulture standards. The grapes must be grown in a manner specified by the law. Only certain kinds of fertilizers and pesticides can be used. Irrigation is prohibited in the *cru* areas. The number of vines per hectare (2.471 acres), pruning, and time of harvest are controlled. In fact, very little from the planting of the grapes to the harvest and care of the vines in the winter is not regulated.

Yield. Only a given amount of wine per hectare can be produced in various locations. In most AC areas, the limit is 40 hectoliters (4,000 liters) per hectare. However, a complicated system of annual re-assessment can allow considerably more production in certain areas. Yield is most strictly controlled in the *Grand Cru* areas and in the Sauternes area, the yield is limited to 25 hectoliters per hectare for AC designated wines. These restrictions on the amount of wine produced per hectare are rigidly enforced. Thus, if one produces more wine than allowed under the AC certification, the AC rating may be denied. One cannot even bottle the legalized amount under an AC label and the remainder under a different label.

Production methods. The manner in which the wine is made is also strictly controlled. Thus, Champagne must be made in a specified manner and labeled accordingly. Sauternes must come from a grape that has developed the "noble rot." Fermenting procedures are precisely prescribed for different kinds of wine and for different regions. Such things as adding or taking away acidity depending on how ripe the grapes are at harvest are also controlled.

Bottling. Some appellations, like Alsace and Champagne, stipulate that bottling must take place in the region of production. Even the kind and shape of the bottle may be regulated (see Exhibit 15.5). Thus, wine from Alsace must be bottled in Alsace and bottled in tall, fluted, greenish glass bottles.

Alcohol content. The minimum alcohol content by volume for different kinds of wine is strictly controlled and specified on the label. Certain wines cannot be made unless the grapes contain at harvest sufficient sugar to produce wine of a specified alcohol content. Some addition of sugar before fermentation to increase alcohol content (chaptalization) is permitted in some cases, but is strictly regulated. Thus, a chablis can be chaptalized but not above a specified naturally fermented alcohol content.

Analysis. All appellation wines since 1979 have to be submitted to a tasting panel which rejects wines it considers faulty or unrepresentative of the "typical" or historic standard of a particular AC designation. Appellation growers/bottlers can present samples two times and if they fail both times, they lose their right to AC designation for that year. (In a "bad" year, many great châteaux will voluntarily forgo bottling part or all of that year's crop under their AC label, opting instead to sell their grapes to bottlers who will use them in the production of generic or other blended wines.)

The VDQS Label. In 1945 France instituted a second rank of appellations under the designation *Vins Délimités de Qualité Supérieure* (VDQS)—literally, "wines from a specifically defined region of superior quality." While generally ranked below AC wines in quality and consistency of quality, some VDQS wines are superior to some AC wines. Sometimes the reason for a particular wine not getting an AC rating is that it is made from the wrong grape in the right place; for example, Sauvignon de St-Bris is VDQS because it is made from the Sauvignon Blanc grape grown in the AC-designated Chardonnay- and Aligote-only Burgundy area.[4] It is possible, over time, for a particular VDQS wine to move up to AC ranking or vice versa; some consider VDQS as a "training ground" for AC status.

The Vin de Pays Label. The label *vin de pays* means, literally, "country wine" and such wines must come from the region of production claimed; one or more classic grape varieties are required; yield is controlled and alcohol levels prescribed and on the label. Again, it is possible for a wine in this group to move up or down in rank. This category was created by the government in 1968 and 1973 in order to recognize the quality of large, anonymous areas of table wine production and give them some geographical identity. Consequently, there are three levels of *vin de pays*:

- *Vins de Pays Régionaux*—Regional classification covering wide areas, such as the Loire valley (Vins de Pays du Jardin de la France)

- *Vins de Pays Départementaux*—Classification restricted to smaller areas (*départements* or "counties")

- *Vins de Pays de Zone*—Classification covers wines from single communes or small areas within a *département*

Vins de pays do have AC-type limits but are the laxest of the three major designations. Below the *vin de pays* designation is the *vin ordinaire* or *vin de table* (ordinary or table wines), which are very basic wines virtually unregulated by the government. About 70% of France's wines are *vins de pays* or *vins de table*.

Exhibit 15.8 How to Read a French Wine Label

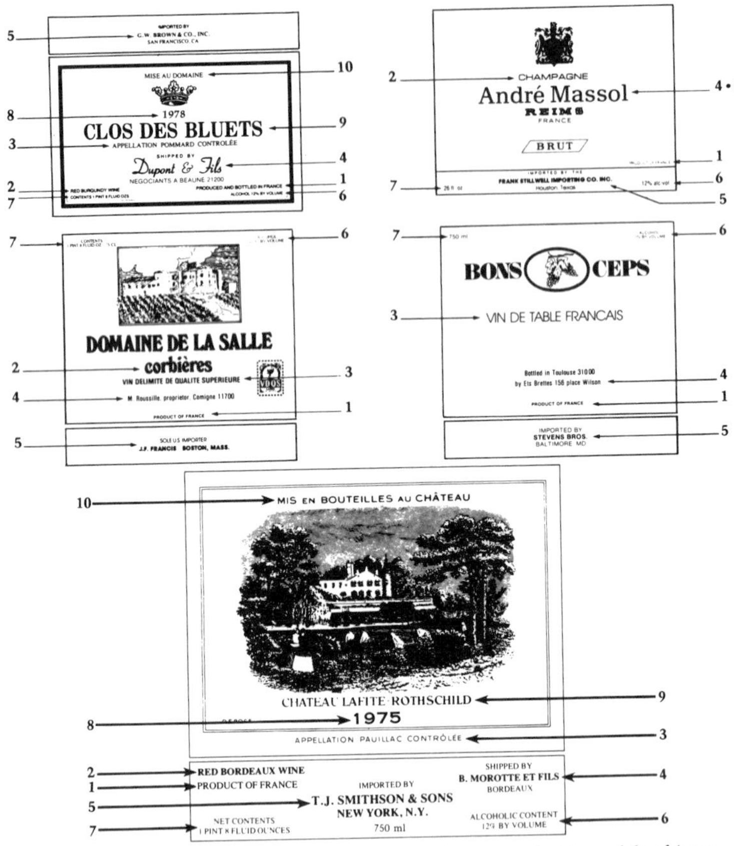

How to Read a Wine Label

Both the American and the French governments have very strict labeling rules to govern the information given on a bottle of wine.

These sample labels are number coded to show you the information that, by law, must be included on a label:

1. The wine is a product of France.
2. The region in which the wine was produced—for example, Burgundy, Bordeaux, Champagne.
3. The appellation for which the wine qualifies: A.O.C. (Appellation d'Origine Contrôlée), V.D.Q.S. (Vins Délimités de Qualité Supérieure), Vin de Pays, or Vin de Table.

4. The name and address of the shipper, except in the case of Champagne where, usually, the Champagne house (brand) is also the shipper.
5. The name and address of the importer.
6. The alcoholic percentage by volume.
7. The net contents of the bottle.

The following is optional information which may appear on the label:

8. Vintage.
9. Brand name or château name.
10. "Estate bottled," "Château bottled" or similar phrase.

Courtesy of Wines of France

Other Labeling Regulations. Exhibit 15.8 indicates how to interpret information on a label of French wine. As noted in this exhibit, both the French and U.S. governments have strict labeling rules. Seven items *must* be on a French label to meet labeling requirements; three are optional:

Bottler. There are four kinds of bottlers in France:

- One is a vineyard of no special note bottling its own wines.

- Another kind is a group of growers and/or vintners (*caves coopératives*) that band together to bottle and even ship their wine.

- A third is known as a *négociant* or *négociant-éleveur* (merchant or merchant-breeder). The *négociant-éleveur* creates the wine by blending different wines for a distinctive and consistent taste which he (or she) will offer under the firm's label. He or she may also age the wine before bottling it. Many Bordeaux reds are bottled this way and may carry on the label *mis en bouteille dans nos chais* (put into the bottle in our place or warehouse) or *mis en bouteille par négociant* (bottled by the merchant or firm). These wines can be quite good, but the only guarantee of quality is a merchant's long-standing reputation.

- The fourth kind of bottler is one who wants the world to know that the wine was produced and bottled on the place where grapes were grown. The bottle will usually state *mis en bouteille au château*, (bottled at the manor house), *mis en bouteille au domaine* (put into the bottle at the place), or *mis en bouteille à la propriété* (put into the bottle at the property). Many wine drinkers, especially Americans, have taken the *mis en bouteille au château* as a sign of quality. It's not. Since the advent of mobile bottling "plants" (semi-sterile bottling facilities in large vans or lorries) in the 1960s, many small and undistinguished growers can claim that their wine was bottled at their château or place.

Vintage. Although the vintage year is optional as far as labeling is concerned, it is a crucial factor when considering wine purchases. It is particularly crucial for the high-quality red Bordeaux wines and some of the finer red Burgundies made from the Pinot Noir grape. Such wines mature in the bottle; some are not ready to drink until 7 to 12 years after bottling. Thus, the vintage year is a decisive purchasing factor. The **vintage year** is the year in which the grapes were grown, and a great or good year for a particular type of wine will be celebrated by including the vintage year on the label. Consumers will decide whether it lives up to its promise.

Brand or château name. Although the brand or château name is legally optional, one or the other will always be present on French wine labels.

Germany

In 1971 Germany revised its wine regulations, making them stricter and broader in application. They covered many factors which related not only to general German viticulture conditions but also to specific local conditions. Labeling was strictly controlled and considerable information was required on the label so consumers could know what they were getting. The major points of the 1971 wine regulations are in effect today—along with subsequent revisions—and are discussed in the sections which follow.

Producing Regions. Eleven major wine-producing regions (*bestimmte Anbaugebiete*) were defined: Ahr, Baden, Hessische-Bergstrasse, Franconia (Franken), Mittelrhein, Mosel-Saar-Ruwer, Nahe, Rheingau, Rheinhessen, Rheinpfalz (Palatinate), and Würtemberg. We will discuss in more detail the 5 major regions of these 11 in Chapter 16.

Within these regions 34 districts (*Bereichen*) were established. The *Bereichen* are divided into *Gemeinden* (villages) and the villages, in turn,

Exhibit 15.9   German "Appellation of Origin"

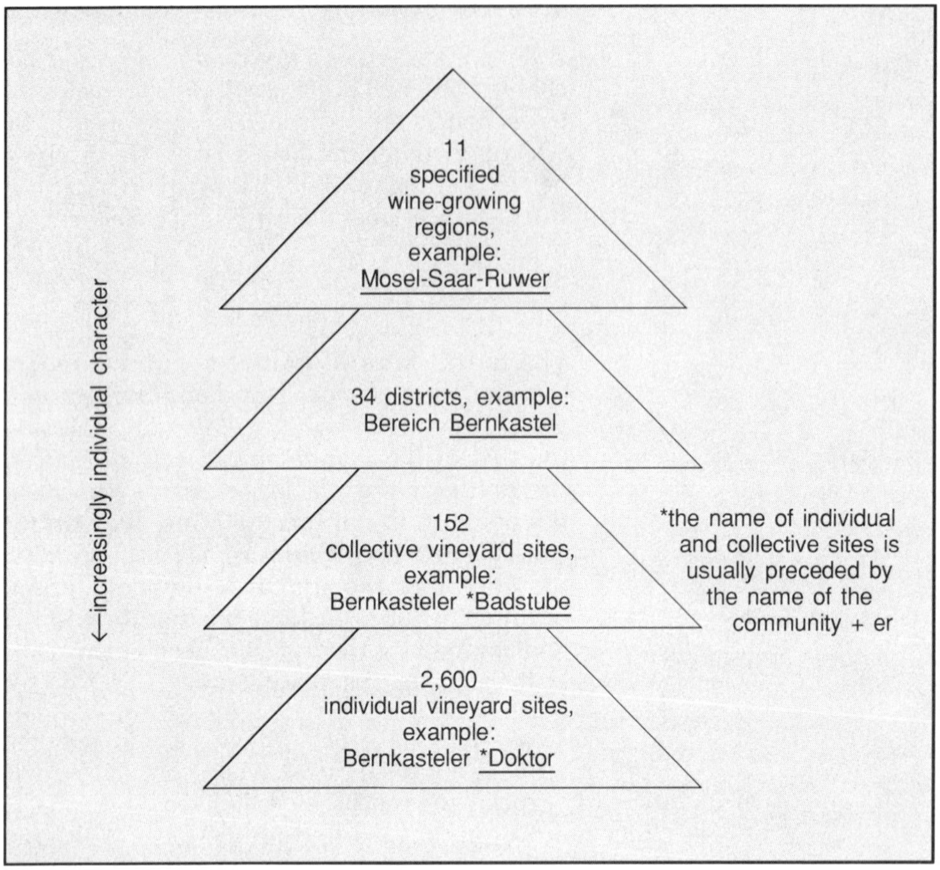

←increasingly individual character

11
specified
wine-growing
regions,
example:
Mosel-Saar-Ruwer

34 districts, example:
Bereich Bernkastel

152
collective vineyard sites,
example:
Bernkasteler *Badstube

*the name of individual
and collective sites is
usually preceded by
the name of the
community + er

2,600
individual vineyard sites,
example:
Bernkasteler *Doktor

German wine laws do not classify quality or vineyards as the French do; nevertheless, the best German wines are more likely than not from individual vineyards.
(Courtesy of the German Wine Institute)

are divided into some 2,600 recognized *Einzellagen* (single sites, or vineyards). Villages and single sites sometimes join together in cooperative units called *Grosslagen*. As with the château designation in French labeling, the smaller the unit, the higher the quality is likely to be. *Einzellagen* corresponds to the French *châteaux* (see Exhibit 15.9).

Quality Levels. Three levels of quality were established in 1971, with a fourth, *Landswein*, created in 1982.

Qualitätswein mit Prädikat (QmP). Stiffly translated as "quality wine with special attributes," QmP wines are the highest quality German wines. The quality of QmP wines is largely rated by the amount of natural sugar in the grape at harvest. Accordingly, QmP wines are further calssified into five categories of quality and natural sweetness:

- *Kabinett*—a wine made from simply ripe grapes picked at the normal harvest time.

- *Spätlese*—literally, "late picking," which means the grapes are picked about three weeks later than the official harvest opening and are riper and, consequently, sweeter.

- *Auslese*—literally, "late selected picking," this category uses selected bunches of the very ripest late harvest grapes. (At this point, the wine will retain some of its natural sweetness after full fermentation.)

- *Beerenauslese*—literally, "selected overripe picking," this category uses individual grapes selected for extreme ripeness and concentration, most often grapes which have been infected by the "noble rot" (*Edelfaüle* in German).

- *Trockenbeerenauslese*—literally, "dry grape, special late picking," this is the rarest of the categories. The grapes are left in the field until the *Edelfaüle* dries up the grape to an almost raisin-like state after which the berries are picked individually. Much less juice is obtained, and the harvest conditions are very rare (about one every ten years), so the wine is costly.

Eiswein (ice wine) is a rare and costly QmP wine made in some years by leaving ripe grapes on the vine until they freeze, then crushing and removing the ice which leaves a heavy concentration of sugar and acid. It is discussed in Chapter 16.

Qualitätswein bestimmter Anbaugebiete (QbA). Literally, "quality wine from designated regions," QbA wines are in the second quality ranking. The basic legal difference between QbA and QmP wines is that sugar may be added to the must to help the QbA wines ferment to required alcohol levels.

Landwein. This "wine of the land" was re-classified from common table wine to recognize some qualitative differences in large regional areas. It corresponds nicely with the French *vins de pays* classification.

Tafelwein. *Tafelwein* (table wine) is a blended wine that compares with *vin ordinaire* of France and is usually consumed young and domestically. It is prohibited from claiming any vineyard origin; it may or may not indicate its origin by giving a township name. It is relatively uncontrolled, often using grapes from Italy. Look for *Deutsche Tafelwein* on the label if you want a good German table wine; it means all of the grapes have been grown in Germany. *Tafelwein* may also be called *Weinstube* (wine of the pub).

Quality dry wines. In 1977 the Germans received approval from the EEC to market two types of wines with a designated standard of sugar content; one was *trocken* (dry) with a maximum residual sugar content of 0.9% (9 g/L) and the other was *halbtrocken* (half-dry) with a maximum residual sugar content of 1.8% (18 g/L). Limits of the acid-sugar ratio in these wines were also set. German producers asked for these classifications because many consumers of German wines have expressed a preference for a wine drier than the quality sweet wines—something similar to the wines of Alsace—wines which would more appropriately accompany food.

Origin. Labels of QmP wines must show either region, district, cooperative, or vineyard. In some cases the village or township (*Gemeinde*) is given and may be combined with the vineyard: Niersteiner-Auflagen, for example. (Nierstein is the township where the Auflagen vineyard is located.

Exhibit 15.10 How to Read a German Wine Label

1) The wine-growing region; one of 11 regions designated by law.

2) The vintage date is the year in which the grapes were harvested. Although different vintages may exhibit subtle differences in taste and style, the German classification system, based on ripeness of the grape at harvest, assures consumers of the quality of each bottle, regardless of whether vintage year is given on the label.

3) The town (first) and the vineyard (sometimes cooperative) from which the grapes came (both, in this example, fictitious).

4) The grape variety. German law controls which grape varieties may be grown in various areas if the grower/wine maker is to receive its quality designations.

5) The taste or style of the wine. In this case, halbtrocken (literally "half-dry") means that the wine maker added a small amount of *Süssreserve* (sweetener) to the wine according to German regulations approved by the EEC. This is not to be confused with ripeness or the classification of sugar content at harvest. *Trocken* means "dry"—all the sugar is fermented into alcohol and little, if any, *Süssreserve* is added.

6) The quality level of the wine (QbA) indicating that the grapes used had a specified ripeness at harvest.

7) The A.P. number is proof that German government inspectors have tested and approved the wine for the quality designation given.

8) Wines grown, produced and bottled by the grower or a cooperative of growers may be labeled *Erzeugerabfüllung*. Other wineries and bottlers are identified as *Abfüller*. (Again, a fictitious name.)

(Courtesy of the German Wine Information Bureau)

Note the addition of "er" to Nierstein, indicating the wine is from that place, just as one would say "Londoner" for a person living in London.) QbA wines *may* show on the label their origin as region, district, township, cooperative, or vineyard. QmP wines must show vineyard (or *grosslagen*), township, and region, such as

> Bernkasteler-Doktor
> Mosel-Saar-Ruwer

The grower, producer, and bottler is not always the same person. There are about 100,000 grape growers in Germany, yet only about a fourth as many producers. If the label indicates *Erzeugerabfüllung* (estate-bottled), it assures you that the grapes were grown and the wine was produced by one and the same grower or cooperative of growers (*Winzergenossenschaft*). The grower or collective group of growers is responsible for and guarantees the quality of the wine. The bottler or shipper whose name is on the label assumes responsibility for the wine's quality, and this fact is identified on the label by the term, *abfüllung*. (See Exhibit 15.10: "How to Read a German Wine Label.")

Wine Name. Many wines, as we have discussed above, are named for their place of origin. However, in Germany as in France, many wines are blends and bear a brand or proprietary name. Proprietary names may be used, such as Moselblümchen (now called Moselthaler), Liebfraumilch (Milk of the Blessed Mother), Schwartze Katz (Black Cat), or Hock, after the township of Hochheim in the Rheingau region.

Vintage Year. The vintage year is generally considered optional for German wines. However, *Tafelwein* and *Deutsche Tafelwein* may not include any quality designation on their labels, including vintage year. Although vintage date on a label is no guarantee of quality, certain vintage years are better than others, particularly among wines of QmP designation.

Sugar Content. Often the growing season in Germany is such that the grapes ripen without adequate sugar to make the amount of alcohol prescribed by German regulations for various kinds of wine. Accordingly, the regulations allow limited sugaring (*anreichern*) of the must prior to fermentation in QbA wine, Landwein, and Tafelwein, but not in QmP wine. *Anreichern* is, in effect, the same as the French *chaptalization* process.

However, sweetening *after* fermentation is not only allowed but is more the rule than not in Germany; the result, when done properly, is an exceptional fruitiness characteristic of the best German wines. The finished wine is sweetened by adding some unfermented grape must (*Süssreserve*). Only a small quantity is usually added. The addition of *Süssreserve* is permitted in QmP as well as other *Qualitätswein*.

It is the sugar content of the grapes at harvest time which is strictly regulated for QmP wines. The legally required sugar content, expressed in degrees Oeschle,[5] is different for the different regions: a *Kabinett* from Ahr must be 67° Oeschle, but 73° Oeschle from Rheingau. The sugar present in the grape at fermentation usually means a higher alcohol content, which is also prescribed for most QmP wines. However, the sweetest (and rarest) of all German wines, the *Trockenbeerenauslese*, requires a grape sweetness of 150°—a degree of sweetness which actually inhibits fermentation to about 6% alcohol.

Grape Varieties. The labels for all wines except Tafelwein must give the grape name. If the label for one of the quality level wines indicates the wine is a varietal wine, 85% of the grapes used to make the wine must be that grape. It is possible to indicate two kinds of grapes as a varietal combination; in this case both grapes must make up 85% of the grapes used, but no ratio of the combination is set. If the label gives a subregion, a village, or vineyard name, 85% of the grapes must come from there. These grape sources may be indicated as from five defined regions: Rhein, Mosel, Oberrhein, Neckar, and Main.

The Riesling grape is the premier grape of Germany—it is the great grape for the great German wines and no hybrids or other variety has yet surpassed it. However, its slow (and thus late) ripening characteristics which undoubtedly bring about its great taste characteristics are also, sometimes, its downfall. Many German wines are made from grapes which ripen earlier and thus avoid being wiped out by killing frosts in the fall. Among the other popular grape varieties are the Sylvaner, Müller-Thurgau, Weissburgunder (French Pinot Noir), Kerner, and Gutedel.

Testing. To be sure a wine meets the QmP or QbA standard, three bottles of the wine must be submitted to regulatory authorities for testing. If approved, the wine is given a certified number called *Amtliche Prüfungsnummer* (AP number). If a wine does not meet a particular standard, it may be put into a lower classification—a QmP wine dropped to a QbA classification, for instance, or an *auslese* re-classified as a *spätlese*.

Italy

In terms of sheer volume, Italy is the greatest wine producer in the world. However, it only exports about a fourth of its output and a great deal of that goes into cheap French and German wine blends. Italy has been relatively slow in establishing standards and regulations to protect and enhance the reputation of its great wines. It was not until 1963 that Italy established new regulations for its wine industry.

Some 220 wine-growing districts and 20 regions are defined and a grading system to note wines of "particular reputation and worth" is established by these new regulations known collectively as the *Denominazione di Origine Controllata* (DOC) (see Exhibit 15.11). The name parallels the French *Appellation d'Origine Contrôlée*, but the DOC is at once more complex and less indicative of quality than the AOC. It controls claims of geographical origin, permissible grape types, permitted yields, pruning methods, alcoholic strength, and aging requirements. Chaptalization is not permitted; the growing season throughout Italy is long enough and warm enough to provide sufficient ripening for sugar content. Even the weight of the grapes that may be harvested and the percentage of that weight which may be processed into wine is regulated. A description of the requirements for Chianti serves as an illustration of the detail covered by a typical DOC regulation:

> It is a red wine from Tuscany, the provinces of Siena, Florence, Arezzo, Pistoia, and Pisa. As for villages, a huge portion of central Tuscany is subdivided into Classico, Colli Aretini, Colli Fiorentini, Colli Pisane, Colli Senesi, Montalbano, and Rufina. The grapes are a blend of Sangiovese (50 to 80%), Canaiolo Nero (10 to 30%), Trebbiano Toscano and Malvasia del Chianti (10 to 30%), and other grapes up to a maximum of 5%. The yield maximum is 87.5 hectoliters per hectare for Chianti and 80.5 hectoliters per hectare for Chianti Classico. The alcohol minimum is 11.5% (Chianti) and 12.0% (Chianti Classico). A *vecchio* (literally, "old") requires aging for two years, and a *riserva* requires three years in wood.[6]

Some of the defined districts are large, covering an entire province, while others are only small local communities or just choice vineyards in an area. Over 800 wines were identified as qualified for DOC ratings. By 1989, 206 wines applied for and received DOC rating while only 5 wines had qualified for the DOCG—the "G" standing for "Garantita" (guaran-

Exhibit 15.11   The 20 DOC Regions of Italy

Courtesy of the Italian Trade Commission

teed). DOCG wines have to undergo a series of tastings by experts in addition to meeting DOC standards. Both DOC and DOCG ratings have to be renewed every year.

Below the DOC and DOCG classifications are the wines called *vini tipici*—wines considered of good quality and typical of the wine of the regions from which they came. *Vini tipici* constitutes a category much like the *vin de pays* of France or the *Landwein* of Germany.

The next category below *vini tipici* is *vino da tavola* (wine of the table) or *vino ordinario* (corresponding to the French *vin ordinaire* or German *Tafelwein*). As in France and Germany, it is that massive category of virtually unregulated wines. It may also be known as *vino da pasto*, indicating its appropriateness as an everyday wine for drinking with pasta. At times a *vino da tavola* may be distinguished by the label term *vino da tavola con indicazione geograficos* which is a *tavola* with an indication of where the grapes were grown and the wine produced. This classification is generally regarded as a slightly better wine than the common table wine. The DOCG, DOC, and *vini tipici* wines meet EEC wine standards. The DOC and DOCG wines, numbered at 211 in 1989, make up about 12% of Italy's wines; the other 88% are from the lower classifications. In France, AC wines total about 20% of production, and EEC regulations require that Italy bring her production of DOC wines up to that level.

Wines with a DOC or DOCG rating indicate this on the label. The lack of such a rating does not necessarily indicate lack of quality; many modern Italian winemakers feel impelled to produce a wine by modern methods not approved by some restrictive DOC regulations which are based on historical methods.

Italian wine names may be classified as generic (place of origin), such as Cirò Rosso (red), a DOC red wine from Cirò of the province of Calabria, or varietal (grape variety), such as Riesling Italico, a DOC wine from Lombardy. They may be proprietary (special distinctive name), such as Lacrima Christi (literally, "Tears of Christ"). At times one may see a wine with a generic and varietal name such as Lambrusco Grasparossa di Castelvetro which bears the name of the grape, *Lambrusco Grasparossa*, and the place of origin, Castel Vetro (not a "castle" actually, but the name of the 14 communes in the Morela district of the Emilia region which grow and produce this popular wine). (See Exhibit 15.12: "How to Read an Italian Wine Label.")

The United States

The United States has been a bit more lenient than European countries in its regulation of the wine industry. The wine producer can decide which particular grape to grow in an area, the time of harvest, the time of aging, the aging process, the kind of fining, and other factors often controlled in other countries. Chaptalization is permitted except in California. The relative lack of regulations has given the industry the liberty to experiment and to conduct extensive research and development which has brought about a highly scientific, modern wine industry. Thus the United States can better control the kind of wine produced as well as its quality.

In the material that follows, some requirements for U.S. wines are omitted because they are discussed later in Chapter 16 in the section dealing with U.S. wines. For the most part, the discussion that follows covers labeling.

United States regulations require that American wine labels give the name of the wine and area of production. These defined regions are called **American Viticulture Areas** (AVAs) and are the beginning of an AC-type system for the United States. The region may be a county, a state, or any geographical area, such as a lake shore. Only one vineyard has been designated an AVA—the Guenoc Winery in Lake County, California (see Exhibit 15.13).

If an AVA is indicated on the label, the major grape in the wine must come from there. If two or three places of origin are given, all the wine must be made from grapes grown in these areas, and the percentage coming from each must be given. If a wine is estate-bottled, 100% of the grapes used must come from there. If a wine bears the name of New York State as the AVA, 75% of grapes used to make it must be grown in the state.

Wine names may be based on grape variety (varietal) or on the type of wine (generic) or be a proprietary name such as "Rancho Yerba Buena," "Royal Occasion," or "Premium Red." A wine with a varietal name such as "Cabernet Sauvignon" must be made from grapes of which 75% must

Exhibit 15.12 How to Read an Italian Wine Label

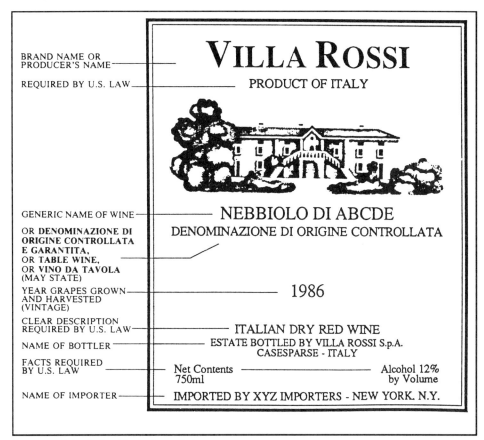

Courtesy of the Italian Trade Commission

be Cabernet Sauvignon. A wine made from a *Vitis labrusca* variety is made from grapes of which only 51% needs to be from that variety.

A vintage date may be given, but there is no requirement that it must be on the label. A wine carrying a vintage date must be made from grapes of which 95% came from the harvest of that year; the 5% allowance is for wines used for topping and blending.

Generic wines such as "Burgundy" or "Chablis" can be made from any grape or grape mixture, but must state origin as in "California Burgundy." Proprietary wines need not meet any specific grape percentage requirements.

Alcohol content by volume must be stated and a 1.5% variation from the stated content is allowed. If a wine is between 7% and 14% alcohol, the label may omit the percentage and just say "table wine" or "light wine."

Labels must also state the amount of wine in the container and the presence of sulfites. (See the discussion on sulfites later in this chapter.) Exhibit 15.14 indicates how to read a label on a bottle of wine produced in the United States.

Labels on wine imported into the United States must meet certain standards. The label must indicate that it is the product of the country where it originated and must show the importer's name and location. The percentage by volume of alcohol, net contents, and name of the wine with

Exhibit 15.13 Guenoc Wine Label

The label of a bottle of wine from the Guenoc Winery, the only single vineyard designated as an AVA (wine-producing region) in the United States. (Courtesy of Guenoc Winery)

some kind of description indicating what it is must be given. The presence of sulfites must be noted. Some specific requirements are required of some nations. For instance, all Italian wines must have a strip label on the back of the bottle bearing "INE," the seal of the agency that approves wines for export.

Spain   In 1972, Spain established new regulations to control its alcoholic beverage industry; they are called, collectively, *Denominaciones de Origen* or *DO*. The *Consejo Regulador* (Control Board) was set up to be the enforcement agency. The law and its enforcement were modeled after the French AC system. Twenty-eight regions were established and each was given the privilege of having specific regulations for the region. The *Instituto Nacional de Denominaciones de Origen* (INDO) was set up to provide regions with assistance in producing and marketing their products and in conforming to the regulations.

Regulatory councils in each region collect wine samples every year from winemakers (*bodegas*) and send them in to the *Consejo Regulador* for analysis and classification. If a wine passes the examination, a special number is assigned which can be placed on the back of every bottle of that lot.

Exhibit 15.14   Decoding a (U.S.) Wine Label: What It Means

Grape Variety. If a wine is labeled as a varietal (Chardonnay, for example), 75% of the wine in the bottle must come from the stated grape variety. This percentage may seem low, but it is actually a marked improvement to the law prior to 1983, when only a surprising 51% had to be of the designated varietal.

Vintage. At least 95% of the wine must be produced from grapes harvested in the vintage indicated. And the other 5%? For wines aged in small oak barrels, for example, "topping up" or adding wine from another vintage is sometimes necessary, given that oak is porous and evaporation occurs within the barrel.

Viticultural Area. In California there are 60-plus geographically-designated viticultural areas; exemplary names include Napa Valley, Sonoma Valley, Santa Cruz Mountains, Carneros, etc. At least 85% of the grapes used to produce the wine must have been grown within the specified area. The other 15% can come from outside sources.

Produced and Bottled By. 75% of the grapes must be fermented, cellared and bottled by the listed producer. The other 25% can come from outside sources and, in this respect, the winery is a form of negociant.

Bonded Winery. All of California's wineries are federally bonded, insuring that taxes will be paid on the wine produced. Federal taxes per gallon are; $0.17 for still wines, $0.67 for dessert wines and $3.40 for sparkling wines.

Contains Sulfites. *All wine contains naturally-occurring sulfites.* Sulphur dioxide is also sprayed on grapes in the vineyards to protect against bacteria and mold, on grapes prior to crushing, and on wine prior to barrel-ageing and bottling to control oxidation. Wines produced without SO_2 tend to be oxidized and "dirty." Although sulfites may cause an allergic reaction in some wine drinkers, most people need not fear a wine's sulfite level. Many foods (dark leafy vegetables, broccoli, dried apricots, for example) contain 2–3 times more sulfite than wine.

Estate Bottled. This means that 100% of the wine is from the property name given on the label. Neither the grapes nor the wine may leave the estate between the harvest and the time of bottling.

Barrel Fermented. This term means that after the grapes were crushed, the juice was fermented in oak barrels instead of stainless steel. The resulting wines are often rounder, smoother and more elegant. The term doesn't necessarily mean that the wine

No matter how many reviews and recommendations you may have at your disposal in selecting a wine, the wine label itself in many cases still remains a major factor in many buying decisions. But a fully descriptive label can be less than helpful if you don't understand the terms used. This brief guide should help clarify the matter.

Chateau Bay Food

Chardonnay
1988
Napa Valley

Produced and Bottled by
Bay Food Vintners, Berkeley, California
Bonded Winery 9999
Contains Sulfites

This Estate Bottled Chardonnay was Barrel Fermented in French oak Barrels. It has undergone malolactic fermentation and had extended barrel aging to create a complex and unforgettable wine.

Alcohol 12.5% by volume
Total Acidity 0.73 gm/100ml
Ph 3.2
Residual Sugar 0.1

Government warning: (1) According to the Surgeon General, women should not drink alcoholic beverages during pregnancy. (2) Your ability to drive a car or operate machinery may be impaired, and may cause health problems.

has been 100% barrel-fermented. There are currently no laws governing the term.

Malolactic Fermentation. This is a biochemical process that converts the "sour" malic acid of unripe grapes into 2 parts "soft" lactic acid and 1 part carbonic acid. Considered by some as a secondary fermentation, malolactic fermentation reduces the wine's acidity, making the wine smoother and creamier on the palate. As in the case of barrel fermentation, the wine may not have undergone 100% malolactic fermentation. There are no set laws concerning the term.

Barrel-Aging. This means that the fermented wine has been aged in wood to give a "lift" to the flavor. As a general rule, red wines are barrel-aged longer than whites. During barrel-aging, different flavors are imparted to the wine (there are over 100 compounds in wood that can influence the wine's flavor), and slow oxidation allows for earlier maturation.

Alcohol. The alcohol in wine is ethyl alcohol, a colorless, flammable liquid. By law, the stated alcohol percentage must be within a 1.5% margin of error. Thus a wine described as "12.5% Alcohol By Volume" can actually be anywhere between 11–14%.

Total Acidity (TA). TA is the total amount of acidity in a wine. Sound, healthy grapes contain natural acidity. Too little natural fruit acid makes a wine dull, flat and short; too much makes it "hot" and sharp. While some agree that .7–.75 gm total acidity is desirable, other factors can make this number meaningless out of context.

Residual Sugar (RS). RS is the grapes' sugar that remains unconverted into alcohol in a finished wine. If too much, the wine may seem cloying and sweet. Anything under .5% is considered reasonably dry. Wines between .5% and 1% are considered "offdry." These numbers are difficult to interpret out of context. A higher acidity level will, theoretically, balance higher R.S. levels to make a "balanced" wine.

Ph. Ph is the commonly used chemical abbreviation of potential hydrogen-ion concentration. After hearing and reading several explanations, I have concluded that it is of interest only to biochemists.

Government Warning Label. As of November 18, 1989, every bottle on your wine merchant's shelf has to carry the 41 word Alcohol Beverage Labeling Act warning. An insult to common sense and intelligence, this new labeling law makes a societal statement: that we are living in a risk-obsessed age of neo-prohibitionism.

Source: Kay Steffey, "Decoding a (U.S.) Wine Label: What It Means," *Bayfood* (Berkeley, California, May, 1990). Reprinted by permission.

Exhibit 15.15 How to Read a Spanish Wine Label

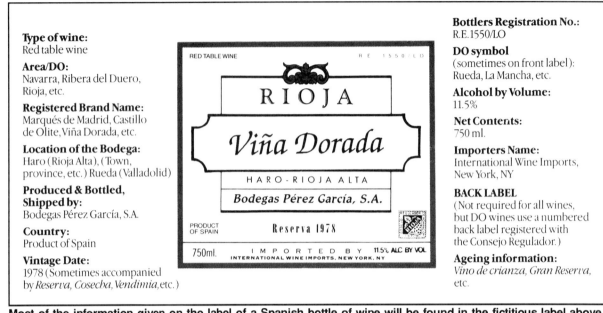

Most of the information given on the label of a Spanish bottle of wine will be found in the fictitious label above.
(Courtesy of Wines of Spain)

All wine exports must be sent to the *Consejo* to be examined; the cases are then wax sealed to ensure they remain authentic.

To meet the EEC codes, Spain established in 1979 two wine categories: *Vino de calidad* (quality wine) and *Vino de coseda* or *vendimia* (wine of special vintage year). (See Exhibit 15.15: "How to Read a Spanish Wine Label.")

Other Countries

Other nations of Europe, such as Portugal, Austria, Hungary, and Yugoslavia, and other nations of the world, such as New Zealand, Australia, Argentina, and Chile, have regulations governing their wine industries. In many respects they resemble the laws discussed above, with special provisions to take care of conditions as they exist in their own regions. For the most part, they serve to protect the consumer and to standardize and stabilize the industry in that nation (see Exhibit 15.16).

Recent Trends in Regulation and Labeling

Organic Wines. As it has in foods, the use of chemicals and other substances in wines has come under scrutiny. The U.S. federal government's GRAS (generally regarded as safe) list permits 75 different additives to be used in wine. Some additives—such as ascorbic acid (vitamin C), egg white, oak chips, carbon dioxide gas, and activated charcoal—are probably harmless. Others may be questionable, running the gamut from acidifiers such as acetic, fumaric, sulfuric and tartaric acids, through bentonite clay and many other fining (clarifying) agents, stabilizers, de-foamers, adjuncts to aid or control fermentation, and precipitators, to bleaching agents and odor removers. The amounts and ways such additives are used are controlled, but those who feel that we are getting too many chemicals in our food and beverages question their use and advocate a more naturally made, organic wine.

Some wine producers have seen a growing and loyal market for these organic wines, and a number of wineries in the United States and several

Exhibit 15.16 How to Read an Austrian Wine Label

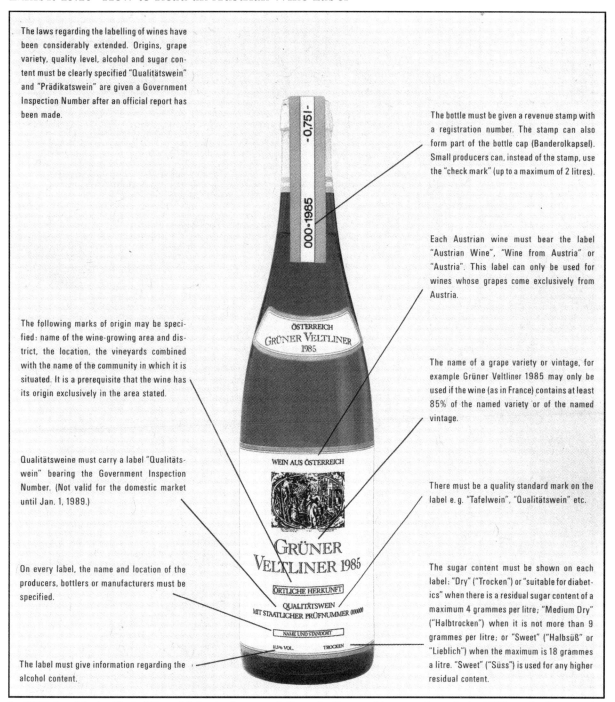

The laws regarding the labelling of wines have been considerably extended. Origins, grape variety, quality level, alcohol and sugar content must be clearly specified "Qualitätswein" and "Prädikatswein" are given a Government Inspection Number after an official report has been made.

The following marks of origin may be specified: name of the wine-growing area and district, the location, the vineyards combined with the name of the community in which it is situated. It is a prerequisite that the wine has its origin exclusively in the area stated.

Qualitätsweine must carry a label "Qualitätswein" bearing the Government Inspection Number. (Not valid for the domestic market until Jan. 1, 1989.)

On every label, the name and location of the producers, bottlers or manufacturers must be specified.

The label must give information regarding the alcohol content.

The bottle must be given a revenue stamp with a registration number. The stamp can also form part of the bottle cap (Banderolkapsel). Small producers can, instead of the stamp, use the "check mark" (up to a maximum of 2 litres).

Each Austrian wine must bear the label "Austrian Wine", "Wine from Austria" or "Austria". This label can only be used for wines whose grapes come exclusively from Austria.

The name of a grape variety or vintage, for example Grüner Veltliner 1985 may only be used if the wine (as in France) contains at least 85% of the named variety or of the named vintage.

There must be a quality standard mark on the label e.g. "Tafelwein", "Qualitätswein" etc.

The sugar content must be shown on each label: "Dry" ("Trocken") or "suitable for diabetics" when there is a residual sugar content of a maximum 4 grammes per litre; "Medium Dry" ("Halbtrocken") when it is not more than 9 grammes per litre; or "Sweet" ("Halbsüß" or "Lieblich") when the maximum is 18 grammes a litre. "Sweet" ("Süss") is used for any higher residual content.

In 1985 Austria instituted the strictest wine regulations in the world; amendments in 1986 made the regulations slightly more lenient. (Courtesy of Oesterreichischer Wien)

hundred in Europe now produce them. In France, the procedure followed is one advocated by the Nature and Progress Association, which obtained approval for their recommended method for organic wine production from the French Ministry of Agriculture. In general, the method calls for the grapes to be grown and the wine made in the traditional manner without the use of synthetic chemicals, pesticides, herbicides, fungicides, chemical fertilizers, metasulfites, hormones, and other additives. The method does allow controlled amounts of "mined sulfur" to be added to help preserve the wine. Otherwise, it is a totally natural process. The vineyards and wineries in France subscribing to this method are inspected regularly to see that they follow the regulations.

Sulfur and Sulfites. One of the main concerns about chemical additives in wine is the use of sulfur as a spray on grape vines to control oïdium—a powdery, destructive mildew. Sulfur, burned to form sulfur dioxide gas, is also widely used to destroy wild yeasts in the must and bacteria in casks and other equipment. All these processes add to the sulfur or sulfite content of the wine.

Sulfites in wine are objectionable for two reasons: they can give a sulfurous flavor to wine, a flavor associated with putrefaction. More importantly, a small percentage of the population is seriously allergic to sulfites, with some cases of death reported. Because of this latter consideration, the U.S. federal government now requires that the presence of sulfites in excess of 100 ppm (parts per million) in foods and beverages be noted on the label.

This means that almost every white wine label today will note that sulfites have been added because most wines, even without the addition of any sulfur, produce at least six ppm of sulfites as a natural part of the fermentation process. In addition, the sulfur used in most processing methods produce an end sulfite content of 80 to 200 ppm—some wines go as high as 350 ppm (with a noticeable sulfur flavor). The French do not permit sulfites in red wines to exceed 90 ppm and in whites, 100 ppm.

Because sulfites are a problem for relatively few people and because almost all wines contain sulfur and sulfites, some wine producers have objected to the labeling requirement. They say it means little. However, the rule is on the books and labels for wine sold today in the United States must adhere to it.

Non-Alcoholic Wine. With the continuing trend toward moderation in drinking, more and more individuals are selecting non-alcoholic beverages as their drink of choice. Today one can find a wide range of whites and reds, as well as rosés and sparkling wines, that are labeled "non-alcoholic." (It must be noted, however, that "non-alcoholic" beverages are not entirely alcohol-free—the legal requirement in the United States is for the label of non-alcoholic beverages to read "contains less than ½ of 1% alcohol by volume.") Many of the currently popular non-alcoholic wines are made from a variety of *Vitis labrusca* grape and so have a slight "grapy" flavor. However, a number of the new non-alcoholic wines are being made from *Vitis vinifera* varieties and thus resemble more closely their European counterparts. We can expect to see more wines of this type on the market and an increase in their consumption.

Tasting and Judging Wine

Not only is a knowledge of the quality of a wine needed to purchase and merchandise wine properly, but service personnel need to know about the quality of the wines on the wine list to sell them. It goes back to the old adage about selling: "If you wanna sell, you gotta know."

There are two essential parts to judging a wine. The first is the basic preparation and the second is the judging itself. In addition, the judge should also understand a few things about judging wine.

Judging is a matter of obtaining sensory stimuli that give a clue as to what the wine is. The most important stimuli come from sight, taste, and smell. Tactile stimuli or feeling sensations are less in number but are often extremely important. The senses of taste and smell are most acute when one is hungry. Thus, about 11:30 a.m. and 4:30 p.m. are often desirable times to judge wine. Smoking, alcohol, a cold, fatigue, emotional upset, or other reasons can dull the senses and make a good judge a poor one. As one gets older, there is a loss of sense acuity, but this may be compensated for through the acuity gained by experience. In judging, one must have a memory which recalls typical flavor and other sensations with which to compare those received from the wine being judged.

While there are only four tastes—sweet, acid, salt and bitter—there are thousands of odors; identifying even several hundred and evaluating them properly when combined with the four tastes can be a challenge. Judging wines relies on experience, because, as one tastes wines one learns to identify various aromatic and taste components and to decide their value. Almost everyone senses the same thing in tasting a wine. It is the experienced judge who knows how to identify the various sensations and to properly interpret their meaning.

Preparing to Judge

Proper preparation is needed if a wine is to be judged properly. Not more than three to five wines should be judged at one time—more will result in tasting fatigue. Usually, low-alcohol and the most delicate wines are selected for judging first. Water and low-salt crackers or bread may be provided to cleanse the palate between judgments. The judging should be in a quiet and well-lighted room. Set a plain, white cloth on the table or surface to be used by the judge, so the wine can be viewed through the glass with the white cloth as backdrop. Use a plain, clear, bell-shaped glass with the top rim smaller than the bowl to help concentrate the bouquet as it rises from the wine. The opening of the glass should be large enough to allow the nose to get into the glass to smell the wine at close quarters. The glass should be large enough to adequately hold the wine and allow it to be swirled.

The amount of wine poured may vary. Some judges feel a small amount—an ounce or two—is enough, while others may desire more because they feel that they are better able to judge the depth of color and also have enough wine to build up a proper aroma in the glass. The wine should be served at a proper temperature. Exhibit 15.17 shows the temperatures recommended for wines to be served at the table.

Judging the Wine

Water makes up from 83% to 90% of unfortified wine. The next component in quantity is alcohol, which can vary from about 6% minimum to 24% in fortified wines. Sugar is next in quantity and may run 2% in some sweet wines; a dry wine will have little sugar. The remainder—about one percent— is acids, glycerine, tannins, color pigments, and some flavoring ingredients and minerals. These components (other than water) have much to do with

Exhibit 15.17 Temperature Chart for Serving Wines

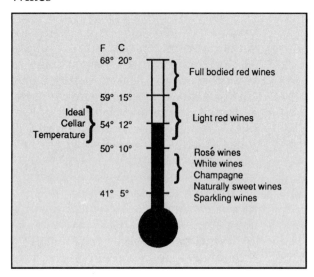

what we call **body**—the degree of consistency, texture, firmness, or viscosity of the liquid.

In judging a sparkling wine, one can get a sense of the effervescence or zest of the wine from its bubbles by holding the glass up and listening to the click of the tiny bubbles as they break. A wine with fine, lively bubbles will have bubbles that click when they reach the surface. A wine that is not as lively or has coarse bubbles will give off less of a clicking sound.

Much information about wine can be gained by just looking at it. It is important in judging wines to have the same kind of glass for each wine and to pour the same amount. Otherwise the color, odor, and other characteristics of the wines may differ not because of the wine but because of the difference in the glass or wine amount. Watch the wine as it is poured into the glass. As it hits the curved sides of the glass, it should curl up and turn over like a wave and one should note a flash of brilliance in a wine of good clarity and clear color. Next, tip the glass so a thin layer of wine is at the edge of the glass; now look at the color as it shows up over the white cloth. The true color of the wine will stand out.

Look at the wine next as it stands level in the middle of the glass. The wine here will have a deeper color than at the edge, but the clarity of the wine will be shown. Swirl the wine and also note the clarity. If the wine has been handled or poured poorly, sediment may harm an otherwise excellent wine. Clarity in wine is an important factor in judging quality. Poor wines are often muddy.

Certain wines should have a specific color at a specific stage of their maturity. White wines when young or with a full body and flavor may have a yellowish-green tinge instead of the typical straw color. As these whites age, they may turn to a light brown, but this color also may indicate that the wine is not up to standard. When a white becomes brown or amber it is probably overage and a poor wine. Sweet whites will usually be somewhat golden in color. Young or immature reds will be somewhat purple but will change on aging to a ruby red or just a rich red; such a wine has had several years of aging. A red that has taken on an amber or brown color has aged prematurely or is just too old. Rosé wines range from a pink to light red to a slightly orange-red. Again, an amber color is an indication that perhaps the wine has "gone over the hill."

Besides denoting clarity, the color of a wine is also an indicator of body. A wine of heavier components will have a deeper color than one of light body. Experts know wines have a typical color governed by the kind of grape, the making of the wine, the age of the wine, and perhaps its care. A wine that doesn't show such color characteristics may be downgraded.

Judges frequently swirl a wine to note the color. They also look to see how the wine clings to the sides of the glass. Small rivulets may show. Called *legs*, these indicate the presence of glycerine and other body-making components which contribute to the texture and smoothness in the wine. As the wine is swirled, the judge can also note the density of the wine, again giving a clue as to body.

The next step in judging a wine is to smell it. Every kind of wine has a typical odor and, depending upon its age, the odor should be typical of that wine. The nose is several thousand times as sensitive as the taste buds and so odors of even the faintest kind are picked up. Off odors should be quickly detected. Defects in wines which the nose can detect are:

Odor Factor	Related Smell
Sulfur dioxide	burnt matches
Acetic acid	vinegar
Acetaldehyde	apple or sherry odor
Ethyl acetate	fingernail polish
Hydrogen sulfide	hot-spring water—rotten eggs
Diacetyl	cheesy or buttery
Yeast (Brettanomyces)	horsey or barnyard odor
Mercaptans	skunky or onion or garlic odor

One can often tell the age of a wine by its odor. Some whites five or more years in the bottle develop a sweetish, honey odor and then later take on a flat, dull, coffee-like odor. A fresh apple smell is usually characteristic of a young wine with excess malic acid and perhaps a poor vintage. Young wines should have the kind of good, solid, fruity smell associated with the smell of ripe fruit in a fruit market. Wine odors mellow with age, becoming more soft and harmonious.

Wine odors can be said to be light, deep, nondescript, superficial, full, or rounded. Such terms describe the degree of development of the wine. A wine that has not developed its odors, but has the potential to do so, may be called *dumb*, a just designation.

Some wine experts like to differentiate between the odors of a young and an old wine by calling the former an "aroma" and the latter a "bouquet." Young wine odors are simple and not too difficult to describe, while an older wine develops a much more complex set of odors.

To smell a wine, if it is cold, warm the glass with your hands. Then swirl it vigorously to build up as much odor as possible in the glass. Put the nose deep down into the glass and sniff hard, drawing in as much air as possible. The judge should know what to expect from various wines,

Exhibit 15.18 Sample Scoring Sheet for Wine Judging

WINE TASTING SCORE SHEET

Date:

WINE	APPEARANCE:	SMELL:	TASTE:	QUALITY:	COMMENTS:
Name:	Color–Clarity	Aroma–Bouquet	Flavors > Finish	(relative)	
Region:					
Year:	1 2 3 4	1 2 3 4	1 3 5 7 9	1 2 3	Total/

WINE	APPEARANCE:	SMELL:	TASTE:	QUALITY:	COMMENTS:
Name:	Color–Clarity	Aroma–Bouquet	Flavors > Finish	(relative)	
Region:					
Year:	1 2 3 4	1 2 3 4	1 3 5 7 9	1 2 3	Total/

WINE	APPEARANCE:	SMELL:	TASTE:	QUALITY:	COMMENTS:
Name:	Color–Clarity	Aroma–Bouquet	Flavors > Finish	(relative)	

and this expectation is gained through experience. For instance, many fine wines are aged in small oak casks; an experienced judge will note a smell of wood among the other smells of such a wine.

By the time the judge is ready to taste the wine, much is known about it, but it is in the tasting that the flavor components of the wine are finally realized. Odor sensations are almost instantly recorded, but there is a time lag in obtaining taste, especially with the bitter taste. Therefore, judges must wait for a time for taste sensations to be fully registered.

All judges should have specific standards by which they judge a specific wine. Each standard may have different elements appropriate to the wine. These elements are judged and their balance evaluated. If there are variations from the standard, these are recorded in the judge's evaluation and a final judgment obtained.

To taste a wine, suck it up with some aggressiveness so there is a spray that pervades the entire mouth. Before swallowing or spitting the wine out, most judges will draw a sharp intake of breath through the mouth over the surface of the wine. This important routine is practiced because, as we have noted, the taste buds provide very limited sensations by themselves; the taste sensations combined simultaneously with the far more complex odors will offer a more precise record of a wine's "taste."

Some wine experts describe tasting as first an attack, then an evolution or development, and finally a finish. Sweet sensations are evident in the attack, acid and salt in the evolution, and bitter in the finish. In tasting, the judge is looking for a balance between the sweet, the acid, and the bitter components. If they are there in balance, along with proper odor, the wine is apt to be scored high. Variations from what the judge considers a desirable balance can downgrade the wine.

In addition to obtaining wine flavor, the tasting sensation will reveal the wine's texture or **body**. Wine contains a number of solids which give it viscosity and body, and often add to the flavor. Some light whites have few solids; their flavor is built up by aromatics which have little density. Some reds are heavy with solids and thus have a very definite body. Wines with body tend to fill the mouth and last, while wines with a light body seem to disappear in the mouth quickly. White wines should be lighter in body than reds, but some whites—Chablis, for instance—will have body equal to that of a light red such as Beaujolais. Judges roll wines around in their mouths to check for body.

It is not necessary to take a lot of wine to obtain the proper taste sensations. A small amount is adequate. Many judges do not swallow; they spit the wine out after tasting. If the judge consumes some, he or she is doing so to get the throat sensations which can provide a clue to aftertaste.

The last set of sensations comes in the aftertaste. The weakest and more quickly dissipated factors have now disappeared, and the most prominent and longest lasting remain. The aftertaste is a blend of final flavors and is, perhaps, one of the biggest contributing factors in a final judgment of a wine's value. The aftertaste can change in time; it can be just sweet at first, then change to cloyingly sweet. The acidity can give an initial "zing" but then become slightly unpleasant. The most interesting wines have a complex aftertaste: the taste lingers on in the mouth and offers a complex variety of taste sensations. Such a wine is said to have length.

In some judging, wines are scored. Exhibit 15.18 is a sample sheet that could be used in such a scoring.

Endnotes

1. Hugh Johnson, *Modern Encyclopedia of Wine*, 2d ed. (New York: Simon & Schuster, 1987), 17.

2. Johnson, 13.

3. Sulfur dioxide has also been used to stop fermentation in order to leave some natural sweetness in a wine. However, this practice has been largely replaced by sterile filtration and the addition of unfermented sweet grape juice to make a wine sweet.

4. Oz Clarke, *The Essential Wine Book* (New York: Simon & Schuster, 1988), 30.

5. One degree Oeschle is each gram by which a liter of grape juice is heavier than a liter of water. Thus, a reading of 73° Oeschle means that a liter of the must is 73 grams heavier than a liter of water. The additional weight is sugar ripeness.

6. Donald A. Bell, *Wine and Beverage Standards* (New York: Van Nostrand Reinhold, 1989), 115.

Key Terms

aging	generic wine
American Viticulture Areas (AVAs)	good year
aperitif wine	lees
appellation contrôlée	maturing
blending	must
body	natural wine
champagne method	noble rot
chaptalization	phylloxera
Charmat (bulk) process	racking
crus	sulfites
dessert wine	sulfur dioxide
fining	varietal wine
fortified wine	vintage year

Discussion Questions

1. What are the basic wine classifications? How is each defined?

2. Why are some wines red?

3. How are most rosé wines made?

4. Why are most European vines grafted to American rootstock?

5. What are the requirements for the labeling of a varietal wine in France? In the United States?

6. What is "noble rot"? What is its significance in wine production?

7. What is the significance of adding sugar before fermentation and what is this process called?

8. Discuss blending—the blending of grapes to make various wines, and the blending of wines to make Champagne, Bordeaux reds, and other wines.

9. What is fortification?

10. Discuss aging—in the cask and in the bottle (maturing). Name some types of wine which definitely improve with age; some wines which are better consumed while young.

11. Discuss the elements of the *appellation contrôlée* system: What is regulated and why?

12. What is the single most important element in conferring the highest quality designation (QmP) to German wines? How is this element regulated?

13. What is the "vintage" year and what is its importance on a wine label? What percentage of grapes must be from the vintage for the vintage date to be shown on a bottle of U.S. wine?

14. Explain the significance of sulfur compounds in winemaking. Why do most labels of U.S. wines contain a sulfite warning?

15. Discuss the importance of odor in tasting a wine. What is the best method to combine taste and odor in judging a wine?

16 Wines of the World

Chapter Outline

France
    Champagne
        The Champagne Process
    Alsace
    Loire
    Burgundy
        Chablis
        Côte d'Or
        Southern Burgundy
    Bordeaux
        Médoc
        St-Emilion
        Pomerol
        Graves
        Sauternes and Barsac
    Côtes du Rhône
        Châteauneuf-du-Pape
Germany
    Mosel-Saar-Ruwer
    Rheingau
    Rheinhessen
    Rheinpfalz
    Nahe
    Schaumwein
    Eiswein
Italy
    Piedmont
    Lombardy
    Veneto
    Emilia-Romagna
    Tuscany
    Latium
    Sicily
Spain
    Sherry
Portugal
    Port
The United States
    California
        Main Grape Varieties (Red)
        Main Grape Varieties (White)
        Vintages
        Growing Regions
    New York

Wines of Other Countries and Areas
    Australia and New Zealand
    Austria
    Bulgaria
    Greece and Cyprus
    Hungary
    Israel
    Madeira
    North Africa
    Romania
    South Africa
    South America
    The Soviet Union
    Yugoslavia

The amount of wine produced in the world each year is immense. In 1983 world production was estimated at 8.0 billion gallons. Italy was the largest producer, contributing 2.17 billion gallons, followed by France with 1.8 billion gallons. The other leading nations were, in billion gallons:

USSR	0.93
Spain	0.80
USA	0.39
West Germany	0.34[1]

Production is worldwide in any temperate area where there are 120 or more frost-free days with fairly warm summers and not overly cold winters. In the last 50 years many countries not traditionally known as wine producers have developed sizable wine industries, and are exporting their wines around the world. At almost any important wine competition today, you can observe a great many nations offering a wide variety of excellent quality wines. Nor is it unusual to see some country not particularly noted for its wines walk off with some of the highest awards. (Exhibit 16.1 shows some of the major wine-growing regions of western Europe).

In the discussion that follows, a short summary of the major wine producing nations is given, along with some indication of the quality and the distinctive characteristics of their major wines. However, it should be noted that entire volumes have been written on the subject; this chapter can only scratch the surface. Unfortunately, this may lead to some important omissions, but, we hope, not too many.

France

While the nation of France is not the world's largest wine producer, it is perhaps the most important. This statement can be supported by the fact that France leads in the variety of wines produced and has more wines of international reputation than any other nation. It has led the world in the promotion of wine and has marketed its wines in more countries than any other. It is the country that has made wine the beverage most closely associated with food. When one says "wine," one thinks of France, and when one thinks of France, one is most apt to think of fine food accompanied by wine.

Wine is produced in all of France except in its most northern part. Exhibit 16.2 shows where the eight major wine-producing districts are located. There are other areas where wines of distinction are produced, but the eight featured stand out because of the amount and the quality of the wine produced.

Champagne

Champagne is one of France's most famous and finest wines. Champagne was first made at the end of the 17th century by a monk named Dom Perignon and others. It is the wine of love, weddings, births and birthdays, ship christenings, dreams, feasts, and festivals.

By law, wine labeled "Champagne" can only come from the triangle formed by the Marne region, Montagne de Reims, and Côte des Blancs (see Exhibit 16.3). Other laws have been established to strictly control the industry, such as defining the vineyards that can produce the grapes,

Exhibit 16.1 Major Wine-Producing Areas of Western Europe

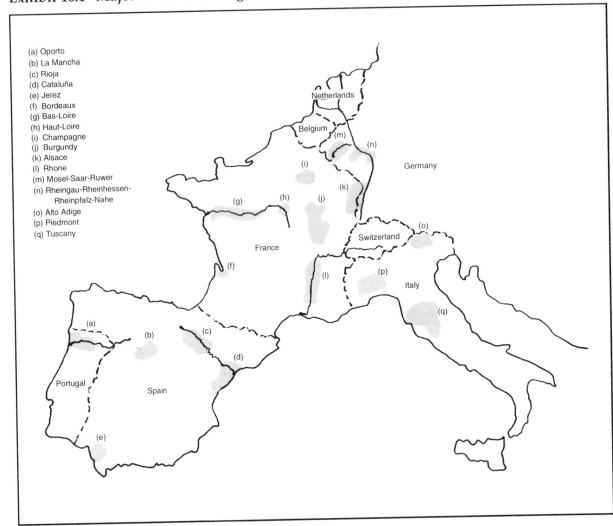

the kinds of grapes, growing and pruning methods, the sugar content of the grapes, yield per hectare, the methods of pressing, fermentation, aging, the method of making the champagne, aging in the bottle and a host of other details. These controls have brought about a stable industry, known for its high quality product.

It is of the essence of Champagne that it is a blend of wines from many growers. Thus, a considerable quantity of Champagne is produced by **Négociant-Manipulants**, firms that purchase wines from growers or cooperatives. The label may note this with the letters "NM." Other labels may show the following as the producer:

RM *Récoltant-Manipulant* (vine grower)
CM *Co-operative de Manipulation* (cooperative)
RC *Récoltant-Cooperateur* (cooperative for a grower)
SR *Société de Récoltants* (family owned firm)
MA *Marque d'Acheteur* (private brand)

Exhibit 16.2 Major Wine-Producing Areas of France

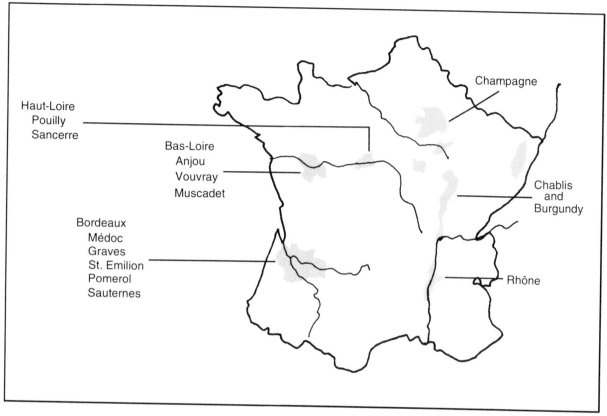

Only three grape varieties can be used to make Champagne: the Chardonnay, a white, giving lightness, elegance, and finesse; the Pinot Noir (red), giving body, strength, and fullness of flavor; and the Pinot Meunier (red), giving freshness and youth. If the Champagne is made from all white (Chardonnay) grapes, it is called **blanc de blancs** (literally, "white from white"); if it is made from all black (red) grapes (with the skins removed before fermentation), it is called **blanc de noir** (literally, *"white from black"*).

To obtain *Grand Cru* classification, 100% of the grapes must come from one of the 12 *Grand Cru* classified villages in the Champagne district; to obtain a *Premier Cru* rating, 90% to 99% of the grapes must come from one of the 41 *Premier Cru* villages.

The Champagne Process. The traditional process of making Champagne is called *méthode champenoise* (champagne method); the label will often read **"fermented in this bottle."** This method is widely practiced for the making of the highest quality sparkling wines. However, French Champagne labels do not carry the designation *méthode champenoise* because, in order to be called "Champagne," the wine *must* be made by that method. (See Exhibit 16.4: "How to Read a French Champagne Label.") Only sparkling wines made outside the Champagne region will note the method on the label.

By international law, only France can use the designation "Champagne." Sparkling wines produced in the United States, for instance (whether made by the champagne method or not), must be labeled

Exhibit 16.3 Champagne Territory—France

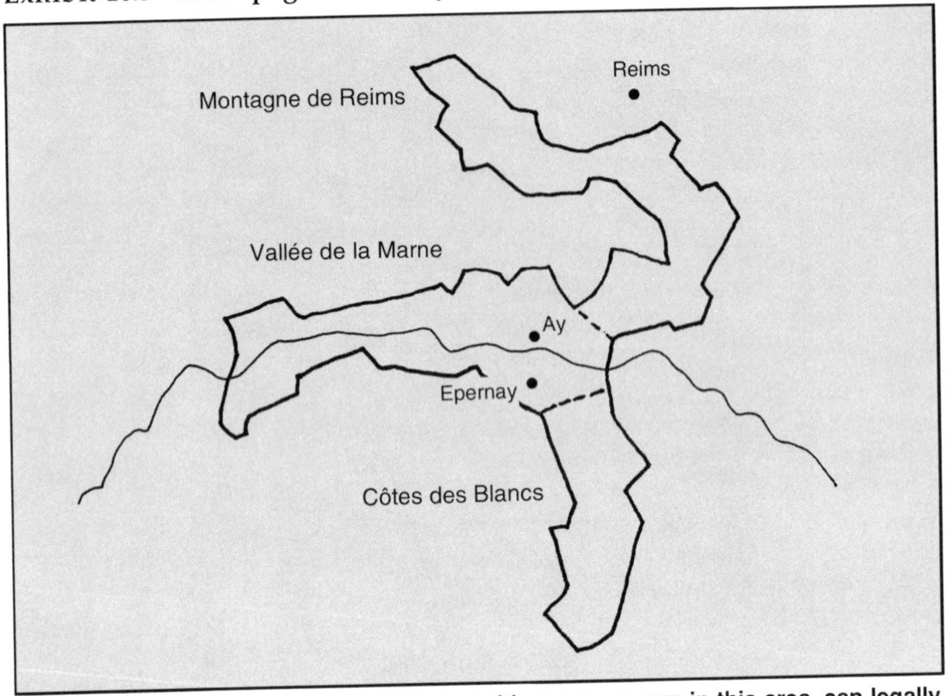

Only wine produced in this area of France, with grapes grown in this area, can legally be called "Champagne." (Courtesy of Food and Wines from France)

"sparkling" or state specific origin as in "American," "New York State," or "California Champagne." In Germany, sparkling wines are called *Schaumwein, Qualitäts Schaumwein,* or *Sekt* (*Prädikat Sekt* or *Deutscher Sekt*) with different requirements for each classification; in Italy, *spumante;* in Spain, *cava;* in Portugal, *espumante.* In France, sparkling wines produced outside the Champagne region are called *vin mousseux* (foamy) or *pétillant* (crackling—a semi-sparkling wine produced naturally with the malolactic secondary fermentation).

In the spring after the first fermentation, the most important step occurs—the blending of wines in what is known as the *cuvée* for the re-fermentation process which produces the characteristic Champagne bubbles. The various wines which will be blended are tasted to judge their flavor and other quality characteristics; as many as 30 or more different wines may be blended together to create the desired taste. Blending formulas are carefully-guarded secrets, since this is what distinguishes one Champagne from others.

The cuvée is then bottled; yeast and some sugar is added and the bottle is plugged with a strong cap. This step in the process is called *le tirage.*

The bottles are now stored in cool (50° to 55° F or 10° to 13° C) chalk caves to slowly ferment, a process called *prise de mousse* (the making of foam). During this second fermentation, more alcohol is made along with carbon dioxide gas which, trapped by the bottle, is forced into the wine. The pressure that builds up is usually 110 psi (pounds per square inch) or 7½ atmospheres. This is the gas that forms the bubbles or sparkle, giving the wine its effervescence. A properly made Champagne has fine bubbles that last a long time.

Exhibit 16.4. How to Read a French Champagne Label

To be sure you are drinking Champagne, the proudest of French wines, look for the following information on the label:

1. The word "Champagne" in prominent letters.
2. The brand name of the Champagne producer.
3. The phrase "produce of France".
4. The contents of the bottle.
5. The location of the producer in the Champagne Region.
6. The degree of dryness: "brut", "extra-dry", "sec" or "demi-sec".

If the Champagne was bottled in a vintage year, the year of the harvest will also appear. The label may also state that the Champagne was blended only with Chardonnay grape wines *(blanc de blancs)* or has been allowed to derive a pink color from the skins of red grapes *(rosé).*

During this second fermentation, the bottles are stored in slanting A-shaped frames called *les pupitres* with the bottle necks down so the yeast and other sediment collect there. To encourage this collection of sediment, a process called *remuage* occurs—professionals *(remueurs)* grab the base of

Two *remueurs* performing *remuage* on bottles of Champagne during re-fermentation. This process, which involves shaking and turning the bottles, is now often done by machines with up to 4,000 bottles at a time. (Courtesy of Food and Wines from France)

each bottle, giving it a slight shake and turn. Gradually this action causes a plug of sediment to form in the neck of the bottle, so it can be removed later in the *dégorgement* process. Today, *remuage* can be done mechanically by large machines processing over 4,000 bottles at a time. As many as three years may be required for this second fermentation, at the end of which time the bottles are brought in from the caves and placed head down into a cold brine (usually propylene glycol) that freezes the sediment in the neck to the cork. Then, with a quick motion, an expert removes the cork along with its plug and the clear wine is left in the bottle. This step is called *dégorgement*. The lost volume is now made up with additional wine, sugar and, in some cases, brandy. This last addition is called **le dosage**.

The amount of sugar added in the *dosage* determines the relative dryness or sweetness of the wine. Depending upon the amount of residual sugar, Champagne labels indicate:

Extra-brut	Driest	0 to 6 grams of sugar/liter
Brut	Less dry	under 15 grams of sugar/liter
Extra-dry	Some dryness	12 to 20 grams of sugar/liter
Sec	Slight sweetness	17 to 35 grams of sugar/liter
Demi-sec	Sweet	35 to 50 grams of sugar/liter
Doux	Very sweet	over 50 grams of sugar/liter

The wine is quickly corked after *dégorgement*, a wire cage called an *agraffe* (or *muselet*) put over the cork to hold it in the bottle, and foil placed

The *dégorgement* process. (Courtesy of Food and Wines from France)

over both. This whole process is called dressing. The bottled Champagne is then put into chalk caves to age. From one to five years of aging is required, depending on the quality of wine, but producers usually exceed this requirement. The following summarizes the aging periods:

	Required Aging	Usual Aging
Non-vintage	1 year	3 years
Vintage	3 years	5 years
Prestige Cuvée		8–9 years

Champagne maturing in chalk caves. (Courtesy of Champagne News and Information Bureau)

Prestige Cuvée is a blend of grapes from the best vineyards in a good year; it is the finest of Champagnes and will cost more because of this quality difference.

Occasionally, a vintage Champagne will have the letters *"RD"* (*Récemment Dégorgé* or "Recently Disgorged") on the label. This means the wine has aged in contact with its yeast deposits longer than usual (gaining additional flavor) and the *dégorgement* takes place shortly before the wine is sold, ensuring freshness.

A "champagne" made in the United States (or a *Sekt* from Germany) may have on the label "**fermented in the bottle**" (not "in *this* bottle") or "Bottle Fermented," which indicates it is made by the transfer process and not by the traditional *champenoise* method. In the transfer process, the second fermentation takes place "in the bottle" as the label says, but the sparkling wine is then transferred to a vat under pressure for settling, clarifying, and fining, then returned under pressure to the bottles, which have been cleaned and sterilized. A *dosage* is added and the bottle is corked.

Exhibit 16.5 Alsace

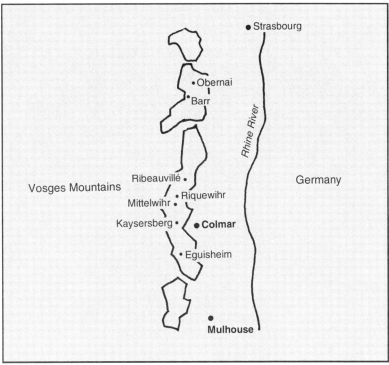

Located on the Rhine River next to Germany, the Alsace produces many traditionally German wines in the French style. (Courtesy of Food and Wines from France)

Another method of making a sparkling wine is called the "Charmat process," the *"cuvée closé"* process, or "bulk fermentation." The still wine is put into a pressurized tank with sugar and yeast to start the second fermentation. After several weeks of second fermentation, the wine is pumped under pressure into another tank where it is clarified. The *dosage* is then added and the wine is bottled and corked. One of the advantages of the Charmat process, according to some tastes, is that the resulting product has a fresher grape flavor. The Italians use this method almost exclusively for the making of *spumante*. Since this method eliminates a lot of highly professional labor, the wine is less costly. However, the bubbles of carbon dioxide are not as fine nor do they last as long as with the traditional method.

Another method of making a sparkling wine is to carbonate a still wine by forcing carbon dioxide into the wine under pressure. Such a wine is usually lowest in cost and quality. The bubbles are usually coarse and come out of the wine rapidly, giving a flat wine.

Alsace   The Alsace region lies along the French bank of the Rhine river; it is known for its dry, fresh, fruity whites, often sold under the grape variety and not vineyard name (see Exhibit 16.5). The major grapes used are the Pinot Gris, Pinot Blanc, Riesling, Muscat, Gewürztraminer, and Sylvaner. The Pinot Gris makes a hearty, full-bodied but lightly fruity, dry white wine. The Pinot Blanc produces a wine of good body and delicate lightness

Exhibit 16.6 The Loire Valley

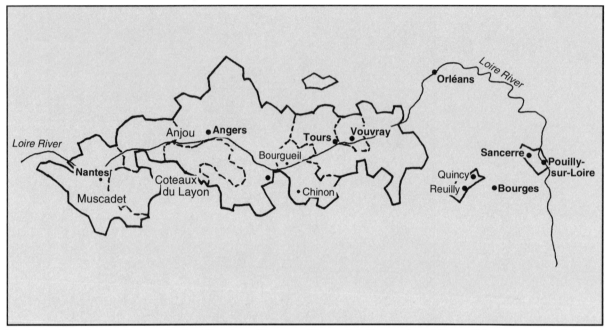

The Loire is noted for its excellent white wines (Vouvray, Muscadet, Saumur) and the well-known rosés of Anjou.
(Courtesy of Food and Wines from France)

and is the primary grape of what are called the Edelzwicker (noble mixture) blends. The Pinot Blanc is also used to produce the excellent dry, fruity, sparkling Crémant d'Alsace. (A *crémant* is a semi-sparkling wine made by the *méthode champenoise*. France makes two other *appellation côntrolée crémants*—the Crémant de Bourgogne and the Crémant de Loire.)

The widely used Riesling makes a very dry, elegant and classic white with a light, delicate bouquet. Normally the Muscat produces enough sugar to make a sweet wine, but in the Alsace it does not; the wine is crisp, light, with the typical Muscat grapy, fruity flavor. Gewürztraminer wines are quite fruity and probably exceed all others in spiciness (*Gewürz* means "spicy" in German). Traminer wine belongs to the same family as the Gewürztraminer but is lighter in bouquet and flavor. Sylvaner wines are fresh, light, and fruity whites.

Some late-harvested wines (*Vendange Tardive*—"tardy harvest") are made that resemble the late harvest wines of Germany. The label will read *Sélection des Grains Nobles* for the sweetest. These wines are rich, full-bodied, and sweet with an exotic bouquet.

Loire   The Loire River drains central France, flowing west to the Atlantic Ocean (see Exhibit 16.6). It is a rich agricultural land, famous for its castles where some of our greatest fairy tales were born. It has two grape growing areas: (1) Bas-Loire (lower Loire) consisting of Anjou, Saumur, Vouvray (Touraine), and Muscadet de Sèvre-et-Maine, and Haute-Loire (upper Loire) consisting of Pouilly-Fumé and Sancerre. Most of the wines are fresh, light, and delicately fruity and meant to be consumed when fairly young. Only the sweet

Exhibit 16.7 Burgundy (Bourgogne)

The heart of Burgundy—the Côte d'Or—produces only one-tenth that of Bordeaux, but its wines are some of the world's finest. (Courtesy of Food and Wines from France)

whites age well and keep for a long time. The best known wines of the region are the dry, still, whites of Pouilly-Fumé and Saumur; the white wines, dry or sweet, of Saumur; the still and sparkling white wines of Vouvray; the whites or rosés (the latter mostly sweet) of Anjou; and the dry whites of Muscadet.

Burgundy

Wine was being made in Burgundy (Bourgogne) when it was conquered by the Romans. Today it is only rivaled by the region of Bordeaux as the producer of the world's greatest wines. The Burgundy region lies between the cities of Dijon and Lyon, a distance of some 225 miles (see Exhibit 16.7). Chablis, the area that produces some of the world's greatest white wines, is considered a part of this region. It is about 75 miles north of Dijon.

Before the French Revolution much of the land was owned by the Church. After the Revolution, the land holdings were divided into small parcels and sold. Thus, today some of the vineyards are owned by a great many owners. The famous Montrachet vineyard of 19 acres has over a dozen owners. The famous Chambertin vineyard is similarly parceled. Sometimes, vineyard or vineyard parcel owners will pool their grapes or their musts, selling them to a shipper. As long as each parcel has the same *cru* ranking under the AC, the resulting wine can qualify for the appropriate *Grand Cru*, *Premier Cru*, or other designation. The shipper then ferments the wine, ages, and bottles it.

If a vineyard produces and bottles its own wine, the label can bear the term *Mise en Bouteille à la Propriété* or *Mise en Bouteille au Domaine*.

The label will usually have the name of the *domaine* under this, such as *Domaine Claude Laret*. In some cases, small owners may join together in a cooperative and blend their musts together to make wine. If a merchant bottles the wine, the name and location of the bottler will be indicated along with a phrase like *Négociant à Vosne-Romanée* or *Propriétaire à Vosne-Romanée*.

Sometimes a label gives just the name of the vineyard or *commune* (township or village) that produces the wine such as Chambertin or La Tâche. Such names are so famous among wine lovers that no other information is needed.

Burgundy has three major wine-producing regions: 1) Chablis, 2) Côte d'Or, which includes Côte de Nuits and Côte de Beaune, and 3) southern Burgundy, which includes Chalonnais, Mâconnais and Beaujolais.

Chablis. The Chablis area, located north of the main Burgundy area, is famous for only one wine, but it is one of the best white wines in the world. It is so popular that vintners in other nations have grown the Chardonnay grape (which, according to French law, must be used to make Chablis) so they could imitate it—they never quite succeed. It is a crisp, fruity, very dry wine with a fresh bouquet and a delicate, refreshing acidity; its color is typically yellow tinged with green.

There are four AC rankings for Chablis which, from highest to lowest are: Chablis Grand Cru, Chablis Premier Cru, Chablis, and Petit Chablis. To qualify for these rankings, the grapes on harvest must, in addition to satisfying other *cru* qualifications, be able to produce, respectively, a wine having an alcoholic content of 11, 10.5, 10, and 9.5 percent. The following is a listing of some Grand and Premier Cru Chablis vineyards:

Chablis Grand Cru	Chablis Premier Cru
Blanchots	Chapelot
Bougros	Côte de Fontenay
Les Clos	Fourchaume
Les Grenouilles	Mont-de-Milieu
Les Preuses	Montée de Tonnerre
Valmur	Vaucoupin
Vaudésir	Vaulorent

Côte d'Or. Côte d'Or means "slope of gold," and richly deserves the name, since some of the world's greatest wines come from there. It is divided into two parts: Côte de Nuits in the north and the Côte de Beaune in the south. The best wines of the Côte d'Or are reds which are beautifully balanced between acid and tannins so they last and last. In fact, a good red is not quite that until it has been about 10 years in the bottle. The Côte de Nuits burgundies are full-bodied and carry an elegant, deeply perfumed bouquet. The Côte de Beaune reds have a warm, fragrant bouquet, but are lighter in body and mature more quickly than those of the Côte de Nuits.

The wines of Côte d'Or are ranked as *Grand Cru*, *Premier Cru*, *Appellation Communale*, and a fourth classification of inferior vineyards which may only be labeled "Bourgogne." *Grand Cru* wines will have on the label only the vineyard name or the village-vineyard name. *Premier Cru* wine is identified by the village plus the vineyard name or the phrase Premier

Cru or often with both. An *Appellation Communale* wine will have only the village (*commune*) name on the label such as Pommard.

In some cases a village name plus that of the most famous vineyard located in it are combined. This practice allows certain growers or bottlers with inferior wine to trade on the name of a justly famed vineyard. The buyer must beware by knowing more about Côte d'Or vineyards and villages than can be ascertained from labels. Thus, the name Chambolle-Musigny is only an indication that the wine comes from the Chambolle area but does not mean the wine is made from the Musigny vineyard grapes.

By law all red wines produced in the Côte d'Or must be made from the Pinot Noir grape. The Pinot Noir grape is difficult to bring to successful harvest year after year, but it does better in the Côte d'Or than in other areas. And when it is brought to ripe harvest, it produces magnificent wines.

Côte d'Or Reds. The map of Burgundy shown in Exhibit 16.7 shows that the northern end of the Côte d'Or where Dijon and Fixin are located is in the shape of a canopy or cap. This area's reds are respectable but are so much overshadowed by those of the more southern areas that we hear little about them.

Next in line to the south is the village of Gevrey-Chambertin, from which come nine *Grand Crus*, all bearing the name of Chambertin in some form or another. One must be alert, however, to know which these are, because a wine bearing the name of Gevrey-Chambertin may not be made from any of the famous vineyard grapes but only be an ordinary red made in the village area of Gevrey-Chambertin.

South of Gevrey-Chambertin is the village of Morey-Saint-Denis, which has similarly elegant reds. Four Morey-Saint-Denis vineyards hold *Grand Cru* rankings.

The next village, Chambolle-Musigny, is noted for reds which are slightly different from those of its more northern neighbors. They are sometimes described as "elegant, delicate, and charmingly feminine." Three of the wines of the area have *Grand Cru* status.

Sandwiched in between Chambolle-Musigny and Vosne-Romanée is the tiny village area of Vougeot where the famous *Grand Cru* vineyard, Clos de Vougeot, is located (see Exhibit 16.8). It was once the property of a monastery, but was divided into many parcels after the Revolution. Today there are over 80 owners holding the property. The wines of the Vosne-Romanée are rich in flavor and full in body and have a tremendous bouquet. When tasted, they are said to "open up like a peacock's tail in the mouth." It is a great wine area with 7 *Grand Crus*, 9 *Premiers Crus*, and the world's most expensive wine—Romanée-Conti.

The southern end of the Côte d'Or, but the biggest area, is that of Nuits-Saint-Georges. While it boasts of no *Grand Crus*, it has a flock of *Premier Crus* and its village red wines are of very high quality.

The Côte de Beaune starts at the villages of Ladoix-Serrigny and Pernand-Vergelesses. After this, to the south, the first red of note produced is in Aloxe-Corton, a *Grand Cru* of the vineyard Corton.

Farther south the area of Savigny-les-Beaunes produces some excellent village reds. The city of Beaune is just south of Savigny-les-Beaunes, and it is here that the Hospices de Beaune, the charity hospital established in 1443 by the Dames Hospitalières, holds its famous wine auction every November. Much of the Burgundy wines are purchased at this auction,

Exhibit 16.8 Clos de Vougeot Wine Label

which finances the charity hospital, by shippers and others. In 1984 the famous white wine Corton-Charlemagne sold for an average of 105,000 francs (about $21,000) per cask (225 liters).

Pommard and Volnay to the south of Beaune produce some respected, delicate, soft red wines of elegant quality. Auxey-Duresses is not particularly known for its reds, but the reds bearing the village names are considered good. Similarly, Meursault and Chassagne Montrachet also produce good reds. The reds of Santenay, the last village of importance in Beaune, produces reds called "pleasant and light."

Côte d'Or Whites. The Côte de Beaune is famed for its whites, although they account for less than 20% of its total output. The great *Grand Crus* Corton-Charlemagne and Charlemagne come from the village of Aloxe-Corton.

Meursault, next in line to the south, produces great whites that are full-bodied, big and round in flavor with a luscious softness. They are dry to the almost crisp stage. None of its wines, red or white, hold *Grand Cru* rank, but it has a number of *Premier Crus*.

Puligny-Montrachet produces only dry whites which are rich in body and flavor and of a green-gold color. It boasts of four *Grand Crus*; since a part of these *Grand Cru* vineyards are in Chassagne-Montrachet, it can also claim these wines as its own. In addition, its famous white Criots-Bâtard-Montrachet is classed as a *Grand Cru*.

Southern Burgundy. The middle part of the Burgundy region is made up of the Côte Chalonnaise and Mâconnais. Their reds are of notably good quality, lighter in body and flavor, with less bouquet than the great reds of the Côte d'Or.

Bouzeron Rouge is a respectable wine after about three years maturity. Bouzeron has also been granted the only single village Aligoté white appellation in all of Burgundy.

Mâconnais reds are well thought of, having a fresh, fruity, light flavor and bouquet which comes from the Gamay grape. However, the area's whites are better known than the reds. Montagny produces whites *any* of which, if 11.5% or more in natural alcohol, can be labeled *Premier Cru.* Most of the dry whites of the Mâconnais are considered plain with few frills but, because of their highly refreshing, agreeable, and charming quality, are considered a bit above the average.

On the very southern border of the Mâconnais, right next to Beaujolais, are the slopes that produce the famous Pouilly-Fuissé, a richly flavored, pale, golden wine. Other excellent whites are produced in this same area such as Mâcon Blanc, Mâcon Supérieur, Mâcon-Villages, Saint-Véran, Pouilly-Vinzelles, and Pouilly-Loché. Mâcon produces a few good rosés.

Beaujolais. Beaujolais, the most southern part of Burgundy, is the region's largest producer of wine. Here, the Gamay is the grape of choice. Gamay reds have less tannin, less body, and a lively, lighter and more delicate, fruity flavor than the heavier Pinot Noir reds. The wine has a rich, full berry aroma. It is often consumed lightly chilled. It does not improve with age—about three years is enough—so most of the production is consumed young. At times, when a more robust red develops, the wine does improve with age—a Moulin-à-Vent in a good year will reach the quality of the best Burgundy reds after 10 years.

Beaujolais reds are ranked in one of four quality levels: Cru Beaujolais, Beaujolais Villages, Beaujolais Supérieur, and Beaujolais. First quality is Cru Beaujolais which comes from nine *communes* (villages) in the north: Brouilly, Chénas, Chiroubles, Côte de Brouilly, Fleurie, Juliénas, Morgon, Moulin-à-Vent and Saint-Amour. These nine are part of the group of 35 villages which make up the second ranking: Beaujolais-Villages. Beaujolais Supérieur, the third rank, is only superior to ordinary Beaujolais because it has an extra degree of natural alcohol content. The name of the bottler is often prominently displayed.

Some of the new, lighter Beaujolais wines—called **Beaujolais Nouveau** or Beaujolais Primeur—are hurried to market as early as the third Thursday in November. Beaujolais Nouveau is a very popular wine with a short life—about nine months. It is light, refreshing, lively, and very fruity.

Only about one percent of Beaujolais' wine is white. It goes by the name of Beaujolais Blanc and is a fruity, refreshing, wine much like the Saint-Véran white. It should also be consumed young.

The AC requires that Beaujolais reds must have 9% alcohol, whites, 9.5%, 10% for Beaujolais Supérieur reds or whites, and 10% for Cru Beaujolais.

Bordeaux   The Bordeaux region is that area of land around the lower Garonne and Dordogne Rivers and some of the area after these two join to form the Gironde River (see Exhibit 16.9). Reds (the famous clarets), rosés, and whites

Exhibit 16.9 **Bordeaux**

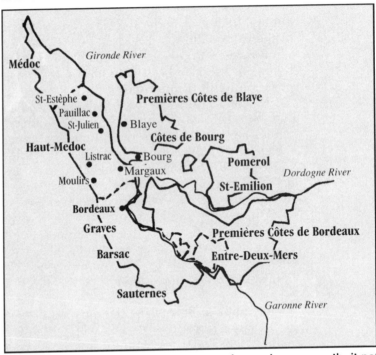

Bordeaux is one of the most important wine regions on earth; it not only produces more wine but more of France's greatest wines.
(Courtesy of Food and Wines from France)

are produced; the reds are primarily dry, while the whites are dry, medium dry, sweet, or very sweet. The Bordeaux region is the most prolific wine producer in France—about one and one-third million gallons of wine in 1983. Reds dominate whites three to one.

The climate favors vine growth—short winters with few frosts and good humidity. The grapes grown to produce the reds are largely the Cabernet Sauvignon and the Cabernet Franc. These give desirable vigor in body and flavor and sufficient acid and tannin to give a wine that usually lasts a long time, and improves with age. Merlot grapes are often used to give softness and suppleness while the Malbec and Petit Verdot varieties are used to give wines a proper balance. The major whites grown are Sauvignon Blanc, Muscadelle, and the Sémillon.

Many Bordeaux wines are bottled under the labels of the châteaux which grow the grapes, produce the wine and bottle it. (See Exhibit 16.10.) Shippers and bottlers, called *négociants*, may purchase different wines and bottle them, putting their own labels on them. Wine labels may disclose a regional or communal name such as Médoc, Graves, or, simply, Bordeaux. Others may feature a varietal grape name which, by law, requires the contents to be made from 100% of that grape.

Monopole labels are those of a merchant-shipper with a brand name and perhaps a regional or communal name attached. The label usually says "Appellation Bordeaux Contrôlée" if labeled just "Bordeaux."

Exhibit 16.10 Bordeaux Wine Labels

One of the original *Grand Cru Classé* **designations under the 1855 law ordered by Napoleon III.** (Courtesy of Food and Wines from France)

The most famous AC-defined regions are: Médoc, St-Emilion, Pomerol, Graves, Sauternes, and Barsac. However, some excellent wines also come from districts such as Cérons, Ste-Croix-du-Mont, Loupiac, Côtes de Bordeaux-Ste-Macaire, Prémieres Côtes de Bordeaux, Ste-Foy-Bordeaux, Entre-Deux-Mers, and Graves de Vayres.

Médoc. The most famous parishes (*communes*) in the Médoc are St-Estèphe, Pauillac, St-Julien, and Margaux. Their wines are beautiful reds, light bodied and elegant, and haunting in fragrance and mellowness. The flavor is delicate and long lasting. Connoisseurs vie to lay down their vintage wines.

St-Estèphe reds have a deep, red color, last a long time and have a succulent and lasting flavor. The reds from this parish are more full-bodied and robust than those of the rest of the Médoc. Their lingering bouquet leaves an impression of pears, apples, peaches, and apricots. They are fairly high in tannin and so last a long time; they mature more slowly than other clarets.

Pauillac, to the south of St-Estèphe, produces reds deep in color and balanced in tannin so they also last a long time. They develop great finesse and an opulent bouquet when mature. The First Growths of the Château Lafite, Château Latour, and Château Mouton-Rothschild are produced here.

St-Julien is next to the south. Its reds are lighter but have excellent harmony and balance. Likewise Moulis and Listrac's dry, fruity reds are light and delicate and mature more quickly than other Bordeaux wines.

Some of the noblest reds of Bordeaux are produced in the parish of Margaux. Its reds are very delicate, yet substantial and full-bodied, lasting a long time. Their great elegance is crowned by a fragrant, lingering bouquet. Château Margaux's First Growth clarets are considered as some of the world's finest. Château Palmer, next door, is a Third Growth but its wine often rivals that of its more prestigious neighbor. Other growths of this area are similarly good and often represent bargains compared to the price charged for Château Margaux.

St-Emilion. The reds of this district are more full-bodied and robust than the other reds of Bordeaux. They also have a flavor all of their own, with a slightly sweet aftertaste. These wines mature fairly quickly; some of the poorer ones will reach their peak in four years, while others may take eight or more. Quality designations of St-Emilion's wines are as follows:

First quality:	St-Emilion
Second quality:	St-Emilion *Grand Crus*
Third quality:	St-Emilion *Grands Crus Classés*
Fourth quality:	St-Emilion *Premiers Grands Crus Classés*

Pomerol. While Pomerol is the smallest of the wine districts of the Bordeaux region, Pomerol's wines are far from small. They are substantial wines, more rugged than St-Emilion's but with some of the same flavor characteristics. The finest taste almost creamy; the color is deep and rich. Buyers select Pomerol wines based on the reputation of the châteaux from which they come.

Graves. About a third of the Graves—named for its gravelly soil—wine production is in reds. They are sturdy wines with a body and flavor typical of the Bordeaux clarets. While some should be consumed fairly young, others carry enough tannin to last well from six to eight years.

The whites of Graves are quite dry, having a crisp, lean, clear taste and well balanced between dryness and bitterness. They have a delicate bouquet and a fruity, aldehyde flavor. A few Grave whites are slightly sweet. The whites of the Graves are considered some of the finest whites produced in the world.

The dry white wines of Bordeaux are usually marketed in green bottles while the sweet whites are usually in clear bottles.

A considerable amount of the dry whites are labeled "Bordeaux Blanc Sec." They are light and refreshing.

Entre-Deux-Mers translates into "between two seas" but it is a triangle set between the Dordogne and Garonne Rivers. The whites of this area are respectable, light, dry, pleasant, and sound.

Sauternes and Barsac. The most southern wine-producing areas of the Bordeaux are Sauternes and Barsac. They get a lot of sun, and the growing period is long so the grapes can remain on the vines for a long time to develop the "noble rot." The wines are mellow, sweet, luscious, and golden in color. They rank among the great sweet wines of the world.

An additional guide to buyers or those merchandising wine is the French ADEB seal affixed on the bottle neck. It is a gold and black seal of the Association pour le Développement de l'Exportation du Vin de

Exhibit 16.11 Côtes du Rhône

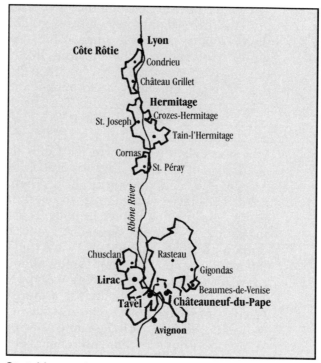

Stretching north to south along the Rhône River, the sunny "slopes of Rhône" produce 90% red wines, the famous Tavel and Lirac rosés and a few interesting white wines.
(Courtesy of Food and Wines from France)

Bordeaux, which seal indicates the wine meets its standards. The seal is respected in the wine trade.

Côtes du Rhône

The Côtes du Rhône wine growing region starts below Beaujolais and follows the Rhône River south to Avignon (see Exhibit 16.11). There is good, long summer warmth so the grapes develop full body and solid alcoholic content. The wines are rich and deep in color and show the vigor of the summer climate. The best wine-growing areas are Côte-Rotie, Condrieu, Hermitage, Cornas, St-Péray, St-Joseph, Lirac and Tavel, and Châteauneuf-du-Pape. Excellent whites, reds and rosés come from this region.

Most of the grapes grown are the Cinsaut and Syrah varieties which develop a deep red wine, full-bodied, possessing vigor and warmth, with a rich bouquet and luscious, rich, deep taste. Southern Rhône uses more grape varieties such as the Grenache and Clairette. Often wines made from the Syrrah have some white grapes blended in to reduce the deep, almost blackish red color and heavy body that grape gives to wine. The wines of the area usually have a consistent quality which makes them quite dependable. The reds when young possess a bit of harshness so they are often aged in the cask several or more years. They mature well in the bottle. The whites of the area also are longer lasting than is usual with whites. This is because of their high alcoholic content as well as other properties.

Only about 10% of the wine produced in the Côtes du Rhône is white. They are so high in alcohol that they are often said to be somewhat heady. Perhaps the most famous white—a golden wine with an intense peach-like flavor—comes from the vineyard of Condrieu. A rare golden, fragrant white of full body and flavor comes from the Château Grillet—rare because the vineyard is so small that less than 20 barrels of the wine is made each year. The golden wines of Hermitage and Crozes-Hermitage are dry, with a delicate flavor and fragrance. They are long-lasting. A similar white wine is produced at St-Joseph but it is lighter in flavor and body. It matures more quickly and is not as long-lasting. Some excellent *crémants* (sparkling wines) are also produced in the Côtes du Rhône.

Two famous rosés are produced in this area, the Tavel and the Lirac. The Tavel is made mostly from the Grenache grape and is orange-pink in color. The flavor is generous, the body medium and the fragrance quite fruity. Lirac rosé is lighter in body and not as well known. It is also primarily made from the Grenache grape, has a similar color and about the same high alcoholic content. While the Tavel is almost as well known as the rosé of Anjou, the Lirac is not, although it deserves to be. Some good rosés are found under the regional appellation of Côtes du Rhône.

If a wine cannot qualify for a more specific appellation, it can be labeled "Côtes du Rhône." Those wines with "Côtes du Rhône Villages" or "Côtes du Rhône" plus the name of a commune hyphenated to it, such as "Côtes du Rhône-Sabon," are of higher quality than those labeled Côtes du Rhône.

Châteauneuf-du-Pape. Châteauneuf-du-Pape is perhaps the most famous of the Côtes du Rhône wines, with a long and distinguished history. In 1305, Clement V became Pope and was pressured into making his residence at Avignon in France instead of the Vatican. A summer castle was built just north of Avignon for him and was called Châteauneuf-du-Pape (new castle of the Pope). Grapes were planted for him, and soon wines of considerable elegance were produced. Today this vineyard is still considered one of France's finest. Its reds are intensely Côte du Rhône in character but more pungent, vigorous, and deeper flavored than others. The Syrrah, Grenache, and Clairette grapes are predominant, but others may also be used. AC has authorized 13 different grapes that can be used for wines bearing the Châteauneuf-du-Pape label. Even some white grapes can be used to reduce the intensity of the Syrrah grape must.

The vineyard of the Châteanueuf-du-Pape's soil is made up of a lot of gravel and large stones. In the summer sun these stones absorb a lot of heat which is radiated back to the vines and causes the grapes to develop a large quantity of sugar. Because of this, the AC set the highest alcohol requirement for any wine in France—12.5%. This, with the high tannin and acid content, gives a wine that matures slowly but holds its age for a long time, being best at five to 10 years. In good years this vineyard produces as much as 100,000 hectoliters of wine.

Germany

Only five of the 11 designated wine-growing areas of Germany produce wines that are found commonly in the United States: these are the

Exhibit 16.12   The 11 Qualitätswein Regions of Germany

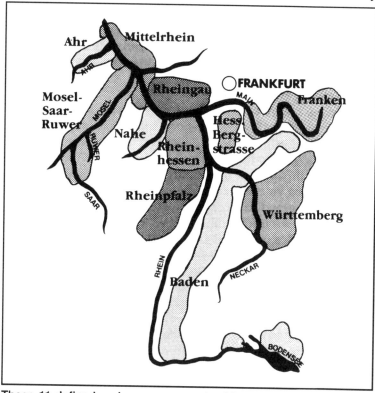

**These 11 defined regions are recognized by statutory regulation as
specially defined quality wine-growing regions.** (Courtesy of the German Wine Institute)

wines of the regions of Mosel-Saar-Ruwer, Rheingau, Rheinhessen (Hes-
sen), Rheinpfalz (Palatinate), and Nahe. These five are grouped together
in the central Rhine River area (see Exhibit 16.12).

Mosel-Saar-Ruwer

The soil of the Mosel-Saar-Ruwer region is high in slate and stones which
capture heat in the day and lose it slowly during the night. The great Riesling
grape predominates in this region, producing excellent wines of light alcoholic content (8% to 10%), with light, crisp body, and a dry, fragrant flavor.

The best wines come from middle Mosel areas such as Piesport,
Bernkastel, Zeltingen, and Erdener Treppchen. As is true with other wine-
producing regions, a famous name can increase price, often over the true
wine value; a wine of equal or almost equal quality produced in a nearby
vineyard may sell for much less.

Rheingau

The Rheingau area is northwest of the Rhine River bend as it moves
toward Koblenz and includes the adjoining west bank of the Main River,
where it flows into the Rhine. The wines come in tall, slim, brown bottles.
Rheingau wines are delicate and have a light body and flavor, a fragrant
bouquet, and a brilliant sparkle, but some may be a bit austere and hard.
They are light in alcohol and may vary in quality from year to year, depending on seasonal and climatic conditions. The labels will usually have the

Exhibit 16.13   Zeller Schwartze Katz

The "Black Cat" wines, governmentally regulated proprietary blends (as the QbA on the label indicates), are popular German exports, particularly to the United States.

name of the village or township with the Schloss name or just the name of the vineyard. The best wines of the area usually come from the villages of Eltville, Erbach, Geisenheim, Hallgarten, Hattenheim, Hochheim (the home of Hock), Johannisberg, Kiedrich, Oestrich, Rauenthal, Rüdesheim, and Winkel. The famous Schloss Johannisberg, Schloss Vollrads, Rüdesheimer Schlossberg, Marcobrunn, and Steinberg wines come from this area.

Rheinhessen   The Rheinhessen runs on the other side of the bend of the Rhine River. Its wines are like those of the Rheingau but are a bit softer and richer. They are apt to have a slightly higher alcoholic content and a heavier bouquet and flavor.

The famed proprietary wine called "**Liebfraumilch**" (Milk of the Blessed Mother) was originally a Hessian wine, but today, regulations allow this blended wine to be made in the Rheingau, Rheinhessen, Rheinpfalz, and Nahe. Liebfraumilch is, legally, a QbA from the four regions mentioned and from three grape varieties: Riesling, Sylvaner, and Müller-Thurgau. The name "Liebfraumilch" cannot be on a label larger than the name of the region. The original Liebfraumilch does not carry the name. Instead, it will be sold under the name of one of the famous vineyards—Liebfrauen, Stift, or Kirchenstück—that surround the Church of Our Beloved Lady (*Liebfrauenkirche*) in the city of Worms. The other imitators are apt to be good if they come under the name of a good shipper and from Nierstein, Nackenheim, or Oppenheim, but many poor Liebfraumilchs are marketed in this country.

Exhibit 16.14 A QmP Auslese Wine Label from Nahe

SCHLINK HAUS™

AUSLESE

1983 Bereich Kreuznach · Nahe

Qualitätswein mit Prädikat · Auslese

A. P. Nr. 1 710 077 067 85 - contains sulfites

alc. 8,5% vol.

White Quality Wine - Product of Germany

750 ml

Bottled and shipped by:

net contents

Qualitätsweinkellerei G. Schlink KG, Bad Kreuznach, Germany

Note the relatively low (8.5% by volume) alcohol content; this is characteristic of most types of German wines.

Niersteiner Domtal is another somewhat popular German export, but also may vary considerably in quality.

The best Hessian wines come from near the Rhine and alongside of it and should be made from the Sylvaner or Riesling grape. Buyers should learn the names of towns and *lagennamen* (vineyard names) from which the best wines come, and purchase them.

Rheinpfalz (Palatinate)

South of Hessia is the Rheinpfalz (Palatinate) region where the grapes develop greater sugar content and the resultant wines are not as dry as most German wines. They also tend to be higher in alcohol. The Mittel-Haardt area between Neustadt and Bad Dürkheim produces the best wine, especially around Wachenheim, Forst, Deidesheim, Ruppertsberg, Bad Dürkheim, Kallstadt, Leistadt, and Königsbach. The better wines have a delicate flavor, rich fruitiness, soft bouquet, and great delicacy. They are less crisp and harsh than the Rheingau wines. In good years, many of the *Beerenauslese* and *Trockenbeerenauslese* wines come from here. The poorest wines from this area are coarse, lack flavor, and may taste heavily of soil (described as *bodeneschmack*).

Nahe

Nahe sits between Rheinpfalz and Alsace. Its wines resemble those of the Rheingau but often carry more fruity bouquet and flavor with a somewhat earthy flavor. The best wines will come from the vineyards located in the villages of Bad Kreuznach, Niederhausen an der Nahe, and Schloss Böckelheim (see Exhibits 16.13 and 16.14).

Exhibit 16.15 Eiswein Label

Although this Eiswein is from Germany's southern neighbor, Austria, its grapes are harvested and produced according to the same regulations as German Eiswein and the wine is just as rare.

Schaumwein   An effervescent wine resembling champagne is made by the Germans and, under 1986 regulations, must be made from German grapes. The label will give the name of **Deutscher Sekt**, but in the United States it may be labeled German Sekt. The label should give an A. P. number. Also one may find on the label the letters b. A. which indicates the wine was produced from grapes from the area named on the label. If only *Deutscher Sekt* appears, the grapes may come from any German area. In the past, much of *Sekt* was made from grapes imported from Italy or France. This is still done and the label will indicate this by having on it only the term *Sekt*. Sparkling Hock and sparkling Moselles are prominent among *Sekt* wines. Most German sparkling wines sell at a lower price than French Champagnes. They also tend to be sweeter than their French counterparts.

Eiswein   An unusual German wine called **Eiswein** ("ice wine") is made only under special conditions which do not occur every year (see Exhibit 16.15). In years (and in areas) where the grapes can ripen without a killing frost before some time in November, the grapes are allowed to stay on the vines to develop maximum sugar. When (and if) a hard frost occurs, freezing the grapes on the vine, the grapes are quickly harvested, rushed frozen to the presses, and pressed while frozen.

The ice, which is pure water, is thus removed, leaving a syrup must heavy in sugar and acidity. Only about a third of the normal grape must is obtained. A special fermentation method is used with special yeasts. A succulent, luscious wine of great fragrance and rich flavor results, a wine that vies in quality with *Beerenauslese* or *Trockenbeerenauslese* wine but without the specific flavor of these "noble rot" wines.

Eiswein is both very sweet and very tart. It is the wine of the connoisseur, often accompanying desserts or enjoyed by itself. Because of the special handling that must be given the grapes, the special production methods, and the fact that so little must is obtained, it is very expensive. Also, only in one year in four do favorable conditions exist for its production.

Italy

Italy's wine industry began in earnest when ancient Greeks planted the grape in Sicily. Today Italy both produces and consumes more wine than any other country in Europe. It is sold everywhere. Even cafeterias have automatic wine dispensing machines where one can drop in a coin and get a large glass of wine. It is said, "Stop in a village and ask for a glass of water, and you'll be more apt to have a glass of wine handed to you." The wine is usually safer to drink than the water.

Almost every area in Italy produces wine. The climate is warm and the grapes get plentiful sun during the ripening period. The climate may even be too warm—Sicilian and some other southern red grapes may get so much warmth that the wine is fiery and harsh and must be softened by either using white grapes or using special production methods to moderate the flavor.

The **DOC** (*Denominazione di Origine Controllata*) established 20 wine-producing regions in Italy; of these the Piedmont, Lombardy, Veneto, Tuscany and Latium are considered the major areas because of either the amount of wine produced or its excellence (see Exhibit 16.16). The following is a short summary of the main wine producing DOC regions:

Piedmont

The Piedmont region in northwest Italy descends from the Alps down into the fertile Po River plain. The main wine producing area is in the Hills of Monferrato, where grapes have been cultivated since ancient times. The Piedmont is known for its great red wines, but also produces a number of excellent whites. The famous Asti Spumante, Italy's answer to Champagne, comes from this region.

One of the best Piedmont reds is the Barolo, a DOCG (*Denominazione di Origine Controllata e Garantita*) wine, made from the Nebbiolo grape. The wine is ruby red in color with amber lights; it is dry, smooth and velvety in taste, carrying to some tasters the perfume of violet and the taste of roses. It is full-bodied and, when aged six to 20 years, is at its best. It does, however cast considerable sediment and often has to be decanted before it is consumed. Two consortiums making dependable Barolo attach their symbols on the bottle necks: one showing a golden lion and the other a helmeted head.

Barbaresco, another DOCG wine, is a rival of Barolo as the best red of the area; it has more smoothness and ages more quickly, but keeps well.

Exhibit 16.16 Italian DOC Wine Regions

Italian DOC Wine Regions
1. Valle d'Aosta
2. Piedmont
3. Lombardy
4. Liguria
5. Emilia-Romagna
6. Trentino Alto Adige
7. Veneto
8. Fruili-Venezia Giulia
9. Tuscany
10. Umbria
11. Marches
12. Abruzzi
13. Molise
14. Latium (Lazio)
15. Campania
16. Apulia (Puglia)
17. Basilicata
18. Calabria
19. Sicily
20. Sardinia

It is best when aged six to 15 years. The consortium that makes the wine has its symbol on the neck of the bottle showing Barbaresco's ancient tower in gold against a blue background. Both Barolo and Barbaresco must be over 12.5% in alcohol.

Other highly respected Piedmont wines are:

- Barbera wines: Barbera d'Alba, Barbera d'Asti, Barbera del Costi Tortonesi, and Barbera del Monterro—all DOC wines.

- Dolcetto wines: Dolcetto d'Aqui, Dolcetto d'Asti, and Dolcetto d'Alba.

- Freisa di Chieri and Freisa d'Asti come from the Freisa grape of Chieri and parts of the provinces of Alessandria, Asti, and Cuneo.

- The Nebbiolo d'Alba has a pleasant bouquet and taste. It can be sweet or dry and is a good keeper.

- Asti Spumante, the "champagne" of Italy, carries with it the typical, rich, delicate flavor of the Muscat grape.

- The Vermouth of Turin (Torino or Gran Torino) is famous as an aromatic aperitif wine. It is light golden yellow or dark orange in color with a brilliant shine.

Lombardy   The wines of Lombardy are well regarded: the area produces a number of DOC wines.

Valtellina wines, coming from the mountainsides near the city, along the shores of Lake Garda, or on the hillsides of southern Lombardy, are highly regarded. Some of the better known Lombardy wines are:

- The bright ruby red, dry, smooth, and harmoniously flavored Sassella from the vineyards around the old church near Sondrio.

- Sfursat or Sforzato is made from the Nebbiolo grapes also, but some are dried until December which helps to make a wine about 14.5% in alcoholic content. It is rich, deep and somewhat bitter in flavor; it has a heavy bouquet.

The Brescia area produces two wines that have received the DOC rating: the Riviera del Garda Bresciano Chiaretto, a rosé, and the Lugana, a white. Both are best consumed young.

Veneto   Many fine wines come from Veneto, especially those from the dusky volcanic hillsides of Verona, the hillsides of Valdobbiandene flanking Monte Grappa, and the hills of Conegliano in the province of Reviso.

The best known white wine from the vineyards around the city of Verona is the DOC Soave, but the Bianco di Custoza, Gambellara and Verduzzo del Piave are also DOC-listed white wines. Soave has a light straw color with greenish highlights, a delicate, fruity, characteristic bouquet, and a dry, suitably acidic, exquisitely bitter, well-balanced flavor.

Verona's two DOC reds are the world-renowned Bardolino and Valpolicella. Both have a delicate, characteristic bouquet and smooth, velvety, dry, slightly bitter flavor, and are light in body. Neither requires much aging; they are best consumed young.

Wines labeled *Recioto* are higher in alcohol and may have just a touch of sweetness. (*Recie* means "ears" which refers, in this case, to the fact that only projecting grapes that are on the outside of a bunch and usually at the top are selected for such wines.) Recioto Veronese has a deep garnet red color, a delicate bouquet, and sweet, velvety, attractive flavor. It has a strong full body that makes it a good dessert wine.

Amarone has a dark, ruby color, a rich bouquet and a velvety, spicy flavor touched with raisins. It should be aged 10 or more years. Prosecco di Conegliano comes from the Treviso Hills. It has a brilliant sparkling golden color and a dry, prickly taste; its tannins give it a slightly bitter taste.

Emilia-Romagna

A number of the best wines of this region are made entirely or for the most part from the Lambrusco grape; they usually carry the grape name on the label. Many are *frizzantes* (slightly sparkling) and some may even be fully sparkling wines (**spumantes**). Three of the Lambruscos have DOC ratings: Lambrusco di Sorbara from the area of Sorbara and Bomporto, a light bodied, brilliant, ruby red wine with characteristic dry or semi-sweet, slightly tart, fresh and fruity flavor; Lambrusco Reggiano from the Reggiano area; and Lambrusco Grasparossa di Castelvetro. Other DOC's are Trebbiano di Romagna (white), Gutturnio (red), and Sangiovese di Romagna (red) from the Hills of Romagna where wines of slightly higher alcoholic content than the other Emilia-Romagna areas are produced. Sangiovese di Romagna is a light garnet red, with a delicate bouquet and slightly bitter, dry flavor. Aging improves its qualities and bouquet. Albana di Romagna (white) has recently been given the rare DOCG rating.

Tuscany

Florence and Sienna are the main cities in this region, a region famous for Chianti, Brunello di Montalcino, and Vino Nobile di Montepulciano. The three Communes of the ancient League of Chianti, along with some neighboring districts, make what is called Chianti Classico (*classico* is the DOC designation reserved for the area which produces the best wine within a DOC-defined region). Chianti Classico is identified by either a neck label showing a white Della Robbia angel (*putto*) or one showing a black and gold seal with a black cock inside.

The first Chianti was made by using red grapes with some whites added to soften the somewhat harsh, tannic flavor and rich body produced by a wine made only of reds. Today DOC-approved Chianti must also be made of 10% white grapes, but many Chianti-like wines are being introduced which are made from all red grapes. A wine made by the famous Antinori family called *Tignanello* is made up of 90% Sangiovese and 10% Cabernet Sauvignon instead of the obligatory white wine. Such wines cannot legally be labeled Chianti.

Chianti has a bright, lively ruby red color, varying in hue and depth according to type. The bouquet is pleasant and the flavor is dry, strong, smooth, velvety and well-balanced. Some Chiantis are best consumed when young; others age well. The best Chiantis are not marketed in the straw-covered flasks but in bottles shaped like Bordeaux wine bottles.

Brunello is a full-bodied, fragrant wine that ages very well—in fact it is best consumed after four to six years of aging.

Other DOC's of the region are:

- Vin Santo—a sweet wine of high alcoholic content made somewhat like sherry and tastes somewhat like it

- Galestro—a delicate white with a distinctive aroma

- Bianco Toscano—a white dry wine of light body and delicate fruity fragrance

Latium (or Lazio)

Latium or Lazio is in south Umbria, the parts surrounding Rome. It is known best for its whites, among which are DOCs like Trebbiano di Aprilla, sweet or dry Frascati, Colli Albani, and Marino. Some good non-DOCs are found bottled under the label of Castelli Romani. Castelli Romani is one of many Italian winemakers who refuse to be restricted by DOC regulations which, they believe, would keep them from making higher quality wines. This region is also the home of the famous Est! Est!! Est!!! This wine got its name when the Bishop Baron Johannes de Fugger of Germany was on his way to Rome and sent his valet ahead to check the wines at di Montefiascone where they were to stay the night. They had heard that the wines there were of great excellence and when the valet tasted a wine served to him, he is reputed to have exclaimed: "Est! Est!! Est!!!" ("It is!"). Evidently the bishop also found it so, because tradition has it that he came to Montefiascone to live and finally died from overindulging in the wine. Today's version is a golden wine with a rich, delightful, fruity bouquet and a pleasing, slightly bitter flavor.

Sicily   The warm climate and bright sunshine of Sicily produces grapes with good sugar, acidity, and other desirable wine properties. Its most famous wine is **Marsala**, which is amber in color, varying in intensity, with a penetrating, characteristic bouquet and a rich, full, warm, velvety taste. It is sweet and an outstanding dessert wine. Long aging gives it finesse and refinement. Marsala contains from 5% to 10% sugar and about 18% alcohol. "Aromatic" Marsala is a Marsala clarified with eggs and almonds or other ingredients added for additional flavor. The following terms refer to the amount of aging the wine gets:

- **Fine**—moderately aged

- **Superior dry** or **Superior sweet**—well-aged

- **Virgin** or **Soleras**—very old

Corvino (Corvo) is from white grapes grown on Mt. Etna's slopes—a fine, dry, white with a somewhat fiery character. A good red, and a sparkling white may also bear this name on the label. Some others of Sicily's best DOCs include Bianco di Alcamo and two reds, Cerasuolo di Vittoria and Etna Rosato.

Spain

Spanish wines have grown in quality over the past 30 years and, today, many have acquired a solid international reputation. In 1972 Spain set up its Instituto de Denominaciones de Origen (INDO) which established 28 wine-producing regions (see Exhibit 16.17). INDO confers the Denominación de Origen (DO) on wines which meet its regulations—regulations which are much like those of the French AC system. Spain has more acreage in vines than Italy but only a third of its production—only 20 hectoliters harvest per hectare—less than half of what France allows for her finest wines!

Another prominent difference between the wine industry in Spain and France is that the wine producers, the powerful bodegas, are generally more important than vineyards or estates. They buy the best grapes from local farmers to supplement the grapes they grow themselves. Estate bottling (estates which produce all the grapes and bottle their own production) is not a factor. Only one vineyard is featured on all the sherries made in Spain. And only one estate, Castillo Ygay, is prominent in Rioja.

Exhibit 16.17 The Winemaking Areas of Spain

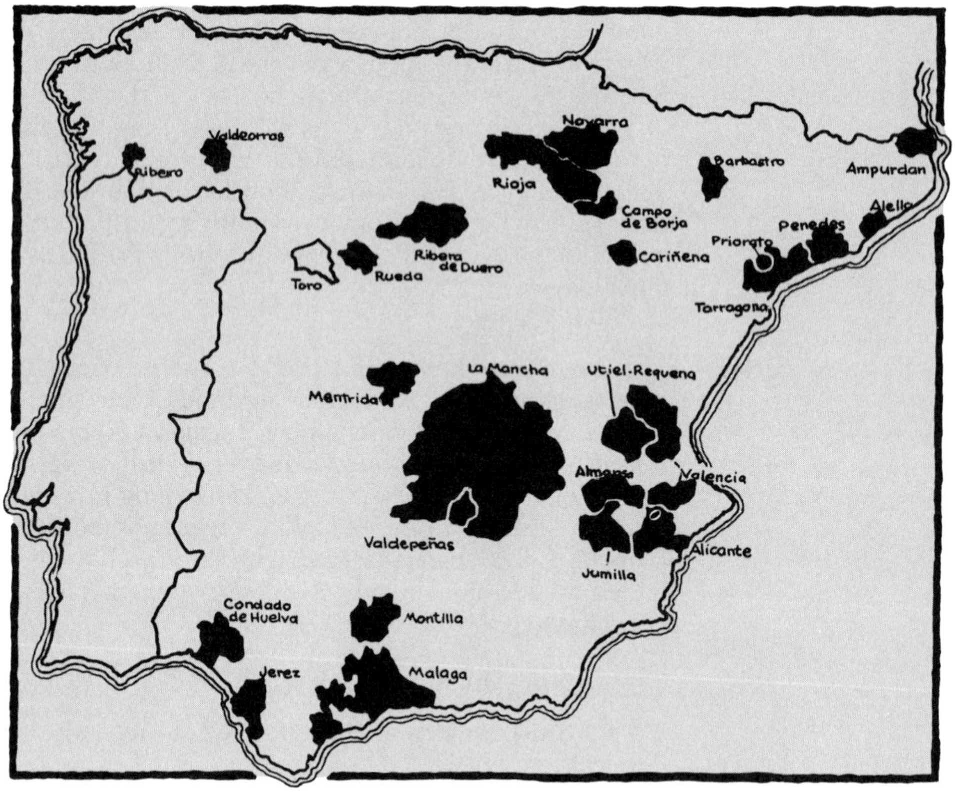

Courtesy of *The Wines of Spain* (prepared by the Instituto Nacional de Fomento de la Exportación)

One of the main growing regions is Rioja, about 200 miles southwest of Bordeaux. In fact, Rioja wines are often favorably compared to those of Bordeaux and Burgundy. Rioja has three growing areas: Rioja Alta, over 2000 feet above sea level, Rioja Alavesa, about 1500 feet above sea level, and Rioja Baja, around 1000 feet high. Alta and Alavesa's wines are usually those exported; Baja's wines are a bit harsher, higher in alcohol, and mostly for local consumption. All the Rioja areas have much sun and warmth during the growing season, so the grapes develop considerable sugar, resulting in wines of fairly high alcohol content.

The red Riojas will be full bodied, balanced in acid with a rich, full flavor, fruity bouquet, and fairly high tannin content. Some are apt to be fiery. The reds are basically of two types: a *tinto* which may be considered Spain's answer to a Burgundy-type wine—deep, full red in color, with a heavy body and full flavor; the other kind is a *rioja* which is lighter in body and flavor and might be compared to a Beaujolais, only heavier in body and flavor.

The whites will also have a rich, fruity bouquet, high alcohol content and rich, full flavor, but are less likely to have some of the harshness sometimes displayed by the reds.

Another region producing good quality wines is Catalonia, especially around the area of Penedés, near Barcelona. The winemaker of note here is Bodega Torres, operated by the Torres family for over three centuries, but fully modernized with stainless steel fermenting vats, and planting non-traditional grapes such as the Pinot Noir, Cabernet, Chardonnay, and Gewürztraminer. Its reds age well, carrying a good balance of acid-tannin-alcohol. They are heavy in body and full in flavor with a velvety feel in the mouth. Their Gran Coronas Black Label is pure Cabernet and carries a fruity bouquet reminiscent of blackberries.

Fermentation in Spain still takes place in clay *tinajas*, but the industry is rapidly converting to stainless steel vats. The finest reds are aged in new oak casks made of American oak, while whites are aged in stainless steel tanks. A wine labeled *reserva* must be aged at least a year in the cask or vat and then two more years in the bottle. If labeled *gran reserva*, it must be aged two years in a cask or vat and bottle-aged for three before being sold. Vintage and release dates are usually given.

Sherry   Spain's most famous wine is sherry, production of which is limited by INDO to Jerez de la Frontera. Originally the town under the Phoenicians was called Xeira, but the Romans changed it to Ceret and the Moors to Scheris, which the Spanish then changed to Jerez and the English mispronounced "sherry." The English got into the act as the most avid importers of this distinctive Spanish wine since the 18th century. Only wine of Spanish origin can truly be labeled sherry; all the imitators must mention the place of origin on the label, such as California sherry.

The first pressing only of the Palomino grape is kept for fermentation in new oak barrels; the other pressing (about 15%) is fermented and distilled into brandy which is used after fermentation to fortify (increase the alcohol content to 15%–18%) the wine.

Aging is accomplished by the *solera* system, an elaborate blending of sherries of similar character according to individual bodega formulas and guided by Spanish law. Rows of casks are stacked in tiers—usually ten tiers maximum and three, minimum. The casks are outside so they are exposed to the full effects of the Spanish sun and warmth. After sufficient aging, sherry from the bottom casks is removed for bottling and wine from the next higher tier is added to the bottom casks, wine from the third tier added to fill up the second tiers, and so on, with new wine topping off the casks in the highest tier. By law, only 33% can be removed from the bottom cask each year. Because there are fewer casks as the tiers go up, more than 33% is removed from the upper tiers, so casks in the top tier will often require about 80% new wine to be completely filled.

Casks are also not tightly bunged so air can enter, encouraging the growth of *flor*, a thin, yeasty, whitish film that forms over the wine, slowing the process of oxidation and helping to give sherry its typical flavor. The longer the sherry remains in contact with the *flor*, the finer the sherry. These finer sherries are, in fact, called *finos*. Some heavier sherries, however, develop little or no *flor* (or are given a stronger dose of fortifying spirit which discourages *flor*) and produce *oloroso* type sherries. A third, rare class of sherry—*palo cortado*—combines the depth and body of an *oloroso* with the finesse of a *fino*.

All sherries are fermented dry, i.e., all the grape sugar is turned into alcohol during fermentation. While coloring sometimes takes place after aging (with a tasteless, blackish wine called *vino de color*), aging in wood darkens color. All sherries come from the cask dry at 13% to 14% alcohol but are sweetened, made deeper in color, or given a higher alcohol content by addition.

Sherry is sweetened by the addition of a heavy grape syrup or *dulce*, a sweetening wine often made from the sweet Muscat grape especially for blending. Alcohol can be increased to 15%, even over 20%, by adding brandy made from the last pressings of grapes.

Beyond solera blending, most sherry is also a further blend of finos, olorosos, coloring, sweeteners, sometimes a little unaged, young wine for freshness, and extremely old, wood-aged sherry used as a flavoring agent. The particular blending formulas not only create the *Amontillados* and cream sherries, but produce the distinctive taste associated with a particular bodega or brand.

The following classifies sherries according to their dryness or sweetness:

Manzanilla	Pale and light bodied; somewhat acid and salty flavor; very dry, fine sherry
Fino	Very pale color; more body but less dry than Manzanillas; light body; distinctive, soft nutty flavor
Amontillado	Dry, golden color with fuller body than finos
Amoroso	Golden to light amber; medium dry; some body
Oloroso	Amber to light brown or tan color; full body; sweet; full, well-balanced, nutty flavor; delicate, rich aroma
Cream	Deep tan to brown; full body; rich, full flavor; very sweet; rich bouquet

Portugal

Portugal was actually the first nation to regulate its wine industry, creating something very much like the French system 25 years before the first French *appellation contrôlée* system went into effect in the mid-19th century. However, control was allowed to lapse and until very recently, one had to look to the brand name of a bottler as the sole indication of quality. Common market (EEC) regulations have probably helped to change that situation, and today, areas of production have been redefined and production regulated by a *Denominação de origem* system. The system requires that all exports bear the government seal of guarantee (*selo de garantia*). The term *reserva* indicates a high quality, aged wine from a good harvest. The term *garrafeira* indicates that the wine is the merchant's best—a cut above a *reserva*, aged in the bottle as well as the barrel. Some of the more well-known exporters of *garrafeira* wines are: Aliança, Arealva, Aveleda, Garcia, Gatao, Gazela, Mesa do Presidente, and Ouro do Minho.

Wines are either *verde* (young) or *maduro* (mature). Most of Portugal's wine is produced in the northern part of the country, known as the Minho, where the wine known as *vinho verde* (literally, "green wine") is made—the "green" refers to the youth of the wine and not its color. The whites are a pale lemon color and the reds, a light ruby. The wine is clean, crisp and refreshing with a slight spritz or fizziness.

Dão is the biggest and most prosperous producer of *vinho maduro* wines. It also produces some excellent fruity, medium-bodied reds, that are smooth and soft to drink even though young. Some very good dry whites also come from the region.

Bucelas produces crisp, dry reds with a fairly high tartness. Bairrada makes excellent rich, dark, full-bodied and full-flavored reds which are high in alcohol. Its whites are delicate, moderate in body, with just a touch of sweetness or the sensation of it.

Colares produces a small amount of some excellent wines. The Algarve in south Portugal and the Carcavelos both produce respectable wines but they must be selected carefully.

Port

Portugal's most famous wine is **port**, as it is known in English or *porto*, as it is known in other countries. It is one of the original trinity of great processed wines which includes champagne and sherry. Port is something of a political creation as it came out of the late 18th century when the British were looking for alternatives to French wine. They found ideal growing conditions in the fertile Douro valley. When the product of the Douro became the sweet, fortified wine we know today in the mid-19th century, it became a favorite throughout the world, but especialy in Great Britain.

Today port is one of the most strictly regulated of all wines—every stage of its production is overseen and controlled. In a few places, crushing is still accomplished by bare feet; however, new crushing machinery is now commonplace. Fermentation takes place in closed concrete tanks where natural carbon dioxide keeps bubbling up, breaking up the cap, and causing the juice to churn in contact with the skins.

When fermentation has reached the stage where half the sugar has been used up, the partially fermented juice is poured into a barrel containing one-fourth brandy. Fermentation stops immediately upon contact with the brandy as the alcohol kills the remaining yeast cells. Port ends up at 18% to 22% alcohol. After it is racked off its gross lees, port is moved to shippers' lodges where it is stored, aged, and blended much like sherry. Barrel aging must be for at least three years; what is called "vintage" port can be wood-aged two years, but must be bottle-aged for many more.

A ruby port is the youngest port; a tawny port is so called because aging for a long time (six to eight years) in the barrels causes a degeneration of the red pigments which turn a brownish purple.

The ultimate port—a vintage port—is not blended but produced from the grapes of an exceptionally good year. About three out of ten years qualify. As mentioned above, vintage port is only aged in the barrel for two years; its significant aging takes place in the bottle where it must be aged 15 to 20 years, but many shippers won't put it on the market until it is at least 25 years old. The wine needs many years of bottle aging to reduce its harshness; adding many more years serves to make it, at its best, one of the world's great wines.

In this impatient age, the slow bottle aging process is often replaced by late bottling. Late bottled vintages ("LBVs" or just "Vs") are aged in the barrel for six years before bottling and are ready to drink much sooner than the vintage ports. Some quality ruby ports which come from close to vintage years are aged for four or five years in the cask and are ready to drink when bottled; these ports are referred to as "vintage character" or "vintage reserve."

Some authorities claim that the greatest wine of Portugal is not port, but Moscatel de Setúbal, rated along with some of the greatest dessert wines of the world as "out of this world." It is made from Muscat grapes and is less fortified than port. It is excellent both young and aged.

Perhaps Portugal's greatest world-wide marketing success was created by Mateus with its semi-sweet, semi-sparkling rosé. The phenomenal success of Mateus led to many other companies producing similar wines. The rosés are made from grapes anywhere in Portugal and made much like rosés anywhere with the red skins in contact with the fermenting must for only a short time. Fermentation is stopped by sulfur dioxide with about 18 grams per liter of original grape sugar unfermented. The wine is blended for consistency and bottled under carbon dioxide pressure for the semi-sparkling effect. Some critics have derisively referred to Mateus rosé as "Portugal's answer to Coca-Cola."

The United States

The first wine in the United States is thought to have been made from Scuppernong grapes by the Huguenots in Florida in 1564. Records also show that missionaries were making sacramental wine in New Mexico in 1609. The first commercial winery was built in 1793. California's wine industry began around 1824. Today there are over a thousand wineries in 40 states.

California has led all other states in the amount of wine produced, in varieties of wine, and in developing a major industry in winemaking. Its wines are of the highest quality and compete with the best in the world. It has over 350,000 acres planted with grapes and produces over 400 million gallons a year, which is 70% of total U.S. production. It is fortunate in having a climate and soil that furthers grape growth.

The climate has historically been consistent year after year and there is adequate rainfall, or, if not, adequate water for irrigation purposes. The climate is usually so reliable and the production of sugar in grapes so consistent that chaptalization is forbidden in California. However, the drought which began in 1985 and continued through the writing of this text may bring changes to the industry.

New York is another state in which wine making had early beginnings. Early colonists found an abundance of grapes suitable for winemaking there and, while some grapes produced fair wines, others did not. Over the years, growers created hybrids and developed clones from the native varieties that made a better product. Today, many New York wines are considered high quality. Although second in wine production in the United States, New York is fast being overtaken by the State of Washington.

While the State of Washington has only begun to seriously produce wine, it is now a factor in the U.S. wine industry. Vineyards existed before the 1900s but not until about 1960 was it realized that the *Vitis vinifera* grew extremely well there. The Yakima Valley and the Columbia River Basin are the main producing areas, with many of the wineries located in the Seattle area. Washington's summers and summer days are long and although there is usually adequate rainfall, most vineyards are irrigated.

The nights are cool. This favors the growth of grapes such as Rieslings, Gewürztraminer, Müller-Thurgau, Chardonnay and others that make good whites.

Oregon is another serious but small producer of wines. Its climate is slightly milder than Washington's but rather similar otherwise. While Oregon has been making wines for a long time, it is not until recently that it has seriously entered into such making and, while what it produces is respectable, one looks more to the future than to the present on what Oregon's contribution will be to the wine industry.

Other areas where wine is produced or where there is a promise of developing some significance are: Virginia, Maryland, Pennsylvania, West Virginia, Kentucky, Massachusetts, Georgia, Tennessee, Ohio, Michigan, Missouri, Arkansas, Texas, Arizona, and New Mexico.

California

California has a variety of climates, from the desert south to the northern coastal regions near San Francisco (see Exhibit 16.18). Wine grapes do well in almost all of California's climatic conditions, but the best wines grow in the famed Napa Valley, where cool nights and morning fog ameliorate the hot summer days and keep the many grape varieties from ripening too soon. Following is a discussion of the main grape varieties grown in California. It should be noted, however, that most California wines are blends of different grape varieties. By law, a named varietal need only make up 75% of the grapes used in that wine, and some of California's best wines are not varietals, but blends.

Main Grape Varieties (Red). The Cabernet Sauvignon grape prospers in California and it is that state's most widely grown grape. It is partial, however, to Napa Valley where it is the primary grape used in the production of a red claret-type wine that rivals those of Bordeaux. It develops a complex flavor of cedar, cassis, and black currants and produces a wine that is balanced in tannins and acid, is full-bodied, and ages into a smooth, brilliant, deep ruby red with a very fragrant bouquet. The best Cabernets are aged in American, French, or Yugoslavian oak barrels, with much discussion about the merits of the taste characteristics of each.

The Zinfandel is another popular red grape variety in California. The grape is a sort of bastard since no one knows its parentage. Some think it derives from a spore from the Italian Primitivo grape that was brought to California. It makes a light and fruity red somewhat like a Beaujolais, a more intense, heavier-bodied and complex red, a delicate, spicy rosé, or a nearly-white wine. All wines made from it carry the typical spicy, raspberry flavor and aroma.

The Merlot grape was originally brought to California to be used in blending, especially with the musts of the Cabernet Sauvignon. But by using the carbonic maceration method described in Chapter 15, a refreshing, well-balanced red with mouth-filling roundness and softness was produced that made it a wine of its own and worthy of bottling. Many say it is much like the wines of the Pomerol in Bordeaux.

The Pinot Noir grape is not too well suited to California's climate, but it does well in certain areas, especially Carneros. It makes a full-bodied, full-flavored red that has a cherry-like aroma and flavor and a silky, satiny,

Exhibit 16.18. The Wine Districts of California

Wine Districts of California

A. Sonoma-Mendocino
B. Napa Valley-Solano
C. Lodi-Sacramento
D. Livermore-Contra Costa
E. Escalon-Modesto in the north portion, Fresno-San Joaquin Valley in the south portion.
F. Santa Clara-San Benito-Santa Cruz
G. Southern California

Courtesy of the U.S. Department of Agriculture

almost oily feel in the mouth. It is the grape used to make the generic wine called Burgundy.

The Gamay and Gamay Beaujolais are used to make a light-bodied, refreshing, fruity wine. The Gamay makes a slightly heavier-bodied wine than the Gamay Beaujolais. Both are used to make good rosés.

The Petite Sirah grape makes a wine of rich, deep red color, with good body and a fresh, spicy, berry-like flavor and aroma. Because it is well-balanced with acid and tannins, the wine ages very well.

The Barbera grape is used more for blending (to provide a good natural acidity to red table wines) than as a varietal wine. However, some Barbera wines are marketed which have a medium to dark color, with a fruity taste and a natural tartness that gives a zestful quality to the wine.

Main Grape Varieties (White). California makes a large quantity of high quality white wines but, with the heavier market demand today for these, producers are moving to step up production even more. The best white and most white wine produced comes from the Chardonnay grape that does well in many places in California, but loves the Alexander Valley. One excellent Chardonnay varietal wine is made by fermenting in stainless steel to obtain the luscious, crisp, apple aroma and flavor, and then aging

Exhibit 16.19 A California Johannisberg Riesling Label

1988
Napa Valley
JOHANNISBERG RIESLING
ALCOHOL 10.5% BY VOLUME

PRODUCED AND BOTTLED BY
ROBERT MONDAVI WINERY
OAKVILLE, CALIFORNIA

Robert Mondavi was one of the first to produce a quality wine from this imported Germany grape variety.

in small oak barrels to develop greater complexity of flavor. A quite different Chardonnay results when the fermentation takes place in a barrel and the fermentation process is continued over a long time. The flavor of wine produced by this process is complex and considered by some the more desirable of the two processes. The California Chardonnays hold their flavor for about six to seven years.

The Chenin Blanc grape makes a wine that is light, delicate, slightly acidic and fruity with a hint of melon in its aftertaste. A dry Chenin Blanc that is given oak-cask aging makes a good table wine, while a slightly sweeter version is served as a refreshment wine.

The Sauvignon Blanc is perhaps California's second most popular white varietal wine. Sometimes it is identified on labels as Fumé Blanc. The wine has great depth with a full, lively, peppery, fruity flavor. A blend with the Sémillon grape is also popular.

The Johannisberg Riesling, sometimes called the White Riesling, does well in California making a delicate, light, slightly tart and slightly sweet, zestful white that is touched with a hint of spring flowers and autumn peaches (see Exhibit 16.19). It can be left to develop the "noble rot" to make a sweet, full-bodied, full-flavored, high alcohol wine reminiscent of the German *Spätlese* or *Auslese*. The label will note "late harvest" or "selected late harvest."

California vintners have developed a variety of the Gewürztraminer grape that has a fruity, flowery, spicy aroma and flavor with a touch of sweetness. It is delicate and light as is typical of the wines made from this grape.

The French Colombard is a grape grown in France primarily to produce cognac. California's vintners have been able to take this grape and make from it a fresh, fruity light- to medium-bodied wine with a slight bit of sweetness balanced by acidity.

The Pinot Blanc grape is used to make unique, dry, crisp, delicate, medium-bodied wines and heavier, oak-aged wines. It is also used to make California champagne.

California's vintners make their rosés by cold fermentation to preserve the freshness and fruitiness of the grape. Many different grape varieties are used for rosés. They can vary from a dry, crisp wine to a slightly sweet one. The Zinfandel and the Gamay grapes are used to make a popular wine called the pink rosé (or, sometimes, Zinfandel white or Gamay white). The distinct character of the grape comes through, giving a pleasant, wholesome wine.

California makes its champagne by the four methods, the traditional champagne method, the bulk fermentation (Charmat) process, the transfer process, and forced carbonation for the lower-priced ones. The traditional grapes of the French Champagne are often used—Pinot Noir and Chardonnay—but other grape varieties such as the Pinot Blanc noted above are also used.

Vintages. Europe's climate is such that the quality of the harvest (and the subsequent wine production) can vary greatly in quality from year to year and from growing region to growing region. This gave rise to the labeling of "vintage year" and the development of quality evaluations of the different regional wines according to their quality for that year. California's remarkably consistent climate, however, produces grapes of about equal ripeness year after year; vintage labeling thus does not convey such crucial information about quality.

California uses vintage labeling more to indicate wines of special character and style. Thus, many vintners chose to give the Zinfandels and Cabernet Sauvignons of 1979 vintage designation because of their refined, medium-intense style, while the same wines were also selected for vintage designation in 1980 and 1982, because the wines of that year were fuller-bodied with more flavor depth than some years. However, it must also be said that knowing how old a wine is is important information, whether a Chenin Blanc is getting a little long in the tooth or a Pinot Noir or Cabernet varietal could use a few more years bottle-aging to achieve the same kind of balance as their French counterparts.

Growing Regions. California's wine-growing regions are usually divided into four major areas: the North coast, consisting of Mendocino County, Lake County, Napa Valley, and Sonoma County; the North-Central coast, consisting of Livermore, Santa Clara and Monterey Counties; the South-Central coast, consisting of San Luis Obispo and Santa Barbara; and the Central Valley, another way of referring to the San Joaquin Valley.

While Mendocino County is the most northern of these growing areas, it is not necessarily the coldest; some excellent wines such as the full-bodied reds are made from the Cabernet, Pinot Noir, Zinfandel, and Petite Sirah grapes. Some of the better known wineries are Parducci, Fetzer, Cresta Blanca and Weibel.

Lake County gets its name from Clear Lake which lies within its boundaries; the best vineyards are located near the lake. Lake County is not particularly known for its fine wines, but the famous Guenoc vineyard, currently the only vineyard given an AVA (American Viticulture Area) designation, is located here.

Napa Valley has a large number of famous wineries such as Stony Hill, Chappellet, Schramsberg, Clos du Val, Stag's Leap, Robert Mondavi, Inglenook, Louis M. Martini, Beaulieu, Beringer, Charles Krug, Freemark Abbey, and Sterling. Wines of almost any kind are produced with the major emphasis on wines made from the Cabernet Sauvignon grape. The Napa Valley is so well thought of as an ideal vineyard location, that Moët and Chandon located their Domaine Chandon winery there in 1973, producing an excellent California champagne. Mumm's of Rheims followed by locating its winery there.

Sonoma County is known for both its whites and its reds. The Cabernets of Kenwood Winery are highly respected. The Chardonnay of Château St. Jean has a similar reputation. The Sebastiani winery is located there, and one of its wines is an especially good Barbera. Los Carneros ("The Sheep Place"), a good wine producer, straddles Napa and Sonoma County, and therefore, wines from its wineries may use the name of Sonoma County, Napa Valley, or Los Carneros on the label as the area of production. The Pinot Noir grape does well there as does the Chardonnay; wines from these two grape varieties are especially good from this area.

The Livermore area is best known for its whites; the Wente Brothers and Concannon vineyards are located there. The high-gravel slopes drain into the east side of San Francisco Bay. Much of the land of this area has been taken out of grape production and sold for home sites. If this trend continues, some wonderful dry, crisp whites, as well as sweet whites, will disappear from the market.

Santa Cruz, Santa Clara, and Monterey Counties lie south of San Francisco Bay. Famous vineyards such as Mirassou, Almadén, Jekel, Taylor, Paul Masson, and Martin Rey are located there.

The San Joaquin Valley produces 80% of California's wine. It is a huge area, 400 miles long, fertile, and flat, and a producer not only of wine grapes, but grapes for raisins and table grapes. Grapes like the Emerald Riesling and the Ruby Cabernet do well in the hot, dry summers. The huge Gallo vineyards and winery (Gallo accounts for one out of every three bottles of California wine production) are located there. Still wholly owned by the Gallo brothers, Ernest and Julio, Gallo also buys grapes from all over the state, particularly the types of grapes that do not do so well in the warm valley vineyards. Two other huge wine corporations—Guild with its Tavola and Winemaster brands and ISC with its Colony, Italian Swiss Colony, Petri Lejon, and Jacques Bonet brands—are located in the San Joaquin Valley. Another large winery, Franzia, is also located there.

The San Joaquin Valley not only grows grapes for its own production but it grows grapes for many other wineries in the state and even ships out of the state. The northern part of the valley near Sacramento is noted for producing the best quality wine of the area. Some respected wines come from the vineyards around Madera such as Almadén, Papagni, Fixin and Quady.

Certain areas of southern California are too warm to produce anything but some very good dessert wines and some fair table wines. Wineries like Brookside, Rancho California (Temecula), Callaway, and San Pasqual have good reputations. In table wines, whites rather than reds are the better wines.

Most of California's sherries are not made by the traditional *solera* method. Instead, they are heated to 140° F (60° C) to give them a nutty, sherry-like flavor and deepened color. However, some sherries are made by the traditional method and are considered good products. California brandies are well thought of, but are considered more suitable for mixed drinks than the traditional after-dinner drink.

New York

The second largest wine-producing state is New York. The primary wine grape of this area is one or more varieties of ***Vitis labrusca*** along with some *Vitis vinifera-Vitis labrusca* hybrids. A few *vinifera*, those that have been found able to stand the more rugged winters that occur there, are grown, but the roots need to be covered by more than a foot of earth after harvest to be safe from the hardest frosts.

The major *Vitis labrusca* varieties used in New York state are the Delaware, the Elvira, and the "Riesling," which has some characteristics of the grape after which it is named but is much like the Elvira. The Catawba is another *labrusca* which is widely grown in Ohio as well as New York and is desirable for the making of sparkling wine.

The main producing regions are the Finger Lakes District which lies south of Syracuse and Rochester. Long, narrow lakes such as Lake Seneca, Keuka, and Canandaigua help to moderate the winters.

Long Island has been suitable for some *Vitis vinifera* varieties and is becoming prominent. A fairly large area west of Buffalo along the Lake Erie shore is another area of some significance.

Wines of Other Countries and Areas

Australia and New Zealand

A Scot, James Busby, is considered the father of the wine industry in these far-away countries. He brought the first plantings of the *Vitis vinifera* to Australia, whence they later made their way to New Zealand. The British, anxious to free its empire from dependence on European wines, whole-heartedly supported the fledgling industry. Today the wines produced in both countries are gaining international recognition.

Australian whites have a better reputation than do the reds. Chardonnay and the Riesling grapes are usually the primary choice. The Rieslings are more like those of the Alsace than those of Germany. The cold fermentation process is used for the whites, which preserves their fresh, fruity flavor.

A few good reds are beginning to be produced and these usually come from the Shiraz or the Cabernet grape (see Exhibit 16.20). The Cabernets may be blended with Merlot, Malbec, or Shiraz grapes.

The wine-producing area is largely that portion of Australia south of a straight line running from Sydney to Adelaide. Only one area outside of this is of importance and this is Hunter Valley and Upper Hunter, north of Sydney.

New Zealand is a bit behind Australia in wine production. Some fairly good reds made from the Cabernet Sauvignon grape are produced. The main producing regions are Hawkes Bay, Gisborne and Blenheim on the South Island.

Exhibit 16.20 An Australian Wine Label

Australia is known more for its white wines, but red varietals are becoming more prevalent.

Austria   While Austrian wines are not well known, some excellent wines come from there. By far, the good whites exceed the reds. As noted in Chapter 15, Austria passed the world's strictest wine regulations in 1985 and 1986. While we cannot hope to cover the regulations in detail, we can outline their primary thrust. They provide for four classes of wine, *Tafelwein, Qualitätswein, Kabinett,* and *Prädikatswein* (the latter divided into *Spätlese, Auslese, Eiswein, Beerenauslese, Ausbruch,* and *Trockenbeerenauslese*).

The first two grades allow sugar enrichment (chaptalization) up to 19° KMW (the Austrian sugar measure—equivalent to 94° Oeschle) with the *Qualitätswein* also requiring that the wine come from a single wine region and be officially tested. *Kabinett* level wines allow for no chaptalization; grapes must have a minimum of natural sugar at harvest of 17° KMW (83.5° Oeschle). Because Austria is south of Germany and its growing regions warmer, most grapes can ripen with a higher sugar content. As a consequence, the requirements for sugar content at harvest are higher for Austrian *Prädikatswein* than for the German counterparts. An Austrian *Auslese,* for instance, must have a sugar content similar to a German *Spätlese* (about 94° Oeschle).

If a vineyard, village, or commune is mentioned on the label, 100% of the grapes must come from that area. However, if vintage or grape variety is stated on the label, only 85% is required. Labels must show unfermented sugar percentages. Finally, in order to receive the Austria Wine Seal, wines must meet two tests: 1) a laboratory test to check for sugar, alcohol, acid, and other properties; and 2) a taste test in which six judges check a sample.

The grapes grown are much like those of Germany. However, wines made from the German Riesling grape bear on the label *Rheinriesling*. If *Riesling* alone is on the label, the poorer Italian Riesling grape is used.

The main growing region is in eastern Austria. Some of the best wines are Ruster Ausbruch, a sweet wine between a *Beerenauslese* and a *Trockenbeerenauslese*, the Grüner Veltliner, Lenz-Moser, and most wines coming from the famous Esterhazy vineyards.

Bulgaria

A significant amount of both red and white wine is exported from Bulgaria. The main grapes are the Cabernet Sauvignon, the Merlot, and the Chardonnay. A fruity, vigorous, well-balanced, claret-like wine is made from the Cabernet. In 1978 the country passed new wine regulations, and this has helped to improve the wines and to provide for more certainty about product quality.

The main producing regions are found all through the central region and in the Southeast, but a few are more north and to the west.

Greece and Cyprus

Greece was probably the first European country to make wine an important drink. Vines from Asia found their way to Greece in ancient times, and wine became a national drink, often diluted with water. Today a large quantity of wine is still being produced but most of it is locally consumed. Good quality whites, reds, and rosés are produced. Much of the whites and some rosés are flavored with resin during fermentation which gives a resinous, turpentine-like flavor to the wine. The Greeks like *retsina*, as they call it, because it goes well with the oily, spicy food they often eat.

The Greek Islands also produce wine. Sweet ones predominate. Some fairly good sherries are made in the islands.

Cyprus makes a considerable amount of its wine from native grapes. Its wines are good and all types are made. Lately its wine industry has picked up with the planting of new types of imported grapes. One of the best known wines is the Commandaria made from dried red and white grapes which gives a very sweet wine, sweeter than port or some of the richer, fortified wines. After the importation of the Palomino grape, sherry was made which is of good to high quality.

Hungary

The Riesling grape grows well in Hungary and some excellent whites are made from it. They are rich in flavor and light in body and almost golden in color. The climate is such that the grapes develop much sugar and so many sweet whites are made. The most famous of the Hungary sweet wines is the **Tokaji Aszú**, a wine referred to as "the wine of kings and the king of wines." Some fine reds and good rosés are also produced.

The main grape growing region is on the northern shore of Europe's largest lake, Lake Balaton. To the northwest is the Ezeno Ator region; and farther to the west, the Matralia Eger. The famed Tokaji region is in the far Northwest. A few significant vineyards are spotted in the southern part near Yugoslavia.

The Riesling and Furmint grapes are the primary grapes from which dry, delicate, whites are produced. Similar wines are produced in the Ezeno Ator. However, the district of Eger is more widely known for its noble, rich, red Bikaver (Blood of the Ox). The wine is a deep, red color and much like a fine Bordeaux except richer in flavor, heavier in body, and a bit fiery in nature. The alcoholic content is high and the wine holds its age well.

Tokay wine is made largely from the Furmint grape which is allowed to stay on the vines until it develops the "noble rot" (*aszú* is Hungarian for grapes infected with noble rot). When the grapes are picked, the ripest grapes are set aside to be crushed into 30-liter butts called *puttonyos*. These *puttonyos* are used to sweeten one-year-old wine which is already a bit sweet. If one *puttonyos* is added to a 140-liter barrel, the result is a wine about as sweet as an *Auslese* (about a 23% original grape sugar), while four or five *puttonyos* give a finished wine as sweet as a *Beerenauslese* (about 30% original grape sugar). The finished Tokay (Tokaji) Aszú must be aged at least three years. Because of all the sugar in the must, fermentation takes a long time and special yeasts must be used. In certain years when the grapes develop a maximum amount of sugar, a special *tokaji* is made called *Tokaji Essencia*; it must be aged at least 10 years. It is the equal of the best *Trockenbeerenauslese* or the finest *sauternes*. It is a sweet, delicate, velvety wine, with a flavor that holds in the mouth for an hour or more. The wine can be stored for decades.

Israel

Few think of Israel as a wine-growing nation, but it has been traditionally so since pre-biblical times. Today it has a thriving, modern wine industry. Israeli wines must meet Kosher law requirements—including one that commands growers to pour the entire production back onto the land every seventh year.

Much foreign capital has gone into modernizing the wine industry; Baron Rothschild himself has given money and much of himself in seeing that wines of good quality are produced. Excellent dry and sweet reds are produced as well as imitations of many other wines of the world. The Israelis are enterprising merchandisers and get their wine around the world. Since it is not high-priced and is of good quality, the purchase is usually very satisfactory.

Madeira

The Portuguese islands of Madeira, Porto Santo, and Desertas are known for only one wine—Madeira. It is made from the Rhine Riesling grape. The grapes develop considerable sugar, and fermentation is stopped midway by the addition of brandy. The result is a sweet wine. The wine is then heated at a steady 120° F (49° C) for four to five months which gives it a slightly caramelized flavor typical of the wine. Madeira actually goes by different names indicating quality and sweetness. These are:

- Malmsey—rich, brown color, fragrant, with a rich flavor, soft, velvety texture.

- Bual—less sweet than Malmsey but with slightly less flavor and richness.

- Verdelho—less sweet than Bual with a flavor somewhat tinged with a bit of smoke.

- Sercial—driest and moderate in body; the flavor is full, fragrant, a bit sharp and often used as an aperitif.

The madeira sold for cooking purposes is not made from the Riesling but from a grape called Tinta Negra Mole.

North Africa   Algeria, Morocco, and Tunisia produce a considerable amount of wine which is usually sold to Europe for use as a blending wine. The climate is such that a wine of good body, high alcoholic content, and good flavor results. When bottled and sold, the wines sell for fairly low prices, and for the quality—the best are usually bottled—the wine is a good bargain.

Romania   Romania produces a significant amount of wine which is not known outside the country. One wine for which it is justly famed, Cotnari, is a dessert wine—delicate in body and flavor, with great fragrance and holding power in the mouth much like Tokay. It comes from the part in Moldavia that was left in Romania after the Russians took the greater part after World War II. This is also the area from which most of Romania's better wines come. Most are whites. Two good whites come from Transylvania: one called Tîrnave, a light, slightly sweet white; and the other called Perla.

Murfatlar is another area known for its sweet, pale, golden brown wine made from the muscat grape. Focsani is Romania's biggest wine producer but nothing of world renown comes from there, although many of the wines are considered respectable.

South Africa   At one time Britain favored the wine industry of South Africa because it wanted wines that could compete with those of Europe, and South Africa's wines met this requirement. However, quality dropped and today, South Africa is seeking to bring the reputation of its wines back to their former prominence. In 1972 new regulations were set up and 14 defined regions of origination were established. These laws conform to EEC regulations. Information on labels such as vintage date, place of origin, grape variety, and terms such as reserve, estate, and superior are all controlled in their use.

The main grape used for reds is the Pinotage, a cross between the Cinsaut and Pinot Noir grapes. Some straight Pinot Noirs and Cabernet Sauvignon are also grown. The main grape grown for the whites is the Chenin Blanc, called Steen in South Africa. It makes excellent dry and sweet whites as well as sherry. The Sémillon and a type of Riesling are also grown for whites. The Palomino is grown for sherry making. Some sweet wines are made from the Muscadel and the Muscat of Alexandria.

The main vineyards are the Olifante and Lower Orange along the Olifants River, a spotted coastal area, and the Breede River Valley, Worcester, Paarl, Robertson, Stellenbosch, Malmesbury and Montagu. Most of the exports go to Canada and to Great Britain.

South America   A tremendous amount of wine is produced in South America, largely in Argentina and Chile. Brazil, Uruguay, and Peru are also fairly large scale producers. South American countries account for about one-seventh of the world's wine production, but are not notable exporters because they consume much of what they grow. Argentina and Chile, however, do export.

The main producing regions in Argentina are Mendoza and San Juan. Excellent varietals are produced. Argentina produces better reds than whites. The main grapes are the Malbec and the Cabernet Sauvignon.

Chile's main wine-producing region is around Santiago. Excellent Cabernet Sauvignons are made; they are fruity, with good tannin-acid balance, deep color, and good body. They are long lasting wines. The white wines are also good, since the producers changed over to refrigerated fermentation and improved methods of aging.

Both Argentina and Chile must use irrigation. Both grow *Vitis vinifera* grapes on natural roots; the *phylloxera* has never reached these countries.

The Soviet Union

In 1983 the Soviet Union produced over 3½ billion liters of wine, making it the third largest producer in the world. It has a modern set of regulations governing the industry, and these meet the regulations of the EEC. From best to last, qualities are: *kollektsionye*, which is a wine from selected areas and named varieties with two years aging in the bottle; *named*, a wine of some maturity with a named place of origin; and *ordinary*, a wine similar to *vin ordinaire* in France. If a grape name is put on the bottle, 85% of the grapes must be of that variety. A majority of the grapes used are *vitis vinifera* varieties common in Europe.

The main producing region is a long area stretching from Moldavia near Romania (it was once part of Romania) westward to the Caspian Sea. This takes it through the Ukraine down through Crimea and all through the huge land mass that sits between the Black and Caspian Seas. It is the second largest amount of land devoted to the wine grapes in the world. Excellent dry reds, whites, and rosés are made, as well as sweet wines. A lot of the wines produced in the wine-growing area along the Caspian Sea are very sweet. Excellent sparkling whites and reds are also produced, as well as sherries, ports and aromatic wines; even a good imitation of a Madeira can be found.

As yet, not much of the total produced is exported, but an aggressive move is being made to increase this with some success. Here in the United States, we are beginning to see these wines occasionally, and many Americans have been surprised by their quality. The Russians themselves are heavy consumers of wine; more wine is served at parties than vodka.

Yugoslavia

The amount of wine produced in Yugoslavia is approximately 300 million gallons a year, with a significant amount being exported at extremely low prices. The east side stretching along the Adriatic Sea and the South produce reds primarily, while the area closer to Hungary and Romania produces whites almost exclusively. Slovenia and the adjoining part of Croatia produce the largest amount of the best wines. Serbia produces the most. The wine industry is regulated by modern laws which meet EEC regulations.

Endnotes

1. The figures given here were interpolated from those given by Hugh Johnson in his famous book, *The World Atlas of Wine* (New York: Simon and Schuster, 1985) : 10.

Key Terms

Beaujolais Nouveau
blanc de blancs
blanc de noir
cuvée
Deutscher Sekt
DOC
Eiswein
fermented in the bottle
fermented in this bottle
le dosage
Liebfraumilch
Marsala

Mise en Bouteille au Domaine
Mise en Bouteille à la Propriété
Négociant-Manipulants
pétillant
port
Sekt
solera system
spumante
Tokaji Aszú
vin mousseux
Vitis labrusca

Discussion Questions

1. While France is not the largest producer of wines, it is universally accepted as the most important producer. Discuss at least three reasons why this is so.

2. Why is the *méthode champenoise* more expensive than other methods of making sparkling wine? Briefly compare the methods.

3. Why does Burgundy produce some of the world's greatest wines? What grape is used exclusively for its famous red wines? What grape is used for Chablis, Burgundy's famous white?

4. Why is Bordeaux considered the greatest of all wine regions in France? What is its historical significance? What districts are noted for sweet, white wines?

5. What is *the* great grape of Germany? Why is it a difficult grape to grow successfully year after year?

6. *"Liebfraumilch."* What does it mean? What are the labeling requirements (what regions, grape varieties, etc.)?

7. Discuss the most significant basis on which quality in German wines is judged.

8. Discuss why many Italian winemakers ignore the requirements of their government's wine regulating organization, the DOC.

9. Discuss the origin and makeup of Chianti. What is Chianti Classico?

10. What is the solera system? What other aspects of making Spanish sherry are distinctive in comparison with the production of other wines?

11. Discuss some of the reasons why California has become a world player in the wine industry. Discuss climate, technology, innovation, etc.

12. Which country is widely noted as having the world's strictest wine regulations? Compare that country with Germany.

13. Where does the Soviet Union rank in terms of world production? Is vodka or wine the favored drink?

Glossary

A

ABSINTHE

Light yellow-green, high-alcohol-content liqueur with a pronounced aroma in which licorice dominates. The primary aromatic is artemisia, or wormwood. Absinthe with wormwood is prohibited in the United States and a number of other countries. Absinthe substitutes are marketed. These are without wormwood, sweeter, and not as strong.

ACOUSTICAL TILE

Tile, usually for covering ceilings and/or walls, designed to absorb or deaden sound.

ACTUAL BEVERAGE COST PERCENTAGE

Net beverage cost divided by total bar sales.

ACTUAL COST

The amount of money or resources of value paid to acquire an asset.

ADDITIVE

Anything added to a product that is not strictly necessary for making the product, but which facilitates the production of or enhances certain qualities considered desirable by the producer; brewers use additives as preservatives to produce a more stable and softer foam, greater clarity, and other qualities.

ADJUNCT

Natural products—most often grains such as rice, corn, and wheat flakes—often added to malted barley before fermentation; soybean flakes, potato starch, and even sugar are sometimes used as adjuncts.

ADVERTISING

A spoken or written announcement designed to attract business from the public or a specific market segment; most forms of advertising require payment.

ADVOKAAT

Creamy thick egg liqueur, similar in taste to prepared eggnog. Made by addition of fresh egg yolks to basic liqueur.

AGING

The storage of spirits and wines that takes place in casks or barrels after fermentation, but before bottling; its purpose is to allow further chemical reactions with a small amount of air and improve quality.

ALE

A brew that is top-fermented at high temperatures and contains more hops than do most beers, resulting in a characteristic bitter taste.

ALT

A brew much like British ale, named from the German word meaning "old," indicating it is made by the ancient method of top-fermenting.

AMARETTO

Delicate, smooth liqueur with a natural, true sweet-almond taste.

AMBIENT AIR TEMPERATURE

The surrounding inside air temperature, usually considered ideal for human comfort at 65° to 75° F (18° to 24° C).

AMBIENT LIGHTING

Lighting which provides atmosphere and holds varied elements of the decor together.

AMERICAN VITICULTURE AREAS (AVAs)

Areas within the United States, designated and defined by government regulation, growing particular types of wine grapes, and producing specific types of wines under specified growing conditions. (See also *APPELLATION CONTRÔLÉE.*)

ANISETTE

Sweet, mild, delicate, aromatic liqueur with pleasant flavor reminiscent of licorice. May be water-clear or red. Produced as a flavor-blend of aniseed and aromatic herbs.

APERITIF WINE

Wines that are traditionally served before meals as an appetizer or cocktail. They are often fortified and herb-flavored (vermouth, for instance, is both fortified and flavored with herbal ingredients).

APPELLATION CONTRÔLÉE

Literally, "name controlled." A wine with this term on the label belongs to the highest classification of French wines and is strictly regulated by an agency of the French government.

AQUAVIT (Akvavit)

Smooth, light, dry, clear liquor with the flavor of caraway; like Kummell, but much drier. National beverage of the Scandinavian countries. A dill-flavored aquavit is also available.

ARMAGNAC

A great grape brandy of France, probably second only to Cognac. Armagnac is produced in a legally delineated region in southwest France. It is dry, less delicate, and less ethereal than Cognac, but compensates with a fuller body.

AUTOMATIC/COMPUTERIZED BAR SYSTEMS

Beverage dispensing systems that improve portion control, inventory control, and quality control, as well as the accuracy of guest checks and the adherence to standard recipes.

B

B & B

Brand name. Prepared blend of Benedictine D.O.M. and Cognac.

BACK

Any beverage a guest orders which is to be served in a separate glass along with his or her drink.

BACKBAR

That part of the back wall of a bar which is used for storage and display.

BACKUP DRINKS

Two drinks purchased at one time by or for one guest.

BAILEY'S IRISH CREAM

Brand name. A cream liqueur containing a blend of Irish whiskey and country cream.

BANK

The amount of money that the bartender and/or service staff begin the shift with, allocated in the types of change the employee will need to conduct business.

BANQUETTES

Benches, usually upholstered, that are built-in along a wall.

BAR

That area of a beverage operation in which drinks are prepared and from which drinks are sold.

BAR AND BEVERAGE OPERATIONS

Term used to refer to all possible combinations of establishments serving alcoholic beverages.

BAR MENU

The primary types of beverages which you will serve your target markets, including all types of mixed drinks you are prepared to serve, draft and/or bottled beers, wine, and specialty drinks you will offer; the bar menu takes into account your target markets and projects their drink preferences.

BARBADOS RUM

Medium-bodied rum, dry, heavier, and more pungent than Puerto Rican rum, but lighter and not as pungent as Jamaica rum. Produced in pot stills; amber in color.

BARLEY

As used in the discussion of brews, refers to the seeds (grains) of the barley plant; with few exceptions, barley is the major ingredient of beers, ales, and other malt beverages throughout the world.

BEAUJOLAIS NOUVEAU

A Beaujolais wine which is notable for being rushed to market within a few months of harvest; it is a fruity, refreshing wine, popular throughout the world for the few months in which it is sold each year.

BEER-CLEAN GLASS

A glass that looks clean may not be clean enough for beer; invisible grease and detergent residue will cause beer to lose its foam too quickly.

BENEDICTINE D.O.M.

Brand name. Liqueur produced with a formula of barks, roots, and herbs dried and macerated in brandy, distilled twice, then blended with cognac and aged in oak casks.

BEVERAGE INVENTORY TURNOVER

An analysis to help you determine how efficiently you convert your liquid assets back into cash; it is calculated by dividing the cost of beverages sold by your average inventory.

BEVERAGE RECEIVING REPORT

A report that provides your accounting department with a detailed breakdown of what is received on a daily basis; generally, the receiving agent transfers the information on the purveyor invoice and credit memos to the receiving report after the order has been carefully checked and moved to storage.

BIN CARDS

Standardized forms attached to the shelf where the product is stored; they maintain a record of product received, product issued, most recent cost, or other important inventory information.

BITTERS

A type of spirit, bitters are usually made from roots, spices, bark, berries, fruit, or herbs steeped in or distilled with a neutral spirit and are used primarily as cocktail ingredients; bitters have a highly flavorful, aromatic, bitter taste.

BLANC DE BLANCS

Literally, "white from whites," it means a white wine, usually Champagne, made solely from white grapes—Chardonnay grapes, in particular.

BLANC DE NOIR

Literally, "white from black," it means a white wine, usually Champagne, made from black (or red) grapes which are fermented with the skins removed.

BLENDED WHISKEY

A light-bodied, soft whiskey, mild in flavor and aroma, made as a mixture or blend of neutral spirits and straight whiskey. By U.S. law, this whiskey must contain a minimum of 20% by volume 100 proof straight whiskey.

BLENDING

With regard to wine: refers to both the use of different grape varieties in making one wine and (more commonly) the practice of blending different wines (wines from different years or with different taste characteristics) to create one brand of wine.

With regard to whiskey: refers to the process of mixing different batches of new whiskey distillates together to achieve a balanced product that is usually better than any of its parts; blending sometimes involves mixing different types of whiskeys, and sometimes mixing whiskeys of the same type but differing in age or character. (see **RECTIFICATION**.)

BLOOD ALCOHOL CONCENTRATION (BAC)

Expresses the weight of alcohol per unit volume of blood, usually in grams per 100 milliliters (or per deciliter).

BOCK

A German beer that is darker, richer, higher in alcohol content, and somewhat sweeter than regular 3.2% beer.

BODY

With regard to wine, the degree of consistency, texture, firmness, or viscosity of a wine.

With regard to spirits, an indication of the amount of aroma and flavor a spirit possesses. Thus, a "heavy"-bodied whiskey is one of full flavour and aroma while a "light"-bodied whiskey has less of these characteristics.

BONA FIDE OCCUPATIONAL QUALIFICATION (BFOQ)

A job qualification which under normal circumstances is illegally discriminatory, but which is not held to be so if you can prove it is necessary to the performance of a job; for example, gender would be a BFOQ for a restroom attendant but not for a bartender.

BONDED SPIRIT (UNITED STATES)

A spirit (not blended) which has been stored continuously in a warehouse under government supervision for at least four years in wooden barrels and which is bottled at 100 proof; it must all be the product of a single distillery, by the same distiller during a single season and year.

BOTTLED IN BOND (CANADA)

Bottled under the Canadian federal government's supervision on the distillery's premises.

BOTTOM-UP APPROACH

An approach to budgeting that starts with the bottom line of the income statement and adds in the costs listed on the statement.

BOURBON

A whiskey produced from a grain mixture containing at least 51% corn. Different bourbons use different grain formulas.

BRANDY

Any distilled spirit made from fruit or fruit derivatives qualifies as a brandy; however, only a spirit distilled from grapes can be called just "brandy"—if distilled from other fruit, the type of fruit must precede the word "brandy" (as in "pear brandy").

BREWING

The brewing process entails putting the wort in huge brew kettles, adding hops, boiling the mixture to sterilize the wort and extract the flavor of the hops, draining off the remaining hops, and cooling the mixture down according to the type of brew desired.

BUILD METHOD

A method of making drinks in which ingredients are poured into the glass in which the drink will be served. (See also **POUSSE-CAFÉ**.)

C

CALL BRAND

A beverage identified by its brand name by guests (a "Beefeater martini," for instance, rather than "a martini"). (See also **WELL BRAND**.)

CALL DRINK

A drink made from a call brand.

CAMPARI

Brand name. Dry, brisk-flavored Italian aperitif; also an ingredient in a number of cocktails.

CANADIAN WHISKY

Distinctive whisky of Canada, characteristically light, mild, and delicate. Most Canadian whiskies are blended whiskies, combining heavy- and light-bodied whiskies. They are distilled from mashes of corn, rye, and malted barley, much like those used by American distillers, and are usually aged in used or re-charred white-oak barrels.

CARBONATION

The addition of carbon dioxide gas to malt beverages, which is responsible for their zestful character and the collar of foam on the top of the glass; a brew with insufficient carbon dioxide is said to be "flat."

CASH BAR

A bar where each guest pays for each drink as it is ordered.

CASH CONTROL

Control elements needed in all aspects of an operation which involve the handling of cash, including any forms of credit extended to guests.

CHAMPAGNE METHOD

The original method of making champagne (French *méthode champenoise*) in which the second fermentation takes place in the bottle in which it is sold—a laborious and exacting process which accounts for the high price of the best champagne.

CHAPTALIZATION

Adding sugar to the must before fermentation, a process often necessary when weather conditions prevent grapes from ripening fully and developing enough natural sugar to convert into the amount of alcohol prescribed (often by law) for certain wines.

CHARMAT (BULK) PROCESS

Much less expensive than the traditional method of making champagne and other sparkling wines, the second fermentation takes place in a vat and the wine is later filtered and bottled under pressure.

CHARTREUSE

Brand name. Aromatic French liqueur of great delicacy, made from private formula of plants, herbs, and spices. Yellow is 86 U.S. proof. Green is 110 U.S. proof. Green is drier and more aromatic.

CHECK CONTROL SHEET

A sheet used to record which guest checks are issued to which employees.

CHERRY HEERING

Brand name. Danish cherry liqueur.

CHOCOLATE MINT

Rich, creamy liqueur blending cocoa-chocolate, vanilla, and mint flavors. Made from selected cacao and vanilla beans and fine grade peppermint.

CHOCOLATE SUISSE

Brand name. Chocolate-flavored Swiss liqueur produced with miniature squares of chocolate floating in the bottle.

CLOSED STATES

(See **MONOPOLY STATES**.)

COGNAC

Superb brandy of France, with great aroma and the bouquet of grapes. Cognac is produced in a legally delineated 150,000-acre area surrounding the ancient city of Cognac in the departments of Charente and Charente-Maritime in the southwest of France. Under French law, only brandy distilled from wine made from grapes grown within this district may be called Cognac.

COINTREAU

Brand name. Rich, subtle orange flavor/Triple Sec character.

COMMON LAW STATE

A state that places major emphasis on using previous court decisions as the basis of saying what the law is. (See also **STATUTORY STATE**.)

COMPETITION ANALYSIS

An analysis that enables you to anticipate your competitors' actions and capitalize on their weaknesses by positioning your operation's competitive strengths.

COMPLEMENTARY (COLORS)

Colors opposite each other on a color wheel (red and green, for instance).

CONDENSER

In a distillation system, a container for cooling the ethanol vapor to a liquid state.

CONGENERS

Those substances other than alcohol and water (for example, acids, glycerine, phenolics, butyl alcohol, propyl alcohol, fusel oil, aldehydes, and esters) which are found in wine and new spirit distillates; they provide flavor and aroma and may be desirable or undesirable.

CONTROL STATES

(See **MONOPOLY STATES**.)

CONTROLLING

The management process of comparing actual performance with established standards and, when necessary, taking corrective action to bring performance up to standards in order to protect assets and income.

CONVERSION

The natural process of changing solubilized grain starches into grain sugars by use of barley malt and/or rye malt.

COOPERAGE

Barrels, casks, and other wooden containers used for aging and storing whiskeys.

COORDINATING

The management function of using resources efficiently to meet organizational goals and objectives.

CORN WHISKEY

Like straight corn whiskey, except for age. When the label says only "corn whiskey" without the word "straight," the whiskey may have any age up to two years. Straight corn whiskey will be a minimum of two years old.

COUNTRY MELON SCHNAPPS

Brand name. The flavor comes from country fresh, wine-ripe watermelons (minus the seeds). The color is watermelon red.

CREAM ALE

A brew which is created by mixing ale with lagered beer, resulting in a smoother, "creamier" taste and texture.

CRÈME DE CACAO (Crème de Cocoa)

Rich, creamy liqueur blending cocoa-chocolate and vanilla flavors: available in brown (regular) and water-white. Made from selected cacao and vanilla beans.

CRÈME DE CASSIS

Sweet reddish-brown liqueur, fairly heavy with the flavor of currants.

CRÈME DE MENTHE

Refreshing, tangy, natural mint-flavored liqueur. Cool, clean, and very pleasant to the taste. Available in green and water-clear.

CRÈME DE NOYA (Crème de Noyaux)

Rich liqueur with nutty flavor. Flavoring derived primarily from the oil of bitter almonds or of apricot kernels.

CRUS

Literally, "growth" areas—areas singled out by French governmental wine regulations as producing the highest quality wines.

CUBAN RUM

Dry, light rum, brandy-like to the taste, with slight molasses flavor. Produced in two labels—white label, more delicate in flavor and aroma, and gold label, a little sweeter and with more pronounced rum flavor. Cuban gold label tends to be slightly bolder than Puerto Rican gold.

CURAÇAO

Light, delicate, orange-flavored liqueur, produced as a flavor blending of the peels of tangy curaçao and sweet oranges. Amber in color, curaçao has a subtle orange character, contains slightly less total flavor than Triple Sec, has more sweet orange-peel taste, contains more sugar, and is lower in alcohol content.

CURTAINS

Window coverings made from lightweight material which allows light to filter through. (See also **DRAPERIES**.)

CUVÉE

A blend of wines, sometimes from many different vintners or different years, which is then re-fermented to make Champagne.

CYNAR

Brand name. Bitter-sweet aperitif with full flavor from macerated artichokes and other botanicals. Amber in color.

D

DARK BEER

Similar in color to bock but not as sweet, it has a rich, creamy taste; like bock, dark beer gets its color and pronounced flavor from malt sprouts roasted at high temperatures.

DEAD STOCK LIST

A list of all products and brands which guests no longer request.

DECANTER

A glass container into which wine is carefully poured in order to separate the wine from any sediment which may be in the bottom of the wine bottle.

DECANTING

The process of gently and carefully pouring the wine from the bottle into another container (a decanter), leaving the sediment behind in the bottle. The wine is then served from the decanter.

DECIBELS

Decibels (db) are the units of measurement for the loudness of sound (the loudness of a normal speaking voice from three feet away is 70 db).

DEMERARA RUM

Full-bodied dark rum made from molasses of sugar cane grown along the Demerara River in Guyana; distilled in pot stills.

DESIGN THEME

A design theme is established to guide the design of interior decor to ensure its overall consistency.

DESSERT WINE

A wine that is meant to be served after dinner with or as dessert; dessert wines are often fortified.

DEUTSCHER SEKT

An effervescent German wine resembling Champagne, which must be made from German grapes.

DIRECT COST

A cost that can be charged directly as a cost of doing business. Also called variable cost.

DISCOUNTING

With regard to alcohol purchasing, a price reduction given by the purveyor when you purchase large volumes.

DISTILLATION

A process, which takes place in a still, that uses heat to extract the alcohol from a liquid that contains both alcohol and water; when an alcoholic liquid is heated, the alcohol turns into a vapor and rises, leaving the water behind. As these alcoholic vapors cool, they condense back into liquid form, becoming concentrated new whiskey distillates.

DISTILLER'S BEER

The liquid distilled for spirits. (See also **WORT**.)

DOC

Acronym for *Denominazione di Origine Controllata*—literally, "the name of origin controlled." The term printed on Italian wine labels which ensures that a given wine meets various government requirements, particularly concerning its origin.

DOUBLES

Double the standard measure of alcohol in one glass.

DRAM SHOP LAWS

Statutory third-party liability laws which make dispensers of alcohol liable if they dispense alcohol irresponsibly, that is, to minors, to anyone who is obviously intoxicated or to an alcohol dependent, or to anyone who becomes intoxicated because of such service.

DRAMBUIE

Brand name. Scotch whisky liqueur delicately honeyed and spiced.

DRAPERIES

Unlike curtains, draperies are made of heavier material and are designed to keep light out; advantages include absorbing sound and keeping heat from escaping through windows.

DRINK INCENTIVES

Two drinks for the price of one, half-price drinks, and so forth during so-called happy hours.

DRINK RAIL

A type of counter, usually placed against a wall, where guests can either stand or sit on high stools while drinking; often found in airport lounges.

DRINK SIZE

The amount of alcohol (in fluid ounces) that is poured into each drink (not the size of the completed drink).

DRY-HOPPED

A brewing process in which the hops are soaked in the brew without boiling in order to extract a lighter, less bitter flavor.

E

EISWEIN

Literally, "ice wine," a rare German wine which can be made only when very ripe grapes are not harvested until late November; the grapes are allowed to freeze on the vine, then quickly harvested, rushed frozen to the presses, and pressed while frozen.

ELEVATIONS

Architectural drawings showing the front, side, and rear views of a proposed building.

EMPLOYEE REFERRALS

A recruitment method in which current employees recommend friends or family for job vacancies.

EMPLOYMENT AT WILL

An employment arrangement which either party can end at any time for any reason.

EXTERNAL RECRUITMENT METHOD

A method whereby management looks outside the company to fill job vacancies; advertising campaigns, placement agencies, and unsolicited walk-ins are typically used by bar and beverage operations.

F

FEASIBILITY STUDY

A study conducted before beginning a new business or constructing a new establishment to determine the likelihood of success, taking into account extensive market research and financial resources.

FERMENTATION

A step, prior to distillation, during which a mash comprising crushed grain (or grapes or sugar cane, etc.) and water is injected with yeasts. The yeasts convert the product into ethyl alcohol and carbon dioxide gas. The gas drifts off, and the remaining mixture contains a fairly low level of alcohol, which can be extracted and concentrated through distillation. Distilled beverage alcohol can be derived from any plant or plant product containing either fermentable sugars or starch that can be converted to such sugars.

FERMENTED IN THE BOTTLE

The term appearing on a bottle of Champagne or sparkling wine when the transfer process is used; that is, the second fermentation takes place "in the bottle" as the label says, but the sparkling wine is then transferred to a vat under pressure for settling, clarifying, and fining, and then returned under pressure to the original bottles.

FERMENTED IN THIS BOTTLE

The term appearing on a bottle of Champagne or sparkling wine when the traditional champagne method is used; that is, the re-fermentation takes place in the bottle in which the Champagne or sparkling wine is sold.

FINING

A process that removes certain microscopic solids still remaining suspended in the wine after racking, usually by adding materials to the wine which draw the suspended solids out of solution, causing both to drop to the bottom.

FIRST-IN, FIRST-OUT (FIFO) SYSTEM

A system in which the most recently acquired stock is not sold until the older existing stock is sold.

FLUORESCENT

Formerly a cool, blue or blue-green light from glass tubes, fluorescent lighting now comes in all shapes and sizes and is capable of delivering a full spectrum of colors; uses much less energy than ordinary (incandescent) light bulbs.

FORTIFIED WINE

Wine to which additional alcohol is added, usually during fermentation, resulting in a wine with a minimum of 15% and maximum of 24% alcohol by volume.

FREE POUR

An unmeasured system where the bartender simply pours freely into a glass.

FRONT BAR

The front bar's primary purpose is to serve beverages to guests who may be seated at seats or bar stools around the bar or sitting at tables in a lounge area.

FULL BOTTLE

A wine bottle that usually contains approximately 25 ounces (750 ml), which could adequately serve three to four persons, but is not too much for two people over the course of a full meal.

FULL BOTTLE SLIP

A control tool used in maintaining bar par. When a full bottle is ordered, management or the point-of-sale system issues a full bottle slip to the bartender to exchange for the full bottle. To requisition these bottles (since there is no empty), the bartender attaches the full bottle slips to the daily bar requisition form.

FUSEL OIL

The term given to a group of heavy, pungent alcohols produced during fermentation; they impart a heavy sweetness to the final product and are necessary in small amounts.

G

GENERIC WINE

Wine made from a blend of wines to resemble a particular wine of an already established region; a California "Burgundy," for instance.

GENEVA GIN (also Genever Gin; Hollands Gin)

A Dutch gin, the national drink of Holland. Unlike mildly flavored London dry gin, Geneva gin is heavy in body and redolent of juniper, with pronounced grain character. Geneva gin is distilled at low alcohol content from a fermented mash of barley malt, rye, and corn. After this distillation, juniper berries, which give the gin its typical flavor, are added to the malt-wine and it is then re-distilled. Geneva gin should always be served ice cold, never at room temperature. It is served straight and, except for the possible addition of a dash of bitters, is never used in mixed drinks.

GIN

A compounded spirit (the basic product flavored by juniper berries) which is usually classified as "dry" or "heavy"; dry gins are light in flavor and body, while heavy gins are heavily flavored and full-bodied.

GIN-HEAD

In distillation, a device through which vapors are passed to pick up flavor.

GINGER-FLAVORED BRANDY

Neutral brandy with the true flavor and aroma of ginger root and other aromatics. Light brown in color.

GLASS RAIL

An area for glasses to be placed while the drinks are being poured.

GOLDWASSER

Sweet water-clear liqueur with a citrus fruit peel and spice flavor and containing tiny flakes of gold leaf so slight they cannot be felt on the tongue. Also called Liqueur D'Or, Gold Liqueur, and Gold Water.

GRAIN NEUTRAL SPIRIT

A colorless, odorless, and tasteless distilled spirit made from a grain mash; it is produced by continuous distillation until it reaches 190 proof, removing a number of harsh congeners in the process.

GRAND MARNIER

Brand name. Golden French liqueur with orange flavor and Cognac base.

GRAPE MUST

(See **MUST**.)

GRAPPA

Brandy distilled from the pulpy residue—the grape pomace—of the wine press. In France, this brandy is called Marc (Eau de Vie de Marc).

GRENADINE

Bright red flavoring syrup blending the tastes of pomegranate, strawberry, and raspberry.

GROSS PROFIT

Drink selling price minus drink cost times the total number of drinks sold.

GUEST PROFILE

A list of characteristics that your guests have in common; the guest profile helps you to identify which market segments you appeal to and to define segments you would like to attract.

H

HALF BOTTLE

A wine bottle that contains approximately 12.5 ounces (375 ml), usually adequate for two guests.

HAPPY HOUR

A period of time, usually between 4 and 7 p.m., during which bar and beverage operations attempt to bring in customers who are on their way home from work.

HERTZ

The unit of measurement for sound frequency, or the number of sound waves per second.

HIGH GROSS ITEM

An item that is sold for a price higher than a formula-based price would suggest.

HOPPING

Refers to the addition of hops to the wort during the brewing process.

HOPS

The dried, scaly fruit of the vine *Humulus lupulus.* Hops are added to malt beverages to give them a slightly bitter and "hoppy" taste, to produce a more stable and softer foam, to supplement aroma and body, and to help preserve the brew.

HOSTED BAR

An event for which the host or hostess pays for all the drinks consumed by the guests. The price, agreed upon ahead of time, may be per bottle, per drink, or per person.

I

ICE BIN

A container located in the underbar with readily available ice for making drinks.

IMMIGRATION AND NATURALIZATION SERVICE (INS)

The U.S. government agency that enforces the Immigration Reform and Control Act of 1986, which makes it unlawful for any employer to hire undocumented immigrants.

INCANDESCENT

The type of light from an ordinary light bulb that uses electrical current to heat a filament to make it glow. Such lights are hotter and use more energy than fluorescent or mercury vapor lights.

INTERNAL RECRUITMENT METHODS

Methods that seek to determine whether qualified individuals are available within the company for open positions.

INVENTORY

A count of the product you have on hand at any given time; inventory controls need to be established both at the point of sale and in the storeroom.

IRISH MIST

Brand name. Irish liqueur; a blend of Irish whiskey, heather honey, and herbal flavorings.

IRISH WHISKEY

Distinctive whiskey of Ireland made principally from barley, both malted and unmalted, together with oats, wheat, and sometimes a small proportion of rye.

ISSUING

The procedure involved in moving products from storage to the bar area.

J

JAMAICA RUM

Full-bodied rum, with a heavy rum flavor, pungent bouquet, rich golden hue, and dark color; distilled in pot stills.

JIGGER

Double-ended measuring devices typically made of stainless steel. Each end of the jigger holds a different amount (for example, three-fourths of an ounce and either an ounce or an ounce and a half).

JOB ANALYSIS

A process of obtaining information about the job to be performed so that the duties and tasks can be determined.

JOB DESCRIPTION

A document which tells each employee what to do in the performance of his or her job, specifically identifying the duties and responsibilities of each job; job descriptions are also called position descriptions or position guides.

JOB INCUMBENT

The person currently filling a particular position.

JOB INVENTORY

A method of job analysis in which employees actually working in a given position are observed or interviewed, and an audit is taken of the job-related tasks they perform.

JOB POSTING

The process of communicating to current employees about new job openings within the company via postings listed on bulletin boards, in circulated newsletters, or in special publications which list vacancies; these postings provide information about the job, including a job description, and job specifications indicating the necessary qualifications.

JOB SPECIFICATION

A document that identifies the education, skills, and qualifications the applicant needs to perform the duties and meet the responsibilities of each position.

K

KAHLUA

Brand name. Mexican coffee liqueur.

KIRSCHWASSER (Kirsch)

Fruit brandy distilled from cherries; smooth, mellow, with the subtle fragrance of cherries. Water-clear.

KOKOMO

Brand name. Yellow-colored liqueur with a unique, tropical tangerine-pineapple taste.

KRAUSENING

A method of adding carbon dioxide by putting the brew through a second fermentation in a pressurized tank.

KUMMEL (Kuemmul)

Clear liqueur with the pleasing, piquant flavor of the caraway seed. Neither too sweet nor too dry. Also comes very dry.

L

LAGER

Bottom-fermented brew.

LAGERING

The slower process of bottom-fermentation. A term derived from the German *lagerbier,* meaning "beer to be stored"; after fermentation, the brew is stored at cold temperatures.

LAST CALL

A time when the bartender "calls out" the information that one more drink may be purchased before the bar is closed.

LE DOSAGE

In the traditional Champagne method, the final step which adds wine, sugar, and, in some cases, brandy to the Champagne.

LEAD TIME

The amount of time between when you order products and when they are delivered; one management objective is to reduce the amount of lead time, so as to reduce the size of the inventory.

LEADING

The process of motivating employees toward the achievement of organizational goals and objectives.

LEES

Flocculent (suspended) material in the wine which settles to the bottom of the cask or vat as sediment—includes some tannins and some tartrates.

LEVEL OF SERVICE

A term that describes the amount and kind of service appropriate to the needs and desires of the types of guests you wish to attract; the level of service should not be so high as to unnecessarily diminish your profit margin.

LICENSE STATES

States allowing you to choose which purveyor you want to work with. Also called open states. In such states, liquor wholesalers, distributors, and manufacturers are licensed by the state to sell their products.

LIEBFRAUMILCH

Old colloquial German term meaning "Milk of the Blessed Mother." A popular German white wine grown in several specified German wine regions, from a combination of grape varieties specified by government regulations.

LIQUEURS

Flavored, usually sweet alcoholic beverages with an alcohol content higher than fortified wine, but lower than most liquors.

LIQUOR

Unsweetened, high-alcohol-content beverages such as gin, vodka, rum, and the various whiskeys, including scotch.

LIQUORE GALLIANO

Brand name. Gold Italian liqueur.

LIQUORE STREGA

Brand name. Italian plant liqueur; century-old formula utilizing more than seventy herbs. Delicate orange flavor.

LONDON DRY GIN

Crisp, clean, clear liquor, aromatic of juniper to the taste. The term "dry" simply means that a gin lacks sweetness. The name "London" has no particular significance except that it designates a dry gin as opposed to the sweet or Old Tom gins.

LOW GROSS ITEM

An item that is sold for a price lower than a formula-based price would suggest.

M

MALT

Any grain which has been sprouted and then dried to prevent further development. Malt, mixed with other grains, acts to convert the starch therein contained into grain sugar, from which yeast makes alcohol.

MALT BEVERAGE

According to the U.S. government, "a beverage containing 0.5% or more of alcohol, brewed or produced from malt, wholly or in part, or from any substance thereof." Beers, ales, stouts, and porters are part of the malt beverage group.

MALT LIQUOR

A brew made (or that should be made) from straight malt with no adjuncts; it has a more pronounced malt flavor, is slightly darker than regular beer, and usually has a higher alcohol content, ranging from 3.2% to 8% by weight.

MALT WHISKEY

Like straight malt whiskey except for age. When the label says only "malt whiskey," the whiskey may have an age of up to two years. Straight malt whiskey will be a minimum of two years old.

MALTOSE

A fermentable sugar produced by conversion of the starch of sprouting barley grains by malt enzymes, principally *diastase.*

MANAGEMENT

A process involving the functions of planning, organizing, coordinating, staffing, leading, and controlling, to achieve organizational goals and objectives. Since all of the functions involve people, it can be said that management is achieving goals through people.

MARASCHINO

Water-clear, aromatic liqueur with the clean, rich taste of marasca cherries.

MARKET RESEARCH

Research which will be used to identify the needs of customers you already serve as well as customers you would like to serve (see **TARGET MARKETS**) and to determine the most effective ways to reach new customers.

MARKET SEGMENTATION

The process of dividing the broad market into various groups of potential guests who share common wants and needs.

MARKETING

A management planning activity whose purpose is to generate sales by conducting business from the consumer's perspective.

MARKETING MIX

An interdependent mix of the now classic four major elements known as the four Ps of marketing: product, place (channels of distribution), price, and promotion; your understanding of the marketing mix will guide the how, when, where, why, and how much money questions of your entire marketing effort.

MARRYING

A process in which a beverage mixes and unifies as it rests after blending.

MARSALA

A famous sweet, fortified wine from Sicily; served as a dessert wine but often noted for its use in cooking (as in veal marsala).

MARTINIQUE RUM

Rum distilled in Martinique and shipped to Bordeaux, France, where it is blended and re-shipped to world markets. Has a pronounced rum flavor. Amber in color.

MASHING

The process of grinding barley malt into a grist along with adjuncts and heated water, cooking, then filtering out any grain residue to produce clear, warm, sugary fluid called wort.

MASTIC

Sweet, water-clear Greek liqueur, licorice-like in flavor. Slightly drier than ouzo, much drier and more potent than anisette. Flavor derived from aniseed and the sap of a cashew tree.

MATURING

The term used for aging in the bottle; it is usually associated with complex, full-bodied reds such as a good red Bordeaux or Burgundy.

MATURING (Whiskey)

The aging of whiskey in charred oak barrels to develop its characteristic, taste, color, and aroma.

MEASURED POURING

In contrast to free pouring, pouring using a shot glass, a jigger, or a measuring device that is part of a pouring spout attached to each bottle.

MERCHANDISING

In-house promotion of products and services; it requires finding more effective ways to influence guests (customers) who are already at your operation to buy more of what you are offering.

METAXA

Brand name. Greek specialty liqueur with distinctive, slightly sweetened taste.

MEZCAL

The primary Mexican spirit, it is, like tequila, made from the heart of a cactus plant, but is made simply from a single distillation and thus is cheaper.

MILLING

The grinding of grain to expose the starch so that it is more easily solubilized in the mashing process.

MINI-BAR

A small, under-the-table unit which can be stocked with liquor, beer, and wine, usually located within a hotel room for guests' convenience.

MINI-DRINK

A drink with the appearance of a regular drink but about a fourth of the alcohol.

MISE EN BOUTEILLE AU DOMAINE

Literally, "bottled at the place (or residence)," it is a term often found on the labels of French wines indicating the origin of the grapes used to make the wine.

MISE EN BOUTEILLE A LA PROPRIETE

Literally, "bottled by the owner (of the vineyard)," it is a term sometimes found on the label of French wines indicating the origin of the grapes used to make the wine.

MIXOLOGY

The art or skill of mixing drinks; bartenders are sometimes referred to as mixologists.

MOCHA

Coffee liqueur; aromatic coffee flavor drawn from mocha nuts and vanilla beans.

MONOPOLY STATES

Certain states of the United States (also known as control or closed states) in which there is no price competition among retail liquor stores; all liquor in such states must be purchased from state-owned stores and typically sold at prices set by the states.

MUDDLING

The process of crushing fruit and sugar together with either a wooden pestle or spoon; notably used in making "Old Fashioneds."

MUST

The juice and often other parts of the grape produced by crushing and pressing the grapes; the must then undergoes fermentation.

N

NATURAL WINE

Basically the product of grape fermentation without the addition of alcohol, sugar (beyond a small amount allowed for certain wines under specified conditions) or other additives except a small amount of sulfur; natural fermentation stops when there is no more sugar to convert to alcohol or when the alcohol reaches 14% by volume.

NEAT

Traditionally, a straight shot of liquor without ice (see also **STRAIGHT UP**).

NEGOCIANT-MANIPULANTS

Firms that purchase wines from growers or cooperatives, usually blending them for consistency and selling the blend under their own label.

NEUTRAL SPIRITS

An alcoholic spirit purified in the still to a minimum of 95% of absolute alcoholic purity. At that point, the spirit is considered to have no important taste and little body. Although neutral spirits may be distilled from many materials, they are almost always distilled from fermented grain mashes. Neutral spirits are used to make blended whiskey. In original distillation, or redistillation, over juniper berries and other aromatics, neutral spirits become dry gin. Filtered through charcoal, neutral spirits become vodka. Neutral spirits are also the base for many cordials and liqueurs.

NEW ENGLAND RUM

Full-bodied rum produced in the United States from molasses shipped from the West Indies; distilled at less than 160 U.S. proof and also a straight rum.

NOBLE ROT (Noble Mold)

A mold, *Botrytis cinerea*, which infects certain types of grapes in late fall, when morning mists and afternoon sun create ideal growing conditions for the mold; it is called "noble" because it creates some of the greatest naturally sweet wines.

O

OLD TOM GIN

Traditional dry gin sweetened by the addition of sugar syrup.

ON THE ROCKS

A drink served in a glass with ice in it.

ON-PREMISE RETAIL DEALER

Official U.S. federal government term for an alcoholic beverage retailer.

ON-THE-JOB TRAINING (OJT)

A training method in which the employee learns job skills while actually performing the tasks of the job he or she was hired for.

OPAL NERA

Brand name. A black-colored sambuca with a rich, smooth anise and elderberry flavor and a subtle hint of lemon.

OPEN STATES

(See **LICENSE STATES**.)

ORGANIZING

The management process of assembling resources and determining the flow of authority and communication.

ORIENTATION PROGRAM

A way of socializing employees into the operation to minimize problems and maximize job performance.

OUZO

Sweet, water-clear Greek liqueur, licorice-like in flavor. Slightly sweeter than mastic, much drier and more potent than anisette. Flavor derived from aniseed.

OVERPOURING

Putting in more alcohol than the standard recipe or measurement calls for.

P

PAR

The amount of liquor to order and keep in the storeroom and the amount to keep at the bar; in the storeroom, the goal is to store just enough product that you don't run out between deliveries or tie up cash in inventory; at the bar, the goal is to avoid running out of a product in the course of a shift or a day. (See also **TWO TIER PAR STOCK**.)

PASTEURIZATION

The process of exposing brew to 140° to 150° F (60° to 65.5° C) heat in order to kill bacteria which causes spoiling; draught beer is not pasteurized.

PATENT STILL

A still that acts as a vaporizer and condenser; its condensing system consists of a number of condensing spaces placed at strategic points. Also called Coffey still, column still, or continuous still.

PERPETUAL INVENTORY

A record of all product in a bar or beverage operation based on receipts and issuances rather than on a physical count; it helps to determine your beverage inventory in terms of both dollar value and number of bottles.

PERSONAL SELLING

A promotional activity in which a salesperson (a staff member) becomes a persuasive communication tool in the sale of your products and services.

PETILLANT

Literally, "crackling." A semi-sparkling wine with less carbonation than Champagne or *vin mousseux*.

PHYLLOXERA

A variety of vine-killing plant lice; it wiped out the vineyards of Europe in the nineteenth century and is still a problem for vintners throughout the world.

PHYSICAL INVENTORY

An inventory performed to verify the information on your perpetual inventory records.

PILSNER

A light, rich, and mellow lager with a dry, crisp, hoppy flavor and a light color; it is made from hops grown in the area around Pilsen, Czechoslovakia.

PLANNING

The management process of considering all resources available and their limitations. Basic resources of a bar and beverage operation include people, money, products, time, procedures, energy, and equipment. All are in limited supply.

PORT

The famous fortified sweet wine from Portugal.

PORTER

A malt beverage named for the English porters (servers) who first served it at Coventry Garden; it is dark brown from the heavily roasted malt used to make it.

POSITION DESCRIPTIONS

(See **JOB DESCRIPTION**.)

POSITION GUIDES

(See **JOB DESCRIPTION**.)

POSITIONING

The process by which management "positions" itself in relation to the competition; if market research determines that a certain segment of the market has not been well served by the competition, for instance, management may take advantage of the opportunity by positioning its operation to capture that segment.

POT STILL

A round pot-shaped still with a tapering funnel at the top where rising vapors can be collected and then be carried off to the condenser through a tube.

POTENTIAL BEVERAGE COST PERCENTAGE

The cost of a bottle of liquor divided by the sales value of that bottle.

POUR COST

The cost of ingredients for a drink or for all drinks.

POURERS

Mechanical devices containing ball bearings that allow the bartender to dispense whatever pour size has been determined to be appropriate. Each time the bartender tips the bottle, the predetermined amount of alcohol is dispensed.

POUSSE-CAFE

A drink built by very carefully floating one layer of liqueur on top of another.

PRALINE

Brand name. Sweet, rich liqueur combining the flavors of brown sugar and pecan nuts into one distinctive flavor.

PRE-MIX

A commercially prepared mix available for cocktails; a bloody mary mix, for instance, with all the tomato juice and various spices mixed proportionally, needing only the addition of vodka.

PRODUCT CONTROL

Control elements established to protect physical assets.

PROMOTION

Any form of communication between you and your current and potential guests—or any special activity you provide for them—that persuades them to buy your products and services.

PROMOTIONAL MIX

All of an operation's promotional communications, including advertising, public relations and publicity, sales promotions, personal selling, and merchandising; the components of the promotional mix should be viewed as the tools you will use to achieve promotional objectives.

PROOF

A method of expressing alcoholic strength or content; in the United States, proof is equal to twice the percentage of alcohol by volume.

PROOF GALLON (CANADA)

An Imperial Gallon on 277.3 cubic inches (4546 cubic centimeters) that is 57.05% ethyl alcohol by volume.

PROOF GALLON (U.S.)

A standard U.S. Gallon of 231 cubic inches that is 50% ethyl alcohol by volume.

PUBLIC RELATIONS

The process of obtaining public goodwill toward an operation; sometimes requires repairing the negative image of a product or service.

PUBLICITY

Public relations in the form of written or spoken communication about an operation that is given at no cost to the operation; newspaper articles or local TV segments about your operation are typical examples.

PUERTO RICAN RUM

Dry, light rum, brandy-like to the taste, with slight molasses flavor. White label is more delicate in aroma and flavor. Gold label is a little sweeter with a more pronounced rum flavor. Distilled at high alcohol content in column stills aged one to three years and blended by traditional methods.

PULL DATE

The date often marked on packages of canned and bottled beer to indicate when their shelf life has expired; even pasteurized beer has a limited shelf life of three to four months.

PURCHASE ORDER

A form used to record the products ordered and to standardize the information about those products.

PURCHASING

The ability to obtain the right quality of products in the right quantity at the right time from the right purveyor at the right price.

R

RACKING

The process of removing wine from the sediment (lees) at the bottom of a cask and pouring it into another container, leaving the lees behind.

RECEIVING

The process of checking delivered items for quality and quantity and matching them against the purchase order.

RECRUITMENT

The process of finding the best-qualified applicant for an existing job vacancy in a cost-efficient manner.

RECTIFICATION

A term, applied to such aspects of the distilled beverage alcohol-making process as blending, coloring, flavoring, or even redistilling, that implies a further treatment of the product beyond distillation. The U.S. government defines rectification as blending a spirit with anything other than water.

RELATIVE HUMIDITY

The ratio of the amount of water vapor actually present in the air to the greatest amount possible at the same temperature.

ROCK & RYE

Sweet, hearty rye whiskey-flavored liqueur. Amber in color. Made by blending rye whiskey with rock candy and fruit—lemons, oranges, and cherries.

RUM

A family of liquors distilled from the fermented juice of sugar cane or molasses. Rum is produced in virtually all of the various sugar countries and in New England (from West Indies molasses). There are many differences in these rums resulting from the methods of distilling, climate, and soil in which the sugar cane grows.

RYE WHISKEY

A whiskey produced from a grain mixture containing at least 51% rye.

S

SALES ANALYSIS

An analysis measuring whether the sales objectives or projections have been met for a designated period of time. This is done by comparing the actual sales figures against the potential sales.

SALES AND PROFITABILITY CONTROL

Looks at the relationships among costs, sales, and profit in the bar or beverage operation. These relationships form the basis for cost control measures.

SALES FORECAST

A prediction of the amount of a product an operation expects to sell over a specific time period; sales forecasts provide information that can help an operation select target markets, anticipate opportunities for new products and services, develop budgets for advertising and promotions, and predict future cash flow.

SALES MIX

A term that refers to the ratio of categories of drinks you are selling to total sales; this information can be useful in determining prices.

SALES POTENTIAL

Refers to the maximum amount of product that an operation could possibly sell to a given market segment during a specified period.

SALES PROMOTION

A promotional activity that attempts to influence guests (customers) to purchase your products or services; sales promotions offer guests an additional incentive for making a purchase.

SALES VALUE PER BOTTLE

The estimated amount of revenue to be derived from a bottle of liquor; determined by multiplying the number of drinks each bottle provides by the price of each drink.

SAMBUCA

Rich, clear liqueur combining the tang of licorice with the freshness of wild elderberries.

SCHEMATIC PLAN

A representive floor plan, drawn to scale, upon which planners can move scaled representations of interior features to help gauge effective placement.

SCOTCH

A distinctive spirit from Scotland with at least 80 proof alcohol content, manufactured in compliance with British laws; it is sold (and must be labeled) as "blended" or "single malt."

SEDIMENT (Lees)

Naturally occurring solid particles which are heavy or dense enough to collect at the bottom of a bottle of wine (or on the side, if the wine is stored on its side).

SEKT

Ordinary sparkling wine from Germany.

SELECTION

A process in which all job applicants are screened (in compliance with all legal restrictions) to identify the best candidates from the available applicants.

SELLING BY SUGGESTION

(See **SUGGESTIVE SELLING.**)

SEPARATION OF DUTIES

A control policy making employees interdependent in order to reduce the chance of employee theft; that is, no one person is given responsibility for more than one function. Hence, the person responsible for purchasing is not responsible for receiving, storage, inventory, or issuing.

SEQUENCING

Establishing a system by which servers order batches of drinks in a particular sequence, and bartenders co-ordinate the ordering sequence with the sequence in which they prepare those drink orders.

SERVICE BAR

Strictly speaking, a relatively small bar designed solely to prepare beverages for servers to serve to guests in the dining area.

SHAKE/BLEND METHOD

A method of preparing cocktails that use cream, eggs, or fruit juices (along with the alcohol portion of the recipe) which cannot be mixed to the desired texture (usually smooth and foamy) by stirring; such cocktails are either shaken vigorously in hand shakers or (more often) shaken in electric blenders.

SHOPPERS

People hired to observe the bartender and servers while posing as guests. Also called spotters.

SHOT GLASS

Glass used for measuring the liquor required for a particular drink.

SIMPLE SYRUP

A syrup made simply from sugar and water; used instead of sugar by itself because granulated sugar takes too long to dissolve in cold drinks.

SLIVOVITZ

Fruity brandy, distilled from plums. Soft, pleasant, with mellow plum fragrance.

SLOE GIN

Rich red liqueur with delicate bouquet and tangy fruity flavor resembling wild cherries. Made generally from a blend of sloe berries, from which it derives its primary flavor and other fruit flavors.

SOLERA SYSTEM

An elaborate blending of sherries of similar character according to individual bodega formulas and guided by Spanish law.

SOMMELIER

The employee (also called the wine steward) who selects the wines for the wine list, maintains the wine inventory, and is responsible for the storage, handling, and conditions of the wine cellar; must be familiar with wine and food combinations, and may be called upon to help guests with their selection of wines.

SOUR MASH

Term often used in connection with straight whiskey; identifies a production process, distinguished from the "sweet mash" technique of distillation. The name has nothing to do with the taste of the whiskey—sour mash whiskeys are rich and mellow.

SOUTHERN COMFORT

Brand name. American liqueur, amber colored, rich tasting. A combination of fruit flavors; primarily peaches and bourbon base.

SPACE ALLOCATION

The assignment of spaces—spaces between tables, workspaces, and other interior elements—in planning an interior design; functional and aesthetic considerations are important.

SPECIFICATIONS

With regard to the construction or remodeling of a building, a detailed list of all the qualities and quantities required by the architect for every item to be used.

SPEED RACK

A stainless steel rack which contains all well brands, located in the well under the center of the work station for quick and easy access by the bartender.

SPIRIT

Any alcoholic beverage containing a significant amount of distilled ethanol; spirits are classified according to either their alcoholic source or their processing method.

SPLIT

A wine bottle that contains about 6 ounces (187 ml) and is suitable for one person.

SPOTTERS

People hired to observe the bartender and servers while posing as guests. Also called shoppers.

SPUMANTE

The Italian word for sparkling wine.

STAFFING

The recruitment and hiring of employees.

STANDARD RECIPE

A drink recipe with clearly defined ("standardized") measurements for all the ingredients.

STANDARDS

With regard to the purchasing cycle, guidelines established to ensure that each step is conducted in the same manner every time an order is placed; such standards establish consistency, which leads to predictable costs, quality, and profit.

STANDARDS OF IDENTITY

U.S. federal standards which state exactly what a product must be to bear a particular name (for example, a gin, a vodka).

STATUTORY STATE

A state in which the emphasis is on laws created by legislation. (See also **COMMON LAW STATE**.)

STEAM BEER

A malt beverage brewed predominantly from malt with very little adjunct, originally made in San Francisco; it is top-fermented and receives a second fermentation which produces a creamy foam and high carbon dioxide content.

STERILE FILTRATION

A process in which the fermentation of wine and beer is stopped and the product is passed through filters fine enough to remove yeasts, bacteria, and other microorganisms. No further fermentation can occur because all organisms that might cause it have been removed.

STILL

The apparatus in which distillation takes place; there are two basic types of stills: (1) the old-fashioned pot still, which generally yields no more than 140 proof alcohol; and (2) the column or continuous still, which can be used almost continuously day and night and which can easily produce 190 proof alcohol in large volumes.

STIR METHOD

A method of making cocktails which contain liquors and other ingredients that require stirring with a bar spoon for proper mixture.

STOUT

Similar to porter but more "stout"—that is, higher in alcohol content than porter; it is top-fermented and has a dark color, acquired from roasted unmalted barley.

STRAIGHT UP

Any drink served without ice. (See also **NEAT**.)

STRAIGHT WHISKEY

An alcoholic distillate of a fermented mash of grain, identified by characteristic taste, body, and aroma, and bottled exactly as it comes from the barrel in which it has matured, except for the addition of pure water to reduce the proof to bottle proof. By U.S. law, straight whiskey is aged a minimum of two years in new charred oak barrels. The distiller may call this product straight whiskey without a grain tag, or may use the grain tag (such as straight bourbon whiskey or straight rye whiskey) when 51% or more of the grain from which the whiskey is fermented consists of that grain. Straight corn whiskey, an exception, is made from a mash containing at least 80% corn.

SUGGESTIVE SELLING

Putting your sales approach, statement, or question in such a way as to avoid an automatic "no" and to encourage a "yes" response.

SULFITE

A sulfur compound found in wines and other foods, it is dangerous to the health of a relatively small proportion of people allergic to it; the U.S. federal government now requires that the presence of sulfites in excess of 100 parts per million in foods and beverages be noted on the label.

SULFUR DIOXIDE

A sulfur compound widely used in the making of wine to kill the wild yeasts present on the skins of grapes and thus prevent premature and uncontrolled fermentation; it is also used to prevent oxidation and rarely used to stop fermentation.

SWISS CHOCOLATE ALMOND

Brand name. Rich, smooth, velvety liqueur combining the flavors of cocoa, almonds, and true vanilla into one distinctive flavor of chocolate and almonds.

SWIZZLE STICK

A thin plastic tube made available to guests so they can stir their drinks themselves.

T

TANNINS

The chemical name of one group of substances which are found in wine and aged whiskey. A natural product in grapes, but can be added by wood of the aging barrels.

TAPPING

The process of inserting the line from the dispensing system into a barrel or keg of beer under pressure.

TARGET MARKETING

The process of selecting target markets; each manager must decide, based on market research, what particu-

lar market segments his or her operation wants to attract (target).

TARGET MARKETS

Groups of potential guests (customers), defined by market research, who share common wants and needs.

TASK LIGHTING

Lighting designed to facilitate job functions.

TEQUILA

A distinctive Mexican liquor distilled from the fermented juice of the blue variety of the agave plant; its fermentation and distillation process is complex and strictly controlled by the Mexican government.

THERMOVINIFICATION

A process that helps reduce the formation of undesirable components produced in wine fermentation, such as fusel oil and excess acids and tannins.

THIRD-PARTY LIABILITY LAWS

Laws which hold that a third party can be a contributing factor in the injury of others.

TIA MARIA

Brand name. Jamaican coffee liqueur.

TIED-HOUSE AGREEMENT

Illegal arrangement in the United States in which a supplier has a financial or legal interest in the business of an on-premise retail dealer.

TOKAJI ASZU

A famous sweet wine from Hungary made by an elaborate blending process from wines made from grapes infected by the noble rot.

TOP-FERMENTATION

A fast and vigorous process of brew fermentation; it takes only a few days and produces a heavy foam on the top of the brew; the most common top-fermented brews are ales, porters, and stouts.

TRIPLE SEC

Clear, orange-flavored liqueur made from a flavor-blend of the peels of tangy curaçao and sweet oranges.

TUACA

Brand name. An Italian liqueur with a unique brandy and fruit flavor created from a centuries-old recipe.

TWIST

A strip of lemon peel twisted over a drink to flavor it with lemon oil (often followed by dropping the twisted peel into the drink).

TWO TIER PAR STOCK

Establishing a par (the right amount of inventory) for both the storeroom and the bar area.

U

UNDERBAR

The primary working space for the bartender; it is that area of the bar that is in front of the bartender as he or she faces the guests and, as the name would indicate, mostly (but not entirely) below the level of the bar itself.

V

VANDERMINT

Brand name. Minted chocolate liqueur from Holland.

VARIABLE COST

A cost that varies directly as sales go up or down. Also called direct cost.

VARIETAL WINE

A wine produced from a single variety of grape.

VIN MOUSSEUX

Literally, "foamy wine," the name used for sparkling wines made in France outside of the Champagne district.

VINTAGE

The year the grapes for a wine were grown.

VINTAGE YEAR

The year in which the wine was fermented.

VITIS LABRUSCA

A variety of grape vine, native to North America, which thrives in colder areas and which is resistant to phylloxera.

VODKA

A clear, colorless, flavorless spirit made by passing highly refined neutral spirits through charcoal, by re-distillation, or by other government-approved processes.

VOID CONTROL SHEET

A cash handling control sheet used to record all voids rung up at the cash register.

W

WATER (SODA) BACK

A glass of water (or soda) served along with an alcoholic beverage—most often intended to be drunk after consuming a straight alcoholic beverage.

WATER ON THE SIDE

A glass of water served along with any alcoholic beverage—often used interchangeably with "water back."

WEDGE

A piece of fruit, usually lime or lemon.

WELL BRANDS

Those liquors which are poured when the guest does not specify a particular brand; they are less expensive than call brands.

WELL DRINKS

Drinks made from inexpensive house brands, usually kept in a "well" below the bar where customers can't see the labels.

WELL STOCK

Consists of the assortment of bottles of those brands from which well drinks are poured or mixed—usually the most popular liquors such as gin, vodka, rum, bourbon, and whiskey.

WHISKEY (WHISKY)

The generic term for a family of spirits made from grains, which include Scotch, Irish, American (bourbon), and Canadian among the foremost examples; each type of whiskey will vary according to the grain used, fermentation process, distillation, and processing after distillation.

WINE

The fermented juice of fruit, usually grapes.

WINE STEWARD

(See *SOMMELIER.*)

WISNIOWKA

A wild cherry liqueur produced mainly in the Slavic countries of Europe.

WORT

A fermented, cooked mash made from carbohydrates which have been converted into sugars, such as glucose, maltose, or some form of dextrin. It is used in making beer and spirits. The liquid is distilled for spirits. Also called distiller's beer.

Y

YEASTS

Living organisms that convert starches or other sugars into glucose; in the process of metabolizing glucose, yeasts produce carbon dioxide and ethyl alcohol.

YUKON JACK

Brand name. Rich, sweet, slight orange character; Canadian whisky base. Amber in color.

Z

ZONE LIGHTING

Lighting designed to facilitate traffic from one space to another.

Bibliography

This list is a selection of books that may be of further interest to readers. It supplements works cited in the endnotes throughout this text, but it is not a comprehensive list of all sources used in researching the text.

Anheuser-Busch. *The Modern Bartender.* St. Louis, Mo., 1990.

———. *Bartender's Guide.* St. Louis, Mo., 1965.

———. *Fact Book, 1989–90.* St. Louis, Mo., 1991.

Bell, Donald A. *Wine and Beverage Standards.* New York: Van Nostrand Reinhold, 1989.

Coltman, Michael M. *Beverage Management.* New York: Van Nostrand Reinhold, 1989.

Cotton, Leo. *The Official Bartender's Guide.* Boston: Mr. Boston Distillers, Inc., 1960.

Dittmer, Paul R., and Gerald G. Griffin. 4th ed. *Principles of Food, Beverage, and Labor Cost Controls.* New York: Van Nostrand Reinhold, 1989.

Educational Institute of the American Hotel & Motel Association. *Serving Alcohol with Care.* 2d ed. East Lansing, Mich., 1988.

Grossman, Harold L. *Grossman's Guide.* New York: Scribner, 1955.

Johnson, Hugh. *The World Atlas of Wine.* New York: Simon and Schuster, 1985.

———. *The History of Wine.* New York: Simon and Schuster, 1990.

Katsigris, Costas, and Mary Porter. *The Bar and Beverage Book.* 2d ed. New York: Wiley, 1991.

Kubicki, Victor J. *Distillery Training Course Manual.* 14th ed. Detroit, Mich.: Hiram Walker, 1990.

Lipinski, Robert A., and Kathleen A. Lipinski. *Professional Guide to Alcoholic Beverages.* New York: Van Nostrand Reinhold, 1989.

Marvel, Tom. *A Pocket Dictionary of Wines.* New York: Party Book Publishers, 1963.

Ninemeier, Jack D. *Planning and Control for Food and Beverage Operations.* 2d ed. East Lansing, Mich.: Educational Institute of the American Hotel & Motel Association, 1991.

Osterland, Edmund. *Wine and the Bottom Line.* Washington, D.C.: National Restaurant Association, 1980.

Roncari, Bruno. *Viva Vina—200+,* London: Wine and Spirit Publishers, 1986.

Index

A

acoustical materials, 80
    tiles, 73–74
actual cost, 269
additives, 367
adjuncts, 366–367
advertising, 208–211
agave plant, 352
aging, 330–334
    brandy, 354–355
agraffe, 301
air
    control, 78–79
    pressure, 79
aisles, 66
alcohol
    abuse, 22
    alcoholism, 22
    awareness, 115–117, 210
    changing consumption patterns, 9–10,
        31–33
    consumption during pregnancy, 34
    dependence, 22, 34
    effects of, 38–41
    health concerns, 33–34
    other drugs and, 40–42
    per capita consumption, 31–32
    physical effects of, 33–34
    social cost of abuse, 26–30
    use policy, 300
alcohol service, 37–50
    causing intoxication, 22
    monitoring consumption, 47–50
    primary legal concerns, 22–30
    server intervention, 41–50
    to known dependents, 25
alcoholic beverages
    calorie content, 320–322
    characteristics of, 319–322
    classifications of, 318–319
    history of, 307–318
    production of, 322–335
    weight/volume conversion, 319–320
ale, 369, 370
alembic, 311

aliens, 293–294
Alsace region, 437–438
ambience, 60
ambient air temperature, 79
ambient lighting, 81
American proof standard, 319–320
American Viticulture Areas, 414
American whiskeys, 344–346
amylase, 367–368
angel's share, 354
Anreichern, 411
aperitifs, 360–361
appellation contrôlée, 357, 403
applejack, 359
aquavit, 351
architecture, 55–83
Armagnac, 356–357
Auslese, 409
AVA, 414

B

BAC, 30, 38–40
backbar, 91–93
backup drinks, 115
bank, 279
banquets
    beverage control sheet, 270
    product control, 266–268
banquettes, 61–62
bar
    basic types, 6–7, 91–100
    equipment, 100–105
    flooring, 96
    layout, 87–100
    menu, 88–89
    sanitation, 105–106
    tools, 105, 106
Barack Palinka, 358
barley, 341, 365–366
Barsac region, 446–447
bartender, 109–117
    job description, 112–113
    manual, 126–130
    theft, 260–262

    various roles of, 111–117
Bartenders Against Drunk Driving
    (BADD), 115
BATF, 290
Bavarian beer, 371
Beaujolais, 443
beer, 143–148. *See also* malt beverages
    draft, 96, 372–375
    fermentation, 325–326
    glassware, 147–148
    light, 9
    pouring techniques, 146
    selection, 218–219
    serving temperatures, 144
    storage, 238–239
Beerenauslese, 409
beverage cost percentage, 271–273
beverage inventory turnover, 242–244
beverage receiving report, 234, 235
BFOQ, 174–175
bin card, 236–237
bitters, 361
blanc de blancs, 431
blanc de noir, 431
blending, 334–335
    brandy, 355
    wine, 397–398
blood alcohol concentration. *See* BAC
blueprints, 56
bock, 370–371
bodegas, 457
bona fide occupational qualification,
    174–175
bonded spirits, 332–333
booths, 62–63, 65
Bordeaux region, 443–447
botanicals, 350
Botrytis cinerea, 314, 389
bottle sickness, 398
bottle stamps, 234
bottled water, 32
bottom-up pricing, 275–276
bourbon, 344–345
brandy, 352–359
    labeling, 355
brewing, 368
British proof standard, 319–320
build method, 125

bulk fermentation, 382–383, 437
Bureau of Alcohol, Tobacco and Firearms, 290
Burgundy region, 439–443

C

call brands, 114, 222
calvados, 357
Campari, 360
Canadian whisky, 346
carbonation, 369–370
carbonic maceration, 394
carpeting and floor coverings, 70
cash bar, 266–268
cash control, 279–283
cashier check-out procedures, 280, 283
ceilings, 72–74
Chablis area, 440
chairs, 75
champagne, 148–149, 155–156, 323, 383, 429–437, 466
   method, 314, 382, 431–437
chaptalization, 392, 411, 412, 414
Charmat process, 382–383, 437
check averages, 13
check control sheet, 280
cider, 318
cirrhosis, 34
citizen's arrest, 296
Civil Rights Act, 293
closed states. *See* control states
cocktails, 117–124
coffee, effect of, 40
cognac, 355
color scheme, 77
common law, 26
common law states, 289
competition analysis, 193–195
competitive bids, 59
complementary colors, 77
complimentary drinks, 259
congeners, 324
consignment sales, 292
control, 12–16, 251
   cash control, 279–282
   payment, 143
   purchasing, 226
   product control, 252–269
   sales/profitability control, 269–278
   states, 224–225, 295, 318
   systems, 251–287
coordinating, 12
cordials, 359–360
cork, 239, 398–399
corn whiskey, 346
cost control. *See* sales/profitability control
cost percentage, 271–273
costs, 269–271
   hidden, 198
Côte d'Or, 387–389, 440–443
Côtes du Rhône, 447–448
counters, 75–76
cream ale, 370
credit memo, 231, 233
cru, 311, 389, 402, 403
curtains, 72
cuvée, 432
cuvée closé process, 437

D

dark beer, 371
dead stock list, 228
decanting, 151
decibels, 80
dégorgement, 434
demographics, 165–166, 188–189
design
   exterior, 82–83
   interior, 59–77
   theme, 60
designated driver, 41, 45, 195
diastase, 323, 367
digestives, 360
direct cost, 269
discharge, wrongful, 294, 297–298
discounting, 229
discrimination, 293–294
dispensing systems, 256, 263–266
   pressurized, 121–122
distillation, 311, 327–333
   brandy, 354
distiller's beer, 324–325
DOC, 412, 414
DOCG, 412–413, 414
Dom Perignon, 314
doppelbocks, 371
Dortmunder, 371
dosage, 434
doubles, 115
draft beer, 372–375
dram shop laws, 25–26
Drambuie, 360
drapery, 72
drink
   incentives, 116
   preparation methods, 124–126
   rail, 76
   size, 254–255
drug abuse, symptoms of, 42
drug use policy, 300
drunk driving, 3–4, 115–117
dry areas, 298–299
dry-hopped beer, 376

E

Eiswein, 409, 452–453
elevations, 58
Emilia-Romagna region, 456
employee referrals, 173
employment at will, 297–298
employment discrimination, 293–294
employment laws, 293–294
empty-for-full replacement, 258
energy costs, windows and, 71
enzymes, 323, 366, 367
European Economic Community, 403
evaluating, 13
excise taxes, 291

F

FAAA, 290–292, 319
feasibility study, 57
Federal Alcohol Administration Act. *See* FAAA
fermentation, 322–327
   carbonic maceration, 394
   champagne, 431–437
   in the bottle, 436
   in this bottle, 431
   malolactic, 393, 432
   malt beverages, 369
   port, 461–462
   sherry, 459–460
   wine, 392–394
FIFO system, 238
fights, 47
filtration, 326, 369
   wine, 395–397
fining, 395–397
fire codes, 73
flaming drinks, 116–117
flocculent matter, 394
floors, 68–70
fluorescent lighting, 81
forcible ejection, 296, 299
Fraboise, 358
fraud, 260–263
free pouring, 255
front bar, 91–97
fruit fly, 395
full bottle slip, 258
Fundador, 358

G

garnishes, 123
Gay-Lussac standard, 319–320
gin, 350–351
glass rail, 94
glassware, 103–104
   arranging, 100
   beer, 147–148
   standards, 256
   washing, 95–96
   wine, 152
glycerine, 324, 395
grain neutral spirit, 329, 346
grape must, 324
grapes, brandy, 353–354
grappa, 357
Graves region, 446
green-yellow-red program, 43, 45–46
gross profit, 271–273
guest checks, 280
guest profiles, 188
guest-oriented approach, 135–136, 197

H

half and half, 319
handicapper issues, 83
   parking and access, 59

happy hours, 116, 274
hek, 307
Hertz, 80
hopping, 368
hops, 366
hosted bar, 268
Humulus lupulus, 366

I

ice bin, 94
ice-making machines, 100–103
identification, 23–24
Immigration and Naturalization Service, 174, 294
Immigration Reform and Control Act, 174, 293–294
incandescent lighting, 81
INDO, 457
INS, 174, 294
insurance rates, 30
interior design, 56, 59–77
    aisles, 66
    ceilings, 72–74
    curtains and drapery, 72
    environmental planning, 77–82
    floors, 68–70
    furniture and equipment, 74–76
    traffic flow, 65–68
    walls, 71–72
    windows, 70–71
interviewing, 172, 175–177
intoxication, signs of, 38
inventory, 240–244
Irish Mist, 360
Irish whiskey, 344
issuing, 244–246

J

jigger, 255
job
    analysis, 90, 166–168
    descriptions, 168–171
    inventory method, 166–168
    posting, 173
    specifications, 171

K

Kabinett, 408
Karaoke, 6
Kirsch, 357
krausening, 370

L

labeling. *See* regulation
labor
    pools, 172
    supply, 165–166

lagering, 369
landscaping, 83
Landwein, 409
last call, 115
Latium region, 456–457
lautering tub, 368
laws/regulations, 289–304
    federal, 289–294
    local, 298–299
    state, 294–298
    wide interpretations, 301–303
lead time, 227
leading, 12
lees, 394
level of service, 137
liability, 297, 299–301
    flaming drinks, 116–117
    preparing for, 303
license states, 224, 295, 318
licenses, 59, 295, 299
Liebfraumilch, 450
lighting, 80–82
    safety and security issue, 83
liqueurs, 359–360
Loire region, 438–439
Lombardy region, 455
lounges, 7–9
low-alcohol drinks, 50

M

maceration, 357
MADD, 3–4, 27, 35, 193
madeira, 382
malt beverages, 365–378. *See also* beer
    alcohol content, 371–372
    ingredients, 365–367
    judging quality, 376–377
    liquor, 371
    production, 367–370
    types, 370–371
maltase, 323
malting, 367
maltose, 367
management
    functions, 10–13
    resources, 10
    social concerns, 21–50
    styles, 13–14
Marc, 357
marketing, 14–16, 187–213
    four P's, 196–208
    glassware and, 103
    market analysis, 157
    market research, 55–56, 190
    market segmentation, 189
    marketing mix, 196–208
    social/ethical issues, 192–193, 210
    target markets, 189, 190–191
marrying, 335
Marsala, 457
mashing, 367–368
measured pouring, 255–256
Médoc region, 445–446
merchandising, 212–213
Metaxa, 358
méthode champenoise. See champagne
    method

mezcal, 352
mini-bar, 100
mini-drink, 50
minimum age, 23
minimum/maximum par, 227–228
minors, service to, 23–25
Mirabelle, 358
mirrors, 71
mis en bouteille, 398, 407
mixes, 120–122
mixology, 109, 117–126
monopoly states. *See* control states
Mosel-Saar-Ruwer region, 449
Mothers Against Drunk Drivers. *See* MADD
muddling, 120
Münchner, 371
must, 324, 390, 392

N

Nahe region, 451
Napoleonic Code, 289
Nation, Carry, 317
National Bartenders Association, 115
National Fire Protection Association, 76
National Institute on Alcohol Abuse and Alcoholism, 32
National Sanitation Foundation, 105–106
neat, 119–120
négociant, 407
noble mold/rot, 314, 389
non-alcoholic beverages
    brews, 372
    recipes, 15

O

Occupational Safety and Health Administration, 59
off-hour sales, 22–23
on-premise retail dealers, 290
on-the-job training, 181
open bar, 48–50
open states. *See* license states
organizing, 11–12
orientation programs, 177
OSHA, 59
ouzo, 358
overage/shortage report, 284
overpouring, 119

P

paint, 71
par, 226–229, 256–258, 268–269
pasteurization, 369
patent still, 328
permits, 59, 295, 299
perpetual inventory, 241–242
perry, 318
personal selling, 212
phylloxera, 315, 384

physical inventory, 242
Piedmont region, 453–455
pilferage, 260–263
pilsner, 371
pisco, 358
planning, 10–11
    color, 77
      four viewpoints, 56–59
      interior environment, 77–82
point-of-sale system, 279
Poire Williams, 357
policies and procedures, 10–11, 41–43
Pomerol region, 446
port, 382, 461–462
porter, 369, 370
position descriptions, 171
position guides, 171
positioning, 191
pot still, 327
pour cost, 276
pousse-café, 125
pre-check register, 279
predictions, 16–18
pregnancy, 34
pricing, 198–202, 260, 273–278
    categories, 200
prise de mousse, 432
problem guests, 296–297
product control, 252–269
    setting standards, 253–260
product selection, 217–224
Prohibition, 5, 317–318
promotions, 202–213, 274
    promotional mix, 208–213
proof, 319–320
prostitution, 296
protease, 368
public policy, violations, 298
public relations, 211
publicity, 211
pull date, 369
purchase order, 229–230
purchasing, 224–231
purveyor invoice, 231, 233
purveyor selection, 224–225

Q

QbA, 409
QmP, 408–409
Quetsch, 358

R

racking, 394–395
receiving, 231–235
recruitment, 171–174
    methods, 173–174
rectification, 329–330
references, 175
regulation, wine, 401–420
    appellation contrôlée, 403
    AVA, 414
    decoding U.S. label, 417
    DO, 416

DOC, 412
    French, 402–407
    German, 407–412
    INDO, 416
    Italy, 412–414
    labeling, 401–420, 429–473 *passim*
    Landwein, 409
    QbA, 409
    QmP, 408–409
    recent trends, 418–420
    Spanish, 416–418
    sulfites, 420
Tafelwein, 409
    U.S., 414–416
    VDQS, 405
    vin de pays, 405
    vintage, 407
regulatory compliance, 59
relative humidity, 79
renovation, 83
requisition form, 244–245
respondeat superior, 300
Rheingau region, 449–450
Rheinhessen region, 450–451
Rheinpfalz region, 451
room service, 100
rosé, 393
rum, 351–352
rye whiskey, 345–346

S

sake, 319
sales
    analysis, 271–273
    forecast, 195–196
    mix, 201–202
    potential, 196
    reports, 265–268
    sales value per bottle, 199–200, 285–286
sales/profitability control, 269–278
saloons, 315–316
sanitation
    bar procedures, 128–129
    beer-clean glass, 147
Sauternes region, 446–447
Schaumwein, 452
schematic plan, 57
schnapps, 350
scotch, 339–344
screening methods, 174
seating arrangements, 61–65
selection
    employee, 174–177
    product, 217–224
    purveyor, 224–225
selling
    by suggestion, 157–158
    techniques, 157–161
separation of duties, 217, 226, 260–261
sequencing, 99, 129–130
server
    intervention programs, 41–50
    characteristics, 158–159
service
    bar, 97–100
    beer, 143–148
    employee manual, 138

industry characteristics, 191–192
    level of, 137
    orientation, 133–136
    procedures, 137–156
    wine, 148–156
sexual harassment/discrimination, 293
shake/blend method, 125–126
sherry, 382, 390–391, 459, 468
shipment sickness, 240, 401
shoppers, 263
shot glass, 255
Sicily, 457
simple syrup, 120
SIRR, 43
Slivovitz, 358
sloe gin, 351
social legislation, 30
soda back, 120
solera system, 459
sommelier, 150
sound control, 78, 79–80
sour mash whiskey, 344
Southern Comfort, 360
space allocation, 60–65
Spätlese, 408
speakeasies, 5, 317–318
specifications, 56, 58
speed rack, 94
spillage report, 259
spirits, 339–363
    aging, 331–333
    aperitifs, 360–361
    bitters, 361
    compounded, 350–351
    defined, 318
    fruit, 352–359
    grain, 339–351
    judging quality, 361–362
    liqueurs, 359–360
    plant, 351–352
    selection, 222–224
spotters, 263
St-Emilion region, 446
staffing, 12
standard recipes, 119
standards, 13, 253–260
    glassware, 256
    of identity, 290
    recipes, 119, 254–255
    portion control, 255–256
    service, 136–137
statutory states, 289
steam beer, 371
sterile filtration, 326, 369
stills, 327–329
stir method, 124–125
storage, 88, 235–240
    wine, 401
stout, 369, 370
straight up, 119–120
sugar enrichment. *See* chaptalization
suggestion boxes, 190
suggestive selling, 157–158
sulfites, 415, 420
sulfur dioxide, 392
Surgeon General, 34
swizzle stick, 125

T

tables, 75
  arrangements, 61–65
Tafelwein, 409
tannins, 395
tapping, 372
target marketing, 189, 190–191
task lighting, 81
taxation, 290, 291
temperance movement, 5, 316, 317–318
tequila, 352
thermovinification, 326
third-party liability, 25–30, 300–301
Tia Maria, 360
tied-house agreements, 291–292
tip jar, 262–263
torula, 354
traffic flow, interior, 65–68, 90
training, 178–184
  alcohol service, 37–50
  sales and, 182–184
  trainers, 181–182
  wine sales, 159
transfer process, 382, 436
Treasury Department, U.S., 290
trespassing, 296
Trockenbeerenauslese, 409
Tuscany region, 456
twist, 120
two tier par stock, 226–227

U

U.S. Census Bureau, 165
underbar, 93–94
upholstery, 76

V

variable cost, 269
VDQS, 405
Veneto region, 455
vermouth, 360
vin de table, 405
vin mousseux, 432
vin ordinaire, 405

vini tipici, 413, 414
vino da pasto, 413
vino da tavola, 413
vino ordinario, 413
vintage, 327, 395, 407, 411, 415, 466
viticulture standards, French, 404
Vitis labrusca, 384
Vitis vinifera, 383, 384
vodka, 346–350
void control sheet, 279, 281

W

walls and coverings, 71–72
warning label, 34
water
  back, 120
  bottled, 32
wedges, 123
Weinstube, 409
Weissbier, 371
Weizenbier, 371
well brands, 114, 222
whiskey, 339–346
  consumption, 32
  light, 9
  Whiskey Rebellion, 290
white goods, 9
wholesaler regulations, 290–292
windows, 70–71
wines, 381–475
  aging, 333–334, 394–395
  aperitif, 382
  basic classifications, 381–383
  blending, 397–398
  bottling/corking, 398–400
  cellar, 221
  decanting, 151
  defined, 318–319
  dessert, 382
  exploding bottles, 301
  fermentation, 326–327, 392–394
  fining, 395–397
  food and, 149–150
  fortified, 382
  generic, 385
  grafting vines, 384
  growing/harvesting grapes, 383–389
  house, 221–222
  hybridization, 386
  judging quality, 420–425

  maturing, 400–401
  natural, 382
  noble rot, 314, 389
  non-alcoholic, 420
  of France, 429–448
  of Germany, 448–453
  of Italy, 453–457
  of Portugal, 460–462
  of Spain, 457–460
  of U.S., 462–468
  of various countries/areas, 468–473
  organic, 418–420
  pressing, 390–392
  pricing, 202
  production, 389–401
  pruning, 384
  racking, 394–395
  regulation/labeling, 401–420, 429–473
    passim
  scions, 384
  selection, 219–222
  selling, 159–161
  serving temperatures, 150–151
  shipment sickness, 240, 401
  sommelier, 150
  sparkling, 155–156, 382
  steward, 150
  storage, 239–240, 401
  table, 381–382
  varietal, 385
  wine coolers, 9, 381
  wine list, 161, 219
  wine tastings, 300–301
work station setup, 127–130
wort, 324–325
wrongful discharge, 294, 297–298

Y

yeast, 324, 366

Z

zone lighting, 81
Zwetschgenwasser, 358
zymase, 323